NATURAL REGIONS
OF THE
UNITED STATES AND CANADA

A Series of Books in Geology

Editors
 James Gilluly
 A. O. Woodford

NATURAL REGIONS OF THE UNITED STATES AND CANADA

Charles B. Hunt
The Johns Hopkins University

W. H. FREEMAN AND COMPANY
San Francisco

Cover design from a photograph by John S. Shelton.

The photograph shows an aerial view of compound
alluvial fans, east side of Death Valley, California.

Library of Congress Cataloging in Publication Data
Hunt, Charles Butler, 1906–
Natural regions of the United States and Canada.
    Includes bibliographies.
    1. Physical geography—United States.   I. Title.
GB121.H79   917'.02   73–12030
ISBN 0-7167-0255-X

The present work is an expansion and revision of PHYSIOGRAPHY
OF THE UNITED STATES, published in 1967.

Printed in the United States of America

9 8 7 6 5 4

PREFACE

My purpose in this book, as it was in the earlier version, published as *Physiography of the United States,* is to present a broad view of the natural features and resources of the United States and, this time, Canada. The book is an outgrowth of a course offered at The Johns Hopkins University for students not majoring in the earth sciences. The course introduces the subjects of physical geography, geology, climate, landforms, soils, vegetation, resources and related phenomona and describes the several natural regions in those terms. This book has two main purposes: to remind us that we are greatly favored over the rest of the world by our natural environment, and to introduce non-earth scientists to the art of appreciating the landscape. To accomplish the first, it is necessary to emphasize our material resources and to inquire whether we are making the best use of them. The second purpose is of the spirit—to contribute to enjoyment of the outdoors.

I first felt the need for such a book while serving as Executive Director of the American Geological Institute in the mid-1950's. That position increased my appreciation of the general public's wide interest in the natural environment and the need for an authoritative account of it in language as nontechnical as possible. A manuscript was started, and it served as the basis for the lectures presented at The Johns Hopkins University, and from them developed the book *Physiography of the United States.*

In this new and enlarged version, the title has been changed. This was done in response to the criticisms of geologists, who have altered the original meaning of the word *physiography* by using it as a synonym for *geomorphology.*

It would be naive to suppose that the book is without errors, but the number would be very much greater had I not had the benefit of careful technical review by the geology editors of W. H. Freeman and Company—James Gilluly, A. O. Woodford, and Thane H. McCulloh. For forty years Jim Gilluly has been shooting his famed barbs at my writing efforts, and his marksmanship continues to be good. I emerge, as usual, bloody, and next time may try acupuncture.

This new version has had the benefit of suggestions and criticisms of not only my students, but of professors who used the original book at other schools. I am happy to acknowledge assistance from James C. Albrecht of the University of Delaware,

Donald J. Bogucki of the State University of New York at Plattsburgh, C. C. Carney
of Trenton State College, Stanford E. Demars of Utah State University, James W. Dixon
of Baylor University, John A. Enman of Bloomsburg State College, Donald F. Eschman
of the University of Michigan, H. Bowman Hawkes of The University of Utah, S. Roger
Kirkpatrick of Marietta College, Paul D. Knuth of Edinboro State College, M. John
Loeffler of the University of Colorado, Harold A. Meeks of The University of Vermont,
Robert C. Palmquist of Iowa State University of Science and Technology, Bruce M. C.
Pape of Central Michigan University, Nolan G. Shaw of Centenary College, Albert W.
Smith of the University of Colorado, David R. Williams, Jr., of Santa Barbara City
College, and James F. Woodruff of the University of Georgia.

I hope that readers will find no major errors and few minor ones. Any that remain
are mine.

August 1973   *Charles B. Hunt*

CONTENTS

vii

PART TWO   THE PROVINCES

APPENDIXES

NATURAL REGIONS
OF THE
UNITED STATES AND CANADA

PART ONE

GENERAL FEATURES AND PROCESSES

Most of the natural regions have sharply defined boundaries, like this one along the
eastern front of the Sierra Nevada, which separates the Sierra from the Basin and Range
Province to the east (foreground). [Courtesy of Robert Ishi.]

1
.....

THE NATURAL REGIONS

The face of our land is the net result of a complex of processes and changes that occurred in the past and continue to occur today, but the basic differences between various parts of the land surface are structural. The natural regions into which the earth's surface is divided are controlled mostly by the kinds of structural members that make up the different parts of the earth's crust and by their relationship to one another. These structural differences may be further accentuated by differences in climate, which governs the processes that shape the landscape—weathering, erosion, and sedimentation. But the structural differences prevail even where the regimens of climate, erosion, and sedimentation are similar.

The United States and Canada are divided, primarily on the basis of structure, into 40 natural regions called physiographic provinces, which are grouped in 11 major divisions. Each province has characteristics peculiar to itself—a distinctive structural framework giving rise to distinctive landforms expressing their structure and, for the most part, distinctive climate, vegetation, soils, water, and other resources.

Engineers find each physiographic province to have its distinctive kinds of ground with distinctive construction problems and materials. Social scientists and economists find differences between the people and their cultural traits in each of the provinces—differences in ethnology, dialects, educational levels, religions, wealth, industrial or agricultural pursuits, and politics. One may also see differences in architecture despite the continent-wide similarities in appearances of roadside business places and billboards.

Table 1.1 lists the major divisions and the provinces in the United States and Canada, and briefly describes some of their outstanding characteristics (see Fig. 1.1; for Alaska and the Yukon, Fig. 19.1,A,B). Some provinces are divided into *sections;* these will be discussed as the provinces are described in Part II.

The boundaries between the provinces, for the most part, are sharp, reflecting the fact that the chief differences are structural. Some examples are: the break marked by a line of falls between the Coastal Plain and the higher Piedmont Province; the foot of the Blue Ridge, which forms the inner boundary of the Piedmont Province; the so-called knob belt that forms the western edge of the Appalachian Plateaus; the foot of the Front Range in the Southern Rocky Mountains, which marks the western edge of the Great Plains; the southern rim of the Colorado Plateau, which overlooks the much lower Basin and Range Province in central and western Arizona; the northern edge of the Snake River Plains at the foot of the Northern Rocky Mountains in Idaho; the east base of the Rocky Mountains in Canada; and the base of the mountains on both the east and the west sides of the Cascade-Sierra Nevada Province.

A few boundaries, however, are not sharp but gradational over wide areas, even though the provinces are structurally distinct. Examples are the boundaries of the Middle Rocky Mountains and the Basin and Range Province, for these provinces grade into the mountains, plateaus, and basins of neighboring provinces. Such boundaries are necessarily arbitrary.

Plains make up most of Canada and almost half of the United States. The central part of the continent is a vast plain that extends northward to the Arctic Ocean and southward to the Gulf of Mexico. Northward along the Atlantic coast, the Coastal Plain narrows and becomes fragmented where it slopes northeastward under the Atlantic Ocean. The northeastward slope is the result of tilting of the surface by earth movements. This tilting is responsible for the drowned valleys at Chesapeake, Delaware, and New York bays. East of New York only the tops of the highest hills remain above sea level, as islands; beyond Cape Cod the plain is wholly submerged. Other less extensive plains are in the structural basins that separate some of the western mountains, like the broad valley of the Sacramento and San Joaquin rivers in California, many of the basins in the Basin and Range Province, and the Wyoming Basin.

About 15 percent of the continent is made up of plateaus. In order of increasing height the six major plateaus in the United States are: the Piedmont Plateau, the Interior Low Plateaus, and the Ozark, Appalachian, Columbia, and Colorado plateaus; in Canada an extensive plateau separates the Canadian Rockies from the Coast Ranges, and north of it is the Yukon Plateau, which extends westward into Alaska. No two of these are alike; not only have earth movements raised them to different heights, but their rock formations are different. The four eastern plateaus are much older than the western and northern ones; the eastern plateaus are humid, the others semiarid, and there are consequent differences in the weathering and erosional processes that have shaped the landforms.

Mountains make up about 20 percent of the continent. The central plains are flanked on the east by the Appalachian Highlands and on the west by the Rocky Mountain System. The western mountains and plateaus differ from the eastern ones in many ways and for many reasons. The kinds of rocks and their structures are different; the western mountains and plateaus are younger and higher; they are less worn down, partly because they are younger. The landforms differ partly for these reasons and partly because the processes of erosion are mostly those of a semiarid rather than humid climate.

Structural differences are reflected too in the great differences between the shorelines along the three sides of the continent. The Atlantic and Gulf coasts south of New England are plains with extensive, sandy beaches; the Pacific Coast from California to Alaska is mountainous with comparatively few beaches. The coast of southeastern Alaska is mountainous with glaciers and fjords. The Arctic coast is mostly low-ground—coastal plain in Alaska, and fragmented shoreline with bedrock islands in Canada.

The offshore areas differ too. Off the Atlantic Coast the continental shelf is more than a hundred miles wide, but along the Pacific Coast it is quite narrow. The south shore of the Alaska Peninsula, the Aleutian Islands, and the north shore of Puerto Rico are bordered by oceanic trenches several miles deep.

The continental shelf off the west and northwest coast of Alaska is wider than that along the Atlantic Coast. Northernmost Canada is an archipelago of large and small islands. The ground on these islands is permanently frozen, and the straits that separate them are frozen much of the year. At the edge of the archipelago the shelf slopes steeply into the abyss occupied by the Arctic Ocean and its pack of polar ice.

Table 1.1

Major Divisions and Physiographic Provinces, United States and Canada

Major Divisions	Provinces	Characteristics
Canadian Shield	Superior Upland	An upland with altitudes up to 2,000 feet, but without much local relief; drainage irregular; many lakes; extends far north in Canada around both sides of Hudson Bay.
	Laurentian Highlands	Highlands of southeastern Canada; extensive areas higher than 1,500 feet altitude and numerous summits more than 3,000 feet; surface hilly rather than mountainous; drainage mostly to the Gulf of St. Lawrence.
	Labrador Highlands	Mountains in northern Labrador; highest part of the Shield; ground permanently frozen.
	Hudson Bay Lowlands	Plain rising southward from the south shore of Hudson Bay to altitude of about 500 feet; also includes plain at Southampton Island and the other islands at the north end of the Bay; ground in the north plain permanently frozen.
	Athabasca Plain	Plain south of Lake Athabasca; altitude about 1,000 feet; rises southward.
	Thelon Plain and Back River Lowland	Plain rising southward from the Arctic coast to about 1,000 feet near the Thelon River; ground permanently frozen.
Atlantic Plain	Continental Shelf	Submarine plain sloping seaward to depth of about 600 feet; the submerged part of the Coastal Plain.
	Coastal Plain	Broad plain rising inland; shores mostly sandy beaches backed by estuaries and marshes; mud flats at mouth of Mississippi River; some limestone bluffs on west coast of Florida; inland ridges parallel the coast; altitudes less than 500 feet; along Atlantic coast the surface slopes northeast and northern valleys are tidal inlets.
Appalachian Provinces	Piedmont Plateau	Rolling upland; altitudes mostly 500 to 1,000 feet in the south: surface slopes northeast (like the Coastal Plain) and altitudes at the north are below 500 feet.
	Blue Ridge	Easternmost ridge of the Appalachian Highlands; maximum altitudes above 5,000 feet.
	Valley and Ridge Province	Parallel valleys and mountainous ridges; altitudes mostly between 1,000 and 3,000 feet; lower to the north, like the Coastal Plain and Piedmont provinces.
	Appalachian Plateaus	Plateau; surface mostly 2,000 to 3,000 feet; slopes west; deeply incised by winding stream valleys; considerable local relief; hillsides steep.
	New England, the Maritime Provinces, and Newfoundland	Mostly hilly upland with altitudes below 1,500 feet; locally mountainous with altitudes above 5,000 feet; coast irregular and rocky.
	Adirondack Mountains	Mountains rising to more than 5,000 feet.
	St. Lawrence Valley	Rolling lowland with altitudes below 500 feet.

(Continued)

Table 1.1 *(Continued)*

Major Divisions	Provinces	Characteristics
Interior Plains	Central Lowland	Vast plain, 500 to 2,000 feet; the agricultural heart of the continent.
	Great Plains Province	Western extension of the Central Lowland rising westward from 2,000 to 5,000 feet; semiarid.
Interior Highlands	Interior Low Plateaus	Plateaus; less than 1,000 feet; rolling uplands with moderate relief.
	Ozark Plateaus	Rolling upland; mostly above 1,000 feet.
	Ouachita Province	Like the Valley and Ridge Province; altitudes 500 to 2,000 feet.
Rocky Mountain System	Southern Rocky Mountains	A series of mountain ranges and intermontane basins, mostly trending north; high part of the continental divide; altitudes 5,000 to more than 14,000 feet.
	Wyoming Basin	Elevated semiarid basins; isolated low mountains; altitudes mostly between 5,000 and 7,000 feet.
	Middle Rocky Mountains	An assortment of different kinds of mountains with differing trends and semiarid intermontane basins; features here resemble those of the neighboring provinces; altitudes mostly 5,000 to about 12,000 feet.
	Rocky Mountains in Montana and Canada	Linear blocky mountains with long, straight valleys, including the 500-mile long Rocky Mountain Trench. Altitudes mostly between 4,000 and 10,000 feet.
	Idaho batholith and neighboring granitic uplands	Highly irregular granitic mountains without linear trends; altitudes mostly between 3,000 and 7,000 feet.
Intermontane Provinces	Colorado Plateau	Highest plateaus in the continent; surface mostly above 5,000 feet and up to 11,000 feet; canyons; semiarid; crossed by the Colorado River in deep canyons.
	Basin and Range Province	Mostly elongate, blocky mountains separated by desert basins and trending north; pattern more irregular in the south; altitudes from below sea level (Death Valley, Salton Sea) to more than 12,000 feet, but relief between mountains and adjoining basins generally no more than about 5,000 feet; most basins in the north are without exterior drainage.
	Columbia and Snake River plateaus	Mostly plateaus of lava flows; altitudes mostly below 5,000 feet; semiarid but crossed by two major rivers, the Columbia and Snake.
	Fraser Plateau	Mostly a plateau of lava flows; higher than the Columbia Plateau; semiarid but crossed by the Fraser River.
	Yukon Plateau and delta	Delta at west; eastward along the Yukon River in Alaska and Yukon territory a dissected plateau; uplands 1,000 to 2,000 feet higher than the river.
Pacific Mountain System	Cascade-Sierra Nevada	Northerly trending mountains; Cascades a series of volcanos; Sierra Nevada a blocky mass of granite with steep eastern slope and long gentle western slope; some altitudes more than 14,000 feet; western slopes humid, eastern slopes semiarid.

Major Divisions	Provinces	Characteristics
Pacific Mountain System (Continued)	Pacific Border Province	Coastal Ranges with altitudes mostly below 2,000 feet and separated from the high Cascade-Sierra Nevada Province by troughs less than 500 feet in altitude.
	Lower California Province	Northern end of the granitic ridge forming the Baja California Peninsula.
	Coast Mountains of British Columbia and Southeast Alaska	Rugged coastal mountains and insular mountains; peaks up to 13,000 feet; glaciers, fjords.
Alaska, and Canada west of Mackenzie River	Southeastern Coast Mountains	See Pacific Mountain System.
	Glaciered Coast	Coastal Mountains up to 20,000 feet in altitude; 5,000 square miles of glaciers; perpetual snow above 2,500 feet.
	South-central Alaska	Mountain ranges and troughs in arcs curving around the Gulf of Alaska; altitudes up to 20,000 feet.
	Alaska Peninsula and Aleutian Islands	Chiefly a chain of volcanoes; altitudes mostly less than 6,000 feet except at the north; bordered on the south by the Aleutian trough, an oceanic trench 20,000 feet deep.
	Yukon Basin	Plateaus and lowlands in the Yukon River basin, including the delta; some mountains and the Tintina and Shakwak Trenches in Yukon Territory; extensive areas of permanently frozen ground.
	Seward Peninsula and Bering Coast Uplands	Rugged plateau, mostly 1,000 to 2,500 feet in altitude; most ground is permanently frozen.
	Arctic Slope	Nearly featureless coastal plain as much as 100 miles wide; ground permanently frozen.
	Brooks and Mackenzie Mountains	Mountain ranges and plateaus along the northeast side of the Yukon Basin.
Hawaii	Hawaii	Oceanic volcanic islands in part bordered by coral reef; altitudes up to 13,000 feet.
Puerto Rico	Puerto Rico	Oceanic island bordered on north by a trench more than 30,000 feet deep; an east-west trending ridge extends the length of the island; long slope to north; shorter, more-precipitous slope to south; shores partly bordered by coral reef.

8

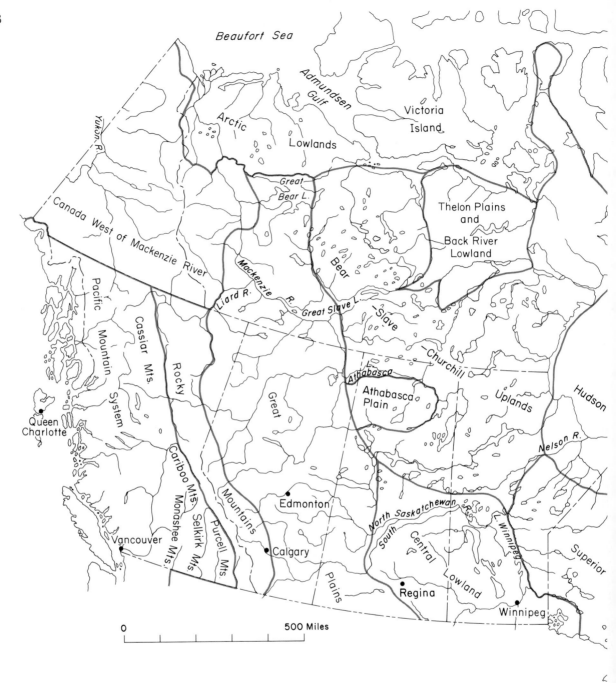

Figure 1.1 (A) Canada, outline map and physiographic provinces.

Arctic

Baffin

Baffin Island

Upland

Lowlands

Foxe Channel

Hudson Strait

Ungava Bay

Labrador

Hudson Bay

Bay Lowland

Belcher I.

Labrador

Highlands

James Bay

Upland

Highlands

St. Lawrence Lowland

Newfoundland

Gulf of St. Lawrence

Laurentian

Quebec

Sable I.

Nova Scotia

Montreal

Halifax

Ottawa

Gulf of Fundy

New England

L. Superior

Toronto

L. Ontario

L. Huron

L. Michigan

Detroit

Windsor L. Erie

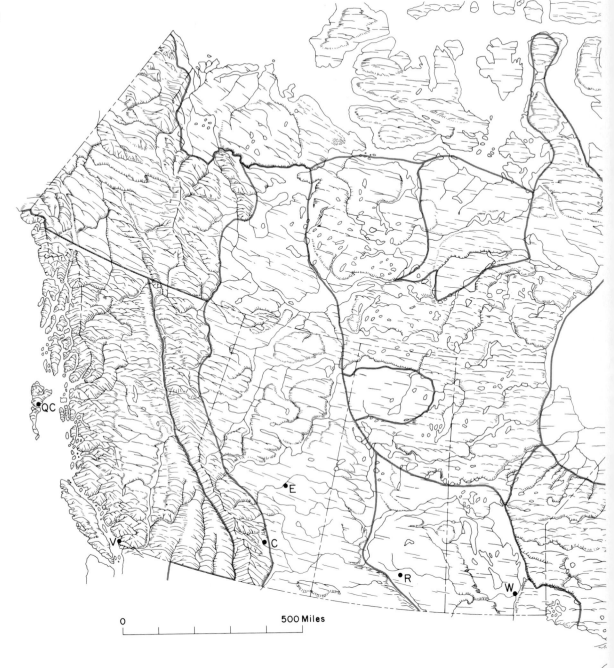

(B) *Canada, landforms and physiographic provinces.*

12

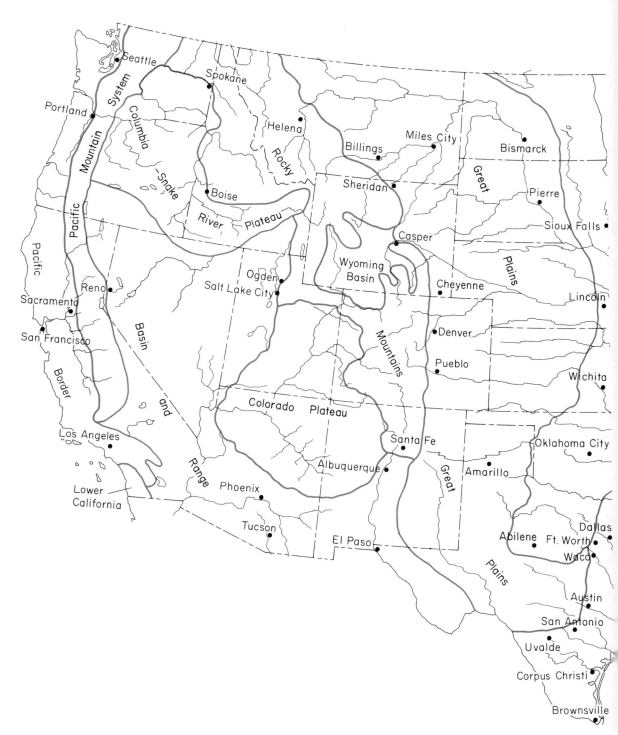

(C) United States, outline map and physiographic provinces.

14

(D) United States, landforms and physiographic provinces.

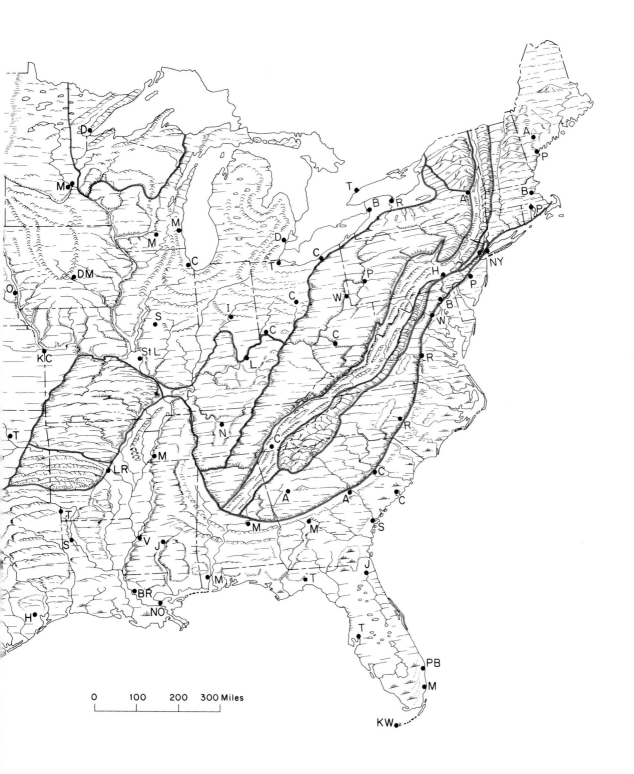

Drawing Maps—The Way To Learn Physiography

Studying physiography involves studying maps, and for many this will mean acquiring new habits and techniques. Gazing at maps is not enough; one must draw them. In the study of physiography, drawing maps serves the same purpose as dissection does in the study of anatomy. The spatial relationships must be drawn to be understood clearly.

Drawing the map of the United States is not difficult if one divides the country into quarters (Fig. 1.2). Drawing the map of North America is not difficult if one first draws the construction lines indicated in Figure 1.3.

Figure 1.1, the map that shows the physiographic provinces, is basic to our study. One must know clearly and exactly the positions of those boundaries, not only relative to state and province boundaries but to each other; such understanding can be acquired by drawing the provinces on an outline map.

There is reason for so much emphasis on this map, for it is *the basic physiographic map.* If this map is thoroughly known, most of the others will be easy to master, for to a considerable degree they are derived from it. The pattern of boundaries of the physiographic provinces reappears prominently in the other physiographic maps. The one to be looked at next is a good example.

Figure 1.2 *To draw a map of the United States, divide the job into fourths along the 100th meridian and 40th parallel. The intersection is near the center of the country, and each quarter can then be completed.*

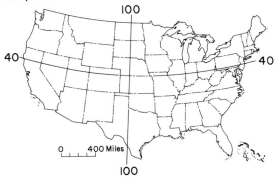

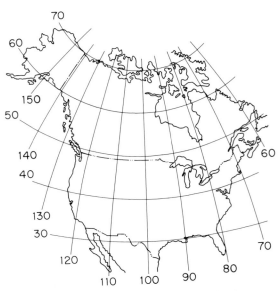

Figure 1.3 *A map of North America can be drawn without much difficulty by building a grid of the parallels and meridians at 10-degree intervals. The map can then be drawn block by block.*

TOPOGRAPHY AND TOPOGRAPHIC MAPS

Topographic maps (see also Appendix A) show the configuration of the land surface by *contour lines,* which represent imaginary lines on the ground, each at a constant elevation above sea level. Figure 1.4, which shows ranges of altitude in the United States and Canada, is a form of contour map. The shoreline is a contour at sea level; it is the zero contour. If sea level were to rise 500 feet, the shoreline would be along the 500-foot contour. This is not entirely fanciful either, because sea level along the Atlantic and Gulf Coastal plains was at about that position in the not very distant geologic past (see Chapter 10). Every contour represents such a level line.

Contours show the slope of the land surface. For example, where the Missouri River joins the Mississippi the altitude is just under 500 feet (Fig. 1.4), but 500 miles west the altitude is 2,000 feet. This 1,500-foot difference in altitude represents an average slope of 3 feet per mile. Two hundred miles farther west, on the Great Plains in Colorado, the altitude is 5,000 feet; in this 200 miles the slope averages 15 feet per mile. From the foot

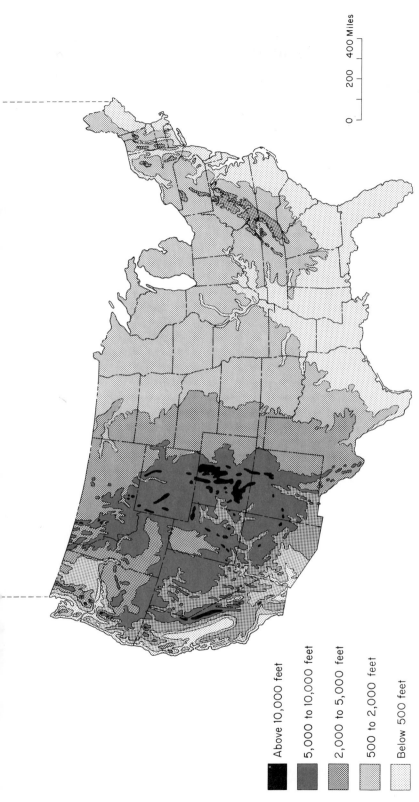

Figure 1.4 *Map showing ranges of altitude in the United States and Canada. For Hawaii, Fig. 20.3; for Puerto Rico, Fig. 20.6.*

Above 10,000 feet

5,000 to 10,000 feet

2,000 to 5,000 feet

500 to 2,000 feet

Below 500 feet

0   200   400 Miles

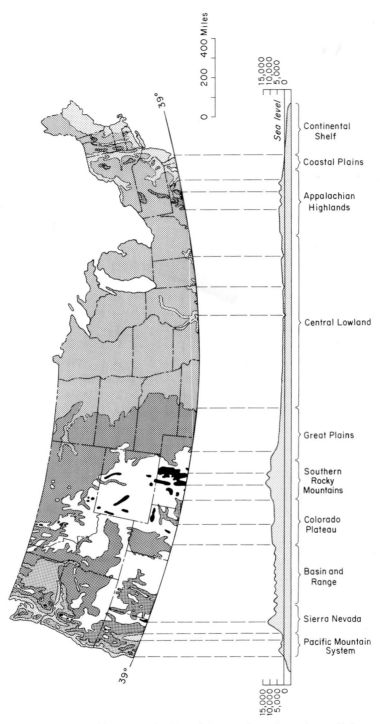

Figure 1.5 *Profile across the United States along the 39th parallel.*

of the Rocky Mountains, say at Denver, to the summit, the rise is about 9,000 feet in 30 miles, which is an average slope of 300 feet per mile.

With contours as widely spaced as those in Figure 1.4, one cannot know whether the actual configuration of the surface is smooth or irregular, but such differences show on more detailed maps that have closely spaced contours.

Figure 1.5 illustrates how slopes determined from contour maps are projected and plotted to scale to obtain a topographic *profile* across an area. The projected contours provide the control points along the profile. Known topographic irregularities that do not have sufficient relief to show between the contours, like some indicated in the Basin and Range Province, can be added by sketching. But the relief on such irregularities must be less than the difference in height of the contours on either side.

Altitudes differ from province to province. Figure 1.4 shows that the Colorado Plateaus are higher than the Columbia Plateau and that these are higher than the Ozark and Appalachian plateaus. To a considerable degree the province boundaries coincide with contours.

The 500-foot contour almost coincides with the inner edge of the Coastal Plain from Virginia to the Rio Grande. The contour has a serrate pattern where the province boundary is smooth because where contours cross valleys they curve upstream, but this need not obscure the general accordance of the contour and the province boundary. This 500-foot contour along the inner boundary of the Coastal Plain is a clear indication that altitudes on the plain are below 500 feet.

The 500-foot contour also outlines the St. Lawrence Valley and the extension of the Valley and Ridge Province along the Hudson River Valley. On the Canadian Shield it outlines the Hudson Bay Lowlands. On the Pacific Coast it outlines the physiographic sections at Puget Trough in Washington, Willamette Trough in Oregon, Central Valley in California, and the Salton Sink at the north end of the depression occupied by the Gulf of California.

The boundary between the Central Lowland and the Great Plains coincides roughly with the 2,000-foot contour in that area. Along the Pacific

coast this contour and the 5,000-foot contour outline the Cascade-Sierra Nevada Province.

These relationships and others that the student can find by comparing the maps illustrate that if the physiographic provinces are known, it is not difficult to draw a topographic map of the continent.

In addition to contours, relief is shown on some maps by means of shading, which gives a pictorial, three-dimensional effect. Some topographic maps are published as relief models. In looking at such models, or at the profile in Figure 1.5, one must remember that the vertical scale is greatly exaggerated, about 40 times in Figure 1.5. The earth's relief is insignificant in comparison with its diameter. The earth, if reduced to the size of a billiard ball, would be equally smooth.

Figure 1.4 has been used to illustrate some principles about topographic maps, but it is hardly representative of the topographic maps prepared and distributed by the Geological Survey of Canada and the United States Geological Survey. The maps are issued as quadrangles bounded by meridians of longitude and parallels of latitude. Some of the quadrangle maps cover one degree, others 15 minutes of latitude and longitude. The most recent and most detailed quadrangle maps cover $7\frac{1}{2}$ minutes of latitude and longitude. These different maps are drawn at different scales.

Scale (Fig. 1.6) can be indicated by a bar or a fraction. The bar scales need no explanation, but the fractional scales are not widely understood. The fraction 1/62,500 means that one unit on the map equals 62,500 of the same units on the ground—for example, 1 inch on the map equals 62,500 inches on the ground. If the fraction were 1/63,360 the scale would be 1 inch equals 1 mile (1 mile equals 63,360 inches). A scale of 1/31,680 means that 1 inch on the map equals 31,680 inches on the ground; that is, 1 inch equals $\frac{1}{2}$ mile. Map scales are commonly referred to as large or small, but this refers to the size of the fraction and not to the area covered.

Parts of numerous topographic quadrangle maps are reproduced in this book to illustrate details of the physiographic provinces. It should be noted that where the land is nearly flat a small

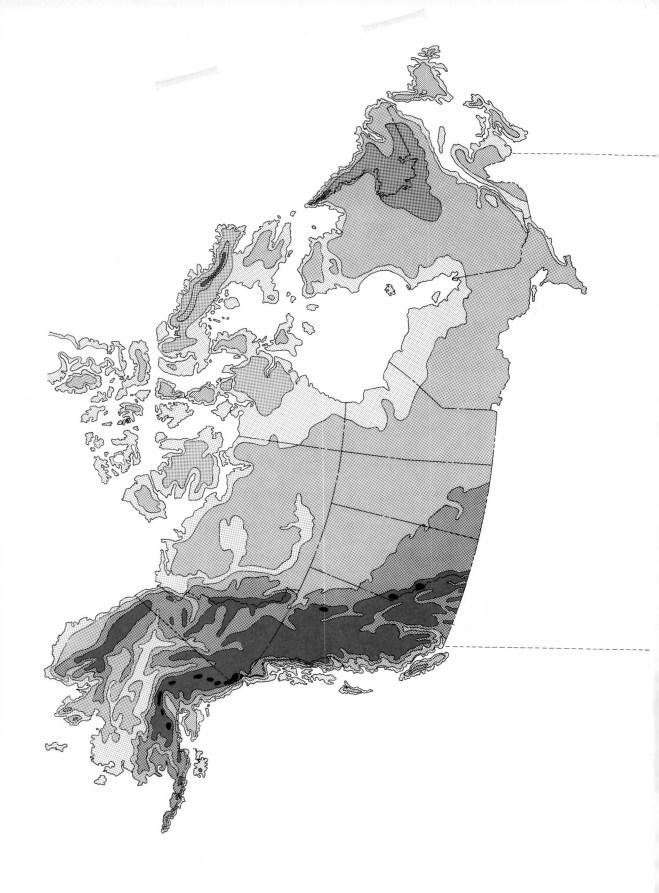

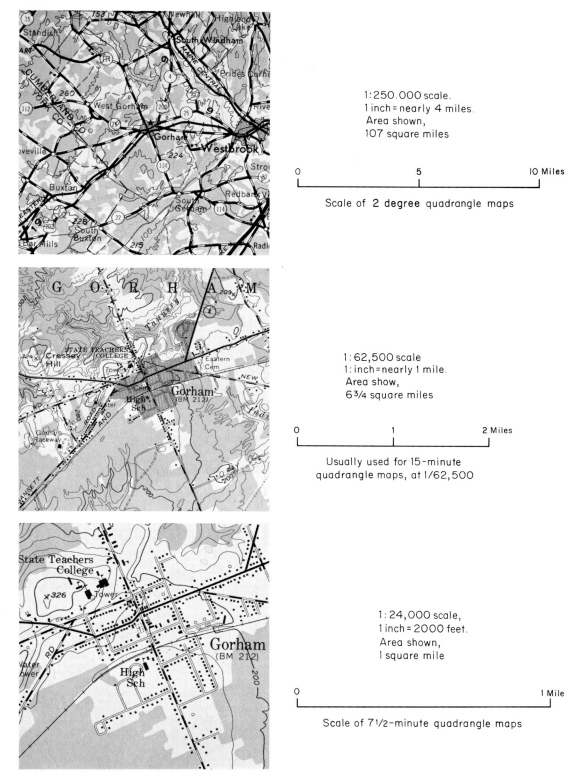

1:250.000 scale.
1 inch = nearly 4 miles.
Area shown,
107 square miles

0   5   10 Miles

Scale of 2 degree quadrangle maps

1:62,500 scale
1:inch = nearly 1 mile.
Area show,
6¾ square miles

0   1   2 Miles

Usually used for 15-minute
quadrangle maps, at 1/62,500

1:24,000 scale,
1 inch = 2000 feet.
Area shown,
1 square mile

0   1 Mile

Scale of 7½-minute quadrangle maps

Figure 1.6 *Three commonly used map scales. Other fractional scales are 1/15,000,000, roughly the scale of Figures 1.1 and 1.2; 1/2,500,000, commonly used for wall maps; 1/500,000, used for state maps; 1/125,000, the scale of 30-minute quadrangle maps; and 1/31,680, one inch equals a half mile.*

contour interval of 5 feet is used, as on contour maps that show parts of the bottom lands along the Mississippi River. In hummocky areas a contour interval of 10 feet may be used, as in Figure 13.5, which shows some glacial features in the Central Lowland. Topographic maps of the eastern mountains and plateaus commonly have a contour interval of 20 feet, as in Figures 13.24 and

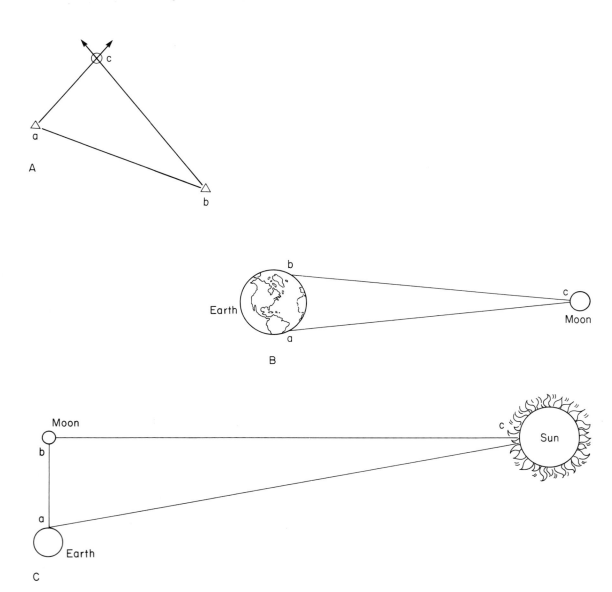

Figure 1.7 *Examples of triangulation, a major tool in surveying and mapping. (A) On the ground, by measuring the distance a to b, the location of c can be determined by knowing the angles CAB and ABC. (B) The distance from the earth to the moon (240,000 miles) can be determined by knowing the distance a to b and determining the angles. (C) When there is a half moon, the distance to the sun (ca. 94,500,000 miles) can be measured by determining the angle BAC (the distance to the moon is known, and angle ABC is known to be a right angle).*

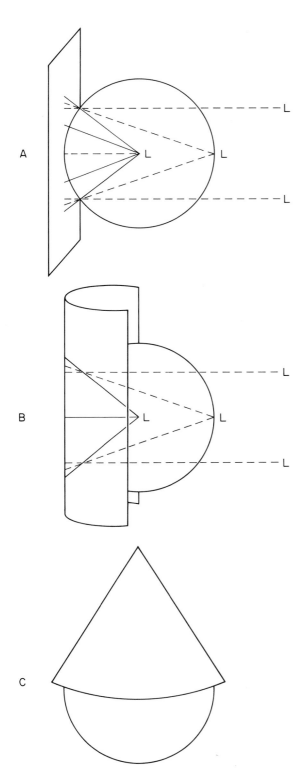

13.19; those showing the more rugged western mountains may have contour intervals of 40 feet (Fig. 18.12), 50 feet (Fig. 14.8), or even more.

In this book the geologic and topographic maps are reproduced in black and white, but the originals are printed in color, and a standard series of colors is used for distinguishing different classes of map features. Place names and such man-made features (cultural features) as roads, buildings, and boundaries are shown in black. Lakes, rivers, canals, glaciers and other water features are shown in blue. Contours are brown. Woodland cover is shown in green, and patterns of green are used to distinguish orchards from natural growth. Important roads and urban areas are shown in red.

Information about available topographic maps can be obtained by request addressed to The Geological Survey of Canada, Ottawa, Canada KIA OE8, or to the United States Geological Survey, Washington, D.C., 20242.

MAKING MAPS

Making topographic or other maps requires making horizontal and vertical measurements of the earth's surface. Theoretically, the methods are simple enough, as they depend only upon plane trigonometry. Distances can be measured by many sophisticated photogrammetric or electronic methods; they can also be measured by tape and by pacing. One of the most used methods is triangulation. Figure 1.7 illustrates how triangulation may be used to locate places in one's back yard or pasture, or to measure the distance to the moon and to the sun.

Figure 1.8 *Principal kinds of map projections. (A) Planar projection is done by projecting onto a plane from a light source at the center of the globe, at the opposite side of the globe, or from infinity. (B) Cylindrical projection is done by projecting onto a cylinder that can be unfolded. (C) Conical projection is done by projecting onto a cone that can be unfolded.*

Vertical measurements, to determine altitude and to draw contours, also can be made by photogrammetric and electronic methods or by triangulation in a vertical plane to measure vertical angles. Vertical measurements can also be made by leveling, including hand leveling. In this method one sights a point level with the eye, moves there and sights the next higher point, and counts the number of times this leveling must be repeated to reach the top of the hill or the top of the stairs.

But no matter how sophisticated the equipment and the measurements, it is not possible to make an accurate flat map of the earth's curved surface. One can approach true accuracy of shape, area, distance, or direction, but it is not possible to achieve all four kinds of accuracy. One must choose the sort of accuracy he most needs and then select the particular kind of map projection. Figure 1.8 illustrates some of the principal kinds of map projection, each of which has particular advantages.

General Physiographic References

Physical Divisions

Atwood, W. W., 1940, The physiographic provinces of North America: Boston, Ginn. Includes map by Raisz showing landforms in the United States.

Bird, J. B., 1972, The natural landscapes of Canada: New York, Wiley.

Bostock, H. S., 1970, Physiographic subdivisions of Canada, *in* Geology and economic minerals of Canada: Geological Survey of Canada, pp. 10–30. Includes map showing physiographic divisions at 1/5,000,000.

Bowman, Isaiah, 1909, Forest physiography: New York, Wiley.

Farb, P., 1964, The face of North America—The natural history of a continent: New York, Harper & Row.

Fenneman, N. M., 1931, Physiography of western United States: New York, McGraw-Hill.

———, 1948, Physiography of eastern United States: New York, McGraw-Hill.

Kroeber, A. L., 1947, Cultural and natural areas of native North America: Berkeley, Univ. California Press.

Loomis, F. B., 1938, Physiography of the United States: New York, Doubleday.

Paterson, J. H., 1970, North America—A Geography of Canada and the United States: Oxford Univ. Press.

Powers, W. E., 1966, Physical geography: New York, Appleton-Century-Crofts.

Salisbury, R. D., and Atwood, W. W., 1908, The interpretation of topographic maps: U.S. Geol. Survey Prof. Paper 60, 84 pp.

Thornbury, W. D., 1965, Regional geomorphology of the United States: New York, Wiley.

Maps

Baird, D. M., 1964, Geology and landforms as illustrated by selected Canadian topographic maps: Geol. Survey of Canada Paper 64-21.

Geological Survey of Canada, 1970, Physiographic regions of Canada: scale 1/5,000,000.

Raisz, E., 1957, Landforms of the United States: scale about 1/4,000,000.

U.S. Geological Survey, 1930, Physical divisions of the United States: scale 1/7,000,000. U.S. Geol. Survey.

U.S. Geological Survey, 1970, The National Atlas of the United States of America: Washington, U.S. Geol. Survey.

U.S. Geological Survey, 1955. Set of 100 topographic maps illustrating specified physiographic features. Washington, U.S. Geol. Survey.

Cartography

Denny, C. S., and others, 1968, A descriptive catalogue of selected aerial photographs of geologic features in the United States: U.S. Geol. Survey Prof. Paper 590.

Dietz, C. H., and Adams, O. S., 1945, Elements of map projection: U.S. Coast and Geodetic Survey Spec. Pub. 68, 226 pp.

Greenhood, D., 1964, Mapping: Univ. Chicago Press.

Raisz, E., 1962, Principles of cartography: New York, McGraw-Hill.

Ray, R. G., 1960, Aerial photographs in geologic interpretation and mapping: U.S. Geol. Survey Prof. Paper 373.

Geology controls topography, water supply, soils, vegetation, and land use. This vertical aerial view of part of the Colorado Plateau shows nearly horizontal formations eroded to form mesas and badlands; in the upper left, the same formations dip steeply to form hogbacks. The flat mesa tops are suitable for grazing; the badlands are practically without vegetation. Settlement and farmed lands are restricted to the alluvial flood plain. [From U.S.G.S.]

2

STRUCTURAL FRAMEWORK OF THE PROVINCES

Bedrock Geology

The structural framework of each physiographic province is determined by its bedrock geology, and the landforms of one province differ from those of another mainly because of the differences in the geologic structures that control them. A map of the bedrock geology of the United States and part of Canada is shown in Figure 2.1. The general geologic structure and resulting landforms are illustrated in Figure 2.2.

Although most people find geologic maps to be pretty much a hodge-podge of color patterns and not very meaningful, one does not have to be a geologist to read a great deal from them. We need first to distinguish the three principal types of rocks—sedimentary, igneous, and metamorphic—and to distinguish between rocks and minerals. A mineral has a definite chemical composition and a definite molecular structure; for these reasons, it also has a well-defined crystal shape, orderly planes of parting or fracturing, and a particular density, hardness, and color. Rocks are mixtures of minerals.

SEDIMENTARY ROCKS

Many rocks are consolidated sediments. If we were to visit the outcrops of the geological formations on the Coastal Plain, we would find that the Cretaceous formations (K in Fig. 2.1) overlie the formations on the landward side but extend under the Tertiary formations (T) that crop out on the seaward side. The Tertiary formations overlie the Cretaceous, but they extend seaward under the Quaternary (Q).

These formations were deposited mostly as nearshore marine sediments, although some nonmarine sediments were deposited in brackish-water or freshwater environments, such as estuaries or deltas. They were derived by erosion of older rocks inland from the Coastal Plain. The youngest strata, or layers, are at the top. From the superposition of strata it is ascertained that the Cretaceous formations are younger than those on the landward side; the Tertiary are still younger, and the Quaternary are the youngest. The geologic time table, derived in just this manner, by observing relationships between rock formations all over the world, is given in Table 2.1. Learning this time table is no more difficult than learning the seasons and months of the year. A year is divided into 4 seasons; geologic time is divided into 4 *eras*. A year is further divided into 12 months; geologic time, after the Precambrian, is divided into 12 *periods*. The periods are divided into *epochs*, but only those of the Cenozoic need concern us (Table 2.2).

The original sediments of the Coastal Plain Province—mud and sand, together with their

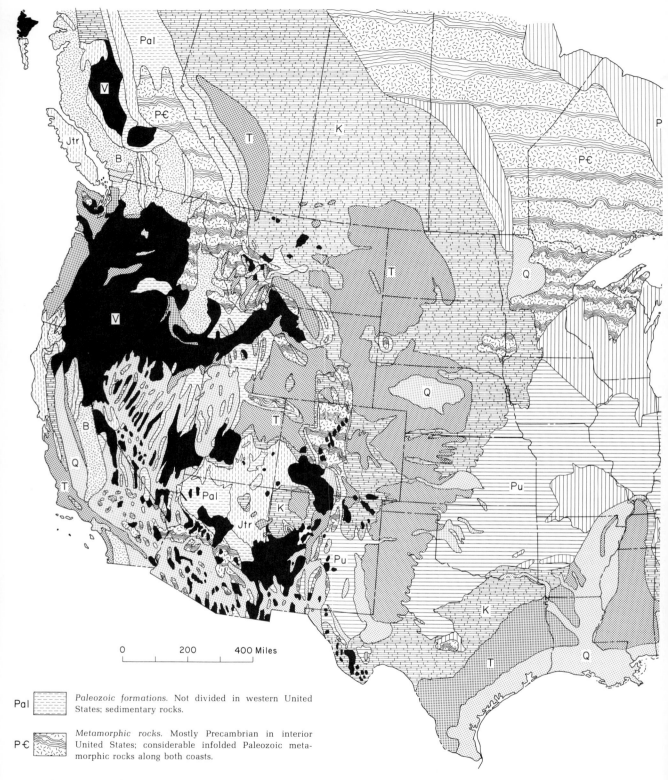

Pal ░░░   *Paleozoic formations.* Not divided in western United States; sedimentary rocks.

P€ ▒▒▒   *Metamorphic rocks.* Mostly Precambrian in interior United States; considerable infolded Paleozoic metamorphic rocks along both coasts.

Figure 2.1   *Bedrock geology of the United States and part of Canada. (After U.S.G.S.)*

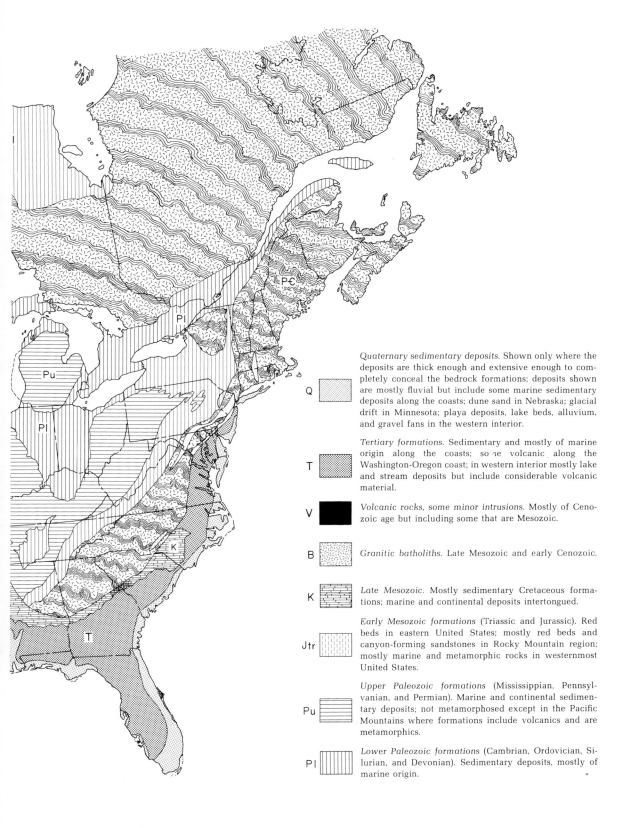

PÉ

Pl

Pu

Pl

K

T

Q — *Quaternary sedimentary deposits.* Shown only where the deposits are thick enough and extensive enough to completely conceal the bedrock formations; deposits shown are mostly fluvial but include some marine sedimentary deposits along the coasts; dune sand in Nebraska; glacial drift in Minnesota; playa deposits, lake beds, alluvium, and gravel fans in the western interior.

T — *Tertiary formations.* Sedimentary and mostly of marine origin along the coasts; some volcanic along the Washington-Oregon coast; in western interior mostly lake and stream deposits but include considerable volcanic material.

V — *Volcanic rocks, some minor intrusions.* Mostly of Cenozoic age but including some that are Mesozoic.

B — *Granitic batholiths.* Late Mesozoic and early Cenozoic.

K — *Late Mesozoic.* Mostly sedimentary Cretaceous formations; marine and continental deposits intertongued.

Jtr — *Early Mesozoic formations* (Triassic and Jurassic). Red beds in eastern United States; mostly red beds and canyon-forming sandstones in Rocky Mountain region; mostly marine and metamorphic rocks in westernmost United States.

Pu — *Upper Paleozoic formations* (Mississippian, Pennsylvanian, and Permian). Marine and continental sedimentary deposits; not metamorphosed except in the Pacific Mountains where formations include volcanics and are metamorphics.

Pl — *Lower Paleozoic formations* (Cambrian, Ordovician, Silurian, and Devonian). Sedimentary deposits, mostly of marine origin.

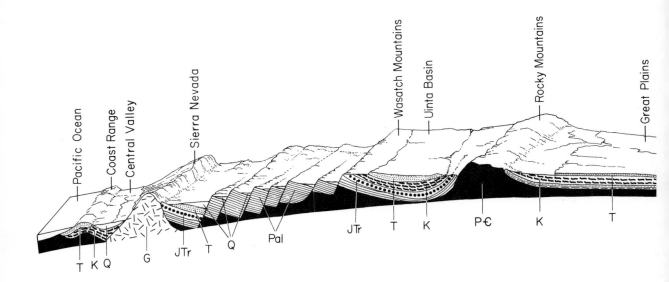

Figure 2.2 *Geologic cross section of the United States, showing structural control of the major topographic features. Q, Quaternary; T, Tertiary; K, Cretaceous; JTr, Jurassic and Triassic; Pu,*

Table 2.1

Major Divisions of Geologic History

Era	Period	Estimated Ages of Time Boundaries in Millions of Years
Cenozoic (Age of mammals)	Quaternary (Age of man)	
		2.5–3
	Tertiary	
		65
Mesozoic (Age of reptiles, notably the dinosaurs; first appearance of birds)	Cretaceous	
		135
	Jurassic	
		180
	Triassic	
		225
Paleozoic (Invertebrate forms abundant and varied; first appearance of fishes, amphibians, and land plants)	Permian	
		270
	Pennsylvanian	
		310
	Mississippian	
		350
	Devonian	
		400
	Silurian	
		440
	Ordovician	
		500
	Cambrian	
		600
Precambrian (Primitive life forms)		Age of the earth 4,600

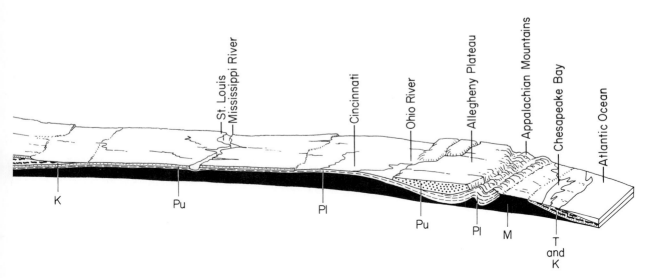

upper Paleozoic; Pl, lower Paleozoic; Pal, Paleozoic undivided; M, metamorphic rocks, mostly Precambrian; G, granite.

contained sea shells—became firm rocks by compaction and cementation. Shells became fossils. Gravels consolidated into *conglomerates;* sands consolidated into *sandstones;* fine-grained muds consolidated into *shales;* the sediments composed of intermediate-size grains became *siltstones, shaly sandstones,* or *sandy shales.* Marls, or calcareous oozes (composed of calcium carbonate), consolidated largely into impure *limestones* (limestone containing much magnesium is called *dolomite*). In addition there are deposits of salts, such as gypsum (calcium sulfate) and rock salt (sodium chloride). Peat and related swamp deposits compacted and altered to *lignite* and then to *coal.* All these are now sedimentary rocks; they were once squishy sediments.

These different kinds of sediments grade laterally into each other. For example, sands deposited near shore grade into muds deposited offshore, and the muds in turn grade into marls deposited in very quiet water. The different kinds of deposits are referred to as *facies,* and each contains remains of the fauna or flora peculiar to the particular environment and time.

Sediment transported by running water, either in suspension or by rolling along the bottom (e.g.,

sand, mud), is referred to as *clastic.* Other sediments are *precipitates,* and were formed by precipitation (e.g., rock salt, limestone). Still other sediments are *organic residues* (e.g., peat).

Fragmental material deposited as volcanic ash produced by the explosive eruption of volcanoes is *pyroclastic.* During violent eruptions, volcanoes eject particles that vary considerably in size: coarse materials are deposited in a cone around the orifice, and the finer materials are carried

Table 2.2

Epochs of the Tertiary and Quaternary Periods

Period	Epoch	Estimated Ages of the Time Boundaries in Millions of Years
Quaternary	Holocene	
	Pleistocene	
		2.5–3
	Pliocene	
		11
	Miocene	
		25
Tertiary	Oligocene	
		40
	Eocene	
		60
	Paleocene	
		65

downwind. Some of these materials are nonvolcanic rocks fragmented by the explosion; others are globules formed from droplets of lava that congealed in the air while falling. Coarse globules of lava are called *bombs,* or *lapilli;* coarse nonvolcanic rock fragments form *volcanic breccia,* or *agglomerate.* When the fine materials, called volcanic ash, become consolidated, they form what is known as *tuff.* Sedimentary deposits of volcanic origin also are distributed in orderly facies.

At times deposition of the Coastal Plain sediments would be interrupted. An unusual storm, for example, may erode layers already deposited in quiet water, and subsequently deposited beds then rest *unconformably* upon the older. Such discontinuities in the sedimentary sequence may represent brief intervals of time, or if there has been earth movement and deep erosion, the discontinuity may represent considerable time, perhaps an entire period. For example, in northern North Carolina and Virginia, the landward edges of the Cretaceous formations were eroded before the Tertiary beds were deposited, and the Cretaceous formations there do not crop out at the surface, but are buried under the Tertiary formations, which extend across the Cretaceous and overlap onto the much older rocks at the Fall Line (Fig. 2.1).

Figure 2.3 illustrates some different kinds of unconformities. Shown in part A is the kind of unconformity that is found between the Quaternary and Tertiary along the Atlantic Coastal Plain (see Fig. 2.1). Part B shows the kind of unconformity that is found at the base of the Quaternary deposits along the Mississippi Embayment. Part C shows the kind of unconformity that can be seen at the base of the Tertiary on the Great Plains. In the north the Tertiary rests on Cretaceous formations; in the south the Tertiary overlaps the Cretaceous and extends onto the upper Paleozoic. Part D shows the unconformity at the base of the Cretaceous at the southwest end of the Appalachian Highlands, where the folded metamorphic and lower Paleozoic formations plunge southwestward under the Coastal Plain.

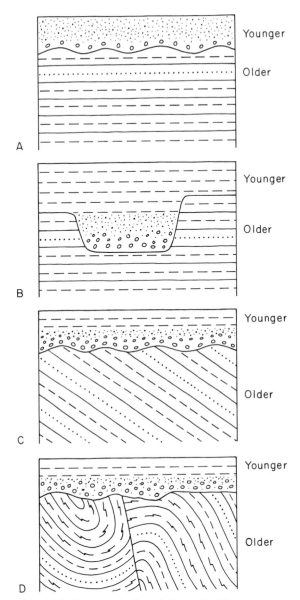

Figure 2.3 *Four examples of discontinuities (unconformities) in sedimentary successions. (A) Deposition of the older formation ended, and its uppermost beds were slightly eroded before becoming buried by the younger formation. (B) Deposition of the older formation ended, and its upper beds were deeply eroded before the younger formation was deposited. (C) Deposition of the older formation ended, and the formation was tilted and eroded before the younger formation was deposited. (D) The older formation was severely folded before the younger formation was deposited.*

During Cretaceous time the edge of the Atlantic was about at the inner boundary of the Cretaceous deposits. The shore gradually shifted seaward and at the beginning of Tertiary time stood about along the boundary between the Cretaceous and Tertiary formations. The shore continued its shift seaward and by Quaternary time stood at the inner edge of the deposits mapped as Quaternary, except in the Mississippi embayment, where there are river deposits called *alluvium*. This retreat of the ocean is shown in Figure 10.7; in a different way the geologic map shows the growth of this part of the United States during approximately the last 100 million years.

Whereas the Coastal Plain deposits are largely marine, other sedimentary deposits are entirely *nonmarine*—for example, the Tertiary formations on the Great Plains. The sediments that formed these deposits were derived by erosion of the Rocky Mountains, which formed as a result of uplift in late Cretaceous and early Tertiary time. These sediments, washed from the mountains onto the plains, are mostly stream, or *fluviatile*, deposits.

Another kind of nonmarine sedimentary deposit is exemplified by the Tertiary and Quaternary fills in the western basins, like those in the Basin and Range Province. In the central part of the basins are lake, or *lacustrine*, deposits, laid down in ancient ephemeral lakes. As these basins are situated in what are now desert or near-desert environments, the former lakes are bare mud flats, except in wet seasons; they are playas. Fluviatile deposits are represented by gravel fans that spread basinward from the foot of the adjoining mountains. These gravel deposits grade laterally into the muds of the playas; gradational sandy belts between the fans and playas supply sand that winds collect into dunes.

Many of the basins contain brines, natural solutions of salts concentrated by evaporation. Upon evaporation, these brines form chemical precipitates, called *evaporites*, which are much like those that form in an evaporating dish in a chemical laboratory, and consist of an outer carbonate zone, an intermediate sulfate zone, and a central chloride zone (Fig. 2.4). The natural

A

B

Figure 2.4 *Zonation of the salts and history of a salt pan. The example could be in Death Valley, California, or the Great Salt Lake desert, Utah. As a brine is evaporated, the least-soluble salts precipitate first (A). These are mostly calcium and magnesium carbonates (c). As the brine evaporates further and the salinity continues to increase, sodium and potassium sulfates are deposited (s). Finally, when maximum salinity is reached, sodium and potassium chlorides and magnesium sulfate are deposited in the interior (h). Both in Death Valley and the Great Salt Lake desert, while the salts were being deposited, the pans were tilted, and the salts are crowded against one side of the valley (B).*

basins in which they form differ from the chemist's evaporating dish only in size; the evaporating dish covers a few square inches, whereas the natural basins cover scores or hundreds of square miles.

Other and older sedimentary deposits are the Mesozoic formations on the Colorado Plateau. Still older ones are the Paleozoic formations in the Valley and Ridge Province and westward to the Great Plains. As can be seen in Figure 2.2 these Paleozoic formations extend under the

Cretaceous and Tertiary formations on the Great Plains and reappear where they are turned up against the uplifted Rocky Mountains.

IGNEOUS ROCKS

Igneous rocks were once molten, but subsequently froze and crystallized to become rock, though it must be remembered that this freezing temperature is hot as Hell, 600° to more than 1,000°C. Some igneous rocks occur as *extrusions* at the surface, like lavas. Volcanic ash, previously referred to, includes material that once was molten, but is generally considered with the sedimentary rocks because of the mode of formation.

Other igneous rocks occur as *intrusions*, masses of molten rock that formed below the surface. Intrusions, in large part at least, were physically injected into the surrounding rocks. Most granites are intrusions. Where erosion has removed the overlying rocks, intrusions have become exposed at the surface. The Columbia Plateau and the Cascade Province are vast fields of extrusive rocks; central Idaho, the Sierra Nevada, and the Coast Mountains of British Columbia and southern Alaska consist largely of intrusive granitic rocks (Fig. 2.1). Igneous rocks also are extensive in the Southern Rocky Mountains, Colorado Plateau, Basin and Range Province, and Alaska. The Hawaiian Islands are wholly of volcanic origin.

Igneous rocks are of many kinds, depending on the composition of the original molten mass, or *magma*, the pressures and temperatures that caused the igneous activity, and the physical conditions that prevailed where the magma froze. Magmas that cool rapidly may freeze to form a glass, such as *obsidian*. If a magma cools slowly, minerals grow large enough to be seen with the naked eye, and the resulting crystalline rock may have a texture like that of granite. Still other rocks, known as *porphyries*, also consist of large crystals in a matrix of fine-grained ones.

The magmas, and the rocks developed from them, generally contain more than 45 percent silica (SiO_2); some igneous rocks contain as much as 75 percent silica. The chief other constituents are iron, aluminum, magnesium, calcium, sodium, and potassium; in fact, these eight elements make up 99 percent of the earth's crust:

O, 47%   Al, 8%   Ca, 3.5%   K, 2.5%
Si, 28%   Fe, 5%   Na, 3%   Mg, 2%

In general, the igneous rocks low in silica are dark—for example, *gabbro* and its eruptive equivalents *basalt* and *diabase*. The lavas of the Columbia Plateau are largely basalt. Igneous rocks containing much silica tend to be light in color, like granite and its eruptive equivalent *rhyolite*.

As a magma cools, the minerals that form crystallize in a definite order that reflects their relative solubilities under the particular temperature and pressure. The general sequence in which the more common rock-forming minerals crystallize is shown in Table 2.3. This sequence illustrates several related features.

1. The minerals that form early contain less silica than those that form late.

2. The early-forming, dark minerals generally occur with the early-forming, light ones; the late-forming, dark minerals generally occur with the late-forming, light ones.

3. The dark igneous rocks, like basalt and gabbro, are composed of early-forming minerals. The light igneous rocks, like rhyolite and granite, are composed of late-forming minerals.

4. The susceptibility of these minerals to weathering and to soil formation is in the same order as the sequence of crystallization (see p. 35).

With Table 2.3 in mind one can infer a lot about the composition of the large granitic masses shown on the geologic map (B in Fig. 2.1). They are composed principally of the light minerals, whereas the basaltic lavas of the Columbia Plateau are composed chiefly of dark minerals.

Table 2.3

The Common Rock-forming Silicate Minerals and their Compositions. The minerals are arranged in their general order of crystallization from molten magmas, their susceptibility to weathering, and their occurrence in various rock types.

Sequence of Crystallization	Susceptibility to Weathering	Dark Minerals	Light Minerals	Rock Types	
				Volcanic (fine-grained or glassy)	Intrusive (coarsely crystalline)
Early	Least resistant	Olivine $(Mg,Fe)_2SiO_4$	Calcic plagioclase $CaAl_2Si_2O_8$	Basalt (Mostly dark minerals)	Gabbro
		Augite $Ca(Mg,Fe,Al)(Al,Si)_2O_6$	Calcic plagioclase with sodium		
			Sodic plagioclase with calcium	Andesite	Diorite
		Hornblende $(Ca,Na,Fe,Mg,Al)_7(Al,Si)_8O_{22}(OH)_2$	Sodic plagioclase $NaAlSi_3O_8$	Latite	Monzonite
		Biotite (dark mica) $K(Mg,Fe)_3(Al,Si_3)O_{10}(OH,F)_2$	Potash feldspar $KAlSi_3O_8$		
			Muscovite (white mica) $KAl_2(Al,Si_3)O_{10}(OH,F)_2$	Rhyolite (Mostly light minerals)	Granite
Late	Most resistant		Quartz SiO_2		

GRANITE AND BASALT. Granite and basalt are the most common kinds of igneous rocks. Most granites are the result of older rocks being melted and the magma being intruded into another part of the crust (p. 38); some granites, however, have formed as a result of metamorphism (p. 38).

The term "granite" is applied to many kinds of rock used for facing stone on large buildings and for monuments, curbstones, paving blocks, riprap, road materials, ballast, and even poultry grits. A few kinds of granite, especially the very coarse-grained forms (*pegmatite*), are useful as a source of certain kinds of minerals.

Different kinds of granites are distinguished by their mineral composition and texture. True granite consists of quartz and alkali feldspar, especially potash feldspar (orthoclase). Mica (biotite or muscovite) is usually present along with hornblende (see Table 2.3).

Granitic rocks composed chiefly of sodic-calcic feldspar and with little or no potash feldspar are known as diorite (Table 2.3). If quartz is present, the rock is known as quartz diorite. Instead of mica, diorite generally contains hornblende or augite (Table 2.3) and magnetite (magnetic iron oxide, Fe_3O_4).

Most of the volcanic rocks shown in Figure 2.1 are basalt. The Columbia and Fraser plateaus and the Hawaiian Islands are almost entirely basalt. Basalt also occurs in the Triassic formations (JTr on Fig. 2.1) of the Piedmont Province.

Basalt, the least siliceous of the common igneous rocks, is composed chiefly of dark minerals (Table 2.3)—silicates of iron and magnesium (olivine and augite) and oxides of iron (magnetite and hematite). The major light mineral in basalt is plagioclase feldspar. Basalts are remarkably uniform in composition, both mineralogically and chemically.

The contrast in the average chemical compositions of granite, diorite, and basalt is given in Table 2.4.

STRUCTURAL FORMS OF IGNEOUS ROCKS. Volcanoes are the most familiar examples of igneous activity. They may be of the central type, which produces volcanic cones (Figs. 2.5,C), or of the

Table 2.4

Differences in Average Compositions (in percent) of Granite, Diorite, and Basalt. (The "other" 3.5 percent in basalt includes 1.5 percent TiO_2 and 1.5 percent H_2O, the latter chemically combined in the minerals.)

	Granite	Diorite	Basalt
SiO_2	70	58	49
Al_2O_3	15	16.5	16
Fe_2O_3	1.5	3	5.5
FeO	1.5	4.5	6.5
CaO	2.25	6.75	9
MgO	1.0	4	6
K_2O	4.0	2	1.5
Na_2O	3.25	3.5	3
Other	1.5	1.75	3.5

fissure type, which produces lava ridges (Fig. 2.5,D). Erosion of the central type may expose a basaltic plug (*volcanic neck*), like Devils Tower in Wyoming (Fig. 2.5,A), or like some on the Colorado Plateau (Fig. 15.7). Erosion of the fissure type may expose vertical sheets, or *dikes*, of the igneous rock (Fig. 2.5,B). Basaltic necks and dikes are well exposed on the Colorado Plateau, but are scarce on the Columbia Plateau because erosion is so minimal that few have been exposed.

Basaltic magmas are fluid enough so that the lavas may spread for miles in flows only 10 to 15 feet thick. Quiet eruptions of basaltic lava form broad low cones, but these eruptions are interrupted by explosive ones that produce steep-sided cinder cones. The cinders are like the porous cinders, or clinker, from a blast furnace—glassy rock frothed by air or gas bubbles. Some cinders are as porous as cotton and nearly as light (pumice).

Highly explosive eruptions, which produce fragments rather than lavas, throw out quantities of hot, finely comminuted rock together with liquid magma that becomes spun out in fine threads that quickly freeze to glass. These fall to the ground as fine threads, like cotton fibers, or as dust-size particles to form beds of *volcanic ash* or *tuff*. The term "ash" is misleading, because

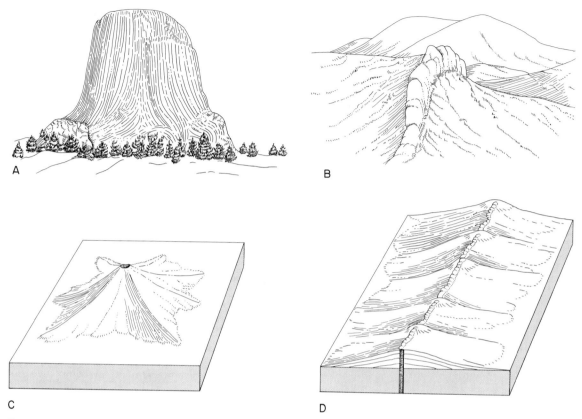

Figure 2.5 *Some topographic forms that express different kinds of volcanic structures. (A) Devils Tower, Wyoming, a volcanic neck. (B) Dike forming a rock wall that extends across the countryside, Spanish Peaks area, Colorado. (C) Central type volcano. (D) Fissure type volcano.*

volcanic ash is not the waste product of combustion, which is the usual sense in which the word is used. Crater Lake (Fig. 18.15) in the Cascade Range is the product of an explosive eruption that produced an extensive ash deposit; the 1912 eruption of Mount Katmai in Alaska (p. 627) is another recent and well-documented example of this kind of eruption.

In places a crust may form over a lava flow and the underlying liquid drain out to leave a tunnel or cave in the lava. The surface of the lava may be slabby if the crust is broken. It may be smooth and wavy (*pahoehoe type*) or rough and cindery (*aa type*). Some lavas on the Columbia Plateau flowed into lakes and developed rounded structures about the size and shape of pillows, and are called *pillow lavas*; but most flowed on

the land and, as they cooled, developed columnar jointing, a highly characteristic and physiographically important feature of basaltic lavas.

The columns are generally 4- to 6-sided, 18 to 36 inches in diameter, and many feet long. They developed at right angles to the cooling surface. In a lava flow they are vertical, with a main set extending downward from the top of the flow and a smaller set extending upward from the base (Fig. 2.6,A). In a dike they are horizontal and in two sets that meet in the middle (Fig. 2.6,B). In a volcanic neck they are radial in ground plan, and they curve upward in the interior of the neck (Fig. 2.6,C). These patterns of jointing provide an important structural control for the landforms developed from basaltic rocks. The lava flows tend to form cliffs as the columnar blocks spall

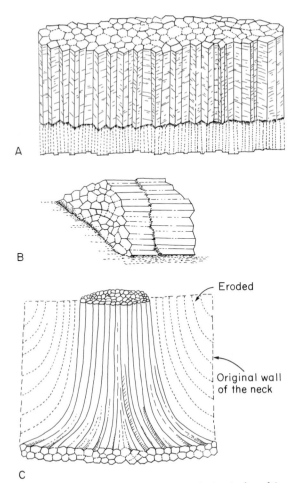

A

B

Eroded

Original wall
of the neck

C

Figure 2.6 *Structure of columnar jointing in basaltic lava flows (A), dikes (B), and volcanic necks (C). The surfaces of flows and the tops of necks generally are cindery (scoriaceous) and lack columnar joints. Along the walls of dikes and necks there is a narrow selvage of platy joints parallel to the walls. These layers have been omitted in order to emphasize the columns.*

away. Dikes generally form walls with vertical sides (Fig. 2.5,B). Volcanic necks narrow upward because of the curvature of the joints (Fig. 2.5,A).

Until basaltic lavas are softened by weathering and by an overgrowth of vegetation, they form a somber, forbidding terrain. Washington Irving, in his account of the travels of Captain Bonneville, described fresh lava surfaces in the Snake River Plain as ground "where nothing meets the eye but a desolate and awful waste; where no grass grows nor water runs, and where nothing is to be seen but lava." In warm humid areas like Hawaii, lava flows may become overgrown with vegetation in 50 years, but on the Columbia Plateau, and in other semiarid provinces, the lavas remain barren for hundreds of years.

Intrusive rocks also may assume a variety of forms, depending on the structure of the surrounding rocks, the viscosity of the magma, and the rate of its injection. The feeders to volcanoes are intrusions, like the cylindrical necks of central-type volcanoes and the dikes of fissure-type volcanoes.

An intrusion being squeezed upward may encounter the base of a strong formation, and if unable to penetrate it, may spread laterally along the base of the layer. Intrusive sheets of more or less uniform thickness are termed *sills;* highly bulged ones that dome the overlying rocks are termed *laccoliths.* Viscous magmas, or those injected rapidly, generally form laccoliths; fluid magmas, or those injected slowly, form sills.

Another common form of intrusion, roughly cylindrical but much larger than a volcanic neck, is referred to as a *stock.* Stocks may be a mile or several miles in diameter. Many stocks—probably most—were formed by magmas that penetrated the surrounding rocks and domed them upward (Fig. 15.11), just as a nail punched into a book will penetrate many pages and dome those that it does not penetrate.

The tremendous bodies of granite in central Idaho, the Sierra Nevada, and the Coast Ranges of Canada and southeastern Alaska cover thousands of square miles and are called *batholiths.* The three-dimensional form of these vast intrusions is poorly known, and how they became emplaced is a matter of much speculation. They appear to be a complex of stocks.

METAMORPHIC ROCKS

The Piedmont Province (Fig. 2.1) consists largely of the third major class of rocks—*metamorphic rocks.* These originally were sedimentary or igneous rocks, but have been subjected to pressures and temperatures so great that

not only have the constituent minerals been recrystallized to form new kinds but the new minerals have been arranged in bands or layers—a
textural pattern called *foliation*. These rocks are
extensively exposed in the Piedmont Province,
New England, the Maritime Provinces, Newfoundland, and the Canadian Shield, in central
Texas, in the cores of several of the mountain
uplifts in the Rocky Mountain region and Alaska,
and in the bottom of Grand Canyon. Rocks of
Precambrian age generally are highly metamorphosed; they constitute the basement complex
underlying the sedimentary rocks of Paleozoic,
Mesozoic, and Cenozoic age (Fig. 2.2).

Metamorphic equivalents of some of the rocks
already described are listed below.

Original Rock	Metamorphic Equivalent
sandstone	quartzite
shale	slate, phyllite, schist
limestone	marble
basalt	greenstone
granite	gneiss
lignite	bituminous coal, anthracite, graphite

Folding and Faulting

Although rocks are hard and brittle in masses of
the size that might be quarried, the same rock
in a slab miles thick and covering the area of a
state would bend if a corner could be raised, just
as a large sheet of glass can be bent without
breaking. Rocks are pliable when acted upon in
large masses and over long periods of time. The
bending of rocks is called *folding*. If folding progresses fast enough, or far enough, breaks occur;
the resulting fractures are called *faults*. Upfolds
are called *anticlines;* downfolds are called *synclines* (Fig. 2.7).

The degree of folding in an area is measured
by the number and spacing of the anticlines and
synclines and by the steepness, or dip, of their
flanks (Fig. 2.8). Strata may be gently dipping,
steeply dipping, vertical, or even overturned (Fig.
2.8,B).

The rock formations in all the physiographic
provinces are, to some degree, folded and faulted.
Folding is well illustrated in the Valley and Ridge
Province. In this province the rock formations,
mostly of Lower Paleozoic age, are strongly
folded, and south of New York State these folded
rocks form elongate fold mountains paralleling
the trend of the province. Immediately to the east
are the folded, faulted, and metamorphosed rocks
of the Blue Ridge, Piedmont, and New England
provinces. West of the folded belt is a broad
structural basin containing Upper Paleozoic formations that are folded parallel to those of the
Valley and Ridge Province, but not nearly so
intensely. The intensity of the structural deformation decreases westward; rock formations in
the eastern provinces are more deformed than
those in the Valley and Ridge, and the formations
in the Valley and Ridge are more deformed than
those in the Appalachian Plateaus. Moreover, the
three quite different structural belts, and the in-

Figure 2.7 *Two kinds of folding. (A) Folding due to
horizontal compression, as if by a piston shoving
against a set of beds contained in a box. (B) Folding
due to vertically directed forces.*

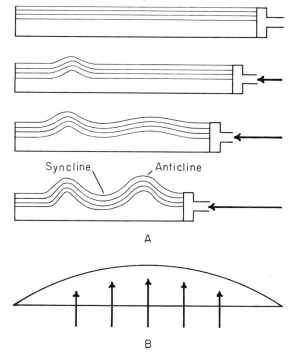

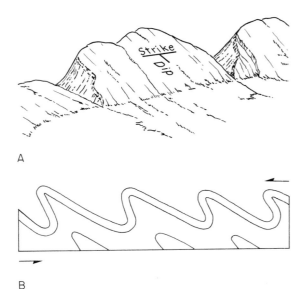

A

B

Figure 2.8 (A) Dip, measured in degrees from the horizontal, indicates the steepest slope of a tilted stratum; strike of a bed refers to its trend at the intersection with a horizontal surface. Dip and strike are at right angles to one another. (B) Asymmetrical folding. One flank is gently dipping, the other steep. In this example the steep flank is overturned.

dividual structures within them, are overlapped and cut off at the south by the Cretaceous and younger formations in Alabama (Fig. 2.1). The geologic map shows the relative age of these rocks and of the major structures—the structural features of the Appalachian Highlands formed before the Cretaceous formations were deposited. From other evidence we know that the principal structural features of the Appalachians formed at the end of the Paleozoic.

The structural features that control mountains like the Appalachians are partly regional in extent and partly local. Regions that have been elevated, such as the Rocky Mountain region and the adjoining Colorado Plateau and High Plains (Fig. 2.2), are called *geanticlines*. Regions that are *linearly* downfolded below sea level are called *geosynclines*. The Gulf of Mexico, the Aleutian Trench, and the Puerto Rico Trench are present-day examples. The Mediterranean Sea is another. The more localized earth movements produce the folds and faults within the geanticline and geosyncline.

In some places, such as along the Appalachians, the folding of the rocks progresses far beyond mere wrinkling. The rocks may be strongly folded and the folds asymmetrical (Fig. 2.8). The folding may be accompanied by fracturing—that is, by faulting. Faults are classed as *normal* faults, *tear* faults, and *thrust* faults, depending on the relationship between the blocks on opposite sides of the plane of fracture (Fig. 2.9 and 2.10). On a much smaller scale, closely spaced fractures along which there has been little or no slippage are known as *joints*.

The displacements due to folding and to faulting may be measurable in scores of miles, although in most individual folds and faults the displacements are moderate and are measurable in hundreds or thousands of feet. The displacements result from intermittent small movements, as can be seen along the active San Andreas fault in California.

Movement on this fault caused the great earthquake in California in April, 1906. The displacement was almost entirely horizontal, the western block moving northward with respect to the eastern block, as is clearly shown by offsets in roads, fences, orchards, and natural features. The maximum displacement was about 20 feet. Older features along the fault, however, are displaced much more than that; the older the fea-

Figure 2.9 (A) Normal fault with mostly vertical movement; the fault plane dips toward the downthrown block (B) Tear fault with mostly horizontal movement. (C) Reverse fault plane dips toward the upthrown block, as if the upthrown block had been pushed onto the downthrown block.

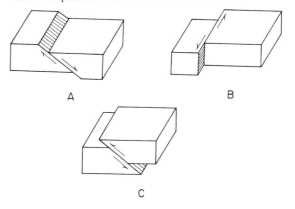

A

B

C

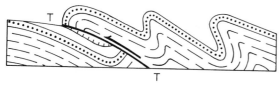

Figure 2.10 *Continued deformation at asymmetrical folds, like those shown on Fig. 2.8, may lead to the development of thrust faults (T-T) by which one set of beds is thrust laterally onto another.*

ture, the greater the displacement (Fig. 2.11). The courses of small streams, for example, may have been offset hundreds or even thousands of feet. Offsets in still older features, such as some rock formations, are measurable in miles. Formations as old as Cretaceous are offset more than a hundred miles, implying an average movement of only a foot or so in a hundred years.

Displacement is going on at the present time, but the fracture generally remains sealed because of friction between the two earth blocks. Locally, however, the stress occasionally exceeds the friction, and the rocks that have been bending suddenly slip along the fracture, producing an earthquake.

Crustal and Subcrustal Structure

The earth consists of three main parts. An outer shell consists of the continental land masses, which are about 20 to 30 miles thick, and the ocean floors, which are about 5 miles thick. This shell has density between that of granite (about 2.7) and that of basalt (about 3.3). Although it is composed of many kinds of rocks, this is called the granitic shell, or *crust* (Fig. 2.12).

Below the crust, and extending to a depth of about 2,000 miles, is a denser layer called the *mantle*. Below this is a *core* of still denser material. The dimensions and certain physical properties of these layers can be estimated by the manner in which they transmit earthquake waves and by their gravitational and magnetic effects.

The differences in seismic, gravitational, and magnetic properties between the materials at the surface and those at depth probably are due

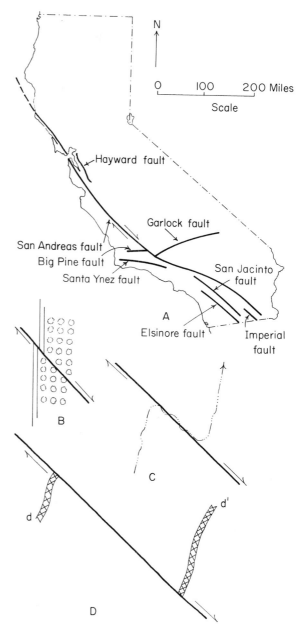

Figure 2.11 *(A) The San Andreas fault system, California. The dramatic horizontal displacement along this fault is the result of many small movements over a long period of time. (B) Recent displacements took place in 1906 and 1964, when roads and orchards were offset as much as 20 feet. (C) Earlier movements on the fault are recorded by stream courses, some of which have been offset hundreds of feet. (D) Displacements of rock formations, older than the streams, are measurable in miles.*

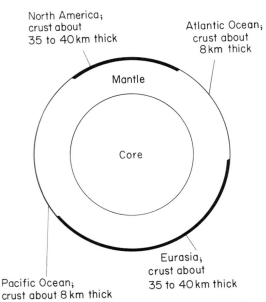

North America;
crust about
35 to 40 km thick

Atlantic Ocean;
crust about
8 km thick

Pacific Ocean;
crust about 8 km thick

Eurasia;
crust about
35 to 40 km thick

Figure 2.12 *Section through the earth, showing the core, mantle, and crust. The crust makes up less than 1 percent of the earth by volume and about 0.4 percent by weight. The mantle is 84 percent by volume and 67 percent by weight, and the core 15 percent by volume and 32 percent by weight.*

partly to differences in composition and partly to differences in temperature and pressure. Temperatures in the outer 500 kilometers of the mantle have been estimated to exceed 1500°C and may exceed 2000°C. Pressures at a depth of 500 kilometers have been estimated to be about 20 million atmospheres. Rock at such temperatures and pressures behaves very differently from the rocks we know at the surface, where the temperature averages perhaps 30°C and the pressure is 1 atmosphere (14.7 pounds per square inch).

The continents can be thought of as slabs of light rock floating on the denser mantle. Being light, at least comparatively, they rise higher than the ocean basins, and their base is deep in the mantle, like an iceberg in the sea.

STRUCTURE OF A CONTINENT

North America, like each of the other continents, is a slab of light granitic rock floating on the denser mantle. Like the other continents, it

has a nucleus of ancient, highly metamorphosed Precambrian rocks. In North America these rocks crop out in the Canadian Shield, which centers on Hudson Bay and covers most of Canada westward to a line connecting Lakes Winnipeg and Athabasca and the MacKenzie River. The shield extends southward into the United States at Lake Superior. Since the beginning of Paleozoic time, about 600 million years ago, the shields of the continents have been stable and subject to little deformation.

Bordering the Canadian Shield on the south and west is a broad structural platform that also has remained stable but has been repeatedly submerged, although shallowly, under epicontinental seas. The platform is covered by sequences of sedimentary rocks about $1\frac{1}{2}$ miles thick deposited during the Paleozoic, Mesozoic, and Cenozoic.

Along the margins of the platform, geosynclines formed in which shallow-water sediments were deposited. Although the sediments accumulated to thicknesses of 6 to 8 miles, the geosynclines were never that deep, for the troughs slowly subsided as sediments accumulated. Curiously, most of the sediments in the geosynclines were derived, not from the shield, but from mountains that were subsequently lost under the oceans bordering the continents. The geosynclines and the mountains that supplied the sediments to them constitute mobile belts around the stable platform—belts along which the continents became much deformed by folding and faulting commonly accompanied by intrusion of granitic batholiths and by volcanism. Figure 2.13 illustrates the continent in cross section.

While the geosynclines were sinking, the sedimentary rocks that had been deposited in them became folded as the sides of the troughs were pushed together. After 6 to 8 miles of sediments had accumulated, each geosyncline was terminated by strong folding and uplift, forming our mountains. At least four such geosynclines (Fig. 2.14) have left their distinctive marks on North America.

With this general structural background, the geologic map (Fig. 2.1) should be easier to read. Moreover, North America and the other continents are adrift, and the crust has yielded where the continental plates of granitic rock have pushed against the basaltic plates of the ocean bottoms, as discussed in Chapter 20.

In the central United States the Paleozoic formations are thinner than under the Appalachians (Fig. 2.2) and, mostly form broad shallow synclines (structural basins) and broad, low anticlines (structural upwarps). The bluegrass area of central Kentucky and the Nashville area in Tennessee are structural domes that expose lower Paleozoic rocks flanked by upper Paleozoic formations dipping off the domes. Southern Illinois and Michigan are broad structural basins which still preserve the upper Paleozoic formations. The Lake Superior region consists of Precambrian rocks at the south end of the Canadian Shield. Other small areas of Precambrian rocks that mark uplifts are found in the Ozark Plateau of Missouri and in central Texas.

Westward, on the plains, these Paleozoic formations and their structures are unconformably overlapped by Cretaceous formations of marine origin, and farther west on the plains these are overlapped unconformably by Tertiary formations of continental origin that were derived from the Rocky Mountains. Accordingly, the Rocky Mountains are younger than the Cretaceous deposits and older than the Tertiary ones. The mountains are formed of uplifts of Precambrian rocks flanked by Paleozoic and Mesozoic (including the Cretaceous) formations, which are turned up steeply at the edges of those uplifts. (Fig. 2.2).

The continuity of the Rocky Mountains is broken in Wyoming by a structural basin partly filled with Tertiary formations like those on the Great Plains. Similar but smaller Tertiary basins in Utah (Uinta Basin) and in New Mexico (San Juan Basin) contain deposits washed from the western slopes of the Rocky Mountains. These basins are part of the Colorado Plateau.

Between the Colorado Plateau and the Sierra Nevada is a highly faulted area, the Basin and Range Province, which consists of elongate mountain ranges and intervening valleys. There and to the west, in California, considerable earth movements are continuing.

How might such structures have developed? Stresses that cause movement in the mantle could produce folds and faults in the overlying, more-rigid crust. According to one theory on crustal movements, the convection-cell hypothesis, differences between the densities of the inner and outer parts of the mantle develop as a result of slow heat transfer, which causes convection currents like those resulting from unequal heating of air in a room or of water in a pan, a process illustrated in Figure 2.15,A. Two adjoining units in the mantle, rotating in opposite directions like geared wheels, could cause a wedge of the crust to be dragged downward or raised, depending on the direction of rotation. The part dragged downward could become the site of a geosyncline, like those referred to earlier.

Another theory holds that the crust is drifting across the top of the mantle. This, the theory of

Figure 2.13 *Diagrammatic cross section illustrating the principal structural elements of North America. The continent, floating on the denser mantle, has a stable nucleus formed by the Shield and the platform around it. Bordering the platform are mobile belts where geosynclines and mountains ranges were formed during the Paleozoic and later eras.*

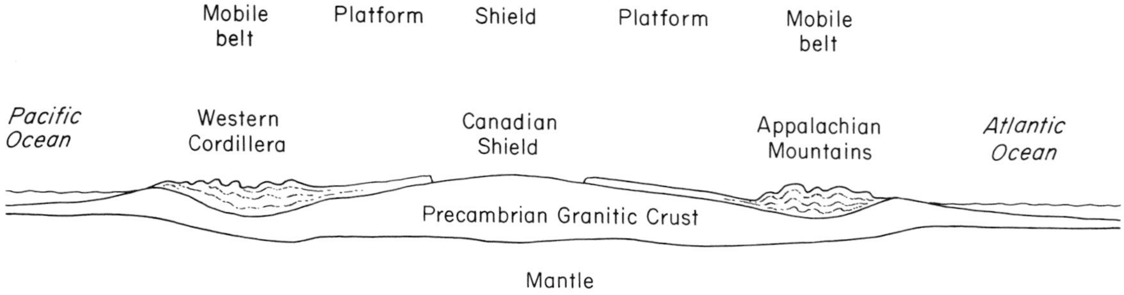

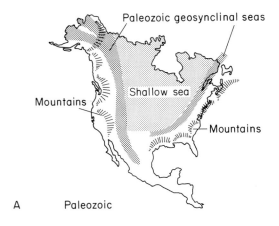

A   Paleozoic

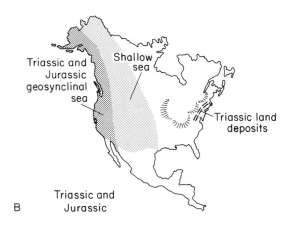

B   Triassic and Jurassic

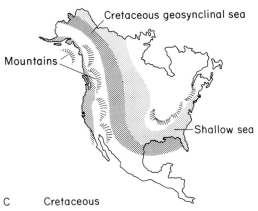

C   Cretaceous

Figure 2.14 *Paleogeographic maps of North America, showing principal Paleozoic and Mesozoic mountains, geosynclinal seas, and the shallow seas that intermittently flooded the stable platform around the shield. During the Paleozoic the Canadian Shield was flooded by shallow seas.*

continental drift, attributes the bends in the Cordillera of western North America to clockwise rotation of the continent, and the bends in the Cordillera in South America to counterclockwise rotation (Fig. 2.15,B). Probably neither theory is wholly right, but either one would account for the kinds of forces required to create mountains and to move them, and to that extent we may rest easier. Figure 2.16 shows an early concept of the continents as they began to slide apart during the latter part of the Mesozoic.

Earthquakes—Seismicity

If all the faults and other fractures in the rocks of the crust were lubricated to eliminate friction, perhaps movement would be continuous, and there would be no major earthquakes. Earthquakes and volcanic eruptions commonly are thought of as occurring together, but earthquakes may be caused by earth movements that are not at all related to volcanic action. The association, however, has some basis, in that most volcanic eruptions are accompanied by earth tremors.

An earthquake actually originates at a point within the earth's crust. This point is called the *focus,* and the point on the surface directly above it is called the *epicenter.* From the epicenter outward in all directions the intensity of the earthquake diminishes, and around the epicenter can be drawn lines, called *isoseismals,* connecting the points of equal intensity of the shock. Intensities of earthquakes are expressed in terms of various scales. A simple but very understandable one, called the Modified Mercalli scale, has been much used:

Modified Mercalli Intensity Scale for Earthquakes (1956 version, abridged)

I. Not felt; detected by seismographs.

II. Felt by some persons at rest.

III. Felt indoors. Hanging objects swing. Vibrations like passing of light trucks. May not be recognized as an earthquake.

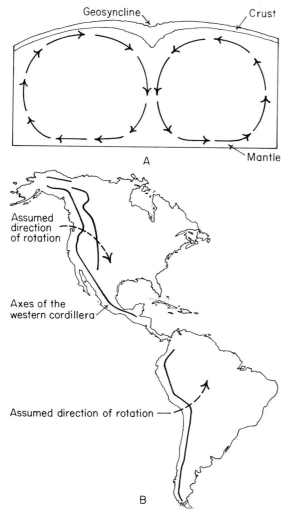

Figure 2.15 *Two hypothetical crustal structures that would explain the forces required to cause crustal warping and folding. (A) The convection-cell hypothesis. (B) The hypothesis of continental drifting assumes that the crust is drifting on top of the mantle.*

broken. Pictures off walls. Furniture moved or overturned. Plaster and weak masonry cracked. Trees, bushes shake and rustle.

VII. Difficult to stand. Noticed by drivers of motor cars. Furniture broken. Weak chimneys broken. Fall of plaster. Waves on ponds. Small slides along sand and gravel banks. Large bells ring.

VIII. Steering of motor cars affected. Fall of stucco and some masonry walls. Twisting and falling of chimney, monuments, and elevated tanks. Some frame houses moved on foundations. Branches broken from trees. Cracks in wet ground and on steep slopes.

IX. General panic. Most masonry seriously damaged. Some frame structures shifted off their foundations. Underground pipes broken. Conspicuous cracks in ground.

Figure 2.16 *(A) Wegener's concept of the continents as they began to slide apart during the latter part of the Mesozoic Era. (B) Present position of the continents and the oceanic ridges (broken lines) that are interpreted as the result of upwelling of the mantle.*

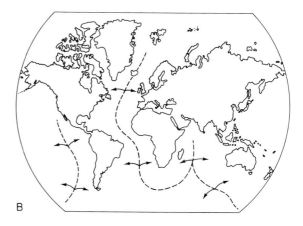

IV. Hanging objects swing. Vibrations like passing of heavy trucks. Windows, dishes, doors rattle.

V. Felt outdoors. Sleepers awakened. Liquids spilled. Small objects displaced or upset. Doors, shutters, pictures move.

VI. Felt by all. Many frightened. Persons walk unsteadily. Windows, dishes, glassware

X. Most masonry and frame structures destroyed. Large landslides. Rails bent slightly.

XI. Rails bent greatly. Underground pipelines completely out of service.

XII. Damage nearly total.

Earthquake *intensity* refers to the effects on the works of man; earthquake *magnitude* refers to the energy released by the earth movement. Magnitude (Richter scale) is measured by the effects on the seismograph, the amplitude of swing of the arms; each unit increase in magnitude represents a 10-fold increase in effect on the seismograph. Thus an earthquake of magnitude 8 is a hundred times greater than an earthquake of magnitude 6.

Although the 1906 earthquake in California and the resulting fire in San Francisco caused much damage and the loss of hundreds of lives, the losses were small compared to those caused by other major earthquakes and the resulting fires or other disasters. The table below lists some of the major earthquakes that have occurred during this century.

By comparison, the United States and Canada have suffered only minor losses due to earthquakes. Even in this respect we have been favored, partly by our physiography and partly because we have been able to afford better construction.

Figures 2.17 and 19.12 show the epicenters of the principal earthquakes that have been recorded in North America (see also Fig. 2.25).

Country	Date	Number of Deaths
India	1905	20,000
Italy	1908	75,000
Italy	1915	30,000
China	1920	180,000
China	1932	70,000
Japan	1923	143,000
Turkey	1939	thousands
India	1935	60,000
Morocco	1960	12,000
Chile	1960	5,700
Iran	1957	2,500
Iran	1962	8,000

Earth Magnetism

Two manifestations of earth magnetism that are significant physiographically are the earth's general magnetic field and the magnetic properties of certain rock masses that cause deviations in the earth's general field. The north magnetic pole is in the northern part of Prince of Wales Island, Canada, at about longitude 100°W, latitude 73°. A compass needle points to the north magnetic pole, not to the north geographic pole, and the angular difference between these two directions is referred to as the *declination*. In the United States magnetic north coincides with true north along a line near the 85th meridian. East of this line the compass points west of north; west of it the compass points east of north. The declination in various parts of the United States is shown in Figure 2.18. A compass taken across the country must be corrected for declination.

Another correction must be made if a compass is taken north. As the pole is approached the needle increasingly dips toward the ground, and at the magnetic poles stands vertically. In the central United States the needle dips about 65 degrees to the north. Compass needles in the northern hemisphere must have a weight on the south end to keep them level.

An effect of declination may be seen in the street pattern in Baltimore, which is not noted for having an orderly system of streets. Baltimore streets that supposedly lead north are aligned about 3 degrees west of north, and the east-west system is similarly misoriented. The survey evidently was not corrected properly for declination.

Rocks containing magnetic minerals affect both the direction and dip of a compass needle. This property can be used to locate such formations, thus serving as an aid to the study of buried rock structures. Deviations caused by magnetic rocks are *magnetic anomalies*. Weakly magnetic masses or strongly magnetic ones that are deeply buried produce anomalies with low amplitude; depth of burial and the nature of the edges of the magnetic masses—that is, whether gradational with or sharply separated from sur-

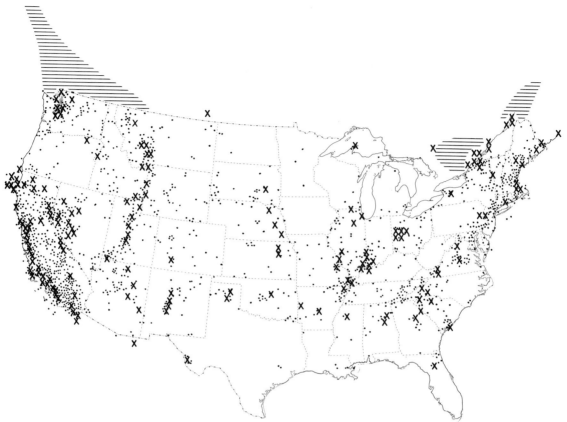

X Destructive and near destructive earthquakes (after C and GS)
· Minor earthquakes (after American Geophysical Union)

Figure 2.17 *Epicenters of earthquakes in the United States and Canada. Horizontal ruling indicates areas in southern Canada subject to minor earthquakes.*

rounding nonmagnetic rock—determine the magnetic gradient or the steepness of the sides of the anomalies. Some examples are given in Figure 2.19, which illustrates some of the kinds of magnetic anomalies in the United States and their relation to exposed and buried rock masses.

The metamorphic and igneous rocks in the Piedmont and New England Provinces give sharp, high-amplitude anomalies; on the Coastal Plain, similar anomalies, except for having low amplitude, leave no doubt about the continuity of the metamorphic and igneous rocks beneath the Coastal Plain formations.

Iron-bearing formations in the Superior Upland produce high-amplitude linear anomalies trending southwestward. Similar anomalies, ex-

cept for having low amplitude, extend southwestward to Nebraska and leave no doubt that the Superior Upland formations extend at least that far under the cover of Paleozoic and Cretaceous formations (Fig. 2.1).

The magnetic properties of some kinds of rock formations also can be used to determine shifts in the positions of the magnetic poles, or possible crustal changes, in the geologic past. For example, in some intrusions and lava flows, as the magma solidified, the magnetic minerals oriented themselves in the earth's magnetic field as it existed at the time the rock body formed. This so-called *relict magnetism* can be determined and used to measure the difference between an earlier magnetic field and that of the present.

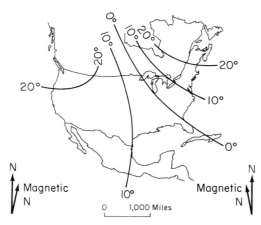

Figure 2.18 *Lines of equal magnetic declination (isogonic lines) are given for each 10 degrees (declinations as of 1960). In the northern United States the north ends of compass needles are drifting westward roughly 2 to 4 minutes annually; in the southern United States they are drifting eastward at a maximum of about 2 minutes annually.*

Gravity

All matter exerts a force that attracts other matter, and this force varies as the product of the masses and inversely as the square of the distance between them. The force of gravity is the attraction that the earth exerts upon matter around it. If the earth were homogeneous and had a smooth surface, the force of gravity would be uniform all over the surface. But the earth is not homogeneous; some rock masses are denser than others and exert a greater pull.

Surveys that measure these gravity differences indicate that the rocks under the ocean basins are more dense than those of the continents. Seismic surveys reveal irregularities in the continental slabs. Figure 2.20 illustrates the great thickness of crustal rocks inferred under the Sierra Nevada as compared with either the Great Basin to the east or the Pacific Ocean to the west. The base of this mass of light rock has slopes as steep as 25 percent, which does not make for a stable foundation and could contribute to the crustal instability of that region.

Figure 2.21 shows irregularities in the force of gravity in the United States. The gravity contours are calculated for sea level. The milligal, the unit by which gravity is measured, is roughly a millionth of the gravitational acceleration at sea level. Masses of light rock, like those under the western physiographic provinces, give negative values; masses of dense rock give positive values. Figure 2.22 shows diagrammatically an interpretation of the possible structural significance of the variation in gravity across the country.

The blocks of light rock floating on the mantle are like icebergs floating on water; the higher and thicker ones have the deeper roots. The blocks are in hydrostatic balance; in geological parlance, they are in *isostatic* equilibrium. If the top of the high block is lowered by erosion, and the sediment transferred to the surface of a neighboring, lower block, the high block would rise isostatically in response to the reduced load, whereas the other block would sink because of the increased load. Such balancing is *isostatic adjustment*. Large segments of the crust are in approximate isostatic adjustment, but because of friction and rigidity, the adjustment is only approximate.

Figure 2.23 offers an interpretation of the configuration of the base of the crust beneath the United States. The high mountains and plateaus in the western United States have deep roots. The Appalachians, which are lower, have shallow roots. Seismic studies show that the still lower mountains of the Lake Superior region do not have roots of light rock, although this seems to be expressed in Figure 2.21. These differences may be related to differences in the ages and histories of the mountains as well as to isostatic adjustment because of differences in their heights; the western mountains are Cenozoic, the Appalachians are Paleozoic, and the mountains of the Superior Upland are Precambrian. If the continents are drifting across the mantle, as suggested in Figs. 2.15 and 2.16, perhaps the roots of the older mountains have been sheared off.

A quite different kind of gravity effect, important in physiography, is the one that the moon exerts, which causes tides. The moon's density, 3.3, is about that of basalt. Its diameter is about

49

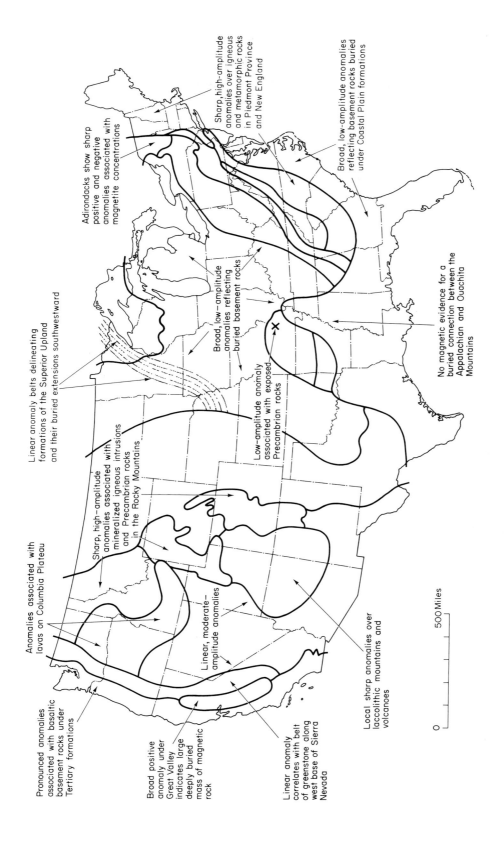

Figure 2.19 *Some magnetic anomalies in the United States. (Generalized from U.S.G.S.)*

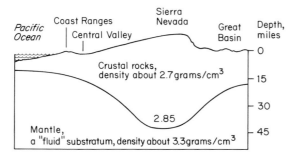

Figure 2.20 *Diagrammatic cross section through the Sierra Nevada from the Great Basin to the Pacific Ocean. Under the Sierra Nevada the layer of light crustal rocks is believed to be about seven times as thick as under the ocean, and about twice as thick as under the western part of the Great Basin.*

half that of the core of the earth, and it is 240,000 miles away. This mass is large enough and near enough to produce a high tide that travels around the earth with the passage of the moon. The

vastly greater mass of the sun also produces a tide, but because the sun is so far away (average, 93,000,000 miles) the effect is small compared to that of the moon. When the sun, moon, and earth are in a line, the tidal bulge is greatest, producing what are called *spring tides*. When the three form a right triangle the tidal bulge is least, producing *neap tides*. Tides also rise on the side of the earth away from the moon. This is because the two bodies, earth and moon, are rotating together around a center of their combined masses. The resulting centrifugal force on earth is away from the moon; this force is less than the gravity effect of the moon on the side facing the moon, and greater on the opposite side. High tides, which occur every 12 hours, are the result of a combination of the two forces. Both the atmosphere and the solid crust also are affected by these tidal forces.

In brief, our knowledge about the structural framework of this planet on which we are pas-

Figure 2.21 *Gravity map of the United States. Contour interval 100 millegals. The continent is light rock and gives negative values; off the coasts dense rocks give positive values. The high-altitude western states have extensive areas with values less than −200 milligals, and evidently are underlain by a thick layer of light rock. (From U.S.G.S.)*

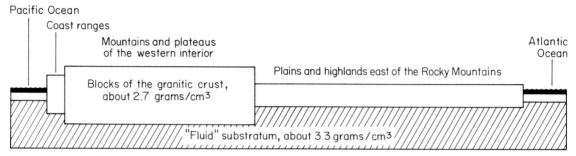

Figure 2.22 *Simplified interpretation of the gravity map of the United States envisages blocks of the granitic crust (density about 2.7) floating in a denser substratum. The crustal blocks are thin under the oceans, but they are thick and sink deeply into the substratum under the high mountains and plateaus in the western United States.*

sengers is based on a combination of different kinds of observations and measurements, each involving highly specialized techniques.

Estimating the Duration of Geologic Time

The most satisfactory methods for estimating the age of a geologic event are radiometric. The principle is disarmingly simple. Certain elements decay radioactively to daughter elements. The decay rate is constant, regardless of changes in temperature, pressure, or other conditions. The

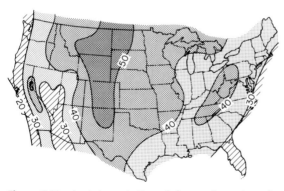

Figure 2.23 *An interpretation of the configuration of the base of the crust under the United States. Contours show the inferred depths of the base in kilometers below sea level. Depths are greatest under the Southern and Middle Rocky Mountains, the northern Great Plains, and the Sierra Nevada. Depths are least under the Pacific coast and under the Atlantic coast. (From U.S.G.S.)*

rate is usually expressed in terms of the half-life of an element, meaning the time period in which half the parent element decays to a daughter element. No two elements have the same half-life. Knowing the decay rate, one need only measure the proportions of parent and daughter elements to determine the age of the material being used to date an event. The major difficulty in applying the method to rocks and minerals or to surface deposits and soils is in the assumption that there has been neither depletion nor enrichment of either parent or daughter element during its geologic history. Although the analytical methods (mass spectroscopy) are highly refined, only samples that have been preserved under conditions simulating those of a sealed test tube will give accurate dates. Such preservation is uncommon in the natural environment.

Among the radiometric methods that have been widely used are those based upon uranium-lead, thorium-lead, potassium-argon, and radiocarbon. In the uranium-lead and thorium-lead method, measurements are made on three pairs of elements that occur together and have different decay rates:

$U^{238} \longrightarrow Pb^{206}$, half-life 4.5 billion years.
$U^{235} \longrightarrow Pb^{207}$, half-life 700 million years.
$Th^{232} \longrightarrow Pb^{208}$, half-life 13.5 billion years.

Although the method has the advantage of measuring three different decay rates, it is not suitable for sedimentary deposits or soils, for the minerals that contain these radioactive elements are largely restricted to igneous and metamorphic rocks.

The potassium-argon method, based upon the transformation of K^{40} to Ar^{40} with a half-life of 1,310 million years, has the great advantage that potassium-bearing minerals are abundant in the crust and in sedimentary deposits.

The radiocarbon method is based upon the transformation of carbon-14 to nitrogen-14 with a half life of about 5,000 years. The amount of carbon-14 is measured against the amount of the stable carbon-12. Because of the short half-life the method is useful for dating events of the past 50,000 years, those of the Holocene and latest Pleistocene. The method was excitedly received when samples from Egyptian tombs, dated by historic records, were correctly dated by measuring the ratio of carbon 14 to carbon 12. Samples from open sites, however, are subject to many kinds of contamination, beause the weathering of organic matter fundamentally is a biochemical process involving alteration by micro-organisms, and to the degree that they derive any of their carbon from soil moisture or soil air, they introduce younger carbon into the system.

Geologic History

In attempting to summarize the major events of earth history that have controlled the structural framework of the physiographic provinces, we will assume the earth to be 4.6 billion years old. This is based on radioactive age determinations on meteorites and on ancient rocks in the crust. But until we know *how* the earth was formed, we cannot be sure what event we should take for the beginning. It could be that the earth is many times older than 4.6 billion years, and perhaps that date merely represents the last time the earth's inhabitants became sufficiently civilized to demolish the planet!

The beginning of the earth is as uncertain and mysterious as the limits, if there are any, to outer space, but if we limit our attention to the last 4.6 billion years, we can keep things comparatively simple and under reasonable control.

The ages and durations of the eras and periods are shown in Table 2.1. The relative duration of the eras is more clearly emphasized by proportions on a linear scale (Fig. 2.24).

The system of dividing geologic time into eras and periods is adopted because, for measuring geologic time, the year is an unsatisfactory unit, and for the same reason and to the same degree that the mile is unsatisfactory for measuring stellar space. Our planet is only a speck of dust in stellar space, and a year is only a split second in geologic time.

Geological processes operate exceedingly slowly, but they cause tremendous changes because they operate for so long a time. A foot of uplift in a thousand years is not a breathtaking rate of earth movement. Indeed, many parts of the United States are moving today at rates greater than that. But uplift continued at that rate for 10 million years—which is not a long time geologically speaking—can build a 10,000 foot mountain range. Slow and easy does it!.

The basis for subdividing geologic history lies in the fossil record, the subject of the science called *paleontology*. Species change from one era or period to another, because extinct species never reappear, and new species that evolve are never quite like more ancient ones. As we look backward into older and older formations, the faunas increasingly differ from those of the present.

Since some species survive without change longer than others, an individual fossil may be misleading. Rather, the whole *fauna*, not the individual fossil or individual species, must be considered. By analogy, a modern kitchen may contain colonial antiques, but one has little difficulty identifying the age of the kitchen on the basis of the total assemblage of utensils and equipment.

Differences may also exist between contemporaneous faunas, because of differences in environment within a depositional basin. For example, noticeable differences in shellfish faunas may be noted between the Mississippi River, its mouth, and the deeper and saltier offshore water. These differences, which are analogous to the differences between a kitchen, a dining room, and

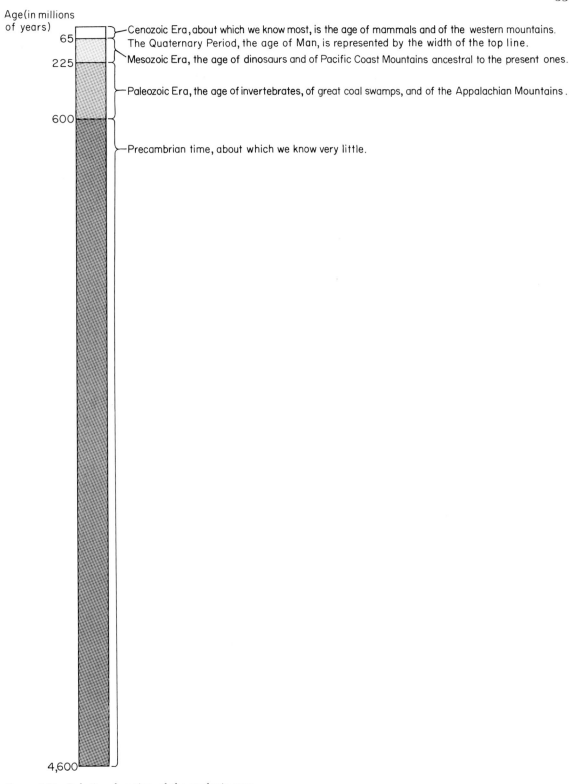

Age(in millions of years)

65

225

600

4,600

Cenozoic Era, about which we know most, is the age of mammals and of the western mountains. The Quaternary Period, the age of Man, is represented by the width of the top line.

Mesozoic Era, the age of dinosaurs and of Pacific Coast Mountains ancestral to the present ones.

Paleozoic Era, the age of invertebrates, of great coal swamps, and of the Appalachian Mountains.

Precambrian time, about which we know very little.

Figure 2.24 *Relative duration of the geologic eras.*

a living room, usually can be correctly identified and understood by noting the changes in texture and composition of the fossil-bearing formation as it is traced away from or toward the original source of the sediments. Such studies are the concern of *paleogeography* and *paleoecology*.

The Precambrian is noteworthy because of the vast time represented by it, almost 90 percent of all geologic time. Precambrian rocks, extensive in the Canadian Shield, are poorly exposed elsewhere—in the Appalachian Highlands, Lake Superior Region, central Texas, and in parts of the Rocky Mountain region, the West Coast, and Alaska. The record preserved in these rocks is not only fragmentary but is difficult to decipher. Many of the rocks are so altered that one cannot be sure what they were like originally. Precambrian history was inscribed on a vast number of pages, of which only a few are preserved for our inspection. Moreover, the writing on many of those pages is illegible, and we cannot be sure of the sequence of the pages we have recovered.

The beginning of the Precambrian, which is the beginning of geologic time, is assumed to be that time when solid crust first formed. Earlier earth history is *astronomical history*. The origin of the earth is in some way related to the origin of the solar system. It is assumed that the earth, and the other planets, began as clouds of dust orbiting the sun. The dust cloud had the composition of outer space, about half hydrogen and half helium and less than 1 percent terrestrial elements. Gravity would have caused the heavier particles to collect toward the center of the cloud. More and more the relatively heavy terrestrial elements would be collected there and the hydrogen and helium lost to outer space.

When the crust began to form, the earth's surface may have looked about like that of the moon, and its composition may have been similar to that of stoney meteorites. As the crust developed, so did the atmosphere; water vapor, nitrogen, carbon dioxide, and other gases gradually escaped from the earth's interior through vents in the slowly cooling crust. Water vapor may have formed clouds, but neither precipitation nor accumulation of water could have occurred until the surface had cooled to less than 100°C. When the rains did come, water running off high ground collected to form the first streams and accumulated in depressions to form the first lakes and seas.

Igneous rocks contain 1 percent water. If the melts from which they formed contained more than that, then the rains must have started early. Even without additions of water from the mantle, the oceans could easily have been filled if a crustal layer 30 miles thick yielded a water content of 3 percent.

The nitrogen and hydrogen in the atmosphere could form amino acids and other substances potentially useful biologically, and at some early stage in the primitive seas, the first organism developed. That these early stages in the primitive earth began about 4.6 billion years ago is judged on the basis of the radiometric age of meteorites, age of moon rocks, and various astronomical calculations. We will assume that these primitive stages lasted no more than a half billion years because rocks in the shields have been dated as old as 3.9 billion years, and these rocks are in the midst of *older* metamorphosed sedimentary rocks. Precambrian stratigraphy begins with these rocks.

For our purpose the Precambrian rocks are important chiefly because they form the nucleus of the continent and provide the basement foundation for the Paleozoic, Mesozoic, and Cenozoic rocks and structures. These ancient basement rocks also contain the world's largest iron, gold, nickel, and cobalt deposits plus a variety of other valuable metals.

Fossil remains in Precambrian rocks are those of primitive forms (algae, radiolaria, sponges, and possible foraminifera), but the absence of higher-order forms does not necessarily mean that all living things were primitive. Soft parts of animals rarely are preserved, and the fossil record must be reconstructed largely from hard parts, such as shells and bones. Late Precambrian animals may have included large and complex forms that were composed wholly of soft, nonmineral tissue. The still-unknown ancestor of the fish may have been a complex organism without hard parts.

Paleozoic rocks, which represent the next 8 percent of geologic time, are widespread, from the Appalachians to the Rocky Mountains. During this time there were uplands and probably mountains along the Atlantic seaboard, and a mediterranean sea occupied a trough, or geosyncline, along the site of the Appalachian Mountains (Fig. 2.14,A). Other uplands or mountains existed at or near the site of the Gulf Coast, and there were seas north of them. Still other uplands existed at the western edge of the continent, and a mediterranean sea occupied a geosyncline that extended northward across western United States and Canada to Alaska (Fig. 2.14). Most of the central United States and the plains in western Canada were part of the stable platform and were alternately slightly below and slightly above sea level, and apparently then, as now, had little relief.

Sediments eroded from the mountains and uplands were deposited in the geosynclines to a thickness of about 40,000 feet. This does not mean that the seas were 8 miles deep. On the contrary, both the fossils and the physical geology indicate that much of the time the seas were shallow. Evidently the sea floors gradually sank as sediments accumulated in them. And during the same long period, the bordering mountains must have been maintained, despite erosion, by a prolonged series of small uplifts.

Numerous episodes of mountain building interrupted the development of the geosynclines. When the Paleozoic ended, the sediments that filled the geosynclines became folded and uplifted; the Appalachian Mountains were formed at this time.

In the central and eastern states the Paleozoic deposits are noted for their mineral fuels—oil, gas, and coal. Other important mineral deposits of this age are the salt beds in New York, West Virginia, Michigan, Ohio, Illinois, Kansas, and southeast New Mexico, and the Clinton iron beds that extend along the Appalachians from New York to Alabama.

In the Mesozoic Era, which represents about 3 percent of geologic time, there were dinosaurs, and toward the close of the Mesozoic the first suckling mammals and toothless birds appeared.

In Cretaceous time, flowering plants appear in abundance for the first time, and perhaps bees and wasps date from then.

The principal areas of Mesozoic rocks in the United States are shown in Figure 2.1. These rocks are a rich source of the energy-producing minerals—coal, oil, gas, and uranium. The principal geosynclinal seas and bordering mounains indicated by the Mesozoic rocks are shown in Figure 2.14,B and C. In Triassic and Jurassic time (Fig. 2.14,B), a geosynclinal sea extended along much of the Pacific coast of the United States, and a thin sheet of sediments was deposited far to the east that was alternately land and shallow sea. In the eastern United States terrestrial deposits of Triassic age were laid down along the eastern foot of the Appalachians, which had risen where the Paleozoic sea had been. This kind of history was repeated in western North America in Cretaceous time (Fig. 2.14,C), when mountains rose at the site of what had been the Triassic and Jurassic sea, and happened again at the beginning of Cenozoic time when the Rocky Mountains were formed aiong the position occupied by the Cretaceous geosynclinal sea. In geology, evidently, what goes down must come up!

Uplift of the Rocky Mountains at the site of the Cretaceous geosynclinical sea occurred 65 million years ago. The time since then, embracing the Cenozoic, is about 1 percent of geologic time. The western mountains had begun forming in California and Nevada during Jurassic time, but did not occupy the positions of present-day mountains, nor did they look like them. At the end of Cretaceous time, the mountain-making movements extended eastward to central Colorado, and for the first time the physical geography of the country, including the outline of the continent, began assuming the shapes we know today. Although the Rocky Mountains began forming in early Tertiary time, the general uplift to their present high altitudes occurred during the latter part of the Tertiary.

During the Tertiary Period, mammals became dominant. These were small and strange ones at first, like *Eohippus*, an ancestral horse that was little bigger than a dog and had five toes. By the middle Tertiary they had become much larger.

The number of toes had been reduced to three, and they stood on the tip of the middle one. By Quaternary time, they were as large as those we know today, and stood on one toe, the laterals being reduced to small splints. The change in foot structure was accompanied by an evolution in the dentition. The early Tertiary horses had short-crowned teeth fitted for browsing rather than for grazing. The change came in the middle Tertiary, when grasses first appeared in abundance. The evolution of the horse and the general proliferation of the mammals during the Tertiary was probably both a cause and an effect of the development during the Cenozoic of the seed- and nut-bearing trees, shrubs, and grasses.

During the first part of the Tertiary Period, the coastal plain along the Atlantic and Gulf coasts was partly submerged (Fig. 10.7). It emerged to take approximately its present form in late Terti-

ary time, and that area is blanketed with Cenozoic rocks, as are the Great Plains and western basins, where sediments eroded from the newly formed mountains were deposited. Many of these sedimentary deposits are rich in mineral fuels, particularly oil and gas in California and along the Gulf Coast in Texas and Louisiana. The tremendous oil-shale deposits in the western interior are of Tertiary age.

During the periods of mountain building in the western United States, there was much volcanic and other igneous activity (p. 34), and as a result, extensive areas there are blanketed by volcanic and related rocks (Fig. 2.1). The great volcanoes of the Cascade Range and southwestern Alaska are part of a volcanic belt that surrounds the Pacific Ocean (Fig. 2.25).

At the end of Pliocene time, roughly 2 million years ago, *Australopithecus, Pithecanthropus,*

Figure 2.25 *Belt of volcanic and tectonic activity surrounding the Pacific Ocean. Active earth movement is indicated by the frequent earthquakes.*

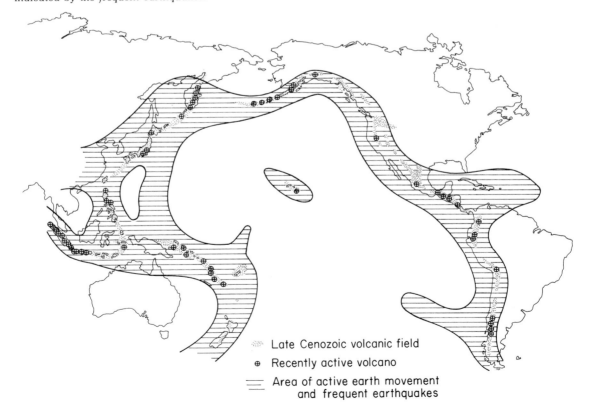

⊕ Late Cenozoic volcanic field

⊕ Recently active volcano

≡ Area of active earth movement and frequent earthquakes

and other primitive ape-men appeared in the eastern hemisphere. *Homo sapiens* appeared no earlier than a few hundred thousand years ago. During this last period, the Quaternary, continental glaciers spread southward into Europe and North America. The deposits left by the gla-ciers, called *glacial drift,* record a succession of climatic changes (p. 90). The last big glaciers in North America had retreated into Canada some 10,000 years ago. Before that time man had migrated to North America.

References

General Geology

Gilluly, J., Waters, A. C., and Woodford, A. O., 1968, Principles of geology: 3rd ed., San Francisco, W. H. Freeman and Company.

Grabau, A. W., 1924, Principles of stratigraphy: Seiler, N. Y.; reprinted by Dover Publications.

Holmes, A., 1965, Principles of physical geology: 2nd ed., New York, Ronald Press.

Shelton, J. S., 1966, Geology illustrated: San Francisco, W. H. Freeman and Company.

Strahler, A. N., 1971, The earth sciences: 2nd ed., New York, Harper and Row.

Crustal and Subcrustal Structure

Daly, R. A., 1940, Strength and structure of the earth: Englewood Cliffs, Prentice-Hall; reprinted 1969 by Hafner Publishing Co.

Gutenberg, B., 1951, Internal constitution of the earth: New York, Dover.

Hodgson, J. H., 1964, Earthquakes and earth structure: Englewood Cliffs, Prentice-Hall.

Phillips, O. M., 1968, The heart of the earth: San Francisco, Freeman, Cooper & Co.

Poldervaart, A. (ed.), 1955, Crust of the earth: Geol. Soc. America Spec. Paper 62.

Richter, C. F., 1958, Elementary seismology: San Francisco, W. H. Freeman and Company.

Sunset Staff and Iacopi, R., 1971, Earthquake country: rev. ed., Menlo Park, Calif., Lane Book Co.

Structural Evolution; Geologic History

Clark, T. H., and Stearn, C. W., 1968, The geological evolution of North America: 2nd ed., New York, Ronald Press.

Eardley, A. J., 1962, Structural geology of North America: 2nd ed., New York, Harper and Row.

King, P. B., 1959, The evolution of North America: Princeton Univ. Press.

Kummel, B., 1970, History of the earth: 2nd ed., San Francisco, W. H. Freeman and Company.

Woodford, A. O., 1965, Historical geology: San Francisco, W. H. Freeman and Company.

Mineral Deposits

Francis, W., 1965, Fuels and fuel technology: 2 vols., Pergamon.

Levorsen, A. I., 1967, Geology of petroleum: 2nd ed., San Francisco, W. H. Freeman and Company.

Lindgren, W., 1933, Mineral deposits: 4th ed., New York, McGraw-Hill.

Park, C. F., Jr., and MacDiarmid, R. A., 1970, Ore deposits: 2nd ed., San Francisco, W. H. Freeman and Company.

The differences in shapes of landforms are controlled by the geologic structure of the rocks, the processes of erosion operating on them, and the stage of erosion—that is, whether advanced or just beginning. This scene on the Colorado Plateau illustrates small plateaus (mesas, or buttes) formed by a protective cap of nearly horizontal sandstone over easily eroded shale sculptured into badlands. The erosion has been by fluviatile (stream) processes in an arid climate.

3

·······

LANDFORMS—THE SHAPES OF HILLS AND VALLEYS

General Considerations of Scale and Origin

The term "topography" refers to the configuration—the relief and contours—of the features that give variety to our landscape: our plains, plateaus, valleys, mountains, and other landforms. The study of landforms is the science of *geomorphology*. Any landform records two quite different chapters of earth history. The first reveals the manner in which the bedrock was formed and how its structure developed—whether by uplift, folding, faulting or some combination of the three. The second chapter reveals the processes of weathering and erosion that sculptured the bedrock and produced the landform. These two chapters of earth history may be separated by hundreds of millions of years. Marine fossils are found at high elevations in many mountains, yet the sea never reached such levels. The rocks in which such fossils are found were once sediments that accumulated below sea level. Over vast periods of time they became *lithified* by pressure or heat caused by burial beneath younger sediments, and were subsequently raised to their present heights by movements of the earth's crust.

Landforms and the processes by which they have developed—the subject of *geomorphology*—

may be considered on four very different scales (Fig. 3.1). The largest, represented by the continents and the oceanic deeps, have horizontal dimensions measurable in thousands of miles and a vertical relief of more than 10 miles. The processes by which these developed involve the geologic history of the mantle and crust.

The next smaller scale of landforms is that represented by the physiographic provinces, especially on the continents, although the ocean bottoms can be divided into physiographic provinces too. The provinces, whether on the land or under the sea, are characterized by a distinctive kind of geologic structure, and are scores or hundreds of miles wide. Figure 3.1,B, illustrates the structural differences that control landforms in the provinces along the middle Atlantic seaboard. The processes by which these developed involve the geologic history of the crust.

The next smaller scale of landforms reflects differences in process or position within the physiographic provinces. The differences between valley bottoms, valley sides, and hilltops are examples. Figure 3.1,C, illustrates some landforms in the littoral zone that are attributable to differences in processes operating at various distances from shore. The smallest scale of landforms is measurable in centimeters or inches;

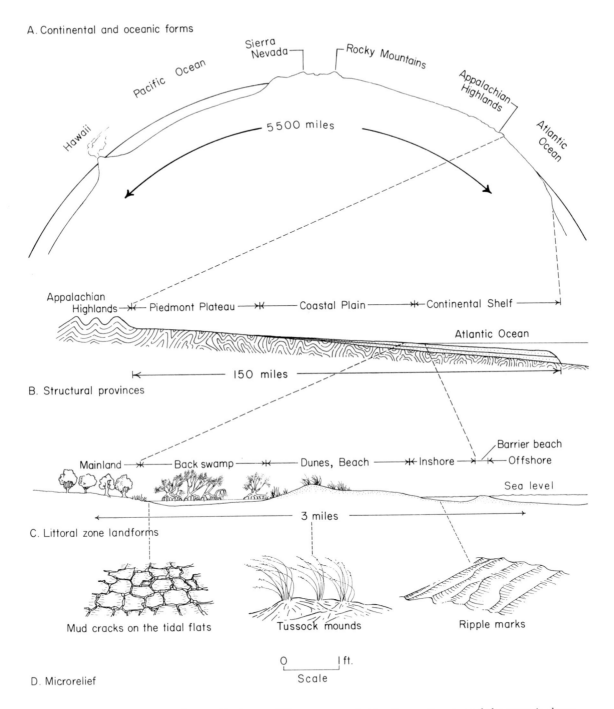

Figure 3.1 *Four scales of landforms. The largest (A) are represented by the continents and the oceanic deeps. Next largest (B) are the physiographic provinces, each characterized by distinctive geologic structure. Within the provinces (C) are smaller differences reflecting differences in local structure or different processes. The smallest features (D) are represented in microrelief.*

every location has its peculiar microrelief, such as mudcracks on the tidal flats, tussock mounds on the sand dunes, and ripple marks where the inshore water is shallow (Fig. 3.1,D). The processes by which these developed involve recent geologic history, that of the surface deposits or soil, the subject of Chapter 6.

Factors that Control
the Shape of Landforms

The three major factors that control the shape of landforms are structure, process, and stage. In the geomorphic sense of the word, *structure* pertains to two quite different properties, one being the resistance of rocks to erosion, and the other being the way in which the rock formations have been deformed—that is, whether they are tilted, folded, faulted, or have remained horizontal though uplifted. For example, landforms developed on folded resistant rocks differ from those developed on similarly folded nonresistant rocks, and both differ from those developed where the

formations are horizontal or gently tilted. Figure 3.2 shows some examples. The two larger scales of landforms are governed primarily by their structures.

Processes that shape landforms are various, and several commonly work together. Some are erosional, others depositional. The agents of erosion and deposition are streams, waves, glacial ice, and wind, and each process tends to develop distinctive landforms. Valleys eroded by streams tend to have V-shaped cross sections; valleys deepened by glaciers have U-shaped cross sections. Streams build alluvial fans, glacial ice builds terminal moraines, and wind builds dunes. Along the coasts wave erosion and shore currents develop cliffs, stacks, and arches. The coastal outline may be straight, like the east coast of Florida; cuspate between spits, like the coast of North Carolina; or built of great capes, like Cape Cod.

The two smaller scales of landforms illustrated in Figure 3.1 are governed partly by their structure but primarily by the processes of erosion and sedimentation that shaped them. These

Figure 3.2 *Some different kinds of landforms reflecting differences in geologic structure. Both A and B are castellate mountains, but A is formed of nearly horizontal resistant beds whereas B is formed of essentially vertical resistant beds. Both C and D have a serrate pattern, but C, a cuesta, is formed of gently dipping resistant beds whereas in D, a hogback, the beds are steeply dipping. Both E and F are needle mountains, but E is a volcanic neck formed of lava that congealed in the throat of the volcano that subsequently has been removed by erosion, and F is a matterhorn due to glacial erosion of the basins (cirques) around its base. [From Geology of Soils by Charles B. Hunt. W. H. Freeman and Company. Copyright © 1972.]*

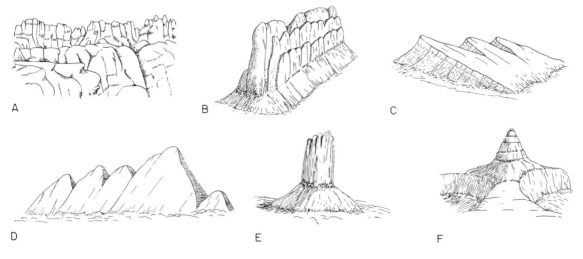

differences in process reflect local differences in environment.

Regional differences in processes reflect differences in climate, whether it is cold-dry, warm-dry, cold-wet, or warm-wet.

Stage pertains to the duration of a particular process and to its intensity—that is, whether the effects are those of a feeble process, one just beginning to operate, or those of a vigorous process that is well advanced.

Differences in the forms of stream valleys have been attributed to stage of erosion. Deep narrow valleys and those having roughened gradients are called *youthful*. Valleys of intermediate width, shape, and longitudinal profile are called *mature*. Valleys that are open and have low gradients are called *old*. This concept, though, is much oversimplified, for the major differences in landforms are due chiefly to structure and process. There is no reason to suppose, for example, that the broad open valleys of the Appalachian Plateaus are older than the deeper and narrower valleys of the main streams. A more extreme example is illustrated by some of our mountains that are formed of resistant igneous rock. The surrounding sedimentary rocks erode more readily, leaving the igneous rock higher and usually more rugged. Such mountains appear more youthful as they become older.

EFFECTS OF CHANGES IN PROCESS

Most landforms have been evolving throughout the latter part of the Cenozoic Era, a period of many millions of years during which the climates have changed greatly. As a result, the capacity of streams to erode and transport debris also has changed greatly; episodes of downcutting have alternated with episodes during which streams were unable to cut downward and instead deposited alluvium in their valleys. Moreover, during the long time that the landforms have been evolving, structural movements have modified stream gradients in many regions and thereby affected their capacity to erode and to transport sediment. Some stream courses have been modified as a result of damming by lava

flows—for example, the one that dammed the outlet from Malheur and Harney Lakes on the Columbia Plateau (p. 547).

Figure 3.12 illustrates a striking example of differences in landform due directly to change in process (see also Figs. 16.32 and 16.33). A delta, with shore bars and terraces, was deposited at the foot of the Wasatch Mountains in Lake Bonneville, a Pleistocene lake that was once 1,000 feet deep and lapped against the side of the mountains. Because the climate has changed, the region is now semiarid; Great Salt Lake is the residue of the Pleistocene lake. Stream erosion in the Wasatch Mountains now extends to the foot of the mountains, and the delta is now being eroded by streams and wind.

Changes in process caused by climatic change also are illustrated by deep, wide, glaciated valleys now occupied by streams too small to cut them; an example is Yosemite Valley in the Sierra Nevada (Fig. 18.10). The alluvial deposits in many western valleys, and the arroyos they fill, record a succession of episodes of downcutting alternating with valley filling.

Much or most of our landscape is the result of processes that have operated during the latter part of the Cenozoic Era. During this time, about 30 million years, there have been earth movements and changes in climates. It follows that most landforms are polygenetic. The landforms evolved while their structure was being changed and while the processes shaping them were changing in intensity or even in kind.

Contrasting the Provinces

STRUCTURE

The distribution of the mountains, plateaus, and plains in the United States (Fig. 3.3) reflects the structure of the continent and the paleogeography of the Paleozoic and Early Mesozoic (Fig. 2.14,A and B) and to a lesser extent that of the Cretaceous (Fig. 2.14,C). The Rocky Mountains in the United States and Canada formed near the axis of a Cretaceous geosyncline. The Coast

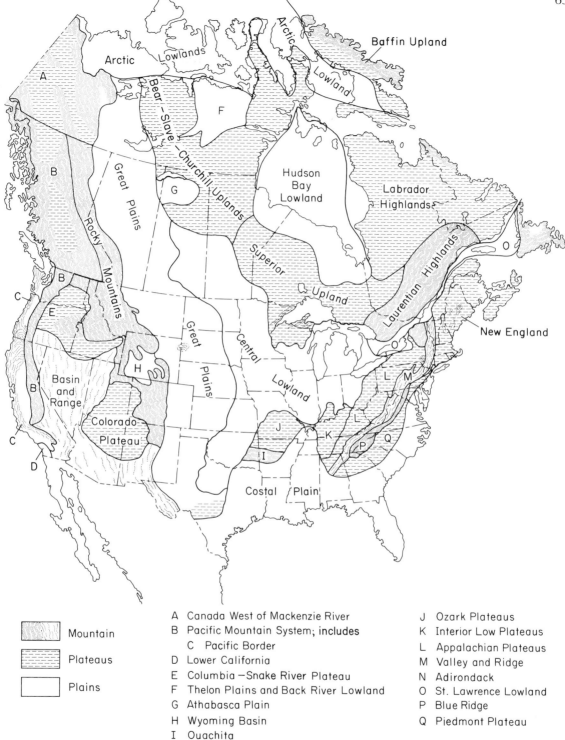

Figure 3.3 *Physiographic regions of the United States and Canada and their dominant landforms. About one-quarter of the land is mountains, one-quarter plateaus, and about half plains.*

Mountain

Plateaus

Plains

A Canada West of Mackenzie River
B Pacific Mountain System; **includes**
 C Pacific Border
D Lower California
E Columbia–Snake River Plateau
F Thelon Plains and Back River Lowland
G Athabasca Plain
H Wyoming Basin
I Ouachita

J Ozark Plateaus
K Interior Low Plateaus
L Appalachian Plateaus
M Valley and Ridge
N Adirondack
O St. Lawrence Lowland
P Blue Ridge
Q Piedmont Plateau

Ranges and the Sierra Nevada developed on the sites of Triassic and Jurassic geosynclines. The Appalachian Highlands and the mountains in Nevada formed along the axes of Paleozoic geosynclines. The plains, both in the interior and along the coast, are the sites of ancient shallow seas (shelf areas on the stable platform bordering the shield) in which thin beds were deposited. In a sense, therefore, the landforms attributed to structure are the product of a series of structures, each dependent upon something that preceded.

The major plateaus in North America are the: Yukon, Fraser River, Columbia, Snake, and Colorado plateaus in the West, and the Ozark, Interior Low, Appalachian, and Piedmont plateaus in the East. In most of these physiographic provinces the rock formations are nearly horizontal; the Piedmont Plateau is exceptional. Each plateau has an upland surface with broad flats but is roughened by dissection, and some have isolated mountains rising above the general surface. The Colorado Plateau, the highest, averages more than 5,000 feet above sea level, and extensive parts of it—the High Plateaus of Utah—are 11,000 feet above sea level.

A small plateau is a *mesa*—a Spanish term commonly used in the Southwest. The difference between a plateau and a mesa is simply one of size, not unlike the difference between a mountain and a hill.

The geologic structure of a plateau is readily seen in the nearly horizontal strata along canyon walls (Fig. 3.4). In the more elevated plateaus the streams are incised deeply, like the Grand Canyon of the Colorado River. Such canyons have been described as "mountains inside out."

The development of plateaus requires not only the uplift of nearly horizontal formations but the presence of resistant formations to maintain the upland surface. In areas where all the formations are easily eroded, the result is badland topography. Similar topography derives from weathering and erosion of homogeneous formations that are resistant enough so that joints, or cracks, in the rock become expressed in the landforms (Fig. 3.2,A,B).

Locally in the plateau provinces the formations are flexed into step folds called *monoclines*, which are expressed topographically by *hogbacks*, like the one shown at s in Figure 3.4,A. Hogbacks are the protruding, eroded edges of steeply dipping, resistant formations. They form some of the spectacular scenery on the Colorado Plateau. One, the Waterpocket Fold, is 1,000 to 1,500 feet high and 75 miles long; only at a few places can its rugged cliffs be crossed, even on foot.

Where the formations dip less steeply than in a hogback, the resistant formations produce *cuestas*, which are ridges that have escarpments facing updip and long, gentle slopes in the down-dip direction (Fig. 3.7, section C-D). Cuestas are characteristic of the Coastal Plain Province and of large areas on the Colorado Plateau and the Great Plains.

Asymmetrical divides, such as cuestas or hogbacks, erode most rapidly on the steep side, where removal of the soft rocks causes undercutting of the resistant ones. The result of this is that the divide retreats *down the dip*—a process called *monoclinal shifting*. As the surface becomes lowered, the hard rocks continue to protrude and the soft rocks continue to form valleys, but the positions of ridges and valleys both shift in the down-dip direction.

On most plateaus the flat upland surface is structurally controlled by the nearly horizontal formations, as is admirably illustrated at Grand Canyon. The flat upland surface of the Piedmont Plateau, however, traverses a great variety of rocks and structures; evidently the Piedmont Plateau was formed by different processes from those that produced most other plateaus. Whatever those processes were, remains obscure.

Plateaus in humid regions (e.g., the Appalachian and Ozark plateaus) are structurally like those in semiarid regions (e.g., the Colorado and the Columbia-Fraser plateaus), yet the landforms are different because differences in climate cause differences in weathering and erosion. In humid plateaus the valley sides generally are smoothly sloped and mantled with loose debris (*colluvium*); in semiarid plateaus valley sides are usually angular, with cliffs and ledges of bare rock.

In humid regions shale formations are reduced to low, gently rounded land surfaces; in arid or

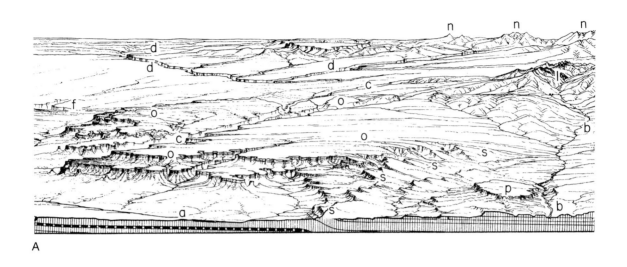

A

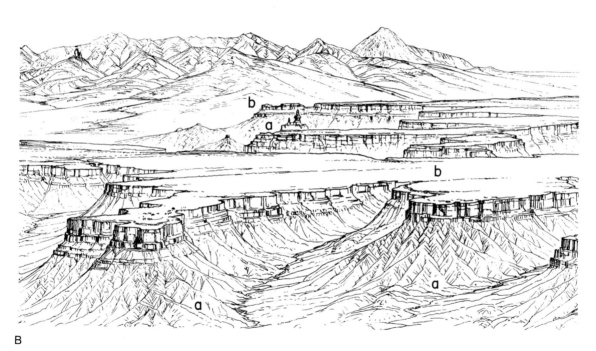

B

Figure 3.4 *Some plateau structures, as sketched by W. H. Holmes. (A) View north across Mesa Verde (o) to the Rio Dolores (d), La Plata Mountains (1), and San Miguel Mountains (n) in southwest Colorado. Other localities: San Juan River (a), Rio La Plata (b), Rio Mancos (c), McElmo Creek (f), hogback (s), Pinon mesa (p). (B) Close view of the Mesa Verde: slopes (a) are shale; the caprock (b) is sandstone (Cretaceous).*

semiarid regions they form distinctive badlands (see chapter frontispiece). Poorly consolidated sandstone formations in arid environments erode to castellate landforms (Figs. 3.2,A), whereas in

humid environments they are reduced to non-descript, low, rounded mounds.

Still another example of differences in land-forms developed on similar structures but in different climates is illustrated by the differences between hogbacks in arid and humid regions (Fig. 3.5).

PLAINS.   The principal plains in North America are developed on the stable central part of the continent—the Canadian Shield (Table 1.1)—and the structural platform around it, which forms the Central Lowland, the Great Plains, and the Arctic Slope of Alaska, and northwestern Canada. Another major plain, the Coastal Plain, is developed on the stable platform along the Atlantic and Gulf coasts of the United States. The Continental Shelf along the Atlantic seaboard is a part of the Coastal Plain that is still submerged.

Structurally, most plains are like plateaus, for their formations are nearly horizontal. The Canadian Shield and the Piedmont Province are exceptional in that the processes that formed them have planed complicated structures in old

Figure 3.5 *Hogbacks, formed by the eroded upturned edges of resistant formations, commonly produce rough, serrate ridges in arid and semiarid environments (A). In humid regions similar structures erode to form long, smooth-topped and smooth-sided ridges (B). In arid and semiarid regions, closely spaced but small washes and gullies are deeply cut into the flanks of the hogbacks, whereas only the main streams disrupt the hogbacks in humid regions.*

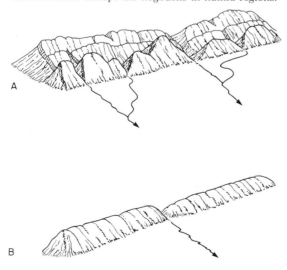

rocks. Landforms on plains are less varied than on plateaus because the plains either have not been elevated much above sea level or they rise very gradually from low altitudes, as do the Great Plains, which are higher than the Appalachian Plateaus. Interstream areas on plains are but little higher than the drainage courses, and there is little topographic relief.

Other plains are formed by the deltas at the mouths of such rivers as the Mississippi, Yukon, and MacKenzie. Other depositional plains are the low, broad, structures that form the Central and Imperial valleys of California and the Willamette Basin-Puget Trough in western Oregon and Washington.

A related but different and special kind of plain is represented by the playas in the valleys separating the block mountains of the Basin and Range Province. Some of these cover thousands of square miles, as does the Great Salt Lake desert, which includes the well-known speed course at the Bonneville Salt Flats. Another large playa, the Carson Sink in Nevada, covers more than a thousand square miles. There are many smaller ones, such as the salt-encrusted floor of Death Valley, which covers about 200 square miles.

MOUNTAINS.   The most complex landforms are the mountains, which are of many different kinds, each reflecting a different geologic structure. Figure 3.6 illustrates four kinds of mountains—dome, volcanic, fold, and block-fault mountains.

Most of the volcanic mountains in North America are along the Pacific coast, especially in the Cascade Range and Aleutian Islands. These are parts of a belt of active volcanoes and numerous earthquake centers surrounding the Pacific Ocean (Fig. 2.25).

Fold mountains, best represented by the Valley and Ridge Province in the Appalachian Province and the Ouachita Mountains in Oklahoma, have been eroded from sedimentary rock formations that were compressed into great folds; the upturned edges of the resistant formations form the mountain ridges.

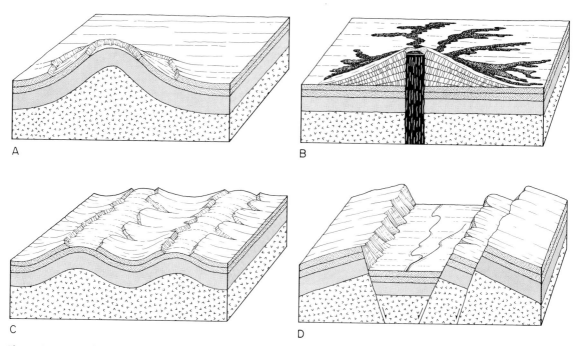

Figure 3.6 *Four kinds of mountains: dome mountain; volcano; fold mountain; block mountain. In dome mountains and fold mountains the escarpments face toward the uplift; in structural basins and synclines the escarpments face away from the downwarps—that is, they face toward the uplifts.*

A dome mountain is a special and local sort of fold mountain, and consists of a single upfold. The resistant formations turned upward around the dome form concentric ridges between the valleys cut in the more easily eroded formations. Examples of dome mountains are the Adirondacks in New York, the Black Hills in Wyoming and South Dakota, the Zuni Mountains in New Mexico, and the Henry Mountains and San Rafael Swell in Utah. Some dome mountains are attributable to folding; others, notably those in the Henry Mountains, are due to igneous intrusions.

In North America the principal area of block mountains, which are formed by faulting, is in the Basin and Range Province. The typical block mountain has an escarpment on the faulted side and a long, comparatively gentle slope away from the fault. The differences in slope on the two sides are illustrated by the profile through the Sierra Nevada (Fig. 2.20), which has been raised along a fault on the east side and tilted downward to the west.

Another important area of block mountains in this country is the belt of Triassic basins in the eastern part of the continent (Figs. 2.1, 3.7). The Triassic formations, mostly red sandstone and conglomerate with interbedded basalt flows and injected basalt sills (Fig. 11.7), occur in the Bay of Fundy, in the Connecticut Valley (Fig. 11.19), and in the Piedmont Province, mostly along its western boundary, from northern New Jersey to North Carolina (Fig. 2.1). In New Jersey, block mountains are represented by the Palisades and Watchung Ridges (Fig. 3.7, section A-B).

Mountains composed of granite develop characteristic landforms. Because granite is both homogeneous and resistant, erosion produces irregular topography without orderly patterns. Granitic mountains are extensive along the Coast Ranges of Canada and southeastern Alaska, in central Idaho, and in the Sierra Nevada. Smaller

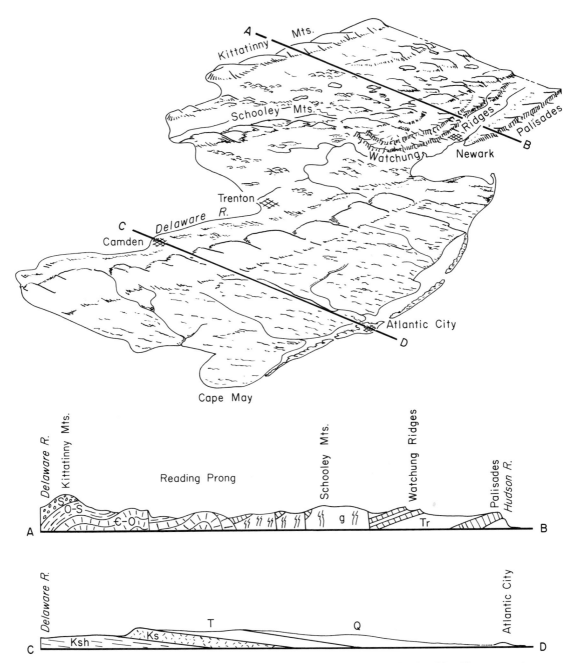

Figure 3.7 *Relief map and cross sections of New Jersey, illustrating several kinds of landforms. Southeastern New Jersey is coastal plain with Cretaceous (K), Tertiary (T), and Quaternary (Q) formations dipping gently seaward. The resistant formations form ridges (cuestas) paralleling the coast. The New Jersey turnpike follows one of the westernmost valleys. Atlantic City is on a barrier beach. The Triassic (Tr) belt of block mountains extends from Newark Bay to Trenton and westward to the Reading Prong, which is a complex (g) of granite, volcanic rocks and Paleozoic formations. To the west are the folded Cambrian (C), Ordovician (O), and Silurian (S) formations.*

granitic masses form the Black Hills, the High-lands of the Hudson, and some mountains in New England. Parts of the Rocky Mountains contain granite, notably the Front Range in Colorado, but the Rockies are complex mountains—partly fold, partly volcanic, and partly block mountains, and partly granitic.

The term "mountain" is used in two senses. One refers to the geologic structure, the other refers to the relief. Geologically the mountains of West Virginia and of eastern Kentucky have a plateau structure and are part of the Appalachian Plateau, yet the topography is mountainous and very well suited to the concealment of back-woods stills. In contrast, the Piedmont Plateau has the structure of mountains: it is the root of an ancient mountain system that has been eroded down to a low plateau. Similarly, the low parts of the Canadian Shield are plains whose structure is that of very ancient mountain roots.

Drainage Patterns

The structural pattern of a physiographic province becomes etched by stream erosion, and each province has its own characteristic drainage pattern. One type of pattern is branched, like a tree, and is called *dendritic.* Drainage systems in plateaus are likely to have this pattern. Examples are the Columbia and Snake rivers on the Columbia Plateau (Fig. 5.2). On plains the drainage pattern tends to be *parallel* in the direction of slope, as on the Coastal Plain and on the Great Plains (Fig. 5.2). Parallel drainage also has developed on the long western slope of the Sierra Nevada. Where the geologic structure consists of long parallel folds or faults, the drainage pattern is like a *trellis,* with long straight stretches parallel to the structures and short stretches at right angles across them, as in the block-faulted Canadian Rockies and the Rocky Mountains in Montana and Colorado, the Valley and Ridge Province, and the Coast Ranges of California. The trellis pattern of drainage in the Valley and Ridge Province in Pennsylvania shows conspicuously even in the state's network of roads. In

isolated mountains, like the Adirondacks and the volcanoes of the Cascade Range, the drainage is *radial.* In the Southern Rocky Mountains the drainage is radial, though on a larger scale.

Although these several kinds of drainage patterns reflect the geologic structure, the history of the drainage courses is highly complex, partly because of changes in climate, partly because of stream diversions such as might be caused by glaciation, and partly because of earth movements. An example of such complexity is illustrated by the riddle of how major rivers have developed and maintained their courses across mountain ranges instead of around them. Examples are legion; seven well-known ones are:

1. Columbia River gorge through the Cascade Range (Figs. 18.14, 18.17).
2. Golden Gate, San Francisco Bay (p. 589).
3. Gorge of the Bighorn River across the Bighorn Mountains, Wyoming-Montana (p. 408).
4. Colorado River gorges at the Black Mountains, Arizona and Nevada. Uncompaghre uplift and White River Plateau, Colorado (p. 424).
5. Royal Gorge of the Arkansas River, Colorado (Fig. 14.1, p. 387).
6. Delaware River at the Water Gap (Fig. 11.40,A).
7. Susquehanna River at Harrisburg (Fig. 11.40,B).

These valleys are all transverse to the mountain structures, and John Wesley Powell distinguished three kinds of relationships depending on whether the stream course was across the fold, in the direction of dip of the formations, or against the dip (Fig. 3.8). Such transverse valleys can originate in three ways—by *antecedence, superposition,* or a combination of those two that has been termed *anteposition* (Fig. 3.9). Antecedence results where uplift of a potential barrier across a drainage course proceeds at a slower rate than that of downcutting by the stream, thus

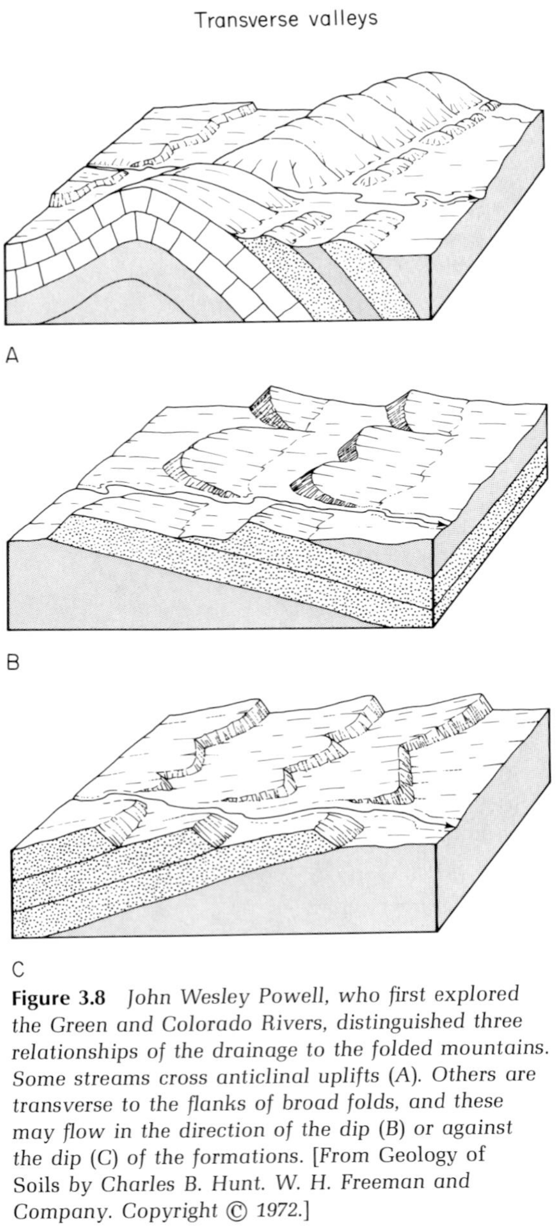

Transverse valleys

A

B

C

Figure 3.8 *John Wesley Powell, who first explored the Green and Colorado Rivers, distinguished three relationships of the drainage to the folded mountains. Some streams cross anticlinal uplifts (A). Others are transverse to the flanks of broad folds, and these may flow in the direction of the dip (B) or against the dip (C) of the formations. [From Geology of Soils by Charles B. Hunt. W. H. Freeman and Company. Copyright © 1972.]*

allowing the stream course to be maintained (Fig. 3.9). Superposition results where a drainage course, flowing on a depositional or erosional surface that covers older, perhaps folded, formations that differ in resistance, cuts through to the older rocks and becomes superimposed on them.

Superposed streams bear no relation to the once-buried rock structures and cut across them (Fig. 3.9,B). These two modes of origin are combined where uplift ponds the drainage for a time but is subsequently overflowed; the effect is that of antecedence downstream from the barrier and superposition upstream from it (Fig. 3.9,C).

Powell also distinguished three kinds of valleys that parallel the mountain structures: those along the crests of anticlines, those along the troughs of synclines, and those along the flanks of broad folds (Fig. 3.10).

LANDFORMS ATTRIBUTABLE
TO DEPOSITION

The converse of erosion is sedimentation, and the conditions that favor erosion, if reversed, favor deposition of sediments. Uplift favors erosion; downwarping favors deposition. An environmental change from arid to humid climate favors deposition; an opposite change favors erosion. Depositional landforms may be produced by the same agents that produce the erosional ones—that is, by streams, glaciers, waves, or wind. The depositional landforms are as varied as the erosional ones, but in general they are less extensive; many are merely local.

Depositional environments are of three major kinds: (1) *continental*—glaciers, streams, lakes, marshes, and dunes; (2) *marine*—shallow seas and deep seas; and (3) *mixed continental and marine*—the littoral zone, tidal lagoons, estuaries, and deltas. The deposits in each of these kinds of environments have characteristic bedding. Glacial till lacks bedding. Stream deposits, even the glaciofluvial ones associated with glacial drift, are stratified but discontinuous because of frequent changes in stream position. Lake deposits and marine deposits are generally thin-bedded, and individual beds may be continuous over long distances.

Among the stream-deposited features are floodplains, deltas, alluvial fans, and talus aprons. Most large rivers have floodplains, even though many are narrow; along many streams there are terraces that record old floodplains at

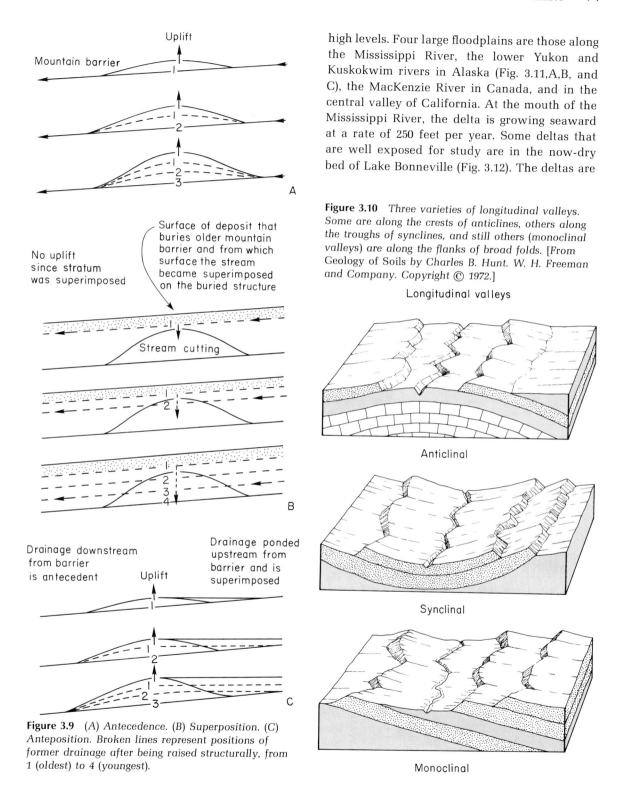

Uplift

Mountain barrier

A

No uplift
since stratum
was superimposed

Surface of deposit that
buries older mountain
barrier and from which
surface the stream
became superimposed
on the buried structure

Stream cutting

B

Drainage downstream
from barrier
is antecedent

Drainage ponded
upstream from
barrier and is
superimposed

Uplift

C

Figure 3.9 (A) Antecedence. (B) Superposition. (C) Anteposition. Broken lines represent positions of former drainage after being raised structurally, from 1 (oldest) to 4 (youngest).

high levels. Four large floodplains are those along the Mississippi River, the lower Yukon and Kuskokwim rivers in Alaska (Fig. 3.11,A,B, and C), the MacKenzie River in Canada, and in the central valley of California. At the mouth of the Mississippi River, the delta is growing seaward at a rate of 250 feet per year. Some deltas that are well exposed for study are in the now-dry bed of Lake Bonneville (Fig. 3.12). The deltas are

Figure 3.10 *Three varieties of longitudinal valleys. Some are along the crests of anticlines, others along the troughs of synclines, and still others (monoclinal valleys) are along the flanks of broad folds. [From Geology of Soils by Charles B. Hunt. W. H. Freeman and Company. Copyright © 1972.]*

Longitudinal valleys

Anticlinal

Synclinal

Monoclinal

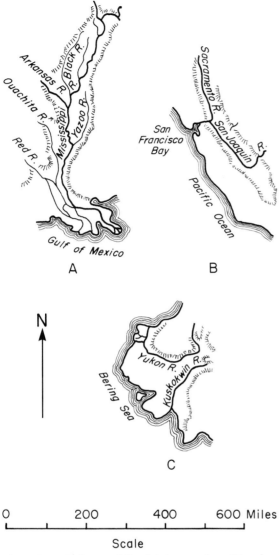

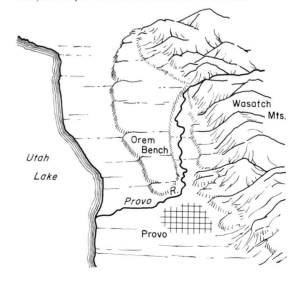

under water. Alluvial fans are particularly conspicuous in arid regions like the Basin and Range Province (Fig. 3.14), where precipitation, though rare, creates flash floods that deposit gravels at the foot of the mountains. The fans slope to a plain, a dry lake bed or playa, in the valley bottom.

Glacial deposits cover most of Canada and the northern United States (Fig. 6.1); they also occur on the high mountains of the western states and even in Hawaii. A few examples of the many different landforms built by glacial deposits are illustrated in Figure 3.15.

At the front, or terminus, of a glacier, gravel and sand are deposited to form a hummocky ridge called a *terminal moraine* (Fig. 11.25). Such ridges extend across valleys that were once occupied by mountain glaciers (Fig. 3.16,C), and many of them now contain lakes. Terminal moraines also formed around the fronts of the lobes of the continental ice sheets. Examples of these are the concentric ridges around the south end of Lake Michigan and around the ends of Lake Erie and Saginaw Bay (Figs. 3.16,A, 13.1). These plains and

Figure 3.12 *Orem Bench, at the foot of the Wasatch Mountains, Utah, is a delta that was deposited in Pleistocene time in a lake (Lake Bonneville) that was 600 feet deeper than its remnant at Utah Lake.*

Figure 3.11 *Deltas and floodplains are depositional landforms.*

flat-topped benches capped by topset beds (Fig. 3.13). Under the topsets are foreset beds that form a steep slope at the front of the delta and grade downward and outward to bottomset beds that form the lake-bottom sediments.

Alluvial fans, another common depositional landform, are related to deltas but were deposited on what is usually dry land rather than

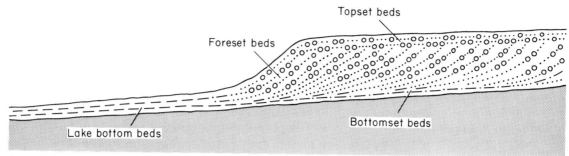

Figure 3.13 *Cross section illustrating the composition and structure of a delta. Fine-grained, commonly clayey to silty lake-bottom beds grade into the bottomset beds of the delta. These grade upward into rather steeply sloping foreset beds composed of sand and gravel washed onto the steep front of the delta; each foreset bed represents a former front of the delta. Topset beds also are sand and gravel and represent the sediment lost in transit across the top of the delta.*

the moraines are hummocky, partly because deposition was caused by short-lived, irregular flooding, and partly because blocks of ice, deposited with the sediments, melted to form depressions known as *kettle holes;* the hillocks are referred to as *kames.* Ice that readvanced over the hillocks reshaped them like teardrops (*drumlins*), elongating and tapering them in the direction of the ice readvance (Figs. 3.16,B, 11.21, 11.24). Many of the hills about Boston, including Bunker Hill, are drumlins.

Another landform attributable to glacial deposition are the ridges (*eskers*) that form where gravels are deposited by streams flowing on or under a glacier; when the ice melts, these gravels are left as meandering ridges.

Other depositional landforms are formed by waves: barrier beaches and beach bars (Figs. 3.1, 3.7, 10.7, 10.9), spits, capes, and hooks (Figs. 3.7, 10.33).

Depositional features attributable to wind include dunes and loess plains. Dunes may be arcuate or elongate and parallel. Some arcuate dunes are concave in the windward direction, others to the leeward. Elongate dunes parallel the wind direction. The dune form depends partly on the availability of sand, strength of wind, and presence or absence of vegetation, which collects and holds the sand. Loess—wind-deposited silt—blankets the middle western plains (Fig. 6.1) and forms the rich soil of that area. The loess dates

from the glacial periods, and originated as dust blown eastward out of the great river valleys, which were left as bare mud flats after floods of glacial melt waters subsided.

Other deposits include *talus,* which collects at the foot of steep slopes as a result of rock falls (Fig. 3.17,A), and *colluvium* (Fig. 3.17,B), which collects on hillsides and moves slowly down gentle slopes—a process called creep.

Finally, some deposits are built by organisms: coral reefs, beaver ponds, peat marshes, gopher mounds, buffalo wallows, and ant hills.

SHORE FEATURES

The shores of the continent exhibit great variety of form, owing to such factors as the hardness and structure of the coastal rocks, slope of the sea floor, recent changes in sea level (or of the height of the land), the effects of glacial activity and wave action, and locally, volcanic activity and coral growth.

The northeastern part of the continent has been tilted northeastward, with the result that the low-lying Coastal Plain formations are embayed by the sea at Chesapeake Bay and to the north. In New England and the Maritime Provinces of Canada, the hard rocks of the Appalachian Province are partly submerged; the coast is rocky and even more irregular than the embayed part of the Coastal Plain. It is a *ria coast.* Beyond

Owlshead Mountains

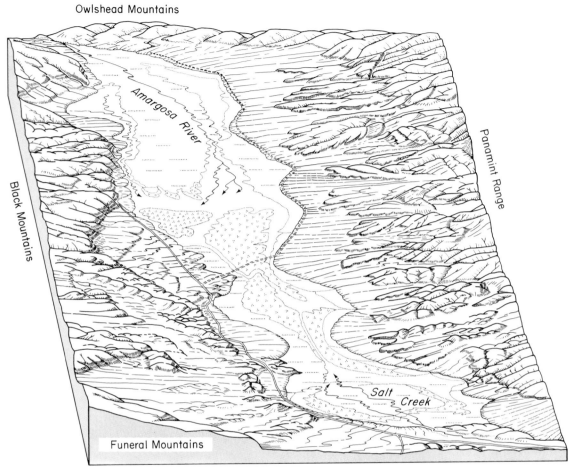

Black Mountains

Panamint Range

Amargosa River

Salt Creek

Funeral Mountains

Figure 3.14 *Death Valley, California, is typical of valleys in the Basin and Range Province in having extensive gravel fans sloping from the mountains to the plain that forms the valley floor. These alluvial fans are several miles long and 1,500 feet high. The valley floor is a salt-crusted, dry lake bed (playa). The flat valley floor consists of rough rock salt (triangular pattern), salt smoothed by washing (horizontal dot pattern), and mud flats subject to flooding (white). [After U.S.G.S.]*

Newfoundland the Appalachians are submerged, as is the Canadian Shield along the Labrador Coast and in Hudson Bay.

Along the glaciated rocky coasts sand and gravel is abundant and may be moved by the waves to build bars across the mouths of valleys (*baymouth bars*) or, depending on the currents and exposure, may be deposited as beaches at the heads of bays (*bayhead bars*). Wave erosion at headlands may develop caves, and their en-

largement and collapse forms *sea stacks,* which are small, steep-sided islands. Stacks or other islands may become connected to the mainland by sand spits, forming what are known as *tombolos.*

Along the Pacific coast of Canada and the southeastern coast of Alaska is *fjord coast* whose valleys were overdeepened by glacial ice and have since been invaded by the ocean. Like other fjords these are on the west side of the continent,

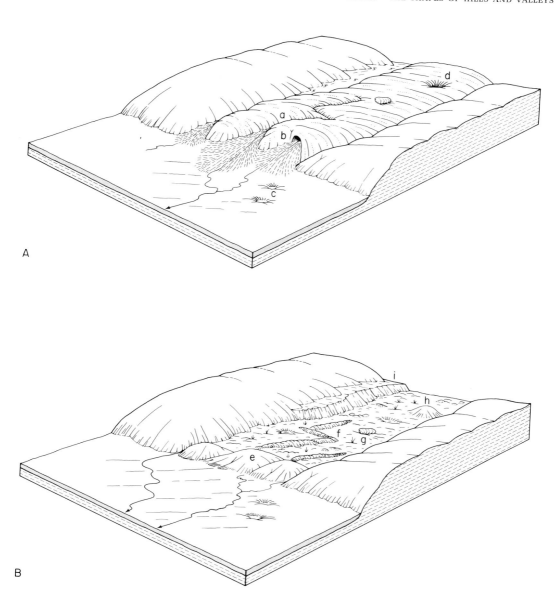

Figure 3.15 *Nomenclature and origin of some glacial landforms. (A) Glacial ice in a valley has streams draining from it in tunnels (b) and crevasses (a) in the ice and from the base of the ice sheet; gravel fans are deposited where these discharge at the ice front. Beyond the ice is a plain of stream-deposited outwash where blocks of ice from the glacier melt and leave depressions, kettle holes (c) in the plain. In and on the ice are boulders from up valley. Shafts (d) with funnel-shaped openings collect gravel and sand. Lakes ponded against the valley walls contain small deltas. (B) When the ice melts the gravel fans in front of the ice collapse and form an end moraine (e); the stream channels on and under the ice are marked by ridges of gravel, eskers (f). The valley floor is hummocky ground moraine on which boulders rest as glacial erratics (g). The gravel and sand deposited in the shafts in the ice form kames (h). Collapsed deltas in the marginal lakes form kame terraces (i).*

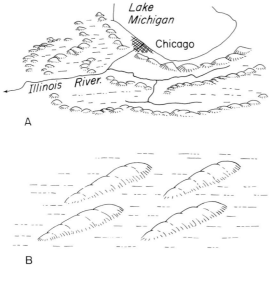

A

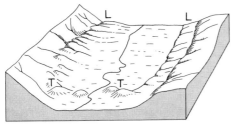

B

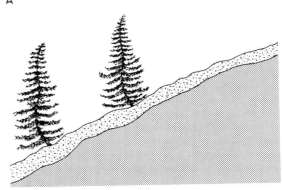

C

Figure 3.16 *Landforms attributable to deposition by glaciers. (A) Terminal moraines south of Lake Michigan form a series of concentric ridges separated by till plains, outwash plains, and lake beds. (B) Drumlins. (C) Lateral (L) and terminal (T) moraines deposited by a former valley glacier.*

in the belt of westerlies—the regions most subject to glacial action during the Pleistocene. Other examples are the west coast of Greenland, the coast of Norway, New Zealand, and the southern coast of Chile.

South of the limit of glaciation the Pacific Coast is hilly or mountainous and is tectonically active. The steep coasts there are largely due to recent earth movements; in some places former beaches have been uplifted a thousand feet above present sea level.

Shores of the Atlantic and Gulf Coastal Plains are very different. The formations there are

mostly flat-lying, easily eroded sandstone and shale having a smooth surface sloping gently seaward. Where submerged, this surface forms the continental shelf; where emerged, it forms the coastal plain. Since Pleistocene time sea level has been rising and advancing landward; at the same time the coast has been broadly warped, yielding a considerable variety of shoreline shapes despite the simplicity of the basic structure: islands east of New York, big bays along the middle Atlantic Coast, smooth cusps and barrier beaches between Cape Hatteras and Cape Fear, numerous small islands along the coast of South Carolina and Georgia, contrasts between the east and west coast of Florida, the palmate delta of the Mississippi River, and barrier beach shores of the East and West Gulf Coastal plains. Reasons for these differences are discussed in Chapter 10.

Figure 3.17 *(A) Talus, coarse debris, accumulates on a slope at the foot of a cliff as a gravity deposit. (B) Colluvium is the mantle of loose material that moves by creep down a hillside. In some places creep is indicated by the bending of trees.*

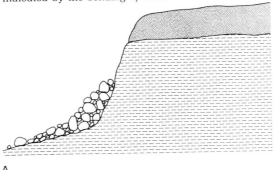

A

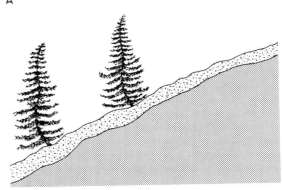

B

References

Baird, D. M., 1964, Geology and landforms as illustrated by selected Canadian topographic maps: Geol. Survey of Canada Paper 64–21.

Bunnett, R. B., 1968, Physical geography in diagrams: New York, Praeger.

Chorley, R. J., Dunn, A. J., and Beckinsale, R. P., 1964, Geomorphology before Davis (The history of the study of landforms, Vol. 1): London, Methuen.

Davis, W. M., 1954, Geographical essays: Dover Publ. (reprinted from 1909 ed.), 777 pp.

Drury, G. H., 1959, The face of the earth: Baltimore, Penguin Books.

Easterbrook, D. J., 1969, Principles of geomorphology: New York, McGraw-Hill.

Jennings, J. N., and Mabbutt, J. A., 1967, Landform studies from Australia and New Guinea: New York, Cambridge Univ. Press.

Lobeck, A. K., 1939, Geomorphology: New York, McGraw-Hill.

Lobeck, A. K., 1958, Block diagrams: Amherst, Mass., Emerson-Trussell Book Co.

Upton, W. B., Jr., 1970, Landforms and topographic maps: New York, Wiley.

See also the general physiographic references at the end of Chapter 1.

Summer rainstorm in the Midwest. [From *Geology Illustrated* by John S. Shelton. W. H. Freeman and Company. Copyright © 1966.]

4
·······

CLIMATES, WEATHER—THE AIR AROUND US

The Atmosphere

The air we breathe is composed of 78 percent nitrogen and 21 percent oxygen; most of the remaining 1 percent is argon. This is the composition of dry air, for water vapor is always present in amounts up to about 5 percent. As we well know, air also contains pollutants.

The atmosphere extends upward about 50 miles from the earth's surface (Fig. 4.1); beyond this, according to some definitions, is outer space, where the commonest elements are hydrogen and helium. The atmosphere has weight. The pressure it exerts at sea level is equal to that exerted by a column of mercury 29.52 inches high ($=760$ millimeters) or by a column of water about 34 feet high. This pressure amounts to roughly 1 ton per square foot, yet we are not crushed. Half the mass of the atmosphere is compressed into a thin layer that is only $3\frac{1}{2}$ miles thick, which is roughly proportional to the thickness of a layer of varnish on a globe.

The atmosphere is layered. The lowermost layer, the *troposphere*, extends from the earth's surface to a height of about 5 miles at the poles and to a height of about 10 miles at the equator. Temperatures in the troposphere decrease uniformly with altitude (to less than $-40°F$ ($-40°C$)); wind velocity increases with height.

The layer next above the troposphere is the stratosphere, of interest to us chiefly because it contains enough ozone (O_3) to absorb the lethal ultraviolet rays entering the atmosphere from outer space.

Temperature and precipitation are the two most important factors controlling climate and weather in the lower troposphere. The four principal kinds of climates are cold-wet, cold-dry, warm-wet, and warm-dry. Extremes of temperature are more important than averages, especially the duration of the frost-free season and the frequency of freeze and thaw in winter. Although the amount of precipitation is important, along with evaporation, of equal importance is the seasonal distribution of precipitation and the extremes, whether of drought or of excess rain or snow.

Climatic Regions

Climates play a major role in controlling physiography all over the world. In the United States, climates are mostly temperate, but they range from polar along the arctic coast of Canada and Alaska to tropical in southern Florida and in Puerto Rico and Hawaii. The major climatic regions are illustrated in Figure 4.2.

Polar climates have a short growing season. In the severest polar climate, at the poles and on the high parts of mountains holding glaciers, even the warmest month averages below freezing, and snow perpetually covers the ground. In the mild-

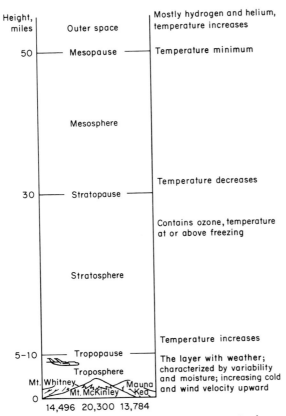

Figure 4.1 *The atmosphere and outer space. In the usual sense of the word, "climate" refers to conditions in the troposphere. Water vapor is almost entirely below the tropopause.*

est polar climate, the warmest month averages above freezing but below 50°F, and the growing season lasts less than about 2 months. This kind of climate prevails along the arctic coasts and also at high altitudes farther south. A 1,000-foot increase in altitude is equivalent roughly to a 3° northward shift in latitude and a $3\frac{1}{2}$°F drop in temperature. Thus, climates on mountain tops in the western United States are the same as those in the polar regions. A person traveling south from the arctic coast can experience polar climate, and enjoy his skiing, by climbing to 3,000 feet in the Alaska Range, 6,500 feet in the Northern Cascades, and 11,500 feet in the Sierra Nevada.

South of the polar region is a rainy belt with severe winters that comprises most of Alaska, most of Canada, and the eastern United States to about latitude 40°. The coldest month averages below freezing, but the warmest averages above 50°F. The growing season lengthens from about 2 months at the north to about 5 months at the south.

The southeastern United States and the Pacific Coast, from San Francisco north to the Panhandle of Alaska, have rainy climates with mild winters. The coldest month averages above freezing. Annual precipitation is more than 40 inches and in some places exceeds 100. The climates differ also on the basis of wet and dry seasons. The Panhandle of Alaska and the western coast of Canada have no dry season. The coast south of Washington has dry summers. In the central United States summers are wet and winters dry. The Gulf and Atlantic coasts have no pronounced dry season. Tropical rainy climates prevail in southern Florida, Hawaii, and Puerto Rico. The coolest month averages more than 65°F.

From the Sierra-Cascade Province eastward to the 100th meridian, the climate is dry; potential evaporation exceeds precipitation, except on some high mountains. Part of this region is desert, with annual precipitation averaging less than 8 inches. The rest is semiarid, and treeless like the steppes of Eurasia, annual precipitation averaging between 8 and 20 inches. The difference in effective moisture in these two climates is even greater than is indicated by the difference in precipitation, because evaporation rates in the arid regions are greater than in the semiarid ones. Permanent throughflowing streams cannot originate in warm regions where annual precipitation is much less than 20 inches.

Temperatures in the interior of the continent may average the same as near the coasts, but temperatures near the coasts vary less because of the modifying influence of the nearby ocean waters. St. Louis and Fort Yukon illustrate *continental climates,* in which the annual variation in temperature is great. At St. Louis January temperatures average 32°F, July temperatures 80°F. At Fort Yukon January temperatures average −21°F, July temperatures 61°F. Hawaii and Puerto Rico illustrate *marine climates,* in which

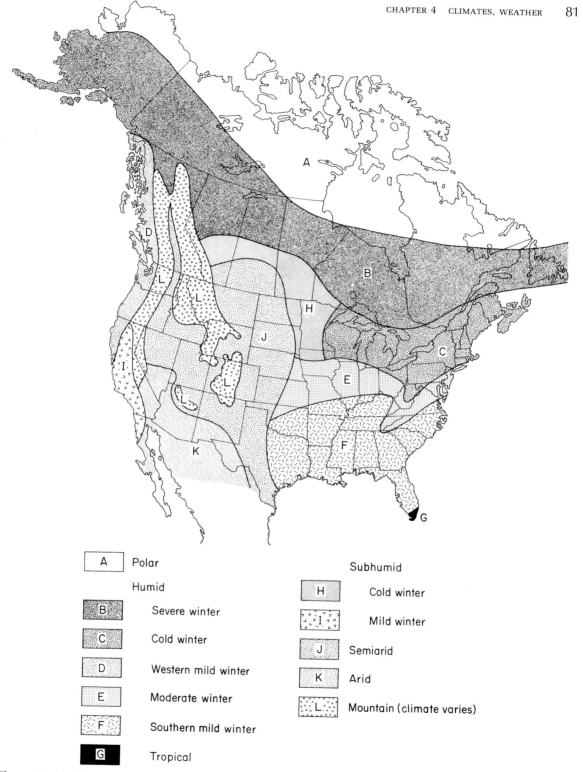

A	Polar
	Humid
B	Severe winter
C	Cold winter
D	Western mild winter
E	Moderate winter
F	Southern mild winter
G	Tropical

Subhumid

H	Cold winter
I	Mild winter
J	Semiarid
K	Arid
L	Mountain (climate varies)

Figure 4.2 *North America climates. [From Geology of Soils by Charles B. Hunt. W. H. Freeman and Company. Copyright © 1972.]*

the annual variation in temperature is small. At Honolulu January temperatures average 71°F, July temperatures 77°F. At San Juan, Puerto Rico, January temperatures average 75°F; July temperatures 80°F.

Urbanization affects climates. Cities average warmer than the countryside around them and commonly are spared freezes that affect the suburbs.

Precipitation—Air and Ground Moisture

Average annual precipitation provides the most readily understood index of moisture availability (Fig. 4.3), but equally significant is the seasonal distribution of that precipitation. As is brought out by Figure 4.4, most precipitation along the Pacific coast (San Francisco record) falls during winter. In the Middle West (St. Louis record) most precipitation falls during the late spring and the summer. Along the Atlantic seaboard (New York record) precipitation is rather evenly spread throughout the year.

Maximum annual precipitation recorded in the United States is in central Kauai, Hawaii, where at 5,075 feet the average rainfall is more than 450 inches. Several stations in Hawaii record more than 200 inches annually. In Alaska the heaviest precipitation has been recorded along the southern coast, where some stations receive more than 150 inches annually; but surely it is even heavier in the coastal mountains. The Olympic Mountains near Seattle receive 140 inches of precipitation annually. At the other extreme is Death Valley, California, where the average precipitation is about 1.6 inches and the evaporation *rate* is about 150 inches annually.

The quantity of moisture that air can hold depends upon the temperature. At freezing, a cubic meter of air can hold about 5 grams of water vapor; at room temperature, 30 grams. When a given volume of air contains the maximum amount of water that it can hold at a particular temperature, it is saturated. The most commonly used measure of atmospheric moisture is *relative humidity*—the actual amount of water vapor in the air expressed as a percentage of the maximum amount the air could hold at the same

temperature. An air mass in New England may have the same amount of water vapor as an equivalent volume of air in the western deserts, but the relative humidity of the air mass in New England would be much higher because that air is cooler and therefore more nearly saturated. Both air masses, however, would have the same *dewpoint,* which is that temperature at which water vapor in the air condenses as liquid.

Temperatures—Heating and Cooling of the Air and Ground

The earth is warmed by solar radiation of which about 35 percent is reflected back into space by the clouds; another 20 percent is absorbed in the atmosphere by water vapor, carbon dioxide, and dust. Most of this absorption is in the lower, compressed layer of the atmosphere. Forty-five percent of the radiation reaches the ground, and almost 90 percent of this is reflected back into the atmosphere. Most of this reflected radiation also is absorbed by the compressed layer of the atmosphere. Only 5 percent of the solar heat goes into the ground, where the heat is transferred by conduction.

Because warm air is lighter than cold air, it rises. During its ascent it expands and cools. Dry air cools about 1°C per 100 meters (1°F per 180 feet); moist air cools about 0.6°C per 100 meters. Conversely, descending air warms as it becomes compressed. These cooling and warming processes are responsible for warm winds that occasionally descend onto the Great Plains from the Rocky Mountains.

Land heats and cools more rapidly than water, which accounts for the alternating land-sea breezes that characterize many coastal and island regions. Water heats slowly and cools slowly; in fact more heat is required to raise the temperature of a mass of water than of any other substance. Moreover, water surfaces reflect more of the solar radiation than do land surfaces, and the radiation that penetrates the water is distributed throughout the surface layers of the water.

The coldest part of North America is in northwest Canada in the Great Slave and Great Bear Lake regions and westward into Alaska. Fort

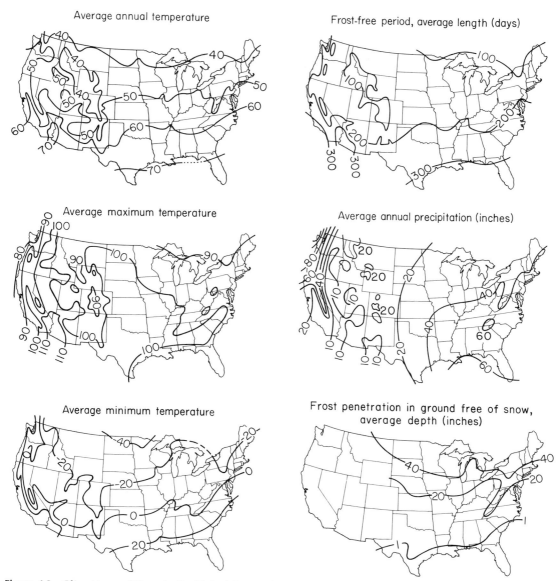

Figure 4.3 *Climatic conditions in the United States. (Data from U.S.D.A.)*

Yukon, Alaska, has recorded a record low of −78°F and a summer maximum of 100°F. Yellowstone Park has the record low for the conterminous states, −66°F. The highest temperature on record in North America is 134°F in Death Valley, California. The central part of the continent, which has a continental climate, shows the greatest variability. In St. Louis, January temperatures have been recorded as high as 74°F and as low as −22°F.

Cloudiness reduces radiation, which is one of the reasons why temperatures are less extreme in humid regions than in deserts. In deserts, the daily temperature range commonly exceeds 30°F, which is about twice the range at inland humid stations.

In northern Canada and northern Alaska the ground is permanently frozen, a condition referred to as *permafrost.* In places the ground ice is more than 1,000 feet deep. In part this condi-

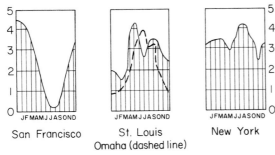

Figure 4.4 *Seasonal variation in precipitation at San Francisco, St. Louis, Omaha, and New York.*

tion is probably a relic from the Pleistocene ice ages. In temperate regions we are accustomed to thinking in terms of depth of winter freezing, but in regions of permafrost one thinks in terms of the depth of summer thaw. Some of the peculiarities of permafrost are described in Chapter 12.

Atmospheric Pressure, Air Circulation

Air tends to move and the winds to blow from high-pressure to low-pressure areas. Land-sea breezes are an easily understood example. The land warms faster than the bordering water surface and as the air warms, the denser, cold air from the sea moves landward. Conversely, at night, the land cools more than the sea, and the air moves seaward. North America is a high-pressure area in winter and a low-pressure area in summer.

Air circulation over the whole earth is due to the combined effects of heating over the equator and cooling over the poles. This combination is modified by the coriolis effect (Fig. 4.5,B), by the distribution of land and sea, by the topography on the land and the currents in the oceans, and by the seasonal shift of the thermal equator. The coriolis force affects ocean currents too. For example, the California Current, which moves southward from the Gulf of Alaska, turns westward into the Pacific, and this addition to the surface of the ocean causes cold water to rise against the coast of the Pacific Northwest, which accounts for much of the fog and high rainfall there. The total complex of atmospheric forces develops *air masses*, which are hundreds of miles

in diameter and many thousands of feet high and have fairly uniform moisture contents and temperatures. Air masses move into the United States from four principal regions. The continental polar air masses bring cold, dry weather. The North Pacific center delivers moist, cold air. The South Pacific and Gulf centers deliver warm, moist air.

The advancing edge of a warm air mass—a warm front—moves more slowly than the advancing edge of a cold air mass, or cold front, because cold air can displace warm air more readily than warm air can displace cold air. For the same reason, cold fronts are steeper than warm fronts (Fig. 4.6). Along cold fronts rain and snow are likely to be heavy but of short duration; along warm fronts the cloudiness is more general and precipitation is more likely to be even and to last longer.

At the fronts the air is turbulent due to the mixing. Most clouds and precipitation occur along the fronts of low-pressure masses because the air is cooled as it rises, causing its relative humidity to increase to saturation. In low-pressure masses the winds spiral toward the center of the low; in high-pressure masses the winds spiral away from the center of the high. Wind velocities depend on the pressure gradients. A scale for estimating wind velocity, developed in 1805 by Admiral Beaufort in England, is summarized in Table 4.1. This scale still has many practical uses.

Pressure decreases with altitude, roughly $\frac{1}{30}$th of the value at the particular altitude per 900 feet of change in altitude. At 5,000 feet the atmospheric pressure is about 20 percent less than at sea level; at 10,000 feet the pressure is a third less than at sea level; and at about 17,500 feet the pressure is only half that at sea level. A practical consequence of this is that airplane runways must be longer at high altitudes than at low ones. Also, because of the lower air pressure, water boils at a lower temperature at high altitudes; a three-minute egg cooked in Denver is really soft.

The unit of atmospheric pressure used on weather maps is the millibar. One thousand millibars equals the pressure exerted by a column of mercury 750 millimeters high, which is equal to 29.53 inches of mercury. The average atmospheric pressure at sea level, 1 atmosphere of pressure, is about 1013 millibars.

When outdoors in the winter, one becomes well aware of the chilling effects of wind. When the temperature is at freezing (32°F), a 25 mile per hour wind has a chilling effect equivalent to zero temperature. When the temperature is zero, a 10 mile per hour wind has a chilling effect equivalent to −22°F, and a 25 mile per hour wind has a chilling effect equivalent to −45°F. Wind chill below −32°F causes freezing of exposed human flesh, depending on one's circulation and physical activity. With wind chill temperatures much below that, survival efforts may be required. As long as the temperature is above 10°F, only gales are dangerous. When the temperature is zero, there is danger of flesh becoming frozen if exposed to a 15 mile per hour wind. When the temperature is −15°F a wind velocity of 10 miles

per hour can be dangerous. At temperatures much below that, it is probably best to remain indoors by the fireside.

Climatic differences between the Atlantic and Pacific coasts illustrate the effect of wind. Because of the prevailing westerly winds, the Pacific Coast has a marine climate with cool summers and mild winters, while the Atlantic coast has a continental climate with hot summers and cold winters. Hawaii and Puerto Rico are in tropical latitudes, but are cooled by the northeast trade winds.

Violent Weather and Other Climatic Hazards

Every part of the continent is subject to occasional combinations of conditions that produce extreme weather. The result may be a record-breaking hot or cold spell, a drenching downpour

Figure 4.5 *Idealized air circulation on the globe. (A) Warm air rises at the equatorial and subpolar lows; cold air descends at the polar and subtropical highs. In moving southward the air masses (and ocean currents) tend to turn right in the northern hemisphere and left in the southern hemisphere—the so-called coriolis effect. (B) A mass of air moving south from a toward b has a component of force toward the east because of the earth's rotation. Let this force be represented by the distance of a-c, which equals b-d. But since point b has moved to position e, the air mass has therefore moved west to the position d. Likewise, an air mass moving north from b would move right and masses in the southern hemisphere move left.*

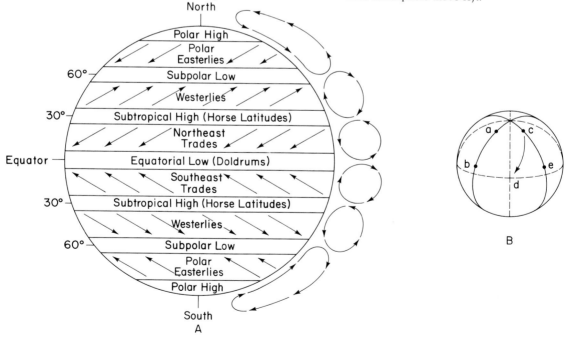

Table 4.1

Beaufort Scale of Wind Velocity

Beaufort Number	Name	Velocity (miles per hour)	Effects
0	Calm	<1	Smoke rises vertically.
1	Light	1–3	Wind directions shown by smoke but not by vanes.
2	Light	4–7	Wind felt on face; leaves rustle; vanes move.
3	Gentle	8–12	Leaves in constant motion; light flags extended.
4	Moderate	13–18	Raises dust and loose paper; small branches move.
5	Fresh	19–24	Small trees sway; wavelets on inland waters.
6	Strong	25–31	Large branches move; whistling in telegraph wires; umbrellas used with difficulty.
7	Strong	32–38	Whole trees move; difficult to walk against the wind.
8	Gale	39–46	Twigs break off trees; progress impeded.
9	Gale	47–54	Slight structural damage such as removal of slate and chimney pots.
10	Whole gale	55–63	Considerable structural damage; trees uprooted.
11	Whole gale	64–75	Widespread damage.
12	Hurricane	>75	Widespread damage, devastation.

of rain, an accumulation of snow, or a severe drought. Weather can become violent, like that caused by hurricanes or tornadoes. Some examples of different kinds of climatic hazards in various parts of the United States are illustrated in Figure 4.7. The hazard, however, is not necessarily greatest in the areas that have the greatest frequency of particular conditions. For example, in the United States, electric storms are more frequent in the East than in the West, but forest fires started by lightning are most frequent in the West. This is because so many electric storms in the West are not accompanied by rain that could dowse a fire started by lightning.

Storms that are characterized by high winds include the *hurricanes* that seasonally move northward out of the Caribbean Sea to the Gulf Coast or sweep along the Atlantic seaboard, and the tornadoes of the southern and central United States. Hurricanes are the western-hemisphere equivalent of the typhoons in the western Pacific Ocean, the Willy-Willies of the southwest Pacific, and the cyclones of the Indian Ocean. Such tropical storms average about 400 miles in diameter. Barometric pressure at their centers may be less than 28 inches of mercury. As in other low-pressure areas in the northern hemisphere, the

winds rotate counterclockwise and may attain velocities of 150 miles per hour. Tornadoes, which form over the land, are much smaller but most are more violent. They are usually only a few hundred yards in diameter, but they may

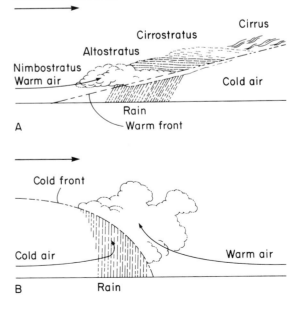

Figure 4.6 *Sequence of cloud forms commonly associated with warm and cold fronts.*

have twice the wind velocity of a hurricane. In a half century more than 6,000 tornadoes have been recorded, and they have caused almost 9,000 deaths and three-quarters of a billion dollars in property loss.

Some Other Factors That Control Climate

Some other factors controlling climate can be illustrated by comparing different regions. Northern Canada and Alaska illustrate the effect of *latitude*. At the winter solstice the sun's rays are tangent to the ground surface at the Arctic Circle, to the north of which there is no sun. Even in summer the sun's rays strike the northern latitudes at a low angle, whereas they strike the southern United States almost perpendicularly. This is shown in Figure 4.8,A, which also illus-

trates the effect of seasons. In winter, the northern hemisphere is tilted away from the sun, and the sun's rays strike this half of the earth at low angles. Less radiation and less heat are received than in summer, and days are shorter.

The effect of altitude, already mentioned, is illustrated by the snow cover on Mount McKinley, for the upper two-thirds of that mountain is enveloped by snow throughout the year.

The deserts east of the Sierra Nevada provide an example of how *topography* can affect climate. The moisture-laden westerly winds must rise to cross the mountains. In doing so they become chilled and drop much of their moisture. The dry area east of the mountains is referred to as a *rain shadow* (Fig. 4.8,B). Other important rain shadows are east of the Cascades, east of the High Plateaus of Utah, and east of the Rocky Mountains. Figure 4.8,B illustrates the close relationships between topography and precipitation

Figure 4.7 *Frequency of some climatic hazards. Ruled areas are those that have the greatest frequency; stippled areas are intermediate; white areas slight.*

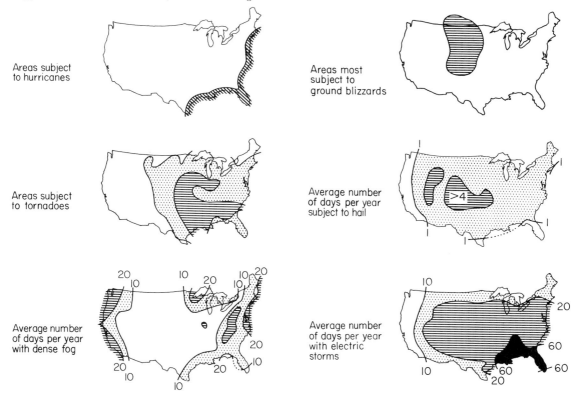

in the mountains, plateaus, and basins of the western United States.

A different effect of topography is the downhill drainage of cold air, which collects in valleys by displacing the lighter warm air. Valley bottoms are colder and have more frequent frosts than nearby hillsides. Most of the apple orchards of Yakima and Wenatchee, Washington, are on hillslopes; only alfalfa is grown in the valley bottoms.

Topography has an important influence on the accumulation of pollutants. When the air is still, stagnant polluted air may become trapped in a valley bottom beneath a blanket of warmer air. Every city in a mountain valley experiences this; Pittsburgh, of course, but also Tucson, Phoenix, and Las Vegas. Polluted air can also be trapped at the windward base of a mountain range; this is the problem in Los Angeles and Salt Lake City.

The effect of *oceanic currents* on climate is illustrated by the North Pacific currents and the Gulf Stream. The Japan Current moves eastward and divides, one branch turning northward and warming the south coast of Alaska, and the other turning southward and causing summer cooling of the coast south of Alaska (Fig. 4.8,C). On the Atlantic seaboard the warm Gulf Stream has a moderating effect as far north as Cape Cod. North of Cape Cod the effects of the cold Labrador Current are felt.

Another factor that affects climate is the composition of the air, never pure, for it contains varying quantities of moisture, dust, soot, and foreign gases. The climate in an industrial city blanketed with smog differs from that in the surrounding countryside.

Microclimate

The climate on and near the ground, referred to as *microclimate,* may differ greatly from the climate a few feet above the ground. The ground may be hotter or colder than the air above it, and may cause moisture to condense from comparatively dry air. At the ground surface air may be almost still while the higher air is in motion. The ground layers of air have more shade than the upper layers because of vegetation, topography,

and buildings. These variations in microclimate modify the general climatic influences on soil processes and on the biota. They greatly influence the use of the land and the design of highway and other foundations. Examples of the effects of microclimate may be seen by comparing the ground on the shaded north side of a house with that on the sunny south side.

Because ground is a poor conductor, the surface becomes intensely heated during the day, and conversely may cool more than the air above it at night. In deserts, the temperature of the ground surface in the sun commonly is nearly twice the air temperature; groundsurface temperatures as high as 190°F have been recorded in Death Valley.

But this surface layer subject to such extreme diurnal temperature changes is only skin deep. In general, the seasonal average temperature for a given locality is reached within a couple of feet of the surface, and for practical purposes the average annual temperature is reached within a few more feet. For example, the limestone caverns in Virginia, Mammoth Cave, and the Carlsbad Caverns are located approximately along the 55°F isotherm (Fig. 4.3), and the temperatures in those caves are nearly constant at about 55°F.

Ground under forest is shaded from sun and protected from the impact of direct fall of raindrops. About 40 to 50 deciduous trees can provide a canopy that, in summer, almost completely shades an acre of ground, so that as little as 5 percent of the radiation reaches the ground. In winter, about 50 percent of the sunlight gets through to such ground, but the ground at that season is covered with a mat of newly fallen leaves. Beneath that is the partly decayed mat of older vegetative material. Wind velocity near a forest floor is only about a third as great as that above the canopy; gusts are moderated. This reduces evaporation, so that the ground remains moist. Air temperatures at the floor may be 5 to 10 degrees colder than the air above the canopy, night or day, but with the protection by the mat of organic matter, the microfauna and microflora continue to thrive.

Because underground microclimates are uniform and their temperatures moderate, farmers

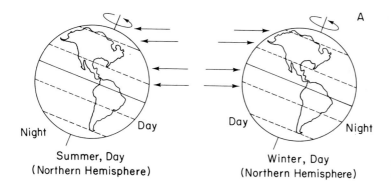

Effect of latitude and season. Direct solar radiation is concentrated in a small area; indirect radiation covers a wide area, and for fewer hours per day. Moreover, radiation that is oblique must penetrate more atmosphere.

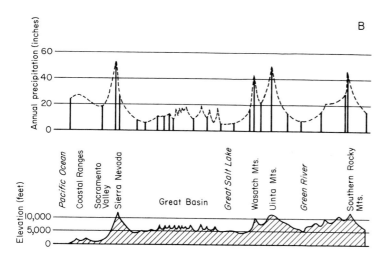

Differences in annual precipitation in the mountains, plateaus, and basins of the western United States. The curve is very similar to the topographic profile because the precipitation varies according to altitude. [From U.S.D.A. Yearbook, 1941.]

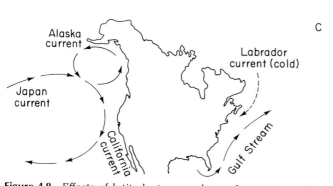

Effect of ocean currents. Our climates are influenced by the Japan Current, the Labrador Current, and the Gulf Stream.

Figure 4.8 *Effects of latitude, topography, and ocean currents on climate.*

have long made use of dug cellars for storing food, especially in those parts of the country where the ground is not excessively moist. Because conduction is slow, some underground limestone quarries and caverns have been artificially refrigerated and used as large freezers.

Climatic Changes

The differences between the climatic regions are of great importance physiographically, but of equal importance are the climates of the past, especially those of the Pleistocene Epoch. Throughout most of North America the various kinds of ground are attributable largely to conditions that prevailed under climates different from those of the present.

As recently as 20,000 years ago an ice sheet covered most of Canada and extended southward to Long Island and northern New Jersey on the east and to the Ohio and Missouri Rivers in the Middle West. The extent of the ice mass was about equal to that of the present Antarctic ice cap. This was the most recent of four glacial stages distinguished in North America, each of which is named for the state in which deposits of the stage are particularly well exposed (see table below).

Glaciers are of three principal kinds. The largest are the ice sheets, or ice caps, like those covering Greenland and Antarctica. During the Pleistocene the Canadian Shield was covered by ice caps centering on the east and west sides of Hudson Bay, the Laurentian Ice Caps to the east and the Keewatin to the west. The glacial ice that was pushed outward from these centers extended to the continental shelf off the Maritime Provinces and New England and southward into the central United States (Fig. 4.9). Such ice sheets bury the topography rather than being molded to it. Toward their thinned edges, however, the glacial ice divides into lobes guided by the topography.

Other, much smaller glaciers develop on mountain tops and descend the valleys. These are known as mountain, alpine, or valley glaciers. These tongues of glacial ice are molded by and reflect the topography. One of the longest, Hubbard Glacier in Alaska, has a length of 120 kilometers. Small glaciers may be little more than ice banks confined to the basins, called *cirques*, where they originate.

Other glaciers develop on plateaus as small ice caps and move off the edges of the plateaus and down the valleys that drain them. Still others, Piedmont Glaciers, form at the foot of mountains, where several valley or plateau glaciers coalesce. The classic example of this kind is the Malaspina Glacier in Alaska.

The evidence for the existence of these ancient glaciers lies in the deposits they left behind. The area covered by the ice (Fig. 4.9) is blanketed with bouldery sand, silt, and clay (Fig. 6.1), and the boulders are of northern types of rocks that have been moved southward. The nonstratified deposits left behind by the melted ice are called *till;* the stratified deposits, formed by glacial streams on or under the ice are *glaciofluvial.* The till and the glaciofluvial deposits are referred to collectively as *drift.*

Other deposits (Figs. 4.10, 6.1) record the past existence of at least three different kinds of lakes.

Period	*Epoch*	*Stages*	
		Glacial	*Interglacial*
Quaternary	Holocene		
	Pleistocene	Wisconsinan Illinoian Kansan Nebraskan	Sangamon Yarmouth Aftonian

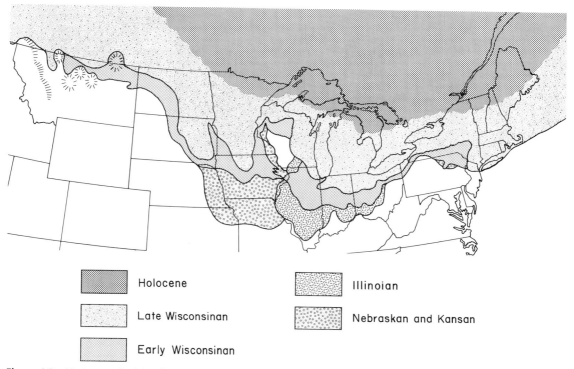

Holocene

Late Wisconsinan

Early Wisconsinan

Illinoian

Nebraskan and Kansan

Figure 4.9 *Limits reached by the continental ice sheets from New Jersey to Montana.*

One kind formed in front of the ice sheets; good examples are in Montana. A second kind formed while the ice melted back and flooded valleys that had been scoured and deepened by the ice; examples are the Finger Lakes, in New York, and the Great Lakes, which are relics of older and larger ones. A third kind flooded closed depressions in the Basin and Range Province and reflect the increased precipitation and decreased evaporation there; two large ones are Lake Bonneville, in Utah, and Lake Lahontan, in Nevada.

Still other deposits related to the glaciation are of eolian (wind) origin. Spring thaws caused rivers to flood, and the silt-laden flood waters made barren wastes of the river valleys. As floods subsided silt blown out of these valleys settled on the adjoining uplands and formed the deposits of loess that compose the rich soils of most of the Middle West farm belt (Fig. 6.1). These deposits thin and become finer grained downwind (eastward) from the valleys that were their sources.

Besides these evidences of the glaciations, the deposits contain the remains of vertebrate and invertebrate animals characteristic of northern latitudes. The interglacial deposits contain remains of faunas characteristic of temperate climates. The faunal changes are paralleled by similar changes in the flora.

Climatic changes during the Quaternary Period also affected sea level. During the glacial stages, a vast amount of water was locked in the ice sheets, and sea level stood a few hundred feet lower than it does now. Furthermore, when the deglaciation was greater than at the present time, the sea stood higher—along the Atlantic Coast, probably about 35 feet higher. These *eustatic* (world-wide) changes in sea level, however, are difficult to study because crustal changes of two kinds also have been taking place. One kind, not related to the climatic changes, is illustrated by the faulting and other earth movement taking place along the coast of California. Another indirect result of the climatic changes, involved

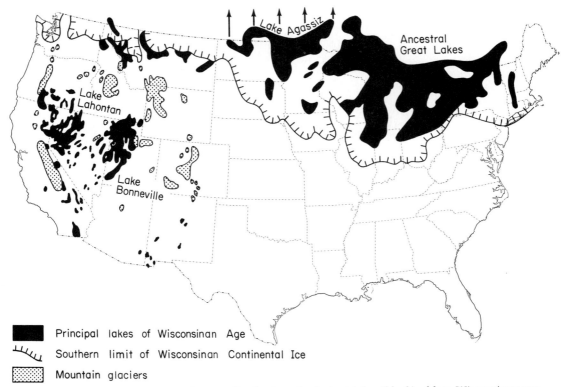

Principal lakes of Wisconsinan Age

Southern limit of Wisconsinan Continental Ice

Mountain glaciers

Figure 4.10 *Paleogeographic map showing distribution of principal lakes (black) of late Wisconsinan age in the United States and their relation to the southern limit of Wisconsinan continental ice (hachured line) and to the mountain glaciers (stippled areas).*

downwarping of the northern United States and Canada because of the weight of ice on that part of the crust. Since that weight has been removed, that area has been uplifted. The differences in the coastline along the Atlantic seaboard may be due in part to such changes. From North Carolina to Long Island the old land surface is partly submerged, and bays and sounds occupy drowned preglacial river valleys. The rocky New England coast is still deeply submerged.

The effects of the glacial and interglacial climates were felt far south of the ice fronts. In the southern and southwestern United States the glacial stages were *pluvial,* or rainy, times, and streams were larger, perhaps because of actual increase in precipitation, or perhaps because of decreased evaporation, caused perhaps by increased cloudiness. The record is clear that during the pluvial times, the effective available moisture was greatly increased. Even Death Val-

ley contained a lake hundreds of feet deep. The Great Salt Lake desert was submerged under a thousand feet of water. The climate was different.

Moreover, the climatic changes are continuing. We seem to be in a period of thaw. Glaciers have been retreating, ground that has been permanently frozen is melting, and the areas of floating ice have decreased. From 1885 to the 1940's world temperatures rose slightly; Arctic winter temperatures rose one to two degrees. Precipitation increased in the arctic parts of this hemisphere but decreased in the temperate latitudes of the United States. This has been accompanied by a drop in the water level of such lakes as the Great Lakes and Great Salt Lake, although this record is obscured by an increase in water use.

Climatic changes in prehistoric time have caused shifts of population and of land use. At about the end of the thirteenth century, there was a period of about twelve years of drought in the southwestern United States, which caused the Pueblo Indians to abandon their towns on the Colorado Plateau and move to the Rio Grande Valley. Although it is doubtful that scarcity of water alone caused the migration, it could be that competition for increasingly scarce food increased, and the agricultural and sedentary Pueblo Indians may have tired of raising farm crops to be plundered by nomadic tribes.

In some western valleys there is archeological evidence that streams dried during the general period A.D. 500 to A.D. 1300 and that Indians inhabiting the valleys moved upstream, evidently as the flow diminished. The physical geology supports the archeological evidence. In Pleistocene time, for example, it is known that streams draining the north side of the Henry Mountains in Utah were capable of transporting coarse gravel to the Dirty Devil River, 20 miles from the mountains. In latest Pleistocene time, only occasional floods were able to move gravel that far, and today the coarse gravel is being deposited 10 miles short of the river.

Death Valley has several dry springs marked by travertine mounds. Some of these can be dated archeologically as having gone dry about A.D. 1, for the artifacts show that the springs were last used about that time.

Causes of Climatic Change

The geological record of how the climates have changed is reasonably clear, but why they changed is not at all clear. A number of hypotheses have been considered.

1. Changes in the earth's orbit about the sun.

2. Changes in the inclination of the earth's axis.

3. Shifts of the continents relative to the poles.

4. Changes in ocean currents due to structural changes in the ocean floor.

5. Changes produced in the atmosphere, such as increased cloudiness.

6. Changes in the sun's radiation.

References

Blair, T. A., and Fite, R. C., 1965, Weather elements: 5th ed., Englewood Cliffs, Prentice-Hall.

Cole, F. W., 1970, Introduction to meteorology: New York, Wiley.

Dunn, G. E., and Miller, B. I., 1964, Atlantic hurricanes: Baton Rouge, Louisiana State Univ. Press.

Flora, S. D. 1954, Tornadoes of the United States: Norman, Univ. Oklahoma Press.
———, 1956, Hailstorms of the United States: Norman, Univ. Oklahoma Press.

Geiger, R., 1965, The climate near the ground: 2nd ed., translated by M. N. Stewart and others, Cambridge, Harvard Univ. Press.

Huntington, E., 1948, Civilization and climate: 3rd ed., New Haven, Yale Univ. Press; reprinted 1971 by Shoe String Press.

Kendrew, W. G., 1941, The climates of the continents: New York, Oxford Univ. Press.

Shapley, H., (ed.), 1953, Climatic change—evidence, causes, effects: Cambridge, Harvard Univ. Press.

Sutton, O. G., 1953, Micrometeorology: New York, McGraw-Hill.

Tannehill, I. R., and others, 1938, Codes for cloud forms and states of the sky: U.S. Dept. Agriculture, Weather Bureau.

Trewartha, G. T., 1968, Introduction to climate: 4th ed., New York, McGraw-Hill.

U.S. Dept. Agriculture, 1941, Climate and Man: *U.S. Dept. of Agriculture Yearbook.*

Stream runoff, including that part stored in lakes and reservoirs, is the principal source of our water supplies. It provides 75 percent of the water used for municipal sources and for irrigation, 90 percent of the freshwater used by industry, and nearly all the water used to generate hydroelectric power. It also provides the major attraction at most recreation areas. This scene is at Letchworth State Park in the Appalachian Plateaus in western New York. [Courtesy of the New York State Department of Environmental Conservation.]

5

......

WATER

The Hydrologic Cycle

The hydrologic cycle begins with precipitation, in the form of rain, hail, snow, frost, or dew. Precipitation on the oceans returns to the atmosphere by evaporation. Precipitation on the land divides four ways:

1. One part, perhaps as much as half, returns to the atmosphere directly by evaporation.

2. A second part, perhaps a sixth, is returned to the atmosphere by transpiration of plants.

3. A third part, perhaps a third, joins streams or glaciers that discharge into the ocean, where it can be returned to the atmosphere.

4. The fourth part, a small but important fraction, enters the ground, but in time returns to the surface, as springs or other groundwater discharge, and from there is returned to the atmosphere.

Over the whole earth, precipitation is equal to evaporation plus transpiration; the hydrologic cycle is a balanced economy. But precipitation, evaporation, and transpiration are three variables that differ greatly from area to area. For example, in the humid parts of the country, less than half the precipitation may be lost by evaporation and transpiration, but in arid regions—for example, along the lower part of the Colorado River—as much as 95 percent may be lost.

Great lakes and great rivers are impressive, and of utmost importance to us, but all the surface water and groundwater on the continents, even including the glaciers, amounts to little more than 0.5 percent of the earth's total water supply. A little more than 2 percent is in the atmosphere; all the remainder, more than 97 percent, is in the ocean.

Oceans, Seas, Bays, and Estuaries

The oceans (Fig. 5.1) cover more than 70 percent of the earth's surface and average more than 2 miles deep. The volume of water they contain is thirteen times greater than the volume of land above sea level. The Atlantic Ocean alone has a volume three times that of all the land above sea level. In fact, the land above sea level has only two to three times the volume of the salt in the oceans. The distinctions between oceans,

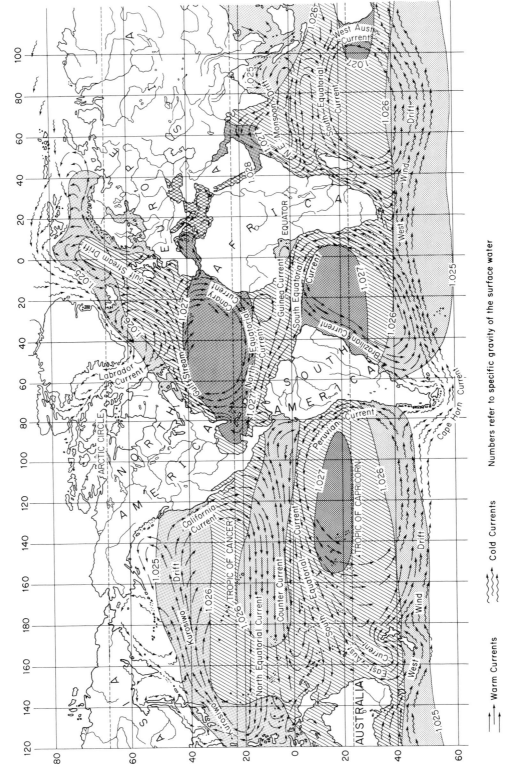

Figure 5.1 Extent and general circulation of the oceans.

⇉ Warm Currents

⟿ Cold Currents

Numbers refer to specific gravity of the surface water

seas, bays, and estuaries are arbitrary and not subject to rigorous definition. Bays and estuaries are where the freshwater from the land mixes with the salt water of the oceans and seas.

Surface Water

Surface water, as that term is used by hydrologists, refers to water on the surface of the land. Oceans are excluded. Surface water is mostly *stream runoff,* and it may be collected by being impounded naturally or artificially in lakes and reservoirs. Quantity of runoff is a function of the precipitation and of the *drainage basins* or *catchment areas.* In North America it is expressed in *acre-feet* (1 acre-foot is the quantity of water that would cover an acre to a depth of one foot: 43,560 cubic feet, or 325,829 gallons). Figure 5.2 shows the average annual discharge of some rivers in the United States and southern Canada.

The discharge of large streams may be expressed in acre-feet per unit of time. Discharge may also be expressed in gallons per minute or cubic feet per second (abbreviated to second-feet). The cubic foot per second (cfs) is the fundamental unit from which others are determined by conversion. It is the discharge of water in a channel of rectangular cross section 1 foot wide and 1 foot deep at an average velocity of 1 foot per second. One cubic foot equals 7.48 gallons.

$$1 \text{ second-foot} = 7.48 \text{ gallons per second}$$
$$= 448.8 \text{ gallons per minute}$$
$$= 1.98 \text{ acre-feet per day}$$
$$= 725 \text{ acre-feet per year.}$$

Measuring the discharge of our streams is a responsibility of the U.S. Geological Survey, although many other agencies, state and federal, collect such data in the areas of their interests. The measurements sometimes are difficult to make accurately, since velocity is not uniform throughout a cross section of stream channel, because of frictional drag along the bottom and

sides or to extreme turbulence at times of flood. Discharge of streams with relatively uniform flow can be estimated roughly by (a) measuring the area of cross section of the channel, (b) selecting a convenient length of channel (10 feet), and (c) timing the rate of flow of a small piece of paper floating on the stream. Discharge (Q) is given by the formula

$$Q = \frac{A \times d}{t},$$

where A is the area of cross section (sq ft), d is the distance (ft), and t is the time required to flow the distance (sec). For most streams this method gives a result that is about a fifth too great, because the measured surface velocity is greater than the average velocity.

Rates of stream flow vary greatly in different streams, and in different stretches of individual streams depending on their stage. At low stage the flow may be $1\frac{1}{2}$ feet per second (about 1 mph), and at flood stage the flow in the same stream may be 10 feet per second (about 7 mph).

Streams may be categorized in many different ways, depending on what factors one wishes to stress—drainage pattern and valley form, origin and relation to the geomorphic surface, age, size, permanence or continuity of flow, relation to groundwater, quality of the water, biota, navigability, or other possible use.

In theory, natural streams contrast sharply with such artificial ones as canals, irrigation ditches, and aqueducts, but in highly industrialized countries today they are not distinct, because almost every stream has been modified by dams for power, flood control, or water diversion, by industrial and municipal wastes, and/or by various kinds of stream-side developments.

Streams may be classed according to permanence as *perennial, intermittent,* or *ephemeral* (Fig. 5.3). Some streams are *continuous,* others are *interrupted*—that is, their perennial stretches may be interrupted by intermittent or ephemeral stretches. Irrespective of permanence, stream channels may be straight, meandering, or

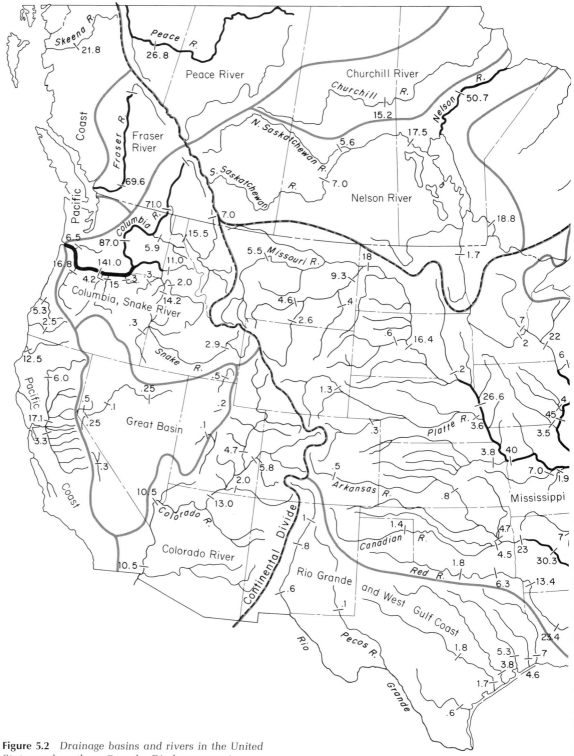

Figure 5.2 *Drainage basins and rivers in the United States and southern Canada. Discharges are in millions of acre-feet per year.*

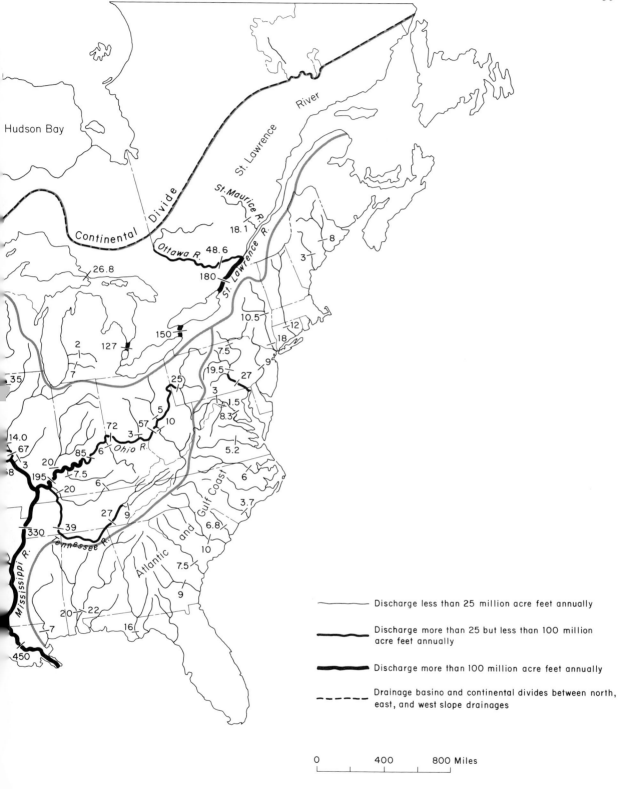

Hudson Bay

Continental Divide

St. Lawrence River

St. Maurice R.
18.1

Ottawa R. 48.6

180

St. Lawrence R.

26.8

8

3

10.5

12

150

18

127

2

7.5

9

7

19.5

27

3

25

1.5

5

8.3

72

57

10

3

85

6

Ohio R.

5.2

14.0

67

20

6

3

195

7.5

6

20

27

9

5.2

6

330

39

3.7

6.8

Mississippi R.

Tennessee R.

10

Atlantic and Gulf Coast

7.5

20

22

9

7

16

450

Discharge less than 25 million acre feet annually

Discharge more than 25 but less than 100 million acre feet annually

Discharge more than 100 million acre feet annually

Drainage basino and continental divides between north, east, and west slope drainages

0   400   800 Miles

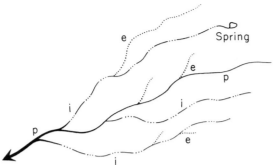

Figure 5.3 *Some categories of streams related to permanence and continuity; p, perennial; i, intermittent, flow is seasonal; e, ephemeral, flow follows local rains.*

braided. Lakes and reservoirs are simply stream runoff in storage.

Stream runoff, including that stored in lakes and reservoirs, provides 75 percent of municipal and irrigation water, 90 percent of the fresh water used by industry, and nearly all the water used to generate hydroelectric power. Knowledge about fluctuations and differences in runoff is important in order that waste and damage during flood seasons be minimized and excess flood waters stored for use when stream discharge is reduced.

Figure 5.4 shows runoff by regions. As might be expected, this runoff correlates rather well with precipitation (compare with Fig. 4.3). Runoff is very much greater in urban areas than in rural areas because of the extensive paving and other surfacing. Figure 5.5, which shows months of peak runoff, illustrates the seasonal variation in discharge of some typical rivers. These variations in stream discharge are much more uniform throughout the country than is the seasonal variation in rainfall (see Fig. 4.4), probably because

Figure 5.4 *Average annual runoff in the United States. [After U.S.G.S.] Each inch of runoff per square mile equals about 17.4 million gallons of water.*

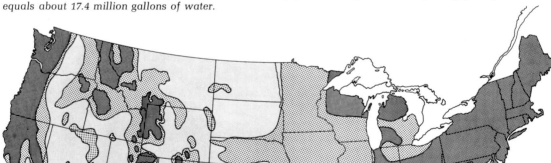

Runoff
in inches

< 1   1- 10   > 10

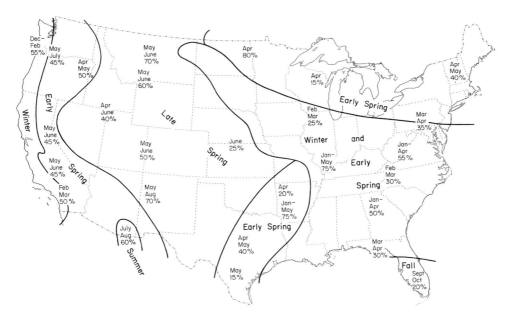

Figure 5.5 *Months and seasons of normal peak runoff, and the percent of annual flow normally discharged during the flood periods at various drainage basins in the United States.* [Data from U.S.G.S.]

the discharge of so many rivers is to a considerable degree controlled by the water stored in the snow pack. Runoff is greatest when the ground is frozen.

In planning for such structures as small bridges or culverts, engineers need to consider the expectable flood stages. For example, a stream in dry season may dwindle to a trickle that barely wets the bed of the channel, and yet every year reach a bankfull stage. Every 10 or 20 years, that same stream might produce floods 2 or 3 feet higher than the banks, and every 50 to 100 years produce floods 10 or 15 feet higher than the banks. Generally it is not feasible to protect against the very infrequent extreme floods, even though they can be expected.

Conversely, in planning use of water for hydroelectric power or irrigation, the expectable low flow is more significant than the average flow. It has been estimated that one day's discharge during the 1936 flood of the Potomac River, if it could have been stored, would have supplied the Washington, D.C., metropolitan area for 4 years.

Waterfalls, Rapids

Waterfalls or rapids of at least four kinds develop where streams cross resistant ledges of rock. At one kind, illustrated by Niagara Falls (Fig. 5.6,A), the stream crosses a nearly horizontal resistant stratum and excavates a deep channel in the easily eroded, underlying formations. Such falls retreat upstream without losing their height. A second kind is illustrated by the Great Falls of the Potomac (Fig. 5.6,B). These falls, formed by nearly vertical ribs of resistant rock athwart the channel, do not retreat upstream, but they are lowered by erosion. A third kind of falls, illustrated by those along the sides of the Yosemite Valley and by those along the sides of the Colorado River canyons (Fig. 5.6,C), develop where the main valley is deeply eroded and the tributary valleys are left hanging. In homogeneous rock these falls both retreat and become lower. Still a fourth kind, rapids, develop where tributary streams deposit more debris in the channel of a main stream than can be moved away immediately by that stream (Fig. 5.6,D). The rapids

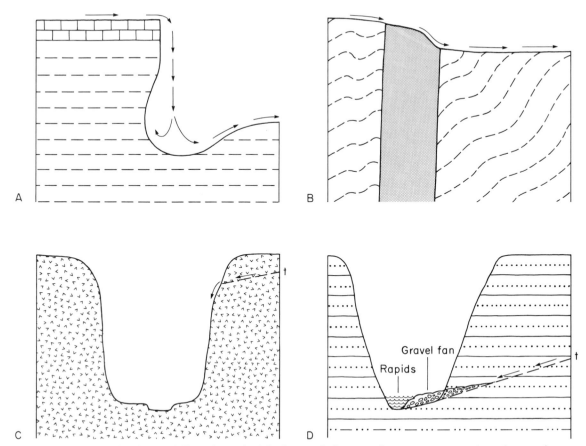

Figure 5.6 *Four kinds of waterfalls and rapids. (A) The nearly horizontal resistant stratum is undercut where stream has eroded into the underlying, easily eroded formation, as at Niagara Falls. (B) Nearly vertical resistant rib of rock, as at Great Falls on the Potomac River. (C) Tributary valleys left hanging because main valley was eroded faster than the tributary streams cut downward, as at Yosemite or Glen Canyon of the Colorado River. (D) Rapids develop at the mouths of tributaries that build alluvial fans into the main valley, as along Cataract Canyon of the Colorado River.*

along the Cataract Canyon of the Colorado River are of this kind; at the mouth of each tributary is a gravel fan that has partly dammed the Colorado River and crowded it into a narrow channel at the far bank.

Lakes, Ponds, Swamps

If Minnesota has 10,000 lakes, as claimed, the total number in North America must exceed 100,000 (Fig. 5.7). For our purpose, a lake is simply an inland body of water, fresh or saline, that is too large to be called a pond. Attempting to quantify the difference between lake and pond is as futile as trying to define the useful but inexact terms mountain and hill. Swamps and marshes are distinguished by abundant vegetation in the water; they may be as large as lakes or as small as ponds.

According to the U.S. Geological Survey, the lakes of North America, including the Great Lakes contain about a quarter of all the world's fresh surface water. This volume of water is

Figure 5.7 *The Great Lakes and Minnesota's 10,000 lakes are at the southern end of a vast lake region covering more than half of Canada. These lakes are centered in the part of the continent that was glaciated in Pleistocene time.*

about 10 times the amount in the atmosphere over the continent and about 100 times the volume of water in North American stream channels at any given moment. Lake water constitutes a substantial part of the continent's water budget. Again we are blessed with more than our share, and should ask ourselves whether we are using the resource wisely. Most of the rest of the world is looking on jealously.

Most of the lakes in North America are in the areas that were covered by the late Pleistocene glaciations. Glacial erosion scoured depressions; glacial deposits blocked valleys and, in general, formed a hummocky surface with many closed depressions. These closed depressions became flooded in those regions where rainfall exceeds evaporation.

Not all lakes formed in this way, of course. Crater Lake, as its name implies, occupies the blown-out crater of an ancient volcano. Malheur and Harney lakes, Oregon, formed behind lava dams. Landslides have also dammed valleys and formed lakes. Some lakes have been formed by

faulting and other earth movements; Reelfoot Lake in the Mississippi Valley, western Tennessee, formed as a result of earth movement that accompanied the New Madrid earthquake of 1811–1812. Great Salt Lake and the lakes in Nevada are in structural depressions, fault valleys. Lake Tahoe also occupies a fault valley that has been somewhat modified by glaciation. Oxbow lakes along the Mississippi River fill cutoff meanders; Florida's lakes occupy limestone sinks.

Geologically speaking, lakes are ephemeral features. A lake may dry as a result of climatic change or it may be emptied if an outlet cuts downward through the barrier that impounds it. Many lakes become filled with sediments that are washed into or blown into them. If a lake becomes shallow enough to be occupied by plants, it becomes a swamp or marsh, which can eventually be completely filled by the accumulation of plant debris.

Limnology, the science of lakes, includes the study of shore processes, shore and bottom currents, lake-bottom sediments, aquatic and shore environments, and the animals and plants living in them.

Subsurface Water

Subsurface water is derived largely from precipitation that filters into the ground. Relatively unimportant physiographically are the small fractions of subsurface water that are chemically combined in minerals or were trapped in sediments at the time of deposition. Water at hot springs commonly is said to be *primitive water*—water escaping for the first time from the earth's interior or water created by the combination of primitive hydrogen with atmospheric oxygen. Most hot springs, however, can be explained simply as groundwater that has circulated deeply enough to have been warmed by the rocks. In many areas the circulation need not be deep. At Yellowstone Park, for example, earth temperatures increase hundreds of degrees (fahrenheit) within a few hundred feet of the surface.

Some of the modes in which water occurs in the ground are shown in Figure 5.8. Water in the ground occupies voids in the soil or other overburden and in the rocks, and its occurrence and movement are controlled largely by the abundance and size of the voids (*porosity*), their shape and continuity—that is, whether the voids are connected or isolated. A rock is saturated with water when all its voids are filled, which is the condition below the water table.

The hydrologic properties of a rock depend on the size and interconnections of its voids. *Capillary interstices* are small enough to cause water to rise above the water table and to be held a considerable height above it—a phenomenon illustrated by the absorption of water upward into a blotter. Larger interstices lack the property of capillarity, and water moves through them in currents. Ground, including the bedrock, is *permeable* if water can move through it—that is, if the voids are of capillary size or larger and connected. Permeability differs from porosity; some fine-grained rocks are highly porous, but the voids are subcapillary in size, and the rock is practically impermeable. Void sizes are determined by the size and shape of the constituent mineral grains, their sorting, cementation, and fractures or other openings in the rock. In northern latitudes, permeable layers may become impermeable in cold seasons because the water in them freezes.

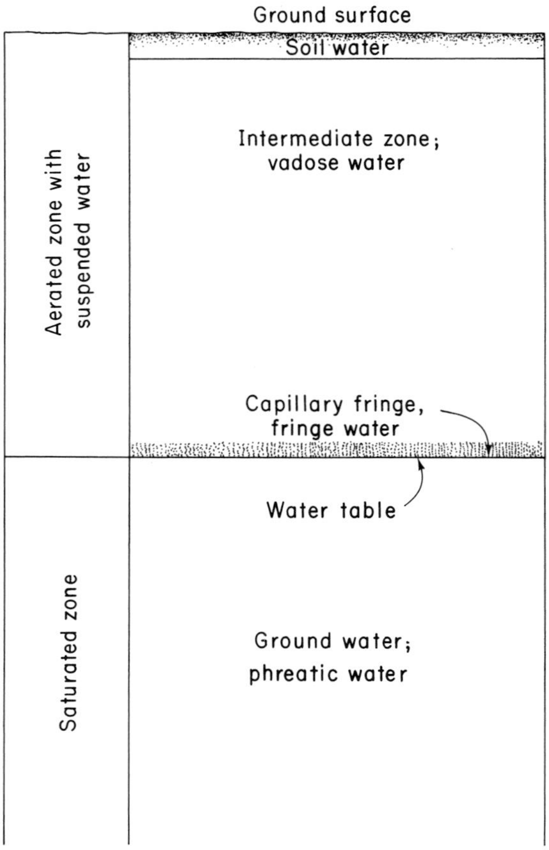

A *water table* is the upper surface of a *zone of saturation*—the upper surface of *groundwater*. Above the water table is a zone called the *capillary fringe*, where water rises from the water table by capillarity. From the capillary fringe upward to the surface is a zone that is alternately wet and dry, a zone of aeration, and its water is called *vadose*, *gravitational*, or *suspended* water (Fig. 5.8). A stratum that yields water is an *aquifer*. Figure 5.9 illustrates the availability of groundwater in the United States. The most abundant groundwater reserves in the United States are in five areas: Atlantic and Gulf Coastal Plain, the alluvial fills in the Basin and Range Province, the glaciated region in Canada and the northern United States, the Tertiary formations of the Great Plains, and the lavas of the Columbia, Snake, and Fraser River plateaus.

Soil water, which is water in the surface layers, is classed according to its availability to plants. The *wilting coefficient* of a soil is the ratio of the weight of water in soil when permanent wilting begins to the weight of the soil when dry. In most soils this is less than half the moisture-holding capacity of the soil. Water in excess of the wilting coefficient is available to plants; water in lesser amounts is not available.

A water table can be represented on maps by contours. The depth one must dig or drill to reach groundwater is measured by the difference in altitude between the topographic contour and the water-table contour at a particular place.

Figure 5.8 *Modes of occurrence of subsurface water.* [*After U.S.G.S.*]

Ground surface

Soil water

Intermediate zone; vadose water

Aerated zone with suspended water

Capillary fringe, fringe water

Water table

Saturated zone

Ground water; phreatic water

105

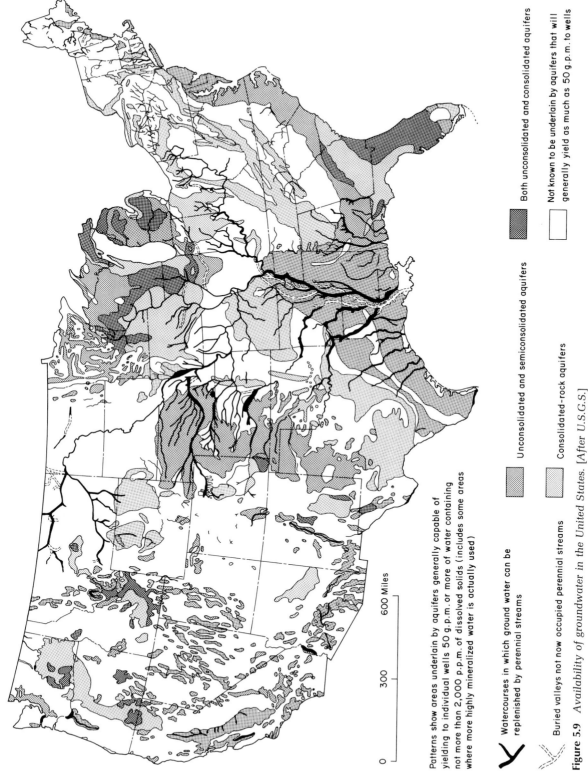

Patterns show areas underlain by aquifers generally capable of
yielding to individual wells 50 g.p.m. or more of water containing
not more than 2,000 p.p.m. of dissolved solids (includes some areas
where more highly mineralized water is actually used)

Watercourses in which ground water can be
replenished by perennial streams

Buried valleys not now occupied perennial streams

Unconsolidated and semiconsolidated aquifers

Consolidated-rock aquifers

Both unconsolidated and consolidated aquifers

Not known to be underlain by aquifers that will
generally yield as much as 50 g.p.m. to wells

Figure 5.9 *Availability of groundwater in the United States.* [*After U.S.G.S.*]

0   300   600 Miles

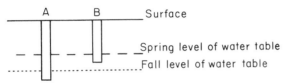

Figure 5.10 *Seasonal fluctuations of a water table. Well A has a perennial water supply; well B becomes dry seasonally. Depending on the kind of ground and recharge, the fluctuation might be 2 or 3 feet.*

Where the water table is a free surface, it may fluctuate daily, seasonally (Fig. 5.10), or over periods of years—when wet years alternate with dry years. Commonly, though, the groundwater is confined beneath an impermeable bed, as in Figure 5.11 (bottom). In such situations the water rises in the wells because of the hydrostatic pressure. The level to which the water rises is the static level, and is called the *piezometric surface.*

Contours drawn to show the static levels in the wells in Figure 5.11 (bottom) would have altitudes lower than those of the ground surface at wells C and D, and higher than the ground surface at well E. The difference between the topographic contours and the contours showing the piezometric surface indicates the height to which water would have to be pumped at C and

D and what the pressure head would be at the surface at E.

Where groundwater occurs above the normal water table, as it does where an impermeable bed prevents downward circulation, the groundwater is said to be *perched,* and the upper surface of such groundwater is called a *perched water table.* Two examples of perched water tables are illustrated in Figure 5.12. The effect of such situations on wells is illustrated in Figure 5.11 (top). A water table may resemble that shown in Figure 5.10 or those shown in Figure 5.11.

In many coastal areas, where fresh water may be underlain by salt water, overpumping causes a cone of salt water to rise into the fresh (Fig. 5.13). This mixes the waters and reduces the quantity of fresh water that can be recovered. Much the same problem exists in oil and gas fields where there may be either an oil-water or

Figure 5.12 *Examples of perched water tables. The barrier formed by the impermeable bed in the upper diagram is a groundwater dam. Spring zones are commonly caused by perched water tables, and this must be determined when estimating potential water yields and water resources.*

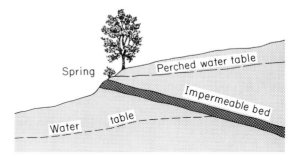

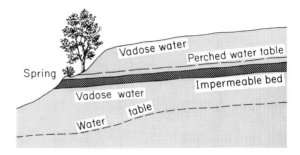

Figure 5.11 *Examples of how impermeable beds affect groundwater. (Top) An aquifer perched on an impermeable bed. The water level in well B driven through this bed will be lower than the water table. (Bottom) An aquifer beneath an impermeable bed. The hydrostatic pressure causes water to rise into wells driven through the bed. Well E would flow without pumping.*

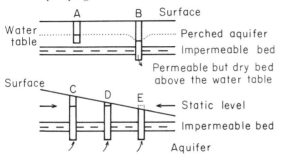

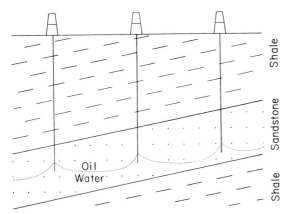

Figure 5.13 *Overpumping in oil fields causes the oil-water interface to rise in a cone at each well. This causes water to rise into the wells before the oil between the wells is recovered. A similar problem occurs in water wells drawing fresh water from a lense above salt water.*

Figure 5.14 *Streams that are above the water table lose water into the ground. Streams that are below the water table receive drainage from it; at flood stage the direction of flow may be reversed.*

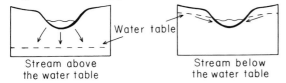

a gas-water interface. Withdrawal of the oil or gas causes the interface to rise, and one of the problems in oil-field development is to raise the interface evenly. Overpumping reduces the quantity of oil that can be recovered (Fig. 5.13).

If a water table is above a stream, groundwater will discharge into it; if it is below a stream, it will receive water from it (Fig. 5.14).

Subsurface water returns to the surface or to the atmosphere in several ways. In semiarid and arid regions, most soil water and vadose water returns directly by evaporation or indirectly by transpiration (Fig. 5.15), whereas in humid regions such water may trickle downward to the water table, from which some discharges into streams (Fig. 5.14), wells (Fig. 5.11), or springs (Fig. 5.12).

Some Physical and Chemical Properties

Undoubtedly the most significant property of water is its high heat capacity—the amount of heat necessary to raise the temperature of a quantity of substance one degree Centigrade. The standard unit of heat, the *calorie,* is defined as the amount of heat necessary to raise the temperature of a gram of water by one degree Centigrade. No other substance has a higher heat capacity than water, which is why water has such a marked effect in modifying climates. The heat of fusion of water is the heat that ice absorbs

Figure 5.15 *Some of the ways subsurface water is returned to the atmosphere and to the surface.*

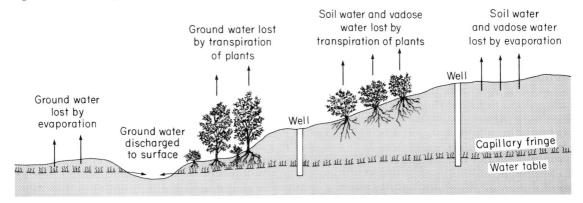

as it melts; to melt a gram of ice requires almost as much heat (80 calories) as is required to heat the gram of water to boiling (100 calories). The heat of vaporization—the heat required to turn the gram of water to steam—is 540 calories, more than five times the amount needed to boil the gram of water. These changes in state (solid to liquid, liquid to vapor) take place at constant temperature (Fig. 5.16). The martini is cooled by ice because the ice absorbs heat as it melts; the desert water bag is kept cool because the water on the outside absorbs heat as it evaporates. A city or field is cooled by a shower chiefly because the rainwater evaporates and absorbs heat; conversely, the condensation of dew or frost on the ground surface has a warming effect.

Because of these physical properties of water, the large water bodies affect the environment on land in two principal ways. First, circulation of

Figure 5.16   *A gram of ice at 0°C absorbs 80 calories in changing to a gram of water at the same temperature—an amount of heat that is only a little less than the 100 calories needed to raise the temperature of the water to boiling. A gram of boiling water absorbs 540 calories in changing to a gram of steam at the same temperature. Evaporation of water at intermediate temperatures similarly absorbs heat and cools the air around it; the amount of cooling depends on the pressure and temperature of the change. [From Geology of Soils by Charles B. Hunt. W. H. Freeman and Company. Copyright © 1972.]*

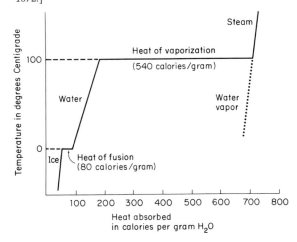

the oceans moves warm water along some coasts and cold water along others (Fig. 5.1). Second, because large bodies of water—lakes, bays, and seas as well as the oceans—are capable of absorbing or releasing great quantities of heat, they tend to warm air that is cool and to cool air that is warm. Marine and mediterranean climates are thus less extreme than continental climates.

Water has other unusual properties, one of which is that it becomes most dense at 4°C. Once the surface water in a pond, lake, or stream has cooled to this temperature, it sinks to the bottom, and warmer water rises to the surface. Between 4°C and 0°C, water undergoes a sharp decrease in density as it expands, which is why ice floats on water. Once a body of water is covered by ice, it is protected from the cold and does not cool below approximately 4°C.

By the time spring arrives, the surface layers beneath the melting ice may be as cold as the bottom layers; that is, the waters may be of uniform density. Once the ice has melted completely, the layers of water are subject to turnover by wind. The water that is built up on the leeward side of a lake or pond is returned by gravity underflow. By the end of summer the whole body of water has warmed. With the onset of winter the cycle is renewed: the surface layers become cooler than the bottom layers, and turnover takes place by convection, recharging oxygen in the bottom. The boundary between the upper and lower layers is called the *thermocline;* the upper layer is the *epilimnion* and the lower one the *hypolimnion* (Fig. 5.17,A).

In estuaries, density differences in the water are caused partly by temperature differences and partly by salinity differences. Where river flow is very large compared to the tidal flow, as in the Mississippi, a wedge of dense salt water moves upstream along the bottom and it has a wavy upper surface where it rises into and mixes with the fresh water (Fig. 5.17,B). Where the fresh water inflow is moderate, say 10 to 100 times the tidal flow (e.g. Chesapeake Bay), the lower wedge of salt water moving up the bottom diffusely mixes with the overlying fresher water. (Fig. 5.17,C).

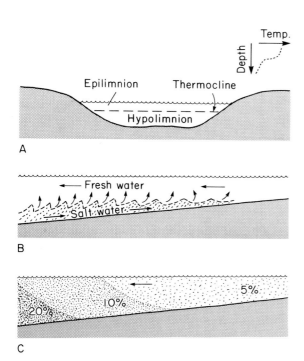

Figure 5.17 *Thermal and salinity stratification of water in lakes and estuaries.*

(A) Cross section showing thermal layering in a fresh-water lake. The epilimnion is the less dense surface layer, which is warmer in summer, as indicated at the right. At the thermocline the temperature abruptly decreases and the density increases. In winter the epilimnion is colder than the hypolimnion.

(B) Cross section showing mixing of fresh and salt water where a large river discharges into an estuary.

(C) Cross section showing mixing of fresh and salt water where a moderate-size river discharges into an estuary; salinities in percent.

(D) Map showing how fresh and salt water are mixed in some estuaries—by inflow of salt water along one bank and outflow of fresh water along the other.

In other water systems fresh water may move seaward along one bank and salt water move inland along the other bank. In these systems the waters mix along the middle of the channel. In other systems the waters may be mixed by turbulence.

The oxygen content of water is important in aquatic environments because it is needed by living organisms. In comparison to the amount of oxygen in air, there is little present in water. A liter of air contains 21 percent of oxygen by volume, or 210 cubic centimeters; a liter of water at 15°C under a pressure of 1 atmosphere contains only 7 cubic centimeters of oxygen. Aquatic animals must therefore take in a volume of water that is thirty times the amount of air that terrestrial animals must breathe in order to get the same amount of oxygen. Plants or animals may survive long periods without food or water, but almost all suffocate quickly if deprived of oxygen.

Recharge of oxygen in lake waters is accomplished mostly by the photosynthesis of green aquatic plants that live in the upper layers. Plant life is concentrated in the upper layers because only they receive enough light for much photosynthesis. Oxygen is depleted in the bottom layers by the plants and animals living there and by the decomposition of dead tissues; the near-surface layers must produce enough oxygen for the entire body of water. In lakes, there must be mechanisms by which the waters are mixed if oxygen is to reach the bottom; in streams, the water becomes oxygenated by aeration as well as by photosynthesis.

Quality of Water

Quality of water refers not to its biology but to its chemistry—the content of dissolved or suspended matter, mostly solids, although dissolved gases may be important locally. Purity of water pertains to its content of living organisms. Rainwater contains almost no dissolved or suspended matter after the first of a fall has cleared the air of dust or smoke, but as soon as the water enters the ground or runs off the surface, it dissolves both organic matter and mineral matter.

The organic residues dissolved or suspended in surface or subsurface water consist in part of carbon dioxide, carbonic acid, and various humic compounds. This organic matter is especially important in soil water, where it is a major factor in the soil-forming processes. The humic compounds also affect the quality of some surface waters to the extent of coloring them brown, especially where drainage is sluggish, as in some ponds.

Most of the dissolved and suspended solids in most water is mineral matter. The quantity and proportions of various mineral constituents are controlled chiefly by the composition of the rocks forming the drainage basin or aquifer and the quality fluctuates seasonally with fluctuations in discharge. The common salts in natural waters are shown in Table 5.1. Water quality is generally described in terms of the anions (Table 5.1).

In addition to these common salts, natural waters contain iron and silica. Waters become acidic chiefly because of carbonic acid (H_2CO_3), and more rarely because of sulfuric acid (H_2SO_4) or hydrochloric acid (HCl).

The common dissolved gases are carbon dioxide (CO_2), nitrogen (N), oxygen (O), methane (CH_4), and hydrogen sulfide (H_2S). Other constitutents are present in minor amounts, yet these amounts may be significant, physiologically or otherwise. Fluorine is an example; in some areas it has even been politically significant.

Ocean water along the shores of the United States contains between 3.3 and 3.6 percent of dissolved salts. In percent of the salt water these are: NaCl, 2.7; $MgCl_2$, 0.4; $MgSO_4$, 0.2; $CaSO_4$, 0.1; K_2SO_4, 0.1; $CaCO_3$ and $MgBr_2$, traces. These principal constituents are present in the following relative abundance (percent):

Na	30.6	Cl	55.0
K	1.1	SO_4	7.7
Mg	3.7	HCO_3	0.4
Ca	1.2	Other	0.3
			100.0

The concentration of salt water is more than twice that of the fluids in the human body, which is why ocean water does not quench thirst. Instead, the salt water, by osmosis, extracts fluids from the body!

The content of dissolved solids in water may be expressed in percent or in parts per million (ppm). One part per million is nearly the same as 1 milligram per liter; 10,000 ppm equals 1 percent. Sea water contains 33,000 to 36,000 ppm of dissolved solids. Great Salt Lake, which is saturated, contains roughly 333,000 ppm. In waters more saline than sea water it is convenient to express the salt content in percent. Most municipal water supplies contain less than 150 ppm of dissolved solids. The Public Health Service recommends that the amount of dissolved solids in drinking water not exceed 500 ppm, which is about equal to a level teaspoon of salt in a gallon of water. More than 1,000 ppm is considered objectionable by persons who have not spent much time in the deserts. Water containing as much as 2,500 ppm can be tolerated for short periods. Such water is suitable for stock but not for irrigation. The compositions of river waters in the United States are given in Figure 5.18.

Table 5.1

Common Salts in Surface Waters

Cations	Anions		
	CO_3^{--} carbonate	SO_4^{--} sulfate	Cl^- chloride
Ca^{++} calcium	$CaCO_3$ limestone	$CaSO_4$ gypsum plus combined water	$CaCl_2$
Mg^{++} magnesium	$MgCO_3$ magnesia	$MgSO_4$ Epsom salt	$MgCl_2$
Na^+ sodium	Na_2CO_3 soda	Na_2SO_4 Glauber salt	NaCl halite (table salt)
K^+ potassium (quantity generally minor)	K_2CO_3	K_2SO_4	KCl
	Alkaline water		Saline water

Hard water / Soft water

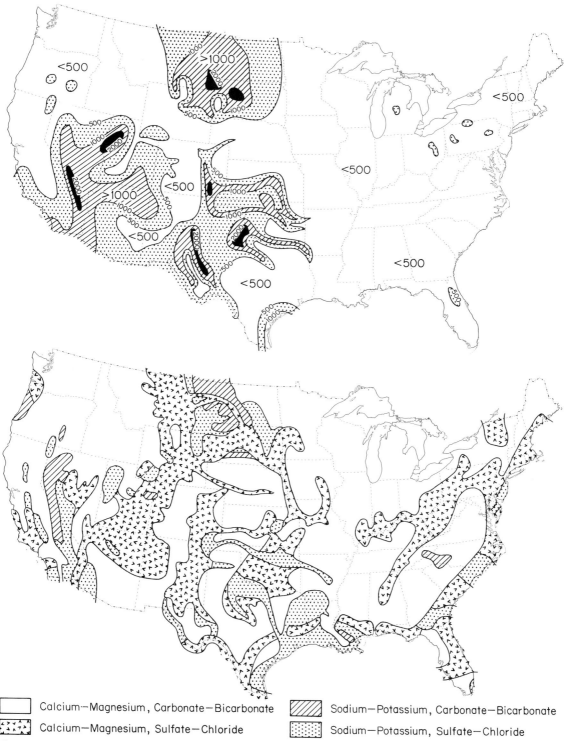

Figure 5.18 *Composition of river waters in the United States. [After U.S.G.S.] (Top) Prevalent total dissolved solids in rivers; figures are in parts per million. (Bottom) Prevalent chemical types of rivers.*

Iron rarely is present in more than minute quantities, but even 0.2 ppm may stain clothing, enamel, and porcelain ware. Quantities above 1 ppm generally precipitate when exposed to air.

In general, waters containing less than 100 ppm of dissolved solids are soft, because, as one water chemist expressed it, where the amounts are less, even the salesmen give up trying to sell water softeners.

What is "hardness" in water? Hardness refers to the property that causes soap to form precipitates rather than to lather, and to the property that causes boiler scale. Hardness is caused by salts of calcium and magnesium, especially the carbonates (Table 5.1). Hardness is measured in parts per million of $CaCO_3$, other salts being converted to equivalents of $CaCO_3$ for this purpose. Waters containing more than 200 ppm of the particular salts are hard. Water containing more than 500 ppm commonly is saline, but may be hard too if it also contains the salts that produce hardness. Carbonate hardness may be reduced by boiling, but noncarbonate hardness requires the addition of chemicals, such as sodium carbonate, slaked lime, or zeolites.

Subsurface water generally contains more dissolved solids than does surface water (Fig. 5.19). Streams in regions of low runoff generally contain more dissolved solids than do streams in regions of high runoff (compare Figs. 5.4 and 5.18).

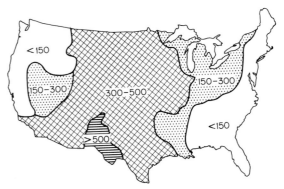

Figure 5.20 *Average dissolved solids in water withdrawn for public supplies in parts per million. [After U.S.G.S.]*

Table 5.2 lists the common dissolved mineral constituents in natural water and their practical effects. Figure 5.20 illustrates regional differences in the average quality of water used for public supplies.

THERMAL WATERS, HOT SPRINGS

Hot springs may be defined arbitrarily as springs with temperatures more than 10°F warmer than the average annual temperature for the locality. In the contiguous United States alone, there are more than a thousand such

Figure 5.19 *Typical differences in quality of water in relation to mode of occurrence. In addition to the five orders of magnitude of salinity illustrated, a sixth would be saturation (10 times the salinity of seawater), as in natural salt pans along a shore, in Great Salt Lake, and in the Dead Sea.*

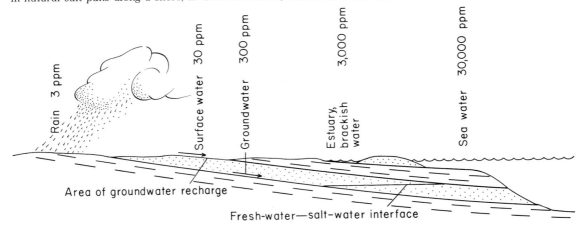

Table 5.2

113

Significance of Dissolved Mineral Constituents and Physical Properties of Natural Water (After U.S.G.S.)

Constituent or Physical Property	Source or Cause	Significance
Silica (SiO_2)	Dissolved from practically all rocks and soils, usually 1 to 30 ppm.	Forms hard scale in pipes and boilers and on blades of steam turbines.
Iron (Fe)	Dissolved from practically all rocks and soils; also derived from iron pipes. More than 1 or 2 ppm of soluble iron in surface water usually indicates acid wastes from mine drainage or other sources.	On exposure to air, iron in groundwater oxidizes to reddish-brown sediment. More than about 0.3 ppm stains laundry and utensils. Objectionable for food processing, Iron and manganese together should not exceed 0.3 ppm because larger quantities cause unpleasant taste and favor growth of iron bacteria.
Manganese (Mn)	Same source as iron but not as common.	Same objectionable features as iron.
Calcium (Ca) and magnesium (Mg)	Dissolved from practically all soils and rocks, but especially from limestone, dolomite, and gypsum.	Cause most of the hardness and scale-forming properties of water (see hardness). Waters low in calcium and magnesium desired in electroplating, tanning, dyeing, and in textile manufacturing.
Sodium (Na) and potassium (K)	Dissolved from practically all rocks and soils.	Large amounts, in combination with chloride, give a salty taste. Sodium salts may cause foaming in steam boilers, and a high sodium ratio may limit the use of water for irrigation.
Bicarbonate (HCO_3) and carbonate (CO_3)	Action of carbon dioxide in water on carbonate rocks.	Produce alkalinity. Bicarbonates of calcium and magnesium decompose in steam boilers and hot water facilities to form scale and release corrosive carbon dioxide gas. In combination with calcium and magnesium cause carbonate hardness.
Sulfate (SO_4)	Dissolved from many rocks and soils.	Sulfate in water containing calcium forms hard scale in steam boilers. The sulfate content should not exceed 250 ppm.
Chloride (Cl)	Dissolved from rocks and soils. Present in sewage and found in large amounts in ancient brines, sea water, and industrial brines.	In large amounts in combination with sodium gives salty taste. In large quantities increases the corrosiveness of water. The chloride content should not exceed 250 ppm.
Fluoride (F)	Dissolved in small to minute quantities from most rocks and soils.	Fluoride in drinking water reduces the incidence of tooth decay when the water is consumed during the period of enamel calcification. In excess, however, it may cause mottling of the teeth.
Nitrate (NO_3) and phosphate (PO_4)	Decaying organic matter and sewage.	Important as fertilizers in soil, these lead to overfertilization in natural water bodies causing eutrophication; concentrations greater than local averages suggest pollution.

(Continued)

Table 5.2   (*Continued*)

Constituent or Physical Property	Source or Cause	Significance
Dissolved solids	Chiefly mineral constituents dissolved from rocks and soils, but includes organic matter.	For drinking water the dissolved solids should not exceed 500 ppm. Waters containing more than 1,000 ppm of dissolved solids are unsuitable for many purposes.
Hardness as $CaCO_3$	In most water, nearly all the hardness is due to calcium and magnesium.	Consumes soap before a lather will form. Deposits soap curd on bathtubs. Hard water forms scale in boilers, water heaters, and pipes. Hardness equivalent to the bicarbonate is called carbonate hardness. Any hardness in excess of this is called noncarbonate hardness.
Acidity or alkalinity (hydrogen ion concentration, pH)	Acids, acid-generating salts, and free carbon dioxide lower the pH. Carbonates, bicarbonates, hydroxides and phosphates, silicates, and borates raise the pH.	A pH of 7.0 indicates neutrality of a solution. Values higher than 7.0 denote increasing alkalinity; values lower than 7.0 indicate increasing acidity. Corrosiveness of water generally increases with decreasing pH.
Dissolved oxygen (O_2)	Dissolved in water from air and from oxygen given off in the process of photosynthesis by aquatic plants.	Dissolved oxygen increases the palatability of water. Under average stream conditions, 4 ppm is usually necessary to maintain a varied fish fauna in good condition. For industrial uses, zero dissolved oxygen is desirable to inhibit corrosion.

springs, or groups of closely spaced springs. They are most abundant and have the highest temperatures where there has been recent faulting and/or volcanic or other igneous activity. That is to say, most of them (more than 95 percent) are in the western part of North America. Hot springs are popular therapeutic resorts, especially for persons with muscular or nervous ailments that are relieved by warm baths. Some hot springs are used for heating; steam springs may be used for power.

The heat sources for hot springs vary. Measurements made in deep mines and wells show that temperatures in the ground increase about 1°F for each 40 to 90 feet increase in depth. Water circulating to a depth of only 500 to 1,000 feet in the ground may therefore become 10° warmer than the average surface temperature. In places where even the rocks at shallow depth are hot because of recent volcanism or other igneous activity, the temperature may greatly increase with depth, and the water may be steaming. Where there has been much recent faulting, deep circulation is favored by the broken rock strata.

In the Appalachians the principal hot springs are in the folded formations of the Valley and Ridge Province, where synclinal folds favor deep artesian water circulation. The springs are most numerous in the Virginia and West Virginia segments of the physiographic province. The most northerly hot spring in the Appalachians is near the north end of the Valley and Ridge Province in the northeast corner of Massachusetts. Warm Springs, Georgia, is in the Piedmont Province, but generally the rocks in the Piedmont Province, New England, and the Atlantic Provinces of Canada are too tightly deformed for deep-water circulation.

The greater part of the continent, including the Atlantic and Gulf Coastal Plain, Interior Low

Plateaus, Appalachian Plateaus, Ozark Plateau, Central Lowland, Great Plains, and Canadian Shield have a few warm springs but almost no hot ones. The Ouachita Province has synclinal structures like those in the Valley Ridge, and at Hot Springs National Park, Arkansas, water issuing from folded Pennsylvanian sandstone is 40–80°F warmer than the average annual temperature. The only other important hot springs east of the Rocky Mountains are in South Dakota at the east foot of the Black Hills uplift; the source of the water is Cambrian sandstone at a depth of only 1,000 feet, and the water temperature is about 50°F warmer than the average annual temperature there. Presumably, at both the Arkansas and South Dakota springs the thermal gradient in the ground is steeper than average or the water has curiously deep circulation.

Of the many hot springs in the western part of the continent, some are obviously related to recent volcanism, like those in Yellowstone and Lassen national parks and the numerous ones in the young lava fields of southeastern Oregon. Many hot springs are clustered in the granitic mass of the Idaho batholith, suggesting that the granite there is still warm at shallow depth. Other springs are distributed linearly along major faults where water can circulate deeply, as along the faulted west edge of the Middle Rockies and Colorado Plateau and in the Death Valley region. Still others are where the mantle is shallow, as in the Salton Trough.

Chemically, most of the springs discharge quite potable carbonate or sulfate water and are marked by deposits of travertine or gypsum. Some are highly sulfurous, and some (e.g., Rotten Egg Spring, Nevada) emit hydrogen sulfide. Many have considerable fluorine. A few that are depositing metals illustrate how some metalliferous vein deposits have been formed.

Water Pollution

Rivers, lakes, bays, and groundwater receive pollutants from a variety of sources: municipal and other sewage systems, industrial wastes, herbi-

cides and pesticides used in agriculture, acid mine waters, and sediment washed from construction sites. By pollution we ordinarily refer to harmful substances or conditions caused by the activities of Man, and we dismiss natural sources of pollution. Herds of buffalo on the Great Plains surely polluted the streams there long before the herds of domestic livestock did so. The problem of Man's contribution to pollution increases exponentially with land use—crowding.

The pollution may merely be obnoxious because of odor or appearance. Banks of many streams and other water bodies are littered with plastic containers, automobile tires, and the suds of detergents. Water may be made unfit for swimming and bathing because of pathogens, or it may be dangerous because of inorganic chemical poisons. Our attitude toward such pollution is likely to be disgust without consideration of the more positive approach that in many cases the pollutants should be thought of as resources out of place.

Raw sewage includes many organic and chemical pollutants that are easily oxidized, and a river or other water system that receives sewage from only a small population cleanses itself by oxidation of the wastes. Where there is much sewage, however, the capacity of the water to oxidize wastes is overwhelmed, the water becomes polluted, and the wastes must be treated. Depletion of oxygen in water may be caused by the breakdown of organic matter by bacteria or by other reducing agents, such as ferrous salts. From the point of sewage infall, the oxygen content of the water sharply decreases and then slowly increases again by aeration at the surface and by photosynthesis of green plants. Rates of reoxidation depend on the rate of flow, depth of water, and amount of photosynthesis, which depends partly on the turbidity and temperature of the water.

Raw sewage may be treated biologically, as in putrefaction by storage in a closed chamber, or cesspool, in which the available oxygen is used up by anaerobic bacteria that produce methane (CH_4) and hydrogen sulfide (H_2S). Much of the organic matter escapes in the form of these gases; the rest, a fluid, percolates into the ground. There are definite limits, however, to the number of cesspools that can be accommodated by particular kinds of ground, and many an affluent suburb has found itself invaded by its own effluents, leading to demand for municipal sewage systems. In municipal systems, aerobic organisms degrade wastes, and sediments are settled out, as illustrated in Figure 5.21. The sediment, or sludge, can be useful as fertilizer and if so used would return nutrients to the ground for reuse by plants and animals. Recycling need not be restricted to the obvious newspapers, tin cans, aluminum cans, and bottles.

Treatment of water for municipal systems involves several steps. One procedure involves filtering to remove suspended solids, followed by the addition of chlorine to help destroy bacteria.

Heavy particles sink in a settling tank. Next, various chemicals are stirred in—alum, which combines with and flocculates some of the impurities; carbon, which helps control taste and odor; and more chlorine. After settling, the water passes through permeable sand filters, and then are added lime and phosphate to lessen pipe corrosion, more chlorine, and in some municipalities fluoride to lessen tooth decay. The product is known as pure water, meaning it is safe to drink, but it contains anywhere from 50 to 500 parts per million of dissolved solids.

Industrial wastes that pollute water are of two quite different kinds, chemicals (e.g., mercury) and heated fluids (thermal pollution). Chemical pollution includes radioactive materials and other elements, especially metals, that are toxic when accumulated in excess. Pollution of surface waters by radioactive materials has not yet been

Figure 5.21 *Schematic flow diagram for one kind of city sewage system. In the example, input from the sewer system and discharge to the river is 150 million gallons a day. At the intake the sewage contains 175 milligrams (mg) per liter of suspended solids and 225 milligrams per liter of biodegradable organic matter (BOD). A bar screen at the intake removes the coarse debris, which is crushed and buried. A mechanical settling tank removes 3 percent solids; the effluent from this step contains 100 mg/liter SS and 200 mg/liter BOD. This effluent, after aeration and seepage through a biochemically active rock pile contains 70 mg/liter SS and 50 mg/liter BOD. This is chlorinated, and after passing through a final settling tank discharges to the river with 25 mg/liter SS and 15 mg/liter BOD. The sludges are used to produce methane, which helps power the plant; the final residue is dried in cakes for fertilizer or fill.*

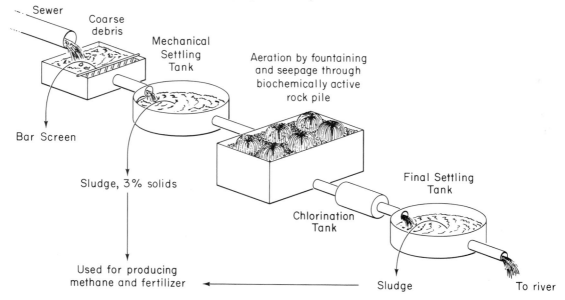

a serious hazard, but with increased use of nuclear power a serious "spill" needs to be anticipated. It can happen, and sooner or later probably will.

Numerous elements are beneficial in small quantities but are toxic when in excess. Fluorine is an example; as already noted (Table 5.2), small quantities slow tooth decay, but excessive fluorine causes mottling of teeth. Mercury compounds, which are known to cause blindness, deafness, or death, accumulate in toxic quantities in the larger animals at the ends of food chains. Such chemical pollutants decrease in concentration downstream from the point of their source, partly because of dilution and partly because the metals become precipitated.

Thermal pollution is caused where large quantities of warm waters are discharged into streams or other water bodies. The heated water speeds organic activity and so increases the rate of deoxygenation. The heat, of course, becomes dissipated by mixing of the waters. If the increase in temperature is not excessive, it can have some benefits, for there are kinds of fish who prefer the warm habitat.

Among the insecticides that pollute, one of the most controversial is DDT (dichloro-diphenyl-trichloro-ethane). This pesticide had a welcome and honorable beginning when it was used effectively to combat mosquitoes, particularly in tropical countries where malaria is a serious health hazard. Subsequently it was found that some strains of mosquitoes developed resistance to DDT and that its effectiveness was thus reduced. Moreover, DDT does not break down readily, and its persistence, combined with its extensive use and mobility, has led to alarming accumulations in quiet waters, where it is especially harmful to the most basic part of the aquatic food chain, the phytoplankton. DDT and other chlorinated hydrocarbons are effective insecticides because they are toxic to most animal life and they are preferentially absorbed from water by living organisms. But these properties combined with the fact that these compounds are persistent and highly mobile—they vaporize with water and adhere to dust—spreads their effects into environments where they become destructive. It would seem prudent at least to be moderate in our use of such weapons; we could be destroying the basis of our food chain.

Other pollutants are nontoxic salts, of which sodium chloride is a good example. Excessive quantities of such salts in the Colorado River water that the United States delivers to Mexico has led to very reasonable international protest by the Mexicans. Excessive withdrawals of groundwater in Southwestern United States have led to salt-water encroachment on the fresh-water resource.

Nutrient salts, such as nitrates, phosphates, and potash, increase biological activity and biological demand for oxygen (BOD), creating the condition called eutrophism. Such salts may originate from the treatment of sewage or be washed in from fertilizers on agricultural lands. Lakes and rivers without such nutrient salts have low biological activity, a condition called oligotrophism. The demand for oxygen must not exceed the supply.

Acid mine waters, notably in the coalfields, result from the alteration of the mineral pyrite, iron sulfide (FeS_2). In the presence of water the pyrite alters to a sulfate, which in turn alters to sulfuric acid and the red iron oxide that stains the streambeds. Such waters are too acid for most fish. The acidity does not persist, however, and within a few miles from the coalfields the waters become diluted, lose their acidity, and become neutral or even alkaline. The effects of acid mine waters, unlike those of many other pollutants, are not felt far downsteam.

Finally may be mentioned the pollution caused by the suspended load in streams. This includes clay and silt washed in from ground laid bare at construction sites and borrow pits or by plowing. Suspended solids make water opaque and reduce plant growth. The suspended solids decrease downstream from their source, partly by settling of the coarser and heavier fraction and partly by oxidation of the organic matter. Deposition of the silt and clay, however, can kill oak trees on the floodplain downstream by suffocating the roots.

It is to be hoped that the foregoing makes it clear that we do not have to live with polluted rivers, lakes, bays, or groundwater. To avoid pollution does require that we understand the mode of occurrence of water, both on and in the ground, and its chemistry and biology. To a considerable degree the cure for particular conditions depends on the local geology, which controls the water circulation—whether the ground is subject to flooding by rise of ground water or surface water, or is well-drained, dry, and stable. Also, whether the pollutant might be converted to a resource by recycling or broken down to harmless compounds depends on the chemistry and biology in particular geologic settings.

City Water Supplies

Americans who dwell in cities and suburbs use an average of about 60 gallons of water per day per person, for drinking, cooking, washing clothes and dishes, bathing, flushing toilets, sprinkling lawns, and washing cars. In the 100 largest cities this totals about 10 billion gallons per day for about 70 million people. Urban use is seven times rural use, but only one seventh the amount used by industry and one seventh the amount used for irrigation. Most cities use surface water, some use ground water, and some use a combination.

About a quarter of the cities use water containing 100 parts per million of dissolved solids or less (Fig. 5.20). About half use water containing between 100 and 250 parts per million, and another quarter use water containing 250 to 500 parts per million. A few cities, totaling more than a million people, use water containing more than 500 parts per million of dissolved solids.

Water shortages on a scale sufficient to force curtailment of city activities are usually the result of combinations of three factors: prolonged periods of below-normal precipitation; inadequate emergency reserves; and pollution that makes many streams unsuitable for city water supplies. The problem of planning for city water supplies is similar to that in planning for the needs of a hydroelectric plant; the important consideration is the minimum rather than the average supply. There always will be the hazard that a period of drought might exceed any in the historical record.

During the 1960's (fall 1961 to fall 1966) the northeastern part of the United States, with its numerous large cities, experienced its worst drought of record. There had been prior periods of similar low precipitation (1879–1883 and 1892–1896), but the effects were less because the population was very much smaller and the pollution was not so extensive. During the 1960's water use had to be regulated and unessential uses curtailed. Even with such restrictions on use, many reservoirs were reduced to one-third their capacity or less. Groundwater supplies became depleted, and as levels of water tables and streamflow declined, wells dried and the increasing concentration of wastes created additional pollution problems. The flow of the Delaware River, for example, decreased to a record low for the 50 years that discharge records had been maintained. The drought was broken in September 1966 by rains that, ironically, caused floods.

References

Coker, R. E., 1954, Streams, lakes, ponds: Chapel Hill, Univ. North Carolina Press; reprinted by Harper and Row.

Durfor, C. N., and Becker, E., 1964, Public water supplies of the 100 largest cities in the United States, 1962: U.S. Geol. Survey Water-Supply Paper 1812.

Grover, N. C., and Harrington, A. W., 1949, Stream flow: New York, Wiley; reprinted 1960 by Dover Publications.

Hynes, H. B. 1970, The biology of polluted waters: University of Toronto Press.

McGuinness, C. L., 1963, The role of ground water in the national water situation: U.S. Geological Survey Water-Supply Paper 1800.

Meinzer, O. E., 1923a, The occurrence of ground water in the United States: U.S. Geol. Survey Water-Supply Paper 489.

——, 1923b, Outline of ground-water hydrology: U.S. Geol. Survey Water-Supply Paper 494.

——, 1942 (ed.), Hydrology: New York, McGraw-Hill; reprinted by Dover Publications.

Stearns, Norah D., and others, 1937, Thermal springs in the United States: U.S. Geological Survey Water-Supply Paper 679-B, pp. 59–206.

U.S. Department of Agriculture, 1955, Water: U.S. Dept. of Agriculture yearbook.

Wisler, C. O., and Brater, E. F., 1959, Hydrology: 2nd ed., New York, John Wiley.

Surface deposits are the loose materials that overlie and mostly conceal the bedrock. Three major kinds are illustrated in this view along the Cache la Poudre River in Colorado. The bouldery deposits in the center and left of center were deposited there by freshets and meltwaters from snowbanks up the gully during the last (Wisconsinan) glaciation. Subsequently, the tow of that deposit was overlapped by alluvial gravel and sand (low terrace at right) deposited by the Cache la Poudre. The hillsides above the alluvium and bouldery deposit are mantled by loose material (colluvium) creeping slowly downhill as a result of a variety of processes known as mass wasting.

6
·······

SURFACE DEPOSITS AND SOILS —THE GROUND AROUND US

What is Soil?

An oft-repeated definition of soil holds that the inorganic part of the material in which plants root is decomposed, by weathering, from bedrock that lies somewhere beneath and which grades upward from hard rock to weathered rock to soil, with characteristic layers developed parallel to the ground. This concept, however, needs clarification, for it is misleadingly oversimplified. Actually few soils have developed from underlying bedrock; most soils are the weathered surface layers of unconsolidated deposits that geologists call "surficial deposits," or more simply, *surface deposits* (Fig. 6.1).

Most surface deposits are sediments weathered from bedrock in one area and transported by water, wind, or ice to another area. The deposits vary greatly depending on their mode of transportation. Some of the different kinds are:

> *Alluvium.* Sediment transported by running water.
> *Dunes* (windblown sand) and *loess* (windblown silt).
> *Till or glacial drift.* Sediment transported by glaciers or their meltwaters.
> *Colluvium.* Sediment moved downhill by gravity.

Some surface deposits are untransported, and are called *sedentary deposits*. The most extensive of these were formed *in situ* by weathering (chemical decomposition and mechanical disintegration) and are called residual deposits. In engineering usage the term soil includes surface deposits.

Transported Surface Deposits

GLACIAL DEPOSITS

The northern part of North America is blanketed with glacial deposits. In hilly or mountainous areas these deposits are confined to valleys and are discontinuous. When the last of the ice sheets were retreating and stood about at the position of the Great Lakes, depressions in front of the ice were occupied by lakes, and some are now marked by dry lake beds. Glacial deposits, and landforms attributable to glaciers, are also found on the lofty western mountains.

The mantle of glacial deposits is called *glacial drift*. Part of it was deposited by the ice and is without bedding; that is, it is *unstratified*. Part was deposited by glacial meltwaters and is bedded, or *stratified*.

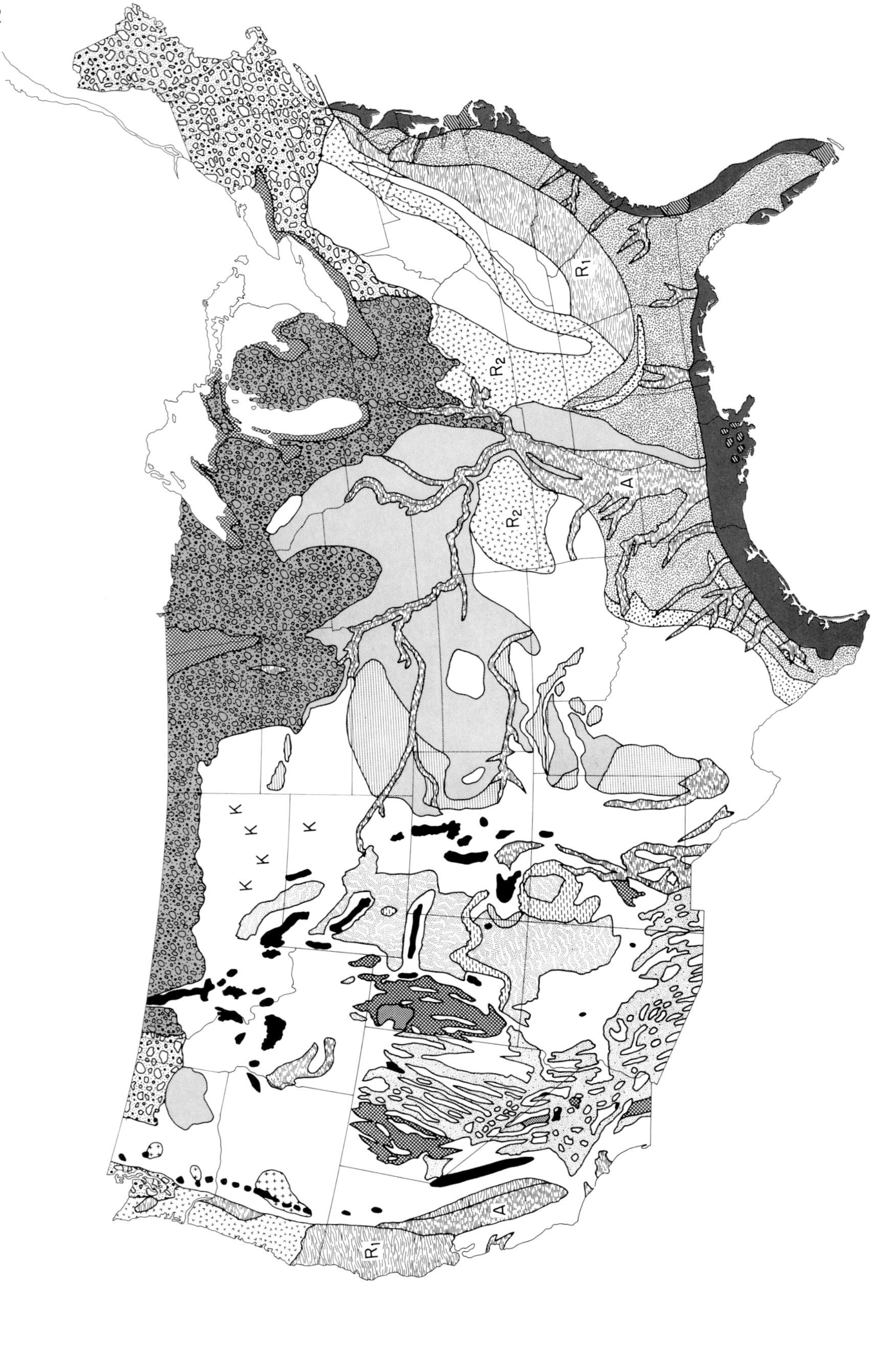
R1
R2
R2
A
K K K K K
A
R1

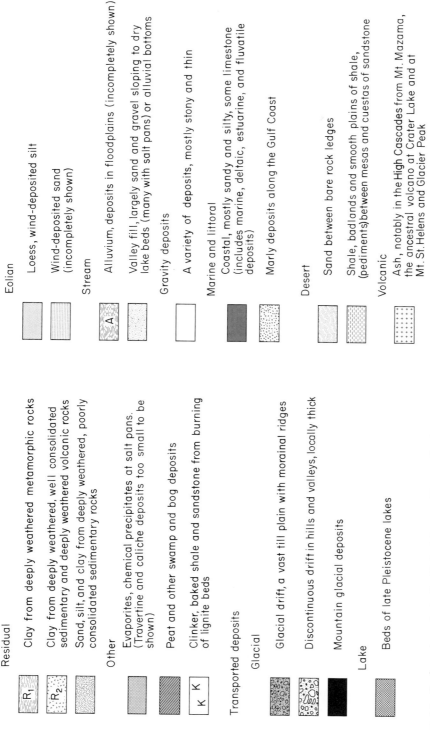

Sedentary deposits

Residual

R₁   Clay from deeply weathered metamorphic rocks

R₂   Clay from deeply weathered, well consolidated
     sedimentary and deeply weathered volcanic rocks

     Sand, silt, and clay from deeply weathered, poorly
     consolidated sedimentary rocks

Other

     Evaporites, chemical precipitates at salt pans.
     (Travertine and caliche deposits too small to be
     shown)

     Peat and other swamp and bog deposits

K   Clinker, baked shale and sandstone from burning
     of lignite beds

Transported deposits

Glacial

     Glacial drift, a vast till plain with morainal ridges

     Discontinuous drift in hills and valleys, locally thick

     Mountain glacial deposits

Lake

     Beds of late Pleistocene lakes

Eolian

     Loess, wind-deposited silt

     Wind-deposited sand
     (incompletely shown)

Stream

A   Alluvium, deposits in floodplains (incompletely shown)

     Valley fill, largely sand and gravel sloping to dry
     lake beds (many with salt pans) or alluvial bottoms

Gravity deposits

     A variety of deposits, mostly stony and thin

Marine and littoral

     Coastal, mostly sandy and silty, some limestone
     (includes marine, deltaic, estuarine, and fluvatile
     deposits)

     Marly deposits along the Gulf Coast

Desert

     Sand between bare rock ledges

     Shale, badlands and smooth plains of shale,
     (pediments) between mesas and cuestas of sandstone

Volcanic

     Ash, notably in the High Cascades from Mt. Mazama,
     the ancestral volcano at Crater Lake and at
     Mt. St. Helens and Glacier Peak

Figure 6.1 *Surface deposits in the United States. Almost all of Canada is blanketed by glacial drift.*

Unstratified drift, referred to as *till*, is a chaotic mixture of stones of all sizes embedded in sand and clay. One form of till, known as *ground moraine*, occurs as a hummocky blanket deposit with marshes and sag ponds between irregular mounds of gravel and sand. Where the glaciers advanced across hills and valleys of resistant rocks, as in New England, boulders plucked from the hillsides were transported far from their source and deposited as *glacial erratics*.

A former ice front is generally marked by a hummocky ridge of gravel and sand, partly stratified and partly unstratified. This is the *end*, or *terminal, moraine* (see Fig. 13.4).

The stratified glacial deposits include glacial outwash deposited in front of the ice (Fig. 3.17) and various ice-contact deposits formed back of the ice front and contained by one or more sidewalls of ice. Among these are isolated mounds of gravel and sand (*kames*), stream deposits along the edges of the ice (*kame terraces*), deltaic deposits in ponds and lakes (*kame deltas*), and smooth plains of water-laid deposits formed between blocks of the melting ice (*kame plains*). Gravels left along the channels of streams beneath the ice became *eskers*.

The stones in most glacial deposits can be identified as to source, and they clearly record the southward advance of the glaciers. Boulders from the White Mountains in New Hampshire have been moved to the southern part of that state; rocks from the Green Mountains in northern Vermont are scattered over the southern part of the state; rocks from the Adirondacks have been transported onto the Catskill Mountains; in Wisconsin, fragments of rocks from the Canadian Shield are contained in drift overlying Paleozoic formations; and on the Missouri Plateau in Montana, igneous rocks plucked from the isolated mountains there have been carried southward and deposited in drift overlying the Cretaceous formations.

EOLIAN DEPOSITS

Meltwaters from the northern glaciers flooded the Mississippi Valley and deposited alluvium there. Valleys discharging meltwaters were deva-

stated during floods, and when the floods ebbed the river flats became a source of silt and sand that was blown from the valleys onto surrounding uplands. Thus was formed the vast expanse of loess in the Central Lowlands and along the east side of the Mississippi Valley (Fig. 6.2). Farther west, similar deposits are sandy.

Other *eolian* (wind-laid) *deposits* include dune sand in various parts of the southwestern deserts and along the coasts. An unusual sort of eolian deposit is the blanket of volcanic ash extending leeward from Crater Lake, Mt. St. Helens, and Glacier Peak in the Cascade Range.

LAKE DEPOSITS

Lakes and ponds and the sediments laid down in them are second only to glacial drift as a characteristic feature of glaciated regions. Northeastern and north-central United States abound with lakes and ponds, including the Great Lakes, and these are only the southernmost parts of the vast lake country that extends northward along both sides of Hudson Bay (Fig. 5.7). During Pleistocene time the lakes were more extensive than today, and they were of many kinds, depending on whether they formed

1. in front of the ice sheets as a result of rivers being dammed by ice;

2. in basins and river valleys overdeepened as a result of glacial scour;

3. in ground moraine;

4. in structural basins, like the more than 100 closed basins in the Basin and Range Province;

5. in sinkholes in readily soluble limestone or gypsiferous ground, as in Florida;

6. along rivers at cut-off meanders or depressions in deltas;

7. back of landslides;

8. back of lava flows or in volcanic craters; or

9. in depressions partly due to wind erosion, as on the Great Plains.

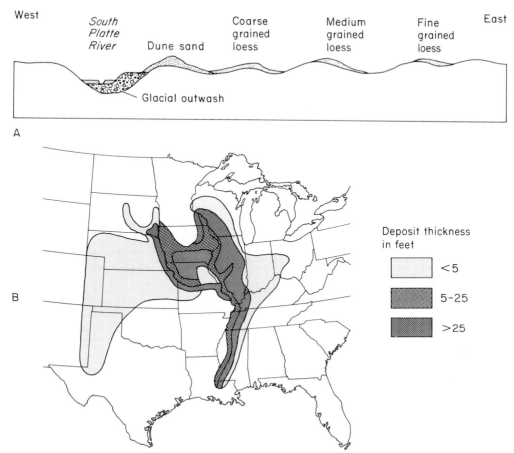

Figure 6.2 (A) Diagrammatic section illustrating how loessial and other eolian deposits thin and become finer grained and discontinuous leeward from their source. Dune sand was deposited on the bluff east of the source, the South Platte River. Farther east, silt (loess) was deposited, particularly on the eastern, lee sides of the hills. (B) Loess and other eolian deposits in the central United States. The loess thins leeward from the sources along the major river valleys that discharged outwash in Pleistocene time. Westward, toward the Rocky Mountains, the eolian deposits on the Great Plains are sandy. (From Geology of Soils by Charles B. Hunt. W. H. Freeman and Company. Copyright © 1972.)

The now-dry beds of the extensive lakes that formed in front of the continental ice sheets, especially in the Great Lakes region, are composed mostly of fine-textured sediments (the lake bottom muds) on flat ground with poor drainage. Swamps are numerous, and many former ones are now represented by deposits of peat. Such ground poses difficult foundation and other engineering and sanitary problems.

In the hillier New England region, lakes were numerous around stagnating blocks of valley ice,

but these lakes were small. Around the sides were deposited coarse deltaic sand and gravel forming kames, kame terraces, and other outwash (Fig. 3.17). The lake bottoms collected muds. This ground is poorly drained and contains small lakes, ponds, or swamps.

The Basin and Range Province consists of three kinds of ground. The ranges, which are rocky fault-block mountains without much soil, are flanked by broad gravel fans that slope from the foot of the mountains to the basins. The interiors of the basins are playas or, in the southern part of the province, broad alluvial floodplains. The extensive dry lake bed around Great Salt Lake is the remnant of Pleistocene Lake Bonneville; another in northwestern Nevada is the remnant of Pleistocene Lake Lahontan. Figure 4.10 shows the distribution and extent of some of the lakes that existed during the Pleistocene.

ALLUVIAL DEPOSITS

Floodplains along rivers and streams are built of *alluvium*, the sediment deposited by streams when they rise over their banks and spread across a flat valley floor. Alluvial floodplains make rich farmland, for the sediment deposited on them is rich in plant nutrients. But the land is subject to repeated flooding. The map, Figure 6.1, shows alluvium only along the principal streams in the central part of the United States; the reader will, of course, recognize that most stream valleys have alluvial floodplains.

GRAVITY DEPOSITS

Another kind of surface deposit is represented by material moving largely by gravity down hillsides. One kind, *talus*, consists of blocks spalled from cliffs and tumbled down the steep face to collect in a heap at the foot of the slope. Another kind, *colluvium*, moves slowly down steep hillsides by *creep*. Downhill creep is caused by frost heaving, pelting by rain or hail, overturning of trees, and dislodgement of particles by animals. Where hillsides become soaked, the ground may move downward as a *mudflow*. Other large masses may move as *landslides*.

Sedentary Surface Deposits

RESIDUAL DEPOSITS

Three widely separated regions in North America are characterized by deep and ancient products of the chemical decomposition of hard rocks—residual deposits called *saprolite*, or resi-

duum. These regions are (1) the Piedmont Province and adjoining areas in the southeastern United States (R_1 in Fig. 6.1), (2) the part of the central United States that lies south of the Ohio and Missouri Rivers, and (3) the Pacific Northwest (R_2 in Fig. 6.1). Many date from Tertiary time, and some from the Cretaceous. Saprolites grade downward from iron-rich aluminous clay at the surface to unaltered bedrock at depth (Fig. 6.3); some are more than a hundred feet deep. Similar deposits are preserved in isolated places elsewhere, mostly south of the limit of Wisconsinan glaciation. The only deposits north of there underlie glacial drift.

The layering that is typical of residual deposits is perhaps best developed in the Piedmont Province, where the parent materials are granite, gneiss, and schist. Above the fresh bedrock is a layer of weathered bedrock. This layer, variable in thickness, is tough enough so that it must be broken with a hammer; when struck by a ham-

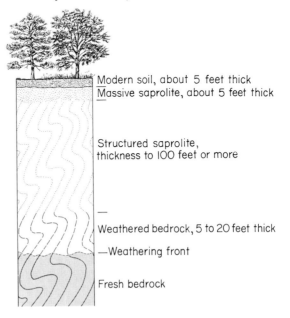

Figure 6.3 *Typical layering in saprolite in the Piedmont Province includes weathered bedrock, structured saprolite, massive saprolite, and the modern soil. Total depth commonly exceeds 50 feet and locally exceeds 100 feet.*

Modern soil, about 5 feet thick
Massive saprolite, about 5 feet thick

Structured saprolite, thickness to 100 feet or more

Weathered bedrock, 5 to 20 feet thick
Weathering front

Fresh bedrock

mer, however, it doesn't ring like fresh rock but gives a dull thud. The weathered layer is stained brown and yellow by hydrated iron oxides, especially along partings. Clayey alteration of minerals can be seen with a microscope, but the parent mineral grains are still firm. The weathered rock is 5 to 10 percent less dense than the fresh rock. The weathered layer is thin in dense rocks; in porous rocks it may be many feet thick.

Above the weathered bedrock is *saprolite,* which perfectly preserves the structure of the parent rock, but is largely altered to clay stained with iron oxide. The density of the saprolite is only half that of the unaltered rock. The alkalis (sodium and potassium) and alkaline earths (calcium and magnesium), which form readily soluble salts, have been almost entirely removed by leaching. More than 90 percent of this layer is alumina, silica, iron, and combined water.

These deposits illustrate the confusion over the term "soil." The saprolite and the underlying layer of weathered bedrock are not soil to agriculturalists because they are far too deep for plant growth. The layer of structured saprolite is soil to an engineer because it can be excavated without blasting, but the underlying weathered bedrock must be blasted and so is not soil in engineering parlance. To geologists, both are layers of an orderly ancient weathering profile, and are therefore considered soil.

On the Coastal Plain, Valley and Ridge Province, Interior Low Plateau, and Ozark Plateau, ancient deep red soils are extensively developed on sedimentary formations. Those developed on limestone formations are brilliant red and similar to the well-known European *terra rossa.* All these soils are pre-Wisconsinan and many are pre-Pleistocene. In the southern Appalachians, on the Cumberland Plateau, remnants of the old soils are moderately extensive, but they become relatively smaller and scarce northward, probably because during the glacial stages the old soils in the north were severely frost heaved and eroded. Some remnants, though, have been found under glacial drift, and these record the considerable antiquity of the weathering; in places the weathering can be shown to be as old as Tertiary.

Of special interest economically as well as scientifically are the bauxite deposits in the southern states. Bauxite, a hydrous aluminum oxide, is valuable as an ore of aluminum. These deposits formed as a result of intensive weathering of the sort that produced the saprolite on the Piedmont Province.

Soils

The term "soil" is used with three very different meanings. Agriculturalists limit the term to the surficial materials that provide a foundation and nutrient substratum for plants. Engineers use the term to refer to all unconsolidated materials, regardless of depth, that may be involved in foundation and excavation problems or be utilized as fill. Geologists use the term to refer to the surficial zone altered by weathering. In this book the term "soil" is used in the geologist's sense, but most terms used in the description of soils are borrowed from the nomenclature of soil scientists, who are agriculturally oriented.

Soils are layered parallel to the surface as a result of weathering (Fig. 6.4). The surface layers are rich in organic matter. The uppermost layer is a mat of leaves and other litter that is only slightly decomposed. Below is a layer of partly decomposed leaves and other organic matter. This organic matter is 99 percent carbon, hydrogen, oxygen, and nitrogen, and it grades downward into a layer of mineral matter blackened with organic matter. Below this is a light-colored layer in which there has been maximum leaching—that is, the transfer of constituents downward, by solution and by physical washing. Decomposition of organic matter in the surface layers produces acids that are carried downward by the soil water and dissolve matter from the layer immediately below the organic-rich one. Part or all of the dissolved matter is deposited in the subsoil (B layer in Fig. 6.4). Below this is the parent material.

Acid soils of the humid provinces differ greatly from alkaline soils of the semiarid and arid provinces. Acid soils (Fig. 6.4) develop where

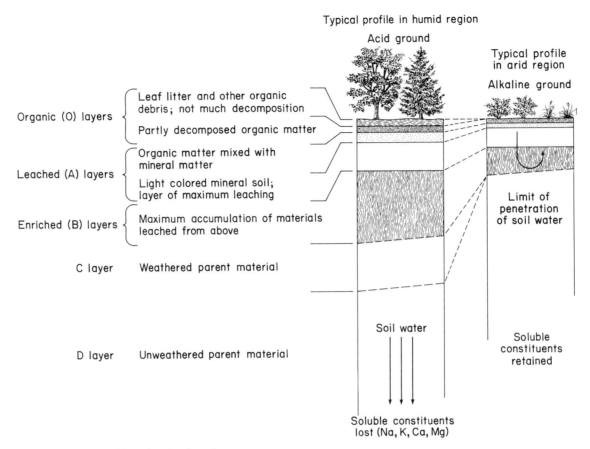

Figure 6.4 *Soil profiles, showing layering.*

moisture is sufficient to penetrate to the water table. Because soil moisture is ample, vegetation is lush and organic matter plentiful; decomposition of the organic matter renders the soils acid, and leaching is intensive. Aluminum, iron, and clays are leached from the upper layer and deposited in the lower layer, which is less acid and may even be chemically neutral. Since moisture is sufficient to drain down to the water table, it also removes silica and the very soluble alkalis and alkali earths from the profile. Continued weathering of acid soils changes their composition toward that of a clay mineral composed of aluminum and silica (kaolinite) and the hydroxides of ferric iron and aluminum.

Alkaline profiles (Fig. 6.4) develop where moisture wets only the upper layers of the ground and does not seep downward to the water table. Vegetation is sparse compared to that of humid regions; organic matter in the soil, and leaching are correspondingly less. Such constituents as are leached are transported downward as far as the water penetrates and are deposited where the water evaporates as the soil dries. Carbonates, whether contributed by organic matter or by the parent material, combine with the alkalis and alkali earths to form soluble salts. Their deposition gives rise to a B layer containing much carbonate, especially calcium carbonate. Alkaline soils have lost no constituents; indeed, carbon (from the organic matter) has been added.

Some of the common soils in North America are described in Table 6.1 and their distribution is shown in Figure 6.5. Figure 6.6 illustrates the

Table 6.1

Modern Soils

Acid ground, wet

I. Organic-rich soils

A. *Tundra Soils; Tundra* and associated *Arctic Brown Soils.*
Dark brown peaty layer over gray layers mottled yellow or brown subsoil permanently frozen. Arctic Brown Soils on well-drained uplands; Tundra Soils on poorly drained ground. Thickness 1 to 2 feet. *Climate:* frigid, humid. *Vegetation:* lichens, mosses, herbs, shrubs. *Weathering process:* decomposition of organic matter slowed by freezing and, in Tundra Soils, excessive wetting; frost-heaving mixes organic and mineral matter. *Age:* Holocene.

B. *Alpine Meadow Soils.*
Soils on mountain tops above timberline; somewhat like Tundra Soils but the subsoil is not permanently frozen and the ground generally is not so wet.

C. *Peat and Bog Soils.*
Brown, dark brown, or black peaty material over buried peat (*Bog Soil*) or over gray and rust mottled soils of mineral matter (*Half Bog Soil*). May be many feet thick. *Climate:* arctic, temperate, or tropic; standing water. *Vegetation:* swamp forest, sedge, or grass. *Weathering process:* decomposition of plant matter slowed by excessive wetting, which also causes development of organic-rich, sticky, compact clayey layer (gley). *Age:* mostly Holocene, rarely late Pleistocene.

Acid ground; mostly open system (i.e. alkalis and alkaline earths removed)

II. Forest soils

A. *Light soils; conspicuous light leached layer; Podzol Soils.*
Surface layer is litter of needles, twigs, and cones over a humus-rich layer containing mineral matter which overlies a conspicuous whitish-gray, leached layer that generally is sandy; layer of deposition clayey and stained brown. Total thickness generally less than 24 inches. Associated with extensive Peat and Bog Soils. *Climate:* cold, humid; annual precipitation mostly between 20 and 40 inches. *Vegetation:* mostly spruce-fir forest. *Weathering process:* acid leaching removes iron and aluminum from the leached layer and redeposits them in the layer of deposition; clay worked downward partly by washing and probably partly by the vigorous freeze and thaw which contributes to the sandiness of the leached layer. *Age:* Holocene.

B. *Dark soils; brown to gray-brown leached layer; Gray-Brown Podzolic Soils, Sol Brun Acide; related soils modified by cultivation are Brown Podzolic Soils.*
Surface layer is mostly litter from broadleaf trees, some conifers; under this is humus-rich layer containing mineral matter and overlying a brown or gray-brown leached layer containing more or less clay (compare above); layer of deposition stained darker brown and contains more clay than does the leached layer; locally it is an acid, clay-rich hardpan. Total thickness commonly about 30 inches. Occurrence generally south of the soils having conspicuous light leached layer and only locally associated with Peat and Bog Soils. *Climate:* temperate, humid; annual precipitation 30 to 40 inches. *Vegetation:* in eastern United States mostly deciduous broadleaf forest, some conifer forest on western mountains. *Weathering process:* the difference in leaching between these soils and those farther north in eastern United States and Canada is attributable to several factors: greater carbonate content of the more southerly ground south of the Precambrian Canadian Shield, greater extent of broadleaf forest, less sandy and less permeable leached layers, and (along the Appalachians) greater extent of steep slopes favoring rapid runoff. *Age:* Late Pleistocene and Holocene.

C. *Dark soils without a noticeable leached layer; Brown Forest Soils.*
Leaf litter over dark brown friable surface soil grading downward through lighter colored soil to calcareous parent material; the layering is obscure because the leaching is slowed by the carbonate matter. *Climate:* cool temperate; annual precipitation about 30 inches. *Vegetation:* mostly northern hardwood forest, some mixed broadleaf and conifer forest. *Weathering process:* same as in the other northeastern forest areas but leaching retarded by the high calcium carbonate content of the parent material. *Age:* Late Pleistocene and Holocene.

(Continued)

Table 6.1   *(Continued)*

Acid ground (continued)

    D. *Red and yellow soils, clayey; Red and Yellow Podzolic Soils.*
Thin, dark colored organic layer at surface over yellow-gray or gray-brown leached layer over a darker clayey layer of deposition which grades downward into deeply weathered parent material brightly colored and generally mottled red, yellow, purple, brown, white, and gray. The deeply weathered parent material may be scores of feet deep; the organic layer, leached layer, and layer of deposition commonly total 3 to 4 feet in thickness. *Climate:* warm temperate to tropical humid. *Vegetation:* southeastern pine forest or mixed broadleaf and pine forest. *Weathering process:* like the more northerly soils but these soil layers are dominated by the deeply weathered, clayey, residual parent material. Depending on the kind of parent residuum, there are 5 principal varieties of these red and yellow soils: 1, residual deposits on the crystalline rocks of the Piedmont Province; 2, residual deposits on the weakly consolidated sedimentary formations of the Coastal Plain; 3, weathered loess of Pre-Wisconsinan age, especially along the east side of the Mississippi River valley; 4, residual deposits in central and eastern United States developed on the Paleozoic formations, particularly the limestones (*Terra Rossa*); and 5, residual deposits on various kinds of rocks in the rainy Northwest. *Age:* the surface layers are late Pleistocene and Holocene; the residual, deeply weathered parent material is the result of much older weathering, early Pleistocene, Tertiary, and locally even older.

    E. *Sandy soils over shallow water table; Ground Water Podzol Soils.*
Thin organic layer over thick (2 to 3 feet) light-colored leached layer, usually sandy, over dark brown layer enriched with organic matter and collected at the top of the water table, which fluctuates. *Climate:* cool to tropical, humid. *Vegetation:* mostly southeastern pine forest. *Weathering process:* intensive acid leaching and transfer of organic matter to water table at bottom of the profile. *Age:* Late Pleistocene and Holocene.

III. Grassland soils

Transitional ground; mostly open system soil profiles; nearly neutral, or partly acid and partly alkaline

    A. *Parent materials noncalcareous or only slightly so; no hardpan; Prairie (Brunizem) Soils.*
Dark brown to nearly black, mildly acid, surface soils over brown, well-oxidized subsoils; reddish brown toward the south. Grades downward to lighter colored parent material with no layer of lime carbonate accumulation. Total thickness about 3 feet. *Climate:* cool to warm temperate, humid; annual precipitation 25 to 30 inches. *Vegetation:* tall grass. *Weathering Process:* acid leaching, but weak. *Age:* Late Pleistocene and Holocene.

    B. *Parent materials noncalcareous or only slightly so; with hardpan; Planosols.*
Leached surface soils over parent material containing clay and developing a clayey hardpan; ground nearly level. *Climate:* cool to warm temperate, humid; annual precipitation 25 to 30 inches. *Vegetation:* tall grasses, some forest. *Weathering process:* acid leaching with gleyization. *Age:* late Pleistocene and Holocene.

    C. *Parent materials calcareous; Rendzina Soils.*
Dark gray or black, organic rich, surface layers over soft, light gray or white calcareous material derived from chalk, soft limestone, or marl; associated with swelling clays, Thickness highly variable. *Climate:* variable. *Vegetation:* mostly tall grasses. *Weathering process:* acid leaching but process slowed by the carbonate in the parent material (cf. II,C, forest soil without noticeable leached layer). *Age:* mostly late Pleistocene and Holocene.

Alkaline ground; mostly closed system (i.e. alkalis and alkaline earths retained)	IV.	*Thin, woodland soils (e.g. chaparral, pinyon-pine, juniper, oak brush); Noncalcic Brown Soils.* Brown to red surface layers over redder and more clayey subsoil; alkaline to about neutral. *Climate:* semiarid; seasonally dry. *Weathering process:* weak acid leaching; little or no calcification; some clay and silica accumulated in layer of deposition.
	V.	*Grassland soils; Chernozem, Chestnut, Brown Soils.* Black to gray-brown, friable soil to depth of 3 or 4 feet under tall grasses and 1 to 3 feet under short grasses; grades downward through lighter colored layer to a layer where lime carbonate has accumulated. *Climate and vegetation:* subhumid, temperate to cool, annual precipitation 20 to 25 inches in belt of tall grasses (Chernozem Soils); 15 to 20 inches in belt of short grasses (Chestnut and Brown Soils). *Weathering process: calcification,* i.e. accumulation of carbonates in the lower layers. *Age:* late Pleistocene and Holocene.
	VI.	*Reddish calcareous soils under grasses or shrubs; Reddish Chestnut, Reddish Brown Soils.* Rather like IV but surface layers are reddish and lime carbonate layer generally thicker and more conspicuous; occur farther south. *Climate and vegetation:* semiarid; annual precipitation 10 to 20 inches; cool to hot; grasses and shrubs. *Weathering process:* calcification. *Age:* mixed ages with late Pleistocene and Holocene weathering profiles superimposed on older Pleistocene ones.
	VII.	*Western forest soils; Chestnut, Brown Soils.* Rather like IV but developed under woodland of oak, pinyon and juniper, or pine forest.
	VIII.	*Desert soils under shrubs; Desert, Sierozem, and Red Desert Soils.* Light gray or brown in north, reddish in south; organic layer thin and may be discontinuous where shrubs are widely spaced; carbonate layer generally within a foot of the surface. *Climate and vegetation:* arid; annual precipitation less than 10 inches; cool to hot. Shrubs, occasional trees; some woodland. *Age:* Late Pleistocene and Holocene soils (shallow, weakly developed profiles); older Pleistocene soils (several feet thick, generally reddish, and with well-developed layers).
	IX.	*Excessively alkaline and saline soils; Solonetz, Solonchak Soils.* Accumulated salts on or near the ground surface due to imperfect drainage; salts more than 0.2 percent. Alkaline ground ("Black Alkali"; Solonetz) usually formed by the less soluble salts (esp. sodium carbonate and sulfate); saline ground ("White alkali"; Solonchak) contains more soluble salts (esp. the chlorides). *Climate and vegetation:* arid, semiarid climates but may occur on saline ground in humid regions; vegetation limited to salt-tolerant species. *Age:* Holocene.
Acid or alkaline ground	X.	*Surface deposits with weakly developed weathering profiles; Skeletal Soils, Lithosols.* (Whether categories X and XI are acid or alkaline depends on parent material.) See Chapter 7.
	XI.	*Disturbed ground.* May be plowed layers on agricultural lands, where the organic and mineral layers would be mixed; may be weathered or unweathered surface deposits heaped in embankments or spread across a surface, or land cleared of top soil.

changes in soil profiles that accompany changes in vegetation and climate along a transect from northeastern Canada to the southwestern United States. The northeast end of the transect is cold and wet, and the soils there are acid; the southwest end is warm and dry, and the soils there are alkaline. The vegetation changes from tundra and conifer forest at the northeast, to grassland on the semiarid plains, to shrubland in the desert at the southwest.

Soils under the conifer forests are *Podzols,* characterized by a thin, ash-gray, leached horizon (A) over a dark-brown (B) horizon. Soils under the deciduous forests are *Gray-Brown Podzols,* characterized by a gray-brown leached horizon (A) over a dark-brown (B) horizon. These are typically acid soils.

Under the tall grass on the plains the A layers become thicker. Near the 100th meridian, where the annual precipitation averages about 20

132

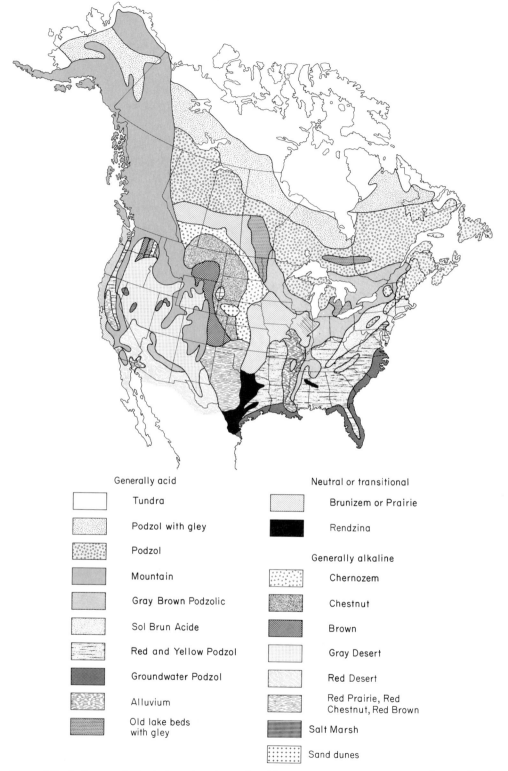

Legend:

Generally acid
- Tundra
- Podzol with gley
- Podzol
- Mountain
- Gray Brown Podzolic
- Sol Brun Acide
- Red and Yellow Podzol
- Groundwater Podzol
- Alluvium
- Old lake beds with gley

Neutral or transitional
- Brunizem or Prairie
- Rendzina

Generally alkaline
- Chernozem
- Chestnut
- Brown
- Gray Desert
- Red Desert
- Red Prairie, Red Chestnut, Red Brown
- Salt Marsh
- Sand dunes

Figure 6.5 *Soil map of North America. Generalized from U.S.D.A., Legget, 1968, and Oxford Atlas.*

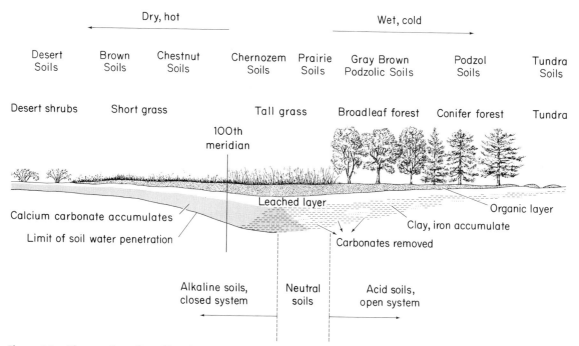

Figure 6.6 *Changes in soil profiles that accompany changes in vegetation and climate between the tundra in northern Canada and the deserts in the southwestern United States.*

inches, the soils are typically alkaline with lime carbonate in the subsoil. Prairie soils have a deep organic layer without a lime zone. Chernozem Soils, farther west but still under deep-rooted tall grass, have a deep layer of black organic material and an underlying zone of lime accumulation. Still farther west, where rainfall is less, the grasses are short and shallow rooted. The organic layer is thinner in the Chestnut Soils and lighter in the Brown Soils; the lime zone of both is more distinct but thinner. Soils in the deserts are thin and the horizons are not well developed.

Differences between soils in the northern and southern physiographic provinces are due partly to differences in climate but chiefly to differences in the ages of the soils. The Red and Yellow Podzols south of the limit of Wisconsinan glaciation owe their principal characteristics to weathering that occurred before the Wisconsinan glaciation. The organic fraction is the product of Holocene vegetation, which has developed a Holocene profile near the surface, but the present mineralogy of the soils is largely inherited from pre-Wisconsinan time, as shown by the fact that the B and the lower horizons are overlapped by and therefore older than the glacial drift and other deposits of Wisconsinan age. These old soils have been leached of silica and are called *lateritic soils,* or *latosols,* because of their similarity to the tropical soils known as laterites.

Most of the red soils of the southwestern United States also are old soils, but the Podzols and the Gray-Brown Podzols, which are developed on glacial drift and other deposits of Wisconsinan age or younger, are young.

Weathering of Mineral and Rock Particles to Form Soil

Weathering generally begins with mechanical rock disintegration. Examples are frost action, splitting of rocks by plant roots, growth of salt crystals, fires, and abrasion during transport by wind, water, or glacial ice. The continental and alpine glaciers produced quantities of rock flour by grinding the rock fragments they transported. Rock disintegration accelerates chemical decomposition by increasing the surface area subject to alteration. Fine-grained materials expose more surface area per unit mass and weather more rapidly than do coarse materials.

Soils are produced by weathering (chiefly chemical decay but including physical disintegration) of the mineral and rock particles in the upper layers of surface deposits. Soils include grains of unaltered, resistant minerals, partly altered minerals, and new minerals composed of the chemical elements dissolved from the altered minerals. The rock-forming minerals differ in susceptibility to weathering (Table 2.3). In general, their relative susceptibility is the same as the order in which they crystallize from silicate melts. The minerals formed early at high temperature and pressure are least resistant to chemical changes at the low temperatures and pressures of weathering; minerals that form late are most resistant to alteration in the soil.

The factors controlling rock weathering, like those controlling erosion, can be considered in terms of structure, process, and stage. Differences in the structure of rocks, including their hardness, permeability, and mineral composition, give rise to differences in the soils derived from them.

Weathering is controlled chiefly by four factors: organisms, climate, geologic setting, and topographic position. Acids derived from decomposition or organic matter on and in the soil are the principal agents of the decay of the minerals and rock particles, and accordingly the biota determines the kind and intensity of the chiefly biochemical processes that alter the mineral matter. Climate affects not only the biota but the abundance and temperature of soil moisture. The geologic setting may affect the soil climate—for example, by controlling the height of the water table. Similarly, the topographic position affects soil processes by controlling surface drainage; hillsides are better drained than flat uplands or valley bottoms.

The alteration of minerals by solutions requires time, and the kind and stage of alteration therefore partly depend on the duration of the process, the geologic history. The organic fraction in soils, largely a function of the present biota, is a product of the Holocene Epoch. But the Holocene has not lasted long enough to have a great affect on the mineral fraction of many soils; the characteristics of this fraction are largely inherited from the Pleistocene and older epochs, when the climate and biota over wide areas differed greatly from those of the present. In brief, then, the weathering of mineral and rock particles to form surface deposits is controlled by structure (parent material), process (biota, climate, topographic setting, geologic environment), and stage (time).

The four principal processes that alter minerals and rock particles in surface deposits are *carbonation, oxidation, hydration,* and *solution.* Carbon dioxide (CO_2) is readily soluble in water (H_2O), forming carbonic acid (H_2CO_3), which dissolves such carbonates as calcite.

$$\underset{\text{carbonic acid}}{H_2CO_3} + \underset{\text{calcite}}{CaCO_3} \longrightarrow \underset{\substack{\text{calcium bicarbonate}\\ \text{(soluble)}}}{H_2Ca(CO_3)_2}$$

Carbon dioxide makes up about 300 ppm of the atmosphere; in the soil atmosphere the CO_2 content is very much greater than in the air above ground because of the intense biochemical activity.

Oxygen, which makes up about 21 percent of the atmosphere, dissolves in rain and groundwater and combines with various bases in the process of oxidation, most notably in connection with alteration of iron-bearing minerals (dark minerals in Table 2.3); the iron becomes oxidized, and the minerals and soils are stained brown or red.

Hydration is the process by which water combines with various compounds. Hydration, carbonation, and solution participate in the alteration of feldspars to clay minerals. A sodic-calcic feldspar, for example, alters to a clay mineral (kaolinite, a hydrated aluminum silicate) and to calcium and sodium bicarbonate:

$$CaAl_2Si_2O_8 \cdot 2NaAlSi_3O_8 + 4H_2CO_3 + 2(nH_2O) \longrightarrow$$

sodic-calcic feldspar   carbonic   water
acid

$$2Al_2(OH)_2Si_4O_{10} \cdot H_2O + Ca(HCO_3)_2 + 2NaHCO_3$$

kaolinite   calcium   sodium
bicarbonate   bicarbonate

The bicarbonates are soluble and are removed in solution; the clays remain behind, so that old soils tend to be enriched in clay.

The stable products of mineral alteration are clay minerals and hydroxides of aluminum and ferric iron. Where weathering is advanced these new minerals become mixed in the soil with the more resistant minerals surviving from the parent rock, especially quartz and muscovite. The alkalis (K, Na) and alkali earths (Ca, Mg) freed by these alterations form carbonates, sulfates, chlorides, nitrates, borates, and other highly soluble salts that can be removed in solution. Silica also is released and may be removed by groundwater; the feldspars and the dark silicates contain more silica than the clay minerals that develop from them.

The rates of weathering and erosion are affected by the climate, but in complex ways. Increased rainfall tends to accelerate both weathering and stream discharge, and so increases erosion. But these effects are partly offset by increase in vegetation, which retards runoff. Increased temperature greatly increases biochemical activity involved in rock weathering and soil development. The rate of chemical reactions, in general, about doubles for every 10°C rise in temperature, which is to say that, other things being equal, rocks in southern United States decompose twice as rapidly as do those in the northern states and four times as rapidly as those in northern Canada. Moreover, the increased rainfall increases the vegetation, which in turn increases the quantity of organic acids for decomposing rocks and minerals.

References

Baldwin, M., Kellogg, C. E., and Thorp, J., 1938, Soil classification, in Soils and men, U.S. Dept. Agriculture yearbook.

Buckman, H. O., and Brady, N. C., 1969, The nature and properties of soils: New York, Macmillan.

Bunting, B. T., 1965, The geography of soil: Chicago, Aldine Publ. Co.

Flint, R. F., 1971, Glacial and Quaternary geology: New York, Wiley.

Foth, H. D., and Turk, L. M., 1972, Fundamentals of soil science: 4th ed., New York, Wiley.

Hunt, Charles B., 1972, Geology of soils—Their Evolution, Classification, and Uses: San Francisco, W. H. Freeman and Company.

Jenny, H., 1941, Factors of soil formation: New York, McGraw-Hill.

Legget, R. F. (ed.), 1968, Soils in Canada: Royal Soc. of Canada Spec. Publ. No. 3, Univ. Toronto Press.

Wright, H. E., Jr., and Frey, D. G., (ed.), 1965, The Quaternary of the United States: Princeton Univ. Press.

Erosion and sedimentation can be considered at various scales and ages. In this view, at Deadhorse Point State Park, Utah, the macro-scale is represented by canyons 2,000 feet deep and perhaps 30 million years old. The micro-scale is represented by the way individual strata have been etched a few inches in relief during the past hundreds or thousands of years. The rocks in the cliffs, roughly 200 million years old (late Paleozoic and early Mesozoic), once were soft sand and mud—sediments deposited in water.

7
·······

EROSION AND SEDIMENTATION—
LAND SCULPTURE

Erosion, like landforms, can be considered on different scales, both in space and in time. Chapter 3 considered the larger-scale features of erosion, the "Grand Canyons" and the watergaps—products of what is commonly called geological erosion. This chapter considers erosion and sedimentation on the scale that affects our farms and fields—the kind that is commonly called soil erosion. Actually, "soil erosion" affects more than just soil; it affects land use and land values, and takes many forms.

In some areas, sheetflooding or wind erodes the topsoil and exposes the subsoil. Elsewhere hillside runoff becomes concentrated and the ground becomes gullied. In still other areas, notably in the Colorado Plateau and Rocky Mountains, floodplains are subject to arroyo-cutting, and in other parts of the country stream banks are even more severely eroded. Erosion of this sort removes more than soil; it also removes the surficial deposits on which the soils have developed. Figure 7.1 shows the extent and relative severity of erosion in the United States.

The most eroded areas in eastern United States are those of the Red and Yellow Podzolic soils; in the Middle West, the most eroded are the loessial soils. The "dust bowl" areas of the southern Great Plains are subject to severe wind erosion, especially when tilled. In the Rocky Moun-

tains and other western provinces, the kinds of ground most susceptible to erosion are alluvial floodplains, loessial soils, and shale deserts. Much of Canada is mantled with glacial deposits, and is therefore not subject to rapid erosion.

Erosion of beaches is serious along much of the Atlantic and Gulf Coastal Plains and along the coast of California, especially in the southern part of the State. Hurricanes cause much erosion along the Atlantic and Gulf coasts, and erosion there is becoming more serious as sea level rises. A rise of as much as 6 inches has been recorded in the past 50 years (see pp. 91, 238).

In California, recent uplift along sections of the coast has developed coastal terraces, some highly unstable and subject to landsliding. Such lands, and the exposed stretches of the Atlantic Coast, obviously are more suitable for park lands than for real estate developments. We need the parks, and can do without the perennial disaster relief that is the price of real estate development in such areas.

On lowlands and plains, where slopes average no more than about 5 feet per mile, the rate of lowering seems to be about a quarter of an inch in a thousand years. Where relief is considerable and slopes are steep, as on mountains and plateaus, the rate may be 10 or 20 times that amount. If we assume that the average rate is 1 inch per

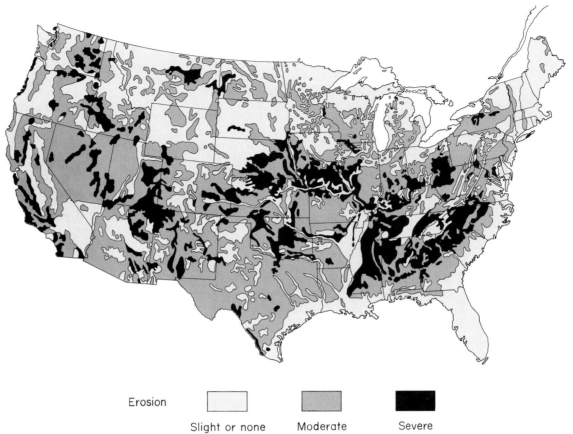

Figure 7.1 *Present-day erosion in the United States. [From U.S.D.A.]*

Erosion   Slight or none   Moderate   Severe

thousand years, North America would be eroded to a low plain in something like 50 million years, approximately the duration of the Cenozoic Era. This has not happened, of course, because structural movements of the crust—folding, faulting, and uplift—have offset the lowering by erosion. In fact, during the Cenozoic Era land has been added to the continent, as represented by the Tertiary and Quaternary formations along both the East and West coasts.

Sediment Transport by Streams

Running water transports sediment in *solution,* *suspension,* and as *bed load.* Constituents transported in *solution* include carbonates and other salts of the alkalis and alkali earths (Table 5.1),

but also silica and certain salts of iron and aluminum. Even the most quietly moving water can transport vast quantities of sediment in solution (see p. 111).

Sediment transported in suspension consists mostly of the fine-grained particles, especially those of clay size. They settle to the bottom in quiet water, but water is sufficiently viscous to hold the particles in suspension where the water is turbulent. The more turbulent the water, the larger the particles that can be suspended.

In slowly moving streams, the individual molecules move in parallel lines, and are smoothly streamlined around obstructions. Such flow is called *laminar flow* (Fig. 7.2,A). In swiftly moving streams, the individual particles swirl in all directions in *turbulent flow* (Fig. 7.2,B). Where the

Laminar flow (A) and turbulent flow (B) (after Gilluly, Waters, and Woodford)

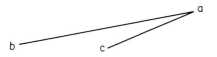

Increasing the gradient ab to ac, while maintaining form of channel and volume, causes:

1. increase in velocity;
2. increase in turbulence;
3. decrease in channel friction (shortening)
4. increase in energy available for sediment transport or corrasion

C

Increasing the volume, while maintaining the form of channel and gradient causes:

1. increase in velocity;
2. increase in turbulence;
3. decrease in channel friction by increasing volume relative to channel surface;
4. increase in energy available for sediment transport and corrasion

D

Channel friction, relates to area of channel surface per unit volume. The channel surface per unit volume is

least in a semicircular channel;

intermediate in a shallow, rectangular channel;

greatest in a deep narrow channel

E

Most stream gradients flatten downstream, the longitudinal profiles are concave upward because steepness bears an inverse relation to volume of water

F

Figure 7.2 *Some energy relationships that affect the capacity of streams to erode and transport sediment.*

flow is laminar, sediment transport is by solution and suspension; where flow is turbulent, sediment is also transported by rolling along the bottom and by saltation—a process in which particles are bounced upward and then being carried in suspension downstream as they settle. Both the velocity and the manner of stream flow control the size of sediment that can be transported.

Roughness of a stream bed also affects the capacity of a stream to transport sediment because increased roughness increases friction along the channel and so reduces the velocity of flow. Friction along a channel varies with the area of contact, being greatest in a deep narrow channel, intermediate in a shallow rectangular channel, and least in a semicircular channel. For a given form of cross section, the area of contact and friction decreases with increase in volume of water, so that the energy available for sediment transport is increased.

The energy consumed in transporting sediment can be measured by the weight of the sediment times the distance travelled as it sinks. Since fine-grained sediment sinks more slowly than coarse sediment, the same energy will move a greater load of fine sediment than of coarse-grained sediment. But increased load decreases the stream velocity, so that a stream fully loaded with fine-grained sediment moves more slowly than one fully loaded with coarse sediment.

Stream energy is measured by the product of its volume times its fall. Increasing either fall or volume increases the energy available for eroding the channel and for transporting sediment (Fig. 7.2,C,D). Moreover, the greater the fall the lower the fraction of stream energy consumed in channel friction, and consequently the more energy available for erosion and sediment transport. Increasing stream gradients, therefore, favors erosion and sediment transport at a greater than simple ratio.

Where a stream is joined by a major tributary and continues at about the same gradient without much change in channel proportions, the velocity is increased. This increases the energy for erosion and sediment transport (Fig. 7.2,D). In general,

though, stream gradients decrease as the volume of water increases, so that stream profiles generally are concave upward (Fig. 7.2,F).

Streams that are fully loaded with sediment have no excess energy left for erosion, whereas streams that do have excess energy actively erode their channels. When the load becomes excessive, some is deposited. Deposition and erosion can occur simultaneously, for a stream may erode the banks along the outer side of meanders, where the current is swift, and deposit sediment on the inner side, where the current is slack.

Because increased velocity increases erosion as well as transportation, changes in grade along a stream course tend to become smoothed, as a result of increased erosion at the steep places. The tendency is for streams to establish smooth gradients that tend to conform to flood stages.

The force of running water varies as the square of the velocity ($f \propto V^2$) because doubling the velocity doubles both the quantity and the momentum of the water. Moreover, the force on a pebble increases as the surface area of the pebble is increased; doubling the surface doubles the force, and since the surface varies as the square of the diameter, the force varies as the square of the diameter ($f \propto d^2$).

The resistance of a stone (its weight) varies as the diameter cubed ($w \propto d^3$), so that when a current is just able to move a stone, the force varies as the weight, ($f \propto w$); that is, $d^3(=w) \propto V^2 \times d^2(=f)$; or, $d \propto V^2$, and therefore $f \propto V^2 \times V^4 = V^6$). This says that the competence of the stream to move particles varies as the sixth power of the velocity.

For example, imagine that a current is just able to move a 1-cubic-inch pebble. If the stream velocity is doubled, it can move stones of 64 cubic inches because the force is increased 16 times on account of the greater surface, and the force against each square inch of surface is increased by the square of the velocity; that is, $4 \times 16 = 64$.

The practical effect of these computations may be illustrated by the following examples of the stream velocities that are required to transport particles of different sizes:

Stream Velocity	Sediment Size that can be Transported
$\frac{1}{6}$ mph	clay
$\frac{1}{3}$ mph	fine sand
1 mph	gravel up to pea size
2 mph	gravel up to thumb size
3 mph	gravel up to size of hen's egg

In the course of their transportation by streams, sediments are corraded, partly by solution but chiefly by abrasion. The effective force is the current; the tools are the sand and stones being moved. The constant comminution of fragments reduces the average size of the particles and the fine ones become separated from the coarse. The degree of corrasion depends partly on the hardness (composition), shape, and size of the particles, and partly on the mode of transportation and distance transported.

Wind Erosion

Wind, like running water, also can transport materials by rolling them along the ground (tumbleweed is a familiar example), by saltation, by suspension (does your city have smog?), and even by solution. Materials in solution are mostly salts in the water vapor or water droplets. The chloride content of the atmosphere, and of the rain and snow, decreases inland from the coasts.

As with water, the capacity of wind to erode and to transport sediment depends on its velocity. Various workers find a linear relationship between wind velocity and sizes of sand grains being transported:

Velocity (meters per second)	Diameter of Grains Suspended (millimeters)
0.5	0.04
1.0	0.08
5.0	0.41
10.0	0.81

Five meters per second is equal to 11 miles per hour.

The roughness and shape of the ground surface affect the velocity and duration of winds. Irregularities favor turbulence and funneling. Blown sand accumulates on the lee sides of hills and lee sides of shrubs. Huge eddies may develop in mountain valleys and create great fields of sand dunes, as at the Great Sand Dunes National Monument in San Luis Valley, Colorado, and the field of dunes at Stovepipe Wells in Death Valley. Sand blown onto the windward side of a hill or mountain forms *climbing dunes;* sand that accumulates on the lee side forms *falling dunes.*

In open, sandy country, where topographic relief is low, characteristic dunes form. Their size and shape depend on the balance between wind velocity, density of vegetation, and supply of sand. Where velocities are great and the supply of sand and vegetation minimal, the sand forms longitudinal ridges. Longitudinal wind cells rotating spirally with a vortex having a diameter equal to the space between the ridges build elongate sand piles; the same explanation has been applied to the lines of seaweed (sargassan lines) on the sea and to similarly spaced lines of clouds. Where wind velocity is small and there is much sand without much vegetation, the dunes are likely to be transverse to the wind direction. Where wind velocity, supply of sand, and density of vegetation are moderate, the dunes are parabolic, giving the appearance of having been scouped out on the windward side.

Solution by rainwater makes a most important contribution to wind erosion, particularly in arid and semiarid regions. Many sandstones are cemented by calcium carbonate, and water that seeps into and through the rock dissolves the cement. Wind can then gradually remove the loosened sand grains, eventually producing niches, alcoves, pedestal rocks, and tanks (Fig. 7.3). Such features commonly are attributed to wind erosion, but their development requires both water and wind.

Corrasion by wind may be caused by sandblasting (Fig. 7.4), mostly by grains of quartz sand. One practical effect of such erosion is the

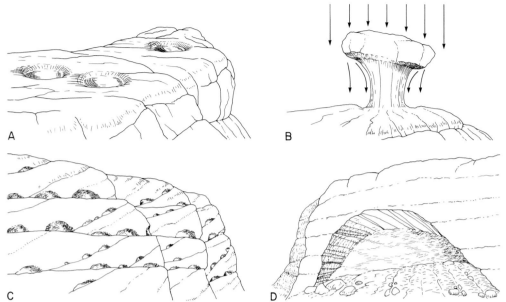

Figure 7.3 *Desert features attributable partly to wind erosion of sandstone. Rain and seep water dissolve the cement (mostly calcium carbonate) that hold the grains of sand together, and the wind removes the loosened sand grains and so develop depressions in flat rock surfaces known as waterpockets or tanks (A). They may be many feet in diameter. Pedestal rocks (B) may develop where resistant beds alternate with easily eroded ones; rain falls on the cap and spills over the side. Part of this drops off the under side as a drip curtain, and part continues as seep adhering to the rock surface. Pedestal rocks may be tens of feet high. Irregular depressions a few inches in diameter known as niches (C) may develop on cliff faces where the cement is irregularly distributed or where there are permeable layers where water entering the rock collects. Large alcoves, some 600 feet long and 300 feet high and 300 feet deep (D) may develop where large seeps or springs discharge from the sandstone cliffs.*

removal of paint from exposed sides of automobiles and the frosting of windshields. Telegraph poles in Cajon Pass, California, had to be protected against sandblasting of their bases. Old bottles that have lain on the ground in arid and

Figure 7.4 *Facetting of stones by sandblast. There is an upper limit of maximum blast, but the stone above that becomes shaped by the saltating grains of quartz sand. Stones may become bevelled by blasting almost down to ground level. Most commonly they develop shapes like the one in the middle diagram.*

Top of maximum blast

semiarid regions are generally frosted on surfaces exposed above ground. Stones that protrude become facetted. Some have irregular shapes (windkanter) whereas others develop a facet at right angles to the wind (einkanter). Still others have several facets (dreikanter etc.), possibly the result of changes in wind direction or of having been turned.

The effects of sandblasting may be seen on a micro scale too. A fragment of obsidian or chert first develops tiny pits, visible only under a microscope. As the number of pits increases the surfaces lose their shineness because they no longer reflect light well. Moreover, the damaged pit walls become hydrated.

The lowering of a surface by wind erosion is called *deflation*. On the Great Plains, there are many shallow depressions, or deflation hollows, where water collects and stands; livestock gather around these to drink, and their trampling loosens the silt and sand, which can be blown away in the dry season. On the Colorado Plateau, alluvial floodplains used for farming in prehistoric as well as historic time have been lowered by wind erosion, and the sand has collected in mounds at the base of such shrubs as greasewood. Such mounds have pedestals of horizontally bedded alluvium and an upper structure of windblown material (Fig. 7.5).

The areas most subject to wind erosion are those having old stabilized dunes or other uncemented sandy ground. Most such ground is in the semiarid and arid parts of the continent, especially the sandy parts of the Great Plains, the sandy delta of the Rio Grande in Texas, the sandy areas of the Basin and Range Province and Colorado and Columbia plateaus.

Wind-deposited sediments generally are well sorted. Fine-grained particles move in suspension and become separated from the coarse ones, which move mostly by rolling and saltation. Dunes, therefore, are sandy rather than silty; the fine sand collects in the troughs of ripples on the dunes, and the coarse sand forms the ridges. Within a particular sand field, the particles exhibit little range in grain size. Similarly, the range in grain size of the silty loessial deposits in the central United States is small; more than 50 percent of the silt particles are in the size range 0.015 to 0.035 mm.

Wind also erodes high mountains at or near the timberline. Strictly speaking, timberline is that line above which trees do not grow because of the shortness of the growing season. But on many mountains timberline is controlled by wind. The summits are so wind-blasted, that trees do not grow there, and consequently timberline may be at quite different altitudes on neighboring ridges depending on exposure.

Mass Wasting

Various processes contribute to the downhill movement, by gravity, of soil or other loose material. Collectively they are referred to as mass wasting.

Freezing and thawing cause slow creep of soil downhill because freezing lifts the soils at right angles to the slope, and thawing allows the frozen ground to settle vertically. Each cycle of freezing and thawing therefore moves the soil a short distance downhill. Likewise, rainstorms knock particles downhill because the trajectory of the splash is greater in that direction than uphill. The toppling of trees turns up roots with soil around them, and this disturbed ground settles downhill. Where snow accumulates on hillsides or where there are torrential rains, the ground may become saturated and slump or slide downhill. The saturated mass may pull away from the surrounding ground and move downhill as an avalanche or as a mudflow.

Figure 7.5 *Example of lowering of a floodplain surface by wind erosion on the Colorado Plateau. The surface has been lowered 8 to 10 inches, and sand has accumulated around the shrubs. The original floodplain surface is marked by the occupation layer under the greasewood mound and by the alluvium hardened by baking at the prehistoric fireplace.*

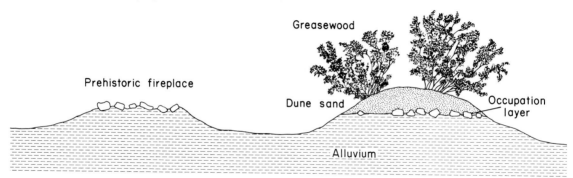

Landslides may move bedrock as well as the mantle of hillside colluvium. In some landslides the oversteepened cliff face falls outward, collapses, and descends as an avalanche. In others, the cliff face slides downward on a sheared surface, generally lubricated by seepage; this surface is concave upward, and the sliding block therefore becomes rotated backward into the plane of shear.

Glacial Erosion

Glaciers and glaciated country provide some of our most spectacular scenery, yet the amount of erosion attributable to glacial action is surprisingly little. Glaciers modify valleys but do not create them. It has been estimated, for example, that the several continental ice sheets that formed on the Canadian Shield have lowered the rock surface there an average of no more than about 25 or 30 feet, yet the ice sheets spread from Canada far southward into the United States and erratics, big isolated boulders, have been carried from Ontario as far south as Missouri. The constructional landforms built of these deposits have been described in Chapter 3.

The continental glaciers derived their load of sediment chiefly from the soil and other unconsolidated deposits overridden by the glaciers, for few hills protruded above the ice to shed debris onto it, except in the northeastern United States. Glaciated areas generally are free of unconsolidated surficial deposits other than those left by the glaciers themselves. Bare rock surfaces are extensive, and these show striations and other signs of gouge caused by rocks frozen into the bottom of the ice. Among the thousands of exposures of bedrock in New Hampshire, only about 50 include rock that is notably chemically decayed.

Most of the debris transported by valley glaciers and deposited in moraines (Fig. 3.17) is derived from the hillsides above the ice, which are subject to severe freezing and thawing and develop mud flows and avalanches during sudden thaws. The sediment falls or is washed onto the ice in the valley and transported down valley by the glacier.

Other sediment moved by valley glaciers is gouged from the valley floor under the ice. Most surficial deposits, when overridden by a glacier, become incorporated in the ice and transported down valley to the terminus, where floods transport the glacial outwash away from the ice front. Although ice movement is responsible for part of the transport by glaciers, much or most of the debris is transported by streams on, in, and under the ice.

In many areas, the striations, or grooves, produced by glacial erosion of bare rock surfaces are oriented in two directions oblique to one another. The two sets of striations might record two glacial advances, but in most areas they probably represent a change in the direction of ice flow as an advance waned. As an ice sheet thins, it molds itself more closely to the underlying topography, and the direction of movement changes.

Hills overridden by glacial ice are likely to have a smoothly sloping stoss slope and a steeper, less regular lee slope. The stoss slope is smoothed by abrasion, like sandpapering, the smoothing being done by stones and grit held in the base of the ice. The steepness of the lee slope can be attributed to release of pressure in the lee direction plucking blocks of rock loosened before the ice arrived, and mechanical quarrying by the overriding ice. Whatever the processes, the molded forms become streamlined in the direction of ice advance. They may be entirely of rock, entirely of glacial drift, or mixed. Well-formed ones, called drumlins, occur in swarms. Those with rock cores are called rock drumlins. There are swarms of drumlins in Nova Scotia, south-central New England, New York south of Lake Ontario, east-central Wisconsin, and northernmost Canada. In each of these regions the drumlins are numbered by the hundreds or thousands.

Much of the rock flour included in glacial till, the very fine clayey fraction, may be of loessial origin. At the time the loess deposits were forming in the central United States, much dust must have been blown onto the ice sheets and mixed with the other debris that was deposited when the ice melted.

Rates of Erosion

Rates of erosion vary greatly from place to place and have varied from time to time in the geologic past as a result of structural movements and climatic changes. Erosion rates vary according to the topography (relief and slope), climate (amount and kind of runoff), and kind of ground (bare rock or easily eroded surface deposits). Present-day erosion can be estimated by comparing the sediment load of streams with the areas drained. Past erosion rates can be estimated by comparing the quantity of sediment contained in the formations in old geosynclines with the areas that were eroded and the duration of the period represented. Such estimates are not very accurate, but they do provide an approximate measure of the forces involved and the times required to modify landforms.

This erosion may remove soil or other surface deposits, or it may remove unweathered bedrock. The relative importance of these in shaping landforms is difficult to assess, but we may assume that channel cutting by streams and by glacial ice is accomplished chiefly by erosion of bedrock, whereas the retreat of hillsides and the lowering of hilltops, at least in the humid provinces, are accomplished chiefly by erosion of the products of weathering—the soil or other surface deposits.

In the humid provinces, where weathering is rapid, valleys are V-shaped. Hillsides are soil covered and tend to rise smoothly, though in places steeply, from valley floors. In the arid provinces, where hillsides are rocky and interrupted by cliffs. Hilltops in humid provinces commonly are soil covered and rounded, but in arid provinces they are mostly bare rock and reflect the structure.

Erosion rates also depend on the toughness of the rock being weathered. Disintegration by corrasion is most rapid in soft rocks, and transportation from the site is favored if the debris

is finely comminuted. Disintegration by frost action depends on climate, permeability of the rock, and its coherence. The mineral and chemical composition determines susceptibility to solution.

Erosion rates also depend somewhat on the climate. Weathering is hastened by abundant moisture; temperature is important chiefly because changes in temperature cause changes in volume. Increased moisture increases the water supply, which both hastens weathering and increases transportation effects because of the great volume of water. Frost action becomes slight where soil depth exceeds the depth of frost penetration. These direct effects of the climate are in part offset by indirect influences of the vegetation, which partly oppose the direct effects.

Measurements of the load carried by streams— the dissolved solids, suspended solids, and bedload—can be used to estimate erosion rates in the stream basins, commonly considered as inches of general lowering of the surface (denudation) per thousand years. Denudation of Continental United States is progressing at 1 to 3 inches per thousand years. The estimated rate, however, varies from one physiographic region to another, as indicated by the following (generalized from various sources):

River Basins	Estimated Denudation, Inches per 1,000 years
North Atlantic rivers, Rapidan River northward to and including the Delaware	0.5
South Atlantic and east Gulf rivers, Roanoke River southward to and including the Chattahooche	1.0
Mississippi River	1.3
Western Gulf rivers, Rio Grande, Pecos, and Colorado (of Texas) Rivers	2.5
Colorado River (of the west)	5.6
San Joaquin and Sacramento Rivers	0.3
Eel, Mad, and Trinity Rivers, California	18.0
Columbia and Snake Rivers	0.6

Beach and Bank Erosion

Three kinds of measures are commonly used to protect shores and river banks against erosion. River banks may be protected by replacing them with walls or by piling coarse stone (riprap) along them. In many places discarded automobiles and refrigerators have been used for this purpose! Along beaches, protective walls are built parallel to the shore and well back from it to protect against storm waves. Heavy structures are called sea walls; lighter ones are called bulkheads or revetments. A common means of protecting beaches from erosion by longshore currents is to construct groynes or jetties at a high angle to the shore. Wave action can be reduced by breakwaters.

Shore erosion along the Atlantic and Gulf Coast is especially severe during hurricanes, which are most damaging at high tide. Vast sums of money are needed to protect private property along the beaches from storm damage and from shifting of the beaches. The money comes mostly from taxes. In the long run it might be less expensive to purchase the private lands and use them as public seashores. Is it sound public policy to permit the erection of costly buildings at exposed sites along the shore, and then commit the public to the protection of that property against obvious storm hazards?

Erosion Control—Soil Conservation

Soil conservation has many purposes besides minimizing erosion. It seeks to help reduce deposition of sediment where it is not wanted, to help maintain proper soil density, to minimize exhaustion of plant nutrients through overleaching, to conserve water by improving infiltration of drainage, and to minimize waterlogging and accumulation of salts or alkalis.

Erosion of farmed land removes the topsoil; unless it is replenished, the ground surface may be lowered to the clayey enriched layer, which is more difficult to farm than the original surface layers. Soil losses increase as slopes steepen.

Ground with a slope of 1 percent might lose 5 tons of soil (about 100 cubic feet) per acre annually, whereas ground with a slope of 10 percent loses 50 tons and ground with a slope of 20 percent loses 100 tons.

Erosion on cropland can be and has been reduced by various conservation practices. One of these is crop rotation, which consists in planting a succession of different crops on the same piece of ground. It is based on the principle that cultivated crops expose the ground to maximum erosion, that small grains cause less exposure, and that grasses or mixed grasses and legumes effectively protect the ground against erosion. A common rotation plan therefore includes a cultivated crop followed by a small grain, and this followed by grasses. Crop rotation not only saves soil, but increases production. Examples of some combinations of rotated crops are:

1. In the northeastern United States: oats, red clover, potatoes.

2. In the southeastern United States: corn with cowpeas, small grain, lespedeza, cotton.

3. In the Ozark Plateau: corn with cowpeas, cotton, small grain, cowpeas.

4. On the Great Plains: sorghum, oats and sweet clover, sweet clover, wheat for 2 years.

Another common practice is contour plowing and the cultivation of row crops along the contour. Runoff is retarded or checked by the furrows. Crop rotation and contour plowing may be combined, and either or both of those practices may be combined with strip-cropping—the practice of alternating row crops with closely growing ones.

Four ways of improving farmed ground in order to retard erosion are: adding vegetable matter to the soil increases its aeration and the spread of roots; terracing sloping ground to minimize runoff and prevent gullying; controlling natural channels artificially by dams, and stabilizing the broad shallow ones with stands of grass or other vegetation; and protecting ground that is subject to washing by runoff from upslope with diversion channels; the runoff might even be saved by collecting it in ponds.

Farmed land can also be protected against erosion by using part of the land for planting permanent buffers in the form of strips of perennial grass or shrubs. Steep slopes generally should not be used for farming; they can be used for growing perennial vegetation.

Other erosion caused by Man's use of the land is caused by quarries, sand and gravel pits, strip mines, and the waste piles at mines and other excavations. The materials obtained from these operations are needed and used, as is the produce from the croplands, but there is no need for the excavations or waste piles to continue muddying streams and scarring the landscape. Highway engineers excavate through hills and fill valleys and contribute greatly to erosion and muddying of streams in the process, but when the construction is completed the scars are covered and healed so well that geologists protest the greenery that covers what had been outcrop. Abandoned quarries, sand and gravel pits, and strip mines could similarly be healed.

References

Brush, L. M., Jr., 1961, Drainage basins, channels and flow characteristics of selected streams in central Pennsylvania: U.S. Geol. Survey Prof. Paper 282-F, pp. 145–181.

Bryan, K., 1923, Erosion and sedimentation in the Papago Country: U.S. Geol. Survey Bull. 730-B, pp.19–20.

Gilbert, G. K., 1909, Convexity of hilltops: Jour. Geology v. 17, pp. 344–350.

———, 1914, The transportation of debris by running waters: U.S. Geol. Survey Prof. Paper 86.

Hack, J. T., 1957, Studies of longitudinal stream profiles in Virginia and Maryland: U.S. Geol. Survey Prof. Paper 294-B, pp. 45–97.

Horton, R. E., 1945, Erosional development of streams and their drainage basins; hydrophysical approach to quantitative morphology: Geol. Soc. America Bull., v. 56, pp. 275–370.

Leopold, L. B., and Wolman, M. G., 1960, River meanders: Bull. Geol. Soc. America, v. 71, pp. 769–794.

Leopold, L. B., Wolman, M. G., and Miller, J. P., 1964, Fluvial processes in geomorphology: San Francisco, W. H. Freeman and Company.

Mackin, J. H., 1948, Concept of the graded stream: Geol. Soc. America Bull., v. 59, pp. 463–512.

Mississippi River Commission, 1935, Studies of river bed materials and their movement with reference to the lower Mississippi River: U.S. Waterways Exper. Sta. Paper 17, Vicksburg, Miss.

Miller, J. P., 1958, High mountain streams: effects of geology on channel characteristics and bed material: New Mexico State Bur. Mines and Min. Resources, Mem. 4, 51 p.

Powell, J. W., 1875, Exploration of the Colorado River of the West and its tributaries: Wash. D.C., Smithsonian Institution.

Schumm, S. A., 1956, The role of creep and rainwash on the retreat of badland slopes: Am. Jour. Sci., v. 254, pp. 693–706.

———, 1960, The shape of alluvial channels in relation to sediment type: U.S. Geol. Survey Prof. Paper 352-B, pp. 17–30.

Wolman, M. G., and Leopold, L. B., 1957, River floodplains—Some observations on their formation: U.S. Geol. Survey Prof. Paper 282-C, pp. 87–109.

Three major North American forests are: the Northern Forest of spruce and fir that extends across Canada from the Maritime Provinces to Alaska; the Western Forests of the United States and southern Canada, which include the Pacific Forest and Rocky Mountain forests; and the Eastern Forests of the United States, which include southern extensions of the Northern Forest in the higher Appalachians and Great Lakes region, Central Forest of hardwoods on the flanks of the Appalachians, and in the Central Lowlands, Southern Pine Forest of the Atlantic and Gulf Coastal Plain, and representatives of Tropical Forest in southernmost Florida and Texas. This view shows redwoods at Humboldt Redwoods State Park, California. [Courtesy of State of California Dept. of Parks and Recreation.]

8
·······

PLANT AND ANIMAL GEOGRAPHY— RESPONSE TO ENVIRONMENT

Life Zones

Along the tropical coast of Florida, one can find mangrove and alligator; around lakes in Canada, spruce and moose; and in northernmost Canada and Alaska, tundra and caribou.

Some like it hot, and some like it cold. Each climatic region has its characteristic flora and fauna, and these regions are referred to as *life zones*. The climatic regions are obviously completely gradational with each other, and their boundaries necessarily arbitrary. The faunal zones also are gradational, but less completely so. The floral zones are still less gradational, and in many places are set apart by surprisingly sharp boundaries.

In North America, seven transcontinental life zones can be recognized (Fig. 8.1). At the north, the *Arctic, Hudsonian,* and *Canadian Zones* constitute the *Boreal Region.* South of this region is the *Transition Zone,* where the Boreal Region grades into the more southerly Austral Region, which is divided into the *Upper* and *Lower Austral Zones.* Farthest south is the *Tropical Zone.* The general arrangement, by latitude, evidently reflects temperature differences; a similar zonation arranged by altitude is found on mountains (Figs. 8.8, 8.9). The more northerly zones extend southward along the tops of the mountains (Fig. 8.1). The Arctic Zone on the mountain tops is referred to as the *Alpine Zone.*

C. Hart Merriam, who introduced the concept of life zones in 1898, suggested that the northward distribution of terrestrial plants is governed by the sum of the temperatures above $32°F (= 0°C)$ for the entire season of growth and reproduction, and that the southward distribution is governed by the mean temperature of a brief period during the hottest part of the year. He suggested that the southern limits of the zones would be at the following isotherms:

Southern limit of Arctic Zone at 50°F,
Southern limit of Hudsonian Zone at 57.2°F,
Southern limit of Boreal Region at 64.4°F.

Although these temperature limits are not generally accepted, some such control seems indicated.

There also are biotic zonations that reflect differences in amount of moisture, especially in the Austral Region. The differences are great enough to require distinction between the Austral Zones of the humid East and those of the arid and the semiarid West, as follows:

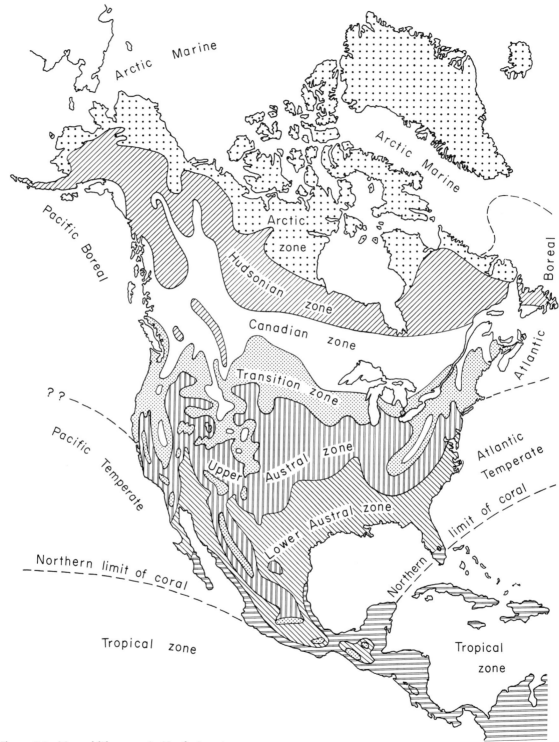

Figure 8.1 *Map of life zones in North America.*

	Semiarid West	Humid East
Austral region	Upper Sonoran Zone	Carolinian Zone
	Lower Sonoran Zone	Austroriparian Zone

Forest Regions of North America

North American forests divide into five regional kinds. Only one, the Northern Conifer Forest, extends across the continent from the Atlantic to the Pacific. This forest is almost entirely in Canada and Alaska. Four prongs, each different, extend southward from it. In the humid, eastern part of the continent are the Appalachian forests, mostly hardwoods—that is, broadleaf trees. A second prong, mostly a pine forest, extends southward along the Rocky Mountains. A third, more varied than that of the Rocky Mountains, although mostly conifer, extends southward along the Cascades and Sierra Nevada. The fourth prong is along the rainy Pacific Coast southward to San Francisco Bay; it includes the coastal redwoods. The Northern Conifer Forest, also referred to as the Boreal Forest, is simplest in composition; its principal species are (Fig. 8.2):

Black spruce
White spruce
Tamarack
Balsam poplar
Aspen
Paper birch

Several other species are restricted to the eastern part of the Northern Conifer Forest: Balsam fir, *Abies balsamea,* and two pines, Red pine, *Pinus resinosa,* which is confined to the southeast, and Jack pine, *P. banksiana,* which extends almost to Alaska. Both pines are two-needle pines. Among the characteristic animals are the lynx, marten, porcupine, red squirrel, snowshoe hare, and moose. Some birds that nest there are the Canada jay, spruce partridge, hawk owl, white-throated sparrow, junco, and hermit thrush.

North of the Boreal Forest is the Hudsonian, or Taiga, Zone, which supports a growth of spruce and lichens. This is the northern limit of forest and northern limit for such mammals as moose, elk, wolverine, marten, and gray wolf. Characteristic birds are the rough-legged hawk, great gray owl, pine grosbeak, and northern shrike.

North of this is the Arctic, or Tundra, Zone, which is treeless except for dwarfed willows and consists of mosses, lichens, and sedges. This is home for the polar bear, musk-ox, caribou, and reindeer and for such characteristic birds as the snowy owl and snow bunting. This zone is circumpolar; most of the fauna, and to a lesser extent the flora, occurs in Eurasia as well as in North America.

The Appalachian Forest is by far the most complex. It has more than 1,000 species of trees, which is more than any other forest on this earth, with the possible exception of the forest in

Figure 8.2 *Some trees characteristic of the Northern Conifer Forest.*

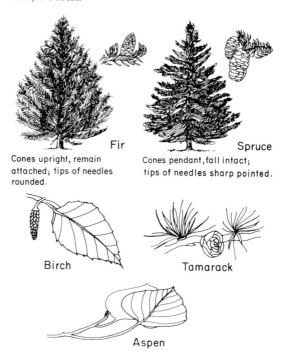

Fir
Cones upright, remain attached; tips of needles rounded.

Spruce
Cones pendant, fall intact; tips of needles sharp pointed.

Birch

Tamarack

Aspen

southeastern China. Needless to say, the description must be generalized. For setting, we begin south of the Appalachians in the Tropical Zone.

The Tropical Zone, represented by a small area at the southern tip of Florida, has mangrove swamps, mostly in the shoals between the islands (keys) and the mainland and along the southern and western borders of the Everglades. Other trees are royal palm, coconut palm, and banana. This area is the home of the alligator and tropical birds, such as the great white heron, everglade kite, and mangrove cuckoo. Coral grows in the warm coastal waters.

Along the Gulf Coast, from the panhandle of Florida to Texas, there are considerable areas of marsh grass. On the seaward side of these areas the water is brackish and the grass salt tolerant (*Spartina*); on the landward side the marshes contain fresh water and are characterized by Indian rice grass (*Zizania*). In southern Louisiana this land is drained and developed for raising rice. These marshes are the breeding ground for numerous species of waterfowl that migrate to the far north during the summer.

North of the coastal belt of grasses is the Southeastern Pine Forest (Figs. 8.3, 8.4), made up of slash, longleaf, and loblolly pines (Fig. 8.5). This is the Lower Austral (Austroriparian) Zone. Poorly drained lowlands in this zone have swamps of cypress, tupelo, and red gum. In Alabama the Southeastern Pine Forest is interrupted by a belt of tall grass that coincides with the limy soils (Rendzina, Table 6.1) on one of the Tertiary formations of the Coastal Plain (Fig. 8.20,B). Some mammals of this zone are the southern woodrat, eastern harvest mouse, cotton mouse, and marsh rabbit. Birds that nest there include the water turkey, black vulture, ivory-billed woodpecker, yellow-throated warbler, and brown-headed nuthatch. Principal crops are cotton, corn, peanuts, sweet potatoes, and beans.

At the inner edge of the Coastal Plain and southern edge of the Appalachian Highlands is Mixed Oak and Pine Forest. Principal oaks are the black, chestnut, post, blackjack, and Spanish. The most abundant pine is the shortleaf. In addition, there are pignut and mockernut hickory.

Principal crops are corn, wheat, cotton, oats, apples, and peaches.

The Upper Austral, or Carolinian, Zone extends north from the Tennessee River. The forests of the Carolinian Zone are referred to as the Central Hardwood Forest (Fig. 8.6). As far north as the Ohio River, this forest was originally populated by chestnut, chestnut oak, and yellow poplar. North of the Ohio River, in western Ohio, Indiana, and southern Michigan, the original forest consisted of oak and hickory. They have largely been cut over and the land cleared for agriculture. Principal agricultural products are livestock, fruit, and tobacco in the south, and corn, soybeans, grains, hay, and potatoes in the north. Among the common trees are:

Eastern red cedar	Ash
Butternut	Sassafras
Black walnut	Witch hazel
Pecan	Sycamore
Hickories—bitternut,	Choke cherry
shagbark, mockernut,	Black cherry
pignut	Redbud
Hop hornbean	Honey locust
River birch	Maples—sugar,
Beech	black, silver, red
Oaks—pin, scarlet,	Buckeye
black, blackjack,	Basswood
shingle, white post,	Black gum
bur, swamp white	Dogwood
Elm	Persimmon
Mulberry	

Some mammals characteristic of the Carolinian Zone are the thirteen-lined squirrel, southern bog lemming, and prairie vole. Some of the birds nesting there include the Acadian flycatcher, cardinal, hooded warbler, chat, Carolina wren, and tufted titmouse.

North of the Upper Austral Zone is the Transition Zone, marked by the Northern Hardwood Forest and originally composed chiefly of birch, beech, maple, and hemlock (Fig. 8.7). This is the northern limit of several Austral species of trees and animals and the southern limit of several species of the Canadian Zone. It is the northern

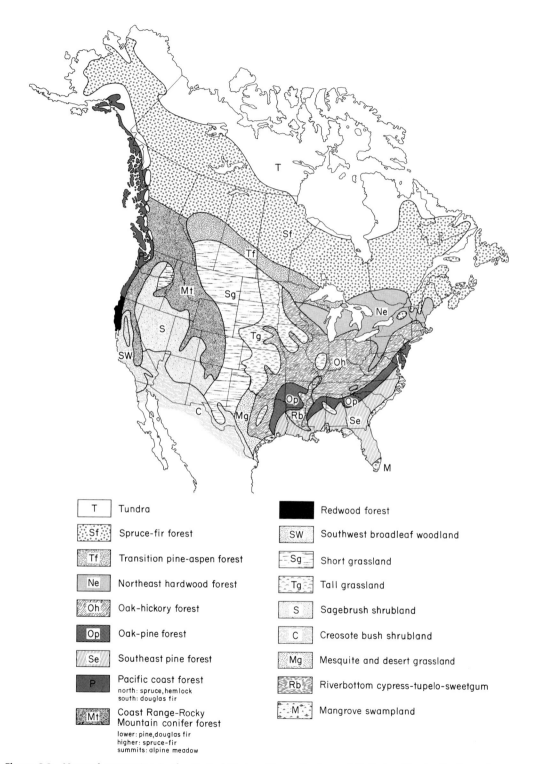

T	Tundra		■	Redwood forest
Sf	Spruce-fir forest		SW	Southwest broadleaf woodland
Tf	Transition pine-aspen forest		Sg	Short grassland
Ne	Northeast hardwood forest		Tg	Tall grassland
Oh	Oak-hickory forest		S	Sagebrush shrubland
Op	Oak-pine forest		C	Creosote bush shrubland
Se	Southeast pine forest		Mg	Mesquite and desert grassland
P	Pacific coast forest north: spruce, hemlock south: douglas fir		Rb	Riverbottom cypress-tupelo-sweetgum
Mt	Coast Range-Rocky Mountain conifer forest lower: pine, douglas fir higher: spruce-fir summits: alpine meadow		M	Mangrove swampland

Figure 8.3 *Natural vegetation in the United States. [From Geology of Soils by Charles B. Hunt. W. H. Freeman and Company. Copyright © 1972.]*

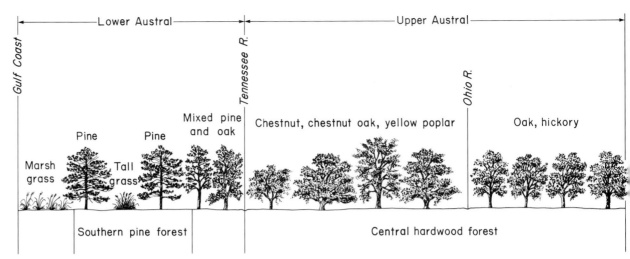

Figure 8.4 *Transect showing principal forest and other vegetation zones between the Gulf Coast and Hudson Bay.*

limit of most snakes and other cold-blooded reptiles. The woodland jumping mouse and yellow-nose vole are characteristic mammals. Among the birds nesting there are the bobwhite, mourning dove, kingbird, crested flycatcher, bobolink, cowbird, meadowlark, Baltimore oriole, chipping sparrow, towhee, catbird, house wren, and wood thrush. The land is used mostly for dairy produce.

The effect of altitude on the distribution of the life zones may be seen in the vegetation patterns in the Appalachian Highlands. On the high mountains the northern zones extend far south of their normal latitudinal range. Spruce-Fir Forest grows at sea level along the Maine coast, but it reaches altitudes of about 3,500 feet in West Virginia and Maryland and 6,000 feet on the Great Smoky Mountains. The boundary between the Carolinian and Transition zones is at sea level in northern New Jersey, about 1,200 feet in western Maryland, 2,500 feet in North Carolina, and about 3,500 feet in Georgia (Fig. 8.8).

The Western Forests

Because of the great height of the mountains in western North America, the life zones there are arranged in two patterns, one conforming to the transcontinental latitudinal zones and the other to altitudinal zones (Figs. 8.9, 8.10). Both of these distribution patterns are controlled largely by temperature, probably duration of the growing season; they differ from the eastern zones chiefly in amount of moisture received. The Rocky Mountains are semiarid, the Sierra Nevada much less so, and the Pacific Coast, north of San Francisco, is rainy and wet.

Again we start at the south. In southern California, Arizona, New Mexico, and western Texas is the Lower Sonoran Zone, characterized chiefly by the creosote bush but including stands of desert holly, mesquite, catclaw acacia, paloverde, and a variety of the picturesque yuccas and cacti (Fig. 8.11). Among the more unusual animals are two large lizards, the gila monster and the chuckwalla; the sidewinder rattlesnake; a considerable population of rodents; a native pig, the peccary; plus badgers, foxes, coyotes, vultures, ravens, and the roadrunner. In most of the Lower Sonoran Zone annual rainfall is less than 10 inches, and the evaporation rates exceed the average rainfall by factors of 10 to 100. Moist locations, where groundwater is at shallow depths, support oases of various species of water-loving plants.

The upper altitudinal limit of the Lower Sonoran Zone is between about 2,500 and 4,000 feet (Fig. 8.9). Its most northerly extent is southern-

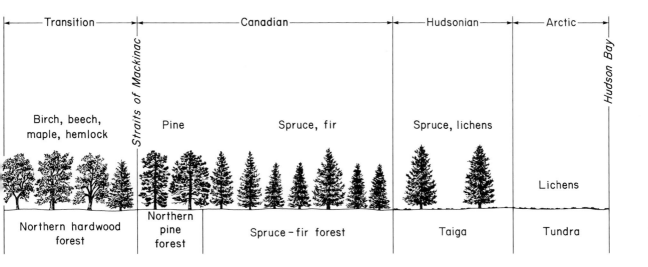

most Nevada and the southwest corner of Utah.

The next higher and cooler zone (Upper Sonoran Zone), which covers much of the western states, is the zone of sagebrush (Fig. 8.12), where annual rainfall averages slightly greater than, and evaporation rates lower than, in the Lower Sonoran Zone. Some of the distinctive stands of plants found in this zone are given in Table 8.1.

Except for the extensive pinyon-juniper woodland, the stands of scrub oak, and the less extensive stands of the Joshua tree, the Upper Sonoran Zone is dominated by shrubs. Plants 10 feet tall are rare, and taller trees are practically nonexistent except along stream courses and at springs. Most of the shrubs are 1 to 3 feet high and are separated by a few feet of bare soil supporting only scattered herbaceous plants. Moist locations, where groundwater is shallow, support oases of greasewood, saltgrass, alkali sacaton, rabbitbrush, or cottonwood.

In southern Arizona and Nevada the upper altitudinal limit of the Upper Sonoran Zone is at about 7,500 feet. In northern Utah and Nevada it is at about 6,500 feet, and still farther north it is at about 5,000 feet.

The Upper Sonoran Zone is inhabited by antelope, coyote, gray fox, the desert rattlesnake, many lizards, kangaroo rats, packrats, and other rodents. The land is used mostly for grazing.

Next upward on the mountains, and next northward is the Transition Zone (Fig. 8.13), which in much of the west is characterized by yellow pine (Pinus ponderosa), and on some dry hillsides by mountain mahogany. In the Pacific Northwest the most characteristic tree is the Douglas fir (Pseudotsuga mucronata). These trees commonly form pure stands, in contrast with the diversified deciduous forests in the eastern states. Toward the south, the upper limit of the Transition Zone is at about 9,000 feet; in the north it is at about 7,000 feet.

On most of the higher mountains in the Rockies, Sierra Nevada, and Southern Cascades, above the yellow-pine–Douglas-fir forest, is the Douglas fir and white fir forest of the Canadian Zone; this grades upward to a belt of Englemann spruce and alpine fir of the Hudsonian Zone. High summits are without trees and have only low-growing plants of the Alpine or Arctic Zone. Many mountain tops lower than 12,000 feet are treeless, but this probably is because of wind rather than temperature.

Vegetation along the Pacific Coast, from south to north, includes in southern California a very dense growth of broadleaf evergreen shrubs known as chaparral. In the vicinity of Monterey Bay and north into Oregon is redwood forest (Fig. 8.14). In Oregon and from there north to British

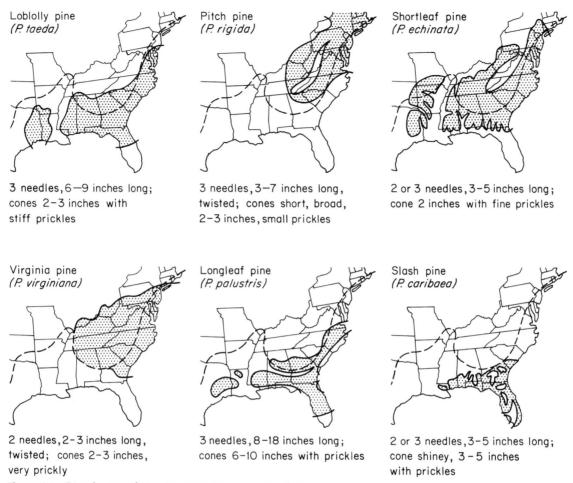

Loblolly pine
(P. taeda)

3 needles, 6—9 inches long;
cones 2-3 inches with
stiff prickles

Pitch pine
(P. rigida)

3 needles, 3-7 inches long,
twisted; cones short, broad,
2-3 inches, small prickles

Shortleaf pine
(P. echinata)

2 or 3 needles, 3-5 inches long;
cone 2 inches with fine prickles

Virginia pine
(P. virginiana)

2 needles, 2-3 inches long,
twisted; cones 2-3 inches,
very prickly

Longleaf pine
(P. palustris)

3 needles, 8-18 inches long;
cones 6-10 inches with prickles

Slash pine
(P. caribaea)

2 or 3 needles, 3-5 inches long;
cone shiney, 3-5 inches
with prickles

Figure 8.5 *Distribution of six pine trees in eastern North America.*

Columbia is coastal forest of Sitka spruce, Western red cedar, and Western Hemlock.

Alaska has four principal types of vegetation: hemlock-spruce forests along the southeastern coast, spruce-birch forests in the interior, grasslands on the Alaska Peninsula and Aleutian Islands, and tundra on the Bering and Arctic Sea slopes (Fig. 19.20).

The Transition and higher zones are summer home for deer, elk, mountain lion, bear, bighorn sheep, beaver, conies, and wildcats. Fish distribution is altitudinally zoned. Various trout and whitefish live in the cold waters of the Transition and higher zones, and channel catfish, yellow perch, sunfish, black bass, walleye, and carp in the warmer waters of the Upper Sonoran Zone. The mountain lands are used mostly for grazing, but produce lumber and other forest products, particularly in the U.S. Pacific Northwest.

In most places the boundary between the vegetation in adjoining altitudinal life zones is sharp, but the position of a boundary varies considerably from place to place depending on the exposure. On cool north slopes the high-altitude zones extend to lower levels than on warm south ones; moreover, the high-altitude vegetation may

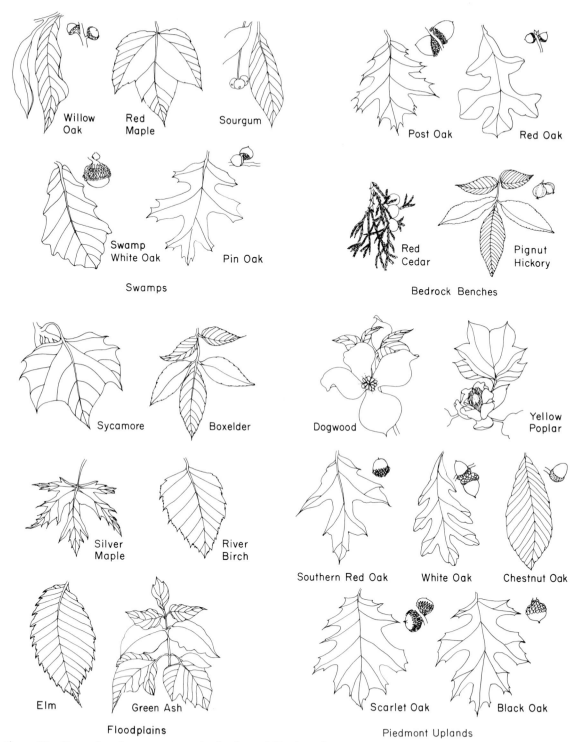

Figure 8.6 *Examples of common trees in the Central Hardwood Forest. The environments indicated as favored by the various species are exemplified by the Potomac River at the Fall Line between Washington, D.C. and Great Falls National Park.*

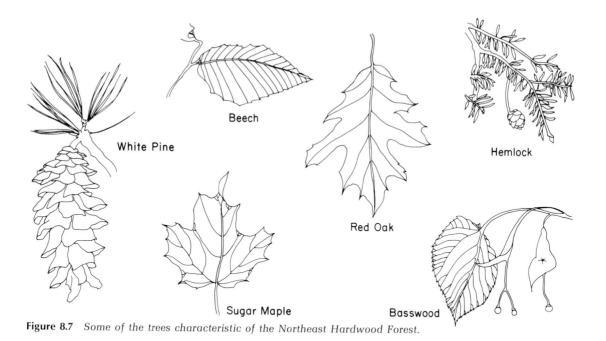

Figure 8.7 *Some of the trees characteristic of the Northeast Hardwood Forest.*

extend far down canyons that drain cold air from high parts of mountains. This causes an inverted arrangement in which the vegetation characteristic of the high altitudes grows in the valley bottoms below the vegetation generally characteristic of low altitudes but growing on the adjoining ridges.

Changes in Vegetation from East to West

Although the life zones just described seem to be controlled largely by temperature (length of growing season?), other regional differences reflect differences in moisture. A transect from the Atlantic Coast to the Pacific Coast can be divided into five parts, each with a distinct complex of vegetative types corresponding to differences in availability of moisture. For example, along the 39th parallel, which corresponds roughly with the 55° isotherm (Fig. 4.2), a transect from the Atlantic Coast first crosses the Central Hard-

wood Forest (Fig. 8.3) of the humid eastern United States. This forest extends to central Missouri. The second region, from there to the Rocky Mountains, is grassland of the subhumid and semiarid belts. The subhumid belt, east of the 100th meridian, is characterized by tall grass; the semiarid belt to the west has short grass.

A third region, described in the preceding section, takes in the Rocky Mountains and the plateaus and deserts westward to the Central Valley of California, where, at the western foot of the Sierra Nevada and eastern foot of the Coast Ranges is another semiarid belt characterized by broadleaf evergreen and broadleaf deciduous trees. The fifth region is the very wet Pacific slope of the coast ranges, location of the redwood forests. The three belts of forest—the eastern, Rocky Mountain, and Pacific Coast forests—extend northward to the northern coniferous forest of spruce, the only forest that extends from coast to coast.

Except across the Rocky Mountains, the average annual temperature along this transect is not much above or below 55°F. The differences in vegetation in the five zones are due chiefly to differences in availability of moisture.

Grasslands

Much of the Central Lowland and almost all of the Great Plains Province was grassland when first settled. East of the 100th meridian, where the annual rainfall averages more than 20 inches, the grasses are tall and deep rooted. West of the 100th meridian, in the semiarid Great Plains, the grasses are short and shallow rooted (Fig. 8.15). Bluestem, which grows to about 4 feet, and needle grass, which grows to about 3 feet, are common tall grasses; blue gramma grass, about 18 inches tall, is one of the common short grasses.

Patches of prairie extend from Kansas and Nebraska eastward across southwestern Minnesota, Iowa, and northern Missouri to Illinois and even into Indiana (Fig. 8.3). This grassland belt, the Prairie Peninsula, is bordered along both the northeast and southeast sides by oak and hickory forest; much of it is occupied by the corn belt (Fig. 9.6). The Prairie Peninsula also coincides with the Prairie and Reddish Prairie Soils (Fig. 6.5), but those soils surely are the result of the grasses rather than the reason why they grow there.

The limits of the Prairie Peninsula may be controlled by the amount and kind of precipitation. The southern limit of the prairie about coincides with the 40-inch rainfall line (Fig. 4.3), which marks the northwest edge of the area affected by warm, moist summer air from the Gulf of Mexico. The northern boundary of the prairie is near the 40-inch annual snowfall line— that is, along the southern and western sides of the area most subject to deep snow. The southern boundary is along the dry side of the area that receives considerable summer rain. The Prairie Peninsula is more subject to summer drought than is the forested land to the east. Although the extent of the grassland is probably controlled basically by climate, there are those who think that the prairies have been preserved and ex-

tended by fire, which could have been man made or ignited by dry electric storms.

The Prairie Peninsula is a postglacial feature. During the last glaciation spruce forest grew there. In Kansas, Nebraska, and South Dakota this boreal forest was succeeded by the prairie grasses; in Illinois boreal forest was succeeded by deciduous forest, which later gave way to the grasses (Fig. 8.16).

In the grasslands most trees grow in the valleys. In the area of short grass the valleys support cottonwood; in the area of tall grass, oak, hickory, ash, black walnut, elm, and box elder— representatives of the Central Hardwood Forests.

Yellow pine, a representative of the Rocky Mountain Forest, grows on high parts of the Great Plains, such as the Raton section, the divide between the Arkansas and South Platte Rivers, the Black Hills, and the high parts of the Missouri Plateau. The mountains on the Missouri Plateau in Montana are forested with lodgepole pine.

Differences in Vegetation Within Climatic Regions

LOCAL DIFFERENCES IN CLIMATE

Plant distribution within climatic regions is controlled partly by climate and partly by geology. The local variations in climate include both those of the macroclimate and microclimate; the four principal factors affecting plant growth are light, temperature, precipitation, and wind.

Some plants require bright light, which controls chlorophyll and photosynthesis; others live in shade. Forests contain both (Fig. 8.17,A). Those that require light reach to the upper canopy, whereas those that can endure shade form the understory. A tree's shape is a result of the light it receives. Many conifers, alone in the open, bear leaves and branches all the way from the ground up, but the same species in a forest may be without branches on its lower parts and bear only a small green crown.

Southwest

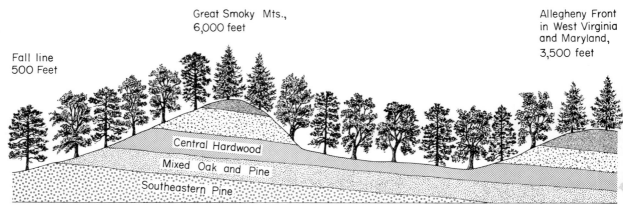

Figure 8.8 *Diagrammatic transect along the Appalachian Highlands, showing the northward slope of the five forest regions.*

North

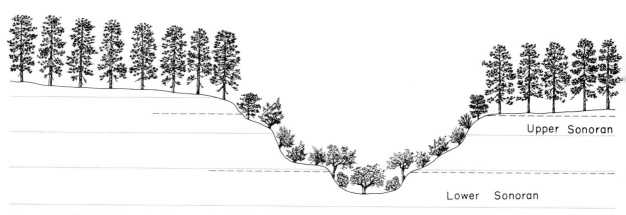

Figure 8.9 *Altitudinal zoning of vegetation in Grand Canyon and on nearby San Francisco Mountain. In the bottom of Grand Canyon is the Lower Sonoran Zone, with creosote bush, catclaw acacia, and mesquite. The Upper Sonoran Zone of sagebrush (S), pinyon and juniper (PJ) and cliffrose extends to the south rim of*

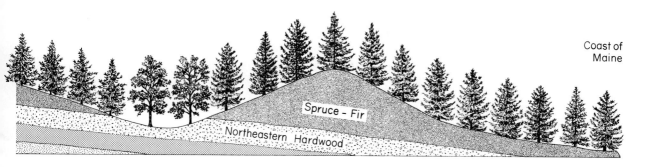

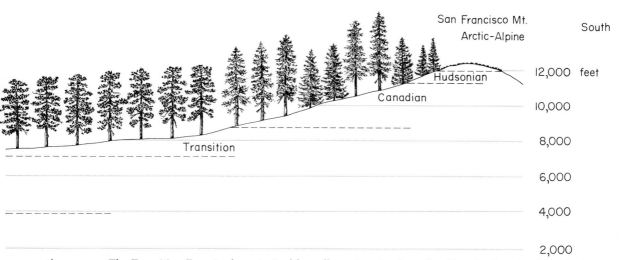

the canyon. The Transition Zone is characterized by yellow pine, the Canadian Zone by Douglas fir and white fir, the Hudsonian Zone by Englemann spruce and alpine fir. The Arctic-Alpine Zone has only low herbs.

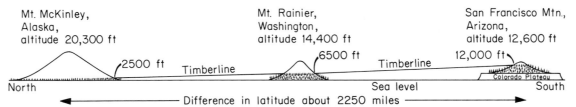

Figure 8.10   *The altitudes reached by the various life zones decrease northward. A thousand feet of altitude is roughly equivalent to 250 miles of latitude.*

Figure 8.11   *Some picturesque plants characteristic of the southern Basin and Range Province, especially the Arizona sections. The Joshua Tree and ocotillo are not cacti, although commonly included with them.*

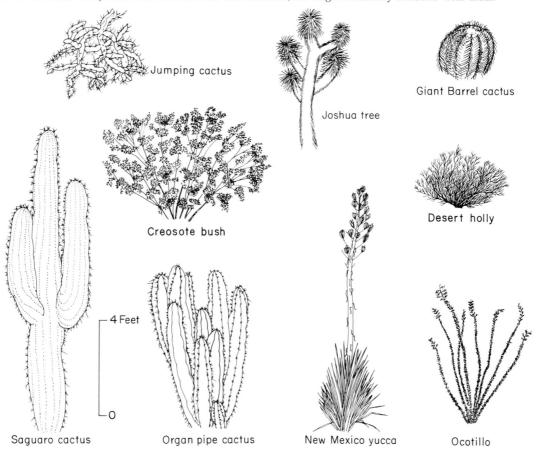

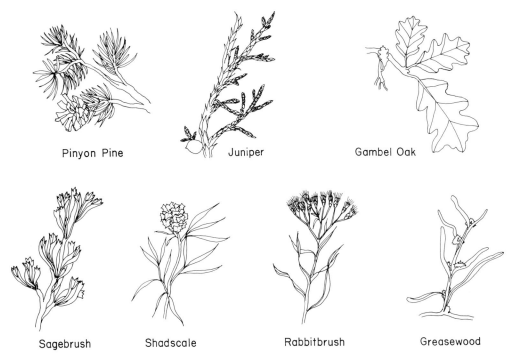

Figure 8.12 *The upper part of the Upper Sonoran Zone is marked in the south by a woodland of piñon pine and juniper and in the north by oak brush. Most of the Upper Sonoran Zone is shrubland, characterized by sagebrush and shadscale with rabbitbrush and greasewood along washes and alluvial plains.*

Table 8.1

Vegetation in the Upper Sonoran Zone Reflects Differences in the Kind of Ground

Altitudinal Position in the Zone	Kind of Ground	Type of Vegetation
Uppermost altitudes	All kinds, but commonly stony	Pinyon and juniper woodland; in north may be replaced by scrub oak.
Next lower altitudes	Stony desert	Sagebrush and grama grass.
Intermediate altitudes	Stony desert	Shadscale and curly grass.
Intermediate altitudes	Sand desert	Sand sagebrush.
Intermediate altitudes	Shale desert	Mat saltbush.
Low altitudes	Loamy desert	Blackbrush; in south replaced by live oak and grass.
Low altitudes	Gravel fans	Joshua tree, in south only.

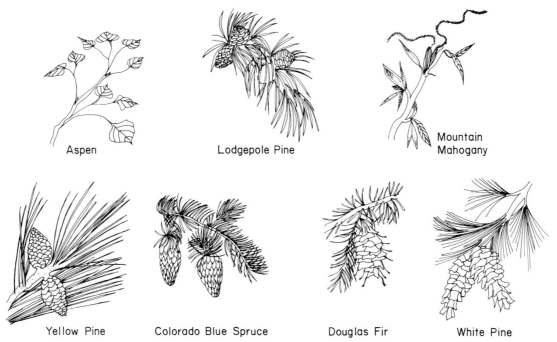

Figure 8.13 *Trees characteristic of the Transition Zone in the Rocky Mountains and eastern slope of the Sierra-Cascades.*

Temperature controls the length of the growing season, and, during growth, the rate of physiological processes. Moreover, for each species there is an upper and a lower critical temperature. Temperature also is a major factor in controlling the differences between north and south slopes (Fig. 8.17,B).

Moisture availability is controlled by many factors, but chiefly by precipitation. Precipitation is important not only in terms of its annual total, but also in terms of its distribution by seasons. For example, the Pacific Coast has dry summers, the Middle West wet summers. Mountain ranges have wet slopes on the windward side, dry slopes to the leeward (Fig. 8.18), and forests on the two sides are different. On the wet western slopes of the Cascades, for example, are found such trees as western red cedar, Pacific yew, western hemlock, red alder, maples, and oaks, wheras the dry eastern slopes have yellow pine, juniper, quaking aspen. On the Sierra Nevada, the sequoia forests are limited to the wet western slope (Fig. 8.18).

On the Coast Ranges the redwood forests are limited for the most part to the wet western slopes.

Wind affects both the distribution and shape of plants. The absence of trees at some exposed situations is due to wind, partly because of physical damage to anything standing upright, partly because of excessive transpiration, and partly because of decrease in soil temperature due to removal of the protective cover of snow. These effects are evident at wind-controlled timberlines: the trees are prostrate, both trunk and boughs are bent with the wind, and the shoots short and mostly on the lee side, resulting in a flag-like unilateral branching (Fig. 8.19).

GROUND INFLUENCES

Although the distribution of the life zones is controlled by the climate, local differences within a zone are controlled chiefly by differences in ground conditions, especially moisture avail-

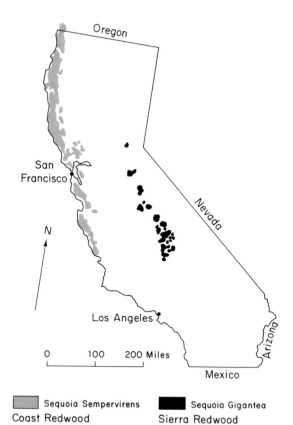

Sequoia Sempervirens
Coast Redwood

Sequoia Gigantea
Sierra Redwood

Figure 8.14 *Ranges of the two California redwoods.* [*After U.S. Forest Service.*]

abity. This is the geologic factor in plant distribution, referred to by ecologists as the *edaphic* factor, and includes effects of the surficial soils and of their substrate.

Soil properties most important for plant growth are: composition and structure of the mineral fraction, the soil atmosphere and soil moisture, content of organic matter, depth, and temperature.

The mineral fraction of a soil may be hard rock, a favorite environment for some lichens. Most soils suitable for the roots of flowering plants consist of various mixtures of gravel, sand, silt, and clay size particles, and the mineral and chemical composition of these determines the availability of elements necessary for plant growth. In general, availability depends on solu-

bility; the more soluble the element and the minerals in which it occurs, the more available it is for absorption by plants. The proportions of the different particle sizes in soils controls pore space, which, controls the availability of soil moisture and soil air. Sandy soils, for example, dry more rapidly than clay soils. Clay soils are more difficult to penetrate but provide more mineral nutrients than do soils that are largely quartz sand.

The principal elements required by plants are oxygen, hydrogen, carbon, nitrogen, phosphorus, sulfur, iron, potassium, calcium, and magnesium. Excesses or deficiences of any of these elements, or of some other minor elements, lead to specialized vegetation adapted to that soil. Some examples are the specialized plant stands on the serpentine (magnesium rich) soils in the California Coast Ranges and the Maryland Piedmont (Fig. 8.20,A). Other examples are the belts of grassland on the lime-rich black belts of Alabama, Mississippi, and Texas (Fig. 8.20,B), and the low, mat saltbush on shale deserts (p. 451) of the Upper Sonoran Zone, which contrast with the upright shrubs on adjoining sandy ground (Fig. 8.20,C).

The soil atmosphere contains more carbon dioxide and less oxygen than the atmosphere above ground, and in a clayey soil, where circulation is slowed, the oxygen necessary for healthy roots may become depleted. Waterlogged soils are anaerobic.

Water available for plant growth occurs in the ground either as vadose or gravitational water (Fig. 5.8) or as groundwater below the water table (Fig. 8.21). *Xerophytes*—plants that live on gravitational water—are capable of surviving periods of protracted drought. *Phreatophytes*—plants that send their roots to the water table—have a permanent water supply, even in deserts.

The drought-resistant and the water-loving kinds of plant stands can be distinguished everywhere. In the southeastern states, cypress, tupelo, and red gum live in the wet bottoms; longleaf, loblolly, and slash pine on the uplands. In the north, spruce, the dominant tree, grows with balsam, tamarack, cedar, and soft maples in swampy areas, and with hard maples, beech, and

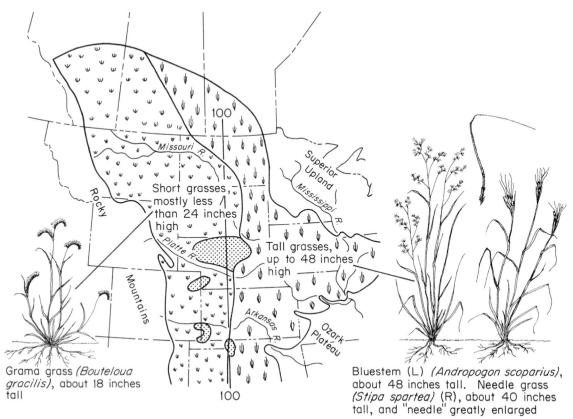

Grama grass *(Bouteloua gracilis)*, about 18 inches tall

Bluestem (L) *(Andropogon scoparius)*, about 48 inches tall. Needle grass *(Stipa spartea)* (R), about 40 inches tall, and "needle" greatly enlarged

Figure 8.15 *The 100th meridian is the approximate boundary between the deep-rooted, tall grasses with large leaves and the shallow-rooted, short grasses with small leaves. Bluestem and needle grass, the characteristic grasses east of the boundary, and grama grass, the characteristic grass west of the boundary, are not confined to the areas indicated here. The stippling indicates sand, covered mostly with tall grasses and shrubs.*

birch on the drier surrounding ground. In the more arid west, shallow groundwater and springs are marked by stands of such trees as cottonwood and willow and a considerable number of shrubs and grasses that are not drought resistant.

The kind and amount of dissolved matter in groundwater also affects plant distribution everywhere. It is especially obvious along coasts and along the edges of desert basins where the water is brackish or saline. Figure 8.22 gives an example from the coast of Florida and another from the salt pan in Death Valley, California.

The organic content of soils includes both the dead organic matter and the organisms living in and on the soil. The vegetative cover and the litter at the surface affect soil temperature, its moisture content and chemistry, compactness, amount of light received, and air movement. Decaying organic matter controls the distribution and abundance of the living microorganisms. But the organic content of soils is largely controlled by the larger flowering plants living on it, and differs greatly under deciduous forest, conifer forest, grassland, and desert shrubland. Plants control the kind of litter that provides the habitat for the microorganisms, which in turn may be deleterious or beneficial for the growth and spread of a particular flowering plant. Pathogens of forest trees—viruses, fungi, or bacteria—may kill by root rot, heart rot, cankers, wilting, leaf

rust, or needle blight. Parasitic insects are familiar to every gardner; some serious pests in the
forests are beetles, budworms, weevils, moths,
sawflies, aphids, and the all-too-familiar tent cat-
erpillar. These insects cause damage by defoliation, boring, or sucking. The virtual elimination
of the chestnut in the United States is perhaps

the best known example of how microorganisms
(and insects) affect plant distribution.

Soil depth, as a factor in plant distribution,
may be controlled by depth to a water table or
depth to bedrock. Vegetation growing along a
stream or pond differs from that growing some
distance away where the depth to the water table

Figure 8.16 *Prairie Peninsula in the Central Lowland. The diagrammatic transect and cross section across the
northern boundary show how the geographical zoning of vegetation becomes duplicated in vertical sections of
the deposit. At A the retreating glacier deposited till, on which grew tundra (t), which became replaced by
spruce forest (s) as the ice retreated farther north. The spruce forest was succeeded by hardwood forest (o),
which in turn was succeeded by grassland.*

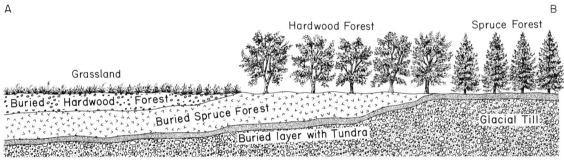

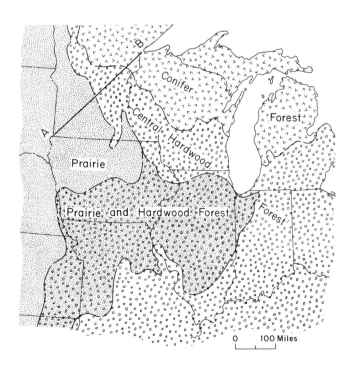

A

B

Figure 8.17 *Light affects plant distribution and plant growth. (A) In a forest (right) shade-tolerant trees form the understory; beneath this understory grow various species of herbs, which are even more shade tolerant. Trees that demand light reach to the upper canopy, and may have live branches only at the crown, whereas in open sites (left) trees of the same species may bear live branches the entire height of the tree. (B) Wooded north slopes contrast with grassy south slopes in a semiarid environment. The vegetation on north-facing slopes commonly differs from that on south facing slopes, especially in semiarid and arid environments where small differences in temperature cause major differences in moisture retention.*

is greater. Examples of the influence of depth to bedrock on plant distribution can be seen in mountainous areas where bare rock surfaces that support only lichens are surrounded by distinctive flowering plants growing where thin soil overlaps the rock, and is, in turn, surrounded by forest where the soil deepens.

Plant distribution also is affected by fire. Fire may burn only the leaf litter, seedlings, and small trees; as a *ground fire,* it may extend into the ground and burn roots; as a *crown fire,* it may burn the tree tops. Climate is important in connection with fire. In the eastern United States, as already noted, electric storms are usually accompanied by rain, and fires caused by lightning are uncommon. In the western United States, lightning is a major cause of forest fires because it is frequently accompanied by only light rain or none at all. In the western United States the fire hazard is greatest during the dry summer months; in the central and eastern United States the hazard is greatest in spring and fall—before the deciduous trees have leafed and after the leaves have fallen.

FORM OF PLANT GROWTH AS CONTROLLED BY CLIMATE AND SOILS

Vegetation differs in many ways between one life zone and another and between one environment and another within a particular life zone. For example, in a given life zone the plants may be mostly trees, shrubs, grasses, mosses, or lichens. Differences between the dominant growth forms of different life zones are perhaps most striking at timberline. Western mountains have upper and lower timberlines: the upper is where the Canadian and Hudsonian zones give way to the Arctic-Alpine Zone, and the lower, the arid timberline, is near the foot of the mountains, where the pinyon-juniper woodland of the Upper Sonoran Zone ends downward against sagebrush or other shrubland.

Also, many conspicuously different ecological types are distinguishable. Aquatic plants, *hydrophytes,* vary according to the dissolved oxygen, exposure to light, water temperature, quality of

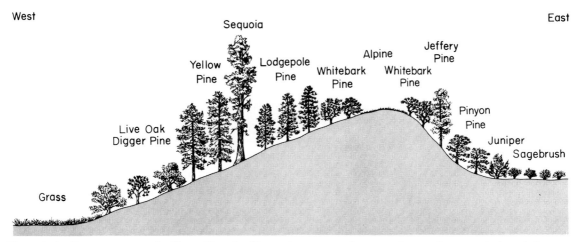

Figure 8.18 *Transect across the Sierra Nevada, illustrating contrast in vegetation on the wet windward slope (west) and the dry leeward slope. Low on the west side is grass with a belt of live oak and digger pine in the foothills. Low on the dry east side is sagebrush with a belt of pinyon and juniper woodland in the foothills. Higher on the west side are belts of yellow pine, sequoia, and lodgepole pine; on the east slope is Jeffrey pine. At high altitudes on both sides is whitebark pine and alpine forms.*

the water, its depth and movement, and the nature of the banks and bottom. Marsh plants, *helophytes,* differ from aquatic plants in having their foliage out of the water; only the roots are submerged. The important environmental factors are about the same as for aquatic plants. Some plants are adapted to moist, highly acid ground, as in peat bogs; others, to cold, moist ground as in tundra. Still other plants are adapted to moist saline ground (*halophytes*), like some along the coasts and parts of the deserts (Fig. 8.22).

Plants adapted to dry ground may grow on bare rock (lichens), on sand and gravel (dune

Figure 8.19 *At a wind-controlled timberline, found on many mountain summits, trees are prostrate and gnarled. The upper branches turn with the wind, forming so-called "flag trees." The wind-blasted summit supports only small herbs.*

grasses), or on impervious, shaly ground (mat saltbush of the Upper Sonoran Zone on the Colorado Plateau) (Fig. 8.20,C). With an increase in moisture during the growing season, shrubs are replaced by grasses, as on the Great Plains. Most forests, whether hardwood or conifer, grow where ground conditions are intermediate.

Other Kinds of Ecological Zoning

Other kinds of ecological zoning, or *biofacies,* may be observed wherever the environment changes notably in short distances. Figure 8.23 illustrates zoning of beach and offshore environments. Figure 8.24 contrasts zoning on a steep, rocky, New England beach with that on a coral sand beach in Florida. Marsh ground in the intertidal zone with prolific vegetation is referred to as wetland.

In estuaries the shore and aquatic life are zoned in accord with changes in salinity from the upper to the lower end of the estuary, as in Delaware Bay (Fig. 8.25). Similar zoning is found in the less-polluted (but threatened!) Chesapeake Bay and the smaller bays along the New England

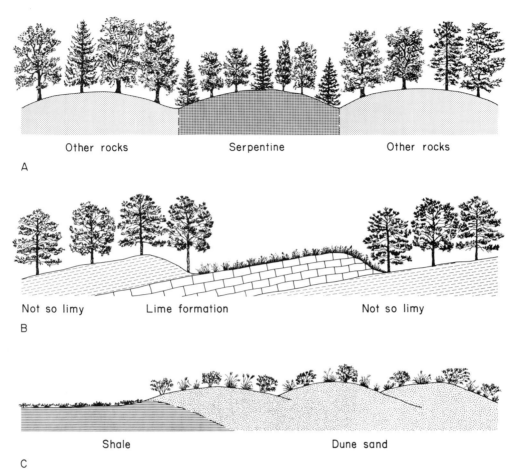

Figure 8.20 *Three examples of vegetation differences that reflect differences in soil composition and texture. On the Maryland Piedmont (A) the vegetation on serpentine formations is dwarfed. Limy formations in Alabama (B) support grasses in the midst of Southern Pine Forest growing on the less limy formations. On the Colorado Plateau (C) shale formations support low, mat saltbush, whereas adjoining sand dunes support grasses and upright shrubs.*

coast. Evaporation of water from estuaries that are nearly blocked by baymouth bars may be great enough to cause salinities to exceed that of sea water (more than 33 parts per thousand). An example is Laguna Madre, back of Padre Island on the southern coast of Texas.

Examples of variation in stream habitats are illustrated in Figure 8.26. The habitats differ depending on whether the current is swift or slow, shallow or deep, interrupted by falls or rapids,

muddy or clear, or salty. Channels and banks may be muddy, sandy, or gravelly; they may also be straight or meandering. Parts of the stream and shore may be shaded and others sunny. Temperatures vary; water issuing from a snowbank at the source is cold, but downstream it warms. Some streams maintain a fairly steady flow, and others fluctuate greatly from season to season. Each habitat is likely to be marked by a unique flora and fauna.

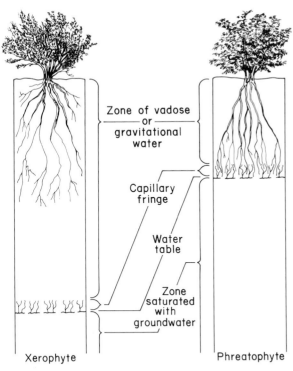

is wet, spongey, peaty ground with leatherleaf and sphagnum moss grading to cranberry and rhododendron. Edges of ponds filled with peat may have a belt of black spruce and larch with broadleaf forest of beech and maple on the surrounding, drier glacial drift. In Canada, this broadleaf forest is replaced by spruce and fir.

Such zoning is accompanied by a zoning of the fauna as well. The larger animals, moose and bear, live mostly on the dry ground. Bog lemming and frogs live on the swampy, peaty hummocks. Dragonflies and ducks prefer the open water.

South of the glacial border, on the deeply weathered saprolite of the Piedmont Province, differences in the stands of trees reflect differences in the thickness and other geological relations of the clayey saprolite. Figure 8.28 illustrates some differences in the species that grow on different kinds of ground there.

Changes in Life Zones

EFFECTS OF CLIMATIC CHANGES

During the Pleistocene Epoch, which ended only about 12,000 years ago, the climate was very different from that of today (pp. 90–93). It was during this epoch of glaciations that ice covered all of Canada and extended southward into the northern United States, and lakes formed in what are now the dry basins of the arid west. During these wet, cold stages the life zones were shifted to more southerly latitudes and, on the mountains, to lower altitudes. Figure 8.29 illustrates an interpretation of how the life zones shifted during the last glaciation.

Overgrown bogs, already described, have a third dimension of ecological zoning. The bottom levels of the peat may record the presence of a spruce-fir forest, and the next overlying layer record a forest of pine. Above the pine forest layer are others that record the transition from broadleaf forest to the present-day bog. This vertical zoning reflects the northward advance of the forest as the glaciers receded and the climate warmed.

Figure 8.21 *Water in the ground is available to plant roots in two ways. The top of the zone saturated with groundwater is referred to as the water table. A capillary fringe rises upward from it. Plants that send their roots down to this zone have a permanent water supply and are known as phreatophytes. The zone above the capillary fringe is wet only when water seeps downward through it, following rains or floods. Plants that root in this zone must be capable of surviving droughts, and are known as xerophytes.*

Ecological zoning because of differences in kind of ground can be seen in the eastern hardwood forests too, but there the zoning is obscured by the tremendous number of plant species. It is truly difficult to see the forest for the trees. In the glaciated northeastern states, differences in the glacial deposits are marked by differences in the kinds of trees (Fig. 8.27). The pond-shore vegetation around the numerous lakes in the glaciated country is zoned with respect to depth of water and wetness of the shore. Vegetation gradually changes from water lilies in the shallow water to loosestrife near the shore. Back of this

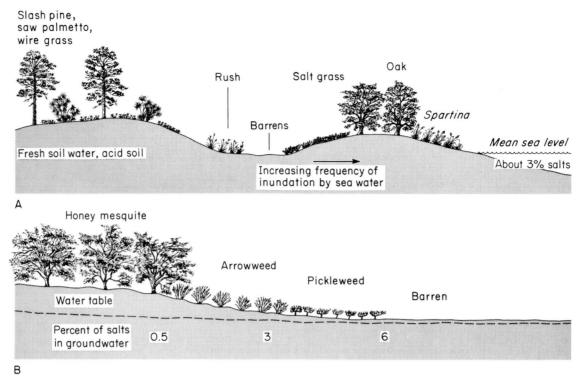

Figure 8.22 *Two examples of plant distribution controlled by salts dissolved in groundwaters. (A) Coast of Florida (generalized after Florida Geological Survey). (B) Edge of salt pan in Death Valley, California.*

Continued climatic change is indicated by the present-day northward migration of warm-latitude species. Spruce forest is advancing into the areas of tundra. The upper part of Mount Washington has been isolated and preserves a relic fauna of arctic species of insects and mice surrounded by warm-latitude species. Marine life is migrating north, too, and mid-Atlantic species (for example, the green crab) have advanced north of Cape Cod. Along the Pacific Coast certain mollusks live 8 to 10 degrees of latitude north of their range in early Pleistocene time. In part of late Pleistocene time their range averaged a degree of latitude north of their present range, perhaps in response to an interglaciation, whereas in latest Pleistocene time their range averaged two degrees south of their present range, perhaps in response to a glaciation. But the Pacific coast evidence is ambiguous because

of the active earth movements there; the differences could reflect crustal movement rather than climatic change.

CHANGES WROUGHT BY MAN

Because Europeans settling this country cleared the land and removed forests, it has been widely assumed that settlement and land use have devastated our soil and vegetation. In much of the country, though, this assumption appears unwarranted. Historical accounts of the original state of the forests in the northeastern United States indicate that present forests are not very different, only less extensive. The forest always has been subject to disturbance—fires by lightning in the west, hurricane winds in the east (like the storm of 1962 in New England).

Figure 8.23 (A) Littoral environments. Principal controlling factors are: frequency and depth of submergence, salinity of the water, exposure to surf, and rockiness, sandiness, or muddiness of the beach. (B) Marine environments vary chiefly according to depth of water and depth of light penetration.

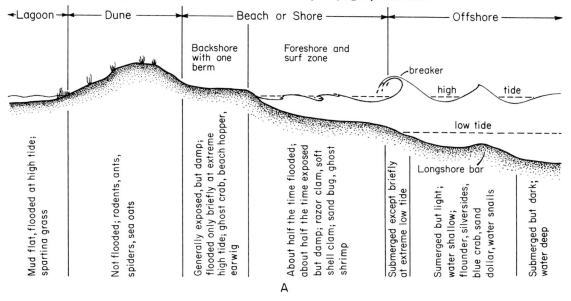

A

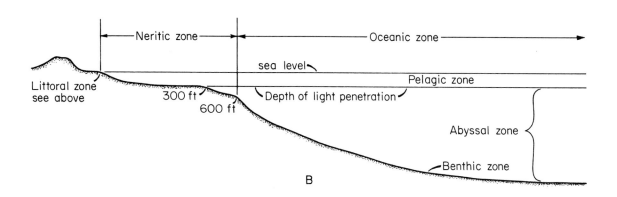

B

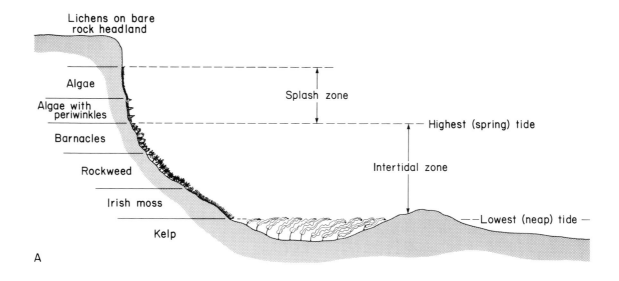

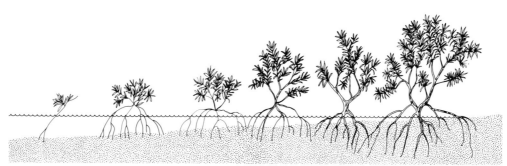

Figure 8.24 (A) Life zones along steep, rocky shores reflect differences in depth of water, frequency of wetting, and salinity. Examples given here are those described by Rachel Carson for a rocky headland on the New England coast. (B) Mangrove along the southern Florida coast builds the land seaward by trapping coral sand around their roots. Farthest seaward are young individuals capable of attaching themselves in isolated pockets of sediment, and progressively older ones grow landward, where the sand has accumulated. Where the sand is very thick or made into land, a second species of mangrove may grow.

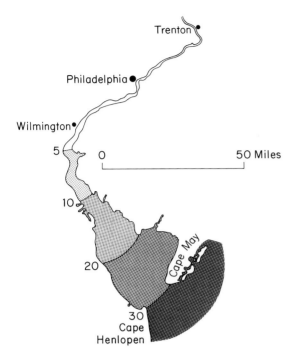

Figure 8.25 *Map of Delaware Bay, showing changes in salinity (in parts per thousand) from about 0 at Philadelphia to the Atlantic Ocean (32 parts per thousand). Marine forms, like the sea star, do not enter the bay. The razor clam extends into that part of the bay where the salinity is greater than about 20 parts per thousand. The oyster drill extends into where the salinity is about 5 parts per thousand, and the oyster extends almost to above Wilmington. An estuarine copepod shrimp lives in all parts of the bay but does not go to sea and does not go into the fresh waters.*

Figure 8.26 *Stream habitats. The sketch illustrates more than two dozen kinds of stream habitats, each having distinctive biotic characteristics. The major controlling factors are: kind of stream flow (swiftness, depth, continuity, and quality of the water); kind of channel and banks (rocky or muddy, straight or meandering, low or high); climate (especially temperature, nature of recharge, and seasonal effects); and the adjoining biota at each particular locality.*

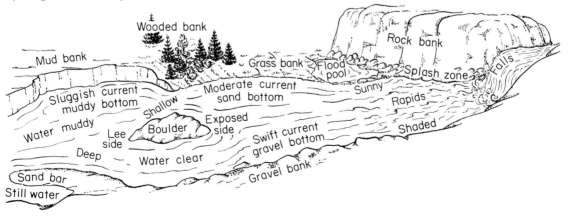

Losses as a result of forest fire make frightening statistics but they need to be viewed in the perspective of other losses. The annual loss due to fire is about half the loss caused by insects and plant disease and about 3 to 4 percent of the annual cut. Moreover, the distribution of loss by fire is regionally very uneven. By far the greatest loss is in the Southeastern Pine Forest, where as much as 1 percent of lands protected by forest agencies burn annually (Fig. 8.30), and a third of that loss is attributed to fires purposely set as part of a long-established practice (whether good or bad) to help establish new crops of pine, to improve grazing, and to reduce the fire hazard. The high rate of burn in California probably reflects the dry summer season. In most of the country 0.1 percent or less of the protected areas are burned annually. With increased use of the forests, however, man's carelessness with fire is increasingly a problem.

Man also has caused changes by introducing new species or by contributing to the spread of others. Tamarisk, or salt cedar, introduced to the Southwest from the Mediterranean, has spread along all the rivers and irrigation ditches of that region (p. 515), adding much to the cost of the irrigation projects. Mesquite has spread along the cattle trails in Texas. Such insects as the Japanese beetle have been introduced. The horse became extinct in North America at the end of the Pleistocene, and was reintroduced by the Spanish in post-Columbian time.

Figure 8.27 *Relationship between vegetation and kind of ground in a glaciated Connecticut valley. Well-drained uplands have mixed hardwoods; excessively drained gravel and sand have oak and pine. Poorly drained ground, on clay, has meadow; upland bogs have black spruce and cedar; bogs in the alluvial valley have red maple and cedar. Rocky promontories have scarlet, chestnut, and black oak. [After Lunt, 1948. From Geology of Soils by Charles B. Hunt. W. H. Freeman and Company. Copyright © 1972.]*

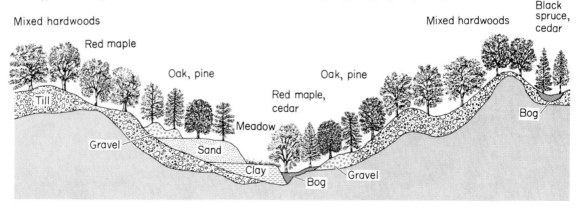

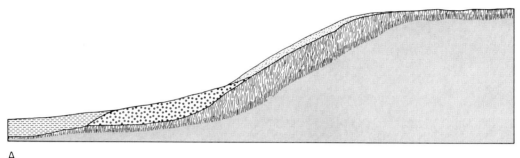

Alluvial floodplain		Gravelly valley side		Colluvium over deep saprolite		Shallow saprolite over gneissic bedrock	
Species	%	Species	%	Species	%	Species	%
Sycamore	30	Red maple	23	Sweet gum	32	Beech	26
Sweet gum	30	Black oak	20	Tulip tree	29	Black oak	16
Red maple	30	Hornbeam	18	Red maple	6	Red maple	13
Others	10	Sweet gum	14	Hickory	6	White oak	13
		Hickory	11	Black oak	6	Hickory	13
		Others	14	Others	21	Dogwood	10
						Others	9

A

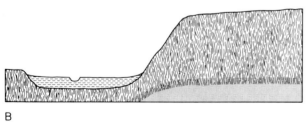
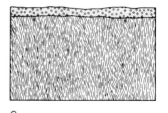

Thin alluvium		Deep saprolite		Thin gravel over deep saprolite	
Species	%	Species	%	Species	%
Hornbeam	32	Hickory	27	Tulip tree	50
Red maple	25	Dogwood	25	Black locust	22
Beech	21	Hornbeam	16	Sweet gum	11
Others	22	Black oak	14	Others	17
		Others	18		

B   C

Figure 8.28 *Differences in percentages of various species, evidently reflecting differences in ground conditions in parts of the Piedmont Province along Kennedy Expressway in Maryland. Geology and plant distribution as revealed during construction in 1962.*

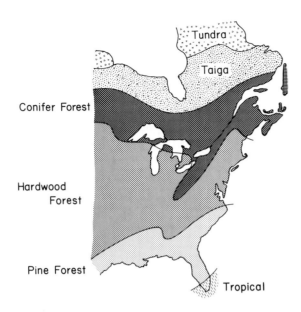

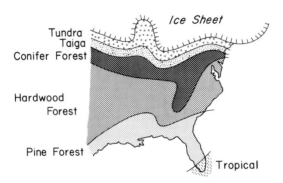

Figure 8.29 *Vegetation zones in eastern North America at the present time (above) and their possible distribution during the Wisconsinan glaciation (below). The shift in position of the zones is continuing. According to many ecologists, beech and sugar maple are moving northward into pine and spruce areas; in Alaska spruce is moving into tundra; trees are migrating westward in Nebraska; and yellow pine of the Rocky Mountains may be spreading eastward on the Great Plains.*

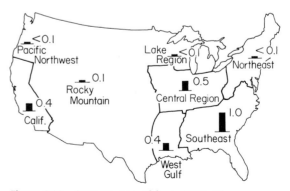

Figure 8.30 *Average annual burn (1941–45) on national forests by regions, in percent of area protected. [After U.S.D.A.]*

References

Cameron, R. E., and G. B. Blank, 1966, Desert algae—Soil crusts and diaphanous substrata as algal habits: National Aeronautics and Space Administration, Technical Report No. 32–971.

Canada Dept. of Forestry, 1963, Native trees of Canada: Ottawa, Queens Printer.

Gleason, H. A., and Cronquist, A., 1964, The natural geography of plants: New York, Columbia Univ. Press.

Hedgpeth, J. W. (ed.), 1957, Treatise on marine ecology and paleoecology: Geol. Soc. America Memoir 67.

Higbee, E., 1958; American agriculture: New York, Wiley.

Hill, A. F., 1952, Economic botany: New York, McGraw-Hill.

Hunt, C. B., 1966, Plant ecology of Death Valley, California: U.S. Geol. Survey Prof. Paper 509.

Janick, J., Schery, R. W., Woods, F. W., and Ruttan, V. W., 1969, Plant science—An introduction to world crops: San Francisco, W. H. Freeman and Company.

Kuchler, A. W., 1964, Potential natural vegetation of the conterminous United States: Am. Geog. Soc. Spec. Publ. 36.

Kurz, H., and Wagner, K., 1957, Tidal marshes of the Gulf and Atlantic Coasts of northern Florida and Chaleston, South Carolina: Florida State Univ. Studies 24.

Meinzer, O. E., 1927, Plants as indicators of ground water. U.S. Geol. Survey Water-Supply Paper 577.

Merriam, C. H., 1898, Life zones and crop zones of the United States: Bull. Div. Biol. Survey, U.S. Dept. of Agriculture, n. 10.

Oosting, H. J., 1956, The study of plant communities—An introduction to plant ecology: 2nd ed., San Francisco, W. H. Freeman and Company.

Our living world of nature, 1966–1967, New York, McGraw-Hill. Ten volumes published with the cooperation of the U.S. Department of the Interior, dealing with the life of the forest, seashore, desert, cave, marsh, ocean, prairies and plains, rivers and streams, the pond, and the mountains; various authors.

Robinson, T. W., 1958. Phreatophytes. U.S.G.S. Water-Supply Paper No. 1423., U.S. Government Printing Office, Washington, D.C.

Sargent, C. S., 1933, Manual of the trees of North America: Houghton Mifflin Company; reprinted by Dover Publications, Inc.

Shantz, H. L., and R. L. Peimeisel. 1940. Types of vegetation in Esialante Valley, Utah, as indicators of soil conditions: USDA Tech. Bull. No. 713, Washington, D.C., U.S. Government Printing Office.

Warming, Eug., 1909, Oecology of plants: Oxford, Clarendon Press.

Weaver, J. E., and Clements, F. E., 1938, Plant ecology: 2nd ed., New York, McGraw-Hill.

Welch, P. S., 1952, Limnology: 2nd ed., New York, McGraw-Hill.

Wilsie, C. P., 1962, Crop adaptation and distribution: San Francisco, W. H. Freeman and Company.

Urbanization at Stone Mountain, near Atlanta, Georgia, an example of the dilemma caused by conflicting interests—parks versus real estate developments and interstate highways? [Courtesy of Stone Mountain Memorial Association.]

9

·······

RESOURCES—CONFLICT OF INTERESTS

At the time of Columbus, the $7\frac{1}{2}$ million square miles of what is now Canada and the United States was occupied by perhaps a million Indians grouped in tribes representing a half dozen linguistic families. Probably a third of the Indians lived along the coasts in the temperate and southern latitudes; most of the rest lived along the interior waterways. But despite an average population density of only 1 person for every $7\frac{1}{2}$ square miles, clean air, plenty of water in streams that were not polluted, no problems of mineral shortages, no need for tariffs, and evident plenty for everyone, the tribes warred with one another, and life for the Indian was still that of the stone age. Clearly, favorable environment does not by itself create good living.

Five-hundred years later, the half of North America represented by the United States had become the world's wealthiest nation. Its population increased to about 10 per square mile. There was a good deal of pollution and there were some shortages, but the old warpaths were now paved. Still the nation found little peace, and lived in fear for its existence. Once again the plentiful resources and favorable environment have not been used for mankind's welfare. The purpose of this chapter is not to assess blame for our failures, but to take a brief inventory of our resources—as a reminder that America really could be beautiful, instead of being the most hated nation on earth.

The Land Resource

UNITED STATES

The spread of settlement and exploration from the Atlantic Coast, the Middle West, and the Southwest followed the natural routes, but the lands as claimed or acquired by the several countries had arbitrary and vague boundaries, perhaps because the acquisitions were made before the lands were well known. To a considerable degree, acquisition came first, and settlement later. The United States now totaling more than 3,700,000 square miles of land and water, was acquired chiefly in ten real estate deals (see also Fig. 9.1):

1. 1782–83, original territory of the United States as recognized by treaties with England (869,735 sq. miles).

Figure 9.1   *Major United States land acquisitions.*

2. 1803, Louisiana Purchase, exclusive of the part that extended north of the 49th parallel (909,130 sq. miles).

3. 1818, Red River Basin and Lake of the Woods drainage, south of the 49th parallel, secured by treaty with England (48,080 sq. miles).

4. 1819, East and West Florida acquired from Spain by trading to Spain about 100,000 sq. miles of land west of the Mississippi River. Value at that time appraised at about the cost of a modern Miami hotel.

5. 1845, Texas annexed (388,687 sq. miles).

6. 1846, Oregon Territory; title established by treaty with England (286,541 sq. miles).

7. 1848, Mexican cession, Treaty of Guadalupe Hidalgo (529,189 sq. miles).

8. 1853, Gadsden Purchase (29,670 sq. miles).

9. 1867, Alaska Purchase (586,400 sq. miles).

10. 1898, Hawaii, Puerto Rico, and Guam (10,144 sq. miles).

Some of the colonies had charters that granted land from ocean to ocean, for the kings had been gracious givers. In the United States, these lands, which were ceded to the federal government when the colonies became states, included the Northwest Territory—the present states of Ohio, Indiana, Illinois, Michigan, Wisconsin, and part of Minnesota. Revenue from sale of the lands was used to pay the public debt, and as the lands became settled new states were created.

By 1750 the population of the colonies numbered about 2,000,000. When George Washington became first president of the United States, the population had doubled to about 4,000,000, but only a half dozen towns had populations greater than 10,000. As United States real estate grew, so did its population. In another 25 years, about 1815, the population had doubled again to 8,000,000, and it doubled again during each quarter of the last century—to 16,000,000 in 1840, to 32,000,000 by the time of the Civil War, and to 64,000,000 in 1890. By 1925 it had doubled again to about 125,000,000, and by that time urban population exceeded the rural. In 1950, 150,000,000 persons were sharing 3,700,000 square miles, and this population reached 200,000,000 by 1970, with 90 percent concentrated in urban areas (Fig. 9.2). As late as 1860 the center of the population still was east of the Plains; today it is at the 100th meridian and continues moving west.

For comparison, the population of Canada has always been about one-tenth that of the United States. Mexico is more crowded than the United States, having a quarter as many people in a fifth of the area. The population of China in 1961 was estimated (United Nations) to be 700,000,000, and their area is about the same as Canada, 3,852,000 square miles. Russia in 1963 had an estimated population of almost 225,000,000 and an area of almost 8,600,000 square miles.

As late as 1890 there were still frontiers in the United States. At that time 50,000,000 people, about 80 percent of the population, resided below 1,000 feet altitude in an area that makes up about one-third of the country. Only 1,500,000 people lived above 2,000 feet in altitude in the vast area that includes most of the West. Land was plentiful, and to a large degree it was this abundance of land that assured democracy in the colonies when attempts to import nobility and to divide the population into classes failed and were replaced by democratic institutions. There was

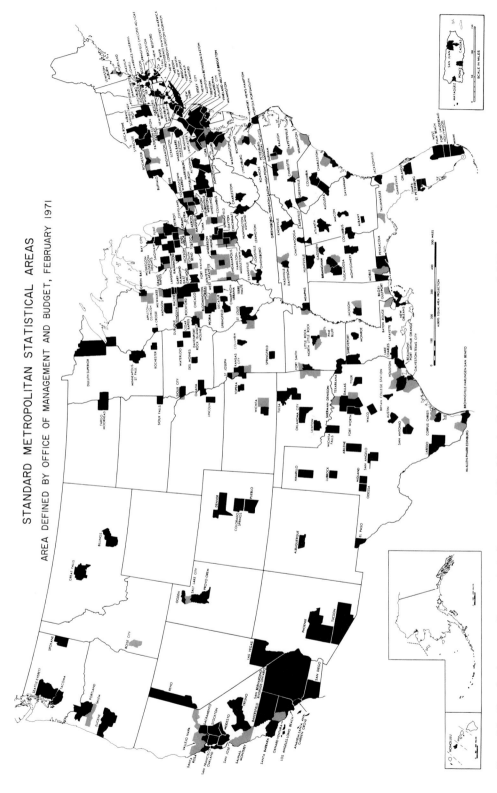

Figure 9.2 *Standard metropolitan statistical areas as defined by the United States government; solid black, as of 1960; stippled are areas added from 1960 to 1971. The map illustrates both the extent and the recent acceleration of urban sprawl, despite the fact that some areas as drawn are quite unrealistic. Few would regard the northwest corner of Nevada, the Mojave Desert, or the south end of Death Valley as urban!*

STANDARD METROPOLITAN STATISTICAL AREAS

AREA DEFINED BY OFFICE OF MANAGEMENT AND BUDGET, FEBRUARY 1971

always free land a little back from the river bank or upstream for those who decided to forego their opportunity of continuing as second-class citizens.

Today, in the forty-eight contiguous states, cheap land is no more. Megalopolis, extending from Boston to Richmond along the Atlantic seaboard, has about 50,000,000 people in about 50,000 square miles—a population density approximately that of sagebrush in Nevada—and a new form of canyon-lands between the high-rise office buildings and apartments. As land becomes more crowded, the importance of understanding its nature and its resources increases.

CANADA

With its 3,852,000 square miles, Canada is larger than the United States. It is divided into 10 provinces and 2 territories as follows (Fig. 9.3):

Alberta	255,000 sq. miles
British Columbia	365,000 sq. miles
Manitoba	245,000 sq. miles
New Brunswick	30,000 sq. miles
Newfoundland	155,000 sq. miles
Nova Scotia	20,000 sq. miles
Ontario	415,000 sq. miles
Prince Edward Island	2,000 sq. miles
Quebec	595,000 sq. miles
Saskatchewan	250,000 sq. miles
Yukon and Northwest Territories	1,520,000 sq. miles

Canada was first controlled by the French, but was ceded to England in the Peace of Paris (1763) at the end of the 7-year's war. Canada was defined then as extending southward to the Ohio River and westward to the Mississippi River. The colony, governed from Quebec, had a population of about 70,000 in 100 communities that, altogether, farmed about a million acres. During the American revolution, efforts to make the revolt continent-wide failed; Canada remained loyal, and became the refuge of many thousands of loyalist Americans who were driven from the 13

Figure 9.3 *Provinces and territories of Canada.*

colonies that revolted. England won their loyalty by grants of land, but that part of Canada south of the Great Lakes became part of the United States.

Canada quickly became two cultures, French and British, and in 1791 the British parliament recognized this fact by creating Lower Canada with French customs below the Ottawa River and Upper Canada with British customs and laws above the river. The separation intensified in the 1830's with an abortive rebellion by the French Canadians, but in 1840 Upper and Lower Canada were united by law if not in fact. The two parts were nearly equal, and a democratic stalemate developed until Nova Scotia, New Brunswick, and Prince Edward Island proposed forming a Federal Union, and this was accomplished July 1, 1867. In 1869 the lands that had been governed by the Hudson Bay Company since 1670 were conveyed to Canada, and in 1878 all of British North America except Newfoundland was conveyed to Canada. Newfoundland remained separate until 1949.

The pattern of Canada's westward growth parallels that of the United States. Manitoba was created in 1879, and the next province to be formed was British Columbia, on the Pacific coast. The interior provinces, Alberta and Saskatchewan, were formed later, as were the western interior states to the south.

Today, 90 percent of the population of Canada lives within 200 miles of its southern border. That part of Canada, about one-sixth of the whole country, is almost—not quite—as crowded as the 48 states to the south. A third of even that most populous belt has fewer than 5 persons per square mile. The remainder of Canada is like most of Alaska—cold wilderness.

Land Surveys—The Basis for Orderly Settlement and Development of the Frontier

The basis for orderly settlement and development of the entire western United States was contained in the Land Ordinance of 1785, which established public land policy and provided for

rectangular surveys of the public lands. Canada devised a similar system.

The lands are divided into townships 6 miles square numbered with reference to principal meridians and base lines (Fig. 9.4,A). The townships (Fig. 9.4,B) are divided into 36 sections (Fig. 9.4,C), each a mile square and containing 640 acres. These are divided into quarters of 160 acres, and the quarters can be further divided into 40-acre tracts (Fig. 9.4,C).

Such squares do not fit the spherical earth's surface, but this difficulty is met by introducing correction lines about every 10 townships where section and township lines are offset in order to restore full measure.

This system allows any tract of land to be precisely identified by location and by size. An air traveler today can scarcely fail to notice the contrast between the crazyquilt pattern of roads and property lines in the Appalachian Provinces and the orderly township and section lines in Ohio and to the west (Fig. 9.5). The flat terrain greatly favored the rectangular surveys, but they were extended later into the mountainous western states also. State boundaries west of the Mississippi are mostly rectangular; many boundaries east of the Mississippi follow natural features.

POLITICAL BOUNDARIES

Political boundaries, between nations or states, may be defined by a water course (stream or lake), by a divide between drainage basins, or by a meridian of longitude or parallel of latitude. Water courses may at first seem like good natural boundaries; a boundary may be defined as either the high- or low-water mark along one bank, as the midline between the banks, or as the center of the main channel. Such definitions, however, can be troublesome, because rivers change their courses. What was a navigable main channel may become silted, and a new channel eroded or dredged in a different position. Many rivers are braided, and if left uncontrolled would change their courses seasonally. Some river courses, particularly those in the arid and semiarid parts of the country, are dry part of the year but are

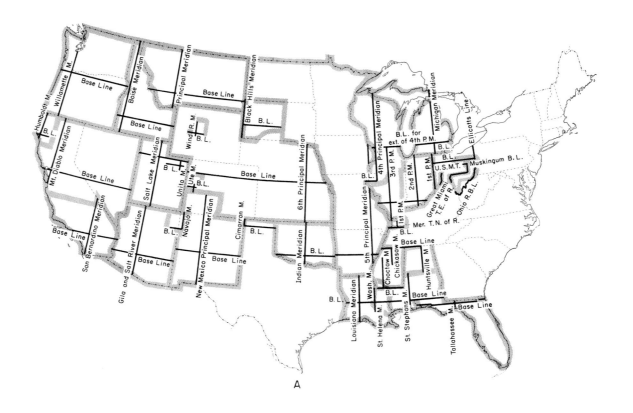

A

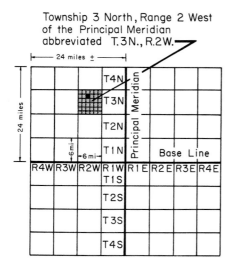

Township 3 North, Range 2 West of the Principal Meridian abbreviated T.3N., R.2W.

B

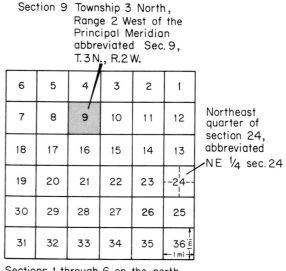

Section 9 Township 3 North, Range 2 West of the Principal Meridian abbreviated Sec. 9, T.3N., R.2W.

Northeast quarter of section 24, abbreviated NE ¼ sec. 24

Sections 1 through 6 on the north side and 7,18,19,30, and 31 on the west side are fractional sections.

C

Figure 9.4 *System of United States rectangular surveys. (A) Location of the several prime meridians and their base lines. (B) Townships are numbered according to their position north or south of a base line and east or west of a principal meridian. (C) Numbering of the sections within a township. [After U.S.D.A.]*

subject to flash floods and the attendant quick changes they produce. Rivers that are actively eroding their banks may cut off meanders. Islands, which are a special legal situation, may come and go. Neither lawyers nor hydrologists have simple answers for these problems, and every river that is a boundary poses problems peculiar to its drainage system.

The law provides that boundary markers on the ground, once legally established, are to be accepted as defining the boundary's location even though a later survey may show that the boundary markers were placed erroneously. For example, the 103rd meridian was defined as the east boundary of New Mexico and the west boundary of the Panhandle of Texas, but the survey was 3 miles too far west in the south and 1½ miles too far west at the north. Nevertheless, the set markers are accepted as defining the boundary, and detailed maps show that the boundary line does not coincide with the meridian.

Several other boundary lines in the western United States also are a little west of the nearest meridians, but for a different reason. The east and west boundaries of Colorado, for example, are about 3 miles west of the 102nd and 109th meridians, respectively. This maladjustment developed because these boundaries were defined on the basis of longitude west of Washington. The Washington meridian was defined as passing through the dome of the old Naval Observatory at 24th and Constitution Avenues in Washington, D.C. It is 77°03'02.3" west of Greenwich. The act adopting the Washington meridian was repealed in 1912, but it figured prominently in setting the meridional boundaries of the western Territories that subsequently became states.

Land Use

About a third of the United States, excluding Alaska, is in forest, and another third is in pasture and range. Almost a third is cropland. The proportions could hardly be better balanced. Figure 9.6 illustrates the geographical distribution of the major categories of agricultural lands in

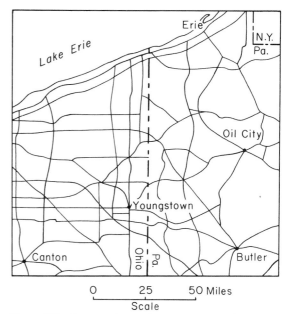

Figure 9.5 *Contrast in road patterns in northwestern Pennsylvania and northeastern Ohio. The rectangular pattern in Ohio is due chiefly to the rectangular surveys that were begun there and continued westward across the United States.*

the United States and southern Canada. The more northerly parts of Canada and almost all of Alaska are forest and tundra. Northern forests are not grazed; southern ones are and are shown as grazing land.

A practical effect of regional differences in the environment is illustrated in Figure 9.7, which shows the great difference in carrying capacity of pasture and range land in different parts of the country. A few acres in the humid eastern states are as productive, on the average, as a square mile in much of the west. In the east, and along the northwest coast, the principal source of grazed forage is provided by cultivated pastures; in the rest of the country and in Canada, native plants are the principal forage.

PUBLIC LANDS

Excluding Alaska, slightly more than 20 percent of the United States is federally owned land. Five percent is owned by state and local govern-

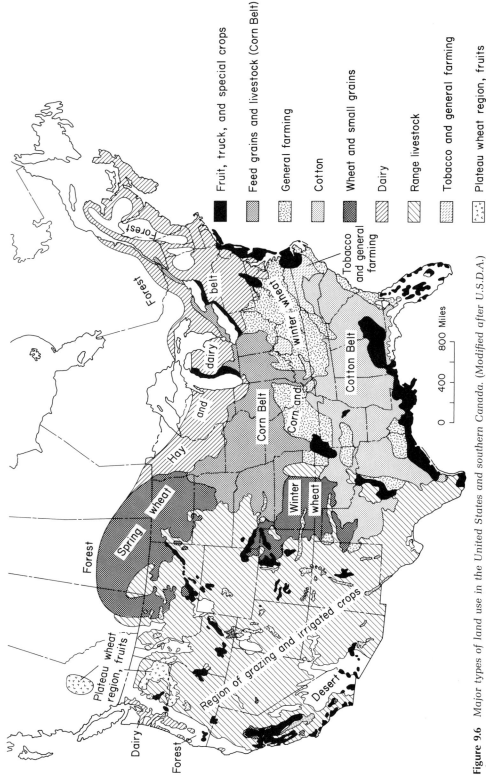

Figure 9.6 *Major types of land use in the United States and southern Canada. (Modified after U.S.D.A.) The Central Lowland includes the corn belt and most of the wheat areas. Although the plains west of the 100th meridian are semiarid, much of that area produces wheat. It also produces dust. The most important crops are (1) corn, which is grown extensively in the cotton belt as well as farther north, (2) wheat, and (3) hay. From 1953 to 1969, the areas producing cotton decreased from 24¼ million to 11 million acres; production declined from 16½ million bales to 10 million. There was corresponding increase in production of synthetic fibers.*

ments; 3 percent is Indian land. Seventy percent is private. Alaska still is about 90 percent federally owned land. Altogether, about one-third of the United States (including Alaska) is federally owned—more than half of four states (Oregon, Idaho, Nevada, and Utah) and between a quarter and half of seven others (Montana, Wyoming, Colorado, New Mexico, Arizona, California, and Washington). Federal lands in states along and east of the 100th meridian range from less than 1 percent to a maximum of 12 percent.

Of the federally owned lands, other than in Alaska, about 40 percent is forest and another 40 percent is nonforested pasture and grazing land. The remaining public lands are those set aside for special uses—parks, wildlife refuges, public reservoirs, and military reservations.

The early policy of the United States was to sell off the public lands and encourage the exploitation of their resources. This policy helped finance the new government. The theory that public lands should be disposed of to private ownership still pervades most of the statutes in force, but that theory is no longer compatible with the needs of the greatly enlarged population and the public demand for land. During the 1960's a comprehensive study of the public land policies of the federal government and of demands made by the various interests upon those lands was made by a Public Land Law Review Commission; the Commission's report to the

Figure 9.7 *Carrying capacity of pasture and range land in the United States, in average number of cows per square mile.* [From U.S.D.A.]

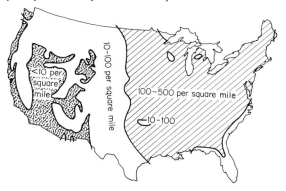

President and Congress was published in 1970 under the title *One Third of the Nation's Land.*

The Commission decided that its consideration of use of public lands must take into account six categories of interest:

1. The national public.

2. The regional public, which has ready access to particular lands.

3. The Federal Government as sovereign, or as the ultimate authority whose responsibility it is to provide for the general welfare.

4. The Federal government as proprietor, with interests that are like those of any other land owner.

5. State and local governments.

6. Users of the public lands and their resources.

The Commission considered all these categories of interest in analyzing the problems that pertain to the principal kinds of resources or uses of the public lands—notably, timber, range (grazing), minerals, water, fish and wildlife, intensive agriculture (as on lands irrigated by a public dam and reservoir)—and to the special problems posed by exploiting the resources of the outer continental shelf and those posed by outdoor recreation.

It was recommended that the policy of large-scale disposal of public lands, as reflected by the majority of statutes in force, should be revised, and that only those lands should be disposed of for which it could be shown that the general public would gain maximum benefit by non-federal ownership—for example, land for a new city, enlargement of an older one, or land for a state or local park.

It also was recommended (1) that a review should be undertaken to determine what best use could be made of all lands not previously designated for a specific use, (2) that consideration be given to all possible uses and to the maximum number of compatible uses that can be permitted within a specified unit of land, (3) that land be classified according to primary uses and managed to provide compatible secondary uses, and (4) that full value should be paid for use of public land, but the payment may be less than so-called market value, provided there is no consumptive use of the land or its resources.

The report also considers possible methods for managing the environment. The conditions to be monitored and managed pertain to water, air quality, maintaining the biosystem, and what is referred to as quality of experience—aesthetics.

Quality of experience refers to visual and aesthetic environments as related to recreational, residential, and travel purposes; cultural, historical, and informational values for recreational and educational purposes; personal and social experiences, escape from crowding, development, and noise; and natural biological and physical features. To achieve this protection may require restraints on noise, numbers of recreation visitors to protect against overuse, restraints on mining, lumbering, and other land use. Among the aims of water management are the protection of fisheries. Fish require high levels of dissolved oxygen, have low tolerances for temperature change, and are sensitive to trace elements and acidity of the water. Obviously, influxes of toxic chemicals, nutrients, silt, and organic matter are harmful to all life. To achieve this protection might require that stringent limitations be imposed upon mining, grading or filling of land, and clearing of vegetation by burning, bulldozing, or use of herbicides. Water used for domestic supplies, swimming, and industrial purposes must be of high quality, but high levels of dissolved oxygen are unnecessary. Standards can be less stringent for water used for secondary purposes, such as irrigation and industrial cooling; controls need only be aimed at minimizing concentrations of salts and toxic materials.

For maintaining the natural biosystem to the fullest extent possible, whether for recreation, education, or scientific study, requires maximum restraints on secondary uses, such as logging, mining, construction, and casual access. Less restrictions would be needed where limited modification of the biosystem is tolerable. Major modification of the biosystem may be needed to maximize output of a particular product or use, such as single-species management for commercial timber production, primary management for elk and other game animals. These practices lead to large scale vegetative changes and major changes of habitat for preferred species. Such intensive use would be undertaken where biosystem losses are offset by value of goods and services.

Air quality requires management for several kinds of tolerances. The most stringent controls would be needed where human health is threatened. The next most stringent controls would be needed to protect the natural biosystem. A third level of control would be needed to protect against corrosion of materials, and last but hardly least is aesthetic protection against haze and odors.

The guidelines recommended for United States public lands could serve equally well as a basis for protection of all lands.

Products from the Land

AGRICULTURE

Because of favorable physiographic factors, North America's agricultural production is prodigious. The United States alone overproduces practically all of the necessary foods—to the absurd degree that landowners have been paid not to grow certain crops. Yet despite this resource, some 11 million American households (assumes family of four) suffer from inadequate diets. Keeping in mind that this malnutrition applies to the wealthiest nation on earth, one can readily imagine how acute the hunger problem is in poor nations. A familiar advertisement reminds us that the underprivileged people in poor nations are not as well fed as an average American pet dog. Still, the United States persists in exporting munitions, and wonders why the world is not appreciative of its generosity.

Even more could be produced by intensive methods, and it would be in the world's best interest to do so and make the surplus food available to those countries that have not been blessed with such a favorable environment. In brief, the answer to agricultural overproduction is *not* to cut back on the produce but to make it available to the many who are hungry. It would be more economical to give the surplus away than to continue a military-oriented program; moreover, the cost-benefit ratios would be vastly more favorable to all.

FORESTS

The most obvious value of forests is to supply wood—for lumber, pulpwood, and fuel. Lumber amounts to about half the value of forest products, pulpwood about a third, and fuel perhaps 5 percent. Other important products are turpentine, pitch, resins, tanbark, and maple syrup. Besides supplying primary wood products, forests serve to control erosion, protect watersheds by storing water, and provide many forms of outdoor recreation.

Erosion in forested areas is minimized partly by the forest canopy, which reduces the impact of hard rains. Moreover, the decaying mat of fallen leaves and fallen timbers absorbs much of the water, keeps it from running off, and allows water to seep into the ground. Tree roots help hold the ground in place too. Because forest floors are generally colder by several degrees than the air above the canopy, and because wind velocities are low, evaporation rates are low. Since snow that collects under forest melts slowly in spring, much of that water also enters the ground.

Between a third and a half of the combined area of Canada and the United States is forested (Fig. 9.8), and these forests constitute about 15 percent of the world's total. With only 6.5 percent of the world's population, North America is blessed with twice its share of forests.

Present lumber production is roughly 50 billion board feet annually, which in North America is about 2 percent of the total reserve of more than 3,000 billion board feet. (A board foot is equivalent to a piece of wood 12 inches by 12 inches and 1 inch thick.) New growth annually

adds more than 135 billion board feet; therefore, with reasonable protection and care we can enjoy an annual crop of forest products without endangering the resource. Indeed, intelligent cutting improves a forest by providing space for new growth.

More than 80 percent of the sawtimber is pine, spruce, fir, and other conifers (so-called softwoods); the remainder consists of the broadleaf trees (so-called hardwoods) such as oak, maple, hickory, elm, cottonwood, and beech. The terms "hardwood" and "softwood" are misleading, for some of the hardwoods (for example, cottonwood) are softer than some of the softwoods.

Standards for classifying stands of timber have varied greatly over the years and from place to place. One set of specifications in recent use classes commercial stands as *sawtimber* if stocked 10 percent or more with trees greater than 11 inches in diameter at breast height. Stands with smaller trees are classed as *poletimber* if stocked 10 percent or more with trees greater than 5 inches in diameter at breast height.

It has been widely assumed that the precolonial "forest primeval" was more productive forest than what remains today and that this forest was devastated by those who settled America. Out of this developed the assumption that the forest could be rehabilitated by sustained-yield management. It was supposed, for example, that the bare rock exposures on the Highlands of the Hudson have been denuded of forest and soil, but accounts of the Highlands left by some of Hendrick Hudson's men indicate that they had as much bare rock then as they have now. Moreover, the forests there were just as stunted then as they are now because of the shallow soil over the rock and its susceptibility to drought. It has been assumed that climax forests existed in other areas before time of settlement, but recent evidence indicates that the pre-settlement forests differed little if any from those that exist today.

Forest lands have gained about 50 million acres since 1910, when lumbering was at its peak. Forest acreage is increasing as a result of the reversion of farmlands to forest, especially in New England. About 16 million acres have been

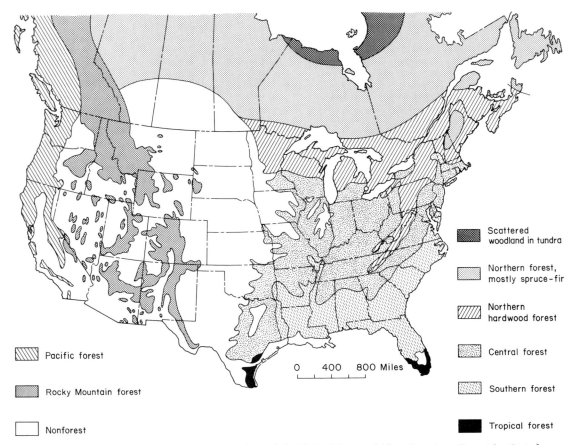

Figure 9.8 *Principal areas of forests in Canada and the United States. [After American Forest Institute.]*

withdrawn from timber production and are used for recreation or other purposes.

Wooded land is classed as forest if the presence of the trees determines land use and if the crowns cover 20 percent or more of the area. Listed here are some of the different kinds of forest.

In Canada and Alaska
Pacific coast forest of Sitka spruce and hemlock
Interior forest of white spruce and birch
Rocky Mountain forests of Engelmann spruce and lodgepole pine
Eastern forests of spruce and fir

In the western United States
Redwood forest   Lodgepole pine
Douglas fir   Sugar pine
Yellow pine   Sitka spruce and
                              hemlock
Pinyon-juniper   Sequoia
Engelmann spruce   Fir and hemlock
  and fir
White pine   Larch and western
                              pine

In the Eastern United States
Spruce and fir   Mixed oak and pine
Northern pine   Southeastern pine
Northern hardwoods   Tupelo
Central hardwoods   Aspen

Of the 760 million acres of forest land in the United States, 510 million acres is classed as commercial forest; 250 million acres is classed as noncommercial.

MANAGING FORESTS.   The potential for conflict between interests competing for different uses of forest lands is high. Logging, watershed protection, grazing, recreation, and mining are the main competing interests. Forest lands can be considered as primarily for timber production if they are capable of efficient, high-quality timber production and are not uniquely valuable for other uses. Land so classified, however, can have secondary uses that are compatible with the primary use. There may be conflict with grazing and, in places, with mining, but conflict with recreation is less than first appears because the highly productive timber areas are at accessible lower altitudes, whereas ground favored for recreation is in large part at high altitudes where the scenery is more spectacular, the ground is more open for hiking, and there is more snow for winter sports. The Public Land Law Review Commission has estimated that a fourth or less of the national forests in the United States should be classified as primarily for timber production.

The time required to grow timber from seed until harvest has usually been determined by the size of log suitable for lumber, but logs of timber size are not needed to meet the increasing demand for pulpwood and related products. In determining the allowable cut, the short-term as well as the long-term rotation must be considered.

The environmental impact of timber cutting also needs to be considered. Strip zones can be left alongside streams, partly for aesthetic reasons and partly for protection against bank erosion. Similar strips can protect aesthetics along roadsides. Logging systems need to be designed to minimize waste as well as the impact upon scenery. Not only must timber cutting be regulated, but the sawmills and pulpmills must be required to maintain satisfactory environmental quality standards—to protect air, soil, and water.

Foresters are not agreed on the best method of cutting timber. Clearcutting is the removal of trees of all ages and sizes in selected areas. Hillsides may be cut in strips adjusted to the contour, which helps reduce runoff and erosion. When clearcut areas are replanted, the trees for the next crop are all of one age. Selective cutting is the removal of large trees, leaving young growth. After being selectively cut, an area will have trees of various ages and sizes.

Trimmings and leftovers from plywood and lumber mills are increasingly being used to manufacture paper goods. This waste wood was formerly burned or otherwise discarded, and its destruction contributed to pollution as smoke or solid waste. Salvaging the leftover wood not only reduces pollution, but conserves trees.

LIVESTOCK

The livestock population on farms and ranches in the United States is about as follows:

Cattle	Almost 100,000,000
Hogs	More than 50,000,000
Sheep	Almost 50,000,000
Chickens	About 500,000,000
Turkeys	About 10,000,000
Horses	About 10,000,000
Mules	Less than 5,000,000

Annual production totals about 20 billion pounds of beef, 20 billion pounds of pork, and 2 billion pounds of lamb and mutton. Other production includes leather goods, wool, butter, eggs, milk, and in the West, cowboys and sheepherders. Lands in the humid central and eastern United States are much more productive for livestock (see Fig. 9.7).

Despite the vast extent of public lands in the western United States, those lands supply only about 12 percent of the total forage for livestock, yet this supply is necessary for the continuation of many ranches. At first the public lands constituted a vast commons for grazing domestic livestock. Control of grazing began when the national forests were created; the first fees for grazing were charged in 1905. In 1934, the Taylor Grazing Act extended the controls to all public lands not otherwise restricted. The reason for this was partly because the effects of overgrazing had been aggravated by drought, and the western range was seriously damaged by deterioration of the feed and by erosion. Eligibility for the grazing permits depends upon the capacity of the ranch to provide necessary feed when the range is not used.

Resources of the Sea—Fish

Most of the open ocean, about 90 percent by area, has too little nutrient matter in the lighted surface layers to support much living matter. In fact, the open ocean has been described as a biological desert. Most of the life of the oceans is concentrated in the remaining 10 percent—the zones near the shore (like the banks off New England, Nova Scotia, and Newfoundland) and in certain offshore areas where upwelling coastal waters bring nutrients from depth. Indeed, in many places estuaries are the principal source of nutrients, which is another reason why such coastal areas need protection against pollution. Although coastal wetlands, constitute but a small proportion of the earth's surface they are said to produce more living matter per acre than any other part of the world. Per acre they are twice as productive as good forest or grassland, four times as productive as a good cornfield, and fifteen times as productive as the oceans. They need protection!

The open ocean annually grows less than 2,000,000 metric tons of fish; coastal waters grow nearly 250,000,000 metric tons. It has been estimated that about half of this total tonnage is available annually for sustained harvesting without depleting the supply. At present the fish harvested total about half that maximum.

Total production of saltwater fisheries around North America each year is about 6 billion pounds, worth about $275 million. About 60 percent of the production comes from the Atlantic and Gulf coasts, and about 40 percent from the Pacific coast. Annual production from commercial fresh-water fisheries is worth only a few million dollars in terms of its market value. The recreational value of fresh-water fisheries is impossible to measure in dollar value; however, it would undoubtedly be many times its commercial value. Millions of persons, both in the United States and Canada, annually spend many days on lakes or along streams—sometimes catching fish and sometimes not, but always catching worthwhile relaxation and enjoyment of the outdoors.

Water Resources

Water resources are needed for personal uses, including recreation, and for industry, agriculture, shipping, and generation of electric power. North America enjoys more than its share. Canada has about a quarter of the world's accessible supply of fresh water, a quantity second only to that in the Soviet Union and eight times the United States supply.

In the United States, annual precipitation averages about 30 inches, of which three-fourths is lost by evaporation and transpiration. The usable part totals about 7,500 gallons per person daily, five times the present demand. Homes use an average of about 50 gallons per day per person. Leaks in municipal systems, including leaky faucets in homes, are responsible for an average loss of about 25 gallons per day per person. Total use for all purposes, including use by the big consumers—agriculture and industry—averages about 1,300 gallons per day per person, and the cost averages about 30¢ per 1,000 gallons. Desalinization costs nearly twice that. The water that is used in the United States is consumed as shown on p. 195.

Not all water that is withdrawn from a stream, lake, or aquifer is consumed, for it may be returned without loss in quantity or important change in quality, as is true of water used by hydroelectric plants. A major nonconsumptive use of water is in navigation. The Great Lakes, together with the St. Lawrence, Mississippi, Ohio,

Use	Total Withdrawn (millions of gallons per day)	Percent of Total
Public supplies	17,000	7
Rural use	3,000	1
Irrigation	110,000	46
Delivered to farms	81,000	
Lost from canals	29,000	
Self-supplied industrial	110,000	46
Total	240,000	100

SOURCE: Data from U.S.G.S.

and Missouri rivers, provide economical transportation to and from the richly productive central states. About 15 percent of the freight moves via inland waterways, compared to 40 percent by railroad, 25 percent by motor vehicle, and 20 percent by pipeline.

The total supply of water in the United States is adequate, but there are problems of distribution, quality, pollution, floods, and dependability (Fig. 9.9). Distribution problems primarily reflect the fact that part of the country is humid and part is arid or semiarid. Some parts are excessively wet and need to be drained for ordinary use (Fig. 9.10,A), like the marshes along the Atlantic and Gulf coasts and the many marshes in the Great Lakes area. In the arid and semiarid parts of the country—that is, in the West—lands need to be irrigated (Fig. 9.10,B). But even around the Great Lakes, because of dense settlement and intensive industrial development, water supplies are not adequate to meet anticipated increases in demand in the next 25 years. The same is true of most of the western United States too.

The water supplies that are consumed include substantial amounts of groundwater. Groundwater supplies must be developed with special

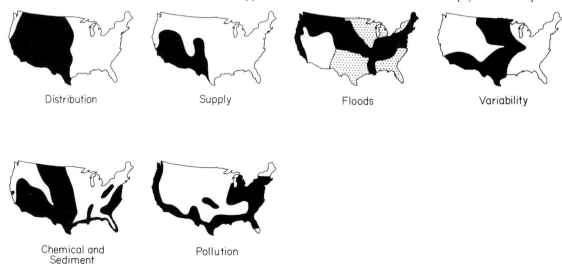

Figure 9.9 *Areas most affected by the major problems of water supply. The problems are particularly troublesome in the black areas, less so in the stippled areas, and least in the white areas.* [After U.S.G.S.]

Distribution   Supply   Floods   Variability

Chemical and Sediment   Pollution

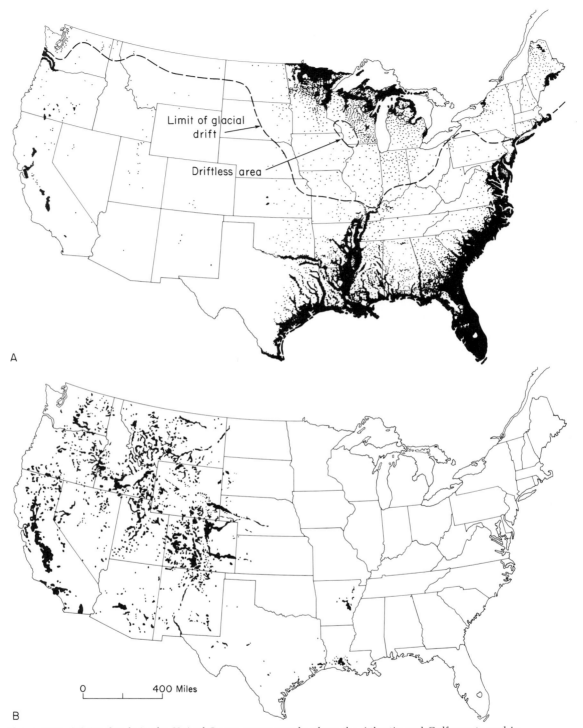

Figure 9.10 (A) *Wetlands in the United States occur mostly along the Atlantic and Gulf coasts and in the glaciated part of the country. (B) Irrigated lands in the United States. In 1954 the total irrigated area was almost 30 million acres of a total cropland area of more than 400 million acres.* [From U.S.D.A.]

Figure 9.11 Areas where significant cones of depression have been developed in the water table or where inferior water has encroached because of overpumping from wells. [From U.S.G.S.]

care, because they can be depleted by overdraft (Fig. 9.11), as is already happening in many parts of the country.

Nonconsumptive uses of surface waters include production of hydroelectricity, navigation, and recreation—boating, waterskiing, fishing, swimming, and other aquatic sports. Waste disposal can be considered a consumptive use if it pollutes or changes the quality of the water sufficiently to affect its use.

Dams in the United States are about evenly distributed between the humid and semiarid parts of the country (Fig. 9.12,A). Those in the East are mostly for flood control; flood losses in the eastern United States are considerable (Fig. 9.12,B). Dams in the West are mostly for irrigation. Whether for flood control, irrigation, or hydroelectricity, we have built more than 200 dams that are more than 200 feet high—175 of them since 1925. Some think the country has gone dam crazy. For example, water losses by evaporation from the reservoirs now exceed the amount used for public supplies in the entire country! Moreover, one can debate the wisdom of building dams for flood control if they permanently flood a substantial area that previously was flooded only seasonally.

The principal water problem in the United States is a self-imposed one—pollution. There is hardly a community in the country that does not face this problem; near some industrial sites, rivers have been so fouled with oil they have been considered a fire hazard. Pollution is a problem in the congested parts of Canada too. When our population was small, we could get by with dumping wastes into streams—disposal by dilution—but with our greatly increased population and industrial activity we can no longer afford to do so. The economic, health, and social problems posed by water pollution are, at last, receiving attention. The problems are great, especially the political problems, because captains of industry and members of the U.S. Chamber of Commerce have been so slow in getting the message. Nevertheless, the problem can be surmounted, and if the effort is continued, we can look forward to the elimination of pollution in

our lakes and rivers so that they may be pleasant for boating, swimming, and even for drinking. It is sobering to recall that in the twelve years of our infamous war in Vietnam, the United States government spent less than 1 billion dollars on water pollution problems.

Nevertheless, there are some bright spots where pollution problems have been overcome, or at least relieved. The Bethlehem Steel facility at Baltimore uses 125 million gallons per day of treated wastewater from the city's sewage treatment plant for cooling purposes. The copper mine at Santa Rita, New Mexico, uses septic-tank effluent for copper processing. Sewage treatment plants at Santee, in southern California, and at Lake Tahoe have succeeded in treating and recycling their effluents to produce recreational lakes. In Southern California, where water costs are high, the Kaiser Steel Plant at Fontana has found it economical to reuse its supplies, with the result that the water requirements are less than 2 percent of the national average per ton of steel. Treated effluent from city sewage plants has been used for irrigation in the Texas Panhandle. The seven-state Sanitation Commission that was organized in 1948 for the Ohio River Valley has improved conditions along many stretches of that river, although much still needs to be done. We can be sure that industry would become progressive about recycling and reusing water and minimizing pollution if the cost of water were increased and if effluents were taxed in proportion to their quantity and potency. This would have to be done on the federal level or at least by interstate compacts in order to meet the standard ploy—a threat to move—that industries use when a particular operation is threatened by local tax or other restrictions.

In order to supply water to those parts of the continent that are living with shortages or are faced with them, a bold plan has been devised by a private engineering firm, the Ralph M. Parsons Company. The plan calls for the creation of a North American Water and Power Alliance (NAWAPA), which would use 15 percent of the runoff from the well-watered Yukon River Basin and join the basin with the Liard, Peace, and

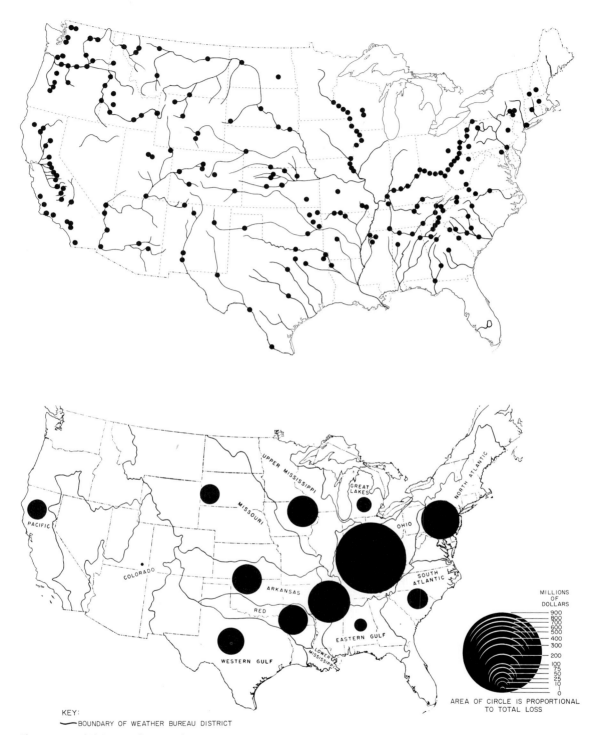

Figure 9.12 (A) Major dams and reservoirs in the United States. (B) Distribution of flood losses by regions, 1902–1937. [From U.S.D.A.]

Fraser rivers. A dam already being built where the Peace River goes through the Canadian Rockies could supply a navigable canal from there to the Great Lakes, and by canalizing the Frazer River a trans-Canada waterway could be developed from Lake Superior to Vancouver.

The divides to be crossed by tunnel or siphon are no higher or more difficult than many already crossed by various water systems in the western mountains. The flow would generate 100 million kilowatts of electricity; one-third would be needed for the pumping stations, and the rest could be sold. Water could be delivered to the parched southwestern United States and to the even more parched northwestern states of Mexico, and it could relieve, or help relieve, a bad hydrologic situation in the Great Lakes. A first estimate of cost is $100 billion dollars. This sum seems large only to those who are not familiar with the United States annual military budget.

The plan certainly is technologically feasible, and it has the benefit of utilizing water that is surplus, and bound to remain so. Whether the vast lake or chain of lakes that would be needed along the Rocky Mountain Trench would have adverse or beneficial ecological effects remain to be determined. And whether the plan is economically and politically feasible also is still to be determined. At the moment the only serious objections to the plan are that it staggers the imagination, and the Canadians have not favored it.

WATER MANAGEMENT

Water management in the United States has evolved through five stages, reflecting changes in the national interest. First, during the first half of the nineteenth century, with the population mostly along the Atlantic seaboard, there was interest in building canals for access to the rivers above the Fall Line, and later, as settlement and commerce increased in the Mississippi River basin, there developed need for improving river channels.

A second stage evolved from the first. As settlement increased in the Mississippi River basin, property became more vulnerable to damage by floods, and during the second half of the nineteenth century there developed increasing need for flood-control measures, the building of levees and floodways. After a disastrous flood in 1874, Congress, in 1879, created the Mississippi River Commission to coordinate the planning. Until 1890, however, federal funds were restricted to channel improvements, and flood control was still considered a local problem. In 1928, after the worst Mississippi River flood to date, flood control became financed wholly by federal funds.

A third stage in water-management practices developed as the semiarid western states became settled; it culminated in the Reclamation Act of 1902 that created the Reclamation Service, which later became the Bureau of Reclamation. This benefitted 17 western states and led to a dichotomy in water management. The Corps of Engineers was the principal water-managing agency during the first two stages and had its clientele of political support in the central and eastern states. The Bureau and the Corps, operating under very different legislation and procedures, became competitive. There are good physiographic reasons for having different water policies in the humid and semiarid parts of the country, but this, unfortunately, was not the basis for the differences in legislation.

A fourth stage in water management concerned the greatly increased demand for hydroelectricity during the 1930's, which culminated in the creation of the Tennessee Valley Authority in 1933. During this stage, increasing numbers of multiple-purpose dams and reservoirs were built, and this led to increasing public interest in and use of the reservoirs for recreation, fish, and wildlife. This surge in public use is partly responsible for the fifth stage—increasing interest in general environmental qualities.

During this stage, which has developed mostly since 1950, we have witnessed increased attention to matters of pollution, soil erosion, and aesthetic qualities. The reservoirs have created new wildlife habitats in place of those now flooded. An experience that I had while assembling this book illustrates the tremendous popularity of these artificial water bodies. Partly to give attention to the system of state parks, I asked state commissions for representative pictures of these parks, and a high percentage of those received turned out to be water scenes at reservoirs. Only a few of these could be used in this book, because many did not illustrate the physiography, but they did illustrate where Americans like to go on weekends.

Still ahead is a sixth stage of water management, which will come when groundwater withdrawals that exceed recharge must be regulated (see Fig. 9.11).

Mineral Deposits, Mining

The mineral industry is and has been widely criticized for defacing the landscape, for polluting streams and the atmosphere, for spilling oil on land and at sea, and for unsafe mining practices. Such criticism is not new; more than 400 years ago, in 1550, Agricola wrote:

". . . the strongest argument of the detractors is that the fields are devastated by mining operations, for which reason formerly Italians were warned by law that no one should dig the earth for metals and so injure their very fertile fields, their vineyards and their olive groves. Also they argue that the woods and groves are cut down, for there is need for an endless amount of wood for timbers, machines, and the smelting of metals. And when the woods and groves are felled, then are exterminated the beasts and birds, very many of which furnish a pleasant and agreeable food for man. Further, when the ores are washed, the water which has been used poisons the brooks and streams, and either destroys the fish or drives them away. Therefore the inhabitants of these regions, on account of the devastation of their fields, woods, groves, brooks, and rivers, find great difficulty in procuring the necessities of life, and by reason of the destruction of the timber they are forced to greater expense in erecting buildings. Thus it is said, it is clear to all that there is greater detriment from mining than the value of the metals which the mining produces."

De Re Metallica, Hoover edition, p. 8.

Ducktown, Tennessee, where copper was extensively mined and smelted around 1900 and later, is commonly cited as an example of the sort of environmental destruction that is associated with mining activities. In the vicinity of the smelters all vegetation was killed by the sulfuric acid fumes. The denuded slopes became gullied to depths of 5 to 12 feet, and as the gullies widened, a badland topography with no soil was created.

Although mining and smelting practices have improved, criticism of the industry still is partly valid. Corporate annual statements proclaim efforts by particular companies to reduce pollution, but too commonly add "Your corporation and every industry has a duty to oppose the establishment of unrealistic standards." And, rather obviously, most proposed standards then become interpreted as unrealistic.

The mineral industry's public image was not helped in 1972 when two major companies, with the connivance of the federal government, openly defied the United Nations Security Council ban on imports (in this case chrome) from white-minority ruled Rhodesia. In the eyes of the rest of the world, that was regarded and labeled as a criminal act, a kind of corporate and governmental anarchy. Most people do not appreciate the fact that America's concept of "law and order" applies only to the man on the street, and not to big business or big government.

The first laws restricting industrial practices in mining and manufacturing industries were adopted in the 1830's, when Great Britain passed the so-called Factory Laws. Among the restrictions were provisions forbidding employment of children underground in mines for more than 9 hours a day. Such "unrealistic standards" forced some mines and other operations to close. Sad? In today's world, a plant that is unable to operate economically without poisoning the people near it, or being offensive to them, should be closed. A century later the world will be better off.

On the other hand, an aroused, frustrated public can defeat its own interests by foolish prohibitions. The problem is illustrated by the dichotomy of public opinion about power plants—we want power for air conditioners, refrigerators, lighting, and heat, but we do not want power plants. Some people would ban nuclear plants, but they do not want strip mining of coal either. It is doubtful if many objectors to strip mining have had to spend their days underground. Emotions to the contrary, the problems of strip mining can be solved by developing means of producing coal from the ground without destroying the land or the watershed. It can be done.

The general public became enraged about strip mining because of the industry's callous disregard for social and environmental values. Many areas were stripped and the abandoned land left upside down. The mines not only disfigured the landscape and left much of it unusable, but waters became acid because pyrite (iron sulfide), which is abundant in many coal deposits, decomposed to form sulfuric acid. These errors by the industry have even led to some legislative moves to ban strip mining altogether, but such prohibition is not the answer.

Most but not all, strip mines should be backfilled, and if pyrite is excessive the fill should be limed. This would be done if backfill performance bonds were high enough to discourage forfeiture. Judgement is needed in zoning areas for strip mining. It makes a great difference whether the formations are flat lying or steeply dipping, and whether the deposit is on flat land or on a steep slope. It makes a difference whether the area is one of low precipitation (like the Colorado Plateau) or high precipitation (like the Appalachian Plateau). Moreover, consideration needs to be given to possible future use of the particular tract of land. Rather than backfilling a stripped area, it might be preferable to use the particular open cut to receive sludge from a sewage treatment plant or to receive solid waste. Some could be used for parks, with ponds and hills. Not every strip mine need be backfilled.

The case for strip mining is that costs are 25 to 35 percent less than for underground mining. Strip mine output per man-day is about 100 percent higher than in underground mining, overall recovery is 60 percent higher, which utilizes the resource more efficiently, and strip mining is obviously the safer method for the worker. The strip mines left abandoned are the proof that rigorous controls are needed, but there can also be no question about the need for strip mining. Prior to 1920 strip mining accounted for only 1 percent of total United States production; by the mid-sixties a third of the production was from strip mines. In recent years Illinois has been the leading state in strip mine production, followed in order by Kentucky, Pennsylvania, Ohio, Indiana, and West Virginia.

By the mid-1960's, power shovels had been developed with capacities of 200 cubic yards (about 300 tons); these are capable of moving about 18,000 tons of overburden per hour. Shovels half again that large are considered feasible. Such machinery can indeed remove overburden efficiently, and the same machinery could be equally efficient in restoring that overburden when the coal has been removed.

Coal beds can be stripped economically where the ratio of overburden to the thickness of coal is as great as 30 to 1. That is, it is feasible to mine a coal bed 2 feet thick under 60 feet of overburden. Other factors besides thickness of overburden need to be taken into account, however, such as density and hardness, quality of the coal, capacity of the machinery, size of the property, selling price of coal from competing sources, distance to transportation facilities and markets, availability of electric power, labor, and supporting facilities. Costs of restoration vary too, depending partly on the slope and erodibility of the ground and partly on the content of iron sulfide in the spoil.

In assessing the need for controls of stripping operations, it must be recalled that underground mining of coal can damage the surface too, not so obviously perhaps but just as seriously. Underground mining causes land subsidence that can break homes or highways apart and lower water tables. Moreover, the waste piles at underground mines contain large quantities of waste coal, from impure layers or from layers too thin to be salvaged, and these waste piles may ignite spontaneously and burn almost indefinitely, adding to the air pollution problem in those areas.

To what extent and by what methods a back-filled strip mine should be landscaped with vegetation to hasten recovery depends on the environment. That it is possible to fully landscape such ground is clear enough from the experience of landscaping steep highway cuts to minimize erosion; it is possible but expensive. Where aesthetics are not an important consideration, erosion might be minimized by contour furrowing, and allowing nature to choose the pioneer plants that take root in the ground. Where aesthetics must be considered, the ground could be reforested or at least screened. The cure for the ills of strip mining is not to be found in simple-minded prohibitions but in flexible rules that can be adapted to particular situations. This, of course, assumes that the regulatory commission is controlled by the citizens rather than by the industry.

Sand and gravel deposits in areas that are becoming urbanized or suburbanized are another example of the need for planning in order to decide the kinds of restrictions that should be adopted. All too commonly sand and gravel operations are prohibited by premature zoning regulations that neglect either or both of two possibilities meriting attention. First, sand and gravel are essential for urban and/or suburban development, and transportation is a major part of the cost. A community may save itself great sums of money if it has nearby sources. Second, if the planners look ahead, they might find that a sand and gravel pit could become the already excavated basement of a large building or an underground parking area. The future of the site could be considered in zoning the ground.

The problem of oil spills is discussed in later chapters (10, 18); mining for metals poses problems too, as Agricola noted. Ducktown, Tennessee, is an infamous example of a landscape that has been deforested and savagely eroded because of bad metal mining practices. The labor strife of a half century ago at Cripple Creek, Colorado, and Coeur de'Alene, Idaho, calls to mind another unsavory side of metal mining. The current resistance to rigorous air pollution standards in the deserts of the Southwest illustrates how slowly progress is made: despite court-documented poisoning of persons living near some big smelters, the copper industry objects to proposed air pollution standards as "unrealistic." The objections would be received more favorably if the industry countered with positive alternatives. An old maxim states that victory is never won from a defensive position, but that has been the stance of the mining industry ever since the first factory laws of the 1830's. With a change in attitude, the industry might find that when the wastes discharged by the chimney stacks are reclaimed, they may have a value as great or greater than the cost of cleaning up.

No continent is self-sufficient in mineral deposits, but some have more than others because of their particular geological heritage. Different kinds of mineral deposits are peculiar to particular geological environments, and we in North America chose our birthplace wisely. For example, the United States consumes almost half the world's total annual coal production, and possesses about a third of the world's reserve. Canada possesses 15 percent of the world's known nickel reserves, and her neighbor, the United States, consumes almost 40 percent of the world's total annual production. The United States has nearly 60 percent of the world's known reserves of molybdenum, and consumes 40 percent of the world's total annual production. Canada and the United States together possess more than half the world's known zinc reserves, and the United States consumes a quarter of the world's annual production. In fact, North America depends on other continents for only 4 metals and only 3 nonmetallic minerals—chromite, ferro-grade manganese, platinum minerals, and tin; industrial diamonds, quartz crystal, and asbestos. No other continent has it so good!

Our mineral production is about 70 percent for fuels, 20 percent for other nonmetals, and about 10 percent for metals. In the United States, mineral production is about 8 percent of the gross national product. The distribution and mode of occurrence of our principal mineral deposits are described in the chapters on the physiographic provinces.

To qualify as a resource mineral, a deposit must be in sufficient quantity and of high enough grade to be commercially produced, a principle illustrated in the words of a prospector who once said: "There's a million dollars in gold in that claim of mine, but there's just too darn much sand and gravel mixed with it." At a higher price for gold, his deposit may have become productive. For example, at normal peacetime prices, we import most of our mercury from foreign countries having deposits richer and, therefore, less costly to produce than ours. But during World War II, because of a considerable increase in the price of mercury, the United States produced practically all it needed. Any appraisal of the mineral resources of a country must consider the size and grade of the deposits, the costs of production, and the market prices of the various products. Technological advances may affect a nation's mineral wealth, as illustrated by the changes in use of various kinds of energy sources (Fig. 9.13).

In comparison with the rest of the world, our mineral resources are prodigious by any yardstick. But can we be proud of the way we are using them? Are we really minimizing waste by recycling? Are we producing with maximum consideration for the environment? And is our mineral production being used chiefly for improving the welfare of mankind or is it being used chiefly for military hardware?

Air—A Resource in Need of Protection

Air pollution is increasingly a national problem. The oxygen we need for breathing is concentrated in a thin layer at the base of the atmosphere, a layer barely reaching to the tops of high mountains. Airplanes flying in the rarefied air above that layer carry supplemental oxygen, and unless we control the air that we breath at ground level, we may need supplemental oxygen there, because this layer of air is being polluted and not merely disagreeably so. In many cases the pollution has been lethal: in 1948, in Donora, Pennsylvania, 20 persons died in a smog; in 1952 some 4,000 persons died in a smog in London; a year later, in New York, 200 deaths were charged to a local smog. Undoubtedly many other deaths in our cities and much illness can be attributed to air pollution.

One of the chief pollutants is carbon dioxide, a product of the combustion of organic fuels. The amount that has been added to the atmosphere is estimated to be enough to raise global temperatures by a degree or two. A related pollutant, carbon monoxide, results when combustion is incomplete. A thousand parts per million can kill quickly; most people are sickened if exposed for a few hours to concentrations of 100 parts per million. Concentrations about this high have been recorded in cities.

Another dangerous pollutant is sulfur dioxide, which oxidizes on contact with water to form sulfuric acid. Normally the concentration of these pollutants is only a few parts per million, but the concentration around some industrial plants is great enough so that whole hillsides may be deforested. Sulfur dioxide and sulfuric acid are exceedingly harmful to the respiratory system.

Nitrogen compounds, also released into the air, give rise to a complex of toxic substances. So do the simple hydrocarbons, like ethylene and the aldehydes (for example, formaldehyde).

A few other pollutants are arsines (a waste product of manufacturing processes in which

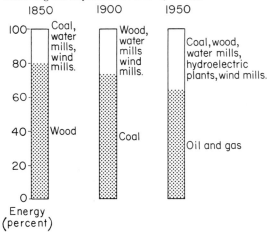

Figure 9.13 *Changes in proportions of energy supplied by different fuels or energy sources as a result of technological advances. Nuclear fuels are becoming an important source of energy.*

arsenical materials are used), phosgenes (carbonyl chloride, a waste product of chemical and dye manufacturing), cyanides, fluorides, and ash, soot, and smoke.

The various air pollutants become concentrated when there is little or no wind. Air chilled at the ground at night is sometimes overlain by a stratum of warm air that acts as a lid and prevents air circulation. This condition is called a thermal inversion. The confined cool layer may be only a few hundred feet thick. Smoke spreads laterally at the base of the layer of warm air and collects beneath it. The smoke and other pollutants continue to accumulate until the inversion is disrupted by wind or by heating of the ground and the lower stratum. The pollutants help keep the trapped air dense and prevent it from rising.

The chief damage, of course, is that people breathe the polluted air. The suggestion that people stop breathing has not been received with favor. In addition to killing people each year, air pollutants cause other damage. They dissolve clothing, stain buildings, corrode metal and paint, rot wood, wither shrubbery, and deforest mountain sides. Moreover, pollutants have sufficiently obscured air navigation as to cause accidents.

The causes? One of the worst offenders is the automobile, and the offense is about proportional to the horsepower. Economy cars not only burn less gasoline, but they contribute less to the polluted air.

The cures? Aesthetic arguments have not been very forceful and, curiously, neither has the health argument. The best argument probably is economic: automobiles, industrial and incinerator stacks, and burning trash piles should be taxed in proportion to their effluent.

Another cure is more grass, which uses the sun's rays to produce synthesizing carbohydrates by carbon dioxide during its green growth. In doing so it gives off oxygen:

$$6CO_2 + 6HO_2 \longrightarrow C_6H_{12}O_6 + 12O$$
$$\text{sugar}$$

A grass lawn 50 by 50 feet is said to release enough oxygen to meet the needs of a family of four, day by day.

Although cities are notoriously subject to smog, even a remote mountain valley with but one industrial plant can have bad smog conditions. With the spread of industry in the West, some Rocky Mountain valleys have been made almost uninhabitable because of air pollution.

And lastly, not only are we blackening our lungs and smarting our eyes with smog, now we also bruise our ears and nerves with noise from jackhammers, outboard motors, power lawn mowers, motorcycles, riveting machines, log cutters, jet engines, and sonic booms. Noise, though, does not kill; it only drives one crazy.

Resources for Outdoor Recreation

In recent years there has been a prodigious increase in the number of visitors to parks, forests, and other recreational areas. The number is expected to double in the next 10 years. The national parks and monuments are by far the best known, for they contain many spectacular examples of major geomorphic features, yet they account for only 10 percent of the visits. National forests account for 25 percent, and the state parks and forests account for 65 percent. Alleghany Park in New York is not widely known outside of the surrounding area, but the number of persons using it each year is nearly as great as the number visiting many of our best-known national parks.

Most of the national parks and forests are located in the West. We need these and more like them. Wilderness Areas are desirable, but most of these are in the West and, under present circumstances, are accessible chiefly to the wealthy. More parks and forests are needed in the eastern United States, where big-city congestion is greatest. The burden there is currently being carried by the comparatively modest state park and forest systems, but their attendance records, like those of Alleghany Park, prove the popularity of parks and forests near home. Development of more of the eastern mountains as parks and forests would provide recreational outlets for the cities and would help relieve poverty in Appalachia.

References

American Heritage, 1966, Pictorial atlas of United States history: New York, American Heritage Publ. Co.

Averitt, Paul, 1968, Stripping-coal resources of the United States: U.S. Geol. Survey Bull. 1251-C.

Cleppen, H., 1971, Professional forestry in the United States: Baltimore, Johns Hopkins Univ. Press.

Deasy, G. F., and Griess, P. R., 1963, An approach to the problem of coal strip mine reclamation: Pennsylvania State Univ. Col. Mineral Industries, v. 33, no. 1, pp. 1-7.

FAO, Department of Fisheries, 1972, Atlas of living resources of the sea: Rome, Italy.

Landesberg, H. H., 1964, Natural resources for United States growth—Resources for the future: Baltimore, Johns Hopkins Univ. Press.

Laporte, L. F., and others on Committee of Geological Sciences, NRC/NAS, 1972, The earth and human affairs: San Francisco, Canfield Press.

Levorsen, A. I., 1967, Geology of petroleum: 2nd ed., San Francisco, W. H. Freeman and Company.

Moss, F. E., 1967, The water crisis: New York, Praeger.

National Academy of Sciences-National Research Council, 1969, Resources and Man—A Study and Recommendations: San Francisco, W. H. Freeman and Company.

Park, C. F., Jr., 1968, Affluence in jeopardy: San Francisco, Freeman, Cooper & Co.

Paterson, J. H., 1970, North America—A geography of Canada and the United States: 4th ed., New York, Oxford Univ. Press.

Public Land Law Review Commission, 1970, One Third of the Nation's Land: Washington, D.C., Government Printing Office.

U.S. Bureau of the Census, 1960, Historical statistics of the United States, Colonial time to 1957: Washington, D.C., Government Printing Office.

U.S. Bureau of Mines, 1970, Mineral facts and figures: U.S. Bur. Mines Bull. 650.

U.S. Geological Survey, 1970, The national atlas of the United States of America: U.S. Geol. Survey.

Van Zandt, F. K., 1966, Boundaries of the United States and the several states: U.S. Geol. Survey Bull. 1212. (see also U.S. Geol. Survey Bull. 817.)

PART TWO

THE PROVINCES

This view west along the south shore of Martha's Vineyard, Massachusetts, illustrates the flatness of the Atlantic Coastal Plain and the broad sandy beaches that here form baymouth bars closing off the inlets. [From *Geology Illustrated* by John S. Shelton. W. H. Freeman and Company. Copyright © 1966.]

10

....

ATLANTIC AND GULF COASTAL PLAINS— EASTERN EDGE OF THE CONTINENT

Along the Gulf Coast and along the Atlantic seaboard northward to Cape Cod is the Coastal Plain, an elevated former sea bottom 100 to 200 miles wide that makes up almost 10 percent of the United States (Fig. 10.1). The still-submerged seaward part of this plain forms the Continental Shelf, which extends another 100 to 200 miles offshore to a depth of 500 to 600 feet below sea level and 1,000 miles northeastward from Cape Cod to the banks off Newfoundland. At the outer margin of the Continental Shelf the ocean bottom plunges downward, forming the steep *continental slope,* which descends to depths of more than 2 miles.

Among the outstanding features of the Coastal Plain are:

1. Because the Coastal Plain is an elevated sea bottom, it has low topographic relief and extensive marshy tracts.

2. With minor exceptions, altitudes are below 500 feet; more than half the plain is below 100 feet, and the half represented by the Continental Shelf is still submerged.

3. The geologic formations—Cretaceous, Tertiary, and Quaternary—are sedimentary deposits representing various onshore, near-

shore, and offshore environments; since the beginning of Cretaceous time the shoreline has receded as the Coastal Plain has been built outward by deposition of sediments and elevated by earth movements.

4. The formations dip gently seaward and crop out in belts forming cuestas and valleys roughly parallel to the inner and outer edges of the plain; the Cretaceous System forms an inland belt, the Tertiary an intermediate belt, and the Quaternary a coastal belt.

5. The surface of the plain slopes northward, and the valleys in the northern part are drowned to form Chesapeake, Delaware, and New York bays and Long Island Sound; northeast of Cape Cod the entire plain is submerged and forms the banks that are world famous for fishing—Georges, Browns, La Have, Sable Island, Banquereau, St. Pierre, and Grand Banks (Fig. 10.2).

6. The shore, more than 3,000 miles long, consists of sandy beaches, several set aside as national seashores; back of some of the beaches are swamps, like the Dismal Swamp in North Carolina and Virginia; there are mud flats at the delta of the Mississippi River, and coral banks at the southern tip of Florida.

210

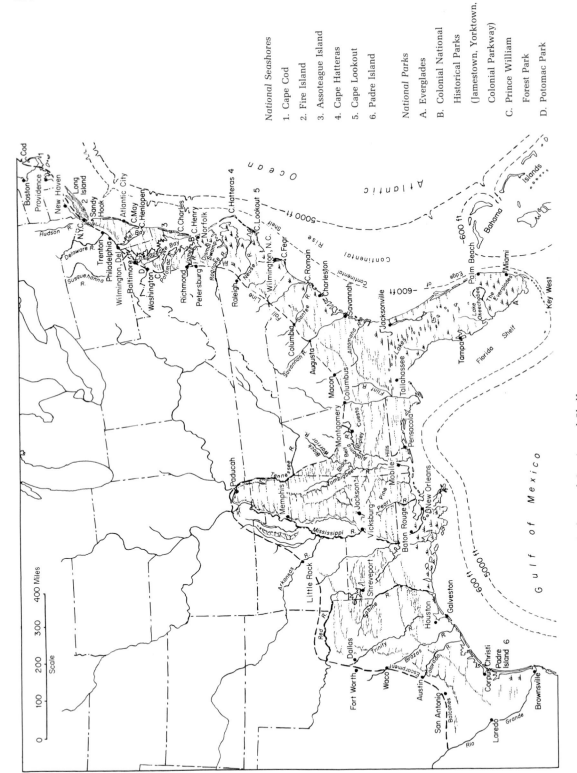

Figure 10.1 *Physiographic map of the Coastal Plain and Continental Shelf.*

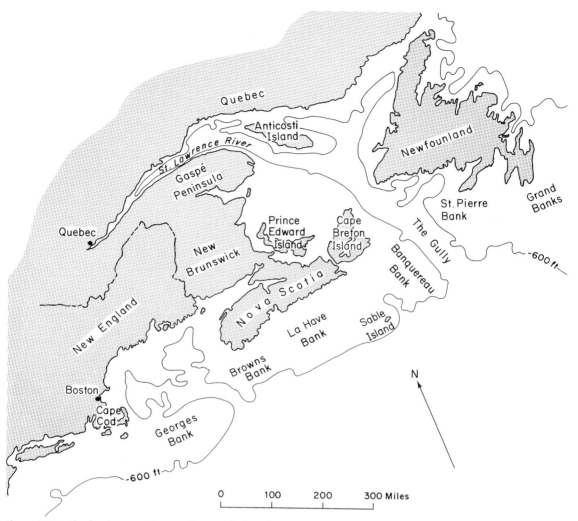

Figure 10.2 *The banks are submerged coastal plain forming the Continental Shelf off New England and the maritime provinces of Canada.*

7. The climate is rainy, except at the southwest, and the winters are mild, except at the northeast.

8. The Gulf Coastal Plain is subject to a high frequency of tornadoes; the Gulf and Atlantic coasts are both subject to fog and hurricanes.

9. Natural resources are varied and of great value. These include:

a. Harbors, some of the world's finest.

b. The Southeastern Pine Forest, which is one of the two principal lumber-producing forests in the United States, the other being in the Pacific Northwest.

c. Agricultural products, which include vegetables in the north; cotton, tobacco, and peanuts in the south; and fruits in Florida and southern Texas.

d. Fisheries, which (including the banks) provide more than half the combined total for Canada and United States.

e. Mineral products, which include oil and gas from the Gulf Coast; also sulfur, salt, and special-use clays, and in Florida, phosphate (for fertilizer).

f. Resort and recreational areas: the Atlantic coast beaches in summer and the Florida and Gulf coasts in winter; an inland waterway that enables small craft to travel safely almost the entire length of the coast.

A notable problem in the southeastern part is the underdeveloped human resource. Despite rich and varied natural resources, Alabama, Mississippi, and Louisiana share the dubious distinction of having the highest illiteracy rate in the country. Even Puerto Rico, crowded and lacking resources, is no worse. Good physical environment favors mankind, but does not determine his destiny.

The physiography has controlled both settlement and development of the Coastal Plain. From Long Island south to Cape Lookout, drowned valleys form the bays and harbors that favored early settlement of these parts of the Atlantic seaboard. The bays and harbors are still important; in fact, about one person in five in the United States lives within commuting distance of them.

From New Jersey to southern Virginia, tidewater extends inland to a line of falls, called the Fall Line, where the Coastal Plain borders the Piedmont Province. Most of the seaboard cities—Trenton, Philadelphia, Wilmington, Baltimore, Washington, Richmond, and Petersburg—are situated along the Fall Line. The growth of these cities was favored partly because each is situated at a head of navigation and partly because they are the most easterly places at which the rivers could be crossed easily. East of the Fall Line the rivers are broad, and twentieth-century technology was required to bridge or to tunnel under such bodies of water as the Hudson River, Delaware Bay, and Chesapeake Bay. The early colonists did not have the 100,000 miles of wire necessary for spinning cables to support suspension bridges across the rivers. Even the Brooklyn Bridge, a small structure by today's standards,

was not built until 1883. Early wagon roads connecting the Fall Line cities—and later the turnpikes and railroads—followed routes near the inner edge of the Coastal Plain, and at each river the roads turned westward to the falls.

South of the region of drowned valleys, the principal cities are located either along the coast (Norfolk, Wilmington, Charleston, Savannah, Jacksonville, Miami, Tampa, Mobile, Galveston, Corpus Christi, and Brownsville) or along the inner edge of the Coastal Plain (Raleigh, Columbia, Augusta, Macon, Montgomery, Little Rock, Dallas, Waco, Austin, and San Antonio). Few cities are located *within* the Coastal Plain; Houston, an exception, has joined itself by canal to the sea. New Orleans, Memphis, and other cities along the Mississippi are joined to the sea by that river.

Sandy beaches, especially barrier beaches (Fig. 10.3), are major features of the Atlantic and Gulf coasts. The barrier beaches are attributed to eustatic rise of sea level which causes them to migrate landward. A number of these have been set aside as national and state parks and beaches. National Sea Shores have been created at Cape Cod, Massachusetts; Fire Island, New York; Assoteague Island, Maryland; Cape Hatteras, North Carolina; and Padre Island, Texas. New York has developed public beaches along the barrier bars on the south side of Long Island. Florida has the Everglades National Park and a recently established marine park off the southern tip of the peninsula, where visitors may observe the ocean bottom and the offshore biota.

Structure, Boundaries, and Subdivisions

The geologic formations that form the surface of the Coastal Plain and at least the inner part of the Continental Shelf are Cretaceous, Tertiary, and Quaternary in age (Table 10.1). Figure 10.4 illustrates their general structure. The basement rocks on which these formations rest are of three kinds. Along the Atlantic seaboard the basement rocks are like those of the Piedmont Plateau, mostly metamorphic rocks but including some

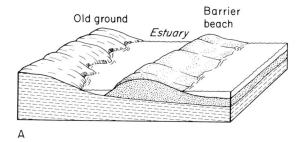

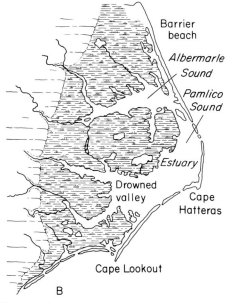

Figure 10.3 *A. Barrier beaches with estuaries behind
them B. Barrier beach islands and capes, drowned
valleys in the estuaries, with marsh and dismal
swamp between [From Geology of Soils by Charles B.
Hunt. W. H. Freeman and Company. Copyright ©
1972.]*

Triassic sedimentary rocks (Figs. 2.1, 2.2). Under
the Mississippi Valley, the basement rocks are
folded Paleozoic formations like those in the Valley and Ridge and Ouachita provinces. In Texas,
the basement is taken arbitrarily at the top of the
Lower Cretaceous formations, which in turn rest
on Jurassic and folded Paleozoic formations.

The basement rocks form the greater part of
the continental crust, and this crust thins seaward under the Coastal Plain and Continental

Shelf (Fig. 2.23). Near the inner edge of the
Coastal Plain the base of the crust is about 35
kilometers below sea level; under the shelf it rises
to about 25 kilometers below sea level.

Along the inner boundary of the Coastal Plain
the top of the basement rocks rises landward
from beneath the Cretaceous and Tertiary formations and forms the line of rapids and falls—the
Fall Line—where the rivers tumble off the Piedmont Plateau onto the Coastal Plain (Fig. 10.5).
The boundary is similar and equally distinct
along each side of the Mississippi Valley. In
Texas, the Lower Cretaceous formations are excluded from the Coastal Plain because they are
much faulted and uplifted, and form a dissected
plateau—the Edwards Plateau.

The Coastal Plain and Continental Shelf are
divided into eight sections (Fig. 10.6):

1. Submerged Section—the continental
shelf northeast of Cape Cod.
2. Embayed Section, where the Coastal
Plain and Continental Shelf slope north
from the Cape Fear Arch.
3. Cape Fear Arch.
4. Sea Islands Downwarp.
5. Peninsular Arch, in Florida.
6. East Gulf Coastal Plain.
7. Mississippi River Alluvial Plain.
8. West Gulf Coastal Plain.

These sections differ in their surface and subsurface geologic structure, geomorphology, soils,
hydrology, and economies.

The Continental Shelf and Coastal Plain together maintain a fairly constant width of about
200 miles from Georgia north to Cape Cod; as the
Coastal Plain narrows northward from Cape
Hatteras, the Continental Shelf widens. In Cretaceous time the Coastal Plain was submerged and
was part of the shelf (Fig. 10.7). In Eocene time,
most of the Coastal Plain still was submerged,
but the Cape Fear Arch had started forming and
that area was coastal plain. During Miocene time
the Coastal Plain was about half its present

Table 10.1

Geologic Formations on the Coastal Plain

Quaternary	Holocene and Pleistocene	Coastal and estuarine sand and gravel; alluvium; in Florida, marine limestone; loess along the east side of the Mississippi River Alluvial Plain.			
	Pliocene	Mostly river and estuarine terrace deposits of gravel, sand, and clay; some sinkhole deposits; marine shell marl and phosphate deposits in Florida and in South Carolina (Cohansey sand in New Jersey).			
Tertiary	Miocene	Yorktown Formation: marine sand, sandy clay, and marl. St. Mary's Formation: marine clay and sand. Choptank Formation: marine sand, clay, and marl. (Called Alum Bluff Group in eastern Gulf Coast; Hawthorn Limestone in Florida.) Calvert Formation: marine sand, clay, marl, and diatomaceous earth; Tampa Limestone in Florida.			
	Oligocene	Vicksburg Group: mostly marine limestone; some bentonite (volcanic ash).			
	Eocene and Paleocene	Jackson Group: marine limestone and nonmarine lignitic clay and sand; some volcanic ash. Claiborne Group: clay, siliceous clay, and clayey sandstone; brown iron ore, limy sandy clay, and clayey sand; phosphatic greensand. Wilcox Group: marine and estuarine sand; clay; some lignite. Midway Group: marine limestone, clay, limy clay, varicolored sand.			

	Upper	Western Gulf	Eastern Gulf	South Atlantic	North Atlantic
Cretaceous		**Gulf Series** — Navarro Formation: clay, chalk, sand, some volcanic ash. Taylor Marl: clay and marl; some volcanic ash. Austin Chalk; impure chalk. Eagle Ford Formation: bituminous clay. Woodbine Sandstone: iron-stained sand and clay.	Ripley Formation and Selma Chalk: chalk grades east and west into clay and sand. Eutaw Formation: limy and phosphatic beds; volcanic ash. Tuscaloosa Formation: sand, gravel, clay.	Peedee Formation: sand and clay. Black Creek Formation: lignitic clay and sand. Tuscaloosa Formation: clay, sand	Monmouth Formation: sand; marine. Matawan Formation dark, micaceous, sandy clay; marine. Magothy Formation: lignitic sand and clay; nonmarine. Raritan Formation: sand, clay; nonmarine.
	Lower	**Comanche Series** — Washita Group: limy, but more shaly and sandy than next older formation. Fredricksburg Group: clay, limestone, chalk, marl. Trinity Group: mostly sand, some thin beds of limestone.		Potomac Group: Patapsco Formation: nonmarine clay and sand. Arundel Formation: clay, lignite, bog iron ores; nonmarine. Patuxent Formation: sand, gravel; nonmarine.	
		Coahuila Series			

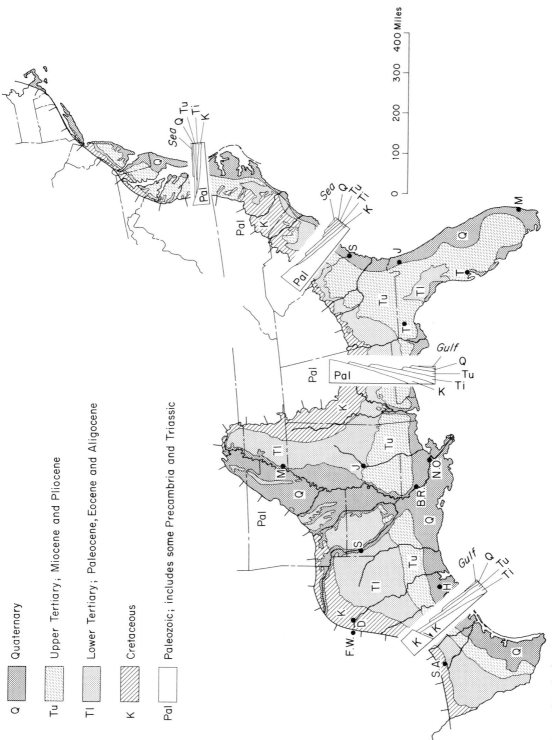

Figure 10.4 *Geologic map of the Coastal Plain Province, showing the position of geologic cross sections given in the text. The formations crop out in belts approximately parallel to the shore. Note that the formations are progressively older in the landward direction; refer to cross sections to understand why.*

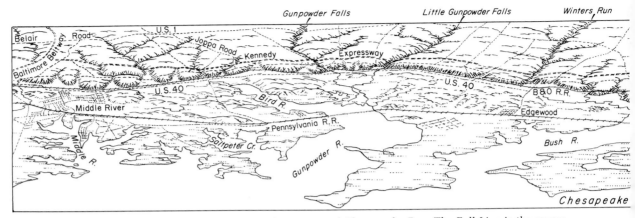

Figure 10.5 *Diagram of the Fall Line along the northwest part of Chesapeake Bay. The Fall Line is the escarpment at the Baltimore and Ohio Railroad. To the northwest is the hilly Piedmont Province; to the southeast is*

width. Even as late as Pleistocene time, parts of the Coastal Plain were still submerged. The present shoreline has developed since the last glacial period. In a sense, Florida is our youngest state, for it did not emerge until very late Tertiary time.

We still cannot be sure about the origin of the Continental Shelf and of the steep break at its outer edge, which has been described as the "world's greatest slope." The shelf probably is some kind of structural unit separated from the abyss and hinged to it by a belt of faulting or

folding. But the surface and the steep slope at the edge have been modified by sedimentation and erosion, including, at least in the shallow parts, alternate submergence and emergence.

SUBMERGED SECTION

The northeast end of the Coastal Plain and Continental Shelf, from Georges Bank to the Grand Banks east of Newfoundland, is almost wholly submerged. The Cretaceous and Tertiary formations that underlie the Coastal Plain formations south of Cape Cod, extend northward to become submerged platforms, known as banks, that lie offshore along the seaward part of the Continental Shelf. The banks are a nearly continuous series of flat-topped plateaus (Fig. 10.2) that occupy an area 300 miles wide and 1,000 miles long, and are separated from the mainland by a trough. Seaward is the continental slope, which is dissected by many submarine canyons; the deepest, known as The Gully, is 25 miles east of Sable Island.

There are three main groups of banks. Georges Bank, at the southwest, ends at a submarine valley opposite the mouth of the Bay of Fundy. Off Nova Scotia are several banks—Browns, La Have, Sable Island, and Banquereau—collectively referred to as the Scotian Banks. These are separated from the Grand Banks off Newfoundland by the Laurentian Channel, which extends

Figure 10.6 *Sections of the Coastal Plain.*

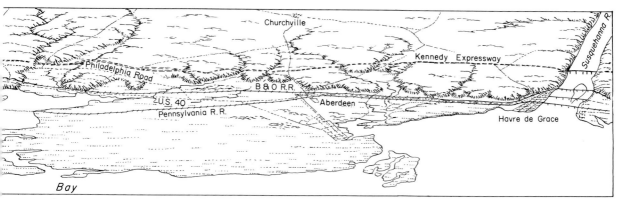

the low-lying Coastal Plain with the drowned valleys and tidewater extending to the Fall Line.

up the Gulf of St. Lawrence and the St. Lawrence River to Quebec. The channel is 600 feet deep near Quebec and more than 1,000 feet deep where it crosses the continental shelf between the Scotian and Grand Banks.

The flat, glaciated surfaces of the banks lie at depths of only 100 to 200 feet, so that the water receives enough light for a prolific growth of phytoplankton, which is the basis for the tremendous schools of fish in the water over the banks.

Although Cretaceous and Tertiary marine sedimentary rocks have been dredged from various places along the banks, the thickness of those formations is not known. Seismic refraction measurements indicate that sediments and sedimentary rocks extend to a depth of about 5 kilometers at the edge of the shelf, but part of this thickness could be pre-Cretaceous. Beneath the sedimentary rocks, crustal rocks of continental type extend to a depth of perhaps 10 kilometers; below that depth are denser oceanic crustal rocks (compare Fig. 2.23).

EMBAYED SECTION

The Embayed Section extends from Cape Cod to about the Neuse River in North Carolina. At the north end, east of the Hudson River, all but the highest parts of the Coastal Plain are submerged and joined with the Continental Shelf.

Cape Cod, Nantucket Island, Martha's Vineyard, Block Island, and Long Island are the tops of ridges formed by Coastal Plain formations and capped by glacial drift (Fig. 10.8). The north end of the Embayed Section, including small areas west of the Hudson River at Staten Island and in northern New Jersey, is the only part of the Coastal Plain that was glaciated. Two terminal moraines form ridges of gravel and sand extending the length of Long Island; these ridges form the "fishtail" extensions at the east end of the Island.

Barrier beaches extend almost the entire length of Long Island and New Jersey (Fig. 10.8). These are popular resort areas, and along the south side of Long Island extensive stretches have wisely been set aside as state parks. Some of the bars have closed the mouths of small bays and converted them into ponds.

The southern part of the Embayed Section also is characterized by barrier beaches, but only the lowermost parts of the valleys are drowned (Fig. 10.9); upstream, as far west as the Fall Line, there are stretches of swampy tidal flats (Fig. 10.10).

The formations in this part of the Embayed Section dip and thicken eastward (Fig. 10.11), but against the north flank of the Cape Fear Arch the younger formations extend landward and unconformably overlap the older ones. At the Fall Line in Delaware and Maryland, Lower Creta-

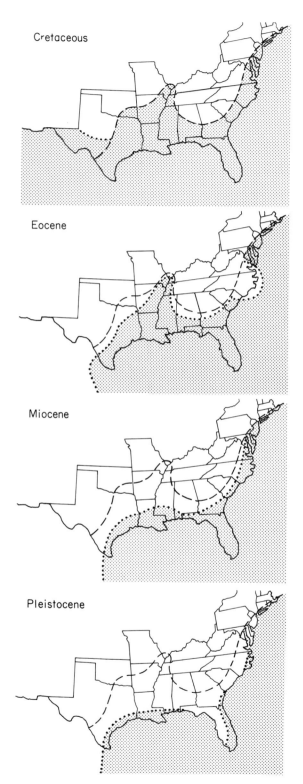

Cretaceous

Eocene

Miocene

Pleistocene

ceous formations overlie the crystalline rocks of the Piedmont Plateau (too thin to be shown in Fig. 10.4), and the Lower Cretaceous is overlain by Upper Cretaceous formations and these, in turn, by Eocene formations. Near the Potomac River the Eocene formations extend unconformably across the Upper Cretaceous and rest on the Lower Cretaceous. South of the Potomac River, the Eocene formations unconformably overlap the Cretaceous and extend onto the crystalline rocks of the Piedmont Plateau. South of Rappahannock River, Miocene formations overlap the Eocene and extend onto the crystalline rocks of the Piedmont Province. These unconformable overlaps are very important in interpreting the geologic history and the subsurface structure because they record structural movements that took place while the formations were being deposited.

North of the Rappahannock River the boundary between the Coastal Plain and the Piedmont Plateau is marked by an escarpment—the Fall Line. South of that river the boundary is not very distinct topographically, being marked chiefly by a difference in kind of topography and soil without much difference in altitude across the boundary, and tidewater does not reach to the Fall Line.

VALLEY-CUTTING IN THE EMBAYED SECTION. Delaware Bay is the submerged channel of the Delaware River, which apparently has followed its present course southward along the inner edge of the Coastal Plain since Pliocene time, because most of the Coastal Plain of New Jersey is blanketed with Pliocene estuarine and littoral deposits. Pleistocene deposits form gravel-covered terraces along the river and these extend southward along the Delmarva Peninsula east of Chesapeake Bay, marking a former more southerly course (Fig. 11.31).

The Susquehanna River may have joined the Delaware on the Delmarva Peninsula near Salisbury, where wells drilled for water encountered

Figure 10.7 *Extent of the Coastal Plain during the Cretaceous, Eocene, Miocene, and Pleistocene. Submerged areas stippled. Compare Figures 2.1 and 10.5.*

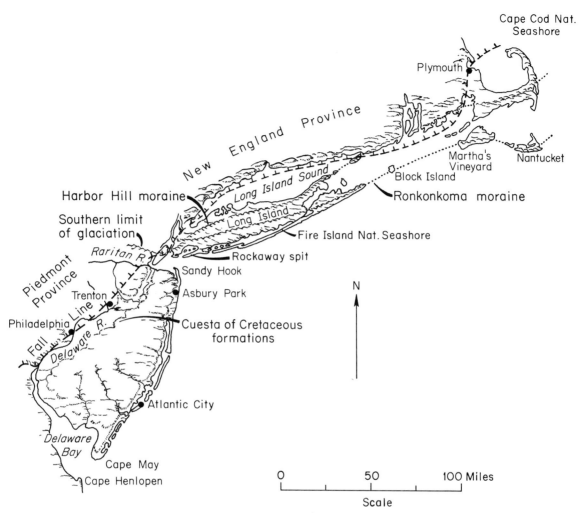

Figure 10.8 *Physiographic diagram of the north end of the Embayed Section of the Coastal Plain. East of the Hudson River all but the highest parts of the Coastal Plain are submerged. Long Island and the islands to the east are ridges of Coastal Plain formations capped by glacial deposits.*

a buried river gravel 200 feet below the surface. The gravel was evidently deposited during one of the Pleistocene glaciations, when sea level was 200 or more feet lower than it is today. Subsequently the Susquehanna was captured by a tributary of the Potomac River and turned southward. Further evidence of the lower stand of sea level are the occurrences of Pleistocene elephant remains and fresh water peat dredged from the bottom of Chesapeake Bay and from the Continental Shelf.

The earliest record of the Potomac River is a gravel deposit on the uplands of the Coastal Plain 15 miles southeast of Washington, D.C. (Figs. 10.12, 10.13). The gravels, 200 to 250 feet above the present river, rest on Miocene deposits and are thought to be Pliocene in age but might be early Pleistocene.

On the Piedmont Plateau, at Great Falls National Park west of Washington, the River crosses a series of steeply dipping, exceedingly resistant rocks in which downcutting progresses slowly

Figure 10.9 *Physiographic diagram of the southern part of the Embayed Section of the Coastal Plain.*

(Fig. 10.14). Downstream from the Falls the rocks are less resistant, and the river has cut a gorge in them. Still farther downstream, in the Coastal Plain, the valley is broad and deep. As sea level was lowered during the Pleistocene glaciations, downcutting must have taken place rapidly in the easily eroded rocks of the Coastal Plain.

CAPE FEAR ARCH

On the Cape Fear Arch the formations are about 2,500 feet higher than in the Embayed Section, which is to say that the structural uplift

there amounts to about 2500 feet. Cretaceous formations are exposed at the surface across most of the arch (Fig. 10.4), but to the north and south these are overlain by Tertiary formations (Figs. 10.12, 10.15). Along the coast, between the Quaternary and the Cretaceous, is a narrow outcrop of marine Pliocene deposits.

The boundary between the Coastal Plain and the Piedmont Plateau at the edge of this section is a well-defined contact between the Cretaceous formations and the crystalline rocks of the Piedmont Plateau but there is little topographic relief across this boundary. Valleys deepen as they enter the Coastal Plain, and are marked by falls. Columbia, South Carolina, is the principal Fall Line city in this section.

The northern boundary of the Cape Fear Arch is taken arbitrarily at about the Neuse River, and the south boundary near the Santee River. Near these rivers the Miocene formations extend far inland and unconformably overlap the Cretaceous formations.

The Cape Fear Section has a distinctive coastline, being marked by three large, smooth scallops between Capes Hatteras, Lookout, Fear, and Romain. The scallops are being eroded and the debris transported to the capes. The smoothness of the scallops and the fact that they are being eroded suggests an emergent, smooth sea floor, as if uplift were continuing.

SEA ISLANDS DOWNWARP

In Georgia the Coastal Plain formations are folded into the Sea Islands Downwarp, between the Cape Fear Arch and the Peninsular Arch in Florida. The Fall Line of the Coastal Plain continues, with Augusta, Macon, and Columbus, Georgia the principal Fall Line cities. The coastline is marked by many islands in a belt about 10 miles wide (Fig. 10.16). Much of the land is salt marsh, but the outermost edges of many islands have firm sandy beaches. In places there are dunes, some of which are moving inland. That the islands are due to very recent downwarping, or rise of sea level, is indicated by stumps of live oak on beaches where they are covered by high tide. Some tidal marshes have

Figure 10.10 *Bald cypress trees with hanging Spanish moss, vegetation typical of Dismal Swamp, may be seen at Seashore State Park, Virginia. [Courtesy Virginia Division of Parks.]*

encroached a quarter mile onto dry land in the last half century.

Curious and still unexplained features of the landscape in this part of the Coastal Plain are the thousands of oval depressions, most of them lakes or marshes. These, the Carolina Bays, are best known in North and South Carolina but are found as far north as Maryland. They range from a few to hundreds of acres in area and from a few feet to more than 30 feet in depth. Most are oriented northwest-southeast. The bays occur on all kinds of ground, including uplands and floodplains. Rims around the bays are sandy, and most are best developed on the southeast side. One theory holds that they are meteorite scars, but no meteorites or fused materials have been found, nor have bays been found west of the Fall Line. Another theory attributes them to the action of storm winds. Another attributes them to spring action, and a few do have springs. Another

theory attributes them to shoreline eddies during oscillations of sea level, although they extend too high for this. Still another theory attributes them to frost action during Pleistocene glacial stages.

PENINSULAR ARCH

Florida is the emerged, highest part of an anticlinal ridge—the Peninsular Arch. Its boundaries with the neighboring sections on the Coastal Plain are arbitrary. The Bahama Shelf southeast of Florida, the Continental Shelf east of Florida, and the Florida Shelf to the west are all part of the arch. The submerged part is twice as long and three times as wide as Florida (Fig. 10.17). Between Florida and the Bahama Islands the arch is broken by a transverse trough through which the Gulf Stream flows.

The arch is underlain by Cretaceous limestone and shale more than 10,000 feet thick under the

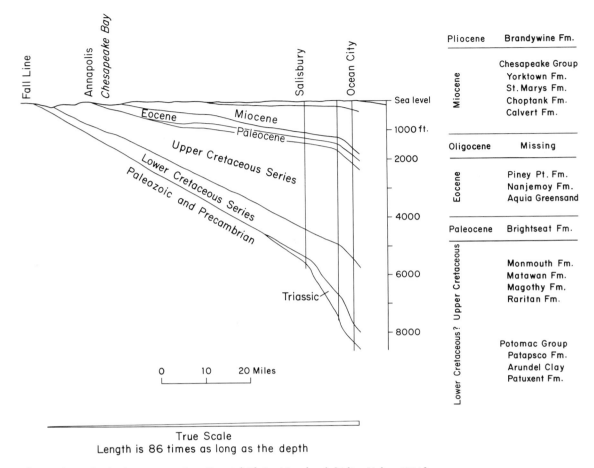

Figure 10.11 *Geologic cross section, Coastal Plain, Maryland. [After Vokes 1961.]*

central and southern part of the peninsula. The formations thin northward toward the Fall Line in Georgia. Resting on the Cretaceous formations are comparatively thin Eocene, Miocene, and Pliocene deposits. During Cretaceous time the site of Florida was a basin in which the 2-mile thickness of sediments was deposited. Since the beginning of Tertiary time, Florida has been a shallow shelf area, and part of the time, as now, elevated above sea level.

Florida is a land of lakes, many occupying sinkholes dissolved in the limestone formations (Fig. 10.18). The limestone is cavernous, especially in central Florida, and has proved troublesome for some whose house foundations have collapsed

into the subterranean cavities. Southern Florida is the site of the Everglades. Lake Okeechobee, about 18 feet above sea level and covering about 750 square miles, has a maximum depth of only about 15 feet.

The peninsula has a varied coastline, with barrier beaches along the Atlantic Coast, rocky stretches between bays protected by barrier beaches along the west coast and by coral reefs and mangrove swamps around the south end. The eastern keys are elongate islands of Pleistocene coral reef flanked by modern coral; the western keys are irregular islands of marine limestone. The coral growths, like others that border continental shores, are known as fringing

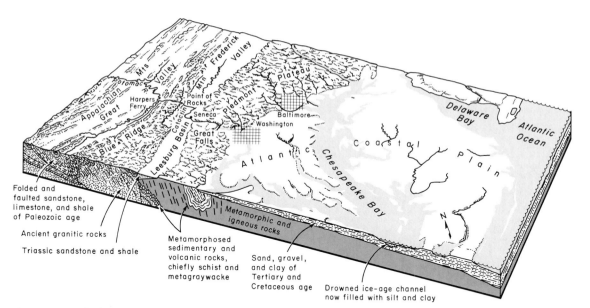

Figure 10.12 *Block diagram of the Washington, D.C., region, showing physiographic provinces and geographic and geologic features. (After U.S.G.S.)*

reefs and are characterized by shallow water, in contrast to the barrier reefs and atolls at oceanic islands (see Chapter 20).

GULF COAST SECTIONS

Along the Gulf Coast the formations are much thicker than those along the Atlantic Coast—about three times as thick. But like the formations along the Atlantic Coast, they thin landward and form belts parallel to the coast; the resistant formations form cuestas, and the easily eroded ones form the valleys (Fig. 10.19).

The East Gulf Coastal Plain is separated from the West Gulf Coastal Plain by the Mississippi Alluvial Plain. In the East Gulf Coastal Plain, the Fall Line swings westward around the south end of the Piedmont, Valley and Ridge, and Appalachian Plateau provinces. In a sense, the Fall Line ends in central Alabama, because the streams farther west have no falls where they flow from the Appalachian Highlands to the Coastal Plain formations. Moreover, there is no abrupt change in topography between the high-

lands and the Fall Line Hills of the Coastal Plain (Fig. 10.19), despite the change in geologic formations and kind of ground.

The Fall Line Hills are sandy ground formed by the Tuscaloosa and Eutaw Formations of Upper Cretaceous age. South of the Fall Line Hills is a lowland, the Black Belt, named for its characteristic black soil, developed on the Selma Chalk, and one of the most fertile areas in the region.

South of the Black Belt is a ridge, the Ripley Cuesta, south of which is lowland developed on formations of the Midway Group (basal Eocene); farther south is another belt of hills formed by the Wilcox and Claiborne groups, also of Eocene age. South of these hills, in eastern Alabama and Georgia, is a plain developed on the uppermost Eocene and dotted with sinkholes. Much of the drainage is underground. South of this plain are the sandy Pine Hills on the Pliocene Citronelle Formation. Along the coast is a lowland developed on Quaternary deposits, mostly sand along the present beaches. The string of low bluffs paralleling the beach apparently marks the site of an elevated former shoreline.

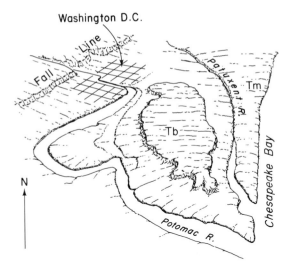

Figure 10.13 *Diagram of upland river gravel (Tb, Brandywine Formation) southeast of Washington, D.C., that represents an ancient (probably Pliocene) alluvial fan of the Potomac River. At the time the gravels were deposited, the river was in its present gorge across the Fall Line, and at the position of Washington the gorge was then perhaps 50 to 100 feet deep. Since then, probably in response to a lowering of sea level during the glacial stages of the Pleistocene, the river cut deeply (another 200–250 feet) into the coastal plain formations (Tm, Miocene), where they were not protected by gravel, and found its course around the south side of the old fan. The course of the Patuxent River is around the north side of the old fan.*

The structure and general topography of the West Gulf Coastal Plain are similar to those in the East Gulf Coastal Plain (Fig. 10.20). The escarpments are less well developed, but the barrier beaches are especially well developed. One of these, Padre Island (Fig. 10.1), extends 125 miles north from the mouth of the Rio Grande. The West Gulf Coastal Plain ends inland at the escarpment formed by the Balcones fault zone, which marks the edge of the Edwards Plateau.

The Mississippi River Alluvial Plain, which is 500 miles long and 50 to 100 miles wide (Fig. 10.21), has an average southward slope of less than 8 inches per mile. At the junction of the Ohio and Mississippi rivers the altitude is about 275 feet. Midway from there to the coast, near

northern Louisiana, the altitude is 100 feet; in the last 250 miles the slope averages less than 6 inches per mile, and because the river follows a meandering course its gradient is only about half that. This is the land of oxbow lakes—the cutoff meanders. According to Mark Twain, cutting off the meanders would so shorten the Mississippi River that Cairo, Illinois, would soon be joined to New Orleans.

The alluvial fill unconformably overlies and conceals the Coastal Plain formations, which in turn overlie and conceal the Paleozoic and other ancient rock formations.

The Mississippi Alluvial Plain is divided into five basins. In Louisiana, west of the river, is the Atchafalaya Basin, which was the site of the Mississippi River delta some hundreds of years ago. West of the river, between Natchez and Vicksburg, is the Tensas Basin. On the east side, above Vicksburg is the Yazoo Basin. Farther upstream, in northeastern Arkansas, there are the basins of the St. Francis and Black rivers. Parts of each basin are lower than the Mississippi River, which is an aggrading stream. For example, the Mississippi River at 100 feet above sea level is 25 to 50 feet higher than the Ouachita River due west in the Tensas Basin. For emergency flood control these basins can be backfilled with flood waters from the Mississippi. The basins probably are due chiefly to irregular deposition by the Mississippi River, but in part they may be due to downfaulting or downfolding of the Coastal Plain formations and basement rocks that underlie the alluvial fill. Such movement took place during the New Madrid earthquake of 1811–1812 (see p. 229).

During the Pleistocene the Mississippi River discharged major floods of meltwaters from the ice sheets, and these deposited a series of gravel and sand formations that now form terraces along the sides of the river and its branches. The oldest and highest, the Williana Formation, forms a terrace about 200 feet above the rivers. It is 50 to 75 feet thick and consists of sand and gravel at the base, a sand member in the middle, and silt beds at the top. The next lower terrace is formed by the Bentley Formation, which aver-

225

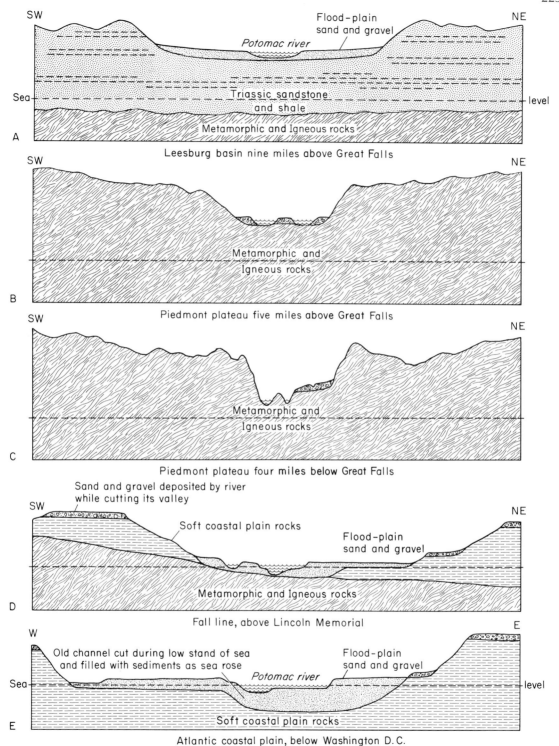

Figure 10.14 *Cross sections of Potomac River Valley, showing typical shape in each landscape province. Each cross section is approximately 4 miles long. (After U.S.G.S.)*

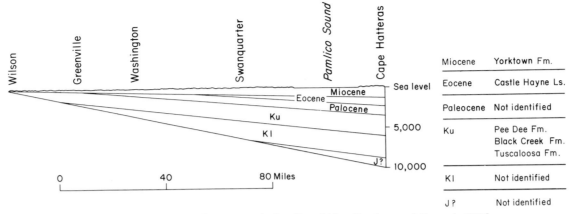

Figure 10.15   *Cross section of coastal plain in North Carolina. [After Stuckey and Conrad, 1958.]*

ages about 60 feet thick. Its surface is about 150 feet higher than the rivers, and also consists of gravels toward the base and increasingly fine sediments toward the top. The next lower terrace, about 100 feet above the rivers, is formed

by the Montgomery Formation, about 115 feet thick. It is mostly clay and sand but increasingly sandy toward the base and gravelly toward the edges of the deposit. The lowest terrace, formed by the Prairie Formation, is 20 feet above the Holocene alluvial floodplain of the rivers. The formation is 20 to more than 50 feet thick and grades from a basal gravel up to silt and clay. The four formations have been correlated with the rises in sea level that are associated with the melting and retreat of the four main continental glaciations—the Prairie correlated with the Wisconsinan, the Montgomery with the Illinoian, the Bentley with the Kansan, and the Williana with the Nebraskan Glaciation.

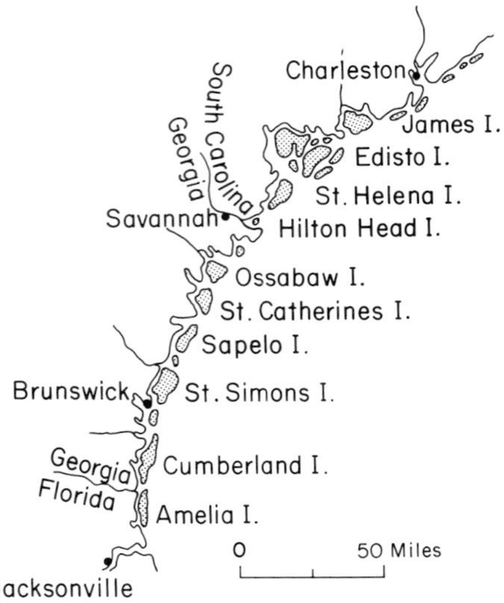

DELTA OF THE MISSISSIPPI RIVER—
LAND OF BAYOUS

The site of New Orleans has been described as the flattest, lowest, and geologically youngest of any major city in the United States. The delta consists of Holocene sediments deposited by the Mississippi River (Fig. 10.22), and the city is built on one of the youngest parts of the delta, a part that was built above sea level about the time of the Battle of Hastings (A.D. 1066).

Some of the stages in the development of the Mississippi River delta over the past 2,000 years are illustrated in Figure 10.22. The big delta is

Figure 10.16   *Sea Islands along the Georgia–South Carolina coast are the result of sea advancing into the downwarp; locally the salt water encroachment is recent enough to have killed oak trees. The rise of sea level here may be accentuated by tectonic downwarping coupled with the eustatic rise.*

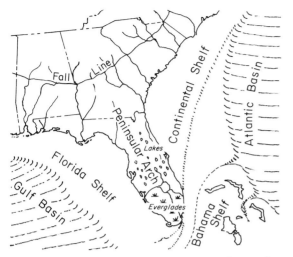

Figure 10.17 *Florida is the highest, emerged part of the Peninsular Arch, which extends southeastward between the Atlantic and Gulf basins.*

composed of coalescing smaller deltas deposited as the river was diverted first one way and then another. It has been described as an area that could not decide whether to be land or water. What *is* land is scarcely a foot or so above high tide, and the tremendous number of winding and dividing waterways, or bayous, are characteristic of the delta. The land has deep back soil that produces three crops a year and sometimes four. The shores are lined with sedges, reed grasses, and palmetto. The brownish waters are the winter home for a vast bird population that in summertime scatters over the entire continent (Fig. 10.23). Most south Louisianans are Acadians, descendants of those who moved from Canada in the eighteenth century.

Floods deposit natural levees on each side of the riverbanks, with the result that most streams flow on ground slightly higher than the ground on either side of the levees. Floods occasionally breach the levees and follow new courses on low ground until the ground is built up too high to contain floods. Parts of New Orleans are 5 feet below sea level (see Appendix B).

Fringing the delta and paralleling the coast are ridges of sand and shell a few feet high, relicts of old barrier beaches. They are known as chênières (French *chen,* oak), as they commonly support stands of live oak. Oaks near the gulf are subject to strong landward winds and salt spray; many are bent landward and partly defoliated.

Another kind of upland feature near the shores of the delta are the hummocks, or so-called islands, on the surface above buried salt plugs (p. 231). The highest, Avery Island, is almost 200 feet higher than the surrounding marshes. Five such mounds form the Five Islands along the shore of the delta from New Iberia to the Atchafalaya. More than 100 salt domes are known in southern Louisiana, but only a few have surface expression. Some of these undoubtedly provided salt licks for Pleistocene animals.

There are three kinds of lakes on the delta: brackish lakes behind barrier beaches, crescentic oxbow lakes along the Mississippi River, and lowland lakes flooded by groundwater. All of these grade into marshes that support grasses and sedges or grade into swamps. Deep swamps are characterized by cypress and tupelo, whereas shallow ones may support a variety of hardwoods.

In the past the delta's wealth involved three seasons of activity: first gathering crabs, then shrimp, and finally trapping muskrat. Today the principal source of wealth is oil, including that

Figure 10.18 *Limestone sinks in Florida. The lake country in Florida is underlain by cavernous limestone (Miocene), and the surface is dotted with sinks caused by solution of the limestone and by collapse of cavern roofs. Sinks deeper than the water table contain lakes; shallower ones (southeast of Lake Starr) are dry. The Florida lakes are much used for recreation and for homesites.*

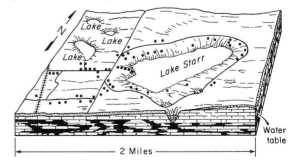

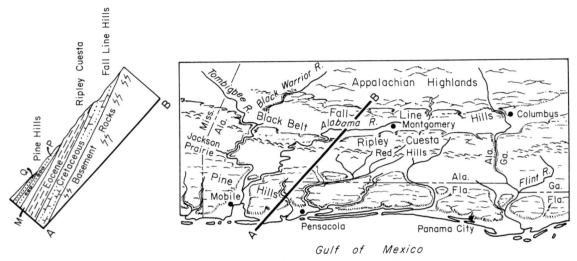

Figure 10.19 *Diagrammatic view and cross section of the East Gulf Coastal Plain. Upper Cretaceous formations form the Fall Line Hills (Tuscaloosa and Eutaw Formations), Black Belt (Selma Chalk), and Ripley Cuesta (Ripley Formation). Eocene formations (Midway Formation, Wilcox and Claiborne Groups, and Jackson Formation) extend from there to the Pine Hills. Pliocene deposits (P, Citronelle Formation) form the Pine Hills and unconformably overlie the Miocene (M). Along the coast are Quaternary (Q) deposits.*

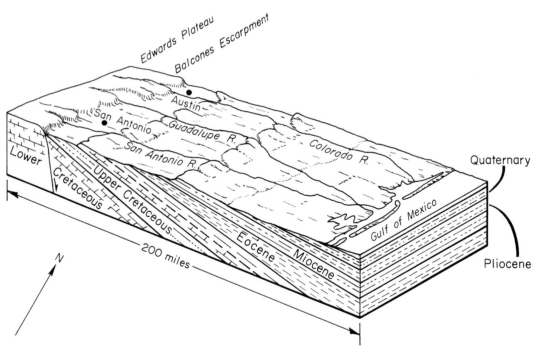

Figure 10.20 *Block diagram illustrating the relation of escarpments and cuestas to the structural geology of part of the West Gulf Coastal Plain.*

produced offshore. Pipelines carry the oil from the offshore rigs to storage tanks on shore. The delta also produces rice and salt. The intracoastal waterway connects bays and bayous about 10 to 20 miles inland from the open waters of the Gulf.

* * *

The Cretaceous and Tertiary formations in the East and West Gulf Coastal Plains, and beneath the Mississippi River Alluvial Plain are thicker than those along the Atlantic Plain and they are more folded and faulted. The principal structural features are illustrated in Figure 10.24. Most of these structural features lie in two belts, one near the inner edge of the Coastal Plain and another along the coast and extending offshore. Some of the folds form broad upwarps, like the Sabine Uplift and Jackson Dome; others form structural basins. The folds are accompanied by faults that trend parallel to the general strike of the formations. Most of the fault blocks are downthrown toward the coast.

Associated structures are formed by salt plugs—masses of salt a mile or more wide that have been plastically squeezed upward from salt beds that probably lie 4 or 5 miles below the surface. As Figure 10.25 shows, the formations penetrated by the salt plugs are dragged upward, and the younger, near-surface formations are domed. Many salt plugs have reached the surface, where they are reflected in the topography and vegetation. The plugs, which consist chiefly of rock salt, are usually capped with gypsum; some with sulfur. Much of the oil produced along the outer part of the Coastal Plain (p. 212) has been obtained from the flanks of the structural domes formed by the plugs. The plugs are also a major source of the world's sulfur and salt.

Earthquakes provide historical evidence about the instability of parts of the Coastal Plain. The head of the Mississippi River Alluvial Plain was the site of one of the most severe earthquakes recorded in the United States—the New Madrid, Missouri, earthquake, which occurred in 1811 and 1812. Despite the fact that some of the land there subsided 9 feet as a result of the earthquake (Fig. 10.26), damage was slight because the region

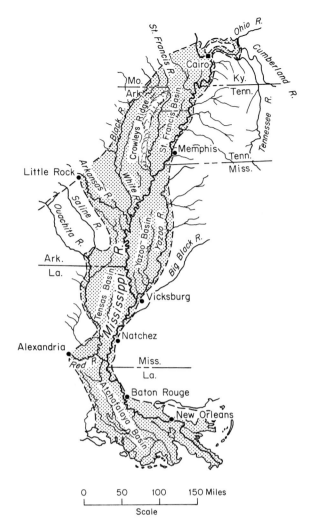

Figure 10.21 *Drainage system of the Mississippi River Alluvial Section. Many of the tributaries have flatter gradients than the Mississippi River, and flood waters can be turned back into them. For example, above its junction with the White River, the Mississippi descends about 25 feet in 45 miles (straight-line distance) whereas the White River descends 25 feet in 60 miles. Much of the Yazoo Basin is as low or lower than the neighboring stretch of the Mississippi River.*

was sparsely settled. The occurrence of a similar earthquake today would be disastrous.

Another major earthquake virtually destroyed Charleston, South Carolina, in 1886. This quake damaged practically every building in Charleston, bent railroad tracks, and produced fissures and depressions.

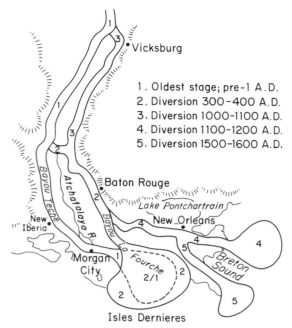

Figure 10.22 *Stages in the development of the Mississippi River delta. (1) Oldest stage, before* A.D. *1. (2) Diversion,* A.D. *300-400. (3) Diversion,* A.D. *1000–1100. (4) Diversion,* A.D. *1100–1200. (5) Diversion,* A.D. *1500–1600.*

Climate

Most of the Coastal Plain Province has a rainy climate, with mild winters, but the southwestern part is semiarid, and the northeastern part, although rainy, has severe winters.

The maximum average annual temperature, 75°F, has been recorded at the southern tip of Florida. The 70° isotherm extends across northern Florida to New Orleans, Galveston, and San Antonio. The 60° isotherm extends from about Norfolk to near the head of the Mississippi River Alluvial Section. The 50° isotherm passes through Long Island and other parts of the north end of the Embayed Section. An effect of proximity to the ocean is shown by the maximum and minimum temperatures recorded. The maxima, between 100 and 110°F, are only 5° to 10° above the average annual maximum temperatures. The minima are only about 10° below the average annual minimum.

The average length of the frost-free period is about 180 days at the north end of the Coastal Plain. The number of frost-free days increases southward to more than 300 along the Gulf Coast (Fig. 4.3). The average depth of frost penetration decreases southward from almost 20 inches on Long Island to less than 1 inch along the Gulf Coast (Fig. 4.3).

Across the West Gulf Coastal Plain precipitation increases from an annual average of 20 inches along the Rio Grande to 60 inches in southern Louisiana and southern Florida. Along most of the Atlantic Coast it is between 40 and 50 inches. This precipitation is distributed rather evenly throughout the year. Annual precipitation has never been less than 20 inches except in the western half of the West Gulf Coastal Plain, where precipitation has been less than 20 inches for 50 percent of the years on record, and high evaporation contributes to the aridity.

Excessive precipitation can be as devastating as drought. Every part of the Coastal Plain has experienced 2.5 inches or more of rain in an hour. Four inches in an hour has been recorded at several places from Virginia southward along the Atlantic Coast and westward across the Gulf

Figure 10.23 *Major flyways along which birds of North America migrate.*

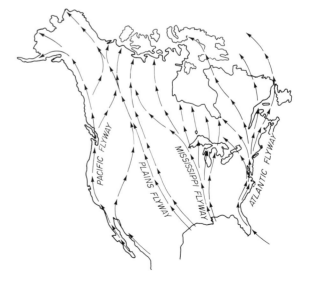

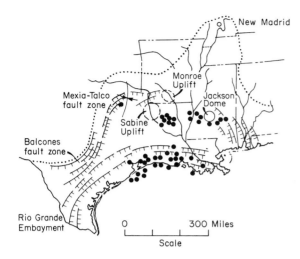

Key

⊤⊤⊤ Fault,
hachures on down–dropped side

• Salt plug

✕ Syncline

Figure 10.24 *Major structural features of the Gulf Coast sections.*

Coast to Galveston. Average annual snowfall is 30 inches on Long Island, 10 inches in Virginia, and less than 1 inch along the Gulf Coast and southernmost part of the Atlantic Coast (Fig. 4.3).

Tornadoes are most common in the Mississippi River Alluvial Section and in the adjoining parts of the East and West Gulf Coastal Plains. During the 30-year period ending in 1950, every 50-mile square of this area was struck by about a dozen tornadoes, and in the whole of that area more than 2,000 persons were killed. During the same period the Embayed Section of the Coastal Plain was struck by about 5 tornadoes per 50-mile square and about 75 persons were killed. Tornado frequency in the Gulf sections of the Coastal Plain is greatest between October and April, and greatest during the afternoon and evening.

Hurricanes (Fig. 10.27) that strike at our Coastal Plain form over the Caribbean Sea, mostly in late summer and fall. They first move westward with the trade winds, but then curve

northward around the west side of the high-pressure areas that prevail over the central Atlantic Ocean. High winds accompanying hurricanes create tides as much as 8 to 10 feet above normal. The winds lose their force as they move inland or to middle latitudes. In an average year the coast is struck by about 5 hurricanes.

The effects of past climates on the Coastal Plain are manifest chiefly in the loessial deposits east of the Mississippi River (Fig. 6.1), the gravel deposits and terraces along the river, the Red and Yellow Podzolic soils, and the eustatic changes in sea level that so greatly affect river histories (pp. 91, 137).

Vegetation, Agriculture

Most of the Coastal Plain is covered by the Southeastern Pine Forest (Fig. 10.28), which extends from eastern Texas to North Carolina. It is bounded on the north by the Mixed Oak and Pine Forest that is transitional northward to the Hardwood Forests (Figs. 8.3, 8.4). The distribution and distinguishing leaf and cone characteristics of

Figure 10.25 *Block diagram of salt plug and dome.*

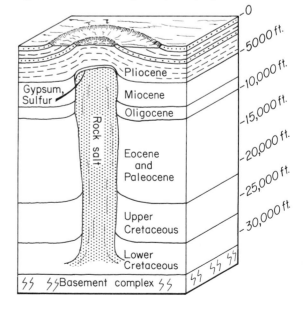

Figure 10.26 *Tree stumps in Reelfoot Lake, Tennessee, where hardwood forest was killed by drowning when the land subsided 3 to 9 feet during the New Madrid earthquake, 1811–1812.*

some common pine trees in these parts of the Coastal Plain are shown in Figure 8.5.

Shortleaf, loblolly, longleaf, and slash pine are important timber trees that provide about a third of the total timber production of the United States. Longleaf and slash pine provide about two-thirds of the world's production of turpentine and rosin, products known as "naval stores" because in the early days tar and pitch were produced chiefly for sailing vessels. This industry figured prominently in our early industrial history. Tar and pitch were needed for the British navy; a bounty was paid for production of naval stores, and their export other than to Britain was prohibited by the Navigation Acts.

The pines grow principally on sandy uplands. The principal other trees on the uplands, in order of their importance or abundance, are, according to the U.S. Forest Service:

Southern red, black, post, laurel, cherrybark, and willow oaks
Sweetgum
Winged, American, and cedar elms

Figure 10.27 *Weather over North America and the Atlantic Ocean, illustrating two hurricanes in the Atlantic, one in the Caribbean Sea, and a front approaching the Mississippi Valley. Photographed by satellite. [Courtesy Environmental Science Services Administration.]*

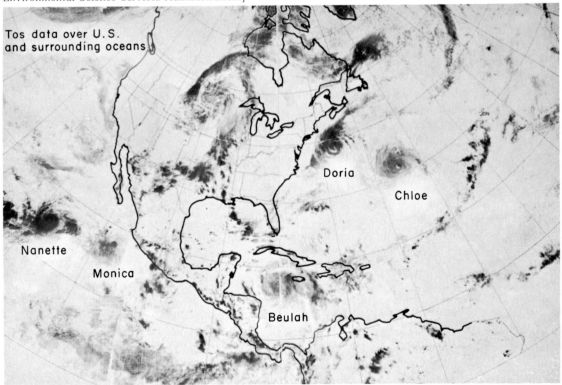

Figure 10.28 *Slash pine, with palmetto, representing the Southern Pine Forest in Florida at Honton Island State Park. [Photograph by Walter J. Kenner, courtesy Florida State Parks.]*

Black, red, sand, and pignut hickories
Eastern and southern red cedars
Basswoods

The principal trees on alluvial bottoms and swamps are:

Sweetgum and tupelo
Water, laurel, live, overcup, Texas, and swamp white oaks
Southern cypress
Pecan, water, and swamp hickories
Beech, river birch, ash
Red and silver maples
Cottonwoods and willows
Sycamore, hackberry, honeylocust, and holly

Red bay and sweet bay
Southern magnolia
Pond and spruce pines
Atlantic white cedar

Northward the Southeastern Pine Forest grades into the Central Hardwood Forest and the pines are mixed with hardwoods, notably oaks. The Mixed Oak and Pine Forest extends northeastward from Texas to the Embayed Section of the Coastal Plain (Fig. 8.3). In the Embayed Section, the shortleaf, pitch, and scrub pines are mixed with white, chestnut, and red oaks, and some hickories.

Southernmost Florida has subtropical forest with mangrove, royal and thatch palms, and

Florida yew. The broadleaf trees are small evergreens. The forest probably covers less than 800 square miles. Other subtropical vegetation grows along the coast of southernmost Texas.

Other quite different vegetation on the Coastal Plain grows in the semiarid part of Texas. Annual rainfall there may be as much as 30 inches, but the evaporation rate is high. The principal tree is mesquite. With it grow thornbushes, cacti, curly grass, buffalo grass, and various shrubs.

The Coastal Plain is bordered in many places along its shores by salt marshes and freshwater marshes. The freshwater marshes are characterized by Indian ricegrass, cattail, and tule, and in Florida, sawgrass. The salt marshes are characterized by marsh grass, *Spartina*. A transect across one of the marsh areas in Florida is illustrated in Figure 8.23,A.

Figure 10.29 illustrates an example of the relationship of vegetation to ground conditions on the Coastal Plain in Maryland. Landward from the shore are found a succession of different environments, each with a distinctive flora. Beachgrass grows on dry dunes along the beaches. Back of these are salt marshes with salt-tolerant grasses, species of *Spartina* in pure stands in the most salty ground, and *Spartina* mixed with salt grass where the salt content is less. These grade into less brackish marshes with salt grass and rush, and then into freshwater marshes with cattail. Farther inland, along streams, are fresh-water marshes and swamps, the latter with bald cypress and white cedar. On the dry uplands, where the ground is loam, the forests are coniferous or deciduous. The coniferous forests consist of loblolly pine mixed with sweet gum, white oak, Spanish oak, and red maple. The deciduous forests are mockernut, pignut, and bitternut hickory with black oak and Spanish oak. Sandy uplands support loblolly and pitch pine.

Agricultural production on the Coastal Plain, other than forest crops, also is zoned from north to south as follows:

1. The Embayed Section produces garden crops, dairy and poultry products for supplying the large northeastern cities.

2. The south end of the Embayed Section produces peanuts and tobacco. Here and southward to South Carolina is the principal area of tobacco production.

3. Cotton, corn, peanuts, and oats are produced in the southern part of the Atlantic Coastal Plain westward across the Mississippi River Alluvial Plain to Texas.

Figure 10.29 *Diagrammatic transect showing relationship between ground conditions and some kinds of plant*

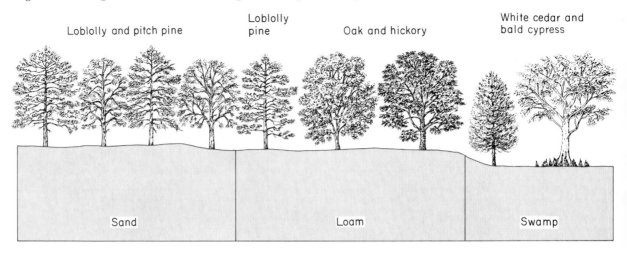

Loblolly and pitch pine   Loblolly pine   Oak and hickory   White cedar and bald cypress

Sand   Loam   Swamp

4. Along the coast of Louisiana and Texas, rice and sugar cane are grown.

5. In Florida, and along the Rio Grande in Texas, citrus fruits and vegetables are the chief crops.

These crops are produced from less than a third of the land. Almost two-thirds of the Coastal Plain is in forest or wooded pasture, which is a higher ratio of the land than was asked for by William Penn, who stated in his Charter of Rights (1681): "Leave one acre of trees for every five acres cleared." The forests provide not only timber and other wood products but watershed protection and parklands for recreation.

Hogs are raised in all parts of the Coastal Plain, but few compared to the corn belt in the Central Lowland. The Coastal Plain in Texas is one of the country's major cattle-raising areas.

Surface Deposits and Soils

Surface deposits on the Coastal Plain include alluvium in the floodplains of the rivers, especially along the Mississippi River; loessial deposits east of the Mississippi River valley; sand and gravel deposits on uplands; and beach sand, dune sand, peat, muck, and marsh deposits along the coasts. The coastal deposits, mostly Holocene in age, are not deeply weathered. Soils on these deposits are weakly developed. The alluvium includes Pleistocene deposits, but much of it is subject to flooding, and the upper layers are mostly Holocene. These deposits are highly productive despite the weak soil development. In the Mississippi Valley well-drained areas produce cotton and corn; poorly drained areas are used for pasture or left in forest.

Recent deposits of peat and muck are extensive along the Atlantic seaboard from Maryland south to Florida. The peat may be woody and derived from the stumps and logs of the cypress-tupelo-gum swamps, or it may be fibrous and derived chiefly from grasses and sedges. The coastal marshes contain fibrous peat deposits that grade from freshwater inland to salt water near the coast (Fig. 10.29). Depending on the geologic history of the location, either the woody or the fibrous peat may contain muds washed in with the organic matter. The lands are used chiefly for timber production and for wildlife refuges. The largest areas are at the Everglades in Florida, the Okefenokee Swamp in southern Georgia, and the Dismal Swamp in Virginia and North Carolina (Fig. 10.10).

stands on the Coastal Plain of Maryland.

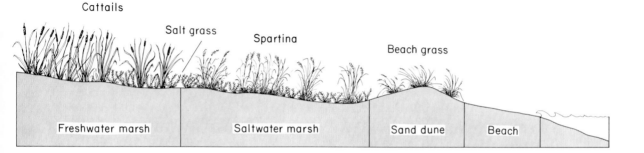

Figure 10.30 *Sea oats and palmetto trees along the sandy beach at Hunting Island State Park, near Beaufort, South Carolina, one of the state's four ocean-front state parks. [Courtesy South Carolina Department of Parks, Recreation, and Tourism.]*

Next older of the Coastal Plain soils is a group known as Ground Water Podzols, developed on sandy Quaternary formations or on older poorly drained formations at low elevations (Fig. 10.31, 10.32,B). The soils have a thin, ashy, organic-rich surface layer over a light-gray, leached layer about $2\frac{1}{2}$ feet thick. Below this is 6 to 20 inches of organic-rich and iron-rich hardpan, generally mottled brown and yellow, but dark brown in some soils. Below the hardpan is the water table. The soils are not very productive, and most are left in pasture or in forest. Many or most of the Ground Water Podzols date from earliest Holocene or late Pleistocene time. They are more than 2,000 years old, for they antedate archeological remains of that age (Figs. 10.31, 10.32,B).

On most of the Coastal Plain the surficial deposits or older formations are deeply weathered. This weathering is older than the latest (Wisconsinan stage) glaciation, because northward the weathered layers, called *residuum* or *saprolite*, are overlapped by the terminal moraines and outwash of that ice sheet (Fig. 10.32,A). Moreover, along the coast the residuum extends under and is overlapped by elevated shell beds of Pleistocene age (Fig. 10.32,B). The soils developed on the residuum are Red and Yellow Podzols.

The Red and Yellow Podzols and underlying residuum are deeply leached, acidic, and low in organic matter and plant nutrients. The near-surface layers, to a depth of 1 to 3 feet, are light in color; the deeper layers are clayey and mottled red and yellow. These soils, related to the laterites, are sometimes referred to as latosols. Leaching has removed alkalis, alkali earths, and silica, leaving behind an excess of iron and alumina. Most of the Red and Yellow Podzols on the Coastal Plain have developed on the Cretaceous and Tertiary formations, but some are developed on the Pleistocene loess east of the Mississippi River Alluvial Plain (Fig. 6.1).

Near the Mississippi River this loess is 100 to 200 feet thick but thins eastward. The loessial soils are fine grained throughout and are leached to a depth of 10 to 20 feet, below which they are still limy in some locations. The southern part of this loessial belt grows cotton; the northern part, corn.

Another soil, Rendzina Soil (Table 6.1), has developed on chalk or marl under native grasses. These are black because, in the presence of lime, humic colloids coagulate and the organic matter is retained. The parent material still dominates the soil profile (Fig. 8.20,B). The soils sometimes are referred to as immature, but may be as old as the neighboring Red and Yellow Podzols. They

are highly productive of corn, cotton, and alfalfa.

In the Embayed Section of the Coastal Plain some soils are Gray-Brown Podzols that in southeastern New Jersey and on Long Island support scrubby oak and pine. Cranberries are cultivated in boggy areas, but agriculturally these soils are among the poorest in the United States.

Long Island is covered with glacial till and glacial outwash of Wisconsinan age, and the soils on them are younger than the Red and Yellow Podzols farther south. The soils closely reflect the texture and composition of the parent materials, and are of four kinds: (1) gravelly, or even bouldery, soils on the terminal moraines and till-covered area to the north; (2) coarse sandy loam on the outwash plain just south of the moraines; (3) fine sandy loam farther south on the outwash plain; and (4) clayey loam on the transition zone between the outwash plains and the salt marshes. Native vegetation of the outwash plain is pitch pine and scrub oak.

At the opposite end of the Coastal Plain, in southern Texas, the soils are alkaline, for that region is semiarid. These soils contain much clay,

Figure 10.31 *Diagrammatic section of Ground Water Podzol, in Florida. Indian shell mounds consisting of unleached debris, and containing pottery and arrow points, overlie the Ground Water Podzols. These mounds range in age from historic time back to about* A.D. *500. The Ground Water Podzols predate the mounds, but seem younger than some earlier, prepottery archeological remains that occur in the subsoil down to the water table.*

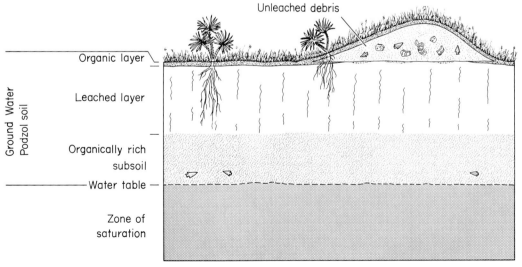

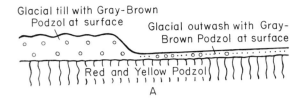

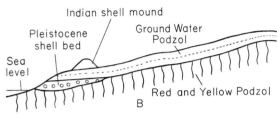

Figure 10.32 *Diagrammatic sections illustrating stratigraphic ages of soils on the Coastal Plain. (A) In the north, the Red and Yellow Podzols are overlain by glacial till and glacial outwash of the Wisconsin stage of glaciation; Gray-Brown Podzols are developed on the glacial deposits. (B) Southward to Florida the Red and Yellow Podzols are overlain by Pleistocene shell beds that are 15 to 25 feet above present sea level; Ground Water Podzols are developed on the shell bed.*

which swells when it is wet, and the swelling closes cracks in the ground, sometimes throwing fences, trees, or telephone poles out of line. Pavements and pipelines may be broken and building foundations cracked. When the ground dries, wide cracks form. The next rains put water into the cracks, wetting the subsoil and causing the cracks to swell; the ground again becomes irregularly heaved.

Soil erosion on the Coastal Plain is most serious on the east side of the Mississippi River; deep ravines have been cut into the fine-grained and much-farmed loessial soils. The Red and Yellow Podzols and residuum are moderately subject to erosion. These, too, are productive, fine-grained soils, but they are clayey, and the general relief is less than in the loessial belt. Elsewhere on the Coastal Plain erosion is slight, because the lands are low lying. Along the valleys the lands are subject to flooding and deposition of muds on the soils.

The Shore

Differences in the kinds of shoreline along the Coastal Plain depend chiefly on whether there has been recent submergence or emergence. The Embayed Section and the Sea Island Downwarp evidently are being submerged; the Mississippi Delta is being extended seaward by deposition. The Cape Fear Arch may be emergent. Sea-level records for numerous stations along the Atlantic and Gulf coasts indicate an average rise of about 6 inches during the last half century. Sea-level measurements are difficult to make, partly because exact low-tide and high-tide levels are necessarily arbitrary, and partly because tidal fluctuations vary greatly along the coasts. The tidal range—the difference between high and low tide—is only a foot or two in parts of Florida but more than 20 feet in parts of New England.

The submergence is attributed chiefly to a world-wide rise in sea level resulting from the melting of ice caps, but crustal movement may be partly responsible; in some places, such as the Mississippi River delta, land may be settling due to compaction of the deposits. Shore features resulting from submergence include the drowned valleys, sea cliffs at headlands truncated by erosion, barrier beaches, spits, and the small sandy islands along the Georgia and South Carolina coasts. Sandy Hook (Fig. 10.33) is an example of a shore feature that has developed as a result of a recent rise in sea level. The spit has been built by shore currents that have cut off headlands and transported sediments northward.

But there are also features of emergence along the shores of the Coastal Plain, such as shell beds and beach bars 15 to 25 feet above sea level (Fig. 10.32). These date from Pleistocene time, and record stages—probably interglacial stages—during which sea level was that much higher than it is today. The Cape Fear Arch may still be rising.

The waves and currents that build a beach are illustrated in Figure 10.34. The maximum height reached by the uprush of water on a beach is usually two or three times the height of the waves. The slope of a beach is controlled partly

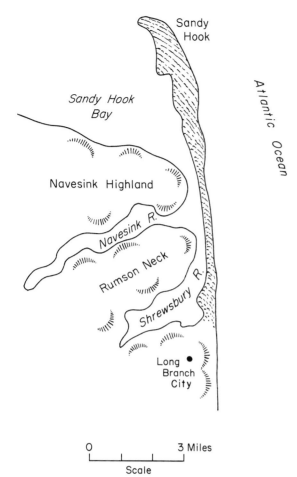

Figure 10.33 *Topography at Sandy Hook, New Jersey. Sediments eroded by longshore currents from cliffs along the shore at Long Branch City have been transported northward and deposited to form the bar and cape. Headlands at Rumson Neck and Navesink Highlands also were eroded as Sandy Hook was built. The hook curves into the bay because it is exposed to the westward sweep of wind and waves from the ocean. Shrewsbury and Navesink rivers are drowned valleys.*

by the coarseness of the sediment; fine sand may slope 3 degrees or less, whereas pebble beaches may slope as much as 15 to 20 degrees. As ocean waves enter shallow water, both their velocity and wavelength decrease, but their height increases. They drag bottom and begin to break when the depth is half the wavelength. As in

streams, sediment is moved by rolling along the bottom, by saltation, and by suspension.

Where waves break at an angle to the shore, as is usual, the waves are refracted producing a longshore component. The waves transport sediment onshore; the longshore currents transport sediment along the shore; rip currents transport sediment offshore. These processes are reflected in the distribution of spits in the Embayed Section, for the spits are at the south sides of the mouths of the bays—at Sandy Hook, Cape Henlopen, and Cape Henry. Shoreline differences reflecting different exposure to the waves and different composition of materials being eroded are illustrated by contrasts between the Connecticut coast and the north and south sides of Long Island (Fig. 10.35).

The sediments on beaches and the shelf illustrate how the sources of sediments can be identified by studying the proportions of different minerals in the deposits. Different streams transport different sediments. All the streams transport sediments composed chiefly of quartz sand and clay, but the other minerals, though minor in amount, account for the differences. Beaches built by sands brought by the rivers draining from the Piedmont Plateau contain minerals characteristic of metamorphic rocks. Beaches along the Texas coast are built of sands brought by rivers draining sedimentary rocks. Sands on Florida beaches also are from sedimentary rocks, but many contain a high percentage of siliceous sponge spicules as well as much carbonate. Beaches on Long Island contain sands derived from glacial deposits brought from New England.

In brief, the various stretches of shore along the Gulf and Atlantic differ because of differences in their Holocene geology. From south to north, they vary as follows:

1. Along the Texas coast, there are drowned valleys in Quaternary alluvial deposits with long barrier beaches protecting the bays.

2. In western Louisiana, the bayou country is eroded late Holocene delta of the Mississippi River.

3. Southeastern Louisiana has the presently forming lobate delta and some slightly older deltaic lobes fronted by barrier beaches.

4. The eastern Gulf Coastal Plain has drowned valleys and short barrier beaches ending eastward at the cuspate delta, and shoals at the mouth of the Appalachicola.

5. The west coast of Florida has bluffs eroded into Tertiary formations.

6. The south tip of Florida has coral and mangrove.

7. The Atlantic shore of Florida is characterized by barrier beaches.

8. Recent submergence along the Georgia and South Carolina coast has developed the sea islands.

9. At the Cape Fear Arch are long arcuate barrier beaches between the sharply pointed capes.

10. The Embayed Section has marshy wetlands along the shores of the bays, and barrier beaches fronting drowned valleys in alluvial deposits along the ocean shore.

11. At Long Island the shore is glacial outwash.

Some other environmental differences along the shores are illustrated in Figure 10.36. There are differences in the salinity of inlets along the Atlantic and Gulf Coasts because of differences in the climate. Where precipitation and runoff are high, salt water is diluted, but where there is little runoff the inlets may become saltier than the ocean. The environments also vary depending

Figure 10.34 *Plan of onshore, longshore, and rip currents along a beach.*

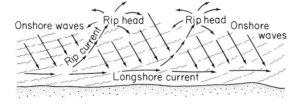

on the width and depth of the inlets and on the width, depth, and spacing of channels through the barrier beaches. These variables affect not only the salinity but also the turbidity of the inlets and their suitability for supporting various kinds of marsh vegetation.

Water Resources

Water supplies along the Atlantic seaboard are adequate for present demand and are believed to be adequate for the demand expected about 1980, but by the end of the century the water supplies for the West Gulf Coastal Plain may be inadequate (Fig. 9.9). It seems likely, however, that by that time satisfactory methods will have been discovered for desalting seawater, and the low altitudes on the Coastal Plain would favor use of such a source.

In the Embayed Section of the Coastal Plain, not much surface water is available for use because brackish water extends up the rivers to the Fall Line. The Fall Line cities are supplied chiefly from surface-water sources on the Piedmont Plateau or other parts of the Appalachian Highlands. East of the Fall Line, however, much use is made of ground-water, and most municipal water systems are supplied by wells. Many of the Coastal Plain formations are important aquifers and yield large supplies of water of good quality, but at depths of about 1,000 feet in some areas the fresh water changes to salt water, and it is necessary to avoid overpumping to avoid mixing the waters. Heavy drafts on the ground-water supply, particularly on Long Island, have caused the fresh-water–salt-water interface to rise and thereby introduced salt water into the aquifers.

On Long Island, glacial drift 25 to more than 100 feet thick overlies the Cretaceous Magothy Formation, which dips southeast and thickens in that direction from 500 feet at Long Island Sound to more than 1,500 feet under the Atlantic Ocean. The Magothy consists of clayey sand and silt; it rests on the Cretaceous Raritan Formation, which is about 500 feet thick and consists of a basal sand and gravel overlain by clay. Permeable beds

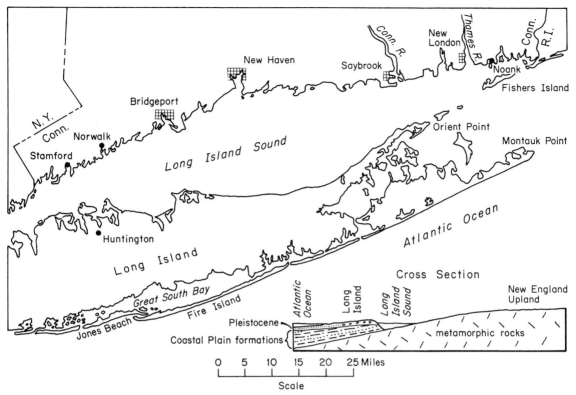

Figure 10.35 *Contrasts in shorelines reflecting differences in process and structure. The south side of Long Island, mostly nonbouldery glacial outwash and exposed to the ocean, has long beach bars and straight, eroded headlands. The north side, composed of bouldery glacial drift and protected from ocean waves, is irregular. The Connecticut coast is rocky with irregular headlands, irregular inlets, and short bars, spits, and narrow beaches. More detailed cross sections of Long Island are given in Figure 10.37.*

in these formations are saturated with fresh water, which forms a lens that rests on heavier salt water.

Before the island was settled, the groundwater circulated as shown by the arrows in Figure 10.37. The thickness of the fresh-water lens is about 40 times the height of the water table above sea level; this means that when the water table was 20 feet above sea level, the lens extended to a depth of about 800 feet. The interface then had the position of the solid line labeled 1,2 in Figure 10.37. Annual precipitation, which recharges the groundwater, totals about 50 inches in the central part of Long Island and about 40 inches at the east and west ends.

During the first phase of groundwater development, shallow wells were dug or drilled into the glacial drift, but wastes from cesspools eventually polluted that aquifer. When it could no longer be used for water supply, deeper wells were drilled to aquifers in the Magothy Formation. Contamination of water in the drift continued, but, more seriously, the deep well caused the interface between fresh and salt water to advance up the dip of the formations, eventually introducing salt water under the south side of the island.

In the next stage, withdrawals from the Magothy continued, but waste waters were instead discharged into sewers, which emptied into the

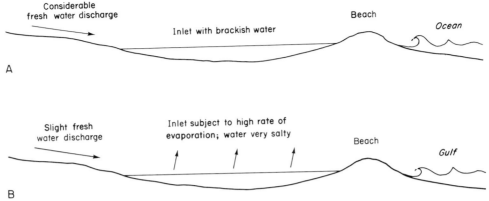

Figure 10.36   *Environments in tidal inlets. (A) Bays and estuaries along the mid-Atlantic seaboard have brackish-water environments because the salt water is diluted by the considerable discharge of fresh water running off the land. (B) Bays and estuaries along the southwestern Gulf Coast are very salty, some more than sea water, because there is considerable evaporation and little fresh water running off the land.*

sound and the ocean. This reduced contamination of the glacial drift, but the recharge of water into the ground was lessened because so much of the surface had become paved. Consequently, the salt-water–fresh-water interface continued moving inland, and the supply of water for the island became seriously threatened. Today, water used for air conditioning and other purposes that do not pollute is pumped back into the ground in an effort to conserve the remaining supply.

The water budget on western Long Island, which is densely settled, is badly out of balance; on eastern Long Island, which is less developed, it is in balance. In addition to recycling water used by industry for cooling purposes, the treated wastes that are now discharged into the sea could be used in barrier injection wells to help hold back the salty groundwater around the edges of the island or it could be collected in shallow recharge basins. If salt water intrusion continues, it will become necessary to resort again to the use of shallow wells that simply skim the fresh water off the top of the salt water.

Despite the fact that the municipal water supplies in the Embayed Section are largely underground, the waters are soft by comparison with most other parts of the country. The waters average less than 100 ppm of dissolved solids (Fig. 10.38). In some cities the content of dissolved solids is high, yet the waters are soft because they contain sodium rather than calcium or magnesium salts. Southward on the Delmarva Peninsula, east of the Chesapeake Bay, sodium and potassium increase while calcium and magnesium decrease.

Along the inner edge of the Coastal Plain the surface waters contain carbonate and bicarbonate, as do those of the Piedmont and other bordering provinces. Toward the coast the waters change to sulfate-chloride types. Along the West Gulf Coastal Plain and parts of the Georgia and South Carolina coasts the surface waters are soft; elsewhere the surface waters contain calcium and magnesium and are hard.

In Texas, as in the Embayed Section, the content of dissolved solids in the surface water is about the same as in the groundwater, but from the East Gulf Coastal Plain northward to the Embayed Section, the content of dissolved solids is higher in the groundwater than in the surface water—three to ten times higher.

On the Florida limestone peninsula, the raw waters are hard, averaging perhaps 150 to 200

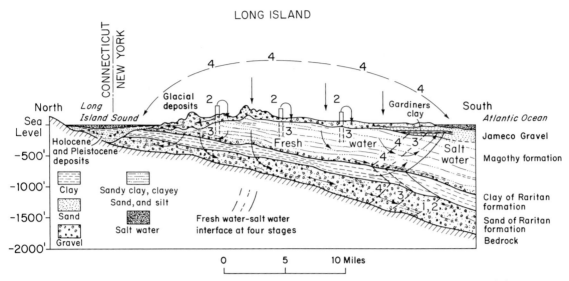

Figure 10.37 *The original circulation of ground water on Long Island was recharged by rain, and the water circulated as indicated by the solid arrows. In the first phase of groundwater development, shallow wells (2) were dug or drilled into the glacial drift, and cesspools discharged waste into that drift. As this shallow water became contaminated, deeper wells were drilled (3). The increased water production and increased waste greatly spread the contamination in the glacial drift; withdrawal of water from the Magothy Formation caused the salt-water front to advance under the island. Now the water is brought to the surface and the waste discharged by sewers (4); much of the runoff now goes into the storm sewers rather than into the ground. The contamination has been reduced in the glacial drift, but ground water recharge has been reduced and the salt water has moved farther inland.*

ppm of $CaCO_3$ equivalent (p. 112), but the waters are treated, and the delivered water is considerably softened. In some parts of Texas—Houston, for example—the water contains sodium, and the hardness is only moderate, even though the content of dissolved solids is considerable. Some water wells in Houston are a half mile deep, and becoming saltier.

A remarkable series of large springs that issue from the Balcones fault zone along the west edge of the West Gulf Coastal Plain (Fig. 10.39) supply much of the water for the cities there, notably San Antonio. The springs are large enough to feed some of the rivers. The water flows from beds of limestone and is hard.

Considerable hydroelectric power is produced at the Fall Line and at falls farther inland, but the Coastal Plain has very little power potential because of the low stream gradients. The rise and fall of tides, however, have been used on estuaries to turn the water wheels of grinding mills.

Marine Environments—Fisheries

One of the more important features of the Coastal Plain is the Gulf Stream (Fig. 5.1). Water from the Caribbean Sea is driven into the Gulf of Mexico by trade winds and the North Equatorial current, and sea level is raised. According to one estimate, sea level in the Gulf is 3 feet higher than in the Atlantic off New York. The water that moves into the Gulf is warmed, and by the time it flows through the Strait of Florida it has a surface temperature above 80°F. The current is 50 miles wide, nearly 2,000 feet deep,

A. Municipalities and principal sources of supply (S, surface water; G, ground-water).

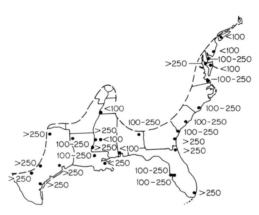

B. Total dissolved solids in the principal source.

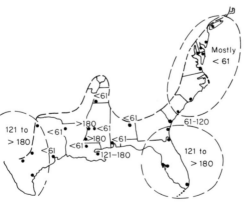

C. Hardness of the untreated water.

and has a velocity of 4 to 5 miles per hour, which is sufficient to keep the bottom free of mud. The flow is about 500 billion acre-feet annually, which is a thousand times the discharge of the Mississippi River.

Northward along the coast the stream widens, and the velocity decreases to about 1½ miles per hour at the latitude of Cape Cod, where westerly winds turn the warm current across the Atlantic. The course of the stream then becomes meandering and divides eastward into distributaries.

At Georges Bank and northeastward to the Grand Banks off Newfoundland, the warmed water is shallow enough (much of it less than 150 feet) for the penetration of light needed to produce an abundant supply of phytoplankton, which are at the bottom of the food chain. In a single day, one crustacean may eat 100,000 phytoplankton, a herring 5,000 of the crustaceans, and a humpback whale 5,000 herring. The abundance of phytoplankton is the basis for the fisheries there, and an international commission is concerned with the ecological balance and the measures needed to protect the fisheries against depletion.

The cold Labrador Current flows southward (Fig. 5.1) and forms a cold body of water between the Gulf Stream and the coast. A consequence of this is frequent fog and storms over the banks, from Grand Bank off Newfoundland to Georges Bank off New England, where, it is said, even the cod get seasick.

Variation in marine environments are the result of differences in the water, the sea bottom, and the marine climate. The water varies in depth, temperature, turbulence, salinity, and bio-

Figure 10.38 *Examples of different kinds of water in municipal systems on the Coastal Plain. Total dissolved solids are generally high in waters on the Peninsular Arch and West Gulf Coastal Plain. Because of the limestone source rocks on the Peninsular Arch and inner edge of the West Gulf Coastal Plain, waters in those areas are hard, and, except at San Antonio, they are alkaline. Water supplies along the Atlantic seaboard are generally soft.*

logical content; bottoms vary depending on the texture of the bottom sediments, rockiness, and topography; and marine climates vary with latitude, exposure, depth, and currents. Figure 8.23,A illustrates some differences in littoral environments.

The principal marine life zones are illustrated in Figure 8.23,B. Differences in depth are accompanied by differences in temperature and illumination. Temperatures in the abyssal zone are as low as 40°F. Depths greater than about 300 feet have little or no illumination. Turbulence is an important environmental factor in the shallow-water zones, and perhaps along the continental rise, where submarine sliding and submarine currents are capable of transporting sediment. Salinity varies most in the inner neritic and intertidal, or littoral, zone, where there is complete gradation from sea water (35,000 ppm of salts), through brackish water (500 to 15,000 ppm), to fresh water (less than about 500 ppm). In Chesapeake Bay, for example, the salinity decreases from 30,000 ppm at the mouth of the bay to 5,000 ppm at Baltimore near the head of the bay. In lagoons, however, where there is considerable evaporation without much inflow of fresh water, salinities may exceed the salinity of sea water, as in Laguna Madre, along the south coast of Texas.

The biota faithfully reflects these differences. Some animals live attached to the bottom, like the oyster. Others are bottom feeders but move about, like the crab, cod, and haddock. Still other animals float on or near the surface, such as the various forms of *plankton,* including the unwelcome sea nettles (stinging jellyfish). Most fish are migratory, and each species has its own habits. Some, like the striped bass, winter off the southern coast and migrate northward for the summer. The summer flounder summers near shore but migrates to deeper water for the winter. Alewife and shad spawn in fresh water; the eel, in deep warm water.

Marine life is zoned both according to latitude (reflecting differences in temperature) and offshore (reflecting differences in salinity, frequency of wetting, and depth of water)(Fig. 10.40).

The following is an example of the variety of kinds of fish that are found, beginning with freshwater on shore, through the brackish tidal zone, to the deeper salt water offshore. The example is from the middle Atlantic seaboard. The list is not intended to be exhaustive:

Fresh Water	Brackish Tidal Water	Salt Water
	Mackerel ←	Mackerel
	Bluefish ←	Bluefish
	Cobia ←	Cobia
	White shad	Sea bass
Northern pike	Channel bass (Red drum)	Flounder
Brown trout	Black Drum	Marlin
Rainbow trout	Rockfish (Striped Bass)	Shark
Brook trout	Norfolk spot	Dolphin
Smallmouth bass	Sea trout	Tautog
White perch →	White perch	Kingfish (Whiting)
Largemouth bass →	Largemouth bass	Bonito (False Albacore)
Bluegill (Sunfish) →	Bluegill (Sunfish)	
Catfish →	Catfish	
Crappie →	Crappie	
Yellow perch →	Yellow perch	
Pickerel →	Pickerel	
Carp →	Carp	

Fish, including shellfish, are one of America's chief resources, and fishing was the earliest industry. Even before the first settlements had been established, European fishing boats crossed the Atlantic and took cod from the banks off Newfoundland. More than half of the present production of commercial fisheries by Canada and United States is from the Atlantic (and Gulf), and the rest is from the Pacific. About a third of the production is canned, a third is sold fresh or frozen, and a third is used for fish meal and oils.

Chesapeake Bay was described by Mencken as "a tremendous protein factory that enabled

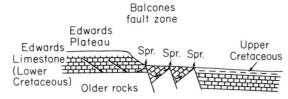

Figure 10.39 *Diagram illustrating springs at the Balcones fault zone. On the Edwards Plateau water seeps into the limestone and emerges in springs at the faults.*

Baltimoreans to eat divinely." About two-thirds of the total value of the production was oysters, about 15 percent crabs, and about 10 percent each of clams and finfish. The salinity range of Chesapeake Bay is such that the Bay is without the starfish, one of the oyster's principal predators, and there are boring snails only in the southern part of the Bay. There are some oyster parasites, but the life expectancy of the Chesapeake Bay oyster is better than most. The natural mortality averages about 10 to 15 percent. The chief threat to the oyster population is pollution.

The Bays and Their Problems

The bays and harbors of the Embayed Section of the Coastal Plain attracted early settlement because of their protection against storms. Today that stretch of coast is almost continuous city from Richmond, Virginia, to New England. The huge population that resides there produces a vast amount of waste, which already has deadened some water bodies and threatens to pollute them all beyond use except for shipping and sewage disposal. These waters receive the waste products of almost half the population of the United States, and despite the large number and large size of the rivers, too many people, too many industries, too many municipalities and too many boats are using them as open sewers.

The pollutants include industrial waste, municipal and other sewage, and pesticides from agricultural land along rivers that drain into the bays. The sewage dumped into Chesapeake Bay alone by the 5,000 ocean-going ships that annu-

ally visit Baltimore about equals the amount that would be produced by a city of 20,000 persons. Electric generating plants cause thermal pollution; people want the power but not the power plants! Sediment is washed into the bays by the all-too-familiar erosion at construction sites, which are characteristically muddy. Owners of waterfront properties contribute wastes in the form of seepage from cesspools, and improvements at waterfront properties contribute to the elimination of the marshes, which are necessary for the spawning of fish, as resting and feeding grounds for numerous species of birds, and for erosion control along the shores.

A hundred years ago Newark Bay had finfish and shellfish, and even then there were complaints that the fish were beginning to taste of coal oil. There is no complaining today: the bay is dead.

The amount of solid waste from the New York metropolitan area is so great that it is hauled by barge to the ocean and dumped there, mostly in the triangular area called "the bight," between Montauk Point, Cape May, and Ambrose Island at the mouth of New York Bay. Four kinds of wastes are dumped there: raw sewage, industrial wastes, dredging spoils, and lethal chemical wastes, the latter being dumped farthest offshore. The dumping ground has become a dead part of the continental shelf and a potential menace to any species that accumulates any of the toxic poisons. This area could recover if it were given a rest and if another dumping ground were used for a while. Ten million people create a lot of waste; are there other ways to dispose of it? Might this waste actually be a resource?

Delaware Bay is almost as dead as Newark Bay. Almost 5 million people live around it, mostly in five large cities in three different states! The complicated, three-state governmental machinery has failed to check the pollution.

Chesapeake Bay is threatened, but most of it is still clean enough to produce safe shellfish and finfish. Near the cities, however, it is no longer attractive for boating or swimming. Most of the pollution is around the edges, but these are the areas of access and greatest use. The danger sig-

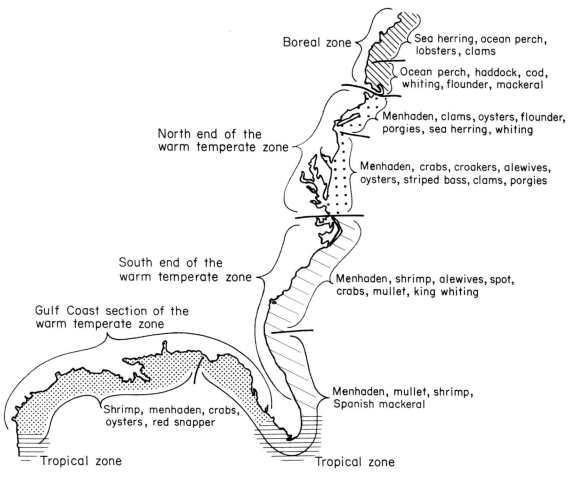

Boreal zone — Sea herring, ocean perch, lobsters, clams

Ocean perch, haddock, cod, whiting, flounder, mackerel

Menhaden, clams, oysters, flounder, porgies, sea herring, whiting

North end of the warm temperate zone — Menhaden, crabs, croakers, alewives, oysters, striped bass, clams, porgies

South end of the warm temperate zone — Menhaden, shrimp, alewives, spot, crabs, mullet, king whiting

Gulf Coast section of the warm temperate zone

Menhaden, mullet, shrimp, Spanish mackerel

Shrimp, menhaden, crabs, oysters, red snapper

Tropical zone   Tropical zone

Figure 10.40 *Latitudinal zoning of fish along the Atlantic and Gulf coasts, as illustrated by the production of some commercial fish. For each stretch of coast, the fish are listed in the order of their weight of commercial production. [Compiled from U.S. Dept. of Commerce statistics.]*

nals are clear: 40,000 acres of what had been prime shellfishing ground have been closed because of pollution, and more than half the public beaches in the Baltimore area and all those in the Washington area have been closed to swimming. Near the cities, most of the streams entering the bay are posted "No wading or swimming"; they simply are dangerous. To prevent the bay from the fate of smaller bays to the north, Maryland and Virginia will have to join in a common effort to save Chesapeake Bay. Those who visit our national capital to see the cherry

blossoms should view the Potomac River too and ask themselves, "Is this the best use of this resource?"

There are problems in connection with canal developments. In Florida, water tables and water supplies are threatened by proposed drainage and shipping canals. The Cross-Florida barge canal, dream of the Army's Corps of Engineers for generations, would connect the Gulf and Atlantic Oceans via Yankeetown, Ocala, and the St. Johns River to Jacksonville. In the early 1800's, it was proposed as a route for avoiding pirates who were operating from the Florida Keys. Some digging was begun in the 1930's to make work, but was suspended when geologists protested about the threat to the water supplies in that cavernous limestone country. During World War II, there were those who argued that completion of the canal would protect oil shipments against German submarines. Supporting the project today are bulk cargo shippers, some landowners along the route, and such companies as the Florida Power Corporation, which stands to gain by commercial development. Opponents include those who would preserve the Oklawaha River as a fast-flowing wild river with abundant game fish, those fearful of oil spills that would contaminate groundwater as well as the canal itself, and many economists who are highly critical of the costs and benefits as presented by the Corps of Engineers. Meanwhile 25 miles of canal have been excavated, and although the project has been halted, a president can order construction resumed at any time. Conservationists are wary; as one expressed it, "I'd rather have 25 miles of ditch that isn't worth anything than 100 miles of ditch that isn't worth anything."

A plan to deepen the Chesapeake and Delaware Canal in order to accomodate larger ships could result in the movement of saline water from Delaware Bay to the head of Chesapeake Bay, which would affect not only the fisheries in Chesapeake Bay but possibly the aquifers that dip eastward under the part of the Coastal Plain between Chesapeake Bay and the Atlantic Ocean.

Additional problems are thermal pollution, the disposal of radioactive wastes from nuclear power plants, and the greater frequency of oil spills from increasingly larger tankers, increasingly numerous pipelines, and increased offshore drilling. Oil washed on a sandy beach forms a continuous layer on the sand that looks quite like oil spilled on pavement. It extends onto the beach as far as the reach of the highest waves at high tide. Waves move the oil along the beach, each surge lifting the layer of oil and moving it a short distance. Sand adheres to the bottom of the layer of oil, which becomes sandier and pastier as it

moves. When sufficiently viscous, the sand separates into platy layers of sandy oil covering tens of square feet and separated by pathways of clean sand. These platy layers of sandy oil, one-half to three-quarters of an inch thick, are lifted and moved along the beach by each surge, and as they become more sandy they break into pads about the size and thickness of pancakes. As these become sandier in their trip along the beach, they become sticky, rounded globs of oily sand about the size of marbles and as sticky as chewing gum. The oil-sand mix is tenacious and would remain until buried by new sand. The oil can be collected, but the volume can be considerable, there is always the question of how to dispose of the waste. Oil spills on the land reach the bays too. Spills from oil trucks in cities are cleaned up by washing the oil down the sewers.

Shore erosion is and has been serious. Altogether Maryland has lost about 30,000 acres to erosion around Chesapeake Bay and has gained about 5,000 acres by deposition of sediments. Prince William Forest Park at Dumfries, Virginia, is something of a national monument to erosion in colonial times. When Dumfries was settled as a port, the mouth of Quantico Creek was a fine harbor. When settlers began farming the surrounding land, however, the hillsides eroded so severely and swiftly that the harbor filled with silt and the port was abandoned. The farmed land was gradually abandoned too, but is once again stabilized by forest.

The kinds of problems that arise in the management of such estuaries are only partly technological; they also are social, economic, and political. The technological problems include:

1. Controlling erosion and sedimentation.

2. Maintaining inputs of fresh water in relation to flow of tidal salt water.

3. Preventing or minimizing the inflow of fertilizers and other nutrients that cause eutrophication.

4. Finding disposal sites for dredging spoils.

5. Eliminating inflows of biologically harmful chemicals.

6. Improving sewage plants.

7. Coping with changes in circulation caused by deepening of channels and canals.

8. Developing efficient, ready means of cleaning up oil and other petrochemicals dumped or spilled into bays.

The political, social, and economic problems arise over conflicts between those who want to use the bays for navigation and shipping; swimming, boating, fishing, and other kinds of recreation; commercial fishing; and thermal sinks. Waterfront property is eagerly sought by real estate and industrial developers.

Reconciling the conflict between actual and potential multiple uses requires making political compromises. Overcoming the technological problems is largely a matter of economics; they can be overcome at a price. Are we willing to pay it? Or, the question might better be asked, can we afford not to?

Mineral Resources

The mineral industry in the United States was started on the Coastal Plain in 1608 when the Jamestown settlers attempted to manufacture glass, probably using sand from the nearby Miocene formations. In 1619 an iron foundry was established on the James River below Richmond. In 1674 iron ore was produced at Shrewsbury, New Jersey. On the Coastal Plain, iron has been deposited in bogs, and also occurs as nodules, called concretions, in the Coastal Plain formations. Such deposits were widely developed by the colonists throughout the Embayed Section but could not compete with other sources after the middle of the eighteenth century.

Today the most important mineral resource on the Coastal Plain is petroleum in Texas and Louisiana. There are two belts of quite different kinds of oil fields, one along the coast and extending offshore, and the other inland (Fig. 10.24).

The coastal oil fields are small but numerous and highly productive; many are salt dome struc-

tures (Fig. 10.25). The inland oil fields are few but large; the East Texas field, one of the world's great oil fields, comprises more than 25,000 wells. At this field, a sandstone (Woodbine Sandstone) thins against the flank of the Sabine uplift (Fig. 10.24) and is unconformably overlapped by a chalk (Austin Chalk), which extends onto the older formations. Oil has been trapped in the thinned edges of the sandstone (Fig. 10.41).

Increasingly, natural gas is being produced at the oil fields. Oil and gas together have accounted for about 95 percent of the half billion dollars worth of minerals annually produced from the Coastal Plain. Practically all the remaining 5 percent is from nonmetals.

The salt domes in the West Gulf Coastal Plain supply about 75 percent of the nation's sulfur. Common salt also is produced for both industrial and table use. Chemical industries thrive by the association of sulfur and salt with nearby oil and gas for hydrocarbon products and fuel.

Offshore drilling is becoming of increasing interest. As of 1968 almost 9,000 wells had been drilled off the Gulf Coast in water depths to slightly more than 300 feet, and rigs for drilling in deeper water are being designed.

Much magnesium, important as a light structural metal, is produced along the Gulf Coast at Freeport, Texas. The metal is obtained from sea water, which contains about 1,300 ppm. Since a cubic mile of sea water contains 6 million tons of magnesium, the supply is virtually inexhaustible.

Figure 10.41 *Diagrammatic section through the East Texas oil field, showing the thinned edge of the productive Woodbine Sandstone where it is overlapped by the impermeable Austin Chalk. [After Internat. Geol. Cong.]*

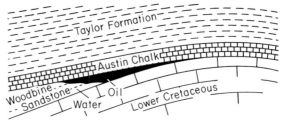

About 70 percent of the nation's phosphate is produced in Florida from the weathered upper part of a Pliocene formation. This weathered layer, an ancient phosphatic soil related to the Red and Yellow Podzols (Fig. 10.32,B), is a near-surface blanket deposit mined by open-pit methods.

Other major resources of the Coastal Plain are the clay deposits, which include bleaching clay and aluminous, or bauxitic, clay. Bleaching clay, mostly the clay mineral montmorillonite, is known as fuller's earth because it was originally used to remove grease from woolen cloth in a process known as fulling; today, a major use of bleaching clays is for decolorizing mineral oils.

The clay deposits are widespread in the Gulf Coast, but the principal production has been from the Hawthorne Formation in Florida and Georgia, from Eocene formations at the head of the Mississippi River Alluvial Plain in Illinois, and from Texas. These areas have supplied about 80 percent of the United States total.

Ceramic clays are of many kinds, such as kaolin (china clay), refractory clay, and pottery and brick clay. Kaolin from the Tuscaloosa Formation in South Carolina and Georgia has been used for making firebrick and for filler in rubber and for coated papers. These two states have accounted for about 90 percent of the United States production of kaolin. Pottery or brick clays

abound in the Coastal Plain and have been widely produced. Bauxite and bauxitic clays that might be a source of alumina are abundant in Arkansas, which has supplied 97 percent of the bauxite produced in the United States.

Building stone is rare, but a gray sandstone quarried from a Cretaceous formation at Aquia, Virginia, was used in 1795 in constructing the White House (painted white) and the central part of the Capitol in Washington, D.C. Among the buildings in Washington, these two are unique for their building stone as well as in other, more familiar ways.

About 5 percent of the Portland cement manufactured in the United States has been produced from Upper Cretaceous chalk or limestone in Texas.

In many parts of the Coastal Plain roads are metalled with oyster shells, quarried in large part from prehistoric Indian shell mounds. Sand is plentiful on the Coastal Plain, but gravel is less abundant, and stone for riprap to control beach erosion must be imported. Other potentially important deposits include heavy beach sands (placer deposits containing monazite, a phosphate of the rare earths containing cerium and thorium) along the Atlantic Coast south of Cape Hatteras; beaches in Florida have yielded concentrates of titanium.

References

Am. Assoc. Petrol. Geol., 1972, Continental shelves—Origin and significance (selected papers reprinted from the Association Bulletin, 1946–1970), Reprint Ser. No. 3.

Bascom, W., 1964, Waves and beaches: New York, Doubleday (Anchor Books).

Carson, Rachel, 1951, The sea around us: New York, Oxford Univ. Press.

———, 1955, The edge of the sea: New York, Houghton Mifflin.

Cohen, P., and others, 1968, An atlas of Long Island's water resources: New York Water Resources Comm. Bull. 62.

Darwin, Geo. H., 1898, The tides and kindred phenomena in the solar system: New York, Houghton Mifflin; reprinted by W. H. Freeman and Company.

Harshberger, J. W., 1916, the vegetation of the New Jersey Pine-Barrens: reprinted by Dover Publications.

Heezen, B. C., Tharp, Marie, and Ewing, E., 1959, The floors of the oceans. I. The North Atlantic: Geol. Soc. America Spec. Paper 65.

Johnson, D. W., 1919, Shore processes and shoreline development: Columbia Univ. Press; reprinted 1965 by Hafner Publishing Co.

Jordan, G. F., 1962, Submarine physiography of the United States continental margins: U.S. Coast and Geodetic Survey Tech. Bull. 18.

Kurz, H., and Wagner, R., 1957, Tidal marshes of the Gulf and Atlantic coasts of North Florida and Charleston, South Carolina: Fla. State Univ. Studies 24.

Murray, G. E., 1961, Geology of the Atlantic and Gulf Provinces of North America: New York, Harper and Bros.

Perkinson, W. J., and others, ca. 1969, The Chesapeake at Bay; Reprinted from The Baltimore Evening Sun.

Prouty, W. F., 1952, Carolina Bays and their origin: Geol. Soc. America Bull. 63, pp. 157–224.

Reid, G. K., 1961, Ecology of inland waters and estuaries: New York, Reinhold Publ. Co.

Shepard, F. P., 1959, The earth beneath the sea: Baltimore, Johns Hopkins Univ. Press.

Strahler, A. N., 1966, A geologist's view of Cape Cod: Garden City, Natural History Press.

U.S. Fish and Wildlife Serice, 1954, Gulf of Mexico—Its origin, waters, and marine life: Fish and Wildlife Service Bull. 89.

Vokes, H. E., 1961, Geography and geology of Maryland: Maryland Geol. Survey Bull. 19.

The folded Appalachians are characterized by long narrow ridges, formed by the protruding edges of the resistant formations, separated by broad valleys in the easily eroded formations. The mountain at the right (Blue Mountain) is formed by the upturned Tuscarora Quartzite (Silurian). The valley to the right of it is in Martinsburg Shale (Ordovician). The canoe-shaped ridge (Cove Mountain), partly a double ridge, is formed by the upturned, resistant Pocono Sandstone and Catskill Formation (Mississippian and Devonian). Easily eroded Devonian shale formations form the valley west of the canoe and the one between it and Blue Mountain. The valley within the canoe is formed of easily eroded Mississippian shale; the rib in the middle, beyond the Susquehanna River, is a synclinal ridge of Pennsylvanian sandstone. [From *Geology Illustrated* by John S. Shelton, W. H. Freeman and Co. Copyright © 1966.]

11
....

APPALACHIAN PROVINCES—
A VARIETY OF MOUNTAINS

The Appalachian Provinces, the mountainous part of the eastern United States, include the Piedmont, Blue Ridge, Valley and Ridge, Appalachian Plateaus, Adirondack, and New England and Maritime provinces, Newfoundland, and the St. Lawrence Lowland (Figs. 11.1, 11.2). The area they cover is about equal to that of the Coastal Plain, and separates the plain of the eastern seaboard from the plains bordering the valleys of the Ohio and Mississippi rivers. The structure here has been inherited from a Paleozoic geosyncline.

In the central Appalachians, fold mountains form the Valley and Ridge Province. In the Piedmont Plateau to the east, the rock structures are also those of fold mountains, but much faulted. The formations have been so eroded and so reduced in height that the landforms are not mountainous except in parts of New England and in the narrow Blue Ridge Province. West of the fold mountains are the Appalachian Plateaus. The formations there are nearly horizontal, a typical plateau structure, but they are so elevated and dissected that the landforms are in large part mountainous. Thus the Appalachian Plateaus are mountainous with a plateau structure, whereas the Piedmont Province is a low plateau devel-

oped on the kind of structures that generally produce mountains. The Adirondack Province consists of a mountainous structural dome with Precambrian rocks at the core.

The differences between the Appalachian Provinces were fully recognized in early American atlases. One, the Carey and Lea Atlas, 1823, distinguished four belts of country along the seaboard. "The first, extending from the sea-coast to the termination of tide water . . . is low and flat . . . The next division extends from the head of tide water to the Blue Ridge . . . The third division is the valley between the Blue Ridge and . . . Allegheny mountains . . . The fourth . . . extends from the Allegheny mountains to the Ohio River and is wild and broken. . . ."

During the Paleozoic Era the site of the Appalachian Provinces was a geosyncline (Fig. 2.14) occupied by a mediterranean sea in which sediments accumulated to a thickness of about 40,000 feet. To the west was stable platform in the interior of the continent, intermittently awash with shallow seas that extended westward from the geosyncline.

The sea never was 40,000 feet deep; the geosynclinal trough sank gradually during the Paleozoic, and the eight miles of sinking and com-

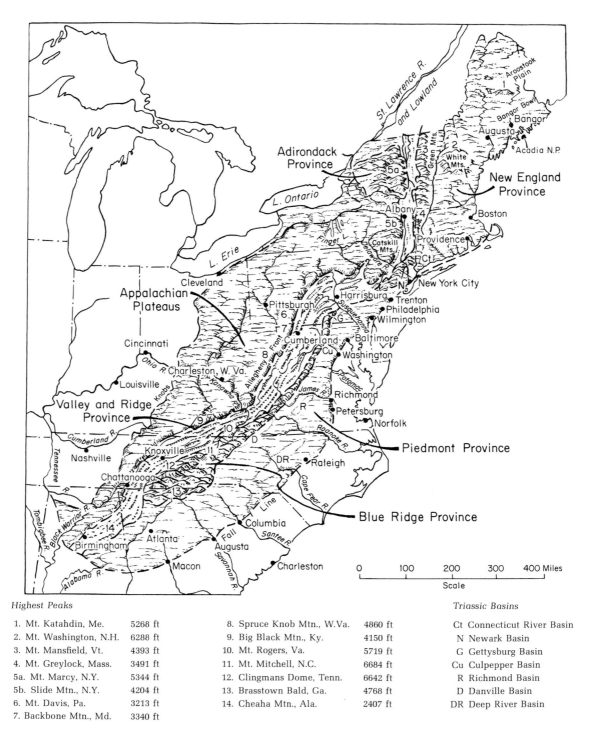

Highest Peaks

1. Mt. Katahdin, Me.	5268 ft
2. Mt. Washington, N.H.	6288 ft
3. Mt. Mansfield, Vt.	4393 ft
4. Mt. Greylock, Mass.	3491 ft
5a. Mt. Marcy, N.Y.	5344 ft
5b. Slide Mtn., N.Y.	4204 ft
6. Mt. Davis, Pa.	3213 ft
7. Backbone Mtn., Md.	3340 ft

8. Spruce Knob Mtn., W.Va.	4860 ft
9. Big Black Mtn., Ky.	4150 ft
10. Mt. Rogers, Va.	5719 ft
11. Mt. Mitchell, N.C.	6684 ft
12. Clingmans Dome, Tenn.	6642 ft
13. Brasstown Bald, Ga.	4768 ft
14. Cheaha Mtn., Ala.	2407 ft

Triassic Basins

Ct	Connecticut River Basin
N	Newark Basin
G	Gettysburg Basin
Cu	Culpepper Basin
R	Richmond Basin
D	Danville Basin
DR	Deep River Basin

Figure 11.1 *Physiographic diagram of the Appalachian Provinces in the United States. The national parks in the region are Acadia (Me.), Great Falls (Potomac River at Washington), Shenandoah (in Blue Ridge Prov., south of the Potomac River), and Great Smoky (11).*

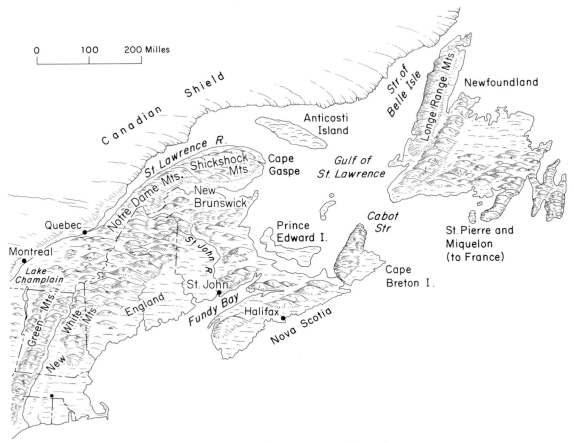

Figure 11.2 *Physiographic diagram of the Appalachian Provinces in Canada.*

parable rise of the mountains to the southeast, from which the sediments were derived, could have averaged only a foot in 10,000 years. Some of the earth movements that occurred repeatedly during the Paleozoic are recorded by unconformities. The hinge line between the area that was uplifted and the area that was depressed seems to have shifted gradually westward. In early Paleozoic time the Piedmont Province was part of the geosyncline, but by late Paleozoic time it became part of the mountain area supplying sediments westward. The hinge line between the geosyncline and stable platform to the west was about at the position of what now is the Allegheny Front.

As already noted, the Piedmont Plateau is the exposed part of the basement rocks that underlie

the Atlantic Coastal Plain. What had been an unstable eugeosyncline during the Paleozoic became a stable platform for deposition of the Cretaceous and younger formations along the coast. It may have become stable platform as early as Jurassic or even Triassic time.

At the end of Paleozoic time, the earth movements reversed, and the sedimentary formations in the geosyncline were folded and uplifted. During the 225 million years since the Paleozoic, the uplifted formations have been subject to erosion, and have supplied the sediments of the Coastal Plain, burying the roots of the Paleozoic mountains that had supplied sediments to the Appalachian geosyncline.

Compared to the Rocky Mountains, the Appalachians are not high. They are more humid, however, and as a consequence the weathering and erosion have produced rounded landforms. The Appalachians lack the sharply angular profiles so common in the western mountains. Fifteen of the highest peaks in the Appalachians, including the highest peaks in fourteen of the states, are indicated in Figure 11.1.

Other outstanding features of the Appalachian provinces are listed below.

1. Winters are cold in the north and mild in the south.

2. Most of the forest is Central Hardwood Forest, but grades northward into Northeastern Hardwood and Spruce-Fir forests.

3. Glacial features that developed during the Pleistocene characterize the northern part.

4. Surface deposits and soils are of four principal kinds: glacial drift in the north, with young (late Pleistocene and Holocene) podzolic soils; ancient and deep residual soils on the Piedmont Plateau and in some valleys of the Valley and Ridge Province; alluvium and alluvial terraces on floodplains; colluvium with weakly developed soils in the mountains. All the soils are acid, open systems.

5. Rivers are numerous and large, and lakes abound in the glaciated areas, providing water supplies considered adequate to meet anticipated increased demand during the next quarter century. These lakes and rivers provided the basis for the country's first transportation boom—the development of shipping by canal—and provided the water power for early industry and for much of today's electric power.

6. Pollution is a major problem chiefly because of dense population. The atmosphere is polluted by industrial stacks and automobiles; streams are polluted by industrial wastes, sewage, acid waters from coal mines, and pesticides washed from agricultural land.

7. Minerals are a major resource of the Highlands, especially the mineral fuels. The abundance of coal, oil, and gas led to intensive industrialization. Other important resources are limestone for cement, building stone, salt, mica, copper, zinc, and sand for glassmaking.

8. Other basic resources include fish and dairy produce in New England, potatoes in Maine, wine-growing in New York, dairies in New York and Pennsylvania, fruit orchards in the Valley and Ridge Province, tobacco and cotton in the southern Piedmont, and corn whiskey in the Appalachian Plateau.

9. The Appalachian Trail (Fig. 11.45), a symbol of the important recreational possibilities of this region, extends along various mountain crests from Georgia to Maine. The national parks (Fig. 11.1) and the more than 200 state and provincial parks in the Appalachians are not enough for its population.

Structural Framework—Relation to Rest of the Continent.

That mountain belts on the continents are situated on the sites of Paleozoic and younger geosynclines (Fig. 2.14) was first recognized after study of the Appalachians. The geosynclines that once bordered the broad stable platform surrounding the Canadian Shield, are characterized by great thicknesses of sedimentary formations, in large part marine, that became greatly folded, faulted, and elevated to form mountains when the geosynclines were terminated.

Curiously, the great bulk of the sediments that accumulated in the geosynclines seems to have been derived chiefly from what is now the oceanic side of the troughs. During the time spans of the Paleozoic and younger geosynclines, the shields appear to have been low plateaus, and their margins were submerged under shallow epicontinental seas. The sources of the sediments are indicated by the changes in facies of the sedimentary deposits—their generally increasing fineness toward the shields and the foreset bedding in deltaic deposits.

Most geosynclines have three major structural parts, with a middle ridge dividing an outer trough on the oceanic side from one on the inner side, bordering the stable platform. The outer member is referred to as a *eugeosyncline;* the inner one is a *miogeosyncline.* Generally the kinds of sediments they received differ greatly.

Eugeosynclinal formations consist chiefly of coarse clastic deposits (poorly sorted conglomerate and sandstone) grading to silty muds, and these deposits include a high proportion of volcanic debris and even submarine lava flows. Because the sediments accumulated in deep water, paleontological remains are not abundant. Miogeosynclinal deposits, on the other hand, generally contain little volcanic debris; they are well-sorted clastic deposits, and even grade to limestone and other precipitates toward the stable platforms. Miogeosynclinal deposits generally are not as thick as those deposited in the eugeosynclines, and the formations thin where they overlap onto the stable platforms.

The various Appalachian Provinces reflect such a complex of Paleozoic geosynclinal structures (Figs. 11.3, 11.4). The Piedmont Plateau New England, and Maritime Provinces of Canada are largely of eugeosynclinal origin. The Blue Ridge, Reading Prong, Berkshires, and Green Mountains occupy the site of the structural ridge that once separated the two troughs of the geosyncline. The Valley and Ridge Province occupies the site of the former miogeosyncline, and the Appalachian Plateaus the site where the formations overlap onto the stable platform.

Structural Divisions

PIEDMONT PLATEAU

The Piedmont Plateau extends almost 1,000 miles from southernmost New York to Alabama and has a maximum width of about 125 miles. To the south, where the province is widest, altitudes range from about 500 feet at the Fall Line to about 1,000 feet at the foot of the mountains to the west. Like the Coastal Plain, the Piedmont Plateau becomes lower northward and is mostly between 100 and 500 feet in altitude in Pennsyl-

vania and New Jersey, although hills near York and Reading are above 1,000 feet.

The rocks are mostly metamorphic with complex structures that generally are truncated by the plateau surface. The landforms therefore only locally reflect the rock structures. The boundary between the Piedmont Plateau and the Coastal Plain is at the Fall Line, where the metamorphic rocks extend under the Cretaceous formations (Fig. 11.5).

The boundary between the Piedmont and the more mountainous province to the west is almost as sharp. To the south, where the Piedmont adjoins the Valley and Ridge Province, the boundary follows an overthrust fault (Cartersville fault), along which the metamorphic rocks have been thrust westward onto folded Paleozoic rocks (Fig. 11.4). The boundary between the Piedmont Plateau and the mountainous Blue Ridge Province is approximately where the metamorphic rocks of the Piedmont end against upthrust Precambrian formations. The thrust faults are directed toward the west—that is, toward the interior of the continent.

Most of the rocks in the Piedmont Plateau are gneiss and schist, with some marble and quartzite. There are many mineralogical varieties of these rocks, and altogether they cover about half the province. In Pennsylvania and Maryland the marble belts form valleys and are the sites of reservoirs; the gneiss, schist, quartzite, and granite form uplands.

Some less intensively metamorphosed rocks, including considerable slate, occur along the eastern part of the province from southern Virginia to Georgia. This, the Carolina slate belt, makes up about 20 percent of the province (Fig. 11.4). Its rocks are somewhat less resistant to erosion than the neighboring formations, and form slightly lower ground with wider valleys. Consequently, the slate belt furnishes reservoir sites on the Saluda River above Columbia, South Carolina, and on the Savannah River above Augusta, Georgia.

Another 20 percent of the Piedmont Plateau is granite, or the metamorphic equivalent, granite gneiss. The granites tend to form uplands, and

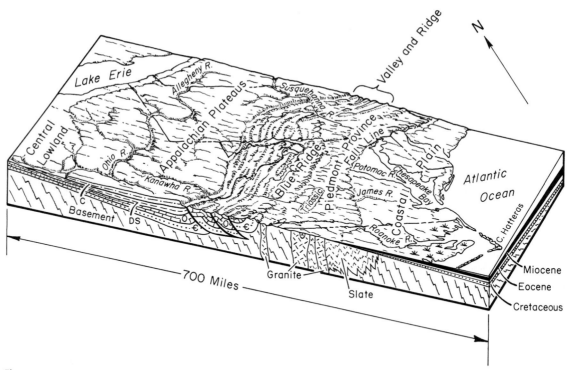

Figure 11.3 *Structural framework of the Appalachian Plateaus, Valley and Ridge, Blue Ridge, and Piedmont Provinces. C, Cambrian; O, Ordovician; DS, Devonian, Silurian; C, Carboniferous (Mississippian, Pennsylvanian, and Permian).*

some form striking, isolated, domical hills are called "balds" (Fig. 11.6).

Other intrusions in this Province consist of gabbro and related rocks with abundant dark minerals. Some of these, especially in Pennsylvania and Maryland, are altered to serpentine, a hydrous magnesium silicate that develops a characteristic and poor soil supporting a distinctive, dwarfed vegetation (Fig. 8.20,A).

In addition to the igneous and metamorphic rocks, about 5 percent of the Piedmont Plateau consists of unmetamorphosed rocks of Triassic age that have been downfaulted into the older metamorphic and igneous formations (Fig. 11.7). The Triassic formations are mostly red beds of sandstone, conglomerate, and silt, but include dikes and sills of diabase. The principal Triassic basins are (see also Fig. 11.4).

1. The Newark Basin (Fig. 11.6), which extends from the Hudson River southwest to the Schuylkill River;

2. The Gettysburg Basin, which extends from the Schuylkill River to Maryland;

3. The Culpepper Basin, which extends from the Potomac River south to Culpepper, Virginia;

4. The Richmond Basin, situated a few miles west of Richmond, Virginia;

5. Danville Basin, southern Virginia;

6. Deep River Basin, North Carolina.

In New England another basin extends along the Connecticut River from New Haven northward almost to the northern boundary of Massachusetts (Fig. 11.16).

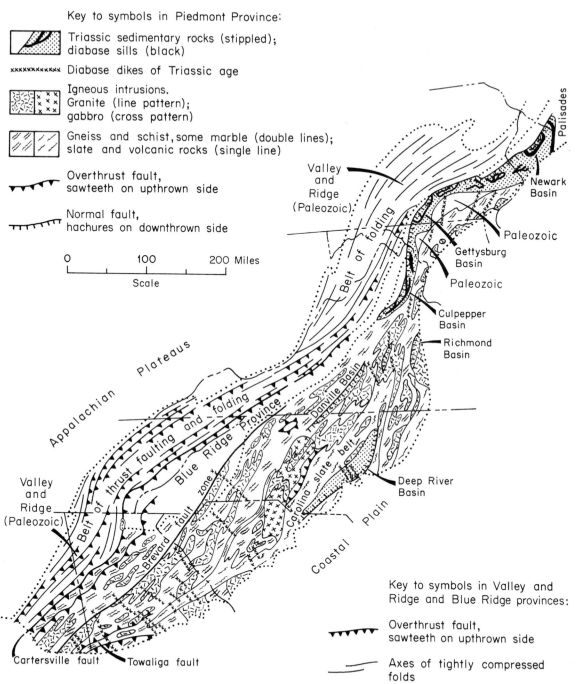

Key to symbols in Piedmont Province:

Triassic sedimentary rocks (stippled);
diabase sills (black)

xxxxxxxxxxx Diabase dikes of Triassic age

Igneous intrusions.
Granite (line pattern);
gabbro (cross pattern)

Gneiss and schist, some marble (double lines);
slate and volcanic rocks (single line)

Overthrust fault,
sawteeth on upthrown side

Normal fault,
hachures on downthrown side

0   100   200 Miles
Scale

Valley and Ridge (Paleozoic)

Belt of folding

Palisades

Newark Basin

Paleozoic

Gettysburg Basin

Paleozoic

Culpepper Basin

Richmond Basin

Appalachian Plateaus

Belt of thrust faulting and folding

Blue Ridge Province

Danville Basin

Brevard fault zone

Carolina slate belt

Coastal Plain

Deep River Basin

Valley and Ridge (Paleozoic)

Cartersville fault   Towaliga fault

Key to symbols in Valley and Ridge and Blue Ridge provinces:

Overthrust fault,
sawteeth on upthrown side

Axes of tightly compressed folds

Figure 11.4 *Map illustrating geologic structure of the Piedmont, Blue Ridge, and Valley and Ridge provinces. Distribution of the principal rock types is indicated in the Piedmont Province. The rocks in the Blue Ridge upthrust, shown without pattern, are mostly Precambrian metamorphic rocks. The rocks in the Valley and Ridge Province are limestone, sandstone, and shale of Paleozoic age. (Generalized from Tectonic Map of U.S. by U.S.G.S. and A.A.P.G.)*

Figure 11.5 *The Fall Line, illustrated by the Great Falls of the Potomac River, where the streams tumble from the Piedmont Plateau to tidewater at the inner edge of the Coastal Plain.*

Cemetery Ridge, at Gettysburg, is a ridge of diabase similar to the Watchung Ridges (Fig. 11.7) but less regular.

BLUE RIDGE PROVINCE

The Blue Ridge Province extends from Georgia to Pennsylvania, and ranges from 5 miles to more than 50 miles in width. In places it is a single ridge; elsewhere a complex of closely spaced ridges. It is the easternmost ridge of the Appalachian Highlands, and overlooks the Piedmont Plateau on the east, rising 1,000 to 5,000 feet above it. It is higher in the south than in the north, and reaches 6,684 feet at Mount Mitchell, North Carolina.

The rocks include Precambrian granite and gneiss, which once formed the basement of the Appalachian geosyncline. The Paleozoic formations of the Valley and Ridge Province are thickest near the Blue Ridge Province, which must therefore be near the location of the deepest part of the Paleozoic geosyncline. Thus, not only has the Blue Ridge Province the highest peaks in the Appalachian Highlands, but it has been uplifted more than any other part.

Besides granite and gneiss, the rocks in the southern part of the Blue Ridge Province include a thick series of late Precambrian sedimentary rocks (Ocoee Series, 20,000 feet thick) consisting of poorly sorted siltstone, sandstone, and conglomerate that grades upward into the Cambrian formations. These late Precambrian formations are metamorphosed, but less so than the formations in the Piedmont Plateau. Northward, in Virginia, there are metamorphosed volcanic rocks of late Precambrian age.

Along the western edge of the Blue Ridge Province, the lower Paleozoic formations of the Valley and Ridge Province turn up steeply at the contact with the uplifted Precambrian rocks. In places this is a fault contact, which makes a sharp structural boundary between the two provinces (Fig. 11.8). Valleys west of the Blue Ridge are only slightly higher than the Piedmont Province.

VALLEY AND RIDGE PROVINCE

The Valley and Ridge Province is divided into three sections: a narrow one, only 25 miles wide, with much shale at the north along the Hudson

River; a second, 75 miles wide, with varied rocks in Pennsylvania, Maryland, and northern Virginia; and a third, about 50 miles wide, which is like the second but more faulted, extending from southern Virginia to the end of the highlands in Alabama.

The Valley and Ridge Province is world famous for its fold mountains (Figs. 11.9, 11.10). The composition of the formations changes westward from the source of the sediments. Sandstone and shale formations in the east grade westward into shale and limestone. The well-known limestone caverns that occur in every state from Pennsylvania to Tennessee are developed in lower Paleozoic limestone formations in the valleys (Fig. 11.8).

Four times during the Paleozoic the geosynclinal trough sank so slowly that coarse, deltaic sandstone and shale deposits were built westward at the expense of the shale and limestone formations—once during the early Cambrian,

again during the early Silurian, a third time during the late Devonian and early Mississippian, and again during latest Mississippian and Pennsylvanian time, when deposits of coastal plain origin, rather like those of our present Coastal Plain, spread westward across the top of the older marine formations. This coastal plain contained swamps, probably not unlike the Dismal Swamp and others along the present Atlantic seaboard, except that the woody plants were tree-like ferns rather than today's broadleaf and coniferous trees. The accumulation of this woody material produced the coal beds of the anthracite fields in the Valley and Ridge Province and the bituminous coalfields of the Appalachian Plateaus.

At the end of Paleozoic time the part of the crust now represented by the Piedmont and Blue Ridge provinces was pushed westward against the side of the geosynclinal trough, squeezing the formations in the trough into great linear folds.

Figure 11.6 *Stone Mountain, Georgia, near Atlanta, is a domical hill of granite about $1\frac{1}{2}$ miles in diameter and 650 feet high. [Photo by Warren Hamilton, U.S.G.S.]*

In the southern section of the Valley and Ridge Province, there was thrust faulting westward as well as folding; in the central section there was folding without much thrust faulting (Fig. 11.4). In the Blue Ridge Province also, there is more thrust faulting in the south than in the north. The northern section, along the Hudson River Valley, seems to have been even more compressed than the southern section. As a result of this folding, the rocks at the site of Washington or Baltimore are about half as far from those under Pittsburgh as they were when first deposited: originally about 400 miles apart, they are now only 200 miles apart.

Four scales of folds are recognized. The biggest are the mio- and eugeosynclines, each 200 to 250 miles wide. Interrupting this are broad upfolds (anticlinoria) and downfolds (synclinoria) about 25 miles wide, on the flanks of which there are individual anticlines and synclines 1 to 5 miles wide. And if one looks on the flanks of the anticlines and synclines he may see that individual beds have microfolds a few inches to a few feet wide.

A representative stratigraphic section of these Paleozoic formations is given in Table 11.1, which describes the principal formations in the Valley and Ridge Province and Appalachian Plateaus in Pennsylvania. In this table can be found the formations that make up the four big deltaic wedges that formed during the period of the geosyncline. Figure 11.10 shows the structural pattern of those formations as they are now exposed.

APPALACHIAN PLATEAUS

The Appalachian Plateaus, approximately equal in area to the Piedmont, Blue Ridge, and Valley and Ridge provinces combined, are an elevated tract of nearly horizontal or gently folded strata. Under the plateaus the deposits overlap the stable platform that lay west of the geosyncline, and the formations are greatly thinned toward the shield.

Altitudes range from about 1,000 feet along the western edge to somewhat more than 3,000 feet at the Allegheny Front, which is a southeast-facing escarpment that overlooks the Valley and Ridge Province and forms the boundary between the two provinces. The Allegheny Front and its extensions form one of the most persistent and most striking topographic breaks in the country. From Alabama to northern Pennsylvania, a distance of 700 miles, the escarpment is 500 to 1,000 feet high (Fig. 11.11). Its extension along the Hudson River Valley, at the eastern front of the Catskill Mountains, is more than 3,000 feet high.

Structurally the north half of the Appalachian Plateaus forms a basin in which each formation has the shape of a saucer (Fig. 11.12). The deepest part of the structural basin is in southwestern Pennsylvania and West Virginia, which is one of the highest and roughest parts of the plateau.

The Appalachian Plateaus can be divided into several sections on the basis of differences in structure and erosional processes. At the north, in New York and northernmost Pennsylvania and Ohio, the Devonian formations that form the plateaus were glaciated, and exhibit such glacial features as the Finger Lakes (Fig. 11.23); otherwise, however, this part of the province differs little from other parts of the province in terms of structure and degree of dissection. At the Catskill Mountains the relief is greater than in any other part of the Appalachian Plateaus. The Catskill Mountains are an exhumed Devonian delta whose coarse, well-cemented rocks have resisted erosion. These gently folded rocks overlook the tightly folded Silurian and Ordovician formations along the Hudson River, in the Valley and Ridge Province. The escarpment continues northward almost to Albany, where it turns westward to Lake Erie. Near Albany, where the Silurian and Ordovician formations extend northward from under the Devonian, they are turned up around the south and west flanks of the structural dome of the Adirondack Mountains. This, the Mohawk Section, consists of a series of cuestas with steep slopes facing the dome and long gentle ones sloping away from it.

From Ohio southward to Alabama, the western edge of the plateaus is an escarpment of Mississippian and Pennsylvanian formations dissected to form scattered buttes and promontories, and is locally referred to as the "Knob Belt" (Fig. 13.12).

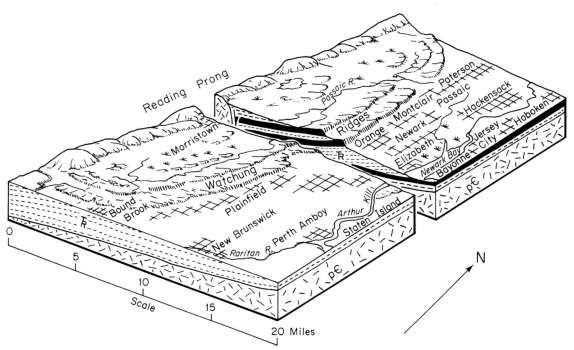

Figure 11.7 *Part of the Newark Basin, showing the topographic expression of the Watchung Ridges, which are diabase lavas (black) interbedded with the Triassic (Tr) red beds of sandstone, shale, and conglomerate that dip westward into a structural basin centering under Morristown. The Triassic formations have been downfaulted against the metamorphic rocks of the Reading Prong; the escarpment forming the east front of the Reading Prong is known as a fault line scarp. The relief along the scarp is due to lowering of the Triassic formations by erosion. Metamorphic rocks also underlie the Triassic formations.*

On the east, from Pennsylvania southward, between the Allegheny Front and the trough of the basin under the Appalachian Plateaus, is a series of open folds parallel to those in the Valley and Ridge Province. This belt of country provides a structural transition from the plateaus to the Valley and Ridge Province. Westward the folds become lower and less steep. Topographically, this belt is part of the plateaus because the folds are broad and open, and not deeply dissected like those in the Valley and Ridge Province.

In Alabama the plateaus slope southwestward and pass unconformably under the Coastal Plain at an altitude of less than 500 feet at Tuscaloosa on the Black Warrior River. That the rock formations and structures of the Appalachian Highlands long antedate the Coastal Plain formations is shown by the unconformable overlap of the Cretaceous and other Coastal Plain formations across those of the highlands (pp. 39–40).

In addition to these sectional differences, attributable mainly to differences in the structure of the rocks or of the process of erosion, other local variations are attributable to differences in stage, or degree, of dissection. Some areas are deeply dissected with closely spaced valleys between narrow ridges (Fig. 11.13,A); others may be equally deeply dissected but by widely spaced valleys that are separated by broad, open uplands (Fig. 11.13,B).

ADIRONDACK PROVINCE

The Adirondack Mountains, in northern New York State, are a nearly circular structural dome, more than 100 miles in diameter (Fig. 11.14). At the center is a core of Precambrian rocks, whose highest peak, Mount Marcy, has an altitude of 5,344 feet. Around the base of the dome, at altitudes of around 500 feet, the Precambrian core

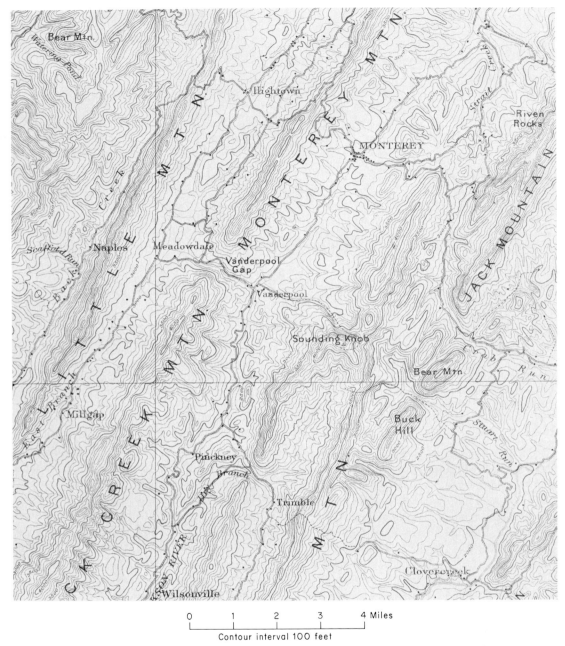

0   1   2   3   4 Miles

Contour interval 100 feet

Figure 11.8 *Topographic map (above) and geologic map with cross sections (facing page), illustrating some relationships between the topography and the structural geology in the Valley and Ridge Province in Virginia. The topographic grain reflects the parallel folds. The ridges have developed along the formations that are resistant to erosion, whether these be at crests of such anticlines as Jack Mountain north of Crab*

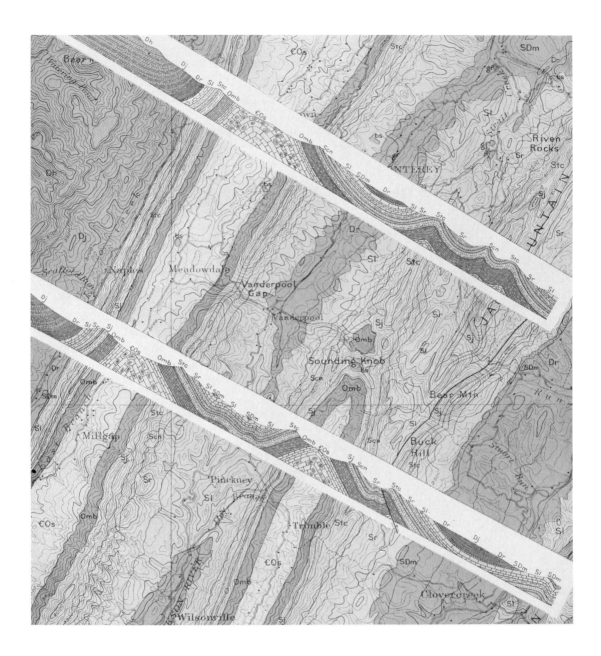

Run or along the flanks of such folds as Little Mtn. The valleys are in the easily eroded formations, whether they form anticlines, like East Branch; synclines, like Jackson River; or the flanks of folds, like Back Creek. Letter symbols on the patterns identify the formations: those beginning Є are Cambrian; those with O, Ordovician; S, Silurian; D, Devonian. [From U.S.G.S.]

Table 11.1

Paleozoic Formations in the Valley and Ridge Province and Appalachian Plateaus in Pennsylvania

Period	Formation or Groups of Formations	Lithology and Thickness
Permian	Dunkard Group	Chiefly shale and shaley sandstone over sandy shale and coarse sandstone; some coal and limestone; 1,200 feet thick.
Pennsylvanian	Monongahela Group	Shale, sandstone, and thick limestone; Pittsburgh Coal bed at base; other workable coal beds; one of the highly productive coal measures; 300 to 460 feet thick.
	Conemaugh Group	Chiefly variegated shale and thick, coarse sandstone; thin coal beds; some limestone; 450 to 900 feet thick.
	Allegheny Group	Shale and sandstone, several workable coal beds including the Kittanning and Freeport Coal beds; some ironstone and limestone; one of the highly productive coal measures; 300 feet thick.
	Pottsville Group	Chiefly coarse sandstone, conglomerate, irregular shale beds, thin coal beds; thickens southwestward to 1,800 feet.
Mississippian	Mauch Chunk Formation	In east, mostly lumpy red and green shale with green sandstone; in west, mostly limestone; as much as 3,000 feet thick in places.
	Pocono Formation	Chiefly thick-bedded coarse-gray sandstone and conglomerate; some red shale toward base; 700 to 1,000 feet thick.
Devonian — Upper	Catskill Formation	Chiefly red sandstone and shale; thickens eastward to 7,500 feet.
	Chemung Group	Chiefly gray sandy shale and blocky sandstone; 1,800 feet thick.
	Portage Group	Dark- to light-gray platy shale; thin beds of sandstone; 1,000 feet thick.
	Genesee Group	Black carbonaceous shale; some limestone; 150 feet thick.
Devonian — Middle	Hamilton Group	Very fossiliferous sandy shale and sandstone; 400 to 2,200 feet thick.
	Marcellus Group	Mostly dark shale, some limestone; 175 feet thick.
	Onondaga Group	Sandstone, grit, cherty limestone; 250 feet or less.
Devonian — Lower	Oriskany Sandstone	Chiefly pure granular sandstone suitable for glass sand; 20 to 200 feet thick.
	Helderberg Group	Mostly limestone and limey shale; 200 feet thick.
Silurian	Cayuga Group	Finely laminated limestone and limey shale; salt beds; 50 to 600 feet thick.

Period	Formation or Groups of Formations	Lithology and Thickness
Silurian (*Continued*)	Clinton Group	Green fossiliferous shale weathers buff; rusty fossiliferous sandstone; hematite iron ore; 250 to 1,300 feet thick.
	Tuscarora Sandstone	Thick-bedded white sandstone; suitable for ganister and sand; 100 to 1,000 feet thick.
Ordovician	Juniata Formation	Red shale and shaley sandstone; 500 to 1,600 feet thick.
	Oswego Group	Gray sandstone with some conglomerate; hard, ridge former; 75 to 1,300 feet thick.
	Martinsburg Shale	Dark gray shale; 1,000 to 3,000 feet thick.
	Trenton Group	Black limestone, becomes shaley eastward; 300 to 400 feet thick.
	Black River and Lowville Groups	Limestone; 1,000 feet thick.
	Beekmantown Limestone	Impure, thick-bedded dolomitic limestone; cherty and sandy; 1,000 to 2,300 feet thick.
	Conococheague Limestone	900 to 2,000 feet thick.
Cambrian	Elbrook Limestone	Bluish-gray magnesian limestone, some shale; cherty; thickness 2,000 to 3,000 feet.
	Waynesboro Formation	Sandy beds with red and purple shale at top; some dolomite; thickness 600 feet.
	Tomstown Group	Mostly dolomite, some interbedded shale; 1,600 feet thick.
	Antietam Sandstone	The oldest fossiliferous formation; 300 feet thick.
Precambrian	Harpers Formation	Partly metamorphosed shale and sandstone; 2,000 feet thick.
	Weverton Quartzite	250 feet.
	Loudoun Formation	Tuffaceous slate, arkosic quartzite, and conglomerate; 300 feet thick.
	Metamorphic	Basement rocks.

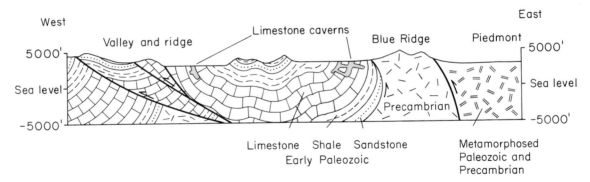

Figure 11.9 *Cross section showing the structural relationship between the Blue Ridge and the Valley and Ridge provinces in Virginia.* [*After Virginia Geol. Survey.*]

is overlapped by early Paleozoic sedimentary formations that dip away from the dome in all directions; they form cuestas with steep slopes facing the uplift and gentle slopes away from it.

The Precambrian rocks that form the core of the dome have been uplifted 2 miles or more.

Some important geologic principles are well illustrated by the structural geology of the Adi-

Figure 11.10 *Geologic map showing the structural pattern of the Paleozoic formations in the Valley and Ridge Province in Pennsylvania.* -€O, *Cambrian and Lower Ordovician;* O, *Upper Ordovician;* S, *Silurian;* D, *Devonian;* M, *Mississippian,* P, *Pennsylvanian.* [*Generalized from Geologic Map of Pennsylvania.*]

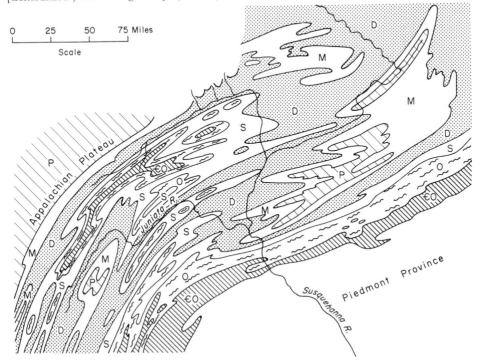

Figure 11.11 *View south along the Allegheny Front near Keyser, West Virginia. Flat-lying Mississippian and Pennsylvanian formations (right) form the east edge of the Appalachian Plateau, and overlook the Valley and Ridge Province. (Compare with chapter frontispiece.)*

rondacks. The formations are oldest near the dome, and progressively younger formations are exposed away from it. This arrangement is opposite to that of a structural basin, as can be seen by comparing Figure 11.14 with 11.12.

Particularly well illustrated around the Adirondack dome are the several successive episodes of uplift, which occurred during the Paleozoic, while the sedimentary formations were being deposited around it. This succession of uplifts is recorded by the unconformities around the flanks of the dome (see Fig. 11.15).

At the south, the Cambrian is overlapped by the Lower Ordovician. On the southwest, both the Cambrian and Lower Ordovician are overlapped by the Middle Ordovician, and the Lower Silurian cuts off the Upper Ordovician. The Lower and Middle Silurian are in turn cut off by the Upper Silurian, which is cut off where the Devonian overlaps onto the Middle Ordovician. This is illustrated in Figure 11.15.

The Adirondacks are related topographically and structurally both to the Appalachians and to the Laurentian Upland of the Canadian Shield. If the Precambrian rocks are emphasized, the Adirondacks relate most closely to the Shield; the Lower Paleozoic formations around the base relate most closely to the Appalachians.

NEW ENGLAND AND THE MARITIME PROVINCES

Structurally, New England resembles the Piedmont Plateau, but the relief is very much greater—as much as 6,000 feet—and the topography is controlled by the structural features to a considerable degree. The distribution of the principal structural members is shown in Figures 11.16 and 11.17. The principal mountain-forming members are gneissic Precambrian rocks. These form the cores of the Green Mountains in western Vermont, the Hoosac Mountains in western Mass-

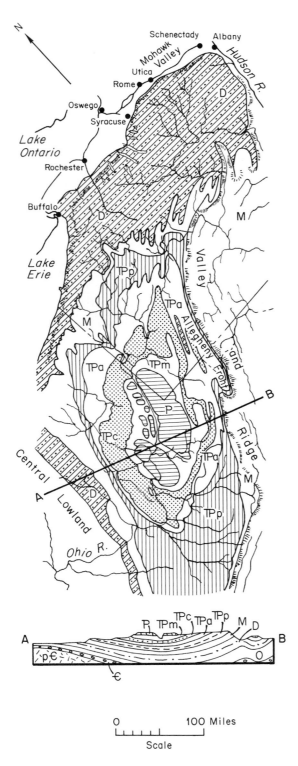

achusetts, the Hudson River Highlands, and the Reading Prong, which extends southwestward across New Jersey to Reading, Pennsylvania. These highland ridges are uplifts of Precambrian rocks, much like the Blue Ridge. To the west of them are folded Paleozoic formations in the Valley and Ridge Province. To the east are folded and faulted, metamorphosed, geosynclinal Paleozoic formations with Triassic formations block-faulted into the Piedmont Plateau (Fig. 11.7).

Granitic rocks that have intruded metamorphic rocks are extensive in a 75-mile-wide belt between the Connecticut Valley and the coast. These rocks form uplands and, in places, mountains, such as the White Mountains in east-central New Hampshire and southwest Maine. Isolated mountains that rise above the general level of the surrounding country are *monadnocks*, named for Mount Monadnock in southern New Hampshire. Many or most of the isolated mountains in New England are granitic, but Mount Monadnock is composed of schist that is not obviously harder than the rocks around it.

Most of New England is underlain by metamorphosed Paleozoic rocks. In much of the region these rocks form a surface lower than the ridges of Precambrian gneiss and granite, but higher than the areas of Paleozoic rocks, which are not metamorphosed, or only slightly so. The unmetamorphosed Paleozoic rocks form basins. Among them are the Narragansett Basin at Providence, Rhode Island. Narragansett Bay is the drowned part of this structural basin. Another partly drowned structural basin is at Boston. Still

Figure 11.12 *Geologic map and cross section of the structural basin under the Appalachian Plateaus. The basin centers under the Permian Dunkard Group (**P**), which is underlain successively by the Monongahela Group (**TPm**), Conemaugh Group (**TPc**), Allegheny Group (**TPa**), and the Pottsville Group (**TPp**) of Pennsylvanian age. Under the Pennsylvanian is the Mississippian (**M**) and Devonian (**D**). In the cross section the Silurian is included with the Devonian. Under this is Ordovician (**O**), Cambrian (**C**), and Precambrian (**pC**). [Geology generalized from U.S.G.S. Geologic Map of the United States.]*

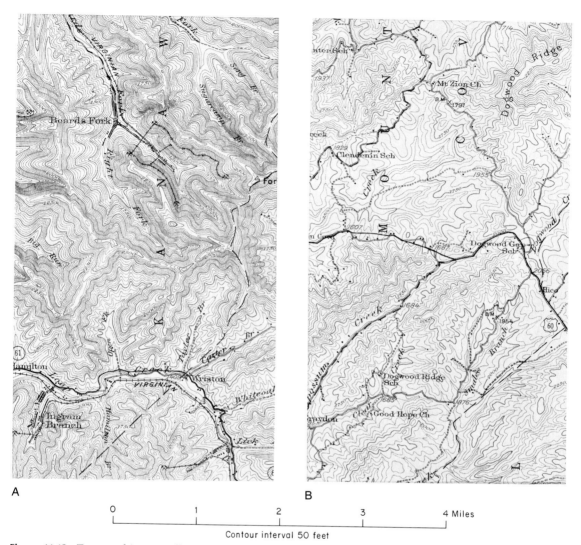

Figure 11.13 *Topographic maps illustrating landforms on the Appalachian Plateaus, where some valleys are closely spaced between narrow, sharp-crested ridges (A) and other valleys are widely spaced and separated by broad, open uplands (B). [From U.S.G.S. Fayetteville, W. Va., quadrangle.]*

a third is along the New Hampshire coast and adjoining part of the coast of Maine. Other lowlands in these formations in Maine are the Bangor Bowl and the Aroostook Plain.

In New England, as in the Piedmont Plateau, the Triassic formations are easily eroded and form topographic, as well as structural, basins (Fig. 11.19). The structures, and even the diabase ridges, are quite like those in the Piedmont, ex-

cept that the faults and dips are in the opposite direction. In the Connecticut Basin the Triassic rocks are downfaulted on the east and dip east. In the Piedmont Province most of the Triassic basins are downfaulted on the west and dip west.

Another structural unit is at the western edge of the New England Province and is represented by the Taconic Mountains along the east side of the Hudson River and Lake Champlain Valley.

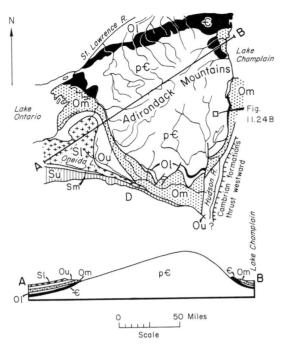

Figure 11.14 *Geologic map and cross section showing the structure of the dome at the Adirondack Mountains, New York. p Є, Precambrian rocks, mostly granite and gneiss, some schist, and some gabbro and other dark rocks. The Paleozoic sedimentary formations overlapping the Precambrian are: Є Cambrian; Ol, Lower Ordovician; Om, Middle Ordovician; Ou, Upper Ordovician; Sl, Lower Silurian; Su, Upper Silurian; and D, Devonian. The Paleozoic formations crop out at altitudes of around 500 feet; high point on the mountains is 5,344 feet. [Generalized from U.S.G.S. Geologic Map of the United States.]*

These mountains consist of Cambrian formations (and some Ordovician formations) that form the upper plate of a westward-directed overthrust fault. The lower plate, consisting of folded rocks of Ordovician age, has been eroded to form the valleys.

The geosynclinal formations and the folding and faulting continue northeastward across the maritime provinces of Canada (Fig. 11.16) to and beyond Newfoundland. The chief difference between this northern segment of the Appalachians and those to the south can be seen along the northwestern edge of the geosynclinal rocks.

South of New York the folded Valley and Ridge Province is as broad as the Piedmont Plateau, and the miogeosynclinal facies end northwestward against the stable platform facies that make up the central United States. In New York State the folded Valley and Ridge belt is narrow along the Hudson River Valley, whereas the New England Province, to the east, is as broad as the Piedmont. To the west is broad, stable platform.

In Canada, the miogeosyncline and the folded Valley and Ridge Province are lost, and near the

Figure 11.15 *The structural history of uplifts can be read by the pattern of the formations on the flanks. (A) Around uplifts that are older than the formations overlapping the flanks, the younger formations extend progressively farther onto the uplift and bury the older formations. (B) Around uplifts that are younger than the formations on the flanks, the dips are away from the uplift, and progressively older formations are exposed toward the uplift. (C) Around uplifts that were raised in stages while the flanking sedimentary formations were being deposited, as at the Adirondacks, combinations of the A and B situations are found. In C there was uplift after Bed 1 was deposited but before Bed 2 was deposited, because the upturned edges of Bed 1 are overlapped by Bed 2. The resulting hill survived without further uplift while Beds 2 and 3 were being deposited, because Bed 3 extends farther onto the flank than does Bed 2. Uplift occurred again after Bed 5 was deposited, because it has been tilted.*

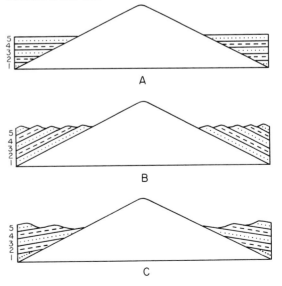

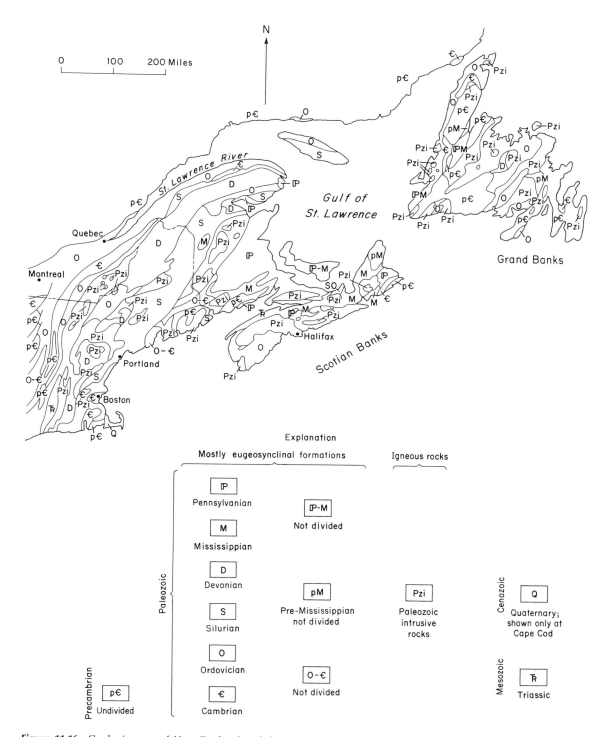

Figure 11.16 *Geologic map of New England and the Atlantic Provinces. [Generalized from Geologic Map of North America by U.S.G.S.]*

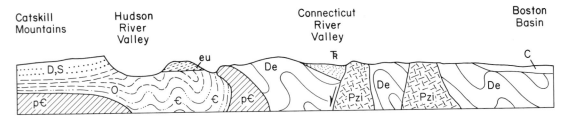

Figure 11.17 *Diagrammatic section across New England and eastern New York. Strongly folded miogeosynclinal Cambrian (€) and Ordovician (O) underlie the Hudson River Valley and thin westward onto the stable platform of Precambrian rocks under the Catskill Mountains, which are composed of thick deltaic Devonian (D) formations overlying thin Silurian (S) rocks. East of the Hudson River Valley, early Paleozoic eugeosynclinal formations (eu) have been thrust faulted westward onto the miogeosynclinal Ordovician. Most of New England consists of very thick, strongly folded, faulted, and highly metamorphosed Devonian eugeosynclinal formations (De) cut by Paleozoic granitic intrusions (Pzi) and, in the Boston Basin, overlain unconformably by Late Devonian and younger (Carboniferous, C) formations. Dionsaur-bearing red beds of Triassic age (Tr) partly fill fault blocks along the Connecticut River Valley.*

city of Quebec the stable platform is cut off. Northeastward from Quebec, highly folded and faulted eugeosynclinal rocks are crowded toward the Precambrian rocks of the Canadian Shield. Fragments of stable platform are preserved in westernmost Newfoundland, Anticosti Island, and in small areas along the north shore of the St. Lawrence River. But the rocks to the southeast are like those in the New England and Piedmont provinces; there is no folded belt like the Valley and Ridge. The deep channel of the St. Lawrence River may be the remains of a trench along which the miogeosynclinal formations have been thrust northwestward under the Canadian Shield or buried under eugeosynclinal rocks overthrust to the northwest.

Near Montreal is an east-west belt of igneous intrusions, the Monteregian Hills, formed of silica-deficient stocks, volcanic plugs, or laccoliths, intruded mainly during early Cretaceous time. Most of the intrusions are in the gently dipping, early Paleozoic platform rocks of the St. Lawrence Lowland. One toward the west intrudes crystalline rocks of the Canadian Shield; some toward the east intrude the folded and faulted middle Paleozoic eugeosynclinal rocks. At the time of the volcanic activity, there were still some Devonian rocks in the St. Lawrence Lowland, because blocks of those rocks were

preserved by being dropped into the volcanic orifices to the level of the surrounding Ordovician formations.

Judging by the thicknesses at Anticosti Island, the St. Lawrence valley has been deepened at least 2,000 feet since early Cretaceous time. The igneous masses rise 1,500 feet or more above the more easily eroded Paleozoic sedimentary rocks of the lowland. This is one of the few places where any limital figure is at hand for estimating Cretaceous and later erosion in the Appalachians.

The rocky coast of the New England Province and the Maritime Provinces (Figs. 11.20 and 11.21) is quite unlike that of the Coastal Plain. The formations that are equivalent to those of the Coastal Plain are submerged and form the Continental Shelf. The ocean extends to the highlands, and the rocky valleys, which are cut into bedrock, are partly filled with glacial deposits, generally more than 100 feet thick, and in some valleys (Narragansett and Passamaquoddy bays) 350 to 400 feet thick. The bedrock floors of some drowned valleys along the Connecticut coast and at Boston are 200 to 250 feet below sea level. Some of this erosion may have occurred below sea level as a result of glacial erosion, but much of it may be attributed to stream erosion that took place when sea level was lower (or the land higher).

Figure 11.18 *Highlands of the Hudson, where Precambrian crystalline rocks extend southwestward from the New England Province to form the Reading Prong in New Jersey and Pennsylvania. The view is up the Hudson River from West Point. Beyond the narrows is open valley in the Valley and Ridge Province.*

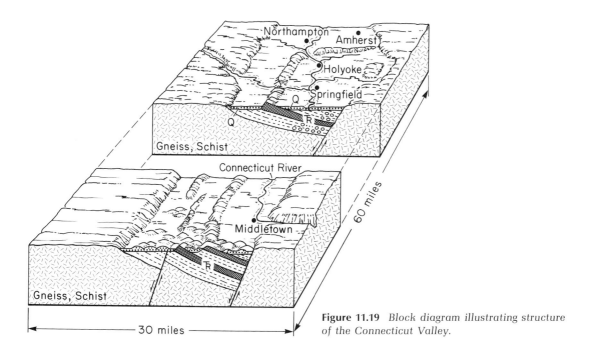

Figure 11.19 *Block diagram illustrating structure of the Connecticut Valley.*

Figure 11.20 *The continent is tilted northeastward, and in New England and the Atlantic Provinces of Canada the Appalachians plunge below sea level, producing drowned valleys along the coast. This view is at Fundy National Park, New Brunswick. [Photograph by T. Clifford Hodgson, courtesy of New Brunswick Travel Bureau.]*

Seismicity

Earthquakes that have been recorded in the Appalachian Provinces during historic time have been of low intensity. Most of the epicenters are in the St. Lawrence Valley, the New England Province, and along or near the Reading Prong and Blue Ridge (Fig. 2.17, 11.22). The locations of these epicenters indicate continued shifting of the major structural members of the Appalachian geosynclines—notably, the structural break along the southeast side of the Canadian Shield, which has evidently controlled the position of the St. Lawrence River, the eastern part of the block of eugeosynclinal formations along the New England coast, and structural ridges dividing ancient eugeosynclinal and miogeosynclinal formations. The very destructive Charleston, South Carolina, earthquake (see p. 229) may have resulted from structural movements in the eugeosynclinal rocks buried there, like the earthquakes in New England. The Appalachian Plateau is almost without earthquake epicenters.

Glacial Effects

All of southeastern Canada plus the New England, Adirondack, and the northern parts of the other Appalachian provinces have been greatly modified by Pleistocene glaciation. Figure 11.23 gives two examples of the glacial features. Ice sheets of the last (Wisconsinan) stage covered the Appalachians as far south as northern Pennsylvania and northern New Jersey (Fig. 4.9). The bedrock geology of the glaciated area is masked by glacial deposits. In places the land has been roughened by glacial action; elsewhere it has been smoothed. The glacial effects are manifested

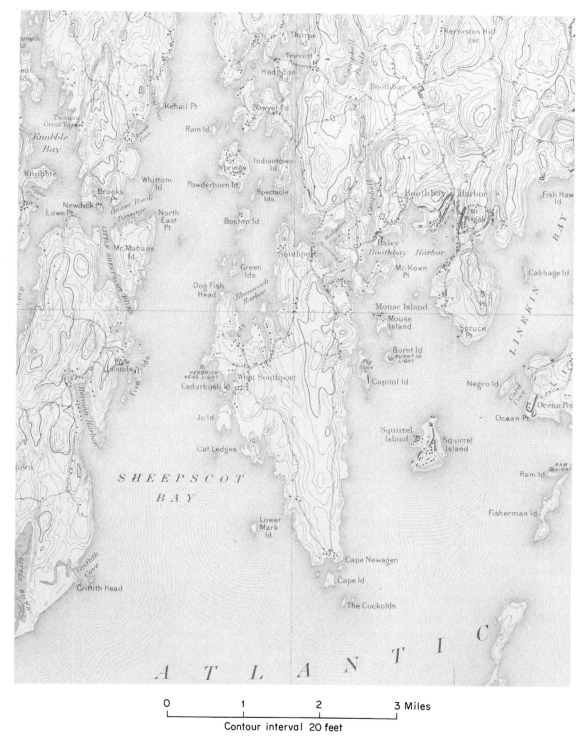

Figure 11.21 Map illustrates the rocky coast of New England. Northeast tilting of this part of the continent submerged the coastal plain and caused the ocean to advance inland. The valleys are drowned like those in the Embayed Section of the Coastal Plain, but because of differences in rock structure the hills are much more irregular, which results in numerous islands. [From U.S.G.S. Boothbay, Me., sheet, 1908.]

Figure 11.22 *Earthquake epicenters in eastern North America are mostly in New England and the Maritime Provinces. Ruled areas indicate locations of epicenters of numerous small earthquakes. Two of the most destructive earthquakes were at New Madrid (1811–1812) and at Charleston (1886).*

also in regional structural upwarping caused by the removal of the ice load that once rested on that part of the crust. The crust was pressed downward under the burden of ice and has risen differentially since the load was removed.

The southern limit of the ice is marked by a terminal moraine, a hummocky ridge of boulders, gravel, sand, and finely ground rock flour. Blocks of ice deposited with the moraine melted and left depressions known as *kettle holes,* many of which are ponds or small lakes. South of the moraine is a smooth plain built of outwash deposited by meltwater streams (Fig. 11.23).

The center from which this glacial ice spread was in Labrador. The directions of motion can be determined and the course of the ice traced back to its source. One method is to map the directions of glacial striae, the scratches left on

bare rock surfaces by rocks dragged along the bottom of the ice. A second method is to trace trains of boulders extending from hills having distinctive rocks. Many such boulder trains have been mapped in New England; igneous rocks from the Adirondack Mountains, for example, were transported southward onto the Catskills, which are Devonian sedimentary rocks. A third method is to map the axes of drumlins (Fig. 11.25), which are parallel to the direction of ice movement. Drumlins are numerous and conspicuous on the lowland bordering Lake Ontario (Fig. 11.24,B), and in the Boston Basin; Bunker Hill is one.

Glacial drift in the northern Appalachians averages between 25 and 50 feet in thickness. In some New England valleys it is 400 feet thick, and in some of the Finger Lakes in New York more than 1,000 feet. Till, the nonstratified mixture of boulders and clay deposited by the ice, mantles the hilltops and hillsides. The valleys are floored by stratified meltwater deposits. The ice sheets in the northern Appalachians seem to have melted without retreating, but by melting at the top as well as from the front and sides—a process referred to as stagnation. The ice became divided into blocks that continued to occupy and dam parts of the valleys, forming a complex of ponds and lakes. Deltas and other stratified deposits in these lakes and ponds were contained partly by an ice wall, which collapsed when the ice melted. The resulting collapsed deposits are *ice-contact deposits.* Ice-contact deposits and outwash abound in the hillier parts of New England and in the Maritime Provinces.

The southern limit of the ice is well marked by terminal moraines, and the various stands of the ice during its retreat are marked by recessional moraines (Fig. 11.25). In many glaciated valleys, there are irregular hills, called *kames,* composed of stratified glacial drift. These formed where streams on the ice discharged into crevasses or other openings along one side of the ice or within it. When the ice melted, the courses of some streams on or under the ice are recognized by long ridges of gravel and sand called *eskers* (Fig. 3.15). These ridges, commonly only

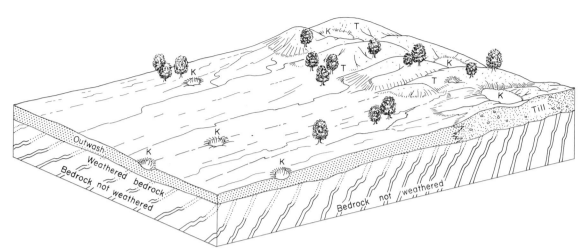

Figure 11.23 *Diagram showing relationship of outwash plain to terminal moraine (T) Both are pitted by kettle holes (K), some containing ponds. Preglacial soils and weathered bedrock commonly are preserved under the stream-deposited outwash, but the till that forms the moraine generally rests on unweathered bedrock because soils there were removed by the ice.*

a hundred feet or so wide, extend for many miles. Some in eastern Maine have been traced for almost 50 miles.

Glacial erratics, the boulders of hard rock carried southward by the ice, are strewn over the New England landscape. Now gathered in neat stone walls, they are characteristic of that region. The ice that covered New England moved across a rough topography having many ridges of resistant rock from which the boulders could be plucked. Erratics are not common in the glaciated parts of the Appalachian Plateaus or Central Lowlands, for those areas lack the ridges of hard rock that could supply boulders.

Bare rock surfaces in the glaciated region tend to be smoothed and show striae as a result of polishing by the ice. South of the glacial border rock surfaces are still rough.

The glacial effects extended far south of the limits of the ice sheet. There must have been snow fields on the mountain summits far to the south, and the effects of freezing and thawing must have been very much more severe then than now, especially in a *periglacial* belt near the ice front and at high altitudes farther south. Accelerated mass wasting (p. 143) in this periglacial zone probably accounts for the huge boulder fields

that occur along many mountain sides south of the glaciated area. The physical geology suggests that there was more effective moisture during the glacial stages than now, and in addition to accelerated mass wasting, there may have been accelerated underground solution of the limestone formations, opening or enlarging the caverns that are so numerous in the limestone formations of the Valley and Ridge Province.

River Systems, Drainage Changes

Preglacial streams became diverted by the glaciers and their deposits. The tributaries of the Ohio River formerly drained north toward Lake Erie. The course of the Ohio River is comparatively young and was eroded by glacial meltwaters escaping to the Mississippi along the front of the ice (p. 358). As a result of such stream diversions, drainage patterns in the glaciated region are highly irregular and haphazard as compared to the drainage patterns in the unglaciated regions.

Some examples of drainage changes caused by the Pleistocene ice sheets are illustrated in Figures 11.26, 11.27, 11.28. Probably because of ice

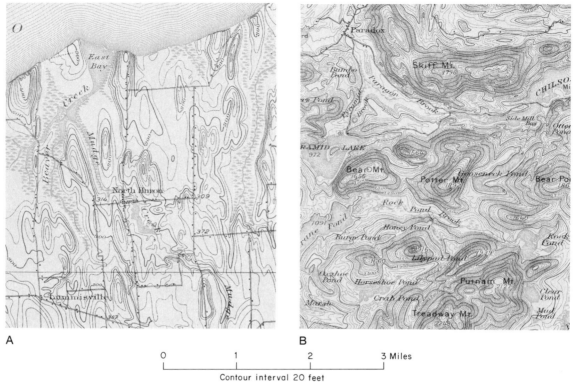

A   B

0 1 2 3 Miles

Contour interval 20 feet

Figure 11.24 *Examples of glacial effects masking the structural geology. (A) South of Lake Ontario, hills of glacially deposited gravels (drumlins) became elongated in the direction of the ice movement when the ice advanced over them. Subsequently, along the shore, waves have cut off the north ends of the drumlins and have built small bars across the mouths of valleys. For location see Figure 11.25. [From U.S.G.S. Sodus Bay and Clyde, N.Y., sheets, 1908.] (B) Lakes characterize the glaciated part of the Appalachian Highlands from Maine to the Finger Lakes in New York. Some lakes occupy valleys deepened by glacial scour; others occupy valleys dammed by glacial deposits. These lakes are in the Adirondaks (see Fig. 11.14). [From U.S.G.S. Paradox Lake, N.Y., sheet, 1908.]*

stagnation in the valley between Middletown and New Haven, Connecticut, the Connecticut River was turned eastward at Middletown, out of the valley it had cut in the Triassic formations and across the upland of hard rocks, into which it cut a gorge (Fig. 11.19). The canyon of Pine Creek at Harrison State Park near Wellsboro, Penn. (Fig. 11.26), was cut when ice dammed the drainage that had gone northward and backed it southward over what had been a divide between that drainage and the Susquehanna. Similar changes occurred along the Genesee River (Fig. 11.27).

The New England Province is nearly bisected by the Connecticut River Valley—a structural valley in Triassic formations that were downfaulted into the Precambrian and Paleozoic formations. The valley trends about south, whereas several of its tributary valleys trend southeast (Fig. 11.28), apparently reflecting bedrock structures. For most of its length, the Hudson River follows the Valley and Ridge, but near West Point it anomalously cuts obliquely across the mountain ridge of resistant rocks that forms the Hudson River Highlands and Reading Prong (Fig. 11.18).

The valley of the St. Lawrence River parallels the southeast flank of the Canadian Shield, a course that was evidently structurally controlled.

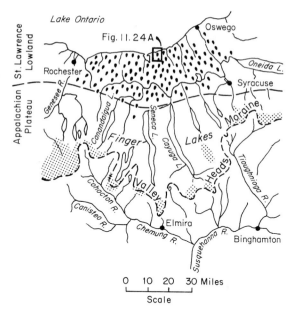

Figure 11.25 *Some glacial features in the Finger Lake country. Bordering Lake Ontario is a lowland belt of drumlins (black; size exaggerated, trends approximate) and buried valleys. South of this is the upland belt of Finger Lakes, which drain northward. At the heads of the valleys is a recessional moraine of late Wisconsin age. South of the valley heads is the drainage basin of the Susquehanna River.*

The drainage system is asymmetric, for all the long tributaries are from the north, off the Shield. The divide between drainage to the St. Lawrence River and that to Hudson Bay is as much as 250 miles northwest of the river, whereas the divide between the same river and the drainage to the Bay of Fundy is only 25 miles away.

When the glaciers melted, sea level rose, and as the load of ice was removed in the north the crust there rebounded, but apparently not to its original height. Evidence of these structural movements is found in the tilted shorelines of lakes that formed during the ice retreat. When the crust was pressed downward, the Hudson River formed a strait that connected the ocean off Long Island with a bay that flooded the St. Lawrence Valley as far as Lake Ontario. Consequently, along both the north and south sides of the St. Lawrence Valley there are wave-cut

benches as high as 400 feet above sea level. Such crustal movements also probably account for the fact that many lake bottoms in the glaciated areas are below sea level.

On the structural dome of the Adirondacks the drainage pattern is radial. Uplift here during the Paleozoic has already been noted. Presumably there was more uplift at the end of the Paleozoic and during the Cretaceous—coincident with the intrusions at the Monteregian Hills. The full mile of relief there, however, is due primarily to faster erosion of the Paleozoic formations around it.

South of the glaciated area, abandoned stream courses are marked by windgaps. One is illustrated in Figure 11.29. In that windgap are gravels deposited by Braddock Run when it joined the master drainage east of Wills Mountain.

The Appalachian drainage system also felt the effects of drowning as a result of the eustatic rise of sea level due to melting of the glaciers. At Boston the bay and rivers have been submerged 16 feet since about 2500 B.C., as indicated by a prehistoric Indian fishweir discovered there during excavation for a building foundation (Fig. 11.30,A). At other places along the New England coast, prehistoric artifacts have been found under peat growing at sea level (Fig. 11.30,B). Other drainage changes are shown by cross sections of the Potomac River (Fig. 10.14).

Only in its later stages can the general geologic history of the Appalachian drainage system be reconstructed; the greater part of that history precedes the glaciations and is lost in obscurity.

Figure 11.26 *Diagram of Pine Creek at Harrison State Park, Pennsylvania.*

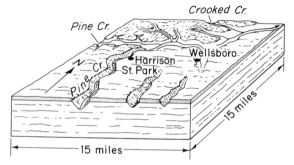

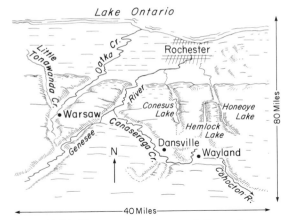

Figure 11.27 *Diagram of drainage relations along Genesee River, New York.*

To a considerable degree the drainage reflects the structural geology, but not entirely.

The divide between the drainage eastward to the Atlantic and westward to the Ohio River cuts obliquely across structural members. In the south, the divide is along the east side of the Blue Ridge. In Virginia it cuts across the Valley and Ridge Province to the Allegheny Front. In Pennsylvania the divide trends nearly north across the northeast-trending Appalachian Plateaus. This was George III's Proclamation Line of 1763, by which he sought to contain the colonists along the Atlantic seaboard and reserve the central United States for the crown. On paper the line seems reasonable, but the fact that it cuts across the structural members made it unrealistic; had he chosen the Allegheny Front, his plan might have succeeded.

The pattern of drainage in the Valley and Ridge Province is that of a trellis; parallel branches between the ridges are connected by right-angle valleys through the ridges. To the east, in the Piedmont Plateau, and to the west, in the Appalachian Plateaus, the patterns are dendritic. The contrast in these drainage patterns shows very distinctly on a road map of Pennsylvania, for the roads generally are along rivers. Right-angle bends in the Delaware and Susquehanna rivers reflect the geologic structure. Formerly, on the Coastal Plain the drainage was more southerly (Fig. 11.31).

Rivers in the Appalachian Highlands are short, only about a fifth as long as those draining the Southern Rocky Mountains (Fig. 5.2), but they are much more numerous and larger in terms of discharge. Nearly a dozen rivers draining the Appalachian Highlands have discharges equal to or greater than the combined discharges of the vastly longer Colorado River and Rio Grande. The rivers provide bountiful water supplies, are a major source of hydroelectric power, and have played a major part in United States transportation history. Unhappily, their potential for recreational uses has been impaired by pollution.

RIVER VALLEYS AS TRANSPORTATION ROUTES

In most parts of the Appalachian Highlands, the river valleys are the favored routes for travel, and a transportation map showing railroads and highways as well as canals has the same pattern as the drainage. An exception is the Pennsylvania Turnpike, which tunnels through the fold mountains of the Valley and Ridge Province. In a few

Figure 11.28 *Diagram of drainage relations in New England (solid lines) and possible older drainage courses (broken).*

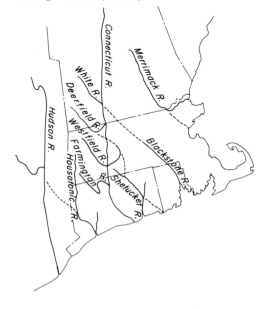

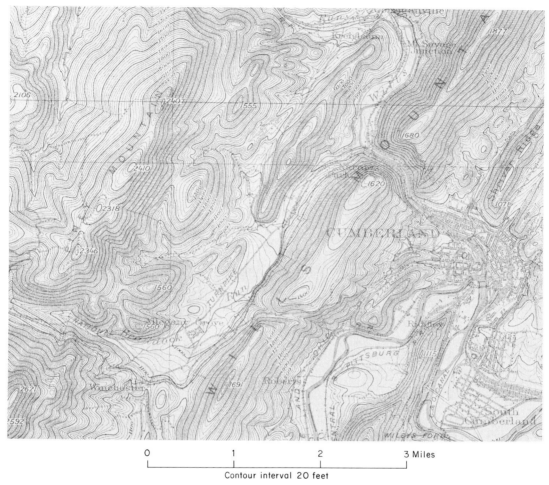

0   1   2   3 Miles

Contour interval 20 feet

Figure 11.29 *Map illustrates water gaps at Wills Creek above Cumberland, Maryland. The gap east of Allegany Grove, referred to as a wind gap, is the former course of Braddock Run; it was captured and turned northward to Wills Creek. [From U.S.G.S. Frostburg sheet, 1908.]*

parts of the Appalachian Plateaus, especially toward the east, the uplands are broad and the valleys narrow. In those places the travel routes are on the uplands, but they parallel the drainage.

Our first transportation boom was based on use of the rivers, and led to an era of canal building. In 1800 transportation in the Appalachian Highlands was accomplished largely by pack animals. A loaded pack train with eight animals might transport a ton. This led to development of roads and the Conestoga wagon, which could transport 4 to 6 tons with four to six horses. Canal boats, a later development, were pulled by

only one or two horses and could transport 40 to 80 tons. Both the automation represented by the Conestoga wagon and the government support of roads necessary for them were protested by the packers. In turn, the wagoners protested the automation represented by canal boats and the government support for construction of canals. Later, it became the canal men's turn to protest competition by the railroads, and, still later, the railroads protested competition by airlines, trucklines, and pipelines.

The canal systems constructed in the eastern United States between 1800 and 1850 are illus-

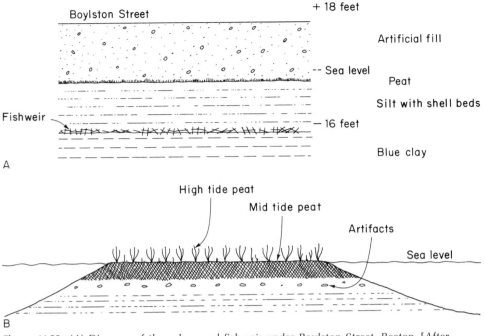

Boylston Street

+ 18 feet

Artificial fill

-- Sea level

Peat

Silt with shell beds

Fishweir

— 16 feet

Blue clay

A

High tide peat

Mid tide peat

Artifacts

Sea level

B

Figure 11.30 (A) Diagram of the submerged fishweir under Boylston Street, Boston. [After Johnson, 1942.] The weir, built about 2500 B.C., covered about 2 acres on a mud flat that probably remained submerged at low tide, but shallow enough to serve as a trap for fish and to collect some peat. As sea level rose, the weir and peat became buried under silt containing shells, on top of which is a second peat. Boylston Street is built on artificial fill on the upper peat. Sea level was much lower when the weir was built. (B) This New England site, with the prehistoric artifacts is buried 2.5 to 3 feet under peat that has built upward and across the island as a result of rise of sea level. [After Johnson and Raup, 1947.]

trated in Fig. 11.32 and listed below. Most of the dates refer to completion of work.

New England Canals

1. Sebago-Portland Canal; Maine, 1830.

2. Middlesex Canal; Merrimac River to Boston, 1803.

3. Blackstone Canal; Worcester, Mass., to Providence, Rhode Island, 1828.

4. Hampshire and Hampden Canal; Northhampton, Mass., to New Haven, Conn., along Farmington River, 1835.

Erie Canal and its Tributary Canals

5. Erie Canal; Albany to Lake Erie, 1824.

6. Champlain Canal, 1819, connecting Lake Champlain and Hudson River.

7. Black River Canal, connecting the Erie Canal and Lake Ontario; authorized 1836, completed 1855.

8. Oswego Canal, connecting Oneida Lake and Lake Ontario; 1828

9. Genesee Valley Canal, from Lake Ontario to the Genesee Valley; authorized 1836, completed ca. 1850.

10. Cayuga and Seneca Canal, ca. 1828.

11. Chemung Canal; connecting Seneca Lake with Susquehanna River ca. 1830.

12. Chenango Canal; authorized 1833, completed after 1863.

Other Atlantic Seaboard Canals

13. Delaware and Hudson Canal, 1826.

14. Morris Canal; from Newark Bay to Paterson and the Delaware River at Easton, 1826.

15. Delaware and Raritan Canal, 1834.

16. Lehigh Canal (1827) and Delaware Division (1832); from the anthracite coal fields to Trenton.

17. Schuylkill Navigation Canal; from anthracite fields at Pottsville to Philadelphia, 1825. First tunnel in the United States.

18. Union Canal; Harrisburg to Reading, 1828. Second tunnel.

19. North Branch Canal; along the Susquehanna River, ca. 1833.

20. West Branch Canal; along West Branch of the Susquehanna River; completed to Williamsport, 1834.

21. Main Line Canal; from Harrisburg via the Juniata River, across the Allegheny Front by the Portage Railway, and down the Conemaugh River to the Ohio River at Pittsburgh, ca. 1829.

22. Susquehanna and Tidewater Canal, 1840.

23. Chesapeake and Delaware Canal, 1829.

24. Chesapeake and Ohio Canal; Washington, D.C., to Cumberland; begun 1828, completed 1850.

25. James River Canal; constructed around falls at Richmond, 1795; completed to Lynchburg, 1840; extended to Lexington and Buchanan, 1851.

26. Dismal Swamp Canal; one of the earliest. Completed for small craft, 1794; completed for flat boats, 1807. Chesapeake Bay to Albemarle and Pamlico Sounds.

27. Santee Canal; from Charleston, South Carolina, to Santee River, 1800.

Canals in the Northwest Territory

28. Ohio and Erie Canal; Cleveland to Portsmouth, Ohio, 1833.

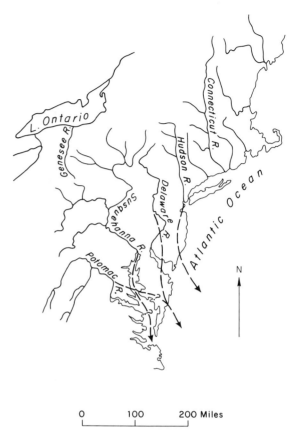

Figure 11.31 *Major rivers in the northeastern United States and possible former courses (broken lines). Gravels in New Jersey include some thought to be from the Adirondacks, and may record a former course of the Hudson River. Gravels in the Delmarva Peninsula east of Chesapeake Bay can be traced to the Delaware River. The Susquehanna River may have joined the Potomac in the southern part of what is now Chesapeake Bay, or turned eastward to join the ancestral Delaware.*

29. Hocking Valley Branch; to coal fields, 1838.

30. Ohio and Pennsylvania Canal; from the Ohio and Erie at Akron to Newcastle and Pittsburgh, 1840.

31. Sandy and Beaver Canal; from the Ohio and Erie to Beaver River and Pittsburgh, 1840.

32. Walhonding Branch Canal, ca. 1836.

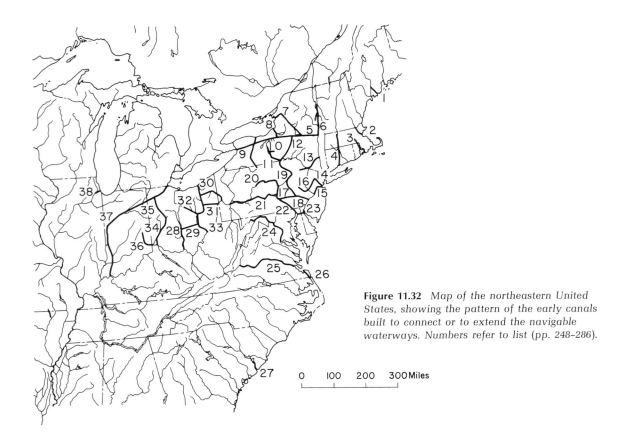

Figure 11.32 *Map of the northeastern United States, showing the pattern of the early canals built to connect or to extend the navigable waterways. Numbers refer to list (pp. 248–286).*

0   100   200   300 Miles

33. Muskingum Canal; to Marietta, ca. 1836.

34. Miami and Erie Canal; from Cincinnati to Dayton (ca. 1831); Maumee and Toledo section completed 1843.

35. Warren County Canal, ca. 1836.

36. White Water Canal, 1846.

37. Wabash and Erie Canal; completed from junction with Miami and Erie to Lafayette, Indiana, 1843; to Evansville, ca. 1855.

38. Illinois and Michigan Canal, 1848.

Lakes

A distinctive feature of the glaciated part of the Appalachians is the abundance of lakes. From the terminal moraine north, there are thousands; south of the moraine, lakes are rare. The lakes formed in many ways. Small ones formed in kettle holes. Larger lakes formed where preglacial valleys were dammed by morainal ridges. Chains of lakes developed in some valleys where irregular deposition of till blocked certain stretches. Still other lakes, like the Finger Lakes in central New York (Figs. 11.25, 11.33), fill valleys that were deepened by ice scour. The bottoms of Cayuga and Seneca lakes are below sea level, and the fill beneath them is hundreds of feet thick. The bottom of Lake Ontario is more than 500 feet below sea level. The bottom of the Hudson River is also below sea level, and is underlain by several hundred feet of fill.

Most of the lakes are shallower than they were originally. Others that are now dry formed in front of the glaciers wherever northward drainage was dammed by the ice. For example in northern New Jersey, a broad lake, known as

Lake Passaic, was formed back of the Watchung Ridges when the Passaic River near Paterson (Figs. 11.7, 11.33,C) was dammed.

Climate

Present-day climates in the Appalachian provinces lands vary greatly from one part to another, much more so than on the Coastal Plain, partly because of distance from the ocean and partly because of the 6,000-foot range in altitude and the 18° range of latitude, from Alabama to Newfoundland.

Average annual temperatures range from below 40°F in northern New England and southeastern Canada to about 65°F at the south end of the highlands. Average annual precipitation is between 30 and 50 inches in most of the highlands, but reaches a maximum of about 80 inches in the Great Smoky Mountains in the southern Blue Ridge Province. Southeast- and south-facing slopes are notably warmer and drier than northwest- and north-facing slopes, because they face the sun and are on the lee side of the ridges. A practical result of this is a greater frequency of forest fires on south-facing slopes.

Precipitation is distributed rather uniformly throughout the year. In those parts of the Highlands that receive an average of about 40 inches of precipitation per year, the averages for the ten driest and the ten wettest years (40-year record) are 30 and 50 inches, respectively. Except for two small areas, one in the lower Muskingum Valley in Ohio and another at the north end of Lake Champlain, no part of the Highlands has recorded less than 20 inches of precipitation in a year.

Maximum precipitation in a 24-hour period on the Appalachian Highlands is only about half that on the Coastal Plain. Maximum precipitation rarely exceeds $2\frac{1}{2}$ inches per hour, and in northern New England is less than 2 inches.

There have been, though, catastrophic floods as a result of heavy rains. In 1969 severe floods occurred in the James River valley in southern Virginia when storms dumped as much as 27

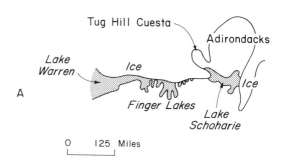

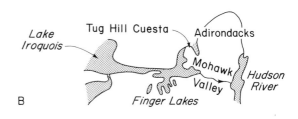

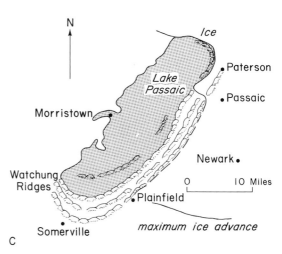

Figure 11.33 *Pleistocene Finger Lakes and Lake Passaic. The Finger Lakes in New York became deepened by ice scour when the glaciers advanced southward to Pennsylvania. As the ice front retreated, the overdeepened valley contained lakes that overflowed first to the west (A) to ancestral Lake Erie, and then to the east (B) via the Mohawk Valley when the ice in the Hudson River Valley melted and drained Lake Schoharie. In northern New Jersey, Lake Passaic (C) formed back of the Watchung Ridges when the glacial ice dammed the valleys draining southwestward through the ridges.*

inches of water in one night in tributaries of the James River in the eastern part of the Piedmont Plateau and the adjoining Blue Ridge. Landslides and debris-avalanches moved soil, boulders, and trees off the hillsides and dumped alluviam, rock rubble, and other debris in the valley bottoms. Many lives were lost as towns were swept away by floods that overtopped the roofs.

In 1972 Hurricane Agnes dumped up to 18 inches of rain in the Susquehanna River Valley in Pennsylvania, and up to 14 inches in the Valley and Ridge and Piedmont Provinces of Maryland and Virginia. At Richmond, Virginia, floodwaters crested about 10 feet higher than the roadbed of the 14th Street Bridge, and a flood at Occuquan, Virginia, near Washington, D.C., was 10 feet higher than a dam 125 feet high. Great Falls, on the Potomac River, together with the high rocks there were hidden under a smoothly cascading sheet of water. Floodwaters reached to the second stories of buildings in the business districts in Ellicott City, Maryland, on the Patapsco River, and in Wilkes-Barre, Pennsylvania, on the Susquehanna River. No respecter of rank, the flood even inundated the Governor's mansion at Harrisburg.

Another kind of flood damage was caused at Chesapeake Bay, where the heavy influx of freshwater killed large numbers of oysters and other shellfish that require salty water.

On June 14, 1972, Hurricane Agnes began developing near the coast of Yucatan, and in three days became a hurricane moving northward across the Gulf of Mexico toward Panama City in the Florida Panhandle. The storm reached there the evening of the 19th. While moving across the Gulf the hurricane winds attained velocities of up to 85 miles per hour, and when the storm reached the coast, there were storm tides—5 feet above normal at Tampa and 6 feet above normal along stretches of the Panhandle.

As the storm moved inland, winds declined, but rains developed in Georgia and the Carolinas, and at least 15 tornadoes were spawned in Florida. Agnes then headed offshore near the mouth of Chesapeake Bay. For several days, until June 22, floods were caused by heavy rains in the mountains and in the Piedmont Plateau in the Carolinas and southern Virginia. By now the swirling cloud of Agnes was 800 miles in diameter, extending from the Gulf Coast to New York and from the west edge of the Appalachian Plateau eastward far into the Atlantic, and the heaviest rains and largest floods were about to come. At Dulles Airport, west of Washington, and at several places in the Maryland Piedmont, $11\frac{1}{2}$ inches of rain were recorded in 24 hours. (The all-time record for 24-hour rainfall in Maryland is 14.75 inches in 1897.) While moving northward along the coast, the storm was accompanied by winds up to 55 miles per hour and by heavy rains in the northern Appalachians and New England.

Still not finished, the storm moved inland again across southern New York, turned back eastward on June 25 and crossed northern New York and southern Quebec; a few days later, it went out to sea at Nova Scotia. It affected shipping until the 7th of July. Altogether about 125 deaths and $3\frac{1}{2}$ billion dollars in property damage are attributed to that one storm.

At any given place, storms of such intensity are rare, occurring only once in a hundred or once in a thousand years, but there is likely to be one every few years somewhere in the Appalachians.

Average annual snowfall is more than 100 inches in southeastern Canada, northern New England, and northern New York, but decreases southward along the mountains to about 30 inches in the Great Smoky Mountains. In northern New England, northern New York and the Maritime Provinces the average annual number of days with more than 1 inch of snow cover exceeds 120.

The average length of the frost-free period is about 100 days on the mountains in the north, and about 220 days on the low, southern parts of the Appalachian Highlands. In most of the Piedmont Plateau frost penetrates to depths of 6 inches to 1 foot; northward, and onto the mountains, frost penetrates to greater depths. In northern New England, land cleared of snow may freeze to a depth of 6 feet; under snow, however, the depth of freezing may be no more than a foot.

Climatic hazards include thunderstorms, tornadoes, hurricanes, fog, and smoke. In the mountain areas, smog is a major problem (Fig. 11.34).

In the narrow valleys, air inversions (cold air trapped under warm air) trap smoke and fumes in the valleys—the condition familiarly known as smog. Practically every community in the Appalachian Mountains is troubled to some degree by smog, and where there is much industry and other settlement, conditions have become acute. There have been occasions when fumes accumulated in valleys in lethal quantities and remained there until winds cleaned out the air, as at Donora, Pennsylvania (p. 204). Such communities become like a garage kept closed with the car motor running. The evidence is plain for all to see—deforested mountainsides leeward from industrial stacks, and smog over every city and town and even over the isolated factories. The air at best is disagreeably smelly and grimy, and at worst is lethal. Industry obviously will remain; it is established, and it is needed. The cure is to develop ways and means of curbing the pollutants and, if possible, put them to use by recycling.

Thunderstorm frequency is greatest in the Great Smoky Mountains, but decreases northward and is least along the northern coasts. Hail storms occur, on the average, only about two days a year. The southern coast of New England is in the hurricane belt, and every few years it experiences a lashing by hard winds, heavy rains, and high waves. The damage can be very great if the high winds and waves coincide with high tide.

Tornadoes are less frequent in the Appalachian Highlands than in the southern part of the Coastal Plain and in the Central Lowland (Fig. 4.7), but nevertheless there have been highly destructive ones. One of the major tornadoes of the century, in terms of destructiveness, struck Worcester, Massachusetts, on June 9, 1953, killing 90 people, injuring more than 1,200 others, and causing more than $50,000,000 in property damage. During the last 50 years Pennsylvania and West Virginia, which have a combined area of about 70,000 square miles, have experienced

Respiratory trouble ?

Maybe you live here

Figure 11.34 *Smog—a major problem in the Appalachian Provinces.*

50 major tornadoes—major in terms of property damage. This seems to be about the average frequency for the Appalachian Highlands.

The coasts of New England and Canada, as well as much of the mountain areas, are subject to frequent, dense fogs. Frequency of fog is considerable in the eastern part of the Appalachian Plateaus, and about half the days each year there are cloudy—a frequency half again as great as on the Coastal Plain.

Forests and Agriculture

Forest vegetation in the Appalachian Highlands is divided into five major regions. From north to south these are (Fig. 8.3):

1. Spruce-Fir forest,
2. Northeastern Hardwood Forest,
3. Central Hardwood Forest,
4. Mixed Oak and Pine,
5. Southeastern Pine Forest.

In addition, in Newfoundland and above timberline on Mount Washington, there is tundra-like growth.

The Spruce-Fir Forest is part of a transcontinental forest that extends from the coast of Maine westward across Canada to the Pacific Coast. Three different forests extend from it southward into the United States—the Appalachian forests, the Rocky Mountain forests, and the Pacific Coast forests. In addition to the Spruce-Fir Forest in southeastern Canada and Maine, outliers are in the Green and Adirondack Mountains and southward along the high part of the Appalachians to the Great Smoky Mountains. The altitudes of these forests rise southward from sea level in the Maritime Provinces to 500 to 1,000 feet in the Adirondacks, 3,000 feet in Maryland and West Virginia, and nearly 6,000 feet in the Great Smoky Mountains (Fig. 8.8). Despite the differences in latitude and length of day, the vegetation is similar at these different altitudes, and the growing conditions are evidently similar.

The Spruce-Fir Forest grows on swamp ground and on well-drained uplands. In the swamps the principal trees are spruce, balsam fir, tamarack, cedar, and soft maples. On the better-drained ground between the swamps, white pine, hemlock, and birch grow with the spruce and fir. On the still drier, mountainous slopes, these species are mixed with hardwood maples, beech, and cherry. The characteristic trees of this forest are, of course, the spruce and fir (Fig. 8.2,A). The spruce, particularly the red spruce, is much used as a source for paper pulp. The balsam fir is a favorite for Christmas trees.

• The Northeastern Hardwood Forest has many more kinds of trees than the Spruce-Fir Forest. The principal trees are birch, beech, maple, hemlock, white pine, elm, red oak, and basswood (Fig. 8.8). White pine, hemlock, hardwood maples, elm, and basswood are important lumber trees. The sugar maple is renowned for its syrup.

The Central Hardwood Forest is chiefly an oak forest, with the white oak and black oak groups (Fig. 8.6) each represented by a dozen important species. The white oak group is characterized by leaves having rounded ends and by acorns that mature at the end of the first season, whereas the black oak group is characterized by leaf tips that are pointed and by acorns that mature after two seasons (Fig. 8.6). About a thousand different kinds of trees grow in this forest. Chestnut formerly was abundant, but a blight has destroyed most of that species. In addition to the oaks, there are poplar, hemlock, basswood, birch, ash, buck-

eye, hickory, black gum, dogwood, white pine, and shortleaf pine (Fig. 11.35).

In the southern part of the Appalachian Highlands the mixed Oak and Pine Forest and the Southeastern Pine Forest resemble their counterparts on the Coastal Plain. In places the plant geography closely reflects the differences in kind of ground (Fig. 11.36).

The principal uses of a few of the more important forest trees in the Appalachian Highlands may be summarized briefly:

Softwoods
  Balsam fir: source of Canada balsam; wood used chiefly for pulp.
  Hemlock: bark used in tanning; wood useful chiefly for coarse work, such as lathing.
  White pine: of major importance as a timber tree.
  Spruce: pulpwood, sounding boards, and light construction.

Hardwoods
  Ash: handles, furniture.
  Basswood: light construction, boxes.
  Beech: boxing, flooring.
  Birch: handles, millwork.
  Cherry: furniture.
  Elm: handles, furniture.
  Hickory: one of the strongest woods; all kinds of construction.
  Maple: furniture; syrup.
  Oak: one of the strongest woods; all kinds of construction.
  Poplar: pulp.

Lumber has been produced for more than three centuries in New England; Maine is credited with the country's first sawmill, built in 1634. Despite continued production for so long, and increasing urbanization, the area of commercial forest land throughout the northeastern United States has been increasing. According to the U.S. Forest Service, commercial forest acreage in New England increased 1.4 percent to 31.5 million acres in the decade 1953 to 1963, and in the mid-

Figure 11.35 *Dense eastern forest and cascades over ledges of the nearly horizontal sedimentary rocks typical of the Appalachian Plateau. This is Falls Creek Falls State Park, Tennessee. [Courtesy of the Tennessee Conservation Department.]*

dle Atlantic States there was a 3.9 percent increase to 43.9 million acres.

Clearing land for farming without protecting it against washing has lead to severe erosion in many places, especially in the Piedmont Plateau. An example, already described (p. 248), is at Dumfries, Virginia, a thriving colonial port until the hillsides were cleared of the forests and intensively farmed; the cleared lands soon became so eroded that the harbor became silted up and had to be abandoned.

Clearing land increases stream runoff. Cleared ground is more subject to landsliding; the flow of springs becomes diminished; floods are more frequent, rise higher, and move downstream more rapidly; and the ensuing stage of low water lasts longer than where the hillsides are forested. How steep a slope can be safely cleared depends upon the kind of ground and the uphill catchment area; generally slopes greater than 15 feet in a hundred—that is, 15 percent—need to be protected by terracing or other means.

Agriculturally the Appalachian provinces are used chiefly for dairying and general farming, with small areas used for special crops. Wine grapes are grown in western New York State. Very little of the Spruce-Fir Forest is farmed; an important exception is the potato-growing area in northernmost Maine. Dairying and poultry farming are the principal agricultural activities in the northern half of the Appalachian Highlands. The chief crops in the Piedmont Plateau south of the Potomac River are: in Virginia, livestock and tobacco; in North Carolina, tobacco; in South Carolina and westward across the south end of the Appalachian Highlands, cotton; in mountain areas west of the southern Piedmont, chiefly fruit, livestock, and general farming.

Surface Deposits and Soils

The principal surface deposits in the Appalachian provinces, as already noted (p. 256), are the glacial deposits, alluvium, colluvium, and the

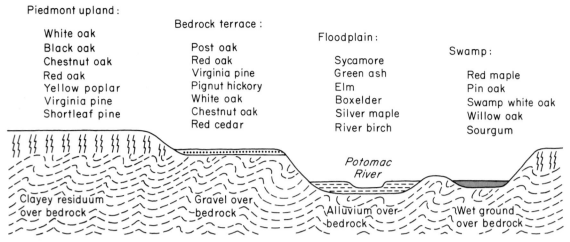

Figure 11.36 *Differences in kinds of ground controlling plant distribution along the Potomac River above Washington, D.C., near the eastern edge of the Piedmont Province.* [*After U.S.G.S.*]

deep residuum, or saprolite. Each gives rise to characteristic soils.

Soils on the glacial drift are mostly Gray-Brown Podzols containing fresh, unweathered rock, even in their upper layers, so they differ from place to place in accord with the parent materials. For example, where the parent material includes much limestone, the soils are limy to within a few feet of the surface. The drift in New England is bouldery; that in New York State is much less so, hence they are correspondingly less stoney.

The Brown Podzols of southern New England (Fig. 11.37), are even less well developed. Podzols, which have well-developed but shallow profiles, are most extensive under coniferous forest. The Podzols, Brown Podzols, and Gray-Brown Podzols differ chiefly in the composition and distribution of their organic matter and in the degree of leaching of sesquioxides. Their development entailed very little chemical alteration of the mineral fraction of the soils.

The alluvium and the soils developed on it are not unlike the alluvial deposits and soils on the Coastal Plain. Podzolic soils have developed on Pleistocene alluvium, but are weakly developed and shallow.

The colluvium is mostly late Pleistocene and Holocene, and much of it is subject to mass wast-

ing at the present time. Where the wasting has been slow, Gray-Brown Podzols have developed.

Saprolite (residuum) is extensive on the Piedmont Plateau and in some of the broad valleys of the Valley and Ridge Province. These residual deposits are the parent material for the Red and Yellow Podzols. Where saprolite has developed on the metamorphic rocks of the Piedmont Plateau, it is more than a hundred feet deep in places. At the base of the saprolite is weathered rock (Fig. 11.38), which grades downward into fresh, unweathered rock. Above the zone of weathered rock is another in which the original appearance of the rock and its structures are perfectly preserved even though the rock has been reduced to clay and to oxides of iron and aluminum (sesquioxides). The density of the original rock has been reduced by 30 or even 40 percent, and the saprolite can be cut by a knife or squeezed between the fingers. In this zone the saprolite is clay that looks like rock!

Above the structured zone the saprolite consists of massive clay. By some process—perhaps by frost heaving during Pleistocene time—the upper layers of the saprolite have been churned and the original structure destroyed.

The mineral fraction of the Red and Yellow Podzols that have developed on this saprolite is inherited, and is not the product of late Pleisto-

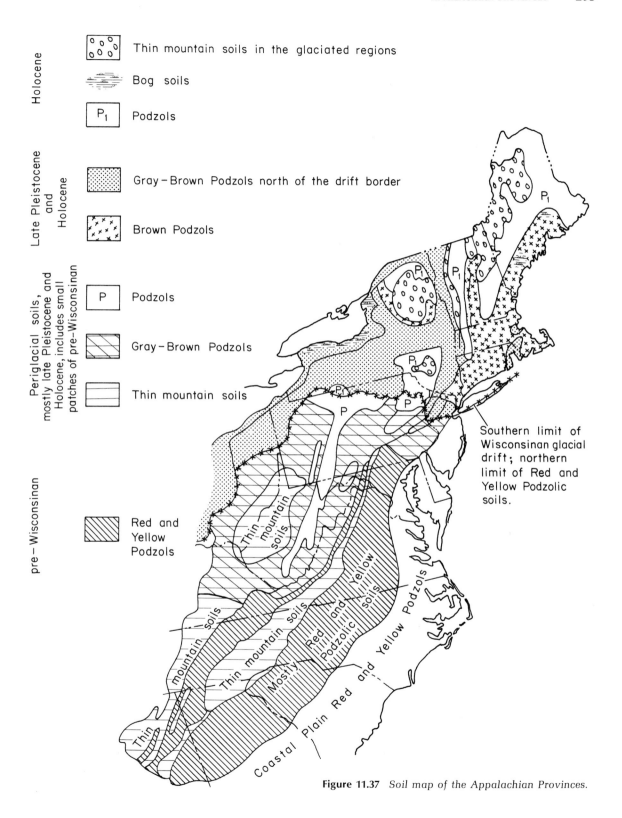

Figure 11.37 *Soil map of the Appalachian Provinces.*

cene or Holocene weathering. The effects of late Pleistocene and Holocene weathering are confined to the upper 3 or 4 feet, which (from top to bottom) consist of (1) an organic rich layer 1 to 2 inches thick; (2) a slightly leached layer that is light in color and extends to depths of 1 to 2 feet; and (3) a clayey B horizon (illuviated layer) about 2 to 3 feet thick. Below the B horizon is saprolite.

Traced northward, the Red and Yellow Podzols and their parent material are overlapped by glacial outwash, or till, as shown in Figures 10.32,A and 11.23. Traced across the Coastal Plain, they extend under Pleistocene shell beds (Fig. 10.32,B). They are not found on glacial drift or glacial outwash of Wisconsinan age, for they date from pre-Wisconsinan time. Some can be dated as early Pleistocene, others seem to be Tertiary, and some are older than the Cretaceous formations that overlap them at the Fall Line, and which are in part derived by reworking of

the saprolite. Saprolite extends under the Cretaceous formations on the Coastal Plain, but some of the weathering that produced the saprolite could be attributed to groundwater weathering that took place after the Cretaceous formations were deposited.

Saprolite probably covered the entire Appalachians in pre-Wisconsinan time. In the glaciated area it would have been largely eroded by the ice. In the mountains south of the glacial border, where slopes are steep and the altitude favors intensive frost action, the old soils were largely eroded. Small remnants are preserved, notably on the Cumberland Plateau. Some remnants are overlapped by younger alluvial or colluvial deposits that contain unweathered rocks even in the upper layers; the soils on these young deposits are classed as Gray-Brown Podzols.

In general, therefore, the soils of the Appalachian provinces form two distinct groups. In one group, chemical decomposition is of little or no consequence. The difference is conspicuous in the contrast between the road cuts in the saprolite along the Kennedy Expressway near Baltimore and those in the hard rocks or bouldery glacial drift along the Connecticut and New York Thruways. The parent rocks may be alike, and there is no gradation between these extremes of weathering. The highly decomposed soils are relics from past climates, but the climatic conditions under which they formed are not known. The climatic and other environmental factors that have operated since the Wisconsinan glacial maximum have not been such as to cause much chemical decomposition of the mineral fraction of the younger soils. The contrast in degree of mineral alteration in the soils is commonly attributed to the difference in their ages, but this is an oversimplified explanation. The degree of difference, and the lack of gradation between the extremes, probably reflects some major differences in the environments under which the soils formed.

Soil erosion in the Appalachian Highlands is severe, or potentially severe, wherever the Red and Yellow Podzols form the surface, and is particularly severe in the southern part of the Pied-

Figure 11.38 *Profile of Red and Yellow Podzol (modern soil) and underlying saprolite. At the surface is an organic layer, commonly no more than an inch thick. The leached layer, about 18 inches thick, is light in color. The B Horizon, about $2\frac{1}{2}$ feet thick, is more clayey, darker brown, and more mottled than the leached layer. It grades downward to the underlying saprolite, which may be tens or scores of feet deep. The saprolite is composed of clay and sesquioxides. The upper part is structureless; the lower part faithfully preserves the structure of the original rock. At the base is a thin zone of weathered rock that grades downward into unweathered rock.*

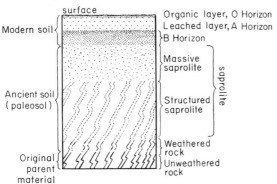

mont Plateau. An explanation that probably accounts, at least in part, for the high susceptibility of these soils to erosion is that they formed in an environmental regimen that no longer exists, and are now out of equilibrium with the environment. The younger soils in the Appalachian provinces are much less subject to erosion, even in the mountainous areas where slopes are steep.

Peneplains

The term peneplain (etymologically, "almost a plain") has special meanings in plant ecology and geology. In plant ecology, the term refers to regions where variations in local climate are minor; in geology, peneplains are considered the ultimate or penultimate product of stream erosion: a plain graded to sea level worn down by the subaerial erosion of mountainous or hilly terrain composed of rocks varying in structure and resistance. The part of the Piedmont Plateau that forms the surface at Harrisburg and extends from there to the Fall Line is a dissected plain and has been called the Harrisburg Peneplain (Fig. 11.39). The erosion surface covers thousands of square miles, and its local relief generally is less than 300 feet. A few isolated monadnocks (p. 270) rise above it.

The erosion surface at Harrisburg, and a similarly dissected one in New England, forms low plateaus whose surfaces truncate structurally complex igneous, sedimentary, and metamorphic rocks. Planation occurred after Triassic time, because Triassic formations are among those truncated. Parts of the Harrisburg Peneplain were eroded and weathered to saprolite before Cretaceous time, because Cretaceous formations locally overlap the surface and the saprolite west of the Fall Line.

In addition to the theory of peneplanation by streams, another theory attributes the erosion surface at Harrisburg to wave action at a time when sea level may have been relatively higher and the ocean may have extended to the Blue Ridge. By either theory the present hills and val-

leys would be the result of later erosion as a result of uplift since planation. The irregularities on the surface seem to be caused by differences in rock hardness, and this forms the basis of a third theory that assumes that the area has always been dissected and has always had about the same relief as now and that the whole area was gradually lowered. Suffice it to say that the erosional history is obscure.

West of the Piedmont Plateau, many ridges appear to rise to accordant heights (Fig. 11.40), and have been interpreted as remnants of an older erosion surface that has been called the Schooley Peneplain.

Water Supply and Water Power

Water supplies in the Appalachian provinces are adequate for present needs and are estimated to be adequate to meet all demands anticipated by the end of the century. The water problems in this region relate not to insufficient supply but to floods and pollution.

The average annual runoff exceeds 10 inches. The months of maximum runoff and greatest flood frequency are February and March in the south, March and April in the central part, and April and May in New England. Towns in the mountain valleys may be inundated by floods where the rivers are not controlled. Figure 11.41 illustrates the network of dams along the Tennessee River; these dams control floods, produce power, and provide recreation.

But dams are not always a blessing, for some have failed, with disastrous results. One such tragedy occurred in the Appalachian Plateau at Johnstown, Pennsylvania, in May 1889. A dam 700 feet long and 100 feet high on a branch of the Conemaugh River about 12 miles above Johnstown gave way during a period of flooding, and released a flood that was 20 feet high as it swept through the city. Other towns and villages in the path of the flood were also swept away. Two thousand persons lost their lives.

Water power resources of the Appalachians are about a third of the total for the United

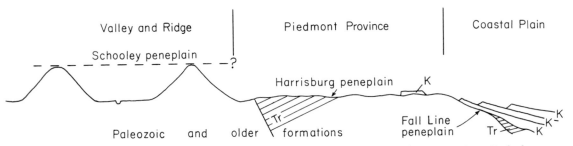

Figure 11.39 *Some interpretations of erosion surfaces (peneplains) along the Piedmont Province. Both the Harrisburg and Fall Line erosion surfaces cut across Triassic (**Tr**) as well as older formations and are overlapped by Cretaceous (**K**). They may be the same surface bent by folding, or developed at different slopes by different processes. The higher Schooley Peneplain has been postulated on the basis of accordant heights of ridges, but there is dispute about the degree of accordance; some regard the ridges as monadnocks.*

States. Some unused capacity remains in New York and northern Pennsylvania, but in other parts of the Highlands the potential is almost fully developed. The growth of New England as a factory area after the American Revolution was due in large part to the ready availability of water power.

Pollution of water supplies by industrial wastes, sewage, and household detergents is a major problem throughout the Appalachian Highlands. The rivers and creeks have been used for disposal of wastes to such a degree that many are discolored and unpleasant to look at, some are unpleasant to smell, and more than a few have to be posted "Stay away—Typhoid!" Floating feces or other waste do not make a pretty sight, nor does the sudsy detergent foam that collects around leaves where branches reach to the water surface. The water in some rivers is so lacking in oxygen that, it is said, nails will not rust. Is all of this really necessary? Not if enough people insist otherwise.

Most municipalities use surface water, because it is plentiful; a few use groundwater. Examples of variations in water quality as a result of mixing of streams having different sources are illustrated in Figure 11.42; examples of the differences in quality of waters in municipal systems are given in Figure 11.43.

Municipal water supplies in New England average less than 100 ppm of dissolved solids. The hardness (noncarbonate hardness attribut-

able to calcium) is correspondingly low. Municipal water supplies of cities in the Piedmont Plateau come mostly from rivers and are equally good. In both regions, groundwater contains, on the average, more dissolved solids and has greater hardness.

Water supplies of cities in the Appalachian Plateaus are variable in quality (Fig. 11.43). Many contain more than 200 ppm of dissolved solids, and are of two kinds. In the north, in New York State, the surface water and groundwater are hard because of their high content of carbonates and calcium. In the bituminous coalfields the total dissolved solids in the surface waters commonly exceeds 200 ppm, but they are not correspondingly hard because they contain sulfate and very little calcium.

Mineral Resources

Mineral production in the Appalachian provinces amounts to almost one and a quarter billion dollars annually. Of this amount, coal, referred to by Emerson as the portable climate, accounts for more than half, oil and gas about a fifth, nonmetals about fifteen percent, and metals 5 percent. The Appalachian Highlands are, par excellence, the place to learn about coal.

Bituminous coalfields are almost coextensive with the Appalachian Plateaus, exclusive of the part in New York. Anthracite coal occurs in the

Valley and Ridge Province in Pennsylvania. These deposits of bituminous and anthracite coal are in Pennsylvanian formations; there is also coal in Triassic formations in Virginia and North Carolina.

The coal beds represent the woody matter accumulated in coastal swamps probably not unlike the present swamps on the Coastal Plain except that the trees were related to the ferns and club mosses. Decomposition of plant matter in swamps evolves carbon dioxide (CO_2), carbon monoxide (CO), and marsh gas (methane, CH_4). As these and other gases escape, the concentration of carbon in the decayed wood increases, and it turns brown and then black. After burial by younger sediments, more volatiles escape. As the carbon content increases, the material changes successively from peat to lignite, to bituminous coal, to anthracite coal, and finally to pure carbon—graphite.

The heat value of coal lies in its content of volatile matter, and this is about 25 percent greater in bituminous coal than in anthracite. It is still greater in lignite, which combusts spontaneously. But the heating value of lignite is less than that of bituminous coal because it retains so much moisture. Bituminous coal is favored for industry because of its efficiency; anthracite was favored for household use because of its relative cleanliness.

From east to west across the provinces, there is an orderly change in the form in which coal occurs (Fig. 11.44). Owing to the westward decrease in folding and other deformation the content of volatile constituents increases in that direction. In the highly deformed Narragansett Basin in New England, there is nearly pure carbon—graphite. In the Valley and Ridge Province there is anthracite. In the eastern part of the plateaus there is bituminous coal with a low content of volatiles; farther west there is bituminous coal with a high content of volatiles.

The earliest coal mines (1750) were in Triassic formations near Richmond, Virginia. Anthracite in Pennsylvania had been discovered before 1803 but was regarded as too difficult to burn and fit only for surfacing roads or walks. Deposits of

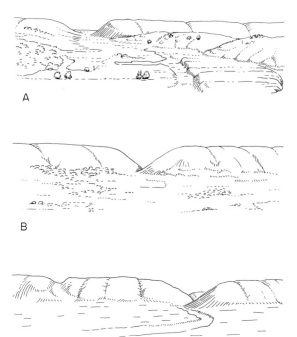

A

B

C

Figure 11.40 *Accordant levels of mountain summits on either side of water gaps in the Appalachian Mountains have been interpreted as the surface of an ancient peneplain. (A) Delaware River water gap. (B) Water gap at Harrisburg, Pennsylvania. (C) Water gap at Cumberland, Maryland.*

anthracite, altered almost to graphite, were mined in Rhode Island as early as 1808, but the foundries along the Atlantic seaboard used bituminous coal imported from England, until the war of 1812 cut off that supply. Thereafter, anthracite was used and found satisfactory under forced draft.

Bituminous coal beds in the Appalachian Plateaus are 8 to 10 feet thick. They are nearly horizontal and can be mined by stripping (turning back the overburden by shovel), or by horizontal workings—tunnels, rooms, and adits. The anthracite coal occurs in the folded rocks of the Valley and Ridge Province, and is mined mostly by vertical or inclined shafts.

Coal yields many by-products. Coke is made by heating coal in ovens without air, and the gases are driven off without burning the coal. The

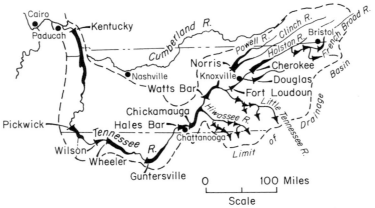

Figure 11.41 *System of dams along the Tennessee River and its tributaries.*

carbon product, coke, is a firm, porous material that can be used in blast furnaces. The gases are collected and distilled to yield more than a thousand useful materials.

Coal mine explosions, one of the major hazards of the industry, are of at least three kinds: explosions of mine gas, explosions of dust, and rock bursts. A combustible solid like coal is explosive when in the form of dust and mixed with the right proportion of air. Rock bursts result from removal of support from a bed that is under tremendous confining pressure; removal of the support may allow the rock to burst into the opened space.

Just as there is an eastward change from bituminous coal to anthracite and graphite, there is an eastward change in the distribution of oil and gas. The oil occurs in the central and western parts of the Appalachian Plateaus. The gas fields extend farther east but barely to the Valley and Ridge Province. The more eastern parts of the highlands, the Piedmont Plateau and New England, are too severely deformed and metamorphosed to retain oil or gas.

The petroleum industry had its beginnings in northern Pennsylvania, where oil had been encountered in wells drilled for salt brine. It was first used for medicinal purposes and sold under the name Seneca Oil. Before the Civil War supplies of sperm oil and whale oil declined, and in 1859 E. L. Drake drilled a well 69 feet deep for oil. This, the first well drilled specifically for oil,

produced 25 barrels a day. Both the production of oil and the development of drilling equipment began with the salt industry. It also led to the first oil pipeline, which was constructed from Butler to near Pittsburgh, Pennsylvania, in 1875.

Gas was first obtained by distillation of bituminous coal, and as early as 1802, gas had been obtained in quantities that made it feasible to consider using gas on a large scale for lighting. Baltimore began using gas for street lights in 1817; New York adopted gas in 1823. By 1891 gas was piped more than 100 miles from fields in Indiana to Chicago. By 1900 the nightly round of the street lighter had become a part of urban culture.

Other mineral products and important reserves of the Appalachian provinces are:

1. Asbestos: Newfoundland, Quebec.

2. Bauxite and highly aluminous clay: From Pennsylvania southward.

3. Building stones such as slate, granite, marble, and flagstone: Widespread in the Piedmont, New England, and Maritime provinces.

4. Cement: A major industry in the limestone belt of the Valley and Ridge Province.

5. Chromite: Minor deposits in the Piedmont Plateau in Pennsylvania, Maryland, and North Carolina.

6. Cobalt: Reserves at Cornwall, Pennsylvania.

7. Copper: Ducktown, Tennessee, Cornwall, Pennsylvania, Quebec, New Brunswick, and Newfoundland.

8. Gold: Piedmont Province in North Carolina; mostly of historic interest.

9. Glass sand: Sandstone formations in the Valley and Ridge Province.

10. Graphite: Low-grade deposits in Rhode Island, New York, Pennsylvania, and Alabama.

11. Gypsum: Newfoundland, Nova Scotia, New Brunswick.

12. Iron: Hematite and limonite deposits in Silurian formations in the Valley and Ridge Province; especially productive in Alabama. Magnetite in metamorphic formations of the Piedmont Province in Pennsylvania and New Jersey, and in the Adirondack Province.

13. Manganese: Numerous small deposits in the Valley and Ridge Province and the western part of the Piedmont Plateau from Virginia southward.

14. Mica: Important deposits in the southern Piedmont and in New England.

15. Molybdenum: Reserves in North Carolina at the eastern edge of the Piedmont Plateau.

16. Salt: beds and brines underlie the Appalachian Plateaus in West Virginia, northern Pennsylvania, New York, and Virginia.

17. Sulfur: Reserves at Ducktown, Tennessee, and in Maine.

18. Talc, from serpentine masses: Piedmont Plateau.

19. Titanium: Reserves in the Adirondacks and in the Piedmont Plateau.

20. Tungsten: Reserves in the Piedmont Plateau in North Carolina and Virginia.

21. Vanadium: In titaniferous magnetite in the Adirondacks, northern New Jersey, and parts of the Piedmont Plateau.

22. Zinc: Valley and Ridge Province in Tennessee and Virginia, in Piedmont Plateau in Pennsylvania, in Reading Prong in northern

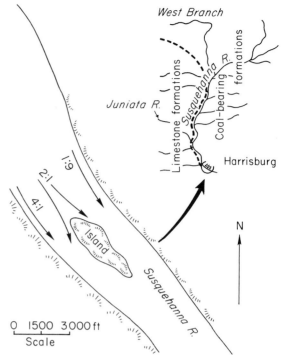

Figure 11.42 *Ratio of bicarbonate to sulfate in the Susquehanna River at Harrisburg, Pa. Water flowing along the west bank is like the water in the western tributaries, which drain limestone formations, and contains a high proportion (4:1) of bicarbonate as compared to sulfate. Water along the east bank is like the water draining the eastern tributaries, and contains a low proportion (1:9) of bicarbonate as compared to sulfate. [Data from U.S.G.S.] There is similar lack of mixing of two very different kinds of river water at Sunbury, Pennsylvania, where the west and North branches of the Susquehanna come together.*

New Jersey; in the Adirondacks; in Quebec, New Brunswick, Nova Scotia, and Newfoundland.

Forests, Parks, and Rivers— The Underdeveloped Resources

The forested mountains, broad rivers, and (in the north) the lakes of the Appalachian Provinces, represent a largely undeveloped major resource that could serve as vacationland. Half of the

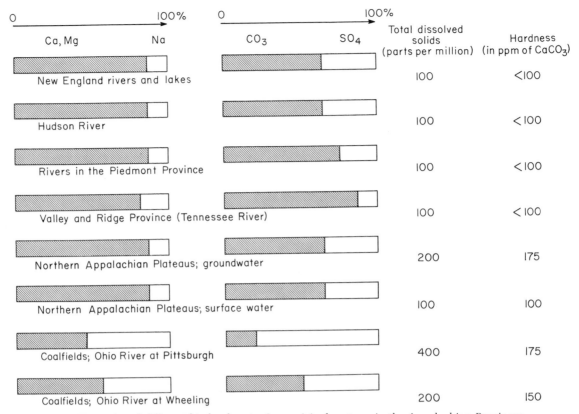

Figure 11.43 *Examples of different kinds of water in municipal systems in the Appalachian Provinces.*

Figure 11.44 *In the central and eastern United States a westward decrease in the intensity of structural deformation controls the form in which coal occurs.*

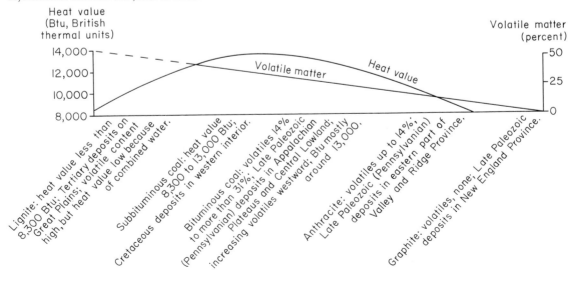

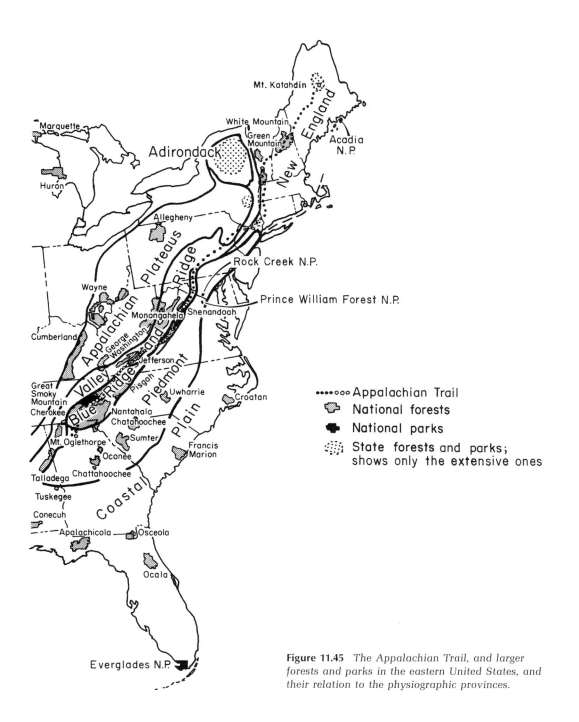

Figure 11.45 *The Appalachian Trail, and larger forests and parks in the eastern United States, and their relation to the physiographic provinces.*

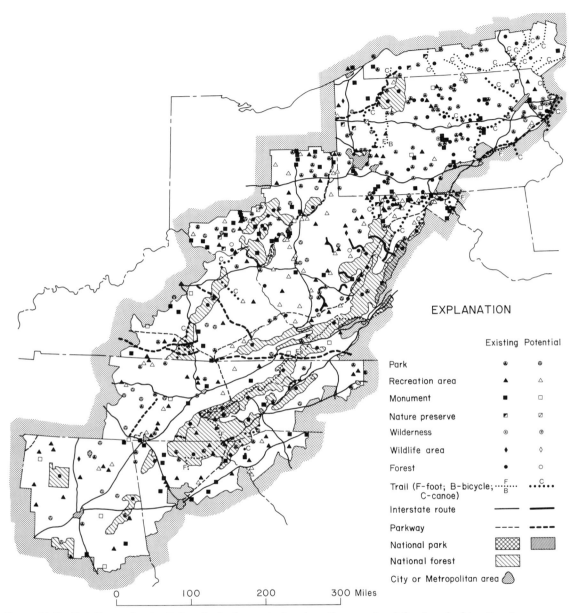

Figure 11.46 *Existing and potential parks in the central and southern parts of the Appalachian Provinces, referred to as Appalachia. [After U.S.G.S. Prof. Paper 580.]*

population of the United States lives within a day's drive of the Appalachian Trail (Fig. 11.45), and as the population increases, the recreational importance of the highlands increases. More land should be set aside, protected from unsightly

development, including billboards, and reserved for camping and other recreational use.

Empty land areas in northern Maine and New Hampshire, the Adirondacks, and plateaus in north-central Pennsylvania are far more suited for multipurpose forests and recreational use than for farming or for industry.

Farther south is Appalachia (Fig. 11.46), a depressed area. Perhaps this area is depressed because we have used it without regard for its total physiographic setting.

Not only is the atmosphere dangerously polluted, but lakes and streams are so contaminated as to be unsafe and unpleasant. These conditions, which arose as an inevitable result of long-term industrial growth, can be corrected and the area restored when enough people recognize that man does not exist to serve industry but that industry exists to serve man.

It would be to our advantage as a nation if most or all of the rougher parts of the Appalachian Provinces were state or national forests, and the land developed for camping, boating, hiking, swimming, golf, tennis, fishing, skiing, and other sports, even including quiet motoring at safe and reasonable speeds. At least 60 million people would be better off! A program of rural renewal should be established that would protect the areas that are still unsettled, reduce the population in the areas already settled, and provide for exporting the products of the forests and mines rather than refining or consuming them there.

References

Billings, M. P., 1956, The geology of New Hampshire. II. Bedrock geology: Concord, New Hampshire Planning and Development Comm.

Cline, M. G., 1963, Soils and soil associations of New York: Ithaca, Cornell Ext. Bull. 930.

Dietrich, R. V., 1970, Geology and Virginia: Charlottesville, Univ. Press of Virginia.

Fisher, G. W., and others, 1970, Studies of Appalachian geology, Central and Southern: New York, Wiley (Interscience).

Glenn, L. G., 1911, Denudation and erosion in the southern Appalachian Mountains: U.S. Geol. Survey Prof. Paper 72.

Goldthwait, J. W., and others, 1951, The geology of New Hampshire. I. Surficial geology: Concord, New Hampshire Planning and Development Comm.

Illick, J. S., 1915, Pennsylvania trees: Harrisburg, Pennsylvania Dept. Forestry.

Johnson, F., 1942, The Boylston Street Fishweir: Andover, Mass., Papers of the Robert S. Peabody Foundation for Archeology, v. 2.

Johnson, F., and Raup, H., 1947, Grassy Island, Mass.: Andover, Mass., Papers of the Robert S. Peabody Foundation for Archeology, v. 1.

King, P. B., 1951, The tectonics of middle North America—Middle North America east of the Cordilleran system: Princeton Univ. Press; reprinted 1969 by Hafner.

MacClintock P., and Stewart, D. P., 1970, Pleistocene geology of the St. Lawrence Lowland: N. Y. State Mus. Bull. 394.

Gadd, N. R., 1971, Pleistocene geology of the Central St. Lawrence Lowland: Geol. Survey Canada Memoir 359.

U.S. Dept. Interior, 1968, The Nation's River (The Department of Interior Official Report on the Potomac): Washington, U.S. Dept. Interior.

U.S. Geol. Survey and U.S. Bur. Mines, 1968, Mineral resources of the Appalachian region: Washington, U.S. Geol. Survey Prof. Paper 580.

Vokes, H. E., 1961, Geography and geology of Maryland: Maryland Geol. Survey Bull. 19.

Zen, E-an and others, 1968, Studies of Appalachian geology—Northern and Maritime: New York, Wiley (Interscience).

The Canadian Shield is characterized by low relief, vast numbers of lakes, ancient metamorphic rocks, and slight weathering of the rocks because of the recency of glaciation. The picture shows metamorphosed sedimentary rocks of one of the Archean geosynclines in the Superior Province. [Courtesy Geological Survey of Canada, No. 117969.]

12

....

CANADIAN SHIELD—
NUCLEUS OF THE CONTINENT

Every continent has a nucleus of ancient Precambrian rocks called a "shield"; in North America this nucleus is the Canadian Shield (Fig. 12.1). It covers about a quarter of the continent, more than 2 million square miles, centering on Hudson Bay and extending into northernmost parts of the United States at Lake Superior and the Adirondacks. The rocks are mostly Precambrian and include some of the oldest (ca. 3.5 billion years) known on the continent. About 1,600,000 square miles of the shield consists of metamorphosed granite batholiths, and these intrusions are separated by highly folded, faulted, and metamorphosed igneous and sedimentary rocks. In addition, there are a few inliers of nearly horizontal Paleozoic rocks. All of these rocks are mantled by extensive and, in places, thick glacial deposits of late Pleistocene age.

Outstanding features of the Shield are its

  1. Ancient rocks, with their record of the earliest geologic history of the continent, including some of the oldest known organisms.

  2. Four kinds of terrain: (a) plains of flat-lying sedimentary rocks of late Precambrian and/or Paleozoic age; (b) hills of folded Precambrian sedimentary rocks and associated

sills; (c) broad uplands of gneissic and other metamorphic rocks; and (d) mountainous terrain on Baffin Island, the coast of Labrador, in Newfoundland, and at the Adirondacks.

  3. Generally low altitudes; a few highlands reach 5,000 feet in altitude, but most are less than 2,000 feet, and more than half of the Shield is below 1,000 feet.

  4. Tremendous mineral deposits, notably iron, nickel, copper, gold, and uranium.

  5. Continental glaciers, which spread far southward into the United States during Pleistocene time.

  6. Extensive mantle of glacial deposits, most of which represent the last glaciation.

  7. Rocks, which are not much weathered because of the recency of the glaciation.

  8. Well-integrated drainage despite the thousands of lakes in basins in the bedrock; the largest are Winnipeg, Athabasca, Great Slave, and Bear lakes along the west edge of the Shield.

  9. Extensive marine deposits of late Pleistocene and Holocene age around Hudson Bay, across the north coast, and in the lowlands bordering the St. Lawrence River.

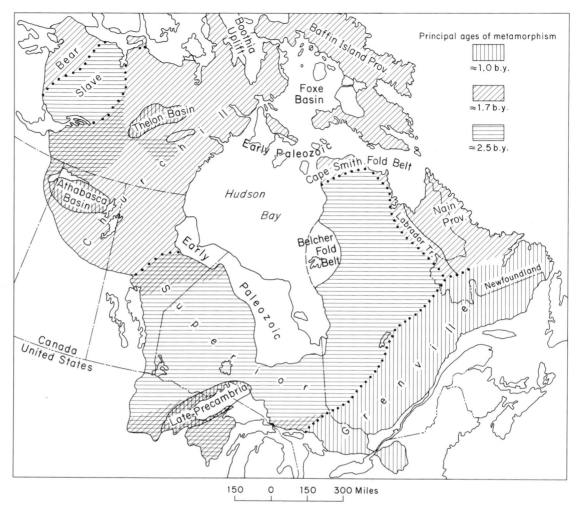

Figure 12.1 *Structural provinces of the Canadian Shield. Combinations of patterns show some principal areas of mixed isotopic ages resulting from overlap of orogenic belts. Boundaries between provinces are shown by dotted lines.*

10. Short growing season lasting less than 3 months except near the Great Lakes; the northwest edge of the Shield from Lake Athabasca to Great Bear Lake is the coldest part of the continent, with minimum temperatures at −70°F.

11. Average annual precipitation, which is less than 10 inches in the north, 10 to 20 inches bordering Hudson Bay, and up to about 40 inches in the southeast.

12. Permanently frozen ground, which on the north half of the Shield reaches to depths

of many hundreds of feet in some localities.

13. Native vegetation: tundra in the north, boreal woodland and coniferous forest south of Hudson Bay, and mixed northern hardwoods and coniferous forest near the Great Lakes.

14. Minor amount of agriculture; considerable fishing and trapping.

15. Sparse population, except near the Great Lakes and along the upper reaches of the St. Lawrence River; 90 percent of the pop-

ulation lives within 100 miles of the border with United States.

Topography

Topographically the Shield is a vast saucer rising outward from Hudson Bay and Foxe Basin. It extends northward to Baffin Island, eastward to the coast of Labrador and Newfoundland, southward to the St. Lawrence River and the Great Lakes, and westward to the interior plains of Canada. The surface is a peneplain with local relief mostly less than 250 feet; even where the relief is mountainous (up to 5,000 feet), as at the Davis Mountains on Baffin Island, at the highlands along the coast of Labrador, and at the Laurentian Highlands overlooking the St. Lawrence, the summits are maturely eroded and smoothed. At the Otish Mountains in the Laurentian Highlands of southeastern Quebec, rounded knobs of resistant rocks rise to 3,700 feet in altitude.

A highland area that borders Lake Superior in southern Ontario, Upper Michigan, Wisconsin, and Minnesota includes the Iron Ranges, which are southwest-trending hills a few hundred feet high (Fig. 12.2). This, the Superior Upland, forms the divide between drainage northward to Hudson Bay, eastward to the Great Lakes, and southward to the Mississippi River. Altitudes are mostly around 1,500 feet, but in a few places reach 2,000 feet.

Hudson Bay is a structural and topographic basin at the center of the Shield; the bay is slightly more than 600 feet deep. Along its south shore is the Hudson Bay Plain, less than 500 feet in altitude and underlain by thin formations of Ordovician, Silurian, and Devonian age that rest unconformably on the Precambrian. Resting unconformably on the Paleozoic are some sediments of Cretaceous age. The early Paleozoic formations reappear in Southampton Island and other islands at the north end of the Bay.

The Precambrian rocks and surface of the Shield rise from under Hudson Bay to uplands rimming the saucer, and the outer slopes of this rim are steeper than the inner slopes. In southern Quebec and Ontario, the rivers that cascade off the rim have been important sources of water power. Along the south and west sides of the Shield, the Precambrian rocks slope into low country and pass under Paleozoic and younger sedimentary formations that form cuestas facing the Shield. The belt of large lakes along the west edge of the Shield occupies that lowland.

Facing the Shield and sloping away from it is a series of cuestas of Paleozoic rocks. (Figs. 12.3, 12.4). One of these, the Niagara Escarpment, defines the arcuate north shores of Lakes Michigan and Huron and extends to Niagara Falls (Fig. 12.5) and eastward across central New York.

Despite the recency of the glaciation and the hummocky surface formed by the glacial deposits, the Shield has a well-developed system of rivers. Many lakes occupy basins eroded in the bedrock.

Structural Framework, Precambrian History

Most of the Shield is composed of granite and gneiss, in large part thought to be granitized sediments. The intrusions are of many ages, at least six different ages radiometrically. Infolded and infaulted with the granite and gneiss are belts of metamorphosed volcanic and sedimentary rocks, remnants of Precambrian geosynclines. They now are isolated from one another, and correlations between the structural basins are subject to considerable uncertainty. The 1965 Geologic Map of North America divides the deposits into Lower, Middle, and Upper Precambrian (Table 12.1).

The Canadian Shield has been divided into several structural provinces (Fig. 12.1) representing the six major episodes of Precambrian and early Paleozoic history. Precambrian rocks of the Shield contain no fossils other than those of very primitive plants. These are of great interest for their bearing on early life but are not useful for stratigraphic dating. It is possible to date the Precambrian crystalline rocks of the Shield by determining the radiometric ages of minerals from igneous and metamorphic rocks supposedly

Figure 12.2 *Even though the linear structures of the Canadian Shield are Precambrian, they are expressed in the landscape because the formations differ in resistance to erosion. As noted in the text, this linearity shows in the outline of Lake Superior; it can be seen in this view of the elongated Lake of the Clouds, in the Porcupine Mountains State Park, Michigan. [Courtesy Michigan Department of Natural Resources.]*

associated with mountain-building episodes, or orogenies. Most of the dating has been done by measuring the potassium-argon ratios in micas. The principal episodes of orogeny and granite intrusion are:

Eon	Orogeny and granite (mean K-Ar mica age, millions of years)
Proterozoic	Post-Grenvillian (955 to 600)
	Grenvillian (955)
	Elsonian (1370)
	Hudsonian (1735)
Archean	Kenoran (2480) Laurentian (3500?)

The reason why igneous intrusions are used to mark the major episodes of Precambrian history, as shown in the table, is because there is no way of correlating the Precambrian rocks in different regions escept by radiometric methods, which can be applied only to the igneous rocks. The sedimentary formations of necessity must be correlated by bracketing them between datable igneous masses.

Within each of the periods between the dated episodes, there are strongly deformed sedimentary and volcanic deposits. The Archean deposits, estimated to be 20,000 to almost 50,000 feet thick, record profound unconformities that cannot be dated because the rocks were altered by later episodes or orogeny or granitic intrusion. The dates represent the episodes that terminated the periods; the number of such episodes must be very much greater than is suggested by the table.

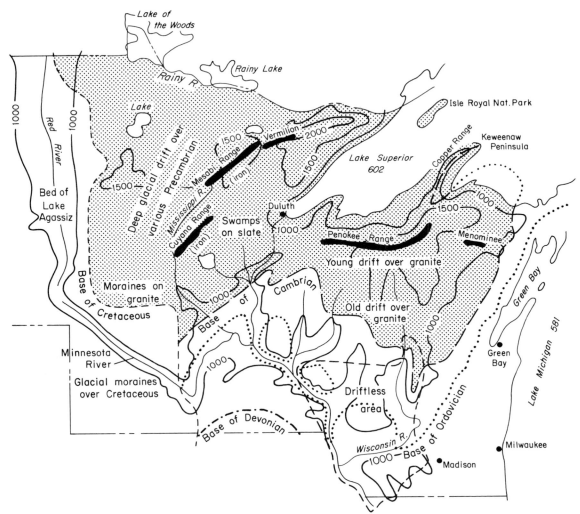

Figure 12.3 *Map of the Superior Upland (stippled area), an anticlinal upwarp. Paleozoic formations on the east and south flanks dip away from the upland and form a series of cuestas. Green Bay lies between two cuestas. On the west, Cretaceous formations overlap the Precambrian rocks and the cuestas of Paleozoic formations south of the upland. Principal ranges are shown in black. Most of the upland is deeply mantled with glacial drift, which obscures the older rocks.*

SUPERIOR PROVINCE

Table 12.1 shows the Precambrian formations and history as currently inferred for the areas bordering Lake Superior. The pre-Kenoran there includes two major depositional series separated by the Laurentian granite and the orogeny with which it was associated. The oldest known rock in North America is Archean granite, which crops out along the Minnesota River; the rock is possibly equivalent to the Laurentian. The older pre-Laurentian depositional series, the Keewatin (Ely Greenstone and Soudan Iron Formation), are geosynclinical deposits of unknown thickness. These were folded and intruded by the Saganaga (Laurentian) granite batholiths and then buried under sediments represented by the Knife Lake Group of slate, graywacke, and conglomerate,

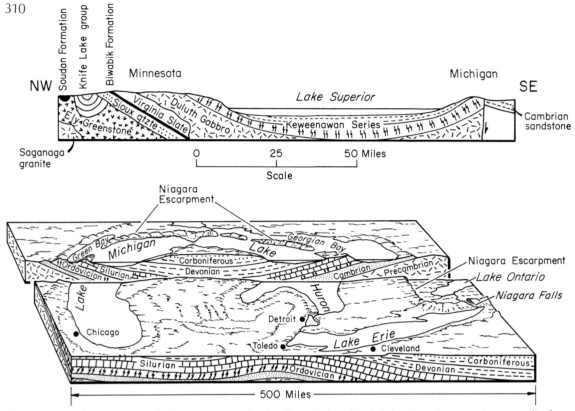

Figure 12.4 *Differences in geologic structure under the Great Lakes. (Top) Lake Superior occupies a synclical basin. (Bottom) Lakes Michigan and Huron occupy strike valleys between cuestas. They are in back of the Niagara Escarpment and flank the structural basin under Michigan. Green Bay and Georgian Bay also occupy strike valleys between cuestas; they are in front of the Escarpment.*

which are at least 11,000 feet thick and also of geosynclinal origin. These in turn were folded and intruded by the Algoman (= Kenoran) granite batholith about 2.5 billion years ago. Clearly, Archean history is long and includes at least two stages of geosynclinal downfolding, each terminated by upfolding and intrusion of granite. Because we are able to date only the episodes of granitic intrusion, the history between those episodes is very uncertain.

The next episode that can be dated is the one that produced the Hudsonian granite, which, in the Lake Superior region, terminated the Huronian geosyncline, in which the Animikie Series was deposited (Table 12.1). This episode is best dated in the Churchill and Bear Provinces and in the central part of the Superior Upland in Minnesota. In all these areas, however, scattered age determinations span the Kenoran-Hudsonian interval. Clearly, the Shield was not structurally

quiescent during those 800 million years, but the igneous activity and metamorphism of the Hudsonian has obscured the age of the later episodes of orogeny and granitic intrusion.

The geosynclinal sediments deposited during the Kenoran-Hudsonian interval are better sorted and contain more limestone than do the pre-Kenoran deposits. Moreover, some of the sediments were deposited as shelf deposits on stable platforms and are only slightly folded or metamorphosed.

The Elsonian Orogeny is even less well documented. It is represented mostly in the western part of the Nain Province, and age determinations made there span most of the Hudsonian-Grenvillian interval. Other age determinations, made on rocks in the Superior Upland and Grenville provinces, also span that interval.

The most extensive Elsonian and Grenvillian rocks are little-deformed shelf deposits that include a wide variety of sedimentary rocks—conglomerate, shale, sandstone, and limestone (or dolomite). These rocks, in places interbedded with lavas, are well represented in the Lake Superior Basin and also in the late-Precambrian Thelon and Athabasca basins of the Churchill Province. In places, Grenvillian formations rest unconformably on Elsonian structures or intrusions. The late-Precambrian formations in the Appalachian geosyncline (p. 260) may be of this age, and there are correlative formations in the Cordilleran geosynclines.

By Cambrian time the complex rocks and structures of the Canadian Shield had been reduced by erosion to a peneplain and were overlapped by Cambrian marine formations. Along the St. Lawrence, Ordovician formations overlap beyond the Cambrian and rest on Shield rocks. Early Paleozoic formations resting on Shield rocks around Hudson Bay have an aggregate thickness of about 3,000 feet; geophysical measurements indicate that the formations may be twice that thick under the Bay. These early Paleozoic formations form the Hudson Bay Lowland at the south end of the Bay. As a result of subsequent uplift the Cambrian and later Paleozoic formations have been stripped from the Superior Upland and the Precambrian rocks again exposed. The present relief, about 1,500 feet, results from later erosion by streams and glaciers that cut deeply into the less resistant of the Precambrian formations. The more resistant formations have again been etched into relief, and control the trend of many of the ranges, peninsulas, and bays of Lake Superior.

CHURCHILL PROVINCE

The Churchill Province includes chiefly middle Precambrian formations. Most of the surface is broad, gently sloping plateau that drains east to Hudson Bay.

On the west side of Hudson Bay, north of Thelon River and the Chesterfield Inlet, is the Wager Plateau, which has one of the few very hilly areas on the Shield; altitudes are only about 2,000 feet, but the terrain is deeply dissected. Some of the rocks are intrusive granites. Between

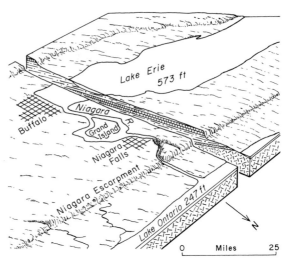

Figure 12.5 *Niagara Falls, view southwest. Niagara River, flowing from Lake Erie, divides at Grand Island, goes over falls almost 200 feet high at the Niagara Escarpment, and discharges in a gorge to Lake Ontario. The escarpment south of Lake Erie is the northern edge of the Appalachian Plateau, here composed of Devonian formations.*

the Wager Plateau and Bear-Slave Upland is the Back Lowland, mostly below 1,000 feet in altitude and composed mainly of Archean Gneiss. This is treeless terrain with post-glacial marine muds up to 675 feet above present sea level.

South of the Back Lowland is the Thelon Plain, formed of gently dipping late Precambrian conglomerate, sandstone, siltstone, limestone, and volcanic rocks. These rocks were not affected by folding. South of this plain is the Kazan Upland; the greatest altitudes are 1,500 to 1,900 feet, and local relief 200 to 300 feet. The greater part of the upland slopes and drains east to Hudson Bay, but a narrow belt on the west drains into the Mackenzie River system. At the west edge, south of Lake Athabasca is another plain of gently dipping sedimentary formations like the Thelon Plain, the Athabasca Plain, which slopes west.

BEAR-SLAVE UPLAND

At the northwest corner of the Shield is upland, with altitudes from a few hundred to about 2,000 feet. Hills are rounded but rocky; the land-

Table 12.1

Precambrian Deposits and Inferred History in the Lake Superior Region

Formation or Event	Lithology and Thickness
Flooding by Cambrian sea	Marine sediments; deposition estimated to have begun 600 million years ago.
Erosion	Truncation of Precambrian structures.
Intrusion of Duluth Gabbro (= Grenville?)	Gabbro intruded at base of Keeweenawan Series and as sills in the Keeweenawan; some granite.
Keeweenawan Series	Deposition of lavas about 3,000 feet thick; some sandstone and conglomerate interbedded with the lavas.
	Deposition of Sioux Quartzite(?)
	Kilarney Granite (Hudsonian, 1.7 b.y.)
Animikie Series	Virginia Slate deposited as clayey mud in Animikie Seaway; 3,000 feet thick.
	Biwabik Formation, an iron-bearing deposit of silica and carbonates; 750 feet thick. This is the iron formation of the Mesabi Range.
	Pokegama Quartzite, 200 feet thick. (cf. Fig. 12.4)
erosion	Truncation of fold structures developed during Algoman orogeny (Ep-Archean interval = Kenoran)
	Algoman (= Kenoran) Orogeny, 2.5 b.y.; folding and volcanism; intrusion of granite batholiths at the Vermillion and Mesabi ranges.
Knife Lake Group, Timiskaming	Slate, quartzite, conglomerate, iron formations, and volcanic tuff and agglomerate; at least 11,000 feet thick.
Erosion	Truncation of fold structures developed during the Laurentian orogeny.
Laurentian orogeny	Uplift with folding and intrusion of the Laurentian granite batholith; possibly 3.5 b.y.
Soudan Formation	Jasper and slate a few hundred feet thick. Subsequent weathering and leaching of the silica have left a deposit enriched in iron—the high grade Vermillion iron ore that has been mined almost continuously since 1884.
Ely Greenstone	Lavas representing flows that accumulated under water; several thousand feet thick.

Left margin labels: Upper Precambrian / Middle Precambrian / Lower Precambrian; Algonquian; (Archean)

scape is treeless and lakes are numerous. The divide between Hudson Bay and MacKenzie River drainage runs approximately through the middle of the upland. The oldest rocks are toward the south, near Great Slave Lake, where volcanic and sedimentary rocks of the Yellowknife Group are intruded by granite of Kenoran age (2.5 b.y.). There also are younger intrusions, some Hudsonian (1.7 b.y.) and others as late as Grenvillian (1.0 b.y.).

In the Bear Province to the northwest, the oldest dates are Hudsonian (1.7 b.y.). The sedimentary formations include miogeosynclinial dolomite, shale, quartzite, and siltstone; to the west are eugeosynclinal red beds and volcanics. Some formations are younger than Grenvillian.

NAIN PROVINCE

In the Nain Province, structural trends are mostly north to northwest. Rocks in the eastern part, along the rugged tundra-covered Labrador coast, are Archean; those in the west have yielded Elsonian dates. Along the southwest edge of the Province is the Labrador Trough, formed of tightly folded Proterozoic geosynclinal sedimentary rocks. Ridges and valleys are parallel like those in the folded Appalachians; the ridges are formed of resistant slate and quartzite, whereas the valleys are in dolomite.

LAURENTIAN HIGHLANDS

The forested Laurentian Highlands rise sharply from the St. Lawrence Lowland along a mountainous front that overlooks the St. Lawrence. The relief is 1,000 to 2,000 feet, but some broad summits reach 3,000 feet in altitude. Tributaries of the St. Lawrence River are deeply incised into the escarpment. Most of the highland has yielded Elsonian or younger dates, but some inliers are of Archean age. The sedimentary rocks are cut by intrusions dated as Grenville.

Climate, Vegetation

The northern part of the Canadian Shield has a polar climate; the warmest month averages above freezing but below 50°F (Fig. 4.2). The duration of the growing season averages less than 2 months. It is cloudy and wet during that "warm" period, and there may be frost at any time. The winter is a time of deep freeze, with temperatures in January *averaging* −20°F. Moreover, the winter is long. It is "dry cold," however. Skies generally are clear, although dark, and there is little snow. Annual precipitation averages less than 10 inches, and in the island north of the Shield the precipitation averages less than 5 inches, most of it falling during the summer months. This polar climate is thus also a desert climate. It has been described as the wettest desert on earth, however, because of the vast amounts of standing water that appear when the usually frozen grounds melts during the summer. Despite the extensive bodies of water that lie across the northern part of the shield, the climate is continental, and daytime temperatures in the summer may be as high as they are in the northeastern United States.

The southern part of the shield has a 3-month growing season, and is very much wetter than the northern part. Around Lake Superior the annual precipitation averages about 30 inches, and in southeastern Quebec averages more than 40 inches.

As a consequence of the climate, growing conditions in the north are too severe for trees. North of a line connecting the middle of the east side of Hudson Bay and the mouth of the Mackenzie River is the Arctic Life Zone (Fig. 8.1), which is characterized by treeless tundra. The tree line at the northern edge of the boreal forest, however, is not the southern limit of tundra, for the two kinds of growth are gradational in a belt as much as 100 miles wide. In the northern part of this gradational belt, islands of boreal forest grow in the midst of extensive open ground with tundra; in the southern part, islands of tundra are surrounded by boreal forest. Ground under the tundra is permanently frozen; that under the forests is not. In this gradational belt, permafrost is discontinuous (see page 319; Fig. 12.9).

The tundra north of the tree line is highly varied depending on local ground conditions, especially the ground drainage. One kind, known as wet tundra, grows where drainage is poor and may approach bog conditions. It consists mostly of grasses and sedges; in the south there may also be shrubs, especially ground birch. The extent of wet tundra decreases northward. Where wet tundra is subject to much frost heaving, the ground becomes hummocky, and the tops of the hummocks may be dry and covered with lichen.

The southern arctic also has heath tundra, characterized by the low evergreen representatives of the heath family and a variety of berry plants.

Northward, the number of species of tundra plants decreases, and mosses and lichens become increasingly abundant. In much of Baffin Island

and westward across the islands immediately north of the shield, shrubs are fewer than they are to the south; the dominant mosses and lichens are associated with sedges, grasses, arctic willow, and avens (species of *Dryas*). Still farther north is polar desert with extensive areas of bare rock or of rock rubble. At protected places within the rocky barrens are stands of tundra consisting especially of lichens accompanied by avens, saxifrage, arctic poppy, and a few other vascular plants that grow chiefly in clumps on comparatively dry hummocks. The most widely known plants of the arctic tundra are species of *Cladonia,* referred to as "reindeer moss," although they are actually lichens.

South of the tundra belt is boreal woodland and coniferous forest consisting of spruce and larch with numerous and extensive areas of bog (Fig. 12.6), which grades southward to the Spruce and Fir Forest, the only forest that extends all the way across the continent. The southernmost part of the Shield has mixed deciduous and coniferous forest—spruce, pine, and hemlock mixed with maple, beech, and other northern hardwoods (Fig. 12.7).

The Superior Upland and the adjoining part of the Central Lowland support four kinds of forests. In the north and on the highlands is the Spruce-Fir Forest of black and white spruce and balsam fir. This is bordered on the south by a mixed pine forest—the Northeastern Pine For-est—composed of jack pine, red pine, northern white pine, and aspen. This grades southward into the Northeastern Hardwood Forest of birch (yellow birch and paper birch), beech, and striped, sugar, and red maples, and hemlock. This in turn gives way farther south to the Central Hardwood Forest, characterized by oaks and hickories.

Although in these northern forests the average annual burn by forest fires is low compared to other forested areas, they have been the scene of three of the most disastrous fires in the history of the United States. The worst, in terms of casualties, occurred on October 9, 1871, at Peshtigo, Wisconsin, where more than 1,200 persons perished in a forest fire that broke out after a protracted drought and raced uncontrolled through the forests west of Green Bay. This fire received little national notice because the telegraph lines had been destroyed, and the news was submerged by news of the great Chicago fire, which had occurred the day before. Yet the Chicago fire took only a fifth as many lives.

Two other major forest fires, both in Minnesota near the tip of Lake Superior, occurred in September 1894, at Hinckley, and in October 1918, at Cloquet. Each of these fires killed about 400 persons.

Such fires create a climate all their own: They exhaust the oxygen to the degree that one may be suffocated without being burned. Warnings by

Figure 12.6 *Cross section illustrating development of a peat bog. Over the surface of a pond of water is a mat of floating and submerged plants on which sedges may be able to take root, and the sedges in turn provide the still thicker substrate for larger plants like alder. As the mat of vegetation thickens, swamp trees may move onto the ground. [From Geology of Soils by Charles B. Hunt. W. H. Freeman and Company. Copyright ©* *1972.]*

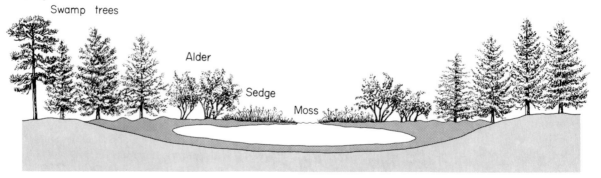

Figure 12.7 *Nistowiak Falls, on the Churchill River, north of La Ronge Provincial Park, Saskatchewan. The Canadian Shield is characterized not only by its Precambrian history but also by its opposite—Quaternary. The forest is the product of the past 10,000 years. Characterized by the sharply peaked spruce and fir, it is the only forest that has extended itself from the Atlantic to the Pacific coasts of the continent. Rivers here, like the Churchill, tumble over falls connecting the glacially scoured beds of the lakes. [Courtesy Saskatchewan Information Service.]*

Smoky the Bear are well based—"Everybody loses when there is a forest fire."

Soils, Weathering

Soils on the Canadian Shield are young, all having formed during the Holocene on late Pleistocene and Holocene glacial, fluvial, lacustrine, colluvial, and beach deposits derived from crystalline rocks. The topography is rather uniform, and consists of well-drained hummocks separated by poorly drained depressions, most of which are bogs, though many have ponds or lakes. Thus three of the factors that control soil development—parent material, topography, and geologic age—are fairly constant over the whole Shield, and the considerable differences in soils between the northern and southern parts chiefly reflect differences in the climate and vegetation.

Soils in the polar deserts, on the islands north of the Shield, are poorly developed and consist largely of unweathered parent material without much humus. The slight weathering shows in the freshness of stones in the parent material and in the extensive surfaces of bare bedrock. Where there are lichens and mosses, a layer of humus develops, but it is thin, and because of the scanty organic matter the soils commonly are neutral or even alkaline. In places this ground has developed salt crusts, alkali flats, and there may even be accumulations of calcium carbonate.

On those parts of the Shield where there is lush tundra, the soils contain correspondingly more organic matter and are highly acid. In places peats have accumulated, and locally as thick as 20 feet, suggesting a rate of accumulation of one or two feet per thousand years. The peats are preserved partly because they are saturated with water (which keeps out oxygen) and partly because they are refrigerated so much of the year.

Extensive parts of the Shield are poorly drained bogs with shrubby marsh tundra. The soils may be Bog Soils if underlain by peat or Half Bog Soils if underlain by mineral matter (see Table 6.1). Marshes having water that circulates may have more or less gley developed in the lower part of the soils.

Although much of the arctic ground is damp or even wet, there are well-drained uplands with lush tundra where the ground is seasonally dry. These upland soils are churned by frost-heaving, hence the organic and mineral matter are thoroughly mixed. The colors are lighter, and the soils are referred to as Arctic Brown.

Another feature of Tundra Soils in the northern part of the Shield is the common occurrence of buried organic layers, which may be decomposed or only slightly so. The layers may be thick or thin and discontinuous, and usually occur at the surface of permanently frozen ground. These layers are not soils that were buried under younger deposits, but, like the organic layer at the groundwater table in a Ground Water Podzol, they became buried by the soil process, partly by mixing of the soil by frost action and partly by hummocks of turf creeping downhill and overriding plant matter growing in depressions between the hummocks. Some of them have been dated by the radiocarbon method as between one and two thousand years old. Evidently their decomposition is very slow—another example of preservation by refrigeration.

In the forested southern part of the Shield, soils on well-drained ground are mostly Podzol Soils; near the Ottawa River and Great Lakes are Gray Brown Podzolic Soils. The Podzol Soils form under spruce-larch-fir forest; the Gray Brown Podzolic Soils, under mixed forest of conifers and northern hardwoods. These forest soils are acidic and have distinct organic layers, leached layers, and layers of deposition. Organic matter is built up chiefly by surface accumulation rather than by decay of roots, and the ground is not subject to such intensive frost heaving and mixing as is tundra ground. Gley soils develop on poorly drained ground in the forested southern part of the Shield.

Glacial History

During the Pleistocene the Canadian Shield was covered by an ice cap, known as the Laurentide Ice Cap. The ice had two centers: one in the highlands of northern Quebec, east of Hudson Bay; the other, in the District of Keewatin, northwest of Hudson Bay. From these centers the ice spread in all directions. It completely covered the Shield and extended southward several hundred miles into the United States and westward across the Interior Plains to the foot of the Canadian Rockies. The retreat from the southern limit of the last advance began 20,000 to 25,000 years ago, and various stages in the retreat are well marked by end moraines. Figure 12.8 shows three stages in the retreat. About 7,500 years ago, there still were residual ice caps at the Laurentide and Keewatin centers and on Baffin Island. Today, the highlands of Baffin Island the islands to the north are capped by permanent ice.

Although the Shield was the center from which the ice caps of the several Pleistocene glaciations spread, only the recessional stages of the last (late Wisconsinan) glaciation are well known. The records of earlier glaciations were largely destroyed by the late-Wisconsinan advance. The younger glaciations also destroyed evidence of Pleistocene and earlier weathering on the Shield. The deposits and soils are young, and

Figure 12.8 *Three stages in the retreat of the last continental ice sheet on the Canadian Shield and bordering areas.* [Generalized from Geol. Survey Canada.]

so is the drainage system and the whole of the landscape, even though they all formed on the oldest rocks known on the continent.

Deposits older than the late Wisconsinan glaciation, including some that are probably pre-Wisconsinan (Sangamon?) have been discovered at several localities south of James Bay, in northern Manitoba, on Baffin Island, and near Toronto. Some of these are between tills. The deposits on Baffin Island record a time when that area was deglaciated, probably during the Sangamon.

The best-known section of pre-Wisconsinan deposits is at Toronto and illustrates the stratigraphic problem of dating the deposits. At the base of the section is an old till that is slightly weathered at the top. The overlying interglacial Toronto Formation consists of two members. The lower one, known as the Don Beds, consists of lake deposits of gravel, sand, and clay with peat. Fossils found in these beds include invertebrates, vertebrates, and species of plants that once grew north of their present range. The assemblage has been interpreted as indicating a climate about 5°F warmer than that of today. The upper member of the Toronto Formation, the Scarborough Beds, consists of well-stratified sand, silt, and clay. The fossil fauna and flora that they contain are indicative of a cooler climate than that of today. These beds are thought to have been deposited while the Wisconsinan ice was advancing southward. They are overlain by till interbedded with stratified sediments that culminate in a sand that may be marine. Above this is the late Wisconsinan Till, which culminates in identifiable lake beds associated with the development of the Great Lakes (Lake Iroquois stage). The Don Beds are generally regarded as Pre-Wisconsinan, but they might be middle Wisconsinan.

In addition to morainal deposits left by the ice, the southern part of the Shield includes extensive lake deposits, some extending far beyond the limits of the Shield. The most extensive of these center on Lake Winnipeg and were deposited by the Pleistocene Lake Agassiz. Lake Agassiz covers most of the south half of Manitoba; it extends southward across North Dakota, eastward into a big area in southwestern Ontario, and westward across Saskatchewan along the Saskatchewan River. It was by far the largest of the glacial lakes. It developed when the drainage northward to Hudson Bay, via the Nelson River, was dammed by the retreating ice cap. The lake overflowed southward via the Minnesota River (see p. 333). When the ice cap had retreated to the mouth of the Nelson River, which drains Lake Winnipeg to Hudson Bay, the lake was 700 miles long and covered about 110,000 square miles.

Lake Ojibway, another extensive lake, developed in front of the ice as it receded into the basin of Hudson Bay from the divide north of the Great Lakes. It overflowed southward via Lake Timiskaming and the Ottawa River. The lake beds cover a crescentic area about 500 miles long and 150 miles wide on the north slope, from the divide toward James Bay.

Lake Ojibway was interrupted by a minor readvance of the glaciers—an advance that deposited the Cochrane till on the lake beds in about 6000 B.C. Thereafter, the ice retreated to its last stand in northern Quebec. The part of the Shield that borders James Bay was still below sea level as a result of the weight of the ice. As the ice load was removed, the ice retreated faster than the Shield rose, so that James Bay extended considerably south of its present position and marine sediments were deposited on the older till and lake beds. This extension of James and Hudson bays is referred to as the Tyrrell Sea. It spread east and west along both sides of Hudson Bay and covered much of the Arctic slope. The high strand lines are more than 600 feet in altitude.

Reconstruction of the rise of the Shield is complicated, for this movement was accompanied by a eustatic rise of sea level. Gravity anomalies over the Shield are negative, which suggests that the Shield has not fully returned to the level it occupied before being loaded by ice.

Very early in the recession of the ice, the southern part of the Shield was depressed below sea level. When the ice in the St. Lawrence Lowland melted, the sea spread along the lowland to form the Champlain Sea, which flooded the lower part of the Ottawa Valley, reached the base of the Adirondack Mountains in New York, flooded the valley of Lake Champlain, and overflowed into the Hudson River. This sea antedates Lake Ojibway; it was receding (due to isostatic rise of the Shield) when Lake Ojibway began to form. These seas and the Holocene lakes were seen by Paleo-Indians who lived along their shores.

Around the Keewatin and Quebec glacial centers are end moraines that collectively form a pattern of crescent-shaped, concentric ridges of gravel and sand. These are discontinous, for the ice front was divided into lobes, some of of which advanced while neighboring ones remained still. Between the end moraines is ground moraine. The large rivers have eroded courses through the end moraines; their tributaries follow irregular courses from one lake to another to join the main streams. Where there is no moraine, the drainage pattern in the bedrock has a trellis pattern.

In addition to morainal deposits over the Shield, there are extensive fields of drumlins whose axes radiate from the ice centers, and there are extensive eskers deposited in channels by meltwaters that flowed in and on the ice, and discharged into Hudson Bay.

Permanently Frozen Ground

North of the 30°F isotherm much of the ground remains permanently frozen (Fig. 12.9), a condition referred to as *permafrost*. The thickness of the permafrost ranges from a few feet at the south to about 1,000 feet at the north. In the north the permafrost layer is practically continuous, but as it thins southward it becomes discontinuous. The interior forests correspond approximately to the zone of discontinuous permafrost; tundra corresponds approximately to the zone of continuous permafrost.

Permafrost is defined on the basis of temperature. The ground may be soil, surface deposit, or bedrock, and may contain no ice, but if its temperature is permanently below freezing it is referred to as *dry permafrost*. More commonly the ground is cemented with ice.

The permafrost layer does not extend to the surface, because the surface layers thaw during the warm season. The surface layers freeze again during the next cold season, but this frozen ground is not part of the permafrost. The layer that freezes and thaws seasonally, the *active layer,* may be 20 feet deep in gravel but only 3 feet or less in silt or under peat (Fig. 12.10). In many places the top of the permafrost layer is deeper than the base of the active layer, and the two are separated by a layer of unfrozen ground (Fig. 12.11).

The freeze-thaw conditions in areas of permafrost are just the reverse of those to which we in temperate climates are conditioned. At temperate latitudes we consider depth of winter freezing; where there is permafrost one considers depth of summer thaw. The substrata remain frozen.

These relations help explain some of the extraordinary frost and ice features of the north country. For example, groundwater commonly becomes trapped between the layer of permafrost and the base of the active layer. When the active layer freezes, the confined water may be

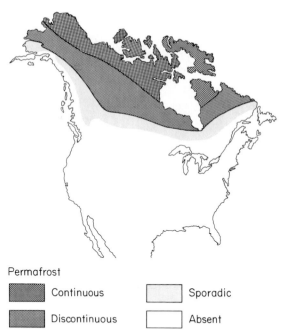

Figure 12.9   *Distribution of permafrost in northern North America. [From Geology of Soils by Charles B. Hunt. W. H. Freeman and Company. Copyright © 1972.]*

Permafrost

▨ Continuous   ☐ Sporadic

▨ Discontinuous   ☐ Absent

squeezed upward to form an ice core that domes the overlying ground, to form steep-sided hillocks as much as 50 feet high, known as *pingos*. They are common in the zone of continuous permafrost, rare elsewhere. If the process continues, the water may be ejected, forming a spring that freezes into a surface mount of ice. This phenomenon may do no harm in a wilderness locale, but in settled areas buildings may be tilted or become engulfed by ice, or the trapped groundwater may convert the unfrozen layer to mud and cause landsliding on slopes. Where the permafrost is shallow, only such shallow-rooted species as black spruce can grow.

In permafrost areas special engineering design is required to avoid foundation failures under buildings, highways, bridge pilings, pipelines, and other structures. The engineer must consider frost heaving of the surface, the depth of the active layer, the depth of the permafrost, and their effects on the ground drainage system.

Abundant fossil remains of animals and plants have been recovered from permafrost, chiefly in

Upland, sandy ground   Swamp over buried peat   Upland, clayey ground

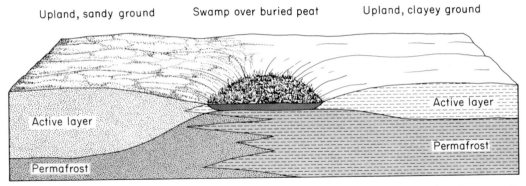

Figure 12.10 *Diagram illustrating differences in depth of the active layer over permafrost because of differences in the kind of ground. Swamps and peat beds are insulators, and the active layer under them is thin. Well-drained ground freezes and thaws more deeply than clayey ground [After Muller, 1943.]*

Alaska as a result of the gold-mining operations. Many of the animal remains are of extinct Pleistocene forms, but remains of entire animals, like the frozen mammoths recovered in Siberia, have not been found. Plant remains found in the permafrost are of the same species that are common today.

Patterned Ground

In the frozen north, where frost action is intensive, much of the ground develops characteristic patterns of regularly spaced, circular or polygonal hummocks, depressions, or ridges (Figs. 12.12, 12.13) a few feet or many feet wide and may be

Figure 12.11 *Diagram of layer of unfrozen ground sealed between the top of the permafrost and base of the seasonally frozen active layer.*

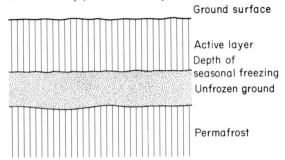

Ground surface

Active layer
Depth of
seasonal freezing
Unfrozen ground

Permafrost

distributed over many square miles. The hummocks range from a few inches to a few feet high. The ground may be uniformly silty or gravelly; where it contains stones, they are likely to be concentrated around the edges of the mound or hummocks, or if the pattern is linear, in ridges. The features become greatly accentuated by the vegetation, which reflects the considerable differences in microclimate, ground texture, and topographic position between the interiors and edges of the mounds, depressions, or ridges.

Similar patterned ground has developed on mountains in the Rocky Mountain and Pacific Coast states, especially those subjected to glaciation and intensive frost action during Pleistocene time. In those mountains the features seem to be in large part relicts from the Pleistocene. Curiously, very similar ground patterns develop in hot, saline deserts. For example, ground patterns in Death Valley, California, are not very different from those on the Arctic Slope.

The conditions necessary for development of patterned ground are freezing and thawing or, in the deserts, solution and recrystallization of salts. Apparently the ground must alternately become soaking wet and then solidify by freezing or by crystallization of salts. In any ground, the alternate freezing and thawing works stones to the surface, but in truly patterned ground the stones are sorted from the silt and arranged in orderly

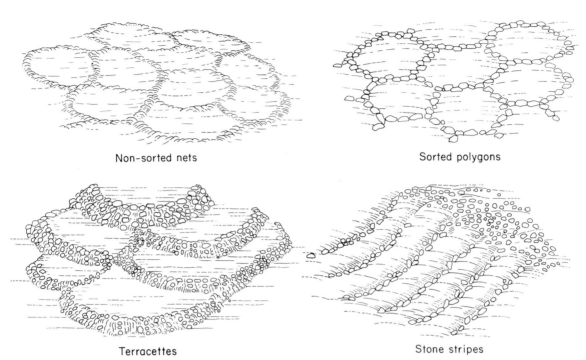

Non-sorted nets

Sorted polygons

Terracettes

Stone stripes

Figure 12.12 *Some common kinds of patterned ground. Heaving of the ground by frost in cold regions or by salts in arid regions produces various kinds of ground patterns. These may be nearly circular and form nets or be polygonal, generally hexagonal. There is a sorting of stones that may be present, which collect in the troughs, and these may be in the central part of the nets of polygons or along their edges. Mass wasting on hillsides may develop terracettes or stone stripes. In terracettes the stones are collected at the risers; the fines form the tread; in stone stripes the stones collect in parallel linear troughs, and the ground between them is heaved. [From Geology of Soils by Charles B. Hunt, W. H. Freeman and Company. Copyright © 1972.]*

patterns, like the depressions around mounds or the ridges around depressions, or in linear ridges. The regularity in the spacing of the features, however, is not well understood. The polygonal patterns commonly are due to a shallow substrate that has cracked polygonally. In the cold country this shallow substrate is a subsurface layer of ice; in the deserts, a subsurface layer of salt.

Mineral Resources

Each physiographic province is characterized by particular suites of rock forming minerals and economic mineral deposits. The mineral deposits of the Shield are those associated with highly

metamorphosed rocks that formed during early stages of the earth's history—notably iron, nickel, cobalt, copper, uranium, and gold. The iron is associated with Precambrian sedimentary rocks, the nickel with Precambrian igneous rocks. The rocks of the Shield are far too severely metamorphosed and far too ancient to contain mineral fuels like those in rocks of the Atlantic and Gulf Coastal plains and the Appalachian Plateau. Not enough organic matter was available when the Shield rocks formed, and any that may have accumulated would have been destroyed by the subsequent metamorphism. The distribution of the principal known mineral deposits on the Canadian Shield is shown in Figure 12.14.

The iron formations are mostly in the Superior and Nain provinces. The ore is mainly hematite

Figure 12.13 *A net of depressions, 50 to 100 feet in diameter, containing ponds and separated by low ridges with crudely polygonal outlines form one kind of ground pattern on the Arctic Slope.*

(Fe_2O_3) with some magnetite (Fe_3O_4) and limonite (approx. $2Fe_2O_3 \cdot 3H_2O$). The ores are believed to have been concentrated by meteoric waters that leached the silica from lean iron-bearing formations that contained chemically precipitated iron carbonates (siderite) and iron silicates. The ores are interbedded with normal clastic sediments such as slate and quartzite.

The iron formations, which range from a few feet to 1,000 feet thick, consist of chert, or quartz, and ferric oxide segregated in bands or sheets and irregularly mixed. The iron also occurs in slates that grade into the ferruginous cherts, cherty iron carbonate and hydrous ferrous silicate (greenalite, which resembles chlorite), and the iron ores themselves.

In places, notably in the Marquette and Mesabi ranges, regional metamorphism has altered the siderite and greenalite rocks to magnetite-amphibole schist and the soft hematite to specularite.

The ores contain about 50 percent iron, 0.1 percent phosphorous, 8.5 percent silica, 0.8 percent manganese, and 10 percent moisture. About 50 million tons of iron (100 million tons of ore) are produced annually. Another 15 million tons of iron is produced from deposits in the Quebec-Labrador iron belt. The mines are partly open pit, as at the Mesabi Range, and partly underground.

About 85 percent of the United States production is from the Superior Upland. The ore occurs in Precambrian rocks as hematite (red iron oxide) in iron-rich cherts, carbonates, slates, and schists. Ore in the deposits mined thus far contains more than 50 percent iron.

Production of iron in the Lake Superior region began in 1854 but was slow in developing because the rich copper deposits in that region were more attractive to miners until after the Civil War. The building of the railroads boomed the iron industry, but the railroads grew faster than the iron mines and steel mills, and a good deal of the trackage had to be imported from England. Steel production began with the development of the Bessemer process in 1855.

The Precambrian rocks in the Lake Superior region, especially in the Keweenaw Peninsula, also contain important deposits of copper. Native copper had been mined there by the Indians, but—to understate the matter—their workings have since been considerably deepened; the Calumet and Hecla Mine, opened in 1846, is now more than a mile deep.

The copper deposits were discovered in 1830, and mining began in 1844. For some years this was one of the leading copper-producing districts in the world, production reaching 80,000 tons during 1900. Since then, production has fallen greatly as the mines have become nearly exhausted.

The major nickel deposits in Canada are at Sudbury, Thompson, and Lynn Lake. Sudbury produces about 75 percent of the world's nickel and is the world's main source of platinum. Nickel is important as an alloy. The ore minerals are sulfides—nickel-bearing pyrrhotite (Fe_nS_{n+1}), nickel-bearing chalcopyrite ($CuFeS_2$), and pentlandite ($(Fe,Ni)S$)—and are associated with a sheet-like intrusion of norite (a coarsely crystalline rock composed chiefly of labradorite and hypersthene) intruded between lower and middle Precambrian sedimentary formations. The middle Precambrian formations are conglomerate, tuff, and slate folded into a syncline 36 miles long and 16 miles wide. These rocks overlie more strongly folded lower Precambrian rocks. The sill is along the contact.

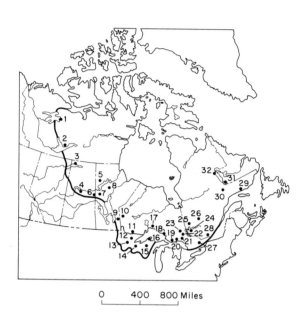

1. Port Radium: silver and copper
2. Yellowknife: gold
3. Uranium City: uranium
4. Waden Bay: copper
5. Lynn Lake: nickel, copper, cobalt
6. Flin Flon: copper, zinc, gold, silver, cadmium, selenium, tellurium
7. Snow, Morton, and Herb lakes: copper, zinc, lead, silver, gold
8. Thompson: nickel, copper, precious-metal residue, sulfur
9. Bird River, Bernic and Werner Lakes: nickel, copper, tantalum
10. Cochenour, Balmertown, Bruce: gold, iron
11. Steep Rock Lake: iron
12. Gunflint, Vermillion: iron
13. Mesabi, Cayuna: iron
14. Penokee: iron
15. Menominee, Iron Mountain: iron
16. Copper range: copper
17. Manitouwadge: zinc, copper, silver, lead
18. Wawa, Pointe Mamainse, Batchawana Bay: iron, copper
19. Elliot Lake: uranium, rare earths
20. Sudbury: nickel, copper, gold, silver, platinum metals, cobalt, selenium, tellurium, iron
21. Cobalt: cobalt, iron, copper, silver
22. Kirkland Lake, Dobie: gold, silver, cobalt, iron
23. Porcupine: copper, gold, zinc, silver, lead
24. Rouyn, Noranda Martic, Norrie: copper, zinc, silver, gold, lead, molybdenum
25. Matagami, Joutel, Normetal: zinc, copper, silver, gold, pyrite
26. Chibougamau: copper, gold, silver, iron
27. Haley, Marmora: magnesium, calcium, iron
28. Oka, Shawville, Lac de Renzy: niobium (columbium) iron, nickel, copper
29. Havre, St. Pierre: iron, titania
30. Gagnon: iron
31. Labrador City: iron
32. New Quebec-Labrador: iron

Figure 12.14 *Major mining areas on the Canadian Shield.*

References

Baer, A. J. (ed.), 1971, Symposium on basins and geosynclines of the Canadian Shield: Geol. Survey of Canada Paper 70-40.

Bird, J. B., 1967, The physiography of arctic Canada: Johns Hopkins Univ. Press.
———, 1972, The natural landscapes of Canada: Rexdale, Ontario, Wiley of Canada.

Canada Department of Forestry, 1963, Native Trees of Canada: Ottawa, Canada Dept. Forestry.

Land, A. H., and others, 1968, Economic minerals of the Canadian Shield, *in* Geology of Canada: Canada Geological Survey, pp. 153–226.

MacClintock, P., and Stewart, D. P., 1970, Pleistocene geology of the St. Lawrence Lowland: New York State Mus. Bull. 394.

Muller, S., 1945, Permafrost, or permanently frozen ground, and related problems: U.S. Engineers Office, Strategic Engineering Study Rept. 62; reprinted by Edwards Bros.

Schwartz, G. M., and Theil, G. A., 1963, Minnesota's rocks and waters: 2nd ed., Minneapolis, Univ. Minnesota Press.

Stockwell, C. M., and others, 1968, Geology of the Canadian Shield: *in* Geology of Canada: Canada Geological Survey, pp. 44–150.

The Great Plains, very nearly as extensive as the Canadian Shield, are mostly grassland on flat-lying Cretaceous and Tertiary formations. In central Saskatchewan and northern Alberta, the grassland is replaced by boreal forest of spruce and fir. This scene is in northwestern Nebraska near Fort Robinson State Park. [NEBRASKAland Magazine Photo, courtesy of Nebraska Game and Parks Commission.]

13
. . . .

INTERIOR PLAINS AND PLATEAUS
—STABLE PLATFORM BORDERING
THE SHIELD

The Central Lowland and Great Plains, extending from the Appalachian Plateaus to the Rocky Mountains, form a vast plain between the two ranges of mountains, and in western Canada the plain extends northward between the Shield and the Canadian Rockies. The largest and lowest part is the Central Lowland; to the west are the Great Plains. To the south are the Interior Low Plateaus and Ozark Plateaus. At the far north are the Arctic Plains, which are separated from the southern ones by plateaus and low ridges. The several provinces (Figs. 13.1, 13.2, 13.3) are distin-guished chiefly on the basis of their geologic structure and geologic history, but there are important climatic differences too. Collectively the provinces make up the stable platform bordering the Canadian Shield and thus constitute the largest member of the continental structural framework (about a third of the land area). The climates range from temperate to arctic and from humid to semiarid.

The Shield and the stable platform surrounding it together make up the craton—the nucleus of the continent. The Precambrian base-

---

Key to Figure 13.1, physiographic map of the Central United States, pp. 326, 327.

Laccolithic Mountains
on the Missouri Plateau

1. Sweetgrass Hills
2. Bearpaw Mts.
3. Little Rocky Mts.
4. Highwood Mts.
5. Moccasin Mts.
6. Judith Mts.

Mountain Ranges in the
Superior Upland

1. Mesabi and Vermilion Ranges
2. Fond du Lac Mts. and North Shore Range
3. South Range and Bayfield Hills
4. Penokee Range
5. Porcupine Mts.
6. Copper Range and Keweenaw Peninsula
7. Huron Mts.
8. Menominee Range

Mountains in the Osage Plains

1. Arbuckle Mts.
2. Wichita Mts.

National Parks and Monuments

A. Mammoth Cave National Park, Ky.
B. Isle Royal Nat. Park, Mich.
C. Pipestone Nat. Mon., Minn.
D. Hot Springs Nat. Park, Ark.
E. Badlands Nat. Mon., S. Dak.
F. Wind Cave and Jewell Cave Nat. Mon's., S. Dak.
G. Devils Tower Nat. Mon., Wyo.
H. Scotts Bluff Nat. Mon., Neb.
I. Capulin Nat. Mon., N. Mex.
J. Carlsbad Nat. Park, N. Mex.
K. Guadalupe Mts. Nat. Park, Texas.

326

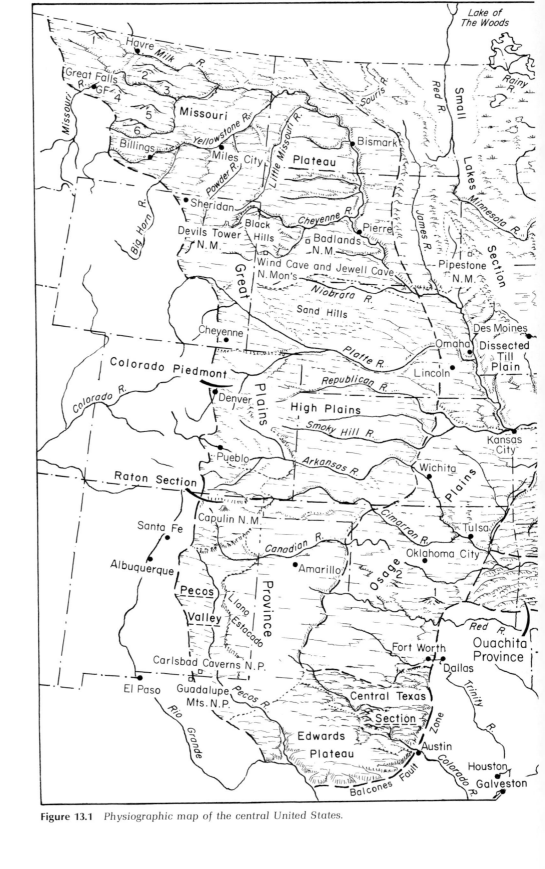

Figure 13.1 *Physiographic map of the central United States.*

0   200   400 Miles

Scale

Isle Royal N.P.

Lake Superior Upland

2

Duluth

602

5 6 7

3

4 *Superior* 8

Lake Huron

Georgian Bay

580

580

Saginaw Bay

Lake Ontario

246

Minneapolis–St. Paul

Rochester

Lake Michigan

Niagara Falls

Driftless

Section

Great   Lakes   Section

572

Madison

Detroit

Lake Erie

Milwaukee

Chicago

Toledo

Cleveland

Pittsburg

Des Moines R.

Till

Plain

Illinois R.

Lowland

Indianapolis

Columbus

Ohio R.

Central

Wabash R.

Cincinnati

Charleston

Missouri R.

St. Louis

Louisville

Lexington

Ozark

Plateaus

Mammoth Cave N.P.

R.

Cumberland

Nashville

Tennessee R.

Memphis

Little Rock

Interior
Low Plateaus

Hot Springs
N.P.

Mississippi R.

Shreveport

Mobile

Baton
Rouge

New Orleans

328

CENTRAL LOWLAND

1. *Manitoba Plain:* southern part is bed of Lake Aggasiz. Underlain by Paleozoic and some Jurassic. Ends eastward against the Shield; ends westward at foot of the Manitoba Escarpment formed by Cretaceous formations. Altitude of the plain is about 800 feet.
2. *Saskatchewan Plain:* Underlain by Cretaceous formations. Ends eastward at rim of Manitoba Escarpment; westward at Missouri Coteau, the edge of the Tertiary formations. Lower and smoother than plains to west (Alberta Plains). Altitudes 1,500 to 2,600 feet. Streams entrenched about 300 feet in open valleys.

GREAT PLAINS

3. *Alberta Plains:* Underlain mostly by Cretaceous formations. Eocene near the foot of the mountains. Rougher than Saskatchewan Plain. Altitudes around 2,500 feet; Cypress Hills reach 4,700 feet and probably were not glaciated. Valleys entrenched 200 to 400 feet.
4. *Alberta Plateau:* Between Athabasca and Liard Rivers. Cretaceous formations in plateaus separated by broad valleys. Plateaus 2,500 to 3,200 feet in altitude. Lowlands along the

Athabasca and Liard Rivers 1,000 to 1,500 feet lower. Near foot of Rocky Mountains altitudes are about 4,300 feet on the plateaus.

GREAT SLAVE AND GREAT BEAR PLAINS

5. *Great Slave Plain:* Underlain by Paleozoic formations. Altitude about 1,000 feet; little relief.
6. *Great Bear Plain:* Underlain by Mesozoic formations. Rolling surface generally lower than 1,000 feet altitude; a few hills up to 500 feet high. Ends at south-facing escarpment overlooking Great Slave Plain.

NORTHERN PROVINCES

7. *MacKenzie Plain, Franklin Mountains, and Colville Hills:* Altitudes near sea level along the MacKenzie River and more than 2,000 feet in the mountains which are ridges of Paleozoic formations.
8. *Arctic Slope, including the MacKenzie Delta:* Slope north from 2,000 feet to sea level. Western part largely covered by glacial drift and slightly lower than eastern part. Streams entrenched increasingly toward the south to about 400 feet.

Figure 13.2 *Interior plains and plateaus in Canada, in relation to those in the United States.*

ment rocks under the platform are exposed at three places in the United States. At the St. Francois Mountains in Missouri and at the Central Texas uplift on the north side of the Edwards Plateau, the exposed rocks are parts of granitic batholiths. At the Black Hills, in southwestern South Dakota, there also is granite along with metamorphosed sedimentary rocks. Presumably the basement rocks under the stable platform are like those of the Canadian Shield, where the area of granitic rocks is about four times that of the metamorphosed, sedimentary, geosynclinal deposits. Ridges presumably formed of gabbroic rocks like those in Minnesota can be traced by

geophysical methods southwestward from Minnesota to Nebraska; they are covered by the Paleozoic and Cretaceous sediments.

Structural Divisions

CENTRAL LOWLAND

The largest of the physiographic provinces is the Central Lowland. At its eastern edge, where it joins the Appalachian Plateaus, the altitude is about 1,000 feet. It slopes westward to about 500 feet along the Mississippi River, a distance of

Figure 13.3 *Map of Alberta, Saskatchewan, and Manitoba Plains.*

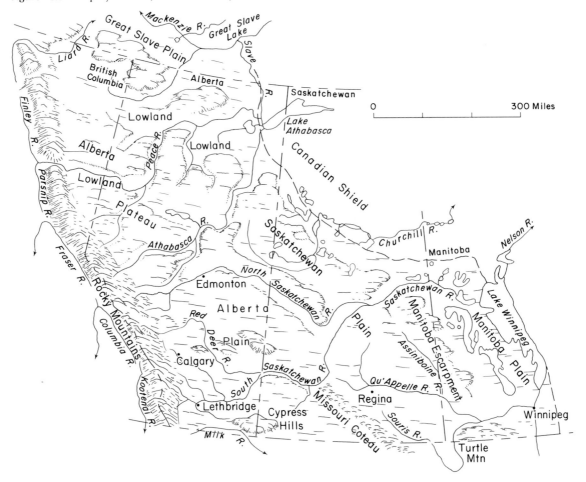

about 400 miles, and it rises again farther west to an altitude of about 2,000 feet at the 100th meridian, which is approximately the western boundary of this province.

The Central Lowland covers 650,000 square miles in the United States and Canada, an area greater than that of Alaska and twice the size of Texas. The low altitude and lack of relief results in scenery that is as plain as the plain is extensive. Scenery in the Central Lowland has a great deal of sameness and plainness, but a few small tracts have been set aside as parks illustrating the physiography, as at Clifty Falls State Park on the Ohio River in Indiana, Starved Rock State Park on the Illinois River in Illinois, Riding Mountain National Park and Duck Mountain and Clearwater Provincial parks in Manitoba, Prince Albert National Park and Nipawin, and Moose Mountain Provincial parks in Saskatchewan.

Outstanding features of the Central Lowland are its

1. Great extent.

2. Low altitude and slight local relief.

3. Continental climate.

4. Great lakes and great rivers.

5. Mantle of glacial deposits that smooth the ground surface and largely conceal the underlying rock formations.

6. Subsurface structure of broadly warped sedimentary rock formations that are thin by comparison with the same formations under the bordering mountain provinces.

7. Rich economy, well balanced between agriculture, minerals, manufacturing, and transportation.

Most of the Central Lowland Province was glaciated, and the sections of the province are distinguished chiefly on the basis of differences in their glacial histories.

The Great Lakes Section is a plain of Wisconsinan glacial till. This plain is interrupted by morainal ridges, mostly about 50 feet high, arranged in concentric arcs around the rounded ends of the lakes (Fig. 13.4). Valleys between the morainal ridges are several miles wide. Parts of the till plains are hummocky with knobs and kettle holes containing lakes, ponds, or swamps (Fig. 13.5).

South of the Great Lakes Section is the Till Plain Section, an area without knob and kettle topography, but consisting of broad level uplands between valleys that have steep sides and broad floodplains (Fig. 13.6). The drainage is integrated, and there are few lakes or ponds. Most of this section lies south of the late Wisconsinan moraines. It includes some early Wisconsinan moraines, but much of it is on Illinoian till and is of pre-Wisconsinan age. The difference in age of the tills accounts in part for the difference in landforms; the young deposits at the north form a rough surface with a drainage system not well integrated. West of the Mississippi River the still older Kansan till forms a plain that is correspondingly more dissected. The valleys are more closely spaced and the uplands more rounded than they are east of the river. Present relief is 100 to 300 feet.

Figure 13.4 *Map illustrating ridges of terminal moraines that curve around the ends of the Great Lakes.*

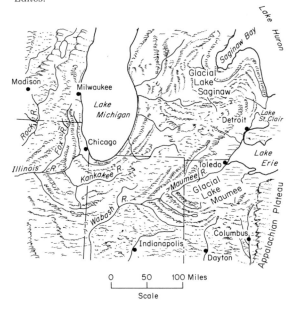

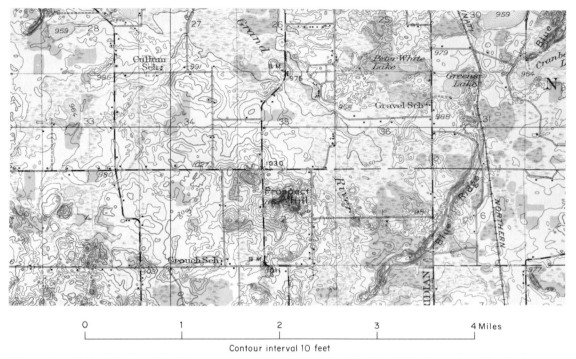

Contour interval 10 feet

Figure 13.5   *Map of knob-and-kettle topography in the Great Lakes Section of the Central Lowland. Blue Ridge is an esker. [From U.S.G.S. Jackson, Michigan, quadrangle map.]*

The differences between the several till plains are in part attributable to differences in the time available for the drainage to become established and in part to differences in the modes of deposition of the till. Differences in landforms built of glacially deposited gravel, sand, and clay may reflect differences in the rates of retreat of the ice. Ice that melted back quickly left deposits differing from those that formed in front of ice that melted back slowly. Other differences depend on whether the rates of melting and retreat were uniform or intermittent, and on the direction and amount of slope of the land surface in front of the ice.

The dissected till plains east and west of the Mississippi River are mantled with loess that commonly is more than 30 feet thick. This blanket of wind-deposited silt resembles that along the east side of the Mississippi Alluvial Section

in the Coastal Plain in origin and texture. The loess thins eastward away from the river beds, which were their source. All these loess-covered areas are subject to severe soil erosion.

The Small Lakes Section in the northwestern part of the Central Lowland (Fig. 13.1) is a plain

Figure 13.6   *Profile across the Little Wabash River near Effingham, Illinois. In the southeastern part of the Central Lowland the uplands are broad and level; the valleys are steep-sided but have broad floodplains. These landforms are developed on glacial deposits that are much older than those bordering the Great Lakes. (Vertical scale is exaggerated about twenty-five times.)*

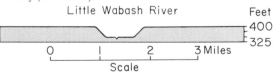

with hummocky moraines of Wisconsinan till. Much of the surface is knob and kettle topography, not unlike that farther east around the Great Lakes (Fig. 13.5) except that the ponds and marshes are smaller and fewer, probably because the annual rainfall here is only about 20 inches, whereas it is 30 inches or more farther east. In this part of the Central Lowland the valleys are parallel to each other and to the former position of the ice front. These valleys are former outwash channels of the retreating ice (Fig. 13.7).

In Canada this province includes the southern half of the Saskatchewan Plain, which consists of glaciated Cretaceous formations at 1,500 to 2,600 feet in altitude. Local relief is mostly less than 300 feet. The province ends eastward at the rim of the Manitoba Escarpment, overlooking the Manitoba Plain.

The Manitoba Plain, at an altitude of about 800 feet, includes Lakes Winnipeg, Winnipegosis, and Manitoba. It is underlain mostly by Paleozoic rocks. The plain, which extends southward

Figure 13.7 *Till plain with knob-and-kettle topography interrupted by parallel valleys representing outwash channels that formed along the ice front as it retreated northeastward. Similar recessional moraines separated by parallel valleys extend northwestward into Saskatchewan. [From U.S.G.S. Lansford, North Dakota, quadrangle.]*

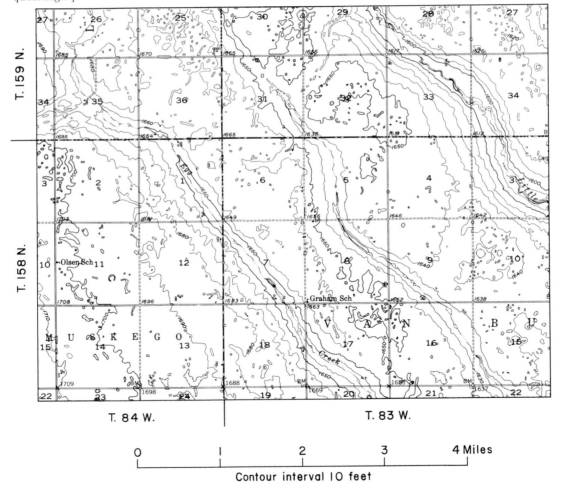

along the Red River on the boundary between Minnesota and North Dakota, is the bed of glacial Lake Agassiz.

The overflow from Lake Agassiz drained southeastward via an outlet channel that was eroded to a depth of 100 to 220 feet and to a width of one mile. This big channel is now occupied by the Minnesota River, a small stream in an oversized valley that was obviously once occupied by a large, vigorous river. As the ice retreated farther northward, Lake Agassiz also discharged into the north side of Lake Superior.

A measure of the extent of poorly drained land in these glaciated areas is provided by Figure 9.10,A. Only the low parts of the Coastal Plain have comparably extensive wet areas.

Two parts of the Central Lowland were not glaciated. One of these, the Driftless Section (Fig. 13.1), comprises the southwestern quarter of Wisconsin and the adjoining 250-mile stretch of the Mississippi River Valley. Not only is this area without glacial deposits and without glacial striae, but it preserves small, fragile landforms, such as natural bridges, arches, buttes, and rock towers (Fig. 13.8), that could not have survived being overriden by glacial ice. The valleys contain stream deposits left by glacial meltwaters, and there are deposits of loess.

The Driftless Section escaped glaciation because of its situation midway between the deep valleys of Lakes Superior and Michigan, and because it is on the lee (south) side of the ridges in the Superior Upland. The glacial lobes became concentrated in the valleys and were diverted to either side of the Driftless Section. The northern and southwestern third of the Driftless Section, however, was covered by one of the pre-Wisconsinan glaciers, and those areas contain deposits of deeply weathered till.

The other part of the Central Lowland that escaped glaciation is the Osage Plain (Fig. 13.1), which lies south of the glacial limit. This section, beginning at the Kansas and Missouri rivers and extending southwestward to central Texas, is underlain by late Paleozoic formations that dip gently westward. In southeastern Kansas these are mostly shale and limestone, and the more

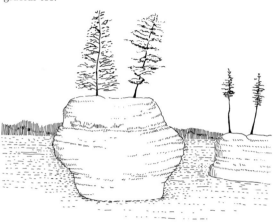

Figure 13.8 *Some landforms in the Driftless Section that would not have survived being overridden by glacial ice.*

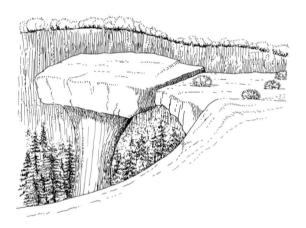

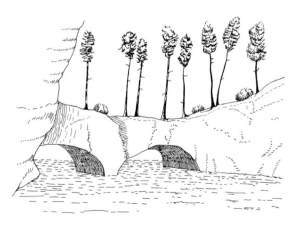

resistant beds, the limestones, form low cuestas facing east. Southward, in Oklahoma, the formations contain less limestone, and the cuestas there are mostly sandstone (Fig. 13.9).

In the southern part of the Osage Plains, the plains form uplands in which the rivers are trenched in gorges a few hundred feet deep. These rivers have sandy beds, and some, notably the Cimarron and Canadian rivers, are bordered on the lee (northeast) side by sand dunes in belts 10 to 15 miles wide.

GREAT PLAINS PROVINCE

The Great Plains Province, including the Alberta Plain, covers about 575,000 square miles and is the semiarid part of the Interior Plains. The plains slope eastward from about 5,500 feet at the foot of the Rocky Mountains to about 2,000 feet at the eastern boundary, which is gradational with the Central Lowland. In the United States, this eastern boundary approximately coincides with the 100th meridian, the 2,000-foot contour, the 20-inch rainfall line, the boundary between tall grass and short grass, and the eastern limit of the Tertiary formations that contain the sediments eroded from the Rocky Mountains and washed eastward onto the plains. The boundary also is parallel to, although a little west of, the boundary between acid and alkaline soils.

In the United States, drainage on the plains is parallel, and the streams flow eastward from the Rocky Mountains to the Missouri and Mississippi rivers. The streams in Canada drain to Hudson Bay via the Saskatchewan and Nelson rivers (Fig. 13.10).

Trees are largely confined to the valleys; the almost-treeless uplands, originally grassland, are now plowed fields or pasture.

Figure 13.9 *Mesas of late Paleozoic formations near the eastern edge of the Great Plains, in Glass Mountains State Park, western Oklahoma. [Courtesy Oklahoma Industrial Development and Park Department.]*

Figure 13.10 *Qu'Appele River, where it is incised into the Cretaceous formations in the eastern part of the Great Plains, near Echo Valley Provincial Park, Saskatchewan. [Courtesy Saskatchewan Government Information Service.]*

The structural geology of the Great Plains differs only in detail from that of the Central Lowland. The formations are nearly horizontal, mostly Mesozoic and Cenozoic overlying slightly warped Paleozoic formations. In the north, the plains are interrupted by dome mountains, such as the Black Hills (Fig. 13.11) and some of the smaller mountains in northern Montana, which are domed upward by laccolithic or other intrusions (Fig. 13.12).

Another important structural feature is the Williston Basin in southern Saskatchewan, northwestern North Dakota, and northeastern Montana. This basin, structurally about 13,000 feet deep, is comparable to the Michigan Basin. At the surface are Paleocene formations that represent coastal plain deposits laid down in the retreating Upper Cretaceous sea (see Fig. 2.14).

The boundary between the Great Plains and the Central Lowland is along a low, east-facing escarpment at the eroded east edge of Cenozoic formations that consist of sediments washed eastward onto the plains from the Rocky Mountains. Their volume provides a minimal measure of the lowering of the Rocky Mountains by erosion during Cenozoic time. Since these sediments roughly equal in volume the mountains that remain, the Rocky Mountains are at least half gone.

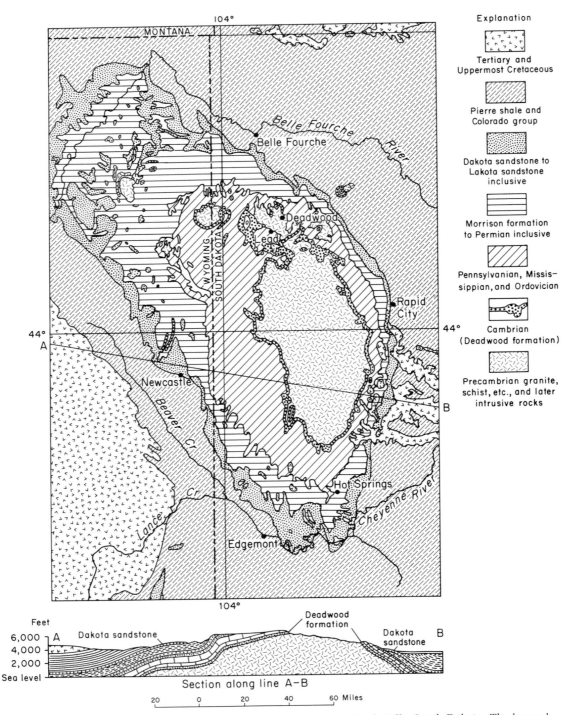

Figure 13.11 *Geologic map and section of the structural dome at the Black Hills, South Dakota. The layered rocks of the dome crop out in concentric bands, with the youngest along the periphery and the oldest at the apex of the dome. [After N. H. Darton, from U.S. Geol. Survey Water-Supply Paper 489, pl. 23.]*

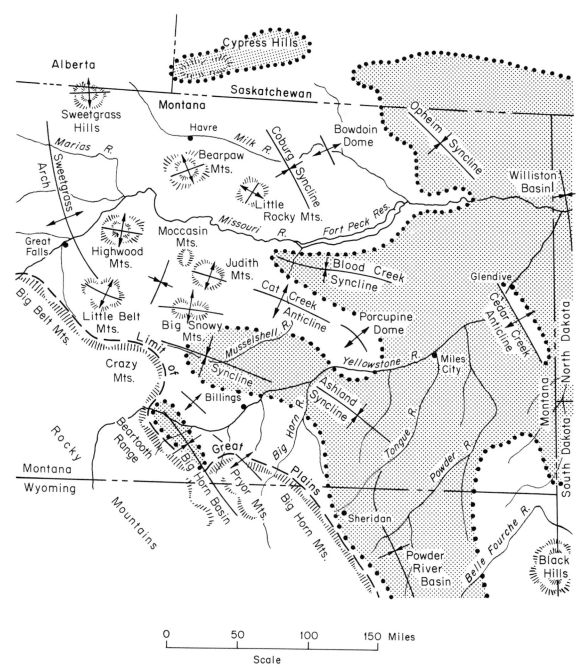

Figure 13.12 *Structural map of the northern part of the Great Plains. Dome mountains on the plains are shown by hachures. Lines indicate the trends of the principal fold axes, and cross-arrows indicate whether dips are toward the axes (synclinal) or away from them (anticlinal). Area covered by Tertiary formations is shown stippled. Except in the mountains, most of the white area is Cretaceous. Older rocks together with some intrusive rocks are exposed in the dome mountains. The youngest formations, those of Tertiary age (Paleocene and Eocene) occupy the basins and synclines. [Data from U.S.G.S.]*

Most of the Mesozoic formations are marine sediments deposited in a broad, shallow geosyncline of Upper Cretaceous age. The axis was at about the position of the western edge of the Great Plains, and the mediterranean sea that occupied it connected the Gulf of Mexico with the Arctic Ocean. The Upper Cretaceous formations are 10,000 to 25,000 feet thick in the central part of the geosyncline. They thin eastward under the Great Plains but extend to the western edge of the Canadian Shield (Fig. 2.14).

Northward in Canada, Paleozoic formations emerge from under the east edge of the Cretaceous and crop out in a lowland belt about 50 to 100 miles wide that separates the Cretaceous from the Precambrian rocks of the Shield.

Cenozoic, Mesozoic, and Palozoic formations extend westward under the Great Plains to the foot of the Rocky Mountains, where they are turned up along the base of that uplift, which began forming in late Cretaceous and early Tertiary time. The formations are listed in Table 14.1. The newly formed Rocky Mountains shed sediments eastward onto the Great Plains. The first formations, of Paleocene and Eocene age (Fort Union and Wasatch formations), included much volcanic debris and were deposited across the northern part of the Great Plains, north of the Black Hills. The next formation, of Oligocene age (White River Formation), was deposited south of the Black Hills, and still farther south was deposited the Miocene Arikaree Formation, which extends into northern Colorado. South of that was deposited the Pliocene Ogallala Formation, centering in eastern Colorado and western Kansas, and still farther south, in Oklahoma and Texas, the late Pliocene or early Pleistocene Blanco Formation. During the 60 million years of Tertiary time, from the Paleocene to the Pliocene, deposition progressed southward. Moreover, these Tertiary formations were laid down on an erosion surface that cut southward across about 10,000 feet of Cretaceous formations and extended southward onto Paleozoic formations (Fig. 2.1), which indicates that uplift in the southern Great Plains has been two miles greater than in the north, despite the fact that these areas now are at about the same altitude.

These differences in the Cenozoic formations and history from north to south control the differences in landforms on the Great Plains and provide the basis for dividing the province into the sections shown in Fig. 13.2. At the north is the Alberta Plain, which grades north to the dissected Alberta Plateau. The Plateau is interrupted by broad valleys at the Fort Nelson and Peace River lowlands. The Alberta Plain, drained by the North and South Saskatchewan Rivers, is mostly around 2,500 to 3,500 feet in altitude. The valleys are incised 200 to 400 feet, and there are hills as high as 4,700 feet. The highest, the Cypress Hills, on the Alberta-Saskatchewan Boundary just north of Montana (Fig. 13.12), are high enough so that they were not overridden by the glacial ice. The eastern boundary of the Alberta Plain and of the Missouri Plateau is at the Missouri Coteau. All the Alberta Plain was glaciated except the Cypress Hills and a narrow belt at the foot of the Rocky Mountains in southern Alberta.

South of the Alberta Plain is the Missouri Plateau Section, the northern part of which was glaciated. Local relief on the Missouri Plateau is greater than in most of the Great Plains. Rivers are entrenched a few hundreds of feet into the plateau (Fig. 13.14), and several dome mountains rise 1,500 and 2,000 feet above it (Fig. 13.12). Largest and highest of them are the Black Hills, properly a separate section. The Black Hills are a domal uplift of Precambrian rocks (Fig. 13.11). Northwest of the Black Hills is a prominent volcanic neck about 1,000 feet high, Devils Tower, a National Monument (Fig. 2.5,A). Other dome mountains—the Sweetgrass Hills, and the Bearpaw, Little Rocky, Highwood, Moccasin, and Judith mountains—are due to laccolithic intrusions.

Between the dome mountains are broad anticlines and synclines (Fig. 13.12), which are well expressed topographically. The anticlines are surrounded by cuestas that face inward; the synclines are surrounded by cuestas facing outward. Shales form badlands at Badlands National Monument and Theodore Roosevelt National Memorial Park in the Dakotas.

The Tertiary formations contain abundant lignite. Many beds have ignited spontaneously and

Figure 13.13 *Badlands in Cretaceous formations at Dinosaur Provincial Park in south-central Alberta.* [*Courtesy Alberta Government Photographic Services.*]

have burned at their outcrops, baking the overlying shale to red clinker—one of the distinctive features of the Missouri Plateau.

South of the Missouri Plateau is the High Plains Section (Fig. 13.15), with a land surface roughly accordant with the top of the Pliocene formations, and, therefore, more of a depositional than erosional surface. Toward the east, such streams as the Republican and Smoky Hill rivers are cut through the Miocene formations and into the Cretaceous. This is the Plains Border Section; it grades into the Central Lowland. On the west, the High Plains are separated from the Rocky Mountains by a structural and topographic basin, the Colorado Piedmont. To the south is the Raton Section, unique among the Great Plains areas in having high mesas or plateaus capped by Tertiary lava flows. Some of these mesas are 6,000 to 7,000 feet in altitude.

Parts of the High Plains Section are sandy, with extensive dunes. One such area lies southeast of Akron, Colorado—an area shown without

drainage in Figure 13.15. The prevailing winds are toward the southeast, and the dunes are aligned in that direction. An even more extensive sand area is in western Nebraska (Fig. 13.1). Still another is along the south side of the Arkansas River at the big bend in Kansas.

In southeastern New Mexico and the Panhandle of Texas are the Staked Plains, the Llano Estacado, one of the most nearly level parts of the United States. This section is a nearly featureless plain, lacking even slight landmarks. The

Figure 13.14 *Diagram of Yellowstone River Valley west of Billings, Montana. The strata are flat lying, and the resistant ones form broad flat uplands.*

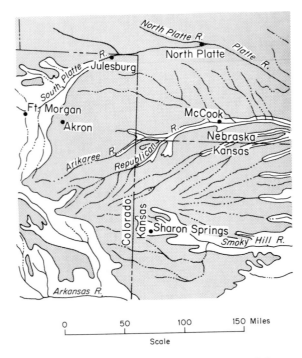

Figure 13.15   *Part of the High Plains Section of the Great Plains Province. Area covered by Tertiary formations, mostly Miocene and Pliocene, is shown stippled. White areas are Cretaceous. The main streams have cut through the Tertiary formations to the underlying Cretaceous. The interstream surfaces are probably little lower than the top of the Tertiary formations, and approximate depositional surfaces. The Tertiary formations are relatively permeable, the Cretaceous formations relatively impermeable. Streams on the Tertiary formations are intermittent; on the Cretaceous, mostly perennial.*

name is supposed to indicate that stakes had to be driven into the ground to mark the trails that crossed the prairie and those that led to water. The surface is dotted with shallow depressions, "buffalo wallows," where rainwater is sometimes ponded. Except for these in the wet season, water is scarce, and there are no hills to guide the traveler. Today there are windmills. These plains, covering about 50,000 square miles, slope southeastward from a maximum altitude of about 5,500 feet to about 2,500 feet at the escarpment overlooking the Osage Plains. The Staked Plains end westward at a west-facing escarpment over-

looking the Pecos Valley, a wide erosional valley from which the Tertiary cover has been stripped, exposing the Paleozoic formations.

Remnants of the late Tertiary formations representative of the Staked Plains are preserved on the east flank of the Sacramento Mountains *west* of the Pecos River. (Fig. 13.16). These remnants indicate that the valley of the Pecos River is no older than early Pleistocene. Before its capture by the Pecos River, the drainage was eastward across the Staked Plains of the Texas Panhandle.

Figure 13.16   *Change in drainage on Texas Plains as result of capture by headward erosion of the Pecos. [Adapted from Plummer, F. B., Bur. Ec. Geol. Univ. Texas, 3232.]*

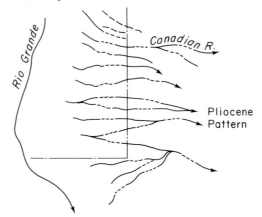

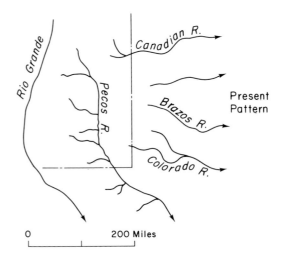

The southern end of the Great Plains is underlain by thick, Lower Cretaceous limestone, which forms the Edwards Plateau in Texas. This limestone extends northward under the Tertiary sediments on the Great Plains, but along the eastern and southern borders forms an escarpment—the Balcones fault zone, overlooking the West Gulf Coastal Plain. Surface streams are few on the Edwards Plateau; drainage is mostly underground and discharges from springs along the Balcones fault zone (Fig. 10.39) that supply the cities along that edge of the Coastal Plain. North of the Edwards Plateau, and slightly lower, is the Central Texas (Llano) uplift, a broad, low structural dome exposing early Paleozoic and Precambrian rocks.

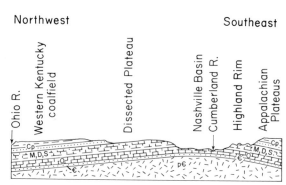

Figure 13.17 *Cross section of the Cincinnati Arch.* p-C, *Precambrian;* C, *Cambrian;* O, *Ordovician;* M, D, S: *Mississippian, Devonian, and Silurian;* Cp, *Pennsylvanian. Section length c. 225 miles.*

INTERIOR LOW PLATEAUS

The Interior Low Plateaus, which lie south of the glaciated area, are part of a broad anticline, known as the Cincinnati Arch, which forms the west flank of the Appalachian geosyncline and the east flank of the broad shallow structural basins under southern Illinois and the Mississippi River Alluvial Section. The axis of the arch approximately parallels the Appalachian Highlands and extends 600 miles from northwestern Alabama to northwestern Ohio. North of the Ohio River these arched Paleozoic formations have been glaciated, and the structure is obscure. The nonglaciated parts of the arch, mostly south of the Ohio River but extending into southern Indiana, reflect the geologic structure and constitute the Interior Low Plateaus (Figs. 13.1 and 13.17), an area of less than 100,000 square miles.

The Lexington Plain, Kentucky's area of bluegrass, and the Nashville Basin are on structural domes where Ordovician formations, mostly limestone, are exposed at the surface. These limestones are cavernous, and the land surface is pitted with sinkholes where caverns have collapsed. Much drainage enters the ground and is discharged in underground rivers (Fig. 13.18). The surface streams are entrenched in steep-walled valleys. Mammoth Cave is in this karst area.

Both the Lexington Plain and Nashville Basin are surrounded by infacing escarpments, or cuestas, as much as 400 feet high; they are topographic basins on the structural domes (Fig. 13.19). The surfaces that slope away from the escarpments make up the Highland Rim. Eastward, the Highland Rim slopes toward the Appalachian Plateaus; westward, it slopes toward the Tennessee and Mississippi rivers. East of the Lexington Plain the Highland Rim coincides with

Figure 13.18 *Underground course (arrows) of Lost River in the nonglaciated Mississippian limestones in southwestern Indiana. The river disappears underground in an open valley about 2½ miles southeast of Orleans, flows underground for 7 miles, and reappears below Orangeville. Floodwaters too great to discharge through the underground channel overflow via the winding valley that has an intermittent stream course. Topographic contours sketched from Vincennes 1/250,000 quadrangle.*

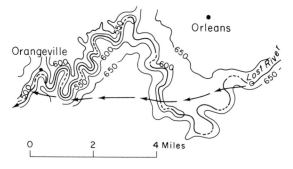

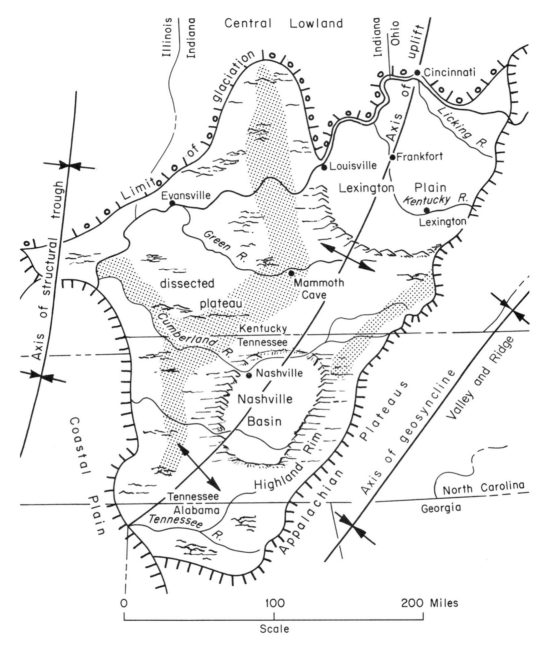

Figure 13.19 *Interior Low Plateaus Province, which lies south of the limit of glaciation and along the axis of the Cincinnati Arch. The Province is divided into four sections. North is the Lexington Plain, corresponding to the bluegrass area of Kentucky. South is the Nashville Basin; the Plateaus around it make up the Highland Rim. The remainder of the province is low, dissected plateau. Areas of limestone sinks (karst topography) on the Highland Rim and dissected plateau are indicated by stippling.*

the west-facing escarpment at the edge of the Appalachian Plateaus, a hilly belt referred to as The Knobs (Fig. 13.20). East of the Nashville Basin the Highland Rim is deeply dissected by valleys, some with steep headwalls attributable to solution.

The dissected plateaus west of the Lexington Plain and Nashville Basin slope slightly westward, but less steeply than the dip of the formations. As a result, the coal-bearing Pennsylvanian formations, which are in the Appalachian Plateaus east of the Cincinnati Arch, reappear at altitudes around 500 feet in western Kentucky. These form the western Kentucky coalfield and the coalfield in the southern Illinois structural basin.

Rivers crossing this dissected plateau are meandering and deeply entrenched. Some meanders are vigorously eroding laterally to produce *undercut walls, slip-off slopes,* and *cut-off meanders* (Fig. 13.21).

Other features of the Interior Low Plateaus are the

1. Temperate continental climate with rainy summer season.

2. Hardwood forests.

3. Residual deposits and Red and Yellow Podzolic Soils.

4. Ample water supplies.

5. Tobacco, corn, coal, bourbon, and, Kentucky Colonels.

OUACHITA PROVINCE
AND OZARK PLATEAUS

Two other highland areas south of the glacial border are the Ouachita Province and the Ozark Plateaus, which together cover less than 100,000 square miles (Fig. 13.1). They resemble the Appalachian Provinces and Interior Low Plateaus in many ways. The Ouachita Mountains are fold mountains of thick Paleozoic formations deposited in a geosyncline. The folds and the mountains trend east-west (Figs. 13.22, 13.23). Northward under the Arkansas River Valley the forma-

Figure 13.20 *The knobs in eastern Kentucky, along the boundary between the Lexington Plain (*back of the observer*) and the Appalachian Plateaus (*distant skyline*).*

tions thin in a structural basin containing coal measures of Pennsylvanian age, somewhat like those in the Appalachian Plateaus but more folded. North of this basin is a broad upwarp, the Ozark Plateaus, exposing early Paleozoic formations like those of the Cincinnati Arch and some Precambrian rocks. North of the Ozark Plateaus is the Illinois coal basin, which extends southeastward into Kentucky on the flank of the Cincinnati Arch.

Altitudes and local relief in the Ouachita Mountains and Ozark Plateaus average lower than in the Appalachian Mountains, but the landforms are similar. The Ouachita Mountains are composed of linear ridges and valleys (Fig. 13.24) that reach maximum altitudes of about 2,600 feet, about 1,500 feet above the adjoining valleys.

The Ozark Plateaus (Figs. 13.25, 13.26) consist of limestone. Altitudes reach 2,000 feet in the south in the Boston Mountains, and about 1,700 feet in the north. Between the Ozark Plateaus and the Ouachita Mountains is the valley of the Arkansas River, at an altitude of less than 500 feet.

As in the Appalachians, the sediments in the geosyncline under the Ouachita Province were derived from what is now the seaward side of the geosyncline. What was once their mountainous source now lies buried under the Coastal Plain and Continental Shelf. In both the Valley and Ridge and Ouachita provinces the thrust that folded and faulted the formations was directed toward the old Precambrian shield area in the interior of the continent.

The Paleozoic history of the geosyncline began with deposition of sands at the edges of the

Cambrian sea, forming sandstones of the Arbuckle and Ouachita mountains, and they overlap the Precambrian rocks in the St. Francois
Mountains (Fig. 13.21) and Lake Superior region.
In the fold mountains of southern Oklahoma
these sandstones are overlain by the Cambro-
Ordovician Arbuckle Limestone, which is a mile
thick; correlative limestone, with some sandstone, in the upper Mississippi Valley (Prairie de
Chien Group and St. Peter Sandstone) is about
250 feet thick. In the geosyncline this is overlain
by the Ordovician Simpson Formation and Viola
Limestone, which together are 3,000 feet thick;
correlative formations of limestone and shale in
the upper Mississippi Valley (Platteville Limestone, Decorah Shale, Galena Dolomite, Maquo-
keta Shale) are about 500 feet thick.

Silurian and Devonian formations in the middle west do not vary in composition or thickness
as much as either the earlier or later Paleozoic
formations. Both in the geosynclinal areas and
on the shelf to the north these rocks are mostly
shale and limestone and together are a few hundred feet thick.

In Mississippian time, however, sinking of the
geosyncline appears to have accelerated again. In
the north, on the shelf area, is shale and limestone less than 1,000 feet thick, but in southeastern Oklahoma and adjoining areas in Arkansas, the Mississippian System is mostly shale and
sandstone (Stanley Shale and Jackfork Sandstone) and is 16,000 feet thick. The Pennsylvanian
similarly is much thicker in the south than in the
north; in southeastern Oklahoma it consists of
15,000 feet of beds. The generalized section is
given in Table 13.1.

The tremendous thickness of Pennsylvanian
formations in the south does not include the
upper Pennsylvanian, which is not represented
there. In the north, the entire Pennsylvanian System is only about 2,000 feet thick, and only the
lower half of it correlates with the 15,000-foot
section in the geosyncline. These Pennsylvanian
formations have supplied much of the Middle
West's coal.

The Permian is not well represented, but at
the end of the Paleozoic, when the Appalachian
Mountains were folded, the rocks that now form

Table 13.1

Formations of Pennsylvania Age in
Southeastern Oklahoma and Western Arkansas

Formation	Description
Thurman Sandstone	Sandstone with con-glomerate and shale; top formation of the coal measures; 200 feet.
Boggy Shale	Alternating beds of shale and sandstone, with coal beds; 3,000 feet.
Savanna Sandstone	Mostly sandstone, some shale; 1,150 feet.
McAlester Shale	Shale and sandstone, with coal beds; 2,000 feet.
Hartshorne Sandstone	Sandstone; 200 feet.
Atoka Formation	Alternating beds of sandstone and shale; basal formation of the coal measures; 7,000 feet.
Wapanucka Limestone	Limestone; 200 feet.
Caney Shale	Upper part only; 250 feet?
Caney Shale	Lower part, and other Mississippian forma-tions.

the Ouachita, Wichita, and Arbuckle mountains
also were folded.

Other features of the Ouachita Province and
Ozark Plateaus include their

1. Continental climate.

2. Residual deposits and Red and Yellow
Podzolic Soils.

3. Hardwood forests.

4. Lack of many metropolitan areas.

5. Mules.

Climate

The climate of the Central Lowland, the plateaus
south of it, and the Great Plains is continental.
Temperature differences between seasons are extreme: winters are cold and blizzards frequent;
summers are hot and subject to tornadoes. Yet

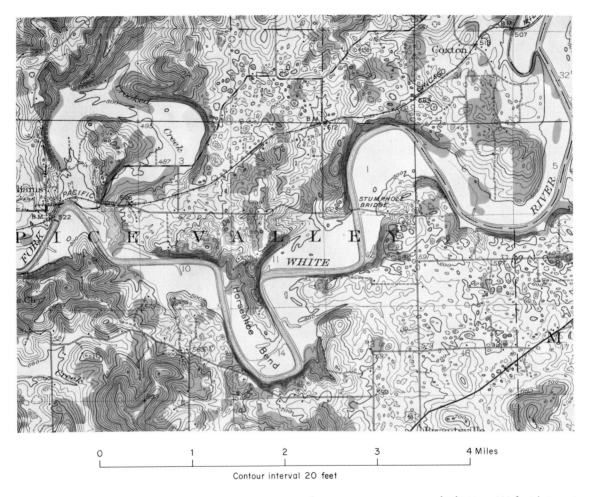

0   1   2   3   4 Miles

Contour interval 20 feet

Figure 13.21 *Dissected plateau in southern Indiana. Meandering streams are entrenched 100 to 300 feet into the plateau. Along the outside of the meanders the valley walls are steep, for they are undercut by the back and forth swing of the meander. Conversely, slopes along the inside are gentle slip-off slopes. Crooked Creek is in a cut-off meander. The plateau surface about 100 feet above the river is limestone and is pitted with sinkholes; hills rising above this part of the surface are shale and sandstone and are smoothly rounded. [From U.S.G.S. Oolitic quadrangle, Indiana.]*

compared to the plains of eastern Europe and western Asia, this climate is mild, for the winters are much less severe. Also, except on the Great Plains, we are favored with more rainfall, and it is better distributed during the growing season.

The climates in the Central Lowland are humid; on the Great Plains they are semiarid. Average annual precipitation in the Great Plains is about 15 inches. This increases eastward to about 20 inches near the 100th meridian, to 40 inches in Ohio, and to 50 inches in Tennessee. Moreover, most of this precipitation takes place during the growing season, which largely explains the tremendous agricultural productivity of this region. One of the effects of the increased aridity westward is the greater frequency of saline lakes and ponds west of the 100th meridian, especially in the Dakotas.

346

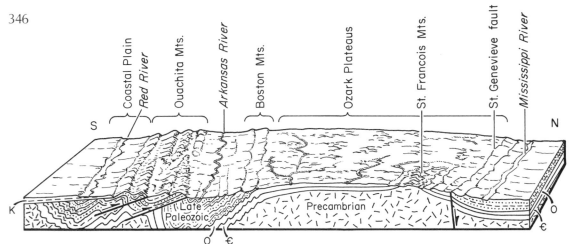

Figure 13.22 *Diagram of the Ouachita Mountains and Ozark Plateaus. The cross section extends from the Coastal Plain in north Texas to the Mississippi River below St. Louis, a distance of about 300 miles. The Ouachita Mountains, composed of Paleozoic formations in folds broken by thrust faults directed toward the core of the continent, developed over a Paleozoic geosyncline where the formations are very thick, as in the Valley and Ridge Province. The south flank of the geosynclinal belt is buried under Coastal Plain formations of Cretaceous age (K). Northward under the Arkansas River the Paleozoic formations thin and form a broad basin containing Pennsylvanian coal measures. The Ozark Plateaus consist of early Paleozoic formations (O, Ordovician; €, Cambrian) and, in the St. Francois Mountains, Precambrian rocks.*

Figure 13.23 *Linear ridges and valleys of folded Paleozoic formations in the Ouachita Province are similar to those of the Valley and Ridge Province in the Appalachians, except that the valleys are generally narrow. The scene here is in Shady Lake State Park, southeast of the skyline drive that extends from near Mena, Arkansas, to Talihina, Oklahoma. [Courtesy of Arkansas Dept. of Parks and Tourism.]*

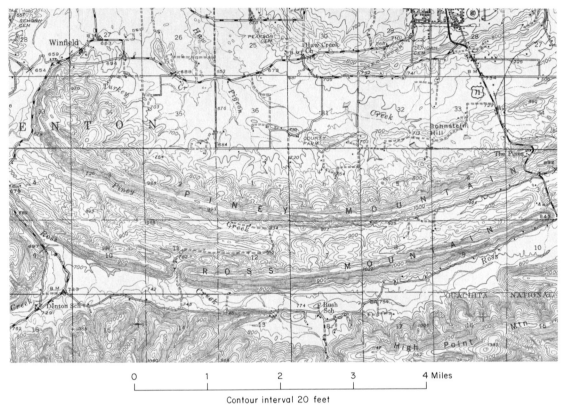

Figure 13.24 *Topography in the Ouachita Mountains is like that of the Valley and Ridge Province.* [*From U.S.G.S. Waldron, Arkansas, quadrangle.*] *Compare with Figure 11.8.*

The Great Plains, like other semiarid areas, is subject to flash floods during occasional hard storms, and, like any other region, every 10 years, 100 years, or 1,000 years, a rare major flood can be expected. Semiarid regions, however, are also subject to drought, and exceptionally serious droughts can be expected every 100 to 1,000 years. Such droughts were experienced on the southern Great Plains during the dust bowl days of the 1930's and again in 1970–1971. The problem with semiarid lands is that they are not half dry and half wet, but they are excessively dry or excessively wet at the wrong times.

Average annual temperatures range from 40°F in the north to somewhat more than 60°F in the south. Average annual temperatures, however, are not very meaningful, because the climate is continental, with extreme seasonal differences. For example, in central Minnesota and the adjoining parts of North and South Dakota, the

average January temperature is 10°F, whereas the *average* July temperature is 70°F. In that same area, the average annual minimum temperature is −40°F, as contrasted with an average annual maximum of more than 100°F. The ranges of temperatures on the Manitoba, Saskatchewan, and Alberta plains are comparable. These extremes are about twice the range of those for equivalent latitudes along the Atlantic and Pacific coasts, where the climates are tempered by the oceans. The great difference between cold-season and warm-season temperatures decreases southward. In southern Oklahoma the difference between average minimum and average maximum temperatures is less than 100°F.

The average frost-free period is about 100 days in northern Minnesota and southern Manitoba, but increases southward to about 225 days in southern Oklahoma (Fig. 13.27). The northern plains in Canada, though, at the Alberta Plateaus

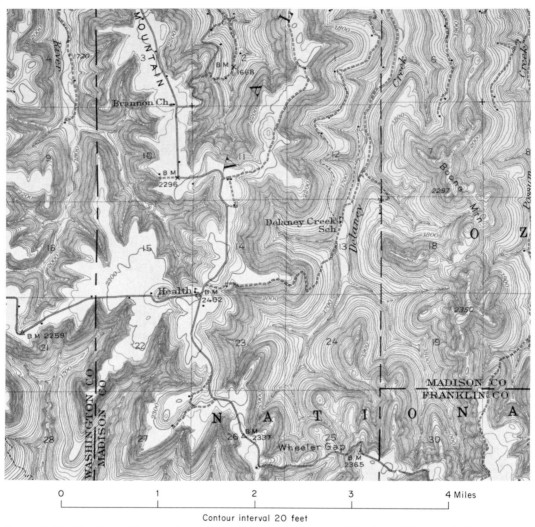

0   1   2   3   4 Miles

Contour interval 20 feet

Figure 13.25   *The Ozark Plateaus have a dendritic drainage pattern like that of the Appalachian Plateaus. In places the uplands are broad flats (western part of the map), but most of the divides are narrow, irregular ridges (eastern part of map).* [*From U.S.G.S. St. Paul, Arkansas, quadrangle.*] *Compare with Figure 11.11.*

and adjoining lowlands, may experience severe frost even in July.

Near the Great Lakes and Lake Winnipeg, especially on the leeward shores, the frost-free period is longer than it is away from them—a result of the tempering effect that bodies of water have on local climate. A good example of this effect is the grape belt of western New York State, which stretches along the southeast shore of Lake Erie.

Important in moderating temperatures on the Great Plains is the Chinook wind. As winds cross the Rocky Mountains, they cool as the air rises on the western slope, loses its moisture at the summit, and is then warmed adiabatically as it descends the eastern slope and spreads on the Great Plains. Six inches of snow may be melted in a day.

The northward cooling affects the average depth of frost penetration—in southwestern

Figure 13.26 *Scene in the Ozark Plateau along the Buffalo River in northern Arkansas. Gently dipping early Paleozoic formations crop out in ledges along the valley sides. [Courtesy of Arkansas Dept. of Parks and Tourism.]*

Texas it is about one inch; at the Canadian border, more than four feet. Under snow the depth of freezing is much less. The northward increase in coldness also affects the natural vegetation, soils, agricultural activity, transportation, engineering problems concerned with foundations, and sales of heavy underwear.

A major climatic hazard in the central United States are the "twisters," or tornadoes, which have wind velocities estimated to be as great as 500 miles per hour. Where they touch ground, tornadoes commonly are about 1,000 feet wide. They extend upward into a funnel-shaped cloud darkened with dust sucked upward, and may reach to 20,000 feet. The storms move at speeds ranging from 5 to 60 miles per hour, and their tracks along the ground extend on the average for about a dozen miles. One tornado left a track more than 100 miles long.

Figure 13.27 *Average length of frost-free period (days) [Generalized from U.S.D.A.] in the central United States.*

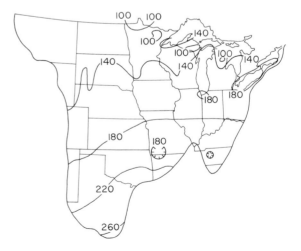

Tornadoes are most frequent in Kansas and Iowa (Fig. 4.7), but property damage is less there and deaths fewer than in some of the more populous states where tornado frequency is less. Although tornadoes may occur in any month of the year, they occur most frequently in spring and early summer. The earliest spring tornadoes generally strike the Gulf Coast; as the season advances, tornadoes strike farther north. The storms may occur at any hour of the day, but usually occur in late afternoon and early evening.

The causes of tornadoes are not very well understood, other than that they are associated with the turbulence accompanying weather fronts. They form in the upper air, commonly between altitudes of 10,000 and 20,000 feet. The whirling column, likened to that of water running out of a bathtub, but inverted, extends itself downward as a lower stratum of air is sucked upward.

The frequency of tornadoes decreases northward and westward. On the Great Plains the principal climatic hazard is provided by hailstorms. Some of the storms produce huge hailstones, many half an inch in diameter and some up to 4 inches. Such storms flatten crops, strip trees, remove paint from buildings, break windows, damage roofs, and collapse the tops on convertibles.

To help provide shelter against strong winds on the Great Plains, windbreaks have been planted on most farms. These consist of several rows of plants, tall trees, such as American elm and silver maple on the inner side near the home, and rows of shorter ones, such as green ash, boxelder, bur oak, or ponderosa pine, in the intermediate rows. The outermost rows are short trees and dense shrubs, to protect the tall ones against defoliation. The short, wind-resistant ones may be common lilac, Russian olive, service berry, red cedar, or Rocky Mountain juniper. Such windbreaks provide some protection for a distance about 20 times the height of the tall trees. Lessening the wind helps protect against excessive wind-chill, reduces snow drift, wind erosion, dust, and losses by evaporation. Large pastures commonly have board windbreaks in

the southeast corners where livestock, drifting with the prevailing wind, can find shelter against winter winds and ground blizzards.

The effects of past climates on the present physiography are perhaps more striking in the central United States and central Canada than in any other large segment of the continent. The direct topographic effects of the deposits left by the glaciers have already been described. In addition, these deposits and the ice are responsible for the great rivers (p. 353), the many thousands of lakes, including the Great Lakes (p. 362), the fertile loessial deposits (p. 352), and the soils. An effect of the present climate on population distribution is illustrated by the following:

State	Average Annual Precipitation	Population Density, Per Square Mile
Indiana	35	130
Iowa	30	48
Nebraska	20	18
Wyoming (plains part)	15	10

For every 20,000 square miles, Indiana has 22 towns with populations more than 10,000, Iowa has 8, Nebraska has 3, and Wyoming has 1.

Agriculture, Vegetation

The Interior Plains, richest of the world's agricultural regions, are favored by a hot and rainy growing season, by rich loessial soils, and by flat land. Production is so lush that some state highway departments collect and bale hay from the highway right-of-ways. It is because of the Interior Plains that so many Americans face the problem of a bulging waistline.

The lake region specializes mostly in hay and dairying. The northern part of the Central Lowland westward onto the Great Plains is the corn and hog belt; parallel to this on the south is a belt used principally for corn and winter wheat.

The two highland areas in the South and the southern part of the Great Plains are in the cotton belt. The central part of the Great Plains is used for winter wheat and the northern part for spring wheat. Lake Michigan provides an example of how local climate influences agricultural practice: fruit can be raised along the leeward (east) side of the lake, but the west side is not suitable.

By 1840 corn was raised in substantial quantities as far west as Missouri and Arkansas, but it was not until the 1870's that Iowa, Illinois, and central Indiana became the heart of the corn belt. About 1890 the pattern of production of wheat in the Plains and Prairie states began to appear as it does today.

The Middle West's impressive growth in agriculture can be illustrated in numerous examples. The center of wheat production began in New York. In 1850 the center had moved to central Ohio. By 1860 it was in Indiana, in 1870 in Illinois, in 1900 in Iowa, and today it is in Kansas. The increase in agriculture was both the cause and the effect of advances in farm machinery. Iron ploughs were not in general use until after 1842. By 1900 large farms used machinery that ploughed, harrowed, and sowed in a single operation. In 1830, 64 hours of labor were needed to produce an acre of wheat; by 1900, only 3 hours of labor were needed. In 1850 the United States had 1,500,000 farms aggregating 300 million acres; soon after 1900 there were 6,000,000 farms with a billion acres. Today there are 3,700,000 farms aggregating 1.1 billion acres. Agriculture today has become big business.

The natural vegetation of the Central Lowland and Great Plains has been largely replaced by the extensive and intensive agriculture practiced there. The general variations from south to north and from east to west across the region have been described in Chapter 8. Because the region is large and the changes considerable, some details are noted here.

The number of species of trees in the Central Hardwood forest decreases westward as forest gives way to grassland. In general, the trees are thought to be advancing westward onto the grassland, but not all species seem to be doing

so. One of the conspicuous dropouts is beech, which is common in the east but barely makes it westward to Illinois. Perhaps it is migrating westward but lagging behind other species, or conceivably it once extended farther west and is now retreating. Along the north edge of the Central Hardwood, the beech, with sugar maple, are reportedly extending their range northward into what has been pine forest.

Similarly, on the western side of the grasslands, yellow pine, which extends eastward from the Rocky Mountain forests, occupies parts of the Great Plains. Precipitation increases eastward and one might suppose that the yellow pine is extending its range in that direction, but this is not at all certain. Likewise one may wonder whether the tall grasses or short grasses are migrating, the one at the expense of the other. Climates change and vegetation can change, but we cannot be sure in what direction present changes are headed—toward an increasingly colder and wetter climate or the reverse. We might know what the recent trends have been if we understood what has happened to the range of particular species. Some species can extend their range when there is a succession of favorable years, and once having occupied new ground, can maintain their growth there although they may be unable to extend themselves farther. Other species can extend their range during a succession of favorable years but are unable to maintain their growth during a succession of unfavorable years following the favorable. In addition, the considerable agriculture practiced on the Central Lowland and Great Plains imposes artificial constraints.

Surface Deposits and Soils

Surface deposits in the central United States and the plains of Canada include the glacial drift; shore and bottom deposits of the Pleistocene lakes; alluvium along the rivers and streams; colluvium where the land is hilly; eolian deposits, the vast blanket of loess and the dune sand; and clayey residual deposits where the sedimentary formations are deeply weathered, especially the limestone formations in the Interior Low Plateaus and Ozark Plateaus.

These differences are reflected in the soils. For example, the clayey residual deposits where the formations are deeply weathered are parent material for Red and Yellow Podzols. These are ancient soils like those in the Appalachian Highlands, and they end northward where they are overlapped and buried by the glacial drift, glacial outwash, or loess of the Wisconsinan stage of glaciation. These ancient soils are most noticeable where they are developed on the Paleozoic formations, but have formed on pre-Wisconsinan glacial drift and loess too.

The soils also reflect the climatic zones—in the same way and to the same degree as does the vegetation. In the conifer forests of the Superior Upland the soils are mostly Podzols. Under the hardwood forest the soils are mostly Gray-Brown Podzols. The eastern part of the tall-grass belt has Prairie Soils, and these grade westward to the Chernozem Soils. The eastern part of the short-grass belt has Chestnut soils, and the western part, near the foot of the Rocky Mountains, has Brown Soils. The changes in soil profile across these belts (Fig. 6.6) are gradual and clearly reflect the decreasing availability of moisture southwestward from the southern part of the Canadian Shield. These soils are of Holocene or late Pleistocene age.

Another group of distinctive soils, the Planosols, which have a clay pan 2 to 3 feet below the surface, have developed on nearly level, poorly drained areas that are most extensive on the loess-covered, pre-Wisconsinan drift in southern Illinois, southern Iowa, and northern Missouri (Figs. 6.1, 6.5). Similar soils on the Osage Plains have developed on shale and sandstone formations, and in Nebraska on loess-covered plains.

The red color of soils south of the Arkansas River commonly is attributed to the increasingly warm climate southward. This is only partly true: Reddish Prairie Soils and the eastern series of the Reddish Chestnut Soils developed in large part from formations that are red, and much or most of their color probably is inherited. Among the

western series of Reddish Chestnut Soils and the Reddish Brown Soils are some soils that are older than the last glaciation. Their properties, including their color, may be inherited from the ancient climates under which they formed, and may have little or no relationship to the present climate. An example of three very different kinds of soil of three different ages in the Great Plains is given in Figure 13.28.

Probably the most important single factor contributing to the composition and fertility of the soils in central United States is the blanket of loess and related deposits covering that region (Fig. 6.1). The loess immediately east of the Mississippi and Missouri rivers is tens of feet thick and covers most of the land. Other thick and extensive deposits cover both sides of the Platte River in Nebraska and extend across Iowa. Along the eastern and southern limits of these deposits the loess is less than 2 feet thick and covers no more than about a third of the land. The eolian deposits in the Great Plains Province are in large part sandy, and some of that area is covered by dunes.

These loessial soils are subject to severe erosion, and sediment load of streams in the loessial areas is about 10 times greater than that of streams northwest and east of the loess. Soils on the southern half of the Great Plains and west of the 100th meridian—the dust bowl—are subject not only to washing but to severe wind erosion. The soils are nutritional enough, but droughts are frequent and the soils are blown off lands where the grass cover has been removed. During the droughts in the 1930's dust was carried eastward to the cities along the Atlantic seaboard. Suitability of these lands for farming is controlled chiefly by climate and topography, and not by the fertility of the soils.

The northern half of the Great Plains has little loess and is less subject to erosion, as is suggested by photographic records covering the last 50 years. The stands of yellow pine growing on the Great Plains have spread, and except in cultivated areas the desirable grasses and shrubs there are maintaining themselves against grazing and other land use. The difference in soil erosion

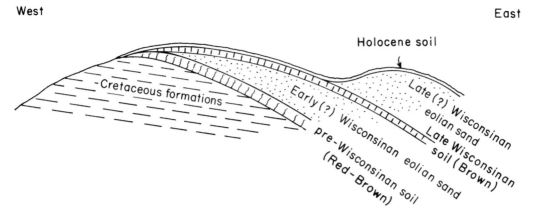

Figure 13.28 *Diagrammatic section through hill in the Great Plains Province, showing eolian sand deposited on the east (lee) side of the hill and soils of three kinds and of three different ages interbedded with the sand. The oldest soil is of pre-Wisconsinan age. This is buried by a bed of wind-deposited sand of Early (?) Wisconsinan age. A Brown Soil developed on this deposit is buried by a sand of Late (?) Wisconsinan age, and the Holocene soil on this sand is feebly developed.*

between the northern and southern Great Plains is in large part a function of the difference in the geology of the soils—specifically, occurrence of loess.

The several soils provide some examples of how soil texture and the availability to plants of chemical elements in the soil affect soil fertility. Some soils contain too little of certain elements necessary for plant growth; others may contain the element in an insoluble form not available for plant use. Some elements are toxic in small quantities; others may be essential in small quantities and become toxic if present in excessive amounts. The Chernozem and Chestnut Soils contain about twice as much phosphorus as do the Red Chestnut Soils, which commonly are deficient in this element. The Red Chestnut and other red soils obviously contain much iron, but evidently not in a very soluble form, because some plants, notably sorghums, show signs of iron deficiency when grown on the red soils. Selenium occurs in toxic quantities in soils developed on some shales of Cretaceous age, and in places selenium poisoning is serious enough to warrant fencing off the affected areas. Such lands can be used for growing fiber or seed crops, but not for growing food.

Great Rivers

The central part of the continent—the Central Lowland and the areas that drain into it—is characterized by great rivers (Fig. 13.29) as well as by the Great Lakes. The region drains in three main directions—northward to Hudson Bay, northeastward via the Great Lakes to the St. Lawrence River, and southward to the Mississippi River. Average discharge of the three river systems totals nearly 700 million acre-feet per year, and of this total more than half discharges via the Mississippi.

The divide between the drainage to Hudson Bay and to the Mississippi crosses North Dakota and northern Minnesota, but in preglacial time the divide was at least 400 miles farther south. Drainage was turned southward by the Pleistocene glaciations; the southward course of the Missouri River across the Dakotas is a result of drainage diversion.

The valley along this stretch of the Missouri River is a deep, narrow trench, quite unlike the broad, open valley upstream in Montana and downstream in Nebraska and Iowa. The plains slope east, but the river flows south. The several large tributaries along this stretch of the river are

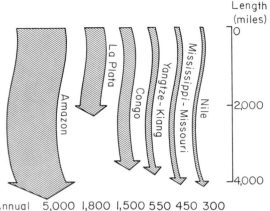

Annual 5,000 1,800 1,500 550 450 300
Discharge
(millions of acre-feet)

Figure 13.29 *Length and discharge of the
Mississippi-Missouri River compared to some other
great rivers in the world. The discharge is greater
than that of the slightly longer Nile River, but less
than that of the Yangtze Kiang, and very much less
than that of the Congo, the comparatively short La
Plata, and the Amazon Rivers. As big as these
streams are, they still are small compared to the
oceanic currents; flow of the Gulf Stream, for
example, is 100 times that of the Amazon River.*

all from the west, and occupy open valleys rather
than deep trenches. Figure 13.30,A illustrates the
probable courses of the streams before they were
diverted. The James River, a postglacial drainage
course known locally as The Jim, has a gradient
of only about 5 inches per mile. It has been
described as the longest unnavigable river in the
United States.

Other examples of major changes in drainage
caused by glaciation are illustrated in Figure
13.30. The Mississippi River drained southeastward to what is now the Illinois River until a
glacial advance pushed it westward to its present
position (Fig. 13.30,B); a preglacial river may have
crossed Iowa to join what is now the Des Moines
River.

Still another major drainage change occurred
along the Missouri River in Montana (Fig.
13.30,C). The river formerly flowed around the
north side of the Bearpaw Mountains (Fig. 13.12)
and along the course of the present Milk River.

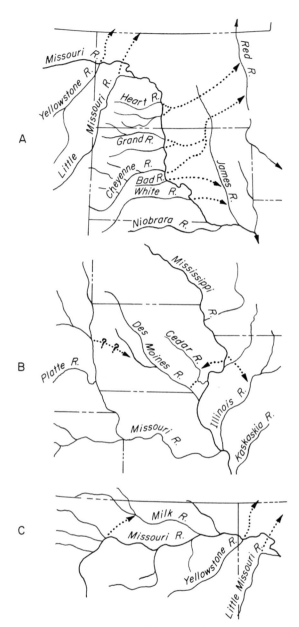

Figure 13.30 *Examples of drainage changes
attributable to glaciation on the Interior Plains.
Present drainage shown by solid lines; supposed
former courses, dotted. (A) Drainage changes along
the Missouri Trench in North and South Dakota. (B)
Drainage changes along the Mississippi River. The
pre-Illinoian course was southeastward to the Illinois
River; the Illinoian glaciation pushed the river west
of its present course. (C) Drainage changes along the
Missouri River in Montana.*

The advance of the glaciers to a position south of the Bearpaw and Little Rocky Mountains diverted the Missouri to its present source.

VALLEY OF THE MISSISSIPPI RIVER

The present Mississippi River crosses three very different kinds of terrain, and the characteristics of the river and its valley differ markedly in the three stretches. There is an upper stretch of roughly 500 miles in glacial drift, a middle stretch of about 1,000 miles from Minneapolis-Saint Paul to the head of the Mississippi Embayment (mostly a broad floodplain between bedrock valley walls), and a lower stretch of about another 1,000 miles in the tremendous alluvial floodplain of the Embayment.

Above the Twin Cities, Minneapolis and St. Paul, the river follows an open valley that winds between morainal lakes and hummocks left by the late Wisconsinan glaciation. The officially designated head of the river is at Lake Itasca, where a sign proclaims: "Here 1475 feet above the ocean the mighty Mississippi begins to flow on its winding way 2552 miles to the Gulf of Mexico."

If they could do so, certain neighboring hills and lakes might dispute this proclamation, because just south of Lake Itasca are hills with ponds and marshes 200 feet higher than it is, and 4 miles to the west there are others up to 500 feet higher. It is not clear, however, whether much of their drainage goes to Lake Itasca and contributes to its overflow: the neighboring hills and lakes remain silent.

For about 150 miles (the distance depends on how one counts), the Mississippi moves from one lake to another in an uncertain course on marshy ground connecting the lakes. At Grand Rapids, Minnesota (Fig. 13.31), at about 1275 feet in altitude, the river crosses the southwest end of the iron formations that extend northeastward from there to form the Mesabi Range. The river then follows a more definite but meandering channel for another 150 miles to the iron formations of the Cuyuna Range, which is buried under glacial

Figure 13.31 *Headward course of the Mississippi River.*

drift. There the river nearly loses itself in a winding course on the flat and otherwise dry bed of a Pleistocene lake (Lake Aitkin) and then crosses another network of lakes at about 1,200 feet in altitude. From there on the river is sure where it is going, and although its channel continues on glacial drift, it is well defined and reasonably straight for another 200 miles to the Twin Cities.

There, at an altitude of 700 feet, the upper stretch of the river ends, for it leaves its bed in glacial drift and enters a valley and channel eroded in bedrock. The river valley above the Twin Cities clearly is younger than the Wisconsinan glacial drift that forms both the river bed and the valley "walls." Downstream from the Twin Cities, below the mouth of the St. Croix River (Figs. 13.32, 13.33), the gorge is in bedrock and is preglacial. Some of the old, preglacial channels, now filled with glacial drift, are shown in Figure 13.33. They record at least three stages of river history. The youngest valleys (3) are those of the present St. Croix and the Mississippi River above its junction with the Minnesota River. An earlier stage (2) is represented by the broad valley of the Minnesota River and the valley of the Mississippi for about 15 miles downstream from that junction. The difference in age of these two stages is illustrated by the contrast between the

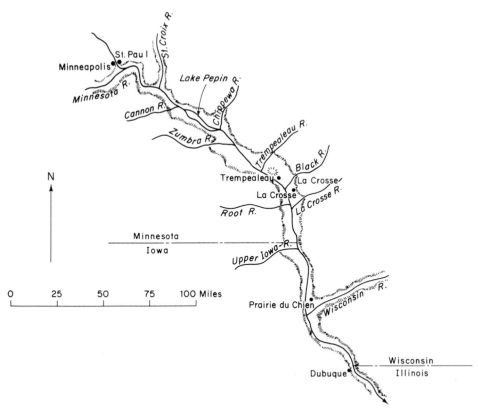

Figure 13.32 *Sketch map illustrating how the Mississippi River is pushed against the opposite side of its gorge at the mouth of each tributary along the gorge crossing the Wisconsin Arch. The gorge is widest near the middle of this stretch, where it crosses the high part of the arch and is in easily eroded sandstone.*

second-stage valley and the present gorge of the Mississippi where it joins that valley, for the gorge of the Mississippi is only about 1,500 feet wide, whereas the valley of the Minnesota River, like that of the Mississippi below the junction, is about 2 miles wide. St. Anthony Falls, 7 miles above the mouth of the gorge, has retreated slightly less than 2½ feet per year in almost 300 years, and at that rate about 6,250 years would have been required for the falls to be cut back to their present position.

The earliest stage (1 in Figure 13.33) in the history of the river valleys in that area is represented by a nearly east-west channel filled with glacial deposits, and by a similarly buried channel thought to represent the ancestral St. Croix

River. Borings indicate that the bedrock floor of the old valley is less than 450 feet above sea level.

For 275 miles below Minneapolis and St. Paul (Fig. 13.32), the Mississippi River follows a deep valley with steep, rocky walls. About 30 miles below the Twin Cities, the river crosses the Wisconsinan terminal moraine, and the valley is cut into the bedrock uplands, which are mantled with older drift deposited during the Kansan or Nebraskan glaciations. Below the Chippewa River and from there to a point below Dubuque, the valley is in the Driftless Area and cuts across the west flank of the Wisconsin Arch, a broad arch of Cambrian and Ordovician formations. Minneapolis and St. Paul are in a structural basin; the base of the Paleozoic formations there is below sea level. From there the formations rise downstream about 500 feet near La Crosse at the mouth of the Black River, and then descend again to about 1,500 feet below sea level near Dubuque. At the crest of the arch near Trempealeau and La Crosse the bluffs are more than 600 feet above the floodplain, but upstream and downstream they are about half that high. The valley is narrow where it passes between bluffs of resistant limestone or dolomite, and widens where it cuts through easily eroded Cambrian sandstones. A good example of this sort of structural control on a smaller scale is provided by a tributary, the Wisconsin River. Its valley greatly narrows downstream, and is only a mile wide where it joins the Mississippi between bluffs of lower Ordovician (Prairie du Chien) dolomite. It widens

to more than 3 miles within 20 miles upstream, where it cuts through easily eroded St. Peter sandstone.

With one notable exception along this stretch of the Mississippi River, each tributary has crowded the big river against the opposite side of the valley by depositing more sediment in it than the main stream could move (Fig. 13.32). The exception is the St. Croix River, which was dammed by sediment deposited on the floodplain by the Mississippi River; the lower stretch of the St. Croix is a lake. The Chippewa River not only crowded the Mississippi against the south bank, but dammed the Mississippi to form Lake Pepin. The Trempealeau and Black rivers from the north, not only crowded the Mississippi against the south bank, but they isolated the river from

Figure 13.33 *The original channel of the Mississippi River south of Minneapolis and St. Paul was at about position 1, and entrenched at least 300 feet into bedrock. During a second stage the Minnesota River Valley was cut deeply by meltwaters from the overflow of Lake Aggasiz. It maintained that course during the 3rd stage, when the Mississippi River, in late Wisconsinan and Holocene time, developed its present course 3. [Generalized after Schwartz and Theil, 1954.]*

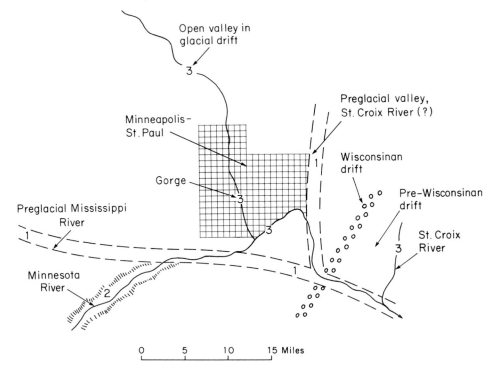

its main valley, which is about 4 miles wide, and forced it into a gorge less than a mile wide in the bedrock.

At La Crosse, Root River joins the Mississippi from the west, and the LaCrosse River joins it from the east; the Mississippi, pressed from both sides, is in the middle of the valley. At the mouth of the Wisconsin River the floodplain is at an altitude of 612 feet; the bedrock floor under the fill in the valley is slightly less than 500 feet in altitude. At the mouth of the Des Moines River the floodplain is at about 500 feet, and is below 350 feet where the river enters the broad alluvial floodplain at the head of the Mississippi Embayment. The bedrock floor under the alluvium there is less than 200 feet in altitude. Several drainage changes along this middle stretch of the Mississippi River are illustrated in Figure 13.30,B.

Near Cairo, Illinois, where the Mississippi is joined by the Ohio River, it enters the broad floodplain of the Mississippi Embayment (p. 224). Between there and the Gulf, the river becomes narrower and deeper. At Cairo the river is a mile wide and 87 feet deep, whereas at the mouth it is a half mile wide and 129 feet deep. The mouth has been extended seaward a third of a mile in 200 years. This lower stretch of the Mississippi is characterized by great sweeping meanders and innumerable ox-bow lakes, formed where meanders have been cut off. In doing this the river shows no respect for the state boundaries that supposedly are along the middle of the river. Where meanders have been cut off, some of the state boundaries have been shifted, by agreement, to the new river course; others have been maintained along the abandoned stretches of river course that form the ox-lakes.

ANCESTRAL OHIO RIVER—A STUDY IN DRAINAGE CHANGE

In preglacial times the Great Lakes probably were river valleys that discharged to the St. Lawrence River. The divide that is supposed to have separated the St. Lawrence drainage from that of the Mississippi was across northern Ohio, northern Indiana, and northeastern Illinois (Fig. 13.34).

The original Ohio River headed a short distance above the Falls of the present Ohio at Louisville. It was joined by the ancestral Wabash, which at that time headed in central Indiana, near Indianapolis. Below its junction with the Wabash, the ancestral Ohio continued at about its present course for 25 miles, after which it turned west into what is now a dry valley. The Mississippi River at that time was 20 miles farther west and flowed into the valley now occupied by the St. Francis River. The Ohio and Mississippi then joined near the present mouth of the St. Francis, about 175 miles south of Cairo.

The main drainage off the west slope of the Appalachian Mountains was by way of a preglacial valley known as the Teays River. This stream (Fig. 13.34) joined the Mississippi in central Illinois. The course of the Teays, northwestward across western Ohio and then westward across northern Indiana and central Illinois, is filled with glacial deposits, and the river's course is not expressed in the topography. It is known, however, from many well borings. Southeast of Chillicothe, the valley of the Teays is marked by the present valley of the Scioto River. Drainage in that segment is now reversed.

The drainage to the St. Lawrence River and to the Teays Valley northwest of Chillicothe became disrupted when the glaciers advanced across that part of the country. The drainage became diverted along the south edge of the ice and into the head of the ancestral Ohio River near Madison. At Louisville, Kentucky, the river meandered widely on glacial fill, and when it began to cut downward it was near the north edge of the fill and encountered a resistant bed of limestone, which now forms the Falls of the Ohio. The present course is superimposed across the limestone ledge, which is 40 feet higher than the bedrock under the fill along the south side of the valley.

In many of the valleys the drainage became reversed. The stretch from New Martinsville to the boundary of Pennsylvania, for example, originally drained northward; glaciers turned it southward, and today it is marked by a narrow valley. The Scioto River was turned southward, as were the Miami River and others near Cincin-

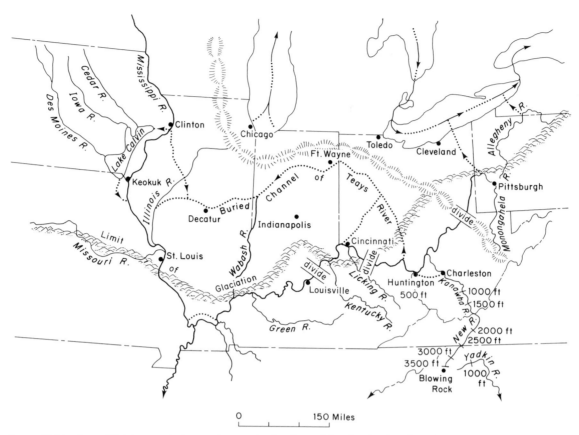

Figure 13.34 *Some Pleistocene drainage changes in the Central Lowland. Abandoned stream courses are shown by broken lines. Before the glaciations, the Teays River drained northwestward from the Blue Ridge at Blowing Rock, North Carolina. Its headwaters are at an altitude of 3,500 feet; draining east in the Piedmont Province is the Yadkin River at an altitude of 1,000 feet. The glaciations blocked the Teays River and filled the valleys with drift. The drainage was pushed southward into what is now the Ohio River Valley, originally a series of short tributaries to the Teays.*

nati. All this drainage was ponded, and overflowed across the divide above Louisville. Figure 13.34 shows the positions of the stream divides before the diversions.

In West Virginia the original course of the Teays was westward from Charleston to Huntington, and that former course, now abandoned, is marked by an open valley. The bedrock floor of the abandoned valley between Charleston and Huntington is 200 feet higher than the Kanawha. It contains rounded stream gravels, including metamorphic rock types, that must have been derived from the Blue Ridge or farther east. Overlying the gravels are silts, known as the

Mimford Silt, probably lake beds deposited when the river system was first dammed. The course of the Kanawha from below Charleston to the Ohio may be a new course cut by overflow from the lake.

Above Charleston the Kanawha and New rivers seem to mark the original course of the Teays. They rise in the Blue Ridge near Blowing Rock, North Carolina, at an altitude of 3,500 feet—2,500 feet higher than the Yadkin, which drains the east slope to the Atlantic. New River enters Virginia at an altitude of about 2,500 feet, and West Virginia at an altitude of about 1,750 feet. At Huntington, where the old course is joined by the Ohio, the altitude is about 500 feet.

The evolution of the Ohio River system from the Teays is generally thought to have occurred during the Kansan Glaciation. The course of the Teays may date from far back in the Tertiary. The so-called New River, therefore, is actually an old one.

OTHER DRAINAGE CHANGES

There have been drainage changes on the High Plains too, but these are not attributable directly to glaciation. For example, the Tertiary formations shown in Figure 13.15 were deposited by streams flowing eastward from the Rocky Mountains. But the old drainage courses have been cut off in the Colorado Piedmont section by the South Platte River and by a tributary of the Arkansas River, both of which have eroded valleys around and below the western edge of the Tertiary formations (Fig. 2.1).

An example of incipient diversion can be seen at Red Lodge, Montana, where the Rock River leaves the mountains and flows onto the plains (Fig. 13.35). A minor tributary, Bear Creek, rising on the plains in front of the mountains, is eroding

Figure 13.35 *Threatened capture of Rock River by Bear Creek at the foot of the Beartooth Mountains. The head of Bear Creek is without gravel and is about 750 feet lower than Rock River. The divide is narrow, although still about 200 feet high. When the divide is breached Bear Creek will become a dumping ground for the gravel being transported by Rock River.*

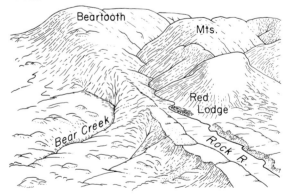

the soft Cretaceous formations, and its channel is 750 feet lower than the channel of Rock River. A narrow divide keeps Rock River on its perched course and when that is breached, the valley of Bear Creek will receive the gravel being transported by Rock River.

Differences in gradients of streams transporting gravel as compared with those transporting sand or silt is illustrated by the change in gradient of the Missouri River where it is joined by the Platte, which introduces coarse sediment to the Missouri (Fig. 13.36). Above this junction the Missouri River has a meandering channel and a gradient of 0.7 feet per mile. Although the Platte is only a tenth as large as the Missouri, the coarse sediment it carries into the main stream causes the Missouri to double its gradient, and the channel is braided.

Another drainage curiosity is the course of the Arkansas River. It flows east from Colorado to central Kansas, where it makes a big bend to the north, as if to join the Smoky Hill and Kansas rivers. But then it turns south again and leaves the plains in a broad valley that crosses the Ouachita Province. The gradient of the Arkansas River across the Ouachita Province is no greater than that of the Mississippi River, which the Arkansas joins.

Actually the Smoky Hill River formerly drained southward to the Arkansas River by way of a now-dry valley, McPherson Valley (Fig. 13.37), and the Saline River was tributary to the southward-flowing Smoky Hill River by way of the abandoned and dry Wilson Valley. Subsequently both rivers were captured by the Kansas River, probably in early or middle Pleistocene time. Both McPherson and Wilson valleys contain Kansan glacial deposits laid down when the drainage was 150 feet below the Pliocene that caps the uplands. Since then the rivers have cut downward another 200 feet.

There have been drainage changes in the course of the Tennessee River too. Its headwaters are in the Valley and Ridge Province. A "sensible" river would continue its course southwestward and join one of the rivers on the East Gulf Coastal Plain, but not the Tennessee. It turns out

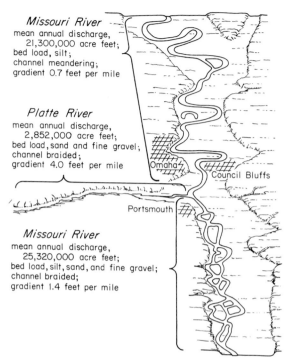

Figure 13.36 *Change in channel and gradient of the Missouri River where it is joined by the Platte River. The Platte River is small compared to the Missouri but transports coarse sediment. The Missouri, below the Platte, has steepened its gradient and is braided.*

of the big valleys into a gorge through the Appalachian Plateaus and then turns north around the west side of the Cincinnati Arch to join the Ohio and Mississippi rivers, a course that is about 700 miles longer than the direct one.

In brief, river courses in the central plains are of several kinds and of different ages. Some rivers are incised deeply into bedrock and have been able to maintain their preglacial courses. Other streams follow courses that antedate one or more of the glaciations and represent reoccupied valleys. In others, the drainage in the reoccupied valley now is in the opposite direction to the preglacial drainage. Other streams have postglacial courses, some of which occupy positions along end moraines whereas others occupy intermoraine swales.

The great rivers have facilitated settlement and trade. Even today, the tonnage handled at

river ports above Memphis, Tennessee, exceeds that of any coastal port except New York. About 2 percent of our national fish production comes from these rivers—carp, buffalo fish, catfish, and mussel. Most of the rivers are muddy, but were so described by early travelers. Farming has not relieved the erosion that causes the muddiness, but is not the main cause of it.

PROBABLE GEOLOGIC HISTORY OF THE MISSISSIPPI RIVER SYSTEM

During the Cretaceous there was no Mississippi River. A Cretaceous geosyncline extended along the site of the Rio Grande valley, and the marine waters that occupied the site of the Rocky Mountains spread eastward at least as far as Minnesota and perhaps farther. The Gulf of Mexico extended up the Mississippi Embayment between the Interior Low Plateaus on the east and the Ozark Plateau and Ouachita Province on the west, and this bay probably connected with the eastern part of the sea that extended eastward from the geosyncline. The Ozark Plateau and Ouachita Mountains would have been islands.

Geologic history of the Mississippi River system begins in early Tertiary time when the sea

Figure 13.37 *Pleistocene drainage changes in east central Kansas; abandoned valleys shown by broken lines.*

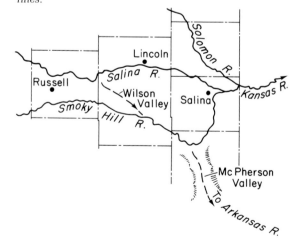

was expelled from the area of the central plains, partly perhaps because of uplift and partly because the sea filled with sediments. We have no record of an early Tertiary ancestral Mississippi River, but presumably drainage westward from the Appalachians found its way to the embayment, and the new land in the western part of what is now the Central Lowland also would have drained there and begun eroding the newly deposited, Cretaceous marine sediments. Minnesota and the country around it was 1,500 feet lower than it is now.

The drainage system eastward from the Rocky Mountains and across the Great Plains has developed within the Cenozoic. Eastward drainage began when the Rocky Mountains were first uplifted, beginning at the end of the Cretaceous Period. During Paleocene and Eocene time the drainage collected in broad basins like the Powder River and Williston basins, where early Tertiary sediments were deposited. There were similar basins west of the Rocky Mountains.

In Oligocene time these basins became filled and began to overflow, and alluvial fans of gravel and sand were deposited by streams discharging eastward onto the Great Plains. These same processes continued during the Miocene, and the Miocene alluvial fans extended beyond the south and east edges of the Oligocene fans. The Miocene drainage probably did not reach the Missouri and Mississippi rivers; it may have been dissipated in innumerable distributary channels and the water lost by seepage and evaporation, for the Great Plains have been semiarid ever since the Rocky Mountains cast their rain shadow eastward.

Meanwhile, the Rocky Mountains continued to be uplifted, and the entire region became raised as the mountains continued growing. When the Cretaceous geosyncline ended at the beginning of the Tertiary, the region was at or near sea level, with the mountains rising above it; today those geosynclinal deposits on the Great Plains are 5,000 feet above sea level. Minnesota was also once at sea level, and has since been elevated 1,500 feet.

As the Central Lowlands and southern part of the Canadian Shield rose, the Great Plains were rising faster, and streams tributary to the ancestral Mississippi River could extend their courses headward toward the Rocky Mountains. As already noted, the southern Great Plains have been uplifted most, more than 10,000 feet, and the Williston and Powder River basins have been uplifted least. Moreover, early Tertiary uplift in the south seems indicated not only by the general absence of early Tertiary formations there, but also by greater erosion of the Cretaceous southward.

The streams draining eastward from the Rockies probably did not extend all the way to the Mississippi River system until late Tertiary time. The Rockies were high above their base and must have cast a rain shadow to the east as they do today. Moreover, much or most of the regional uplift that raised the base of the mountains occurred in the late Tertiary, and until then the stream gradients were less than they are today—perhaps only half as steep. The deposits are alluvial fans, and not those of channelized rivers, which must mean that the drainage dissipated itself by dividing eastward into distributaries; such streams rarely flow far down fans. The probabilities are that runoff from the Rocky Mountains discharged only part way down the fans and that water discharging at the toes of the fans was generated by floods originating at or below the middle of the fans. At least this is the way fan drainage evolves where the extent of the fans is very much greater than the extent of the storms that produce the floods.

The younger fan gravels extend eastward progressively beyond the older ones, suggesting that the fine-grained distal facies of the older gravels became eroded as the younger deposits spread farther eastward. Probably there were two drainage systems, one depositing and extending itself eastward and the other eroding and extending itself westward.

The two systems may have joined in the late Pliocene, after which the drainage from the Rocky Mountains probably became channeled into a few stream courses that could extend all the way to the Mississippi River and cut downward into the Pliocene fans (Ogallala Formation). By Kansan time streams like the Saline and

Smoky Hill rivers had become incised 150 feet below the surface of the Pliocene fan, and have subsequently eroded their channels 200 feet deeper. The distal facies of fine-grained Pliocene sediments has been removed by erosion, and the fan ends in an eastward-facing escarpment. Near the foot of the mountains, rivers like the South Platte and the Arkansas in the Colorado Piedmont had eroded their valleys a thousand feet below the Pliocene fan by Kansan time, and have subsequently eroded them 500 feet further. These river valleys are no older than very late Pliocene. The considerable downcutting there may be attributed to continued uplift of the Great Plains as well as of the mountains, coupled with increased precipitation and runoff associated with the glaciations.

Great Lakes

We look next at the Great Lakes, which, for size, are unusual not only on this continent but in the world. Moreover, they are only a part of a belt of lakes that extends northwest across Canada and includes such other large ones as Lake Winnipeg, Lake Athabasca, Great Slave Lake, Great Bear Lake, and countless smaller ones (Fig. 5.7).

Altitudes and maximum depths of the Great Lakes are summarized below.

Lake	Altitude of Water Surface	Maximum Depth
Superior	602	1333
Michigan	580	923
Huron	580	750
Erie	572	210
Ontario	246	778

Average annual discharge from the Great Lakes is 150 million acre feet at Niagara Falls and 180 million acre feet where Lake Ontario empties into the St. Lawrence River.

Low divides between the tributaries of the Great Lakes and the Ohio and Mississippi rivers facilitated French exploration of the Middle West. Easy portages could be made. One could travel by canoe from Quebec to New Orleans;

canals were later dug along some portage routes followed by early travelers.

The Great Lakes were formed when the Pleistocene glaciers retreated from that area, and several have rounded ends reflecting their glacial history. Figure 13.38 illustrates four stages in the development of the lakes and of the river channels by which they overflowed. The dried parts of the lake beds form some of our best agricultural land, like that of Lake Maumee at the west end of Lake Erie and of glacial Lake Saginaw at the head of Saginaw Bay in Michigan. Between these lacustrine plains is morainal topography.

Niagara Falls came into existence when the retreat of glacial ice allowed the level of lake water in the Ontario Basin to fall below the limestone rim at Lewiston. Thereafter, Lake Erie drained into Lake Ontario via Niagara River and Falls. Because of the undercutting of the shale below the limestone (Fig. 12.5), the falls have receded, at about 4 feet per year, a distance of 7 miles upstream from Lewiston. The rate of retreat, however, has not been constant; part of the time Lake Huron and other lakes to the west drained to the Mississippi River, and the Niagara River drained only Lake Erie.

The earth movements caused by isostatic adjustment to the loading and unloading of the ice sheets (p. 48) are recorded today by the tilt of the shorelines of the ancestral Great Lakes. Such movements are, in fact, still going on; the north shores of Lake Superior and Lake Ontario are tilting southward at the rate of 6 to 12 inches per 100 miles per century.

Shipping at lake ports has been as important as that at coastal ports, despite the fact that they are closed much of the winter. In 1959, canals were deepened and the St. Lawrence Seaway became opened to all but the largest ocean-going vessels. About 80 percent of the world's ships can now go as far as Duluth—more than 2,300 miles inland. However, the lake levels need to be maintained to accommodate the ships. At this writing lake levels are 2 to 3 feet below average; and at such low stages, when water levels drop an inch, an 18,000-ton ship loses 80 tons of cargo space.

The lakes are important too for hydroelectric power and for fisheries (they provide about 2

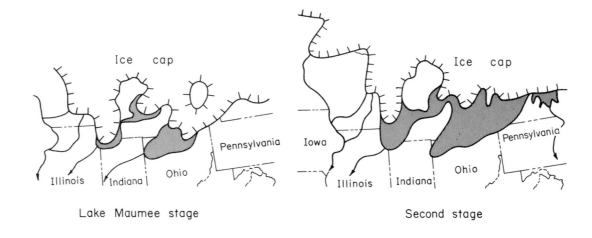

Figure 13.38   *Maps showing four stages in development of the Great Lakes and of the rivers by which they discharged. [After U.S.G.S.]*

percent of the country's production, mostly lake herring, whitefish, lake trout, perch, pike and suckers). Chicago withdraws more than $1\frac{1}{4}$ million gallons a minute for domestic use and to flush its sewage (after treatment) down the Illinois River to the Mississippi. As the saying goes, "Be sure to flush the toilet; folks downstream need the water."

Water Supplies

Water in the Central Lowland is obtained from six sources:

1. Great lakes,
2. Major rivers, excluding the Arkansas,
3. Small rivers and lakes,

4. Groundwater from glacial drift,

5. Groundwater from shallow bedrock (less than 500 feet),

6. Groundwater from deep bedrock (more than 500 feet).

East of the 100th meridian, except around the Great Lakes, the water supplies are adequate to meet present needs and appear adequate to meet anticipated needs in the next 35 years. Around the Great Lakes and west of the 100th meridian, however, the water supplies are not adequate to meet the anticipated increase in demands. A comparison of water uses and water losses in the central United States east and west of the 100th meridian is given in Figure 13.40.

East of the 100th meridian, where annual precipitation exceeds 20 inches, the average annual runoff is more than 1 inch. Where the average

annual rainfall is about 40 inches or more, the average annual runoff is more than 10 inches. Runoff on the Great Plains averages less than 1 inch. Streams crossing the Great Plains lose water by seepage and evaporation, and the losses exceed the gains.

Waters from the six major sources show directional variations in quality. Water in the Great Lakes is carbonate water, and from Lake Superior to Lake Ontario, there is a progressive increase in total dissolved solids (tds) and in the proportion of sulfate (Fig. 13.41,A).

One of the important aquifers in the central United States is the alluvial gravel in an old deep channel eroded into the bedrock along the Ohio River. This gravel thickens from about 25 feet near Ashland, Kentucky, to about 110 feet at the mouth of the River. Along the narrow stretches of the valley, the channel in the bedrock occupies the whole width of the valley; along the wider

Figure 13.39 *Wetlands on the north side of Lake Erie, at Point Pelee National Park, Ontario. [Courtesy of Ontario Dept. of Tourism and Information.]*

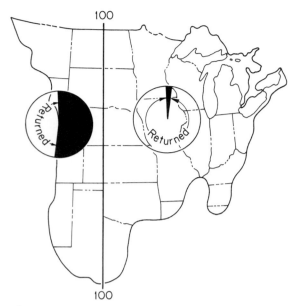

Figure 13.40 *Water withdrawn for irrigation on the Great Plains west of the 100th meridian roughly equals the quantity withdrawn for industrial use in the Central Lowland east of the 100th meridian (quantities represented by areas of circles). Over half the water withdrawn for irrigation is consumed (black); only a small fraction of the water withdrawn for industrial use is consumed.*

stretches, some of which are 10 miles wide, the channel occupies only part of the valley. The alluvial gravel is coarse and cobbly in the upper stretches of the river and decreases to pea size downstream. The channel formed in Pre-Wisconsinan time; the gravel is Wisconsinan outwash. The groundwater is replenished by the river, and the storage capacity of the gravel is estimated at about 20 percent of the volume of gravel; that is, about 1.5 gallons of water per cubic foot of gravel, a large supply of cold, filtered water. It has been overpumped, at times, but the natural recharge by the river could be supplemented by recharge wells at selected places. The good chemical quality of the water could be impaired by careless disposal of chemical or saline wastes, and the temperature could be increased by recharge with heated water, but

properly managed, the supply is large enough to satisfy increased industrial demands and even some irrigation on the floodplain.

Waters in the three major rivers, the Mississippi, Ohio, and Missouri, differ greatly in quality. The Mississippi River, which carries about 200 ppm tds, begins as a carbonate water and becomes increasingly sulfate downstream to Alton (Fig. 13.41,B). The Ohio River at Pittsburgh has 500 ppm tds and is a sulfate water. Downstream the total dissolved solids decrease to less than 200 ppm and the proportion of sulfate progressively decreases (Fig. 13.41,C). The Yellowstone River, a branch of the Missouri in Montana, enters the Great Plains east of Livingston, Montana, with 140 ppm and a hardness of 65. Downstream this river crosses the lignite fields, and the tds increases to 240 ppm at Billings with hardness 140 and to 500 ppm at Miles City with hardness 230. The proportion of sulfate in the water progressively increases downstream (Fig. 13.41,D). The Missouri River below the mouth of the Yellowstone has 250 or more ppm tds and is a sulfo-carbonate water.

Quality of water supplies from the small rivers and lakes in the central United States is illustrated in Fig. 13.41,E. The content of total dissolved solids and, consequently, hardness, is least in the Superior Upland, intermediate in the eastern part of the Central Lowland, and greatest in the western part of the Central Lowland. Groundwater from the glacial drift is similar.

Groundwater from the bedrock formations generally contains more than 400 ppm tds, even in the Superior Upland, where the formations are Precambrian. Farther south, where the groundwater comes from Paleozoic sedimentary rocks, the tds is 800 ppm at shallow depths and exceeds 1,000 ppm in wells 500 feet deep or more. Water in the deep wells has a high content of chlorides and sulfates. To the west, groundwater is obtained from an Upper Cretaceous sandstone formation. Water enters the formation where it is exposed in the uplifts at the Black Hills and Rocky Mountains and seeps eastward under the plains, where it supplies some flowing wells and numerous pumped wells. This water, like other deep groundwater in the central United States, is highly mineralized.

Cities along the western edge of the Great Plains obtain their water from the Rocky Mountains, and these waters commonly contain less than 100 ppm of dissolved solids, mostly carbonates. Eastward and southward, on the Great Plains, the content of dissolved solids increases and the proportion of sulfates and chlorides increases (Fig. 13.41,F).

Floods are a major problem in the extensively settled, rich farmlands of the Central Lowland. An extensive set of dams and levees is being constructed along the rivers, as is illustrated by the network of dams in the Missouri River Basin (Fig. 13.42).

Another major water development program, along the Arkansas River, provides for a channel 9 feet deep and more than 150 feet wide with 18 locks to control the 400-foot drop along the lower 500 miles of the river, from near Tulsa to the junction with the Mississippi. Some opponents of this development contended that it would have

been cheaper to build a double track railroad and to operate it free.

Water power resources in the central United States east of the Mississippi River have been developed almost to capacity. In the Missouri River Basin perhaps a quarter of the capacity remains to be developed, but the potential there is small compared to the western United States and Appalachian Highlands.

Minerals

Mineral production in the interior province, like agricultural production, involves a few commodities produced in tremendous quantities. The most important to the national economy are the mineral fuels (coal, lignite, oil, gas), iron ore, lead and zinc ore, bauxite (aluminum ore), gold, fluorspar, and potash. In addition there are valuable deposits of mercury and salt.

Mineral fuels are abundant in the central United States and have been produced in great quantity. About a fifth of the United States coal

Figure 13.41 *Some variations in quality of water in the central United States (white = carbonate; black = sulfate).*

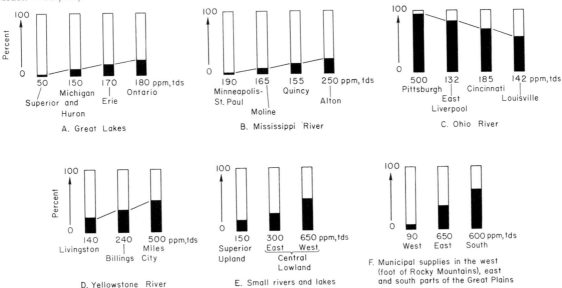

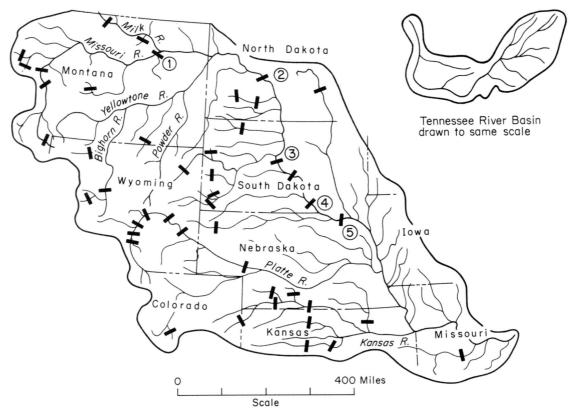

Figure 13.42 *Dams in the Missouri River Basin. Some of these dams, especially those upstream, are multipurpose and provide for irrigation and power, but the system as a whole was designed primarily for flood control. Large dams along the main stem of the Missouri are Fort Peck Dam (1), Garrison Dam (2), Oahe Dam (3) and Big Bend Dam next downstream, Fort Randall Dam (4), and Gavins Point Dam (5).*

production has been from Pennsylvanian rocks in the structural basins bordering the Ozark Plateau and in the Ouachita Mountains. The coal is mostly bituminous, but the Ouachita Mountains contain anthracite. Where the coal is flat-lying, as in the broad structural basins, the mining is done mostly by huge steam shovels operating in open pits—strip-mining methods.

In the past, strip mines were abandoned and left open when the operations ended, leaving a wasteland with pits and mounds. Because of such abuses, strip mining developed a bad reputation, so that increasingly stringent laws now require back-filling and leveling after the coal is mined. Such new ground could be as satisfactory as the original (p. 202).

Cretaceous formations on the Great Plains contain subbituminous coal; the late Cretaceous, Paleocene, and Eocene formations in the northern Great Plains contain vast tonnages of lignite (brown coal). Lignite, a resource for the future, is little used at present, but the deposits are vast and can be produced inexpensively by strip mining and can be transported by pipeline or used at the mines to generate electricity. Some of the deposits are in very thick beds; the one at the WyoDak Coal Mine near Gillette, Wyoming, is almost 100 feet thick.

Oil and gas have been produced from three major areas in the central United States. Greatest production has been from Paleozoic formations in the Mid-Continent region in Kansas, Oklahoma, and Texas, and is about one-sixth the value of the entire mineral production of the United States. A second important producing area is the Illinois Basin; a third is at the western edge of the Great Plains from New Mexico to Montana. Recently a new productive area has been discovered in the Williston Basin of North Dakota. A fourth major producing area is in Alberta.

The principal deposits of lead and zinc are in southwestern Missouri and adjoining corners of Oklahoma and Kansas—the Tri-State district. Other deposits are in southeastern and south-central Missouri, the Illinois-Kentucky district, and the Upper Mississippi Valley district. These were all discovered early. Those in the Upper Mississippi Valley were productive before 1700. The deposits in southeastern Missouri were discovered in 1715, when St. Genevieve was founded. After the Louisiana Purchase the Congress, in 1807, reserved all government lands containing lead ores and provided for leasing them at a royalty.

These ores are found in steeply dipping fissures, along bedding planes, and as irregular pockets in Paleozoic limestone. The lead occurs as a sulfide (galena) and as a carbonate (cerussite); the zinc occurs as a sulfide (sphalerite), a carbonate (smithsonite), and a silicate (calamine). The Tri-State district produces about a quarter of the total zinc mined annually in the United States and between 5 and 10 percent of the lead. The southeast Missouri district produces 40 percent of this country's lead, and the Viburnum district in south-central Missouri is thought to be equally great.

One of the principal gold-producing areas in the United States is in the Black Hills Section of the Great Plains. The deposits occur in Precambrian slate associated with granitic intrusions in the central part of the domal uplift. The gold occurs free; that is, it is not contained in other minerals. The ores are rich and the mines are more than a half mile deep. The Black Hills had been set aside by treaty in 1867 as permanent reservation for the Dakota, Kiowa, and Sioux Indian tribes, but the discovery in 1874 of rich gold placer deposits was too much of a temptation, and the treaty was violated. The Indians fought back as best they could; the massacre of Custer and his troops in 1876 was part of the Indian war that ensued. By 1877 the Indians had been punished for fighting for their rights and the lands were secured. Since then more than 20 million fine ounces of gold have been produced, and about half that amount still remains to be recovered.

When the United States entered World War II, demands made by the aircraft industry caused a sixfold increase in the production of aluminum. This strong, light-weight metal is, by weight, one of the most abundant metallic elements in the earth's crust—half again as abundant as iron. But ores are few. At the present time, the deposits of bauxite (aluminum hydroxide) in Arkansas are the United States' most important source, and supply more than 90 percent of the country's production. The United States has no other known large deposits of bauxite, but in many parts of the country there are immense deposits of lower-grade ores, such as high-alumina clay, aluminous rock known as anorthosite, and alunite (aluminum and potassium sulfate)—all of which could become productive if technological advances reduce production costs. There is no shortage of these low grade sources.

Fluorspar deposits in Paleozoic limestone in southern Illinois and western Kentucky have been the chief source of fluorite in the United States, and until 1898 they were the only domestic source. Fluorite is used for flux in the steel industry, and for making hydrofluoric acid.

Until World War I the United States had to import potash, but in 1913 potash brines were discovered in wells drilled for oil in southeastern New Mexico and west Texas. This was followed by systematic exploration of the area, and such enormous deposits were found that the country is now self-sufficient; 85 percent of the United States' production comes from a few mines in southeastern New Mexico.

Other mineral resources in the central United States include manganese at Batesville, Arkansas. Important nonmetallic deposits include: high-grade ceramic clays in Ohio, Illinois, Missouri, Nebraska, and Colorado; gypsum (calcium sulfate), used in large part for plaster, near Grand Rapids, Michigan, Fort Dodge, Iowa, and in Kansas; salt in brines at Hutchinson, Kansas, and in rock-salt formations that are mined in Kanapolis, Lyons, and Kingman, Kansas; other deposits are in central and southeastern Michigan. The salt mines in Kansas have become a subject of controversy because of a plan to use them for storing radioactive wastes.

Building-stone occurs in numerous formations, but notably the Sioux Quartzite at Sioux Falls, South Dakota, and limestone from Indiana and Iowa; novaculite, an abrasive useful for whetstones, in Arkansas. A soft stone, used by the Indians for making pipes, is obtained in southwestern Minnesota, and the quarry has been set aside as Pipestone National Monument —our only National Monument dedicated to strip mining.

A Misused Resource— The Great Plains

Not quite a hundred years ago John Wesley Powell called attention to the unpleasant fact that lands west of the 100th meridian are not suited for the same kinds of uses as are the lands farther east, because the rainfall in dry years is inadequate to maintain water supplies. The Great Plains have three times the combined areas of Indiana, Illinois, and Iowa, but their effective moisture and total water supply is less than half that for those three Central Lowland states. We still have not faced the dry fact that the Great Plains are semiarid and quite unlike the Central Lowland and should not be used in the same way.

Water supplies on the Great Plains are inadequate to meet demands expected in the next two or three decades. Because irrigation consumes water, only half the water that is used is returned (Fig. 13.40). In the western panhandle of Texas and southeastern New Mexico, groundwater withdrawals are depleting the storage, with virtually no recharge in effect now or even in prospect.

What constitutes sensible use of the Great Plains remains an unanswered question. A start has been made by creating national grasslands, analogous to the national forests. More such steps are needed, for either we find another use for that vast area—a use that preserves its surface when the *inevitable, repeated,* and *protracted* droughts recur—or we must be ready with subsidies and relief programs of one kind or another when it episodically becomes a disaster area.

References

Alden, W. C., 1932, Physiography and glacial geology of eastern Montana and adjacent areas: U.S. Geol. Survey Prof. Paper 174.
———, 1924, Physiographic development of the northern Great Plains: Geol. Soc. America Bull., v. 35, pp. 383–424.
Allen, Durward L., 1967, The life of prairies and plains: New York, McGraw-Hill.
Condra, G. E., Reed, E. C., and Gordon, G. E. (revised by Condra and Reed), 1950, Correlation of the Pleistocene deposits of Nebraska: Neb. Geol. Survey Bull. 15-A.
Dorr, John A., Jr., and Eschman, Donald F., 1970, Geology of Michigan: Ann Arbor, Univ. Michigan Press.
Dort, Wakefield, Jr., and Jones, J. Knox, 1970, Pleistocene and Recent environments of the central Great Plains: Univ. Kansas Press.
Frye, J. C., and Leonard, A. B., 1952, Pleistocene geology of Kansas: State Geol. Survey of Kansas Bull. 99.
Fryxell, F. M., 1927, The physiography of the region of Chicago: Univ. Chicago Press.

Hunt, Chas. B., 1954, Pleistocene and Recent deposits in the Denver area, Colorado: U.S. Geol. Survey Bull. 996-C.

Jennings, J. D., and Norbeck, E. (ed.), 1964, Prehistoric man in the New World: Univ. Chicago Press.

Kraenzel, C. F., 1970, The Great Plains: Univ. Oklahoma Press.

Leverett, F., and Taylor, F. B., 1915, The Pleistocene of Indiana and the history of the Great Lakes: U.S. Geol. Survey Mon. 53.

Lugn, A. L., 1935, The Pleistocene geology of Nebraska: Neb. Geol. Survey Bull. 10.

Martin, L., 1965, The physical geography of Wisconsin: Madison, Univ. Wisconsin Press, 608 p.

Prest, V. K., 1970, Quaternary geology of Canada, in Geology and economic minerals of Canada: Geol. Survey of Canada, pp. 676–764.

Ruhe, R. V., Daniels, R. B., and Cady, John G., 1967, Landscape evolution and soil formation in southwestern Iowa: U.S. Dept. Agri. Tech. Bull. 1349.

Scott, G. R., 1963, Quaternary geology and geomorphic history of the Kassler quadrangle, Colorado: U.S. Geol. Survey Prof. Paper 421-A.

Wormington, Marie, 1957, Ancient man in North America: Denver Mus. Nat. Hist. Popular Ser., n. 4.

Wright, H. E., Jr., and Frey, D. G. (ed.), 1965, The Quaternary of the United States: Princeton University Press.

The Canadian Rockies at Jasper National Park, Alberta. The mountains consist of a series of great imbricated thrust plates; late Precambrian sedimentary formations are thrust eastward onto Paleozoic rocks, and Paleozoic formations are thrust eastward onto Mesozoic formations. In the right center is Jasper, along the Athabasca River. [Photograph courtesy of Alberta Government Photographic Services.]

14

•••••••••••••

ROCKY MOUNTAINS AND WYOMING BASIN —DIVIDING THE CONTINENT

The Rocky Mountains (Figs. 14.1, 14.2) are part of the backbone of the Americas—a backbone that extends 10,000 miles from Alaska to Patagonia. These are young mountains, uplifted high enough to form the continental divide separating the Atlantic and the Pacific drainage systems. Like the Appalachians, the Rockies illustrate the concept of geosynclines, for they developed out of the mobile belts along the western edge of the stable platforms of the cratons both in North America and South America. In this chapter we include the Canadian Rockies south of the Liard River, the Northern, Middle, and Southern Rocky Mountains and the Wyoming Basin in the United States. Outstanding features of the Rocky Mountain System are:

1. High peaks, many above 14,000 feet.

2. Great relief; the summits of many or most of the ranges are 5,000 to 7,000 feet higher than their bases.

3. Ruggedness, which far exceeds that of the Appalachians.

4. Rocks of igneous, metamorphic, and sedimentary origins in diverse kinds of structural uplifts and basins.

5. Shallow soils and extensive areas of bare rock.

6. Forests, which are extensive but much less varied than those of the Appalachians and consisting mostly of conifers.

7. Water supplies; this area is the principal source of water for a quarter of the United States, including the semiarid Great Plains east of the mountains and the deserts to the west.

8. Numerous hot springs.

9. Mineral wealth, which is considerable and varied.

10. Scenery—great vistas showing spectacular landforms with colorful rocks and forests.

Most of the mountains are in national forests. Other mountain areas are dedicated as national parks and monuments. Large and numerous, these include Glacier, Yellowstone, Grand Teton, and Rocky Mountain National Parks and Dinosaur National Monument in the United States and Waterton Lakes, Glacier, Kootenay, Yoho, Banff, Mount Ravelstoke, and Jasper National Parks in Canada.

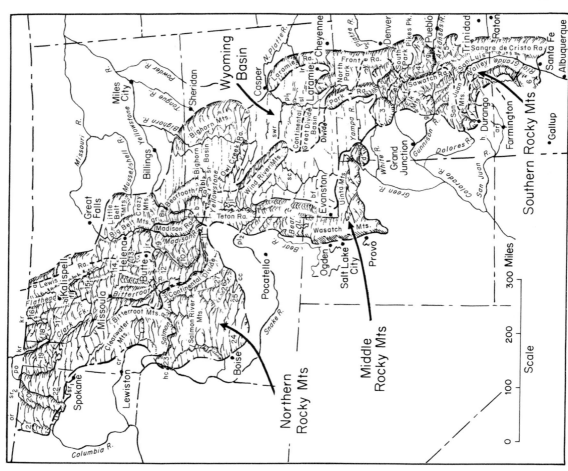

NATIONAL PARKS AND MONUMENTS

a, Glacier Nat. Park; b, Yellowstone Nat. Park; c, Grand Teton Nat. Park; cc, Craters of the Moon Nat. Mon.; d, Dinosaur Nat. Mon.; e, Rocky Mountain Nat. Park; f, Great Sand Dunes Nat. Mon.; g, Black Canyon of the Gunnison Nat. Mon.; h, Mesa Verde Nat. Park

RIVERS AND LAKES

Southern Rocky Mountains: er, Eagle River; rf, Roaring Fork; ar, Animas River; rg, Royal Gorge

Wyoming Basin and Middle Rocky Mountains: swr, Sweet-water River, bf, Blacks Fork; sc, Sandy Creek; jl, Jackson Lake; sl, Seminoe Res.; pl_1, Pathfinder Res.; pl_2, Palisade Res.; bl, Buffalo Bill Res.; sr, Shoshone River; lr, Laramie River

Northern Rocky Mountains: jr, Jefferson River; gr, Gallatin River; fl, Flathead Lake; kr, Kootenai River; po, Pend Oreille River; sr_1, Spokane River; sr_2, Sanpoil River; or, Okanogan River; cr, Clearwater River; hc, Hells Canyon

MOUNTAIN RANGES

Southern Rocky Mountains: 1, Medicine Bow Mts.; 2, Gore Range; 3, White River Plateau; 4, Mosquito Range; 5, Wet Mts.; 6, Jemez Mts.

Middle Rocky Mountains: 7, Absaroka Mts.

Northern Rocky Mountains: 8, Gallatin Range; 9, Tobacco Mts.; 10, Ruby Range; 11, Centennial Range; 12, Pioneer Mts.; 13, Deer Lodge Mts.; 14, Garnet Range; 15, Mission Range; 16, Whitefish Range; 17, Salish Mts.; 18, Purcell Mts.; 19, Selkirk Mts.; 20, Kettle Mts.; 21, Okanogan Range; 22, Pend Oreille Mts.; 23, Seven Devils Mts.; 24, Sawtooth Mts.; 25, Pioneer Mts.; 26, Lost River Range; 27, Lemhi Range

Figure 14.1 Physiographic map of the Rocky Mountains and Wyoming Basin in the United States.

Structural Setting of the System

The structural history of the Rocky Mountains System is illustrated in four paleogeographic maps (Fig. 14.3). Precambrian structural elements on the craton trend generally southwest. In late Precambrian time a geosyncline developed along the eastern edge of the continent, in what are now the Piedmont and Grenville provinces; its counterpart in the west, the Beltian Geosyncline (Fig. 14.3,A), later became the site of the Canadian Rockies and the Rocky Mountains in western Montana and Idaho. The westernmost of the Middle Rocky Mountains were in the eastern part of that geosynclinal structure; its axis was in what is now the Basin and Range Province. This geosyncline was the first one to develop with an axis approximately parallel to the western edge of the continent. Subsequent major structures roughly parallel that geosyncline and the present-day western edge of the continent.

During the Paleozoic a miogeosyncline developed whose axis seems to have been approximately along that of the Beltian geosyncline, or a little west of it. The axis of a new eugeosyncline lay 200 miles west of that. During the Triassic and Jurassic the geosynclinal axes were still farther west; the site of the Rocky Mountains had become stable shelf. During the Devonian, the Transcontinental Arch was uplifted on the stable platform east of the Rocky Mountains, and older Paleozoic rocks were eroded from that part of the platform. During the early Mesozoic the Arch became more definite, and today generally marks the eastern limit of Triassic and Jurassic deposits.

The Gulf of Mexico is at least as old as Jurassic and probably began developing during the Triassic. During the Lower Cretaceous that geosyncline began extending itself northwestward along what is now the valley of the Rio Grande and also into southern New Mexico and Arizona. A second geosyncline, which began developing at about the position of the old Beltian geosyncline in the Canadian Rockies, extended itself southward into what is now the Middle Rocky Mountains. During the Upper Cretaceous, these two geosynclines became one when they were

joined at the site of the Southern Rocky Mountains, connecting the Gulf of Mexico with the Arctic Ocean.

At the site of the Middle and Southern Rocky Mountains, this Upper Cretaceous geosyncline trended obliquely across what had been stable platform and the Transcontinental Arch. In Colorado this geosyncline was 400 miles east of the geosynclines that had previously defined the

Figure 14.2 *Diagram of the Canadian Rockies showing relation of the mountains to the Foothill Belt and Plains Province on the east and to the Rocky Mountain Trench on the west. The Trench is the head of the Liard, Peace, Frazer, Columbia, and Kootenai rivers.*

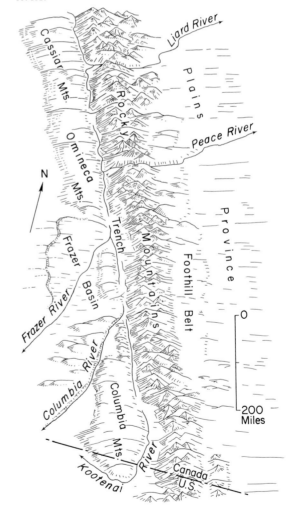

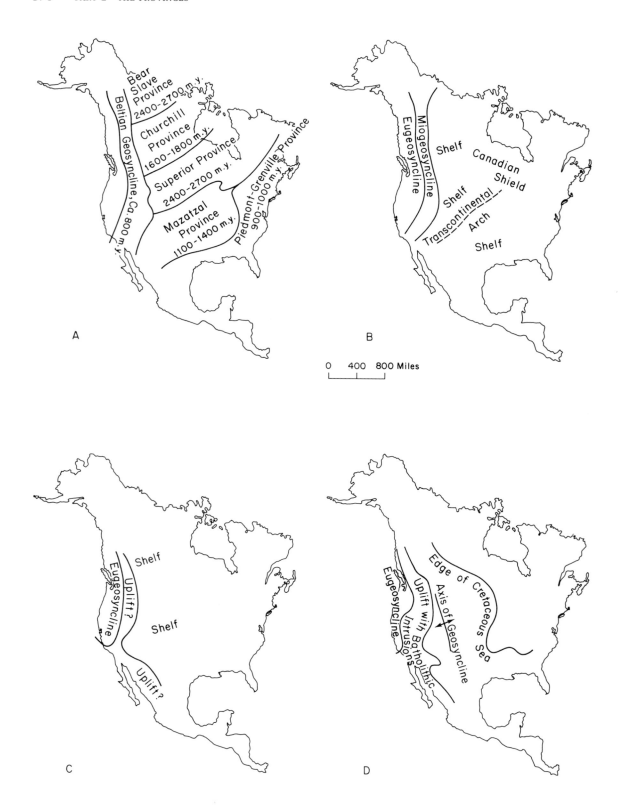

Bear
Slave
Province
2400-2700 m.y.

Churchill
Province
1600-1800 m.y.

Superior Province
2400-2700 m.y.

Mazatzal
Province
1100-1400 m.y.

Beltian Geosyncline, Ca. 800 m.y.

Piedmont-Grenville Province
900-1000 m.y.

A

Miogeosyncline

Eugeosyncline

Shelf

Shelf

Transcontinental Arch

Canadian
Shield

Shelf

B

0   400   800 Miles

Uplift?

Eugeosyncline

Shelf

Shelf

Uplift?

C

Edge of Cretaceous Sea

Eugeosyncline

Uplift with Batholithic Intrusions

Axis of Geosyncline

D

western edge of the continent. The Jurassic and older geosynclinal belts became the mountain area that supplied sediments to the Upper Cretaceous geosyncline.

During Upper Cretaceous and early Tertiary time, the Jurassic and older geosynclinal belts were subjected to eastward thrust-faulting. The Cretaceous geosyncline came to its end by faulting and uplift in the north, where it coincided with the older geosynclinal structures, and by anticlinal uplift without much thrust faulting in either the Southern Rocky Mountains or in that part of the Middle Rocky Mountains where the Cretaceous geosyncline had diagonaled across the stable platform. Differences in the kinds of mountains in different parts of the Rocky Mountains System are therefore inherited from the older geosynclinal and platform structures. The Southern Rocky Mountains and eastern Middle Rockies were derived from what had been stable platform, and they are sharply anticlinal bulges. The western ranges of the Middle Rockies and the eastern ranges of the Northern Rockies were derived from the structural break at the eastern edge of the pre-Cretaceous geosynclines, and those block-faulted mountains are still undergoing deformation, as is indicated by frequent earthquakes there. The Canadian Rockies were derived from the old geosynclines, and those ranges are thrust-faulted mountains.

During the early Tertiary (Paleocene and Eocene) the region seems to have remained nearly at sea level, and sediments eroded from the newly formed Rocky Mountains collected in broad basins, like the San Juan Basin in New Mexico, the Uinta Basin in Utah and Colorado, the Wyoming Basin, and the Williston Basin in Montana, North Dakota, and Saskatchewan. During the Oligocene these became filled and began to overflow.

Beginning in the middle Tertiary, while the mountains continued to be uplifted, the whole region began to be uplifted; the eastern hinge was somewhere near the Mississippi Valley (see Chapter 13). Sediments eroded from the mountains now began forming big fans that, on the Great Plains, built eastward. The Miocene fans overlap eastward beyond the Oligocene, and the Pliocene fans overlap eastward beyond the Miocene. During the Pliocene this eastward drainage became captured by the tributaries of the Missouri and Mississippi, which were eroding headward into the Cretaceous and other formations on the rising Great Plains. The Great Plains at that time may have been about 1,500 feet below their present altitude, because the Pliocene fans are that much higher than the present drainage in the Denver Basin at the foot of the Southern Rocky Mountains.

Now we look more closely at the individual parts of this complex series of structures.

Southern Rocky Mountains

The Southern Rocky Mountains (Fig. 14.1) form a major barrier to travel, for they may be crossed only through high passes, all above 9,000 feet in

Figure 14.3 *Structural setting of the Rocky Mountains and other western structural provinces. (A) Relation of the south-trending Beltian geosyncline to the earlier southwest-trending Precambrian structural elements comprising the craton. (B) The Paleozoic miogeosyncline coincided roughly with the Canadian Rockies and the Rocky Mountains in the northern United States, but was west of the Southern Rockies. The miogeosynclinal rocks are mostly limestone and dolomite. The eugeosynclinal rocks are mostly shale, graywacke, chert, and volcanics and have been thrust eastward out of position onto the miogeosynclinal rocks. (C) Early Mesozoic (Triassic and Jurassic) paleogeography in the western United States and Canada. An uplift seems to have separated the eugeosyncline on the west from mostly shelf deposits on the east. Batholiths began developing in the eugeosynclinal belt. (D) Cretaceous paleogeography. The axis of the geosyncline during the upper Cretaceous was near the site of the Southern Rocky Mountains. The axis probably extended southeastward along the Rio Grande and eastward along the Gulf Coast. Batholiths developed in the western part of the mountainous uplifted belt and in the eugeosyncline to the west.*

altitude and some above 11,000 feet (Fig. 14.4). As a consequence, the emigrant trails to the west followed routes around the northern and southern ends of these mountains. One railroad, the Denver and Rio Grande, crosses the heart of the mountains along a spectacularly scenic route; the railroad's slogan is "Through the Rockies, not around them."

The Southern Rocky Mountains consist of a series of ranges, each with distinctive landforms and scenery reflecting the geologic structure of the ranges. The principal ranges along the eastern slope are the Laramie Range, Front Range, Wet Mountains, and Sangre de Cristo Range (Fig. 14.1). Along the western slope are the Park Range, Gore Range, Sawatch Range, Elk Mountains, San Juan Mountains, and Jemez Mountains. The two groups of ranges are separated at the north by the basin of the North Platte River in North Park, by the valley of the Arkansas River, and at the south by the broad San Luis Valley and the trough of the Rio Grande.

The continental divide follows the crest of the Park Range. At the south end of North Park it swings east around the head of the Colorado River to the Front Range, and then west again around the head of the Arkansas River to the Sawatch Range. It swings far west on the San Juan Mountains around the head of the Rio Grande and extends into the San Juan Basin between the heads of the San Juan and Chama rivers. Two-thirds of the Southern Rocky Mountains drains eastward.

By contrast, about four-fifths of the Northern Rocky Mountains in the United States and southern Canada drains to the Pacific Ocean (Fig. 14.4). The Canadian Rockies, Middle Rocky Mountains, and Wyoming Basin are about equally divided between drainage to the east and to the west.

Most cities are located along the foot of the mountains, where the climate is semiarid but where water can be obtained from the higher country. The population residing along the eastern foot of the Southern Rocky Mountains numbers about 1.5 million, mostly in Colorado along the foot of the Front Range. Only about a tenth as many people live along the western foot of the

mountains; the population there is about 150,000. A few towns are located within the mountains, but none is large, and the total permanent population in the mountains probably is only a little more than 50,000.

Although the population is small, the private lands are, of course, those that are most accessible. As a consequence, the extensive and scenic public lands are nearly surrounded by private lands posted with signs warning, "No Trespassing." Some signs threaten that "survivors will be prosecuted." Colorado's mountain belong to all of us and are needed for national purposes—watershed protection, multiple-use forests, wilderness areas, and parks. It would seem in the interest of the quarter billion owners to purchase much of the acreage now held privately and to return it to the public land system.

The Cretaceous mediterranean sea that extended across what is now the Southern and Middle Rocky Mountains was a thousand miles wide, and its eastern shore lay in what is now the Mississippi Valley in the Central Lowland (Fig. 14.3,D). To the west, in what is now the Basin and Range Province, mountains were shedding sediments into this sea.

The crustal movements that had built the Cretaceous mountains in the west progressed eastward. By middle Cretaceous time the area in western Utah that had been a coastal plain began to be uplifted, and the western shore moved eastward. By the end of Cretaceous time the folding and uplift of the Rocky Mountains had finally expelled the sea from the area they now occupy.

All of Cenozoic time was required for the mountains to develop their present aspect. During the early part of the Tertiary Period the summits of the newly formed mountains may have been a mile or more high, but the bases of the mountains remained near sea level. A large lake, Greenriver Lake, occupied the Wyoming and Uinta Basins; east of the Rocky Mountains coastal plain deposits (Fort Union Formation)

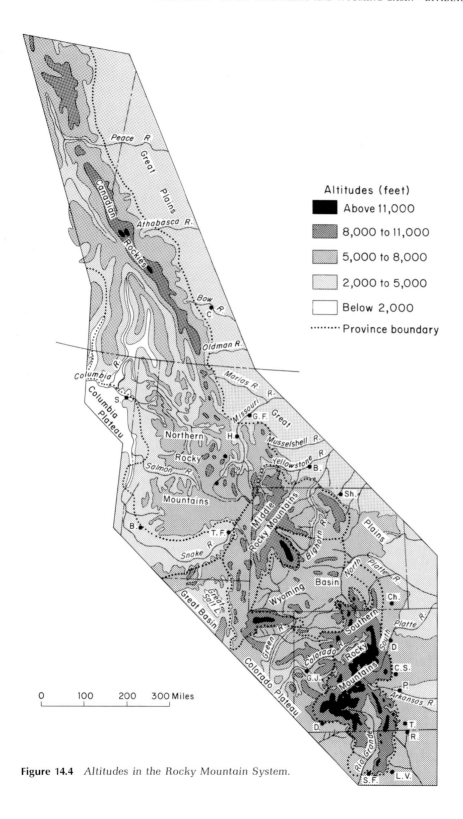

Figure 14.4 *Altitudes in the Rocky Mountain System.*

were laid down between the mountains and a remnant of the former mediterranean sea.

The area now occupied by the San Juan Mountains is the site of a vast accumulation of volcanic materials—lavas, mud flows, and ash. One ash formation (San Juan Tuff) is estimated to include 1,000 cubic miles of ash. Volcanism was extensive in the Northern and Middle Rocky Mountains too, and continues today in the Yellowstone Park region.

The principal formations in the Southern Rocky Mountains, exclusive of the volcanic formations in the San Juans, are given in Table 14.1; Figure 14.5 is a geologic map with cross sections illustrating the structural geology of the mountains.

The Southern Rocky Mountains consist of a series of anticlinal uplifts in most of which Precambrian rocks are exposed in the cores, with Paleozoic and younger formations turned up steeply against the flanks, where the resistant beds form hogbacks (Fig. 14.6). In places, as illustrated in the cross sections in Figure 14.5 the Precambrian rocks have been faulted over the younger formations.

Among the Precambrian rocks are two large granite batholiths, one at Pikes Peak and another in the Laramie Range. The Pikes Peak Granite covers 1,500 square miles; the Sherman Granite in the Laramie Range covers 1,700 square miles. The oldest Precambrian rocks are schists and gneisses of the Idaho Springs Formation, thought to be more than 15,000 feet thick although the folding and metamorphism make this determination uncertain. Younger than the Idaho Springs formation is 6,000 feet of gneiss and 14,000 feet of quartzite. These metamorphosed sedimentary rocks are intruded by the granite batholiths, which are dated at about 1.5 billion years old.

The Pikes Peak and Sherman granites are coarse-grained, and they weather to form two quite different landscapes. In some places the granite has disintegrated to sandy rubble, and the surface is made irregular by rounded masses of residual boulders. At other places the granite forms smoothly rounded summits called "balds."

Although the site of the Southern Rocky Mountains had been stable platform before the Cretaceous, a series of late Paleozoic basins and uplifts trended northwesterly across that part of the platform (Fig. 14.7). During the Pennsylvanian and Permian, the basins collected evaporite deposits while the uplifts became eroded. As a consequence, along parts of the uplifts, Triassic formations rest directly on Precambrian rocks. The basins are sources of various kinds of salts.

During the Tertiary Period a series of large, roughly cylindrical intrusions (stocks), probably related to the volcanic activity in the San Juan Mountains, were pushed upward in a belt that trends northeast across the central part of the Southern Rocky Mountains (Figure 14.5). Mineralization associated with these intrusions gave rise to the Colorado mineral belt. Much of Colorado's production of metals has come from deposits along this belt of stocks.

During Quaternary time snowfields formed on the summits of the Rocky Mountains, and glaciers developed. There was at least one major glaciation before Wisconsinan time, and two during Wisconsinan time. The summit ridges became scored with deep cirques, many with lakes. The alpine glaciers that headed in these cirques extended 5 to 10 miles down the valleys, a few even farther. The glaciated valleys are U-shaped. Many or most of them are partly blocked with terminal moraines deposited at the ice front (Figs. 14.8, 14.9).

Even if the late Pleistocene snow and ice covered only 10 percent of the Southern Rocky Mountains to an average depth of 100 feet, the volume of water held there must have been between a quarter and a half billion acre feet—vastly more than the total annual discharge of the present streams. During the waning of the glacial stage, and even during thaws when the ice was advancing, major floods must have been discharged onto the low country around the mountains. To these floods are attributed the gravel fills along the valleys crossing the Great Plains. The floodplains along these valleys were sources for the deposits of loess that blanket the Great Plains and Central Lowland.

Table 14.1

Geological Formations in and at the Base of the Southern Rocky Mountains

		Western Slope	Eastern Slope
Quaternary		Late Wisconsinan moraines and related deposits, early Wisconsinan moraines and related deposits, pre-Wisconsinan deposits.	
Tertiary	Pliocene		Ogallala Formation: sandstone, shale, gravel, max. 300 feet thick.
	Miocene	Browns Park Formation: sandstone, conglomerate, 1,200 feet thick.	Arikaree Formation: sandstone, shale, gravel, 500 feet thick.
	Oligocene	Duchesne River Formation: sandstone, 1,300 feet thick.	Castle Rock Conglomerate in south; White River Formation in north: 500 feet thick.
	Eocene	Uinta and Bridger Formations: fluviatile deposits, 2,000 feet thick. Green River Formation: lacustrine deposits 4,000 feet thick.	Missing.
	Paleocene	Wasatch Formation: fluviatile deposit 2,000 feet thick.	Denver Formation: fluviatile deposits 1,500 feet thick.
Cretaceous		Mesaverde Formation: coastal plain deposits, 3,000 feet thick. Mancos Shale: marine, 5,000 feet thick. Dakota Sandstone: beach deposit, 100 feet thick.	Arapahoe Formation: fluviatile conglomerate and sandstone, 400 feet thick; contains pebbles from Laramie and older formations. Laramie Formation: coastal plain deposits, 250 feet thick. Fox Hills Sandstone: beach deposit, 500 feet thick. Pierre Shale: marine, 3,000 feet thick. Niobrara Formation: marine shale and limestone, 300 feet thick. Benton Formation: marine shale and limestone, 300 feet thick. Dakota Sandstone: beach deposit, 100 feet thick.
Jurassic		Morrison Formation: fluviatile deposits, 500 feet thick.	
Triassic		Chinle Formation: generally red beds, 500 feet thick.	Lykins Formation: red beds, 500 feet thick.
Permian		Maroon Formation: red beds, 4,000 feet thick	Lyons Formation: sandstone 250 feet thick.
Pennsylvanian		Hermosa Formation: shale and limestone, 1,800 feet thick.	Fountain Formation: red beds, 2,000 feet thick.
Early Paleozoic		Sandstone and limestone, 150 feet thick	
Precambrian		Granite, schist, and gneiss.	

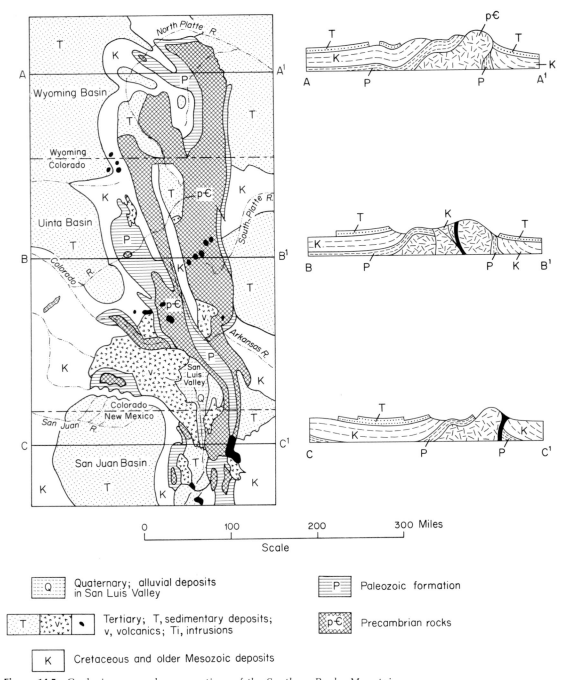

Figure 14.5   *Geologic map and cross sections of the Southern Rocky Mountains.*

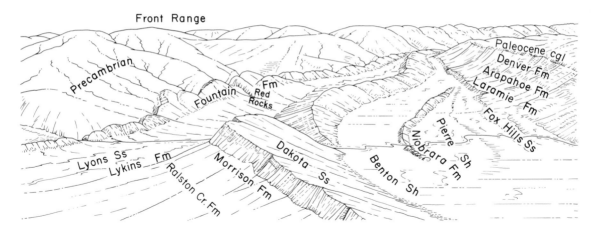

Figure 14.6 *Geology along the foot of the Front Range west of Denver; sketch from aerial photograph. Paleozoic and younger sedimentary formations are turned up in hogbacks along the foot of the anticlinally uplifted Precambrian rocks of the Front Range. A hogback of red rocks of the Fountain Formation (Pennsylvanian-Permian) is the site of Denver's famous Red Rocks Theater. Lyons Sandstone (Permian) and Lykins Formation (Triassic) form the valley back of that hogback. The Ralston Creek and Morrison formations (Jurassic) are dinosaur-bearing beds forming the slope below the hogback of Dakota Sandstone (basal Upper Cretaceous). The overlying formations are Upper Cretaceous to the top of the mountain capped by Paleocene Conglomerate. These sedimentary formations total about 10,000 feet in thickness.*

CENOZOIC IGNEOUS STRUCTURES. Cenozoic igneous structures in the Southern Rocky Mountains are of four principal kinds: cross-cutting stocks; dikes, sills, and laccoliths injected radially from the stocks; fields of basaltic lavas; and cauldron subsidences at volcanic centers.

The stocks are irregular pipe-like intrusions generally 1 to 4 miles in diameter. They are composed chiefly of rocks of intermediate composition—quartz diorite or monzonite—forcibly injected into the older rock formations that form their walls. At many places dikes, sills, and laccoliths were injected laterally into the wall rocks. Around the stocks at Spanish Peaks is a swarm of radial dikes that stand up like vertical walls above the easily eroded shale formations that they intrude. The side walls of the stocks are steep, largely discordant to the older structures, and cut across them. The intrusions were accompanied by considerable amounts of gases and vapors, and these hot fluids greatly altered the wall rocks. The hydrothermal solutions discharged during a late stage in the intrusive activity, and the metals contained in them were

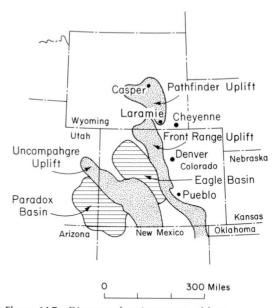

Figure 14.7 *Diagram showing extent of late Paleozoic structural basins (ruled) and uplifts (stippled) in the Southern Rocky Mountains. The basins contain late Paleozoic evaporites; at the uplifts the Paleozoic was eroded, and there the Mesozoic formations rest on the Precambrian. [After U.S.G.S.]*

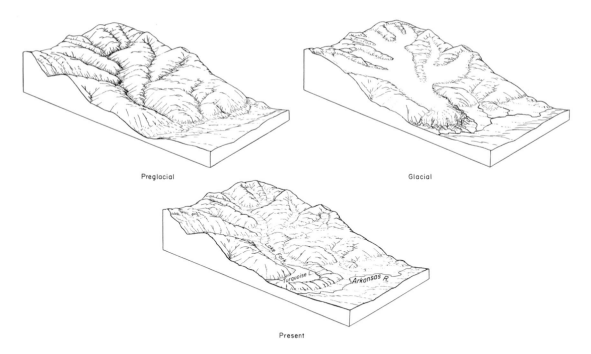

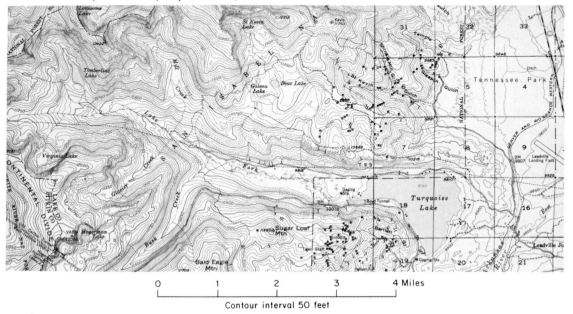

Figure 14.8 *Map showing cirques, U-shaped valleys draining from them, and a terminal moraine along Lake Fork of the Arkansas River, on the east side of the Sawatch Range, Colorado. The diagrams illustrate the evolution of this topography. In preglacial time V-shaped stream valleys were cut into the mountain. In the glacial periods these valleys were filled with ice, which formed a glacier that extended down Lake Fork to the valley of the Arkansas River. Gravel was deposited at the front of the glacier, forming a terminal moraine. When the ice melted, the U-shaped valleys were exposed. The depression behind the terminal moraine has been dammed to form a lake (Turquoise Lake).*

Figure 14.9 *Headward part of the Roaring Fork in the Precambrian core of the Sawatch Range, Colorado. The U-Shaped valley was glaciated during the Pleistocene, and the hanging valleys and faceted spurs were formed at that time. The floor of the valley is covered with hummocky glacial debris. A small stream in so large a valley is "underfit." The forest is spruce and fir at the upper timberline; much of the open ground is subject to average freeze and thaw, and resembles tundra.*

deposited in the shattered surrounding wall rocks and in the intrusive rock. The northeast-trending belt of stocks that forms the Colorado Mineral Belt is where most of the mines, ghost towns, and purple bottles of that region are found. The stocks were intruded early enough in the structural development of the mountains so that a cover of Cretaceous formations still remained. To what degree the stocks reached the surface and erupted is not known. A volcano at Cripple Creek, southeast of Pikes Peak, has been a richly productive mining district.

A second kind of igneous structure in the Southern Rocky Mountains consists of laccoliths clustered around stocks. Four mountain groups are made up of intrusions of this kind—the West Elk, San Miguel, and La Plata mountains, and the

mountains at Rico. These structures are better exposed on the Colorado Plateau, and will be described in the chapter on that province.

Lavas and related eruptive rocks are extensive at several places in the Southern Rocky Mountains. The tremendous volcanic pile at the San Juan Mountains contains a wide variety of volcanic rocks. Many eruptions violently ejected volcanic ash and coarse blocks. Along with these are lava flows, some of basalt and some of rhyolite, but most are of intermediate composition. The eruptions began at least as early as Oligocene, and continued intermittently until the Pleistocene (Fig. 14.10).

At other places in the Southern Rocky Mountains are fields of basaltic lava. Some that cap the White River Plateau are of Miocene age, and

Figure 14.10 *Silverton, Colorado (altitude 9,200 feet), in the San Juan Mountains, which are composed of Tertiary volcanic rocks.*

unconformably overlie the formations that dip off the north flank of the Plateau. This shows that much of the uplift that took place there predated the eruptions. The lavas, however, are part of a similar series that is downfolded into a structural basin at State Bridge, and these show that about 5,000 feet of the uplift of the Plateau was younger. One of the youngest flows in the Mountains is at Dotsero, Colorado, where a very late Pleistocene flow dammed the Eagle River just above its junction with the Colorado and crowded the river against the far wall of the valley.

Other igneous structures in the Southern Rocky Mountains are collapsed sinks at volcanic centers, mostly in the San Juan Mountains. Such structures are called "calderas" (Fig. 14.11). Several of them in the San Juan Mountains are 10 to 12 miles in diameter.

All of the large calderas formed as a result of the withdrawal of support by magma in the lower part of the volcano. The support may be withdrawn several ways:

1. Drainage of the molten support by eruptions of lavas along fissures on the flanks of the volcanic cone.

2. Melting of the lower parts of the cone by heated lavas in the pipe and consequent slid-

ing or avalanching of the fragmented blocks of the cone into the melt and engulfment by it.

3. Change in shape or volume of the magma at depth under the volcano. Although the calderas in the Southern Rockies are circular, others in the world are straight-walled structural depressions, summit grabens (e.g., Haleakala in Hawaii).

DRAINAGE SYSTEM AND ITS GEOLOGIC HISTORY

Figure 14.12 illustrates differences in the gradients of the principal rivers draining the Southern Rocky Mountains. The parts of the courses below about 6,000 feet are outside the mountains; the parts higher than 6,000 feet are in the mountains.

Although two-thirds of the area of the Southern Rocky Mountains drains eastward and only one-third drains westward, the rivers draining to the west have cut their valleys more deeply than those draining east. The Arkansas and Colorado rivers in these mountains are comparable, both in drainage area and discharge, but the valley bottom of the Colorado River averages a thousand feet lower than that of the Arkansas. This seems anomalous, because the plateaus west of the Rocky Mountains average 1,500 to 2,000 feet higher than the Great Plains. The Colorado River is shorter, and therefore its average gradient is steeper than that of the Arkansas River, but the stretches along both rivers down to an altitude of about 500 feet are nearly equal in length.

The rivers cross structural uplifts and structural basins, and the problems of reconstructing their geologic histories are illustrated by the course of Taylor River (Fig. 14.13). The Arkansas River has a structural setting similar to that of the Taylor River. Its basin, on the east side of the Sawatch Range opposite Taylor Park, contains middle and late Tertiary fill representing stages during which the river was ponded by uplifts downstream. To escape its basin, the Arkansas cut Royal Gorge.

The Colorado River (Fig. 14.14) begins on the west slope of the Front Range (an uplift of Precambrian granite), descends into a structural basin at Middle Park, crosses an uplift at the Gore Range (Fig. 14.15), crosses another structural basin at State Bridge and another uplift at the White River Plateau, and then enters the Colorado Plateau. The structural basin at State Bridge and the uplift at the White River Plateau are especially informative about the river's history.

The State Bridge basin is in synclinally folded Miocene lavas and sediments. The syncline extends far to the north along the head of the Yampa River. Downstream from the syncline the Colorado crosses the White River Plateau at Glenwood Canyon. The lavas extend onto that uplift and unconformably overlap domed Paleozoic and Mesozoic formations, showing that part of the doming occurred before the lavas formed. But the lavas are domed too, showing that part of the uplift occurred later, probably in Pliocene time. The position of the river across this uplift surely is due to superposition from the Miocene lavas before they were domed (like the Gunnison River across the Black Canyon; see below). But there is known post-lava uplift at the White River Plateau, and most of the deepening of Glenwood Canyon probably is due to antecedence—that is, continued downcutting during the later episodes of uplift. Across the structural basins above and below Glenwood Canyon, the river's gradient is about 20 feet per mile; through the canyon the gradient is about three times that steep.

Under the lava cap on the north side of White River Plateau, at the head of the White River, are river gravels derived from the Park Range and other ranges east of the structural basin occupied by the Yampa River. The structural basin now isolates the gravels from their source. The ancestral drainage was westward from the Park Range and more or less down the trough of the Uinta Basin, now occupied by the White River. That drainage predated the middle Miocene lavas, and is probably as old as Oligocene. In Miocene time it was disrupted by the basins and ranges at Middle Park, Gore and Park ranges, and State Bridge. In late Miocene or early Pliocene time,

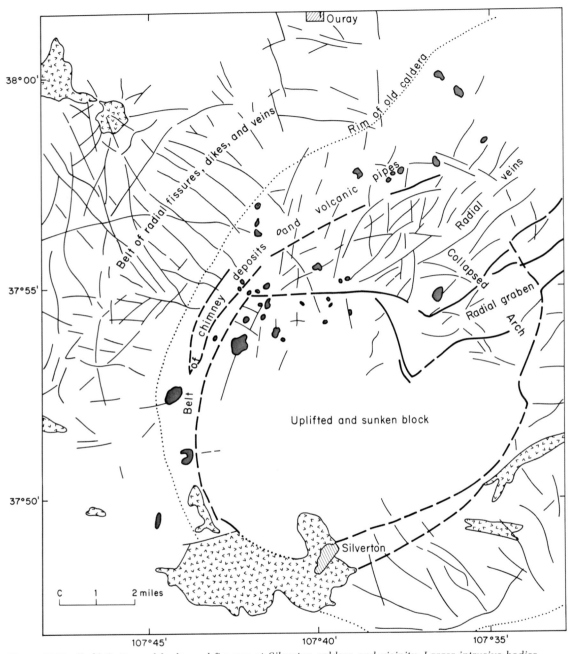

Figure 14.11 (Left) Pattern of faults and fissures at Silverton caldera and vicinity. Larger intrusive bodies, V-pattern; volcanic pipes, stippled pattern; faults, heavy lines; dikes and veins, light lines. Uplift of caldera core and northeast arch and their subsequent collapse caused compression along rim belt. Magmas and ore solutions worked along narrow vertical channels as contrasted with outer belts of tensional stresses. (Right) Schematic sections showing the evolution of the Valles caldera (no vertical exaggeration). *pT*, pre Tertiary; *Tr*, Tertiary volcanics; *rt*, rhyolite tuff; *er, mr, lr*, early, middle, and late rhyolite. [From U.S.G.S.]

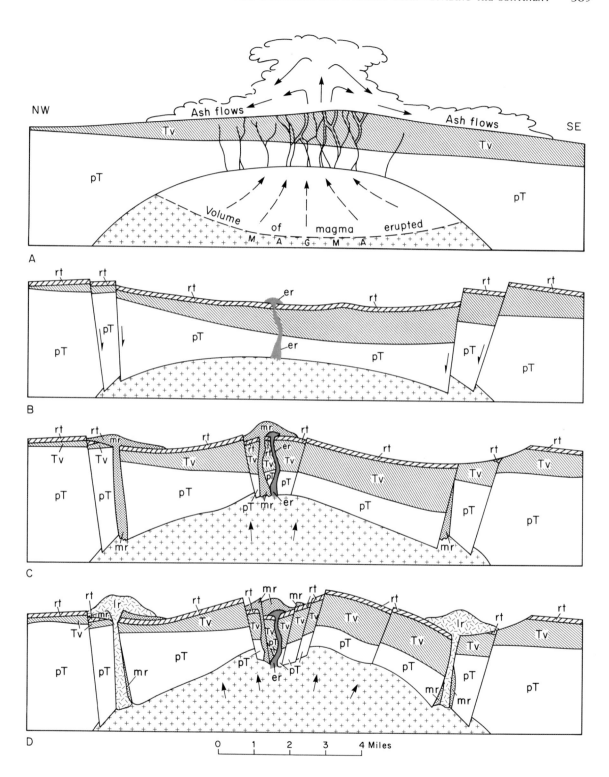

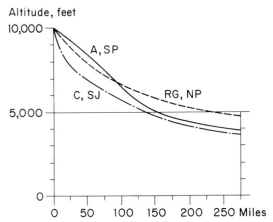

Altitude, feet

Figure 14.12 *Gradients of major streams draining the Southern Rocky Mountains. Broken lines represent streams draining east: A, Arkansas River; SP, South Platte River. Dotted Lines represent streams draining west: C, Colorado River; SJ, San Juan River. Solid lines represent streams draining south or north: RG, Rio Grande; NP, North Platte River.*

the Colorado River spilled southward around the south flank of the White River Plateau to join the Eagle, Fryingpan, Roaring Fork, and Crystal rivers. This stretch of the Colorado River is young—no older than late Miocene.

The oldest valley that can be dated is that of the Gunnison River, on the western slope. It begins in the northeast edge of the Uncompaghre Uplift (Fig. 14.7), where Paleozoic rocks are missing and the Precambrian is overlain by Jurassic formations; the broad, open valley is partly filled with volcanic rocks from the San Juan Mountains on the south and the West Elk Mountains on the north. By Oligocene time, the Gunnison Valley was eroded down to the Precambrian rocks. The youngest lavas are Pliocene, and the Gunnison River and its tributaries are incised into them, hence the inner valley is no older than Pliocene.

The Precambrian floor of the Gunnison River rises westward, and to escape from the broad open valley the river had to cut Black Canyon (Figs. 14.16, 14.17). The course of the river at Black Canyon surely is due to superposition from the lavas that once extended across the uplift and that still flank it, but very probably much or most

of the canyon deepening has been due to renewed uplift and eastward tilting of the valley while the canyon was being cut, as happened along the Colorado River at the White River Plateau. The Gunnison River also illustrates that not much of the downcutting can be attributed to the Quaternary, becase only 200 feet above the river (in the gorge at the head of Black Canyon), there is volcanic ash of middle glacial (Pleistocene) age.

CLIMATE

The difference in mean annual temperature between the mountain tops in the Southern Rocky Mountains and the Great Plains, about 35°F, is as great as the difference between the

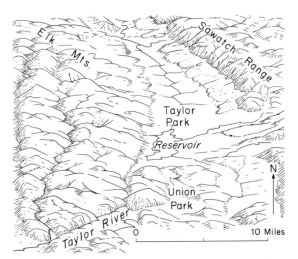

Figure 14.13 *Geologic history of rivers in the Rocky Mountains and elsewhere in the western part of the continent is illustrated by Taylor River in the Southern Rocky Mountains. To discharge from the structural basin of Taylor Park, the river had to erode a canyon through the Elk Mountains. Some rivers have cut downward as the mountain blocks were uplifted—that is, by antecedence; other rivers have been superimposed across uplifted barriers and eroded their canyons while lowering the basins. Most river courses became established by superposition when the uplifts were still low, and the canyons subsequently became deepened as uplift was renewed, a combination of antecedence and superposition referred to as anteposition. [After U.S.G.S. Prof. Paper 669.]*

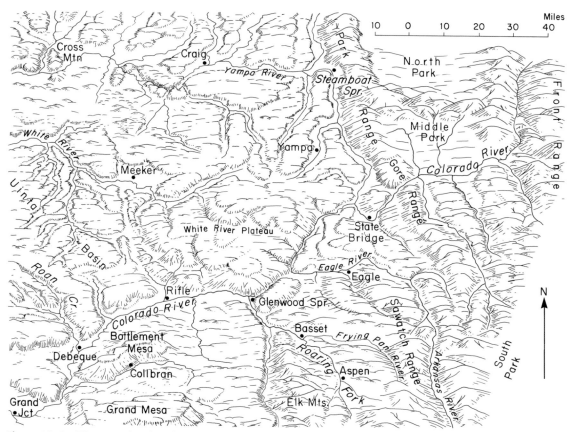

Figure 14.14   *Diagram of Colorado River Basin in the Rocky Mountains. [After U.S.G.S. Prof. Paper 669.]*

mean annual temperature of the plains and that of much of Alaska. In parts of the mountains the growing season is no more than 40 days, about half that of Alaska's Yukon Valley. Average annual snowfall in parts of the San Juan Mountains exceeds 20 feet, and this amount of snow impedes travel on mountainside highways despite numerous and powerful snowplows. Figure 14.18 illustrates the close correlation between annual precipitation and topography. The high-altitude areas have the greatest precipitation and the shortest frost-free period. Conversely, the low-altitude areas have the least precipitation, and the frost-free period, is more than 120 days.

In the Southern Rocky Mountains, 50 percent of the runoff is due to thunderstorms, but this percentage decreases in the physiographic prov-

inces to the west and northwest. Runoff attributable to thunderstorms in the Middle Rockies amounts to about 30 percent, in the Northern Rockies about 15 percent, and in the Sierra-Cascade less than 10 percent.

Along the eastern foot of the Rocky Mountains, the winter climate may suddenly turn mild because of certain westerly winds called *chinooks*, the equivalent of what in Europe is called foehns. A chinook originates when air moves up the western slope across the summit and down the eastern slope to the plains. As it ascends the western slope, the air cools as it expands (about 5.5°F for every thousand feet of rise). When sufficiently cooled, moisture is precipitated, heat is released, and the cooling process is slowed. During its descent, the air becomes

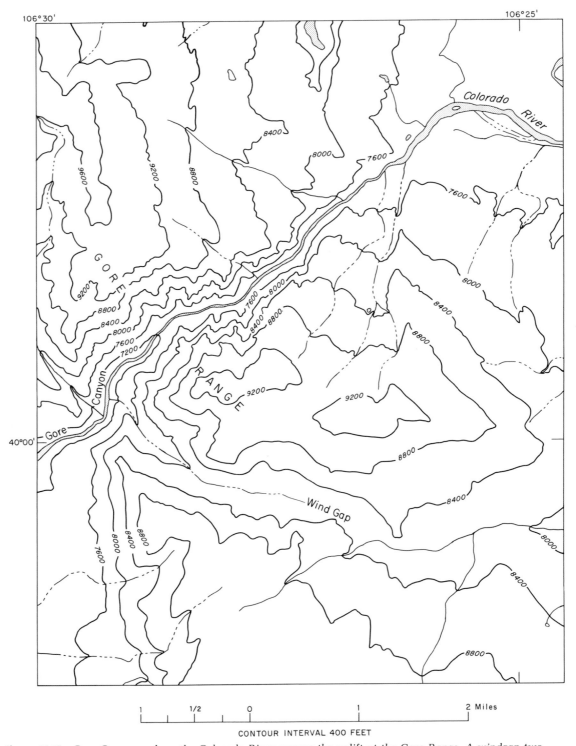

Figure 14.15 *Gore Canyon, where the Colorado River crosses the uplift at the Gore Range. A windgap two miles south probably is the former course of Blue River, which now joins the Colorado in Middle Park, just east of the area shown here. In Middle Park the Colorado River is in an open valley in middle Tertiary sediments evidently deposited when the river was intermittently ponded by uplift of the Gore Range. Gore Canyon, 1,800 feet deep, evidently was cut in a series of stages when the Colorado River overflowed from the basin at Middle Park.* [After U.S.G.S. Prof. Paper 669.]

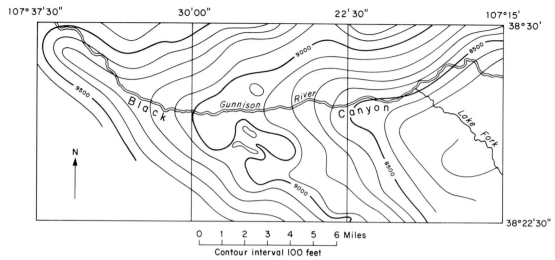

Figure 14.16 *Contours showing configuration of the bedrock surface beneath the Tertiary volcanic fill along the valley of the Gunnison River at Black Canyon and upstream from it. [After U.S.G.S. Bull. 1191.]*

more dense, and it would warm at the same rate at which it had cooled if it were not now dry. If during its descent the air absorbs little or no moisture—a cooling process that would slow the warming—then it reaches the plains much warmer than it was originally. An air mass starting at 50°F at the western foot of the Rocky Mountains may warm to 75°F by the time it reaches the edge of the Great Plains.

The effects of past climates in these and other mountain areas in the west are illustrated chiefly by the empty cirques on the mountain tops, the U-shaped valleys formerly occupied by ice, and the morainal deposits (Figs. 14.8, 14.9).

Forests in the Rocky Mountains region illustrate the climatic influence on the distribution of vegetation. Conversely, however, forests affect climate: they lower the temperature of the air inside and above them—in places, sufficiently so as to increase local precipitation. Temperature ranges in forests are less extreme than on nonforested land. Consequently, frost penetration is less in forest soils—often only half as deep as in nearby, nonforested soils—and the snow melts more slowly there than in the open. Thus, the spring runoff is conserved, and groundwater,

which helps maintain the flow of streams and springs through the summer, is replenished.

VEGETATION

Like the climate, vegetation on the Southern Rocky Mountains is altitudinally zoned (Figs. 14.18, 14.19; Table 14.2). The animal life, including the fish, also is zoned altitudinally (p. 156).

Above timberline (about 11,500 feet), in the Alpine Zone, the vegetation consists of small herbs and grasses. Much ground is bare rock. At timberline, in the Hudsonian Zone, trees are dwarfed and much deformed by wind. Below this, the Canadian Zone supports a dense forest of Englemann spruce and various firs, with considerable lodgepole pine, aspen, and some five-needle pine. This forest extends down to about 9,500 feet on the eastern slope and to about 9,000 feet on the northern and western slopes.

Next lower is the Transition Zone, where forests are open and populated primarily by yellow pine but include considerable Douglas fir and, toward the upper limit of the zone, lodgepole pine and aspen. On the western slope, the lower limit of yellow pine is at about 7,500 feet, but on

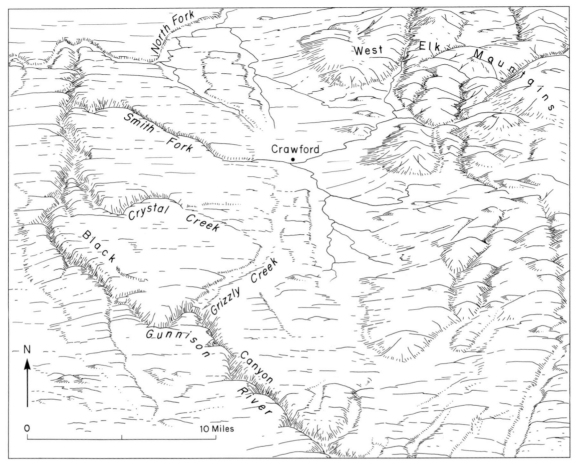

Figure 14.17 *Drainage pattern at the Black Canyon of the Gunnison River. Smith Fork originally drained to the Gunnison River via Grizzly Creek, and later by way of Crystal Creek. As uplift at the Black Canyon continued, the drainage was diverted to the present Smith Fork, and that drainage is about to be diverted again to the north by the tributaries of North Fork that are eroding headward towards Crawford. [After U.S.G.S. Prof. Paper 669.]*

the eastern slope, it extends to the foot of the mountains and onto the Great Plains at altitudes as low as 6,500 feet.

Below the yellow pine forests is woodland of pinyon pine and juniper, representing the upper part of the Upper Sonoran Zone and extending around the southern base of the Southern Rocky Mountains. In the northern part of the zone and at the upper elevations in the southern part of the zone, the pinyon-juniper woodland is replaced by chaparral—a scrubby growth consisting prin-

cipally of Gambel oak, mountain mahogany, and serviceberry. On the western slope the chaparral extends upward into the Transition Zone, and the pinyon-juniper extends downward to about 6,000 feet. Below that level, but still within the Upper Sonoran Zone, sagebrush grows on the west and mostly short grass on the east.

It should not be supposed that the boundaries between these vegetation zones follow contours, for in general the upper altitudinal zones extend far below their normal range along cool, moist

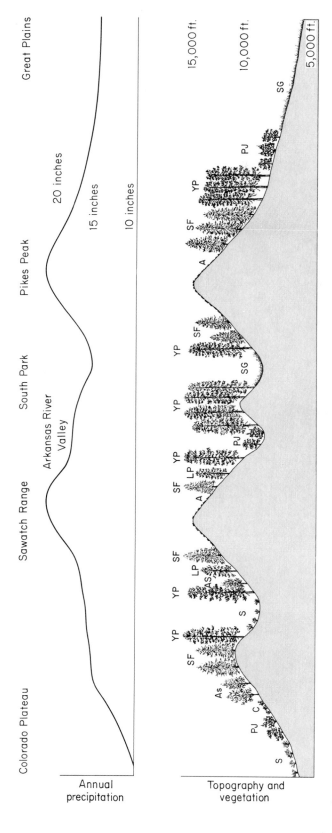

Figure 14.18 *Diagrammatic transect across the Southern Rocky Mountains, illustrating the relationship between topography and precipitation and the altitudinal zoning of the vegetation. Alpine Zone (A); Canadian Zone with spruce-fir forest (SF); Transition Zone, mostly yellow pine (YP) or lodgepole pine forest (LP). Upper Sonoran Zone with pinyon-juniper woodland (PJ), short grass (SG), and sagebrush (S).*

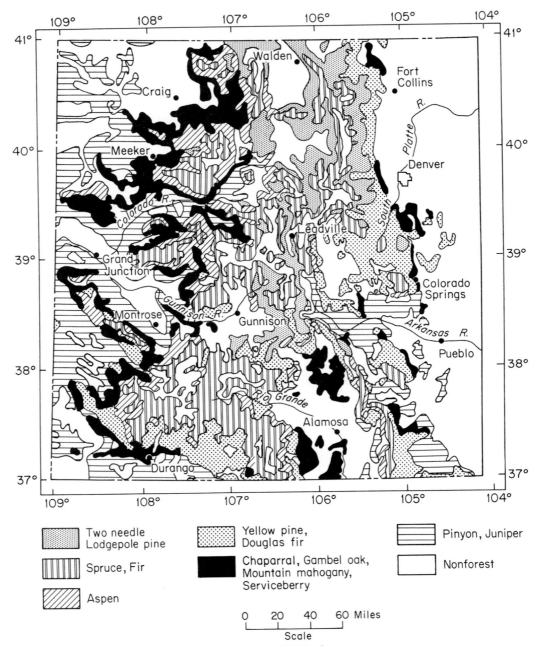

Figure 14.19 *Major forest types in Colorado.* [*From U.S.D.A.*]

Table 14.2

Principal Trees in the Southern Rocky Mountains

Pines
Needles in bundles of 5: Limber pine, Upper Sonoran to Hudsonian Zones; Bristlecone pine, Transition to Hudsonian Zones
Needles in bundles of 3: Ponderosa (Yellow) pine, Transition Zone
Needles in bundles of 2: Lodgepole pine (tall straight), Transition and Canadian Zones
                        Pinyon (Nut) pine (short, scrubby), Upper Sonoran Zone

Spruce (needles stiff, pointed)
Cones 1–$2\frac{1}{2}$ inches long: Engelmann spruce, Hudsonian Zone
Cones $2\frac{1}{4}$–$4\frac{1}{2}$ inches long: Blue spruce, Transition and Canadian Zones

Fir (needles flat, soft)
Cones are upright and lose their scales rather than falling intact; Canadian and Hudsonian Zones

Douglas-fir (needles flat, soft like fir)
Cones 3–$4\frac{1}{4}$ inches long with 3-lobed bracts fall intact

Broadleaf trees
Quaking aspen, Transition to Hudsonian Zone
Narrowleaf cottonwood, Transition Zone
Common (Fremont) cottonwood, Upper Sonoran Zone

valley bottoms; conversely, a particular zone may extend high above its normal range on a dry hillside with southern exposure.

The spruce-fir forests are the major timber resource. Engelmann spruce alone accounts for almost half the total sawtimber production in the Southern Rocky Mountains. Yellow pine was the principal source of sawtimber until recently, because of its lumber qualities and its accessibility. But heavy cutting of yellow pine and improved access to the higher forests have increased the production of spruce and fir.

The volume of timber in these forests, estimated at somewhat more than 50 billion board feet, is about a seventh the volume in all the Rocky Mountains. The annual cut in the Southern Rocky Mountains as of 1965 was about half the annual growth, and attempts are being made to increase the production. Even pulp mill plants are being encouraged, although in such environments these are notorious for polluting both atmosphere and streams. A pulp mill in any of the valleys on the windward side of the mountains could make considerable areas in those lovely mountains unfit for man, other animals, or plants.

Southern Rocky Mountains are grass and shrub rather than forest. North, Middle, and South Parks and the San Luis Valley are examples. Why these areas should be so nearly treeless whereas bordering mountainsides are forested is not clear. There seems to be nothing about the kind of ground or available moisture that would be unfavorable for growth of trees. Possibly the valleys collect too much cold air draining from the bordering mountains to be suitable for trees. Whatever the cause, the vast spread of meadow in the midst of so much forest is a striking contrast.

POISONOUS PLANTS ON
THE WESTERN RANGE

Physiographic setting is a factor in the distribution of plants poisonous to livestock. Poisonous plants grow in all parts of the country; oak, bracken fern, chokecherry, milkweed, sneezeweed, water hemlock, and lupine are examples. Other poisonous plants that grow in semiarid regions include arrowgrass, death camas, greasewood, rubberweed, locoweed, and certain species of larkspur (the beautiful delphinium). Where

feed is plentiful, as it is in humid regions, livestock apparently either avoid most poisonous
plants or do not consume enough to be poisoned.
In the arid and semiarid regions poisonous plants
are a serious menace to livestock because feed is
frequently scarce, at least seasonally, and the poisonous plants may be consumed in toxic amounts.

Since most of the Rocky Mountains and intermontane plateaus and basins are used chiefly for
grazing, the identification and control of poisonous plants are an important aspect of range management in those regions.

SURFICIAL DEPOSITS AND SOILS

Surficial deposits in the Southern Rocky
Mountains include glacial moraines and gravelly
alluvium in valleys: colluvium, landslides (Fig.
14.20), and boulder fields on the mountain sides;
and some sand dunes. These deposits are largely
late Pleistocene and Holocene in age and the soils
developed on them are correspondingly young.

The soils are zoned altitudinally to about the
same degree as the vegetation, and in general, the
sequence of soils encountered upward on the
mountains parallels the sequence encountered
eastward across the Interior Plains, for the climatic zoning is similar (Fig. 6.6). On the Great
Plains, at the foot of the mountains, the soils are
alkaline (Brown Soils) with a thick layer of lime
in the subsoil. Upward on the mountains, in and
near the Transition Zone, rainfall is greater and
the lime zone less well developed; the soils there
are somewhat like the Chestnut Soils in the Great
Plains near the 100th meridian. In the upper part
of the Transition Zone and higher, where the
annual rainfall is 20 inches or more, the soils are
acid and resemble the Gray-Brown Podzols in the
north-central United States.

These shallow soils formed during the very
late Pleistocene and Holocene. Here and there are
remnants of deep, old soils that formed in pre-
Wisconsinan time, but these soils were largely
eroded from the mountains during Wisconsinan
time, when the climate was rigorous. In general,
soil erosion in the Rocky Mountains is severe
only where remnants of the pre-Wisconsinan

soils are extensive. This relationship between soil
age and susceptibility to erosion is similar to that
in the Appalachian Highlands (p. 294).

The differences between the soils of pre-
Wisconsinan, Wisconsinan, and Holocene age on
the Rocky Mountains are best shown by the
differences in weathering of the moraines and
other deposits of those ages. In Holocene deposits, pebbles are fresh. In deposits of Wisconsinan age, pebbles may have a weathered rind.
In deposits of pre-Wisconsinan age, pebbles may
be altered to clay.

Middle Rocky Mountains and Wyoming Basin

The Middle Rocky Mountains and the Wyoming
Basin (Fig.14.1) include a miscellany of landforms
bearing resemblances to all the neighboring
provinces. The Bighorn Basin is nearly sur-
rounded by mountains and is included in the
Middle Rocky Mountains, but it connects with
and is quite like the neighboring parts of the
Great Plains. The eastern part of the Wyoming
Basin connects with and resembles the Great
Plains. To the south the Wyoming Basin connects
with and resembles the adjoining part of the
Colorado Plateau. The Bighorn, Wind River and
Uinta mountains are anticlinal uplifts exposing
Precambrian cores, like the ranges in the Southern Rocky Mountains (Fig. 14.5); the Wasatch and
other mountains on the west are like the block
faulted ranges of Paleozoic rocks in the Basin and
Range Province. The plateau at Yellowstone Park
could as well be included in the Columbia Plateau as in the Middle Rocky Mountains. The
Middle Rocky Mountains and Wyoming Basin
differ from their neighbors chiefly because of
their heterogeneity.

Cities and towns are located around the bases
of the mountains and depend on them for water,
as in the Southern Rocky Mountains. Provo, Salt
Lake City, and Ogden are along the western foot
of the Wasatch Range. Sheridan, Wyoming, is at
the foot of the Bighorn Mountains. Several
towns—Laramie, Rawlins, Rock Springs, Green
River, and Evanston—grew up along the Union

Pacific Railroad and the highway across the southern part of the Wyoming Basin. Other towns have developed along the river valleys—Montpelier on the Bear River, Livingston and Big Timber on the Yellowstone, and Casper on the North Platte. The total population *within* the provinces is probably little more than a quarter of a million.

The resources are considerable and diverse. The region is rich in mineral fuels and other mineral deposits, especially phosphates and salts. It produces livestock, and there is some irrigation farming. It contains two of our best-known national parks, Yellowstone and Grand Teton, and forests popular for camping and dude ranching. The Wyoming Basin, site of the Oregon and Cali-

fornia trails of the last century, is still the major transcontinental route across the Rocky Mountains.

STRUCTURAL FRAMEWORK AND
GEOLOGIC HISTORY

The Middle Rocky Mountains include not only some of the most impressive mountains in the western United States—for example, the Teton Range (Fig. 14.21)—but some of the least impressive and least mountainous ranges in the western United States. Only small parts of the Middle Rocky Mountains are higher than 11,000 feet (Fig. 14.4). Trends of the ranges in the Middle Rockies are so diverse that they nearly box the compass.

Figure 14.20 *Instability in the volcanic rocks of the San Juan Mountains. Slumgullion slide (center) extends for 3 miles and descends 2,000 feet to form the dam for Lake San Cristobal in Lake Fork. Evidently it is an ancient landslide, but movement is indicated by the "crazy forest" of tilted trees.*

A

B

Figure 14.21 *Views of the Teton Range, Wyoming, from the east. In the foreground of both views is the broad valley of the Snake River, an outwash plain of glacial debris. In the lower view the foreground includes part of Jackson Lake, the second largest lake in Wyoming (altitude about 6,700 feet). The high peaks reach to about 12,000 feet.*

Altitudes in the Wyoming Basin are mostly between 6,000 and 8,000 feet and average about 7,000 feet. The continental divide here is scarcely noticeable. In fact, a shallow depression almost 100 miles wide, the Great Divide Basin, lies on it. The basins along the Green, North Platte, and Wind rivers are topographically and geologically like the Powder River Basin on the Great Plains, the Bighorn Basin in the Middle Rocky Mountains, and the Uinta Basin, which is included in the Colorado Plateau (Fig. 14.22). Further, the climate, soils, and vegetation of the several basins are not very different. The Wyoming Basin connects the Great Plains with the Colorado Plateau; one can go from one to the other without crossing a mountain range.

Each individual range and basin in the Middle Rocky Mountains and Wyoming Basin is a structural as well as topographic unit. The Southern Rocky Mountains divide northward into three anticlinal uplifts at the Laramie, Medicine Bow, and Park ranges. They plunge northwestward under the Wyoming Basin and divide it into small

basins like the one at Laramie. Precambrian rocks form the cores of these anticlines. Paleozoic and Mesozoic formations form hogbacks along their flanks, and these formations dip under younger ones of Tertiary age that dip more gently into the basins and form cuestas. The structure of the Tertiary formations is like that of a saucer. If we could see through one of the basins it might look like the idealized cross section in Figure 14.23. The Mesozoic and Paleozoic formations are downfolded more deeply under the basins and have deeper, bowl-like structures. An uncon-

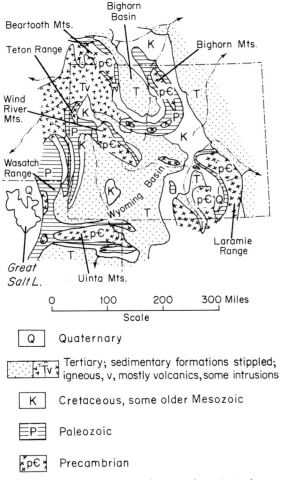

Figure 14.22 *Geologic map showing the principal structural units in the Middle Rocky Mountains and the Wyoming Basin.*

formity between the Tertiary and older formations shows that part of the folding occurred before the Tertiary formations were deposited.

Unconformities separating some Tertiary formations show that the folding was resumed intermittently while they were being deposited. The deposits, of course, began collecting in the basins as soon as the folding started, and the folding progressed intermittently from then on while deposition continued. Unfortunately we see the contacts only around the rims of such basins, and this limited view minimizes the extent of unconformities, which record the amounts of the structural movements.

The Uinta Mountains, which separate the Wyoming Basin from the Uinta Basin, are an anticlinal uplift of Precambrian rocks (Fig. 14.22). The Wind River Mountains are a similar anticline separating the Green River and Wind River Basins. The Owl Creek Mountains, another anticline, separate the Wind River and Bighorn basins, and the Bighorn Mountains similarly separate the Bighorn and Powder River basins.

The mountain ranges west of the Wyoming Basin consist of Paleozoic and Mesozoic formations. Along some of these ranges the Paleozoic formations are thrust eastward onto Cretaceous or older Mesozoic formations. The westernmost range, the Wasatch Range, consists of complexly folded and thrust-faulted Paleozoic formations intruded by granitic stocks and later elevated and rotated in a tremendous fault block, or series of fault blocks, overlooking Great Salt Lake (Fig. 14.24). In all these features the Wasatch Mountains resemble the ranges in the Basin and Range Province. In addition, mineralization associated

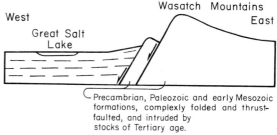

Figure 14.24 *Diagrammatic section through the Wasatch Range in the vicinity of Great Salt Lake. The structural basin occupied by Great Salt Lake is underlain by Tertiary and Quaternary fill eroded from the surrounding mountains.*

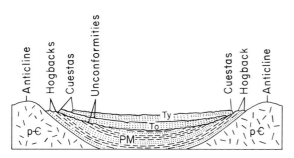

Figure 14.23 *Idealized cross section of a structural basin in Wyoming. pꞒ, Precambrian; PM, Paleozoic and Mesozoic formations; To, older Tertiary deposits; Ty, younger Tertiary deposits. The steeply upturned Paleozoic and Mesozoic formations form cuestas and hogbacks along the flanks of the basin. The older Tertiary formations were first deposited in the center of the basin; as accumulation proceeded, the deposits gradually extended outward onto its flanks. Continued folding during Tertiary deposits to unconformably overlap the older Tertiary deposits. (Compare Fig. 11.12.)*

with the granitic stocks (silver and lead, with some zinc and copper) is like that around many stocks in the Basin and Range Province.

The Teton Mountains in Wyoming are a similar fault block, but it is tilted westward and extends northward under the lavas and other volcanic rocks that cap the Yellowstone Plateau (Fig. 14.25). These volcanic rocks are younger than most of the structural deformation. They are more than 2,000 feet thick, and they spread unconformably across folded and faulted early Tertiary formations.

Volcanism on the Yellowstone volcanic plateau has continued into Holocene time. Yellowstone Park contains thousands of hot springs and geysers. Most of the water is supplied by seepage from the surface. The heat is supplied by shallow intrusive rocks that are still hot. Gases escaping from the heated rocks dissolve in the hot water to form a powerful solvent that can dissolve silica and transport it to the surface, where the water issues from springs and geysers. These are of many kinds, differing in temperature, quantity and mode of discharge, and composition. The springs presumably have open underground passages that permit steady discharge. The geysers are thought to have irregular or constricted underground passages that interrupt the discharge until the accumulated pressure is sufficient to cause violent eruption. Most geysers erupt intermittently; a few, like Old Faithful, erupt periodically. Some springs discharge clear water; others are highly colored. One group, known as the paint pots, discharges a pasty mud. Old Faithful is believed to issue from a U-shaped conduit connected to a higher and empty chamber of heated rock, from which water surges back into the conduit and is converted to steam, which drives out the water.

The activity of the geysers and hot springs is variable. Mud pots, hot springs, and pools may suddenly erupt and throw water or mud tens of feet into the air. Some that have clear water may rapidly change to muddy water. Color of the water may alternate between green and gray. Old Faithful, which normally erupts for 1 to 5 minutes every half hour or hour, can be unfaithful and disappointingly quiet.

Great Divide Basin, between Rawlins and Rock Springs, is unique in being located along the continental divide. As a result, the continental divide is itself divided by a basin! This unusual basin probably is attributable to structural sagging during the Tertiary or Quaternary, either tectonic sagging or sagging caused by the removal of buried salt by solution.

Glaciation during the Pleistocene period was the last geologic event that played a major part in shaping the Middle Rocky Mountains. All the major ranges were glaciated. Although they are not as high as the Southern Rocky Mountains, the snow and ice extended to lower levels because of the more northerly latitude and must

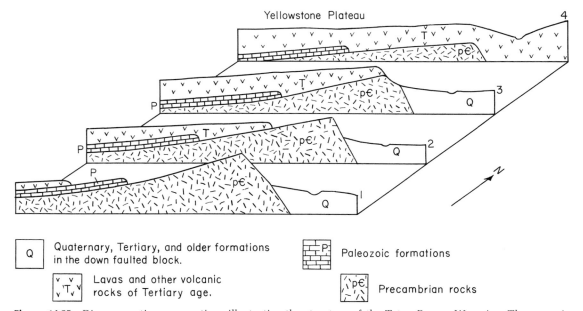

Figure 14.25 *Diagrammatic cross sections illustrating the structure of the Teton Range, Wyoming. The range is a fault block composed largely of Precambrian rocks capped on the western slope by Paleozoic formations (section 1). Lavas and other volcanic rocks overlap the western slope of the range. As the structure plunges northward (sections 2 and 3) the volcanics extend progressively farther onto the western slope and, finally, at the Yellowstone volcanic plateau (section 4), completely bury it.*

have covered most of the mountains above the 8,000-foot level. The alpine glaciers in the Teton Mountains descended to Jackson Hole at 6,500 feet, where they deposited terminal moraines that still contain lakes (Fig. 14.26). On the west front of the Wasatch Mountains and northeast front of the Beartooth Mountains the glaciers extended to the foot of the mountains at an altitude of about 5,000 feet. The extent and volume of the glacial ice and snow probably was as great as in the higher Southern Rocky Mountains.

Figure 14.26 *A lake contained by a terminal moraine at the mouth of a glaciated canyon at the eastern foot of the Teton Range.*

Streams draining from the alpine glaciers in the mountains transported vast quantities of sediments, and most valleys became filled with sand and gravel. These fills are now exposed in gravel terraces along the sides of streams that have excavated new valleys in the fill.

In places the glaciations caused drainage diversions. At the west end of the Uinta Mountains (Fig. 14.27), the upper part of the Provo River, a former tributary of the Weber River, was diverted southward by glacial outwash that filled its original valley at Kamas. Provo River may also have drained west to the Weber River via the valley of Beaver Creek. A cross valley there was dammed by glacial outwash or morainal deposits at the mouth of Shingle Creek. Streams west of Shingle Creek are tributary to Beaver Creek.

RIVERS AND LAKES

Six major rivers drain the Middle Rocky Mountains and Wyoming Basin, and the areas draining east and west are about equal. The North Platte River, which heads in the Southern Rocky Mountains, and its principal tributary, the Sweetwater River, drain eastward. The Green River, and its principal tributaries—the Yampa, Blacks Fork, and Sandy Creek, drain southward. The Bear River drains westward to Great Salt Lake. The Snake River heads in Jackson Lake and drains westward into the Columbia River. The Yellowstone and Bighorn rivers, together with their numerous tributaries, drain northeastward to the Missouri River.

Lakes in the Middle Rocky Mountains and Wyoming Basin are numerous. Some, including the large Yellowstone Lake, occupy depressions in the Yellowstone lava plateau. They have been dammed partly by faulting or tilting, partly by volcanic deposits, and partly by glacial deposits. Yellowstone Lake, which covers 138 square miles and is above 7,500 feet, discharges into the Yellowstone River. This lake, which receives most of its water from the Absaroka Mountains to the east, occupies a glacial valley and was once 160 feet deeper and drained southward to the Snake River. That outlet became dammed, probably by faulting and tilting, and the lake began draining northward to the Yellowstone River. The overflow in that direction has eroded the Grand Canyon of the Yellowstone River and lowered the lake level. Small lakes are abundant in glacial cirques on all the high mountains, especially on the Bighorn, Teton, Wind River, and Uinta mountains. Some cirques in the Tetons contain icefields.

Other lakes have formed along the bases of the Teton and Wind River mountains, where the Pleistocene glaciers reached the low country and built terminal moraines across the mouths of canyons (Fig. 14.26). These lakes are larger than the cirque lakes, and many exceed 100 feet in depth. Such lakes are not found around the bases of the Uinta Mountains and Southern Rocky Mountains because the glaciers there did not extend to the foot of the mountains. In those mountains the terminal moraines are in the canyons, well in from the base of the mountains.

Bear Lake, which covers more than 100 square miles, is situated on the Utah-Idaho boundary at

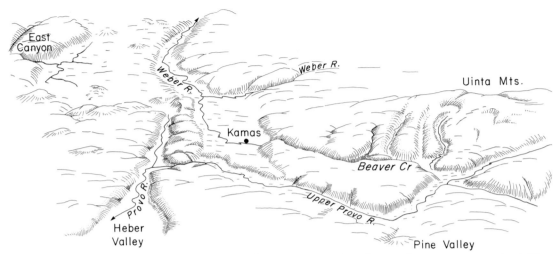

Figure 14.27 *Drainage system at the west end of the Uinta Mountains; view north across an area about 30 by 30 miles. Weber River drains the north side of the Uinta Mountains and collects some drainage (Beaver Creek) from the south side. During the Wisconsinan Glaciation the upper part of the Provo River also was a tributary to the Weber, and filled the broad valley at Kamas with glacial outwash. When this fill overtopped a pass at the head of Heber Valley, the upper part of the Provo River overflowed west and cut a gorge about 100 feet into the fill and into the bedrock at what had been the divide.*

an altitude just under 6,000 feet. The lake is one of several that occupy structural depressions. Bear Lake fills the southern part of a structural valley crossed by the Bear River. The valley was tilted southward and flooded by streams from the surrounding high mountains. A lava flow across the lower, north end of the valley forms a natural spillway for the lake.

Still other lakes occupy small depressions in the southeastern part of the Wyoming Basin. Most cover only a few acres, and are dry, but a few contain small, shallow lakes or ponds. Others are marshy. They seem to have formed in at least four ways. Some of the largest are apparently due to structural downwarping. Some of the smallest ones may be sinkholes due to solution of buried gypsum or other salts. Still others are attributable to wind scour, and are referred to as *deflation hollows*. A few may be due to ponding of washes by sand dunes or by deposits brought in by flash floods from tributaries.

Many water storage reservoirs have been built in the basins and in the mountains. Two major

reservoirs along the North Platte River are the Seminoe and Pathfinder Reservoirs. Several small ones in the Wasatch Mountains store water for cities and farms along the west foot of the range. Irrigation developments along the upper Snake River include the Palisades Reservoir, located where the river turns northwest at the south end of the Teton Range. In the Absaroka Mountains the Buffalo Bill Reservoir on the Shoshone River stores water for irrigation in the Bighorn Basin. Several reservoirs in the Wind River Basin store water for irrigation there and downstream in the Bighorn Basin (Fig. 14.28). No river in Wyoming, maintains its natural flow without artificial controls.

CLIMATE, VEGETATION, AND SOILS

Some climatic data for the Middle Rocky Mountains and Wyoming Basin are given in Figure 14.29. Both temperature and precipitation average slightly lower than in the Southern Rocky Mountains. The basins on the lee (east) side of mountains are favored by chinook winds

Figure 14.28 *Wyoming Basin, at the Alcova Reservoir on the North Platte River. The reservoir is in a structural dome that exposes Mesozoic formations. [Courtesy of Wyoming Travel Commission.]*

during the winter, as are the Great Plains east of the Southern Rocky Mountains. Other, more northerly winds that attain high velocities and give rise to ground blizzards are not regarded so favorably. Ground blizzards are like sand storms; strong winds, for which Wyoming is famous, blow the dry snow along the ground. Ground blizzards not only have a low wind-chill index, they can reduce visibility to nearly zero. It has been said that Wyoming's ground blizzards have snow so dry it can be burned.

Exposure is a major factor controlling plant distribution in the mountains. For example, in the Middle Rockies, at Daniels Canyon southeast of Heber Valley (Fig. 14.27), the south facing north side of the valley has conifer forest with some aspen whereas the shadier and cooler south side supports scrub oak and mountain mahogany. Along the valley bottom are broad leaf trees—cottonwood, boxelder, and willow.

Vegetation on the Middle Rocky Mountains is altitudinally zoned, as it is on other high moun-

tains. Timberline on the high summits rises southward from about 9,500 feet at the northwest end of the Beartooth Mountains to 10,000 feet in the Bighorn Mountains, and to about 11,000 feet in the Uinta Mountains. Above timberline are grasses, sedges, and other low alpine plants. Their total area is only a little less than that of summits above timberline in the lofty Southern Rocky Mountains (Fig. 14.30).

Although timberline, like the other vegetation zones, rises generally southward, its position varies considerably with exposure. On the Beartooth Mountains, for example, timberline is at about 9,300 feet on northern and western slopes and at 9,800 feet on southern slopes.

The highest forest, populated by Englemann spruce with subalpine fir and whitebark pine (Fig. 14.31), extends 1,000 to 1,500 feet downward from timberline, but is much less extensive than its counterpart in the Southern Rocky Mountains. Below it is a forest of lodgepole pine, which extends downward into a lower forest having

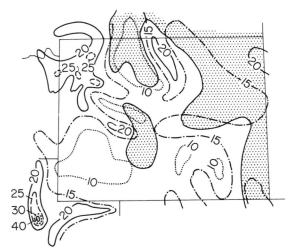

Figure 14.29 *Map showing average annual precipitation in the Middle Rocky Mountains and the Wyoming Basin. The average growing season is more than 120 days in the stippled areas; less than 120 days in the unstippled areas. [From U.S.D.A.]*

Figure 14.30 *Extent of alpine grassland (black) above timberline on the Southern, Middle, and Northern Rocky Mountains. Altitudes are lower in the north than in the south, but so too is timberline.*

Douglas fir. The lodgepole pine forest forms one of the most important timber belts in the Middle Rocky Mountains. At still lower altitudes, and extending onto the Great Plains, far from the foot of the mountains, are scattered stands of yellow pine. On the plains, the yellow pine favors the sandstone ledges; the grasses favor the shale hills. Differences in kind of ground limit the forests also along Jackson Hole, where the valley of the Snake River, mantled with glacial outwash, supports sagebrush, and where forests grow on the moraines and upward onto the mountains.

Pinyon-juniper woodland is hardly represented around either the Wyoming Basin or the Middle Rocky Mountains, although it forms major plant stands farther south. In the Wyoming Basin the chief vegetation is sagebrush.

Moist, alkaline alluvial flats support alkali-tolerant greasewood. Along streams in and near the mountains, where the water is of good quality, valley bottoms are lined with willows and sedges, but farther from the mountains this vegetation gives way to greasewood and other alkali-tolerant plants.

Surficial deposits and soils in the Middle Rocky Mountains are like those in the Southern Rocky Mountains. The Wyoming Basin has extensive alluvial deposits in floodplains of streams and in fans at the foot of mountains. Dry lake beds are numerous, and there are extensive eolian deposits including both dune sand and loess.

Soils in the Wyoming Basin are alkaline and are classed with the desert soils. The surface layer typically contains little organic matter and is calcareous, for leaching is slight. Subsoils are lighter in color and contain a layer enriched with lime and/or gypsum, which may develop into a caliche hardpan. Vegetation on these soils is mostly sagebrush or shadscale. Greasewood and other alkali-tolerant plants grow where there is an excess of alkalis or salts. Because the Wyoming Basin is semiarid and weathering correspondingly slight, the soil textures and compositions are dominated by the parent materials. The sandy formations produce sandy soils; the shale formations produce tight, impermeable, clayey

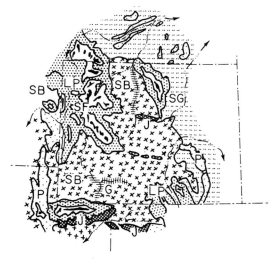

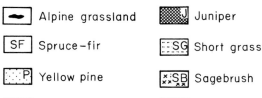

![Alpine grassland]	Alpine grassland	![Juniper]	Juniper
SF	Spruce-fir	SG	Short grass
P	Yellow pine	SB	Sagebrush
LP	Lodgepole pine	G	Greasewood

Figure 14.31 *Principal vegetation zones in the Middle Rocky Mountains and the Wyoming Basin.*

soils. The land is used chiefly for grazing, but where irrigated, as along some floodplains, it can be highly productive for farming.

RANGE LANDS

The Middle and Southern Rocky Mountains and Wyoming Basin, although farmed very little, are extensively used for grazing livestock—in places, too much so. The mountains are used chiefly for summer range; the Wyoming Basin is used for winter range.

Most of the grazed lands belong to the federal government, and are leased to stockmen for grazing. In the past, serious overgrazing of much of the range caused damage, from both erosion and elimination of plant species that provide good forage. Overgrazing is gradually being corrected

by limiting the use of public lands, but such restrictions are politically painful. Ranchers who have become dependent upon the use of public range do not favor measures that might require a reduction in their livestock holdings.

DRAINAGE ANOMALIES

Many rivers in the Middle Rocky Mountains and Wyoming Basin have developed anomalous courses "through the mountains, not around them." The course of the Laramie River is anomalous. It begins in the Laramie Basin and has cut northeastward across the anticlinally raised ridge of Precambrian rocks forming the Laramie Range. Its tributaries, Sybille Creek and Blue Grass Creek, do likewise. All these streams flow through gorges about 500 feet deep and descend 2,000 feet from the Laramie Basin to the Great Plains (Fig. 14.32).

The Laramie Basin (Fig. 14.5, section A–A′) is partly filled with alluvium, brought from the high mountains to the south and west and deposited by the Laramie River and its tributaries. This fill may have raised the river bed to where it could spill over the range to the east.

The North Platte River generally avoids the mountains, but it crosses uplifts also. The river flows northward from North Park and enters a broad structural vally, but instead of staying there the river turns into the side of the Medicine Bow Mountains and is incised into their flank (Fig. 14.33). Forty miles farther north, it flows toward a distant isolated mountain, and then follows a gorge about 1,000 feet deep through it rather than going around it (Fig. 14.34). This situation is repeated 40 miles farther downstream where the river cuts across the northwest tip of the Laramie Range in a gorge with rims about 1,000 feet higher than the lowlands around the tip. The easy route follows the open valleys and lowlands.

Sweetwater River, a western tributary of the North Platte, follows an equally anomalous course, one that has considerable historic interest (Fig. 14.35). The river crosses a granite ridge in a narrow, V-shaped gorge more than 300 feet deep

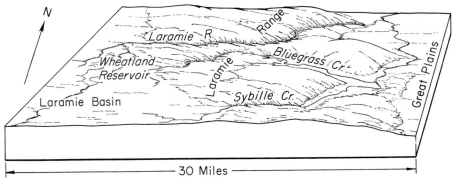

Figure 14.32 *Diagram illustrating the courses of the Laramie River and Sybille Creek across the Laramie Range, Wyoming.*

and only 30 feet wide at river level. The Oregon Trail passed by the foot of Independence Rock, crossed the river, and followed the open valley around the end of Devils Gate Ridge.

The Bighorn River, draining from the Wyoming Basin, takes seemingly difficult routes through mountains rather than across the open, low country to the Powder River Basin and Great Plains. The river crosses two mountain ranges. It leaves the basin north of the Wind River Mountains and passes through a gorge in the Owl

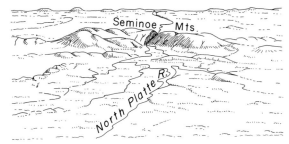

Figure 14.34 *View north (downstream) along the North Platte River to its gorge through the Seminoe Mountains, Wyoming. The lake (Seminoe Lake) is formed by a dam in the gorge.*

Figure 14.33 *The North Platte River, instead of following the broad structural valley separating the Medicine Bow Mountains from the northwest end of the Park Range, turns into a gorge cut into hard rocks forming the flank of the Medicine Bow Mountains. The rim of the gorge is 700 feet higher than the valley at Spring Creek. Length of view, about 25 miles.*

Creek Mountains. Then, instead of continuing north in the open Bighorn Basin and flowing to the Great Plains, it turns into a gorge through the Bighorn Mountains (Fig. 14.1).

Other similarly anomalous stream courses are the Green River gorge (Lodore Canyon) across the Uinta Mountains and Black Canyon of the Gunnison River, which are National Monuments, and the canyons of several rivers crossing the Wasatch Range. The Northern Rocky Mountains provide still other examples.

These anomalies were originally attributed to antecedence (p. 69, Fig. 3.9,A). Later they were attributed to superposition (Fig. 3.9,B). The anomalous courses probably can be explained most easily by anteposition (Fig. 3.9,C)—that is, superposition of the stream while the mountains

Figure 14.35 *Devils Gate, Wyoming, where the Sweetwater River is incised into a granite ridge. The rounded hill in the foreground is Independence Rock. Probably the river was superimposed across the granite during an early stage of uplift, and the canyon deepened when uplift of the granite was resumed.*

were low and antecedent deepening of the canyons when uplift resumed.

Rocky Mountains in Montana and Canada

The Rocky Mountains in Montana and Canada (Fig. 14.2) extend about 1,200 miles along the western border of the Great Plains from southwestern Montana, near Yellowstone Park, to an arbitrary north end at the Liard River in Canada. On the west the mountains are bounded by a remarkably straight structural valley known as the Rocky Mountain Trench, which extends from the Liard River southward into Montana, where it branches into three trenches. The Canadian Rockies average less than about 75 miles wide, but the mountains widen southward in Montana to more than 200 miles.

This part of the Rocky Mountains differs greatly from the Southern Rockies in Colorado. The rocks are different, their structural geology and geologic histories are different, and the scenery is correspondingly different. The basic difference in the rocks and structure is that the Southern Rockies developed from what had been stable platform with a thin cover of Paleozoic and early Mesozoic sedimentary formations, whereas the Rocky Mountains in Montana and Canada developed from what had been the eastern edge of late Precambrian, Paleozoic, and early Mesozoic geosynclines. Whereas pre-Cretaceous sedimentary formations in the Southern Rockies average perhaps 5,000 feet thick, in Mon-

tana and Canada the geosynclinal formations total more than 100,000 feet thick. Whereas the Southern Rocky Mountains were anticlinally folded without much thrust faulting, as were the Middle Rocky Mountains; in the Northern Rocky Mountains, especially in Canada, thrust faulting rather than folding is the rule.

STRUCTURAL FRAMEWORK
AND GEOLOGIC HISTORY

Structurally the mountains are of several kinds (Fig. 14.36), and the province can be divided into four sections with correspondingly different landforms. The Canadian Rockies, which are east of the Rocky Mountain Trench, comprise a belt of great imbricate thrust faults with displacements toward the east (Fig. 14.37). One type, on the high parts of the mountains, is composed of miogeosynclinal Paleozoic strata, which are mostly Devonian and older, and are thrust faulted eastward (Fig. 14.38). On the east is a foothill belt of miogeosynclinal Mesozoic formations, which is also thrust faulted eastward and overridden by thrust plates of Paleozoic formations.

A second structural type of mountain is found west of the Trench in southern British Columbia and extends eastward to the Great Plains in Montana, cutting off the south end of the Canadian Rockies near the international border. These mountains are composed chiefly of late Precambrian geosynclinal formations that are not strongly folded but have been thrust faulted

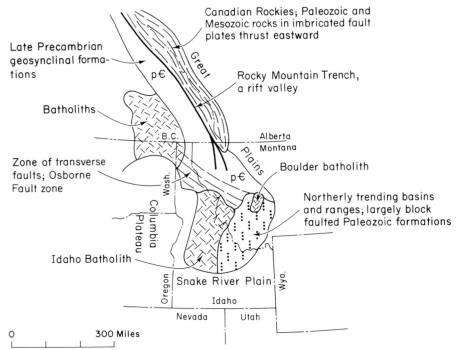

Figure 14.36 *Structural elements in the northern Rocky Mountains. The Rocky Mountain Trench separates the Canadian Rockies from mountains of folded and faulted Precambrian rocks to the west. These three structures end southward at a zone of transverse faults north of the Idaho batholith. In the southeast is an area of block-faulted basins and ranges.*

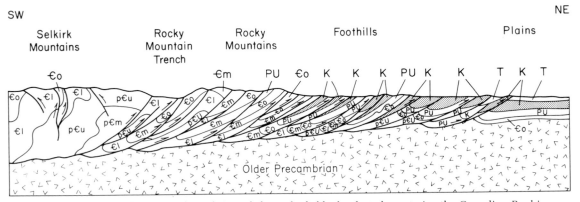

Figure 14.37 *Diagram illustrating the imbricated thrust fault blocks that characterize the Canadian Rockies. [Greatly generalized from Geol. Soc. Canada.] Length of section about 60 miles; position about southwest of Edmonton. T, Tertiary; K, Cretaceous, with some Jurassic and Triassic; Pu, upper Paleozoic (Devonian and Carboniferous); €O, Upper Cambrian and Ordovician, €m, Middle Cambrian; €l, Lower Cambrian; p€u uppermost late Precambrian; p€m, middle late Precambrian; p€l, lowermost late Precambrian.*

eastward onto Cretaceous formations at the eastern edge of the Rocky Mountains in Montana. The thrust plate has been broken into a series of horsts and grabens. The horsts form the mountain ranges and the grabens form the valleys. The structures trend north and the drainage has a trellis pattern. Most of the graben valleys are less than 3,000 feet in altitude; the mountain crests reach 9,000 to 10,000 feet.

These structures and their landforms end southward at a zone of transverse faults. To the southeast are block-faulted mountains very much like those in the Basin and Range Province. Many consist of complexly folded and faulted Paleozoic and Mesozoic formations in north-trending fault blocks (Fig. 14.39). Between these fault-block mountains are structural basins partly filled with debris eroded from the mountains. Other mountains in this section consist of volcanic rocks or granitic intrusions. The largest of these granitic masses, known as the Boulder batholith, extends from Helena to south of Butte. Most of the mountain summits are under 10,500 feet, but a few reach to 12,000 feet; the altitudes of the basins and valleys average about 5,000 feet.

A fourth kind of mountain is represented by the Little Belt Mountains, which are dome mountains formed by the intrusion of laccoliths, like the isolated mountains farther east on the Great Plains in Montana (p. 338).

Most of central Idaho and the Clearwater and Salmon River mountains are formed by the granitic intrusions of Cretaceous age that collectively make up the Idaho batholith (Fig. 14.40), one of the largest batholiths on the continent. It is about 100 miles wide and 300 miles long. Altitudes range between 3,000 and 7,000 feet (Fig. 14.4). The Idaho batholith is a deeply dissected plateau (Fig. 14.41) about 2,000 feet higher than the Columbia Plateau to the west. It is bordered on the east by the Bitterroot Mountains, which rise 1,000 feet above summits on the dissected plateau. The central part of the batholith is homogeneous granite, but the ridges and drainage there tend to be parallel, as if the granite were broken into structures that trend north. Along the eastern and western edges of the batholith are linear ridges of metamorphosed Paleozoic and Precambrian sedimentary rocks that were invaded by the batholith and turned up along its flanks. In these areas, too, the ridges and valleys trend roughly north to south. Over large areas the granite of the batholith is deeply weathered.

West of Spokane, are the Okanogan Highlands, which consist of broad, rounded hills, most less than 5,000 feet in altitude and consisting of granitic rocks intrusive into folded and metamorphosed Paleozoic rocks. The structures trend northerly and drain southward to the Columbia River, where the highlands are cut off by overlap of the Columbia River basaltic lavas, which form the Columbia Plateau.

Figure 14.38 *Mount Robson, eroded in late Precambrian and Cambrian sedimentary formations, is in Mount Robson Provincial Park, in easternmost British Columbia, west of Jasper National Park. [British Columbia Government photograph, courtesy Dept. of Travel Industry.]*

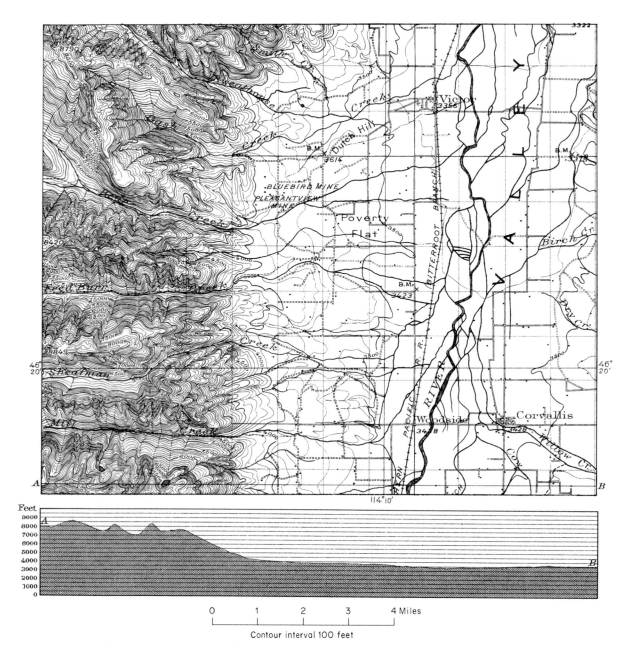

Figure 14.39 *Topographic map and profile across a range and a basin in the southeastern part of the Northern Rocky Mountains. This part of the Northern Rockies resembles parts of the Basin and Range Province and is characterized by three kinds of terrain—mountains, alluvial fans at their bases, and floodplains along the streams draining the valleys.* [*From U.S.G.S. Hamilton, Montana-Idaho, sheet, 1908.*]

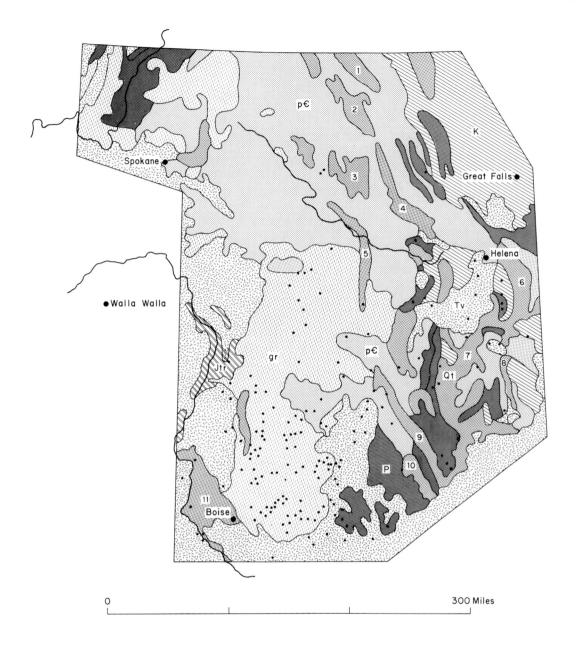

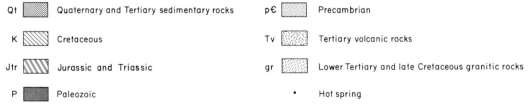

Qt		Quaternary and Tertiary sedimentary rocks	p€		Precambrian
K		Cretaceous	Tv		Tertiary volcanic rocks
Jtr		Jurassic and Triassic	gr		Lower Tertiary and late Cretaceous granitic rocks
P		Paleozoic	•		Hot spring

Figure 14.40 *Geologic map of the northern Rocky Mountains in Idaho, Montana, and Washington. Abundant hot springs in the granitic rock of the Idaho batholith suggest that the lower part of the massive intrusion is still warm. North of the batholith are Precambrian sedimentary rocks; to the east are complexly mixed rocks of many ages, mostly in block mountains. The faulted basins that separate the mountains are numbered as follows: (1) Flathead Valley; (2) Kalispell Valley; (3) Missoula Valley; (4) Flint Creek and Deer Lodge valleys; (5) Bitterroot Valley; (6) Gallatin Valley; (7) Jefferson and Beaverhead valleys; (8) Madison Valley; (9) Lemhi Valley; (10) Pahsimeroi Valley; and (11) lower part of Snake River Valley. [Geology from the National Atlas of the United States of America; hot springs from U.S.G.S. Water-Supply Paper 679-B.]*

Figure 14.41 *View across the Salmon River Mountains, part of the dissected plateau formed by the Idaho Batholith. Ridge tops are accordant; valleys are deep, about 3,000 feet. (From U.S.G.S.)*

In southern British Columbia is the Nelson batholith, and several smaller batholithic intrusions in northern Idaho serve as links between the Idaho, Loon Lake, Colville, and Nelson batholiths. This complex of batholiths is an eastward extension of the more extensive Pacific Coast system of batholiths. Discussion of the details of the structure and age relationships is deferred to Chapter 18.

About 90 percent of the mountains in Montana drain to the Pacific, and the continental divide is crowded against the easternmost part of the province. Not only have the streams draining west eroded farther into the province than those draining east, but they have incised themselves much more deeply. The valley at Kalispell (Fig. 14.40) is about 1,000 feet lower than the Great Plains 50 miles to the east.

Seismic Activity

A seismically active belt extends northward along the western edge of the Middle Rocky Mountains and across the southeastern part of the Northern Rocky Mountains to the Great Plains. This belt has been the site of numerous small earthquakes and two of severe intensity, one in 1925 and another in 1959. Elsewhere in the Rocky Mountains earthquakes have been few and of only moderate intensity.

The epicenter of the 1925 earthquake was east of Helena, Montana. It was felt over an area of 300,000 square miles. Property damage was extensive in an area of 600 square miles. Both the Northern Pacific and the Chicago, Milwaukee, and St. Paul Railroads were blocked by rocks falling from cliffs and by debris from buildings. A rock slide closed one tunnel.

The epicenter of the 1959 earthquake was near the head of the Madison River at Hebgen Lake. Tilting of the lake bed displaced the lake northward (Fig. 14.42). Jetties, docks, and beaches along the north shore were submerged; those along the south shore were stranded high above water. Water in the lake surged back and forth violently, sweeping over the dam that forms the lake and threatening to destroy it. South of the lake a fault more than 10 miles long formed an escarpment 10 feet high facing the lake. Buildings were broken in two, and highways crossed by the fault were displaced 10 feet. In the gorge where the Madison River crosses the Madison Range, a

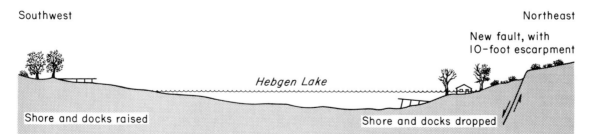

Southwest   Northeast

New fault, with 10-foot escarpment

Hebgen Lake

Shore and docks raised   Shore and docks dropped

Figure 14.42 *Cross section through Hebgen Lake, Montana, shows the tilting and faulting that accompanied the 1959 earthquake. The lake basin was tilted about 20 feet to the northeast along a new fault. A 10-foot escarpment parallels the northeast shore.*

Figure 14.43 *Columbia Icefields at the head of the Athabasca River, Alberta. [Courtesy Alberta Government Photographic Services.]*

tremendous rock slide—38 million cubic yards of rock—broke from the south wall of the gorge, swept across the river, buried about 25 persons camping in the canyon, moved 400 feet up the north wall, and dammed the river, producing what has been named Earthquake Lake.

PLEISTOCENE GLACIATIONS

As in other northern provinces, or in those of high altitude, Pleistocene glaciation played an important part in developing the terrain of the Northern Rocky Mountains. Yet despite the northerly location and high altitude the glaciers extended only about 100 miles into the United States.

A complex of alpine glaciers formed in the Canadian Rockies (Fig. 14.43), and ice pushed southward along the trenches into the United States. The structural origin of the trenches is obscured because they have been gouged by glacial ice and mantled with glacial drift. South of the limit shown in Figure 4.9, only isolated glaciers existed on the highest mountains.

The alpine glaciers pushed down valley to altitudes of about 4,500 feet on the Great Plains and, in the western valleys, to about 3,500 feet, which is a thousand feet lower than the level reached by the ice in the Middle Rockies and 2,500 feet lower than the level reached in the Southern Rockies. This northward decrease in the level reached by the Pleistocene mountain glaciers roughly parallels the northward decrease in altitude of the climatic and vegetational zones.

One important effect of the glaciations was the damming of Clarks Fork by the ice (Fig. 14.44), which formed Pleistocene Lake Missoula. This lake, fed by meltwaters from the ice advancing southward from British Columbia, repeatedly overflowed by way of a gap leading to Spokane. Each time the lake overflowed its ice dam, it

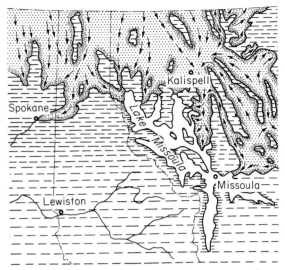

Figure 14.44 *Southern limit of the main mass of late Pleistocene ice in the Northern Rocky Mountains. The ice extended to Clarks Fork near the western border of Montana and dammed it, forming Lake Missoula, which was more than 200 miles long and about 1,000 feet deep; some estimates indicate a depth of 2,000 feet. [From U.S.G.S.]*

quickly cut a deep channel through the ice that emptied the lake in catastrophic floods. These floods swept across the Columbia Plateau lavas, creating the scablands and developing fantastically large canyons, waterfalls (now dry), and other features of flood erosion (see Chapter 17).

CLIMATE, VEGETATION, AND SOILS

Despite the northerly latitudes and the high altitudes, the climates in these northern Rocky Mountains are surprisingly mild. In the mountain valleys in Montana January temperatures average as much as 10 degrees warmer and summer temperatures average about 5 to 10 degrees cooler than on the Great Plains just east of the mountains. The average length of the growing season is about the same, roughly 120 days. Temperatures and snowfall, of course, vary greatly with altitude.

Winds are from the west, and much of the moisture is precipitated where the air masses cross the Bitterroot Mountains (Fig. 14.45). Consequently, most of the Montana portion of the Rocky Mountains is semiarid, with less than 20 inches of rainfall.

As a result of this aridity, the forests on mountains directly east of the Bitterroot Mountains commonly are restricted to the northern and eastern slopes. Although the south-facing and west-facing slopes receive comparable precipitation, they are hotter; they support few trees and are covered with shrubs and grasses.

One of the principal kinds of forests in these Northern Rocky Mountains (Fig. 14.46) consists of larch, a deciduous conifer, and western white pine. This is in the rift-faulted Precambrian blocks along the Purcell and Rocky Mountain trenches. In these forests, areas that have been burned or cut are invaded first by larch. This is followed by white pine, which may crowd out the larch but in turn may be crowded out by hemlock, red cedar, and lowland white fir. The

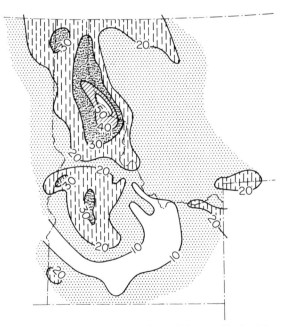

Figure 14.45 *Average annual precipitation (inches) in the Northern Rocky Mountains. In much of the low country the growing season lasts 120 days, about the same as on the Great Plains just east of the mountains. [From U.S.D.A.]*

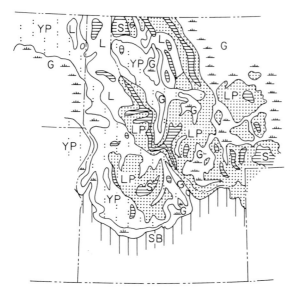

Figure 14.46 *Distribution of the major kinds of vegetation in the Northern Rocky Mountains. SB, sagebrush; G, grasses; YP, yellow pine and Douglas fir; LP, lodgepole pine; L, larch and western pine; S, spruce and fir. [From U.S.D.A.]*

larch is used for ship timber and boxes; white pine for cabinet work and boxes.

Yellow pine and Douglas fir form commercial stands in the Salmon River Mountains, Okanogan Highlands, and along Clarks Fork. Lodgepole pine grows principally in the basins and ranges in the southeastern part of the Northern Rocky Mountains, but it spreads northward and westward too. The high mountain forests of spruce and fir are accessible only with difficulty and are not yet as valuable commercially as the other types.

Forests in Montana and Idaho alone are estimated to contain more than 175 billion board feet of commercial timber. The annual cut is roughly equal to the annual growth, about 2 billion board feet, which is about 5 percent of the United States production.

The most recent estimates of timber reserves are practically double those made in the 1940's. This apparent increase in reserves has been attributed to earlier tendencies to underestimate, but may also result in part from the lowering of specifications for timber grades brought about by changes in the economic situation. The problem of estimating reserves is not peculiar to forestry; comparisons of early and recent estimates of mineral reserves show a similar apparent increase. For the entire Rocky Mountain region in the United States, the relative extent of different kinds of timber are roughly as follows:

> Yellow pine and Douglas fir, about 35 percent;
> Lodgepole pine, about 25 percent;
> Larch and Western White pine, slightly more than 20 percent;
> Spruce and fir, slightly less than 20 percent.

Surficial deposits in the Northern Rocky Mountains are like those in the Middle and Southern Rocky Mountains except for their greater extent and better development of gravel fans. Soils on the fans and valley floors, most of which are below about 2,000 feet, are classed as Chestnut Soils. The upper layers are gravelly loam; at depths of $1\frac{1}{2}$ to 3 feet is a layer of lime-cemented gravel underlain by porous gravel. These soils support sagebrush and bunch grass. Above 2,000 feet, under coniferous forest, the soils are Gray-Brown Podzols.

ROCKY MOUNTAIN SPOTTED FEVER

Rocky Mountain spotted fever is a typhus-like disease caused by an extremely minute microorganism that may be related to bacteria but which is placed in a separate class with the viruses. The pathogen is carried by ticks, in particular the wood tick. Adult ticks may live 4 years or more. The female lays the eggs in soil, where they remain through the winter. In spring the eggs produce larvae which require blood from small animals; the larvae then change to nymphs, in which stage they pass through the next winter, becoming adults during the second spring. The pathogen can be carried by the tick in the larval, nymphal, or adult stage. Man becomes infected by the blood-sucking adult tick. The tick burrows into a blood vessel, passing the pathogen to the person via a fluid that the tick injects to keep the blood from coagulating.

The disease can be treated with antibiotics, and there is a vaccine that protects against it. The best treatment, however, is prevention; during tick season, the outdoorsman would do well to search his clothing and body regularly for ticks. A tick that has bored into a person or pet may be smeared with grease, oil, vaseline, or butter. This causes suffocation, and the tick may even detach itself, or can be removed. Rocky Mountain spotted fever is widespread, but is most prevalent in the Northern Rocky Mountains and the south-eastern United States.

Water

The Middle and Southern Rocky Mountains collect and store the water carried by the rivers crossing the semiarid lands that lie east and west of the mountains. These semiarid lands, ten times the area of the mountains, comprise most of that half of the United States that is west of the 100th meridian. It would be difficult to overestimate the importance of the Rocky Mountains in the water economy of this vast region.

For example, three states wholly outside the Rocky Mountain System—Arizona, California, and Nevada—have been concerned with apportionment of Colorado River water. A decision by the Supreme Court of the United States in 1963 assumed the Colorado River flow to be 15 million acre feet per year and reserved half of this to Colorado, Wyoming, Utah, and New Mexico. The other half was divided 4.4 million acre feet to California, 2.8 million acre feet to Arizona, 0.3 million acre feet to Nevada, and legal provisions were added for dividing surpluses and deficits. Clearly, a major problem in the Rocky Mountains concerns methods for estimating annual and seasonal runoff of surface water and recharge of ground water aquifers.

The runoff chiefly is the water stored as snow and ice in the mountains during the winter. Addi-

tional runoff is provided by groundwater, which in turn is partly recharged by the melting of snow and ice. Still other runoff comes from rain storms.

Runoff from melting snow and ice is estimated by measuring the snow pack at selected places in the mountains. To a considerable degree this also measures the duration and discharge of springs where groundwater feeds streams. By anticipating the runoff from the snow melt it has been possible to predict when maximum flood heights would occur, and some disasters have thus been averted. In 1954 the anticipation by 6 weeks of a flood along the Kootenai River served to hold flood damage to a minimum. Similarly, a deficiency of runoff can be anticipated and steps taken to minimize the effect of drought, such as transferring livestock to other range, maturing crops early, and developing emergency water sources, as was done in Utah in 1934.

An extensive system of reservoirs has been constructed along the rivers in and near the foot of the Rocky Mountains, and the stored water is used for municipal supplies, irrigation, hydroelectric power, flood control, and recreation. Municipal supplies require no more than about 5 percent of all the stored water; most of the rest is lost by evaporation or consumed for irrigation.

The quality of water obtained from the mountains is generally excellent. The total dissolved solids in surface water commonly measures about 100 ppm; the groundwater commonly contains about twice that. Most of the water is bicarbonate water with a carbonate : sulfate ratio of 10 : 1 or more; the hardness of the water is high, considering the low content of dissolved solids. In a few valleys the quality of the surface water has been affected by industrial developments, which have introduced pollutants; further pollution can be expected unless rigorous controls are adopted.

Most water in the Wyoming and Bighorn Basins contains about 500 ppm of dissolved solids, but the carbonate : sulfate ratio is nearly 1 : 1. The hardness of these waters is due more to the presence of calcium and magnesium than to the carbonate (Tables 5.1, 5.2).

Minerals

The Rocky Mountains contain important deposits of metallic minerals, principally copper, gold, silver, lead, zinc, molybdenum, antimony, and tungsten. Mining began there in the the 1850's as a backwash from the California gold rushes. The first deposits to attract attention were the placer gold deposits discovered at the foot of some of the mountains. Tracing these deposits, by gold pan, to their sources led to the discovery of the lode deposits. The history of mineral exploration and mining in the Rocky Mountains forms a major part of the history of the settlement and development of the West. Some of the discoveries involved trespass on lands reserved for the Indians, but when mineral deposits were found it was convenient to draft new treaties that took the mineral lands out of the reservation, as happened in the Black Hills (p. 369). The same thing happened in Idaho in 1861, when gold was discovered on lands that had been reserved for the Nez Percé in 1855, and in the San Juan Mountains, which had been granted to the Ute Indians by treaty in 1868.

Most deposits of the metallic minerals are in the mountainous areas; the Wyoming Basin is important for its petroleum, natural gas, oil-shale, coal, and salines. Of the more than 300 mining districts that have been productive in the mountain provinces, the following are some of the best known (see also Fig. 14.47):

SOUTHERN ROCKY MOUNTAINS

CRIPPLE CREEK, COLORADO. Gold telluride (calaverite) occurs in veins with quartz, fluorite, barite, and calcite in Tertiary volcanic rocks and intrusive Precambrian rocks. Some mines reach to depths of 3,000 feet.

COLORADO MINERAL BELT. This belt includes the mining districts at Breckenridge, Montezuma, Silver Plume, Georgetown, Idaho Springs, Central City, Caribou, Nederland, Ward, Gold Hill, and Jamestown. One of the first mineral-

producing areas in the Rocky Mountains, the belt was discovered after placer gold was found in the Denver area; the gold-bearing gravels were traced upstream to their sources in the mountains. Ores of lead, silver, gold, and tungsten occur in veins that fill faults and fissures.

LEADVILLE, COLORADO. Most ores are mined from flat veins (*blanket veins*) along or near the contacts between sills and dikes of igneous rocks that intrude Paleozoic formations. The principal minerals are sulfides of lead (galena), zinc (sphalerite), and iron (pyrite). Near-surface veins are weathered and oxidized, and the ore minerals in these veins include carbonates of lead (cerrusite) and zinc (smithsonite).

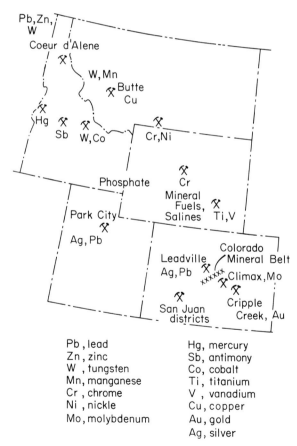

Pb , lead	Hg, mercury
Zn , zinc	Sb, antimony
W , tungsten	Co, cobalt
Mn, manganese	Ti, titanium
Cr , chrome	V , vanadium
Ni , nickle	Cu, copper
Mo, molybdenum	Au, gold
	Ag, silver

Figure 14.47 *Some of the principal mining districts in the Rocky Mountains.*

SAN JUAN REGION, COLORADO. The deposits are in vertical or near-vertical veins (*fissure veins*) and blanket veins in Paleozoic and Mesozoic formations intruded by Tertiary granite rocks, and fissure veins in younger Tertiary volcanic rocks. Since the 1870's major production has been gold, silver, copper, lead, and zinc. Ore minerals are copper- and gold-bearing iron oxide (magnetite), iron sulfide (pyrite), gold telluride (calaverite), silver telluride (sylvanite), zinc sulfide (sphalerite), lead sulfide (galena), and copper-iron sulfide (chalcopyrite).

CLIMAX, COLORADO. Molybdenite occurs in criss-crossing veinlets in a mass of Precambrian rocks cut by intrusions. The veinlets are so closely spaced that the entire mass is mined. Since the middle 1920's, this district has supplied a major part of the world's molybdenum production.

MIDDLE ROCKY MOUNTAINS

PARK CITY AND ALTA DISTRICTS, *Utah*. Ores in these districts yield mainly silver and lead with some copper, zinc, and gold. The ores are in late Paleozoic and early Mesozoic formations that have been fractured and altered by Tertiary granitic intrusions. The principal ore minerals are galena, sphalerite, tetrahedrite (copper, antimony, and sulfur), and chalcopyrite.

UTAH-IDAHO PHOSPHATE REGION. Extensive phosphate deposits occur in southeastern Idaho, northeastern Utah, and western Wyoming. This region has become one of the major phosphate-producing areas, and there remain vast reserves of phosphatic shale in a late Paleozoic formation.

NORTHERN ROCKY MOUNTAINS

BUTTE, MONTANA. One of the world's most productive, this district contains some mines that are a mile deep. The mines produce mostly copper, silver, gold, zinc, and some lead. The ores occur in closely spaced veins cutting a granitic rock and consist mostly of sulfide minerals except within about 400 feet of the surface, where the minerals have been oxidized and leached. Gold and silver remain in the leached zone, but copper has been transported downward and has enriched the deposits with secondary minerals derived from the leaching. The district began as a gold placer camp about 1864.

COEUR D'ALENE DISTRICT, IDAHO. Lead, silver, and zinc are produced from altered Precambrian sedimentary formations near the northern edge of the Idaho batholith.

FOOTHILL BELT OF CANADIAN ROCKIES. Oil and gas production near Calgary and south; coal production as far north as Athabasca River.

SOUTHERN BRITISH COLUMBIA. Numerous mines between the Columbia River and Rocky Mountain Trench produce lead, silver, zinc, and gold.

Fur Trade and Early Trails West

Furs, skins, and hides were the first resources of the Rocky Mountains to be exploited, and trapping and trading began almost immediately after the return of the Lewis and Clark expedition in 1806. The trade that developed became a major business, and it involved Indians as well as whites. It was the fur traders who applied the name Rocky Mountains to the ranges along the continental divide.

Several companies engaged in the business, and their names are prominent in western United States history—the Missouri Fur Company, which had trappers in the Middle Rocky Mountains and Wyoming Basin by 1809; the Pacific Fur Company, which under the direction of John Jacob Astor explored the Columbia River and founded Astoria in 1811; the American Fur Company, another Astor enterprise, which had operated around the Great Lakes as early as 1808 and sent trappers west in the 1820's; and the Rocky Mountain Fur Company and its predecessors, which were active as early as 1832. The northern

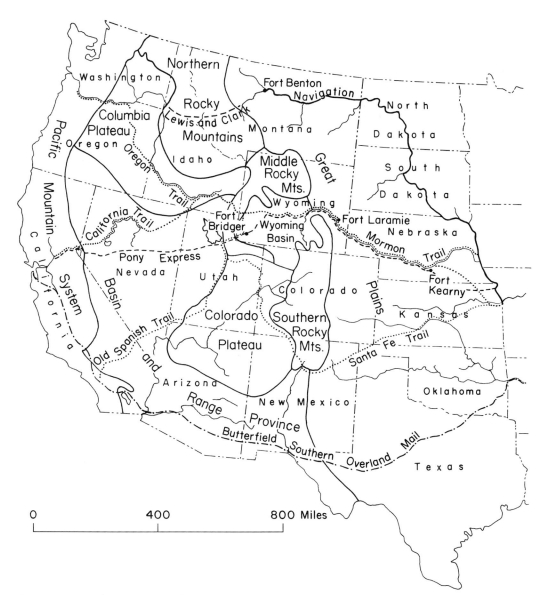

Figure 14.48 *Early trails across the western United States and their relationship to the physiographic provinces.*

areas were visited by the rival British companies, notably the Hudson Bay Company.

The magnitude of the business can perhaps be visualized from the size of the herds of buffalo that once roamed the plains. Clark, in 1806, estimated 80,000 head in one of the herds that he saw. Miles City, on the Great Plains in Montana,

is said to have shipped as many as 250,000 buffalo hides in one season. Yet the principal objective was beaver. By 1845, however, the fur-bearing animals had been greatly reduced in numbers, and the fur trade soon declined.

The routes for travel through the Rocky Mountains were found by the fur traders, and these routes became the trails to Utah, Oregon, California, and Santa Fe (Fig. 14.48). But the trip west was a long one, so much so that some easterners questioned the wisdom of acquiring land in the far west. A senator, arguing in 1825 against acquisition of the Oregon Territory, asked (U.S. Geol. Survey Bull. 612, p. 7):

> But is this Territory of Oregon ever to become a State, a member of the Union? Never. . . . The distance that a Member of Congress of this State of Oregon would be obliged to travel in coming to the seat of government and returning home would be 9,300 miles. . . . If he should travel at the rate of 30 miles per day, it would require 306 days. Allow for Sundays, 44, it would amount to 350 days. This would allow the Member a fortnight to rest himself at Washington before he should commence his journey home.

Some Resource Problems

The land, forest, water, and mineral resources of the Rocky Mountains have become major factors in the national economy, and there is great pressure to utilize them for developing local industries, as has been done elsewhere in the country. But the Rocky Mountains are physiographically different from the rest of the country, and their resources should be utilized in a different way.

For example, it probably is not possible to have factories with smoke-belching chimneys in a Rocky Mountain valley without developing smog and dumping industrial wastes into the streams. These problems are akin to some in the Appalachian Mountains, but with major differences. Industry is well established in the Appalachians, and the population now dependent on that industry is considerable. In the Rocky Mountains, industrial development has barely started, the population is sparse, and most of that great area is still public land, as much the property of those living elsewhere as of those living in it.

Assuming that our population continues to increase, there will be growing need for the water and the recreational facilities that the mountains provide. It would seem better for the nation that these mountains be industrialized as little as possible, limiting development to the production of raw materials and reserving the land primarily for recreational uses and watershed protection. We can have grazing *without* overgrazing. We can have mineral prospecting and mining *without* scarring the landscape or polluting the streams; lumbering *without* destroying the forests; highways *without* having the roadside marred by "No Trespass" signs, billboards, automobile morgues, and unkempt wayside stands. Those of us who share in the ownership of the vast, magnificent Rocky Mountains must insist that they not be spoiled by being placed in the hands of local interests, but that they be preserved and developed to serve the greater national interest. The two interests need not conflict, but the national interest should be the more far-sighted.

References

Alden, W. C., 1953, Physiography and glacial geology of western Montana and adjacent areas: U.S. Geol. Survey Prof. Paper 231.

Atwood, W. W., 1909, Glaciation of the Uinta and Wasatch Mountains: U.S. Geol. Survey Prof. Paper 61.

Atwood, W. W., and Mather, K. F., 1932, Physiography and Quaternary geology of the San Juan Mountains, Colo.: U.S. Geol. Survey Prof. Paper 166.

Bradley, W. H., 1936, Geomorphology of the north flank of the Uinta Mountains: U.S. Geol. Survey Prof. Paper 185-I.

Childs, O. E., and Beebe, B. W. (ed.), 1963, Backbone of the Americas—A symposium: American Assoc. Petrol. Geol., Mem. 2.

Chittenden, H. M., 1902, History of the American fur trade of the far west: reprinted by Academic Reprints, Stanford, 2 vols.

Douglas, R. J. W., and others, 1968, Geology of western Canada, *in* Geology and economic minerals of Canada: Geological Survey of Canada, pp. 366–488.

Fryxell, F. M., 1938, The Tetons: Berkeley, Univ. Calif. Press.

Hansen, W. R., 1965, Geology of the Flaming Gorge area—Utah, Colorado, Wyoming: U.S. Geol. Survey Prof. Paper 490.

Larsen, E. S., Jr., and Cross, Whitman, 1956, Geology and petrology of the San Juan Region, southwestern Colorado: U.S. Geol. Survey Prof. Paper 258.

Lovering, T. S., and Goddard, E. N., 1951, Geology and ore deposits of the Front Range, Colorado: U.S. Geol. Survey Prof. Paper 223.

McCrossan, R. G., and Glaister, R. P. (ed.), 1964, Geological history of western Canada: Alberta Soc. Petrol. Geol.

Preston, R. J., Jr., 1940, Rocky Mountain trees: Iowa State Univ. Press; reprinted 1968 by Dover Publications.

Ross, C. P., 1960, Geology of Glacier National Park and the Flathead region, northwestern Montana: U.S. Geol. Survey Prof. Paper 296.

U.S. Geological Survey, 1959, The Hebgen Lake, Montana, earthquake of August 17, 1959: U.S. Geol. Survey Prof. Paper 435.

Vanderwilt, J. W., and others, 1947, Mineral resources of Colorado: Denver, Colo. Min. Res. Board.

The Colorado Plateau is characterized by canyons. This one, Unaweep Canyon, near Grand Junction, Colorado, is unusual, for it is the abandoned valley of the Colorado and Gunnison Rivers, cut when those streams flowed southward across the Uncompahgre Plateau, an anticlinal uplift exposing Precambrian rocks. These rocks, exposed in the lower half of the canyon walls, are overlain by Mesozoic formations.

15

....

COLORADO PLATEAU—
LAND OF COLORS AND CANYONS

The Colorado Plateau (Fig. 15.1), covering about 130,000 square miles between the Rocky Mountain and Basin and Range provinces, is easily the most colorful part of the United States. It is not just desert; it is Painted Desert with spectacular canyons, high plateaus, volcanic mountains, sand deserts, and shale deserts with grotesque badlands. And along the canyon walls are cross sections of geologic history. These geologic features may be seen in more than a dozen national parks and monuments created expressly for the purpose. It is an area of unusual archeological interest too, and another dozen national parks and monuments protect some of the better known examples of the cliff dwellings and other ruins of the prehistoric Anasazi, ancestors of the Pueblo Indians. Those of special geomorphic, geologic, or archeologic interest are indicated in Figure 15.1. In addition to these there are national recreational areas along the Colorado River at Lake Mead, which extends into the lower part of Grand Canyon, and at Lake Powell in Glen Canyon. Two national monuments of historical interest are El Moro (Inscription Rock) and Pipe Spring.

Outstanding physiographic features of the Colorado Plateau are its:

1. Structural geology, which consists of
    A. extensive areas of nearly horizontal sedimentary formations;
    B. structural upwarps that form striking topographic features;
    C. igneous structures, including some large central-type volcanoes, numerous cinder cones and volcanic necks, high lava-capped plateaus and mesas, and dome mountains caused by intrusion of stocks and laccoliths;
    D. and the whole plateau uplifted as much as 3 miles since the Cretaceous.

2. Great altitude; the general plateau surface is higher than 5,000 feet; some plateaus and several peaks reach to 11,000 feet.

3. Drainage system, which is deeply incised and forming steep-walled canyons, most of which have brilliantly colored walls.

4. Aridity and shortage of water.

5. Extensive areas of bare rock.

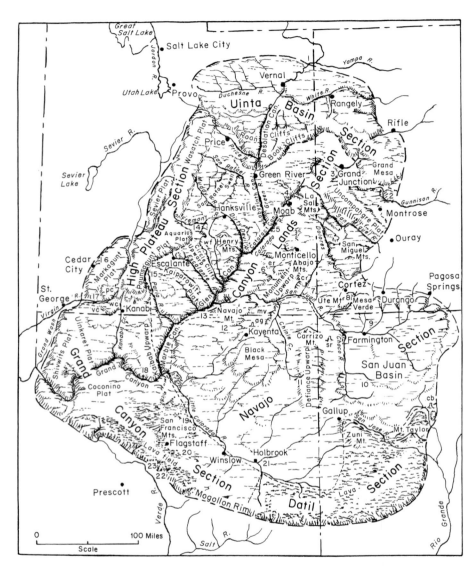

Figure 15.1 *Physiographic map of the Colorado Plateau.*

National Parks and Monuments

1. Dinosaur Nat. Mon.
2. Black Canyon of the Gunnison Nat. Mon.
3. Colorado Nat. Mon.
4. Arches Nat. Mon.
5. Canyonlands Nat. Park
6. Natural Bridges Nat. Mon.
7. Hovenweep Nat. Mon.
8. Mesaverde Nat. Park
9. Aztec Ruins Nat. Mon.
10. Chaco Canyon Nat. Mon.
11. Canyon de Chelly Nat. Mon.
12. Navajo Nat. Mon. (Betatakin and Kiet Seel)
13. Rainbow Bridge Nat. Mon.
14. Capitol Reef Nat. Mon.
15. Bryce Canyon Nat. Park
16. Cedar Breaks Nat. Mon.
17. Zion Nat. Park
18. Grand Canyon Nat. Park
19. Wupatki and Sunset Crater Nat. Mons.
20. Walnut Canyon Nat. Mon.
21. Petrified Forest and Painted Desert Nat. Mon.
22. Montezuma Castle Nat. Mon.
23. Tuzigoot Nat. Mon.

Escarpments at South End of High Plateaus

pc   Pink Cliffs
wc   White Cliffs
vc   Vermilion Cliffs

Other Prominent Features

wf   Waterpocket Fold
er   Elk Ridge
cr   Comb Ridge
mv   Monument Valley
ag   Agathla Peak
sr   Shiprock
cb   Cabezon Peak

6. Sparse vegetation and sparse population (about a half million, an average of about four persons per square mile).

7. Brightly colored and highly varied desert scenery.

Structural Framework

The Colorado Plateau consists of the part of the continent's stable platform that lies west of the Southern Rocky Mountains; the western edge of the Plateau coincides with the ancient flexure along which the platform ended and the basement rocks plunged downward under the late Precambrian, Paleozoic, and early Mesozoic geosynclines from which the Basin and Range Province evolved. The Plateau marks the western edge of the Upper Cretaceous trough, or geosyncline, whose axis was along the site of the Southern Rocky Mountains; the western shore of the Upper Cretaceous sea was at or near the western edge of what is now the Plateau.

This major break in the continental structure is not difficult to see. Grand Canyon, for example, exposes the entire section, only 4,000 feet thick, of Cambrian to Permian epicontinental marine formations that were deposited on the platform (Fig. 15.2). To considerable degree the thickness of this section is typical of the platform all the way eastward to the Appalachian Plateau. Yet just to the west, in the broken-up Basin and Range Province, these formations greatly thicken, and so do the late Precambrian and early Mesozoic formations. At Death Valley the late Precambrian, Paleozoic, and Triassic formations total almost 100,000 feet in thickness.

From the Appalachian geosyncline westward to the Colorado Plateau, the Precambrian basement rocks have formed a stable platform for the Paleozoic and younger formations. This platform was interrupted only by the trough of the Upper Cretaceous geosyncline that crossed it obliquely at the site of the Southern Rocky Mountains. The platform had been stable for about 500 million

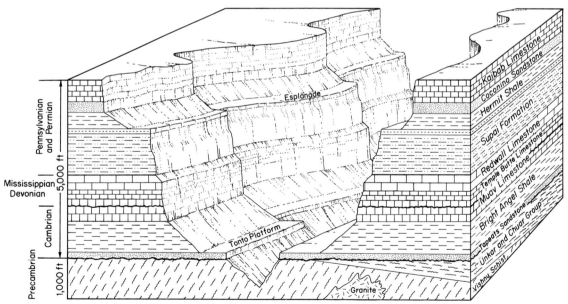

Figure 15.2   *Block diagram illustrating the formations in the Grand Canyon. Vertical scale exaggerated; the canyon is a mile deep, and the rims are 10 to 12 miles apart. In addition to the downcutting of about a mile at the canyon, a thickness of about 2 miles of Triassic, Jurassic, and Cretaceous rocks have been eroded from above the Kaibab Limestone.*

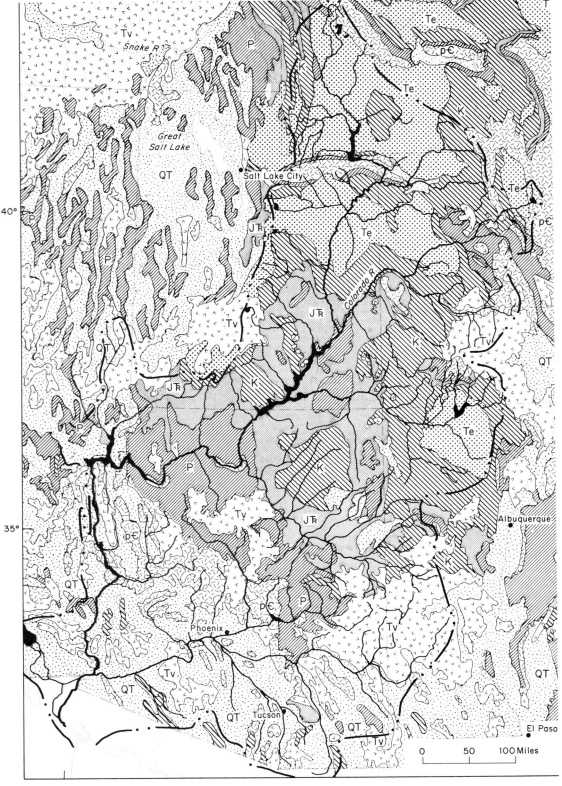

Tv

Snake R.

Great
Salt Lake

QT

Salt Lake City

P

K

Te

pC

Te

Te

pC

40°

P

P

JR̶

U

Te

JR̶

Colorado R.

QT

Tv

K

QT

Tv

QT

P

JR̶

K

K

Te

P

P

JR̶

Albuquerque

35°

pC

Tv

K

QT

QT

pC

P

Tv

Phoenix

Tv

QT

Tv

QT

Tucson

QT

El Paso

QT

Tv

0   50   100 Miles

115°

years during the Paleozoic and early Mesozoic. Moreover, the Precambrian rocks exposed in the Colorado Rockies include extensive areas of granitic batholiths like those on the Canadian Shield, whereas under the Colorado Plateau the Precambrian includes a high percentage of geosynclinal sedimentary rocks, as in the Northern and Middle Rockies. Apparently during the late Precambrian a northerly trending trough or geosyncline developed at about 45 degrees to those that had formed on the Shield and around it. The east edge of this old geosyncline extended southward across what is now the Colorado Plateau; its eastern boundary may have played a part in controlling the position of the boundary between the Colorado Plateau and the Southern Rocky Mountains.

The Colorado Plateau has the general structure of a stack of saucers, tilted toward the northeast. Curiously, the plateau adjoins the Rocky Mountains along the low northeastern part of the structure. As a consequence of this structure, young rocks (Tertiary) crop out in basins on the north and east sides of the plateau, and old rocks (Paleozoic and Precambrian) crop out along the southwest rim (Fig. 15.3), overlooking the much lower Basin and Range Province. The formations are listed and described in Table 15.1.

Although the major structural elements that define the Colorado Plateau are inherited from ancient Cretaceous and older continental structures, the Plateau itself is the product of Cenozoic earth movements and igneous activity. The Plateau and the Southern Rocky Mountains are the high part of a tremendous Cenozoic arch—a geanticline that extends from the central United States westward nearly to the Pacific Coast. The Great Basin, a block-faulted area, is the collapsed western flank of the arch. The Colorado Plateau is a mildly faulted segment of this flank that remains structurally attached to the Rocky Mountain geanticline. This Cenozoic history is summarized on pages 440 to 445. We look next at the structural units that were developed during that history and at the topographic effects that have been produced by the accompanying erosion.

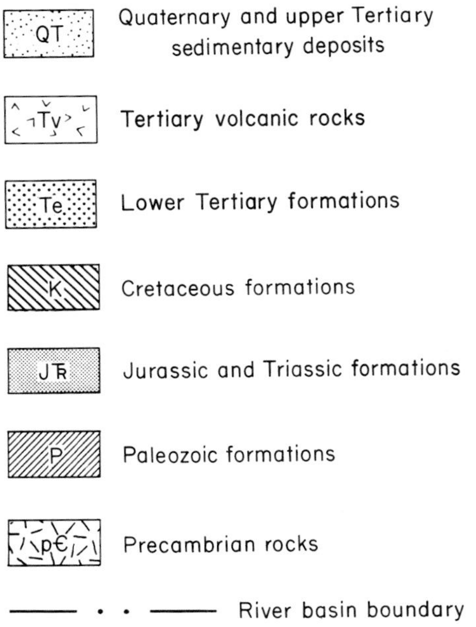

QT   Quaternary and upper Tertiary sedimentary deposits

Tv   Tertiary volcanic rocks

Te   Lower Tertiary formations

K   Cretaceous formations

JŦ   Jurassic and Triassic formations

P   Paleozoic formations

pЄ   Precambrian rocks

—— · · ——   River basin boundary

Figure 15.3 *Geologic map of the Colorado Plateau.* [*From U.S.G.S. Prof. Paper 669.*]

Table 15.1

Geological Formations on the Colorado Plateau

System	Series	Lithology and Thickness
Tertiary	Holocene	Alluvium, colluvium, sand dunes; mostly less than 50 feet thick.
	Pleistocene	Glacial moraines, outwash, terrace gravels, alluvium; periglacial deposits, avalanche deposits; mostly less than 100 feet thick.
	Pliocene	Bidahochi Formation (Little Colorado River valley): playa and fluviatile deposits of calcareous clay and sand with tuff and interbedded lavas, 400 feet thick; *conglomerate in Castle Valley,* at foot of LaSal Mountains, 1,000 feet; Bishop Conglomerate and Browns Park Formation: north side of Uinta Basin, fluviatile deposits (Miocene or Pliocene), 1,500 feet thick; Sevier River and Parunuweap Formations, in High Plateaus Section, conglomerate and lacustrine or alluvial silt mixed with volcanics. 200 feet; age uncertain; *gravel on Kaibito Plateau,* Navajo Reservation, may be late Miocene, gravel deposited by ancestral San Juan River, 50 feet; Datil Formation, in the Datil Section, interbedded volcanics and sandstone 2,000 feet thick, age uncertain.
	Miocene	Muddy Creek Formation: fill in ancient canyon at Peach Springs, Arizona, interbedded fluviatile sediments and volcanics, dated at 18.3 million years, more than 100 feet at that locality but much thicker westward in Basin and Range Province; Brian Head Formation, in High Plateaus, limestone, volcanic ash, and volcanic agglomerate, 500 to 1,000 feet thick, age uncertain; Chuska Sandstone, eastern Navajo Reservation, 700 feet, age uncertain. Gravel on Mogollon Rim.
	Oligocene	Duchesne River Formation: Uinta Basin, playa deposits grading to fanglomerate, may be late Eocene.
	Eocene	In Uinta Basin: Uinta Formation: fluviatile deposit 1,000 feet thick. Bridger Formation: fluviatile deposit like Uinta, 1,000 feet. Green River Formation: oil shale and other lake deposits, 3,000 feet. Colton and Wasatch Formations: fluviatile deposits that grade laterally to lake beds of the Green River formation, 2,000 feet.
	Paleocene	Flagstaff Limestone, Wasatch Plateau, lacustrine limestone, 1,000 feet thick; Tuscher Formation and Ohio Creek Conglomerate, conglomeratic sandstone in eastern part of Uinta Basin, 400 feet thick; upper part of North Horn Formation (see below); Nacimiento Formation in San Juan Basin, fluviatile beds of brown conglomerate interbedded with red and gray shale, 1,000 feet.
Upper Cretaceous		In High Plateaus and Western Uinta Basin: North Horn Formation: lower part (see above): fluviatile and lacustrine deposits of shale, sandstone, conglomerate, and limestone, 2,000 feet. In San Juan Basin: Animas Formation: fluviatile conglomerate overlain by shale and sandstone, high proportion of volcanic material, 2,000 feet. Ojo Alamo Sandstone: cross-bedded conglomeratic sandstone, 100 feet. McDermott Formation: lenticular shale, sandstone, and conglomerate containing much volcanic debris, 300 feet.

System	Series	Lithology and Thickness
Upper Cretaceous (*Continued*)		In San Juan Basin: (*Continued*) Fruitland Formation and Kirtland Shale: deltaic deposits of sandstone, shale, and coal, increasing shale upward, 1,300 feet. Pictured Cliffs Sandstone: littoral sandstone, 250 feet. Lewis Shale: mostly marine shale, 1,500 feet, thins southward by basal beds grading to Mesaverde Formation. Mesaverde Formation: deltaic, littoral, and coastal plain deposits of sandstone, shale, and coal, 1,000 feet, upper and lower parts grade northward to marine shale. Mancos Shale: marine shale, 2,000 feet thick in north, thins southward by intertonguing with Mesaverde Formation. Dakota Sandstone: littoral sand 100 feet thick. In Canyonlands Section, High Plateaus, and Uinta Basin: Mesaverde Formation: deltaic, littoral, and coastal plain deposits, 2,500 feet thick, grades eastward to marine shale. Mancos Shale: mostly marine shale but includes tongues of deltaic and littoral deposits that grade eastward to marine shale, 4,000 feet thick. Dakota Sandstone: littoral sandstone, 100 feet thick.
Jurassic		Morrison Formation: fluviatile deposits of clay and shale, variegated, sandstone, conglomerate, and locally gypsum and limestone, 500 feet. San Rafael Group: Summerville Formation: evenly bedded, reddish brown sandstone and sandy shale, 250 feet, estuarine (?). Curtis Formation: marine, evenly bedded gray sandstone and shaly sandstone, 200 feet. Entrada Sandstone: thick bedded, cross-bedded buff sandstone, thinner bedded and earthy northward, 500 feet. Carmel Formation: thin-bedded red sandstone, shaly sandstone and shale, thin limestone and locally thick beds of gypsum, 500 feet.
Triassic		Glen Canyon Group: Navajo Sandstone: tan to light gray, massive cross bedded sandstone, eolian (?), 600 feet; may be Jurassic. Kayenta Formation: sandstone and shaly sandstone, minor amounts of red shale and green clay, fluviatile (?), 300 feet. Wingate Sandstone: massive, cross-bedded, cliff-forming sandstone, 300 feet. Chinle Formation: variegated sandstone, shale, limestone, and conglomerate, well-bedded but beds lenticular, 500 feet. Shinarump Conglomerate: cross-bedded sandstone and conglomerate, much petrified wood, 100 feet. Moenkopi Formation: red and buff sandstone and red shale, some limestone, abundant ripple marks, 600 feet.

(Continued)

Table 15.1 (Continued)

System	Series	Lithology and Thickness	
		Southwest sequence	Northeast sequence
Permian		Kaibab Limestone: white buff and light gray limestone and limy sandstone, 800 feet. Coconino Sandstone: light colored sandstone, 300 feet. Hermit Shale: red beds, 400 feet.	Cutler Formation: bright red sandstone and lighter red or pink grit and conglomerate alternating with sandy shale or sandy limestone, generally about 1,000 feet.
Pennsylvanian		Supai Formation: red sandstone and shale, 1,000 feet; upper part Permian.	Rico Formation: dark maroon sandstone, and conglomerate alternating with sandy shale and sandy limestone, 300 feet. Hermosa Formation: shale, limestone, evaporites, generally about 2,500 feet but in salt anticlines thickens to 14,000 feet. Molas Formation: red calcareous shale, limestone, 100 feet.
Mississippian		Redwall Limestone: bluish gray crystalline limestone, 600 feet.	Pre-Pennsylvanian Paleozoic rocks, 2,000 feet.
Devonian		Temple Butte Limestone: purple and cream colored limestone and sandstone, 100 feet.	
Cambrian		Tonto Group: Muav Limestone: mottled limestone, 450 feet. Bright Angel Shale: marine shale, 375 feet. Tapeats Sandstone: brown slabby crossbedded sandstone, 275 feet.	
Precambrian		Grand Canyon Series: Chuar Group, sandstone, shale, basalt, minor limestone, 5,000 feet. Unkar Group, quartzite, shale, limestone, conglomerate, 2,500 feet. - - - - - Unconformity - - - - - Vishnu Series, schist, quartzite, and metavolcanics, 25,000 feet.	

STRUCTURAL AND TOPOGRAPHIC UNITS

GRAND CANYON SECTION.   The high southwest part of the Colorado Plateau is called the Grand Canyon Section. The oldest rocks there are complexly deformed Precambrian formations. These are overlain by about 4,000 feet of Paleozoic formations. The Precambrian and Paleozoic formations (Table 15.1) are exposed in the Grand Canyon (Fig. 15.2) and along the southwestern edge of the Plateau. The topography of Grand Canyon is illustrated in Figures 15.4 and 15.5.

The western part of the Grand Canyon Section is divided into a series of blocks by the northerly trending Grand Wash, Hurricane, and Sevier faults (Fig. 15.6). Along each of these faults

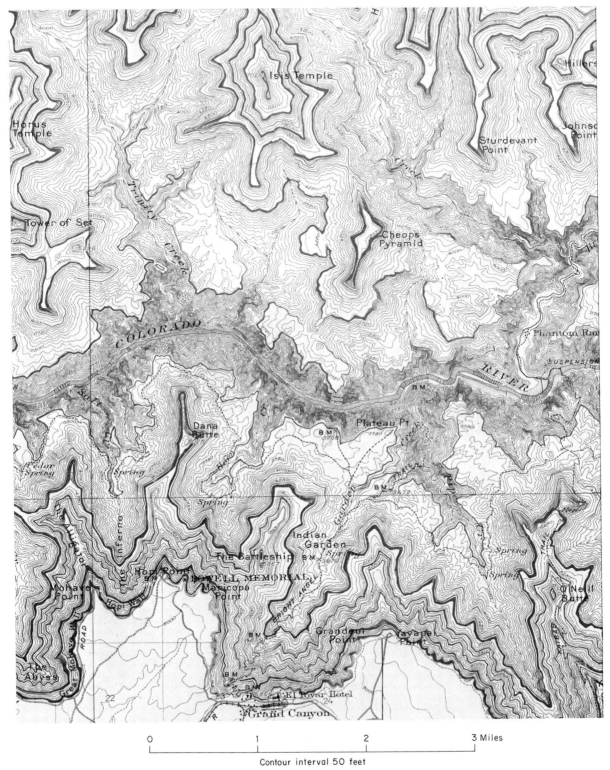

Figure 15.4 *Topographic map of Grand Canyon.* [*From U.S.G.S.*]

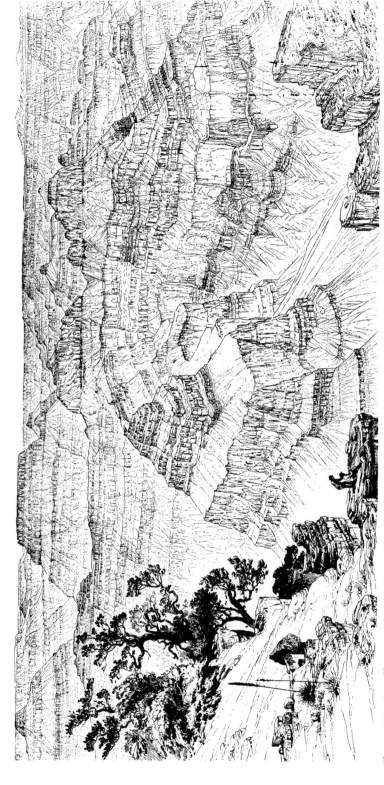

Figure 15.5 *Powell's antecedent Colorado River in Grand Canyon, as seen from Point Sublime, looking east. The sketch is by W. H. Holmes, whose artistic ability for drawing landscapes realistically and showing their geology accurately was appreciated and encouraged by Powell, who provided opportunity for Holmes to use his great talent.*

the blocks to the west have dropped downward relative to the blocks to the east. This structure is transitional between the Colorado Plateau, which in general is little faulted, and the much-faulted Basin and Range Province.

In general, the formations in these fault blocks and those farther east dip northeastward, but about 75 miles from the rim, the northeast dip is interrupted by the Kaibab Plateau (Fig. 15.6) Upwarp, one of several upwarps that characterize the Colorado Plateau. These upwarps are asymmetric anticlines with gently dipping west flanks and steeply dipping east flanks. They represent a mile or more of vertical structural displacement. These folds may be the surface expression of faults deep in the crust.

About a third of the Grand Canyon Section is covered by Tertiary and Quaternary lavas from the San Francisco Mountain volcanic field and from some isolated volcanoes north of Grand Canyon. These lavas unconformably overlie Paleozoic and later formations, which had been faulted, folded, tilted northeastward, and exposed by erosion long before the earliest lavas (Tertiary) were erupted. Enough time elapsed after the deformation and before the eruptions to permit the removal by erosion of thousands of feet of Mesozoic formations that once extended across this part of the Colorado Plateau.

The ancestral river had already cut deeply into Grand Canyon by the time the first lavas were erupted, and some of the later lavas poured down the walls and into the bottom of Grand Canyon. Radiometric dating of the lavas indicates that the Grand Canyon was within 50 feet of its present depth about 1.5 million years ago.

One of the most recent eruptions on the Colorado Plateau took place in about the middle of the eleventh century A.D. at Sunset Crater, east of San Francisco Mountain. Volcanic cinders from the eruption buried a Pueblo Indian village very much in the way that Vesuvius buried Pompeii.

DATIL SECTION.   The south rim of the Colorado Plateau in New Mexico and eastern Arizona is known as the Datil Section (Fig. 15.1), an exten-

sive area covered by thick lavas. The earliest lavas there probably are of middle Tertiary age, but the volcanism continued intermittently into Holocene times. One Late Pleistocene or Holocene lava flow in the San Jose Valley is so fresh that it still looks hot. Santa Fe Railroad conductors tell yarns about being on the last train through before the lava covered the tracks!

Principal structural features in this section are the upwarp at the Zuni Mountains, the large central-type volcano at Mount Taylor, the numerous smaller volcanic centers and volcanic necks (Fig. 15.7) around it, and the extensive lava-covered mesas and valleys to the south. The lavas at Mount Taylor, among the oldest in this section, unconformably overlap the tilted formations on the southern flank of the San Juan Basin. The folding, much older than the volcanism, is early Tertiary in age.

Erosion of the high mesas has, in some places, exposed natural cross sections of the lavas, the volcanic cones, and the feeder vents (Fig. 15.7,A). Elsewhere, continued erosion has completely exposed and isolated the plugs that filled the vents to form volcanic necks (Fig. 15.7,B). The surface onto which these lavas erupted was about 2,000 feet higher than the present surface; thus the surface there has been lowered that much by erosion since the earliest volcanism in that area.

These lavas extend southward into the Basin and Range Province, and consequently that boundary of the Colorado Plateau is arbitrary. Along the eastern edge of the Datil Section, the Basin and Range Province extends northward along the Rio Grande depression to the Southern Rocky Mountains, and the boundary between this depression and the uplifted Colorado Plateau is sharply defined by the westernmost faults of the depression.

NAVAJO SECTION.   North of the Grand Canyon and Datil Sections is a structural depression referred to as the Navajo Section, about half of which is in the Navajo Indian Reservation. The deepest part of the depression, the San Juan Basin, forms an embayment in the southwest

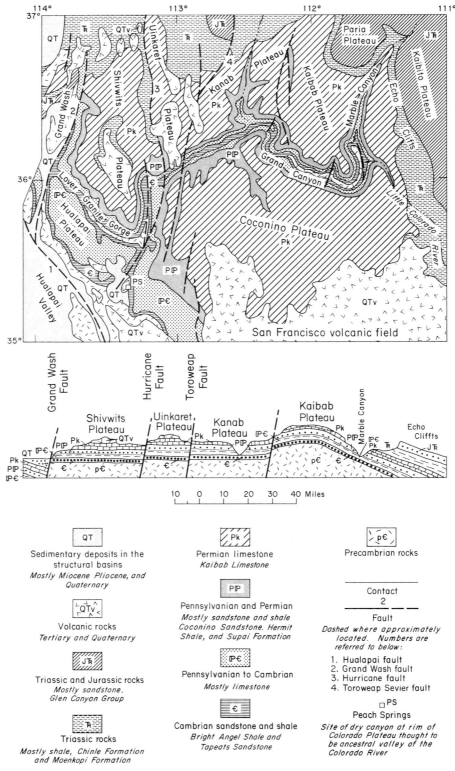

Figure 15.6 Geologic map and cross section at Grand Canyon. [From *U.S.G.S. Prof. Paper 669*.]

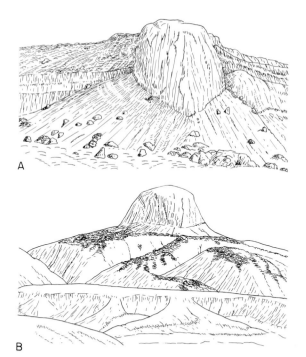

A

B

Figure 15.7 *(A) Natural cross section of a volcano and of the vent feeding it near Mount Taylor, New Mexico. The half-exposed plug in the vent is 500 feet in diameter and about 1,000 feet high. A cone 400 feet high was built at the surface, and lava flows extend $7\frac{1}{2}$ miles from it. (B) Volcanic neck (Cabezon Peak), also near Mount Taylor. This neck is 2,000 feet in diameter. The benches below are formed by Cretaceous sedimentary formations. The volcanic cone and lava flows have been completely removed by erosion from this volcanic center, and only the plug remains.*

corner of the Southern Rocky Mountains. Structurally, this basin is more than two miles lower than the rim of the Plateau at the southern edge of the Grand Canyon and Datil sections (Fig. 15.16). Paleozoic rocks form the rim of the Plateau, but under the San Juan Basin these same rocks are overlain by more than 5,000 feet of Mesozoic formations and about 5,000 feet of Tertiary formations. The Defiance Upwarp separates the San Juan Basin from a shallower basin that lies to the west under Black Mesa.

The Navajo Section is characterized by broad flats on the shaly formations separated by low cuestas where the more resistant sandstones crop out. Colorful Triassic formations produce the Painted Desert, which extends far northwest of the national monument. In the San Juan Basin, the Tertiary and Cretaceous formations resemble a series of stacked saucers that get progressively smaller toward the top and form cuestas that face outward. Erosion of volcanic formations in the Navajo Section has produced numerous volcanic necks, like the frequently illustrated ones at Shiprock, New Mexico, and Agathla Peak in Monument Valley (see also Fig. 15.7).

CANYON LANDS SECTION. North of the Navajo Section is the Canyon Lands Section of the Colorado Plateau, where, as the name implies, canyons are the dominant feature. This section has four large upwarps: the Uncompahgre Upwarp, the Monument Upwarp, the Circle Cliffs Upwarp (Fig. 15.8), and the San Rafael Swell (Figs. 15.15, 15.16). Between the upwarps are structural basins; there is a big one under the Henry Mountains and another big one between the Kaibab and Circle Cliffs upwarps. Very little faulting is associated with these structural upwarps and basins or with those in the Navajo Section, except in the northwest-trending basin south of and parallel to the Uncompahgre Upwarp. This basin differs from the others in that it contains thick deposits of salt. In the course of the deformation that produced the basin, the salt deposits, of late Paleozoic age, were squeezed around like taffy, and the overlying formations were folded in northwest-trending anticlines and synclines that became faulted.

The canyons in the Canyon Lands Section have been carved mostly in sandstones in the upper Paleozoic and lower Mesozoic formations (Fig. 15.9). Jurassic and Cretaceous formations include thick shale units that form badlands arranged in belts between cuestas and benches formed by resistant beds of sandstone.

Where the resistant, canyon-forming sandstones are turned up steeply along the flanks of the asymmetric, anticlinal upwarps, they form great ridges generally known as hogbacks but referred to locally as "reefs." These form nearly

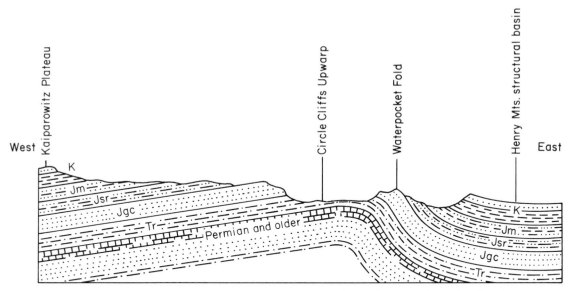

Figure 15.8 *Cross section of the Circle Cliffs Upwarp.* **Tr,** *Triassic formations;* **Jgc,** *Jurassic, Glen Canyon Group, cliff-forming sandstone formations;* **Jsr,** *San Rafael Group;* **Jm,** *Jurassic, Morrison formation;* **K,** *Cretaceous formations. The structural relief is about 6,500 feet; length of section approximately 40 miles.*

impassable barriers, as do the canyons. The thick sandstones erode into characteristic dome-like forms; Capitol Reef (a national monument) was so-named because its domes are suggestive of the dome on the capitol building in Washington, D.C. Back from the rims of canyons, nearly flat-lying sandstone formations form bare, knobby rock surfaces deeply dissected by narrow, rock-walled gulches or small canyons. Friable and earthy sandstones that extend across broad areas form a sandy desert with dunes.

Other distinctive structural features of the Canyon Lands Section are the laccolithic Henry Mountains (Fig. 15.10), La Sal Mountains, and others. These are structural domes produced by the forceful upward injection of molten igneous rock, which formed stocks. The injection of these plug-like masses domed the overlying rocks and those adjacent to them. As the stocks rose higher, they widened; the wider the stock, the steeper and higher the dome (Fig. 15.11). Where the stocks encountered weak shales, the magma was squeezed sideways into them to form laccoliths. The overlying beds were folded into anticlines

radiating from the stocks. Some stocks may have reached the surface and erupted (Fig. 15.12).

During the glacial stages the higher mountains lay within the zone of intensive frost action (p. 461) and are consequently rounded. The lower parts of the mountains faithfully reflect the geologic structure. The contrast reflects the difference in the processes of erosion. Still other erosion forms distinctive of the Canyon Lands Section are the pediments, alcoves, arches, bridges, spires, and pedestal rocks, described later.

UINTA BASIN SECTION. North of the Canyon Lands Section is the Uinta Basin Section, which forms an embayment between the Middle and Southern Rocky Mountains. This, the deepest part of the structural bowl, contains the uppermost of the saucers and is structurally four miles lower than the southwest rim of the Grand Canyon Section (Fig. 15.16). Paleozoic formations under the basin are overlain by about two miles of Mesozoic and another two miles of Tertiary formations. Figure 15.13 shows the formations

Figure 15.9 *Canyons of the Colorado River, where it crosses an anticline in late Paleozoic and Mesozoic red beds at Canyonlands National Park.*

rising gently southward (to the Canyon Lands Section) and rising steeply northward onto the southern flank of the Uinta Mountains. The Tertiary formations in the Uinta Basin form broad hilly benches that slope north, and form the south-facing escarpment known as the Roan

Cliffs (Fig. 15.11). Cretaceous formations, rising southward from under the Tertiary formations, form the south-facing Book Cliffs, an escarpment that is about 2,000 feet high and extends about 100 miles across the southern edge of the basin, overlooking the Canyon Lands.

HIGH PLATEAUS SECTION. At the western edge of the Colorado Plateau is the High Plateaus Section, which consists of northerly trending fault blocks (Fig. 15.14). Many are lava capped and form plateaus, all of which are higher than 9,000 feet and some as high as 11,000 feet. Mesozoic and Tertiary formations underlie the lavas. The plateaus are separated by wide, flat-bottomed structural valleys (grabens) trending north to south. The colorful Tertiary sedimentary formations have been eroded into badlands at Bryce Canyon National Park and Cedar Breaks National Monument. Zion Canyon, at the southern end of the High Plateaus, is similar to many of the canyons in the Canyon Lands Section.

The High Plateaus end southward in three great escarpments that face southward and overlook the Grand Canyon Section. The northern escarpment, the Pink Cliffs, is formed by Tertiary formations (Fig. 15.3). The middle escarpment, the White Cliffs, is formed by upper Mesozoic

Figure 15.10 *Diagrammatic view of the Henry Mountains region, Utah. Mounts Ellen, Pennell, Hillers, Holmes, and Ellsworth are dome mountains produced by intrusion of stocks and laccoliths into the sedimentary formations. In the foreground are the canyons of the Colorado River and its tributary, the Dirty Devil. In the distance is the Waterpocket Fold.*

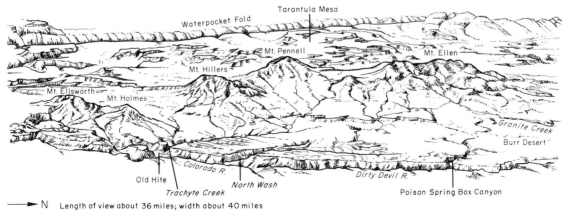

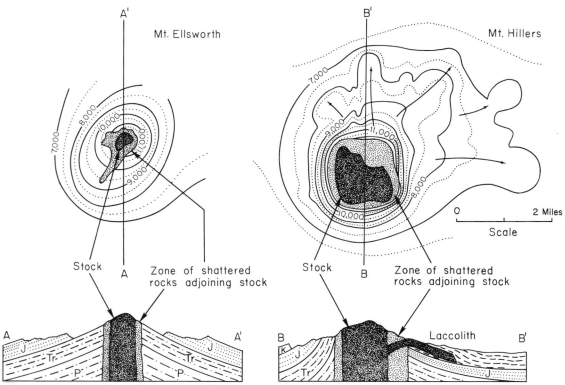

Figure 15.11 *Structure contour maps and diagrammatic cross sections of two laccolithic mountains on the Colorado Plateau. The sedimentary formations (P, Permian; Tr, Triassic; J, Jurrassic, and K, Cretaceous) are turned up steeply around wide stocks like the one at Mt. Hillers (15.9), and where these stocks reached the thick shale formations (K), tongue-like intrusions (laccoliths) were injected laterally between the sedimentary beds, forming anticlines whose axes (represented by arrows) radiate from the stock. Smaller stocks, like the one at Mt. Ellsworth (Fig. 15.9), caused less doming, less shattering of the wall rocks, and produced few, if any, laccoliths.*

sandstone. The southern escarpment, the Vermillion Cliffs, is formed by lower Mesozoic formations. This is known as the Grand Staircase of Utah.

This Section is a structurally high rim of the Colorado Plateau, but it differs from the high southwestern and southern rims in having been raised by faulting (Fig. 15.14). Deformation began in late Cretaceous time and continued intermittently throughout Tertiary and Quaternary time. The recency of some of the faulting, together with the fact that the western edge of the High Plateaus coincides with an active seismic belt (Fig. 2.17), suggests that these fault blocks may still be moving.

CENOZOIC STRUCTURAL AND
IGNEOUS HISTORY

In late Cretaceous time, the Colorado Plateau had become a coastal plain, and the Cretaceous sea lay to the east (Fig. 15.15,A). In Paleocene time, folding, which had started much earlier in western Utah, progressed eastward to the area that was to become the Colorado Plateau. Flagstaff Lake (Fig. 15.15,B) developed at the site of the High Plateaus, and the deposits that accumulated in that lake truncate the folded beds of the Circle Cliffs Upwarp. The upwarp had formed in early Paleocene time, and probably the other upwarps began forming early in the Tertiary,

Figure 15.12   *Structural dome at Mount Ellsworth, one of the laccolithic Henry Mountains. Most of the dark rock at the center of the mountain is intrusive igneous rock that has domed the Mesozoic formations. In the distance can be seen one of the big monoclinal folds, the Waterpocket Fold, and on the skyline are the High Plateaus. [Photograph by Fairchild Aerial Surveys for the U.S.G.S.]*

Figure 15.13   *Cross section of the Uinta Basin, showing thick Tertiary formations overlying the Cretaceous and older strata. Toward the south, the Tertiary formations are conformable with one another, but against the steep flank of the Uinta Mountain uplift, unconformities between these formations record a series of structural movements that began in latest Cretaceous time and did not end until sometime after the Oligocene—that is, in middle or late Tertiary time. General uplift of the Uinta Basin, along with the rest of the Colorado Plateau and Rocky Mountains, occurred in late Cenozoic time and may be continuing.*

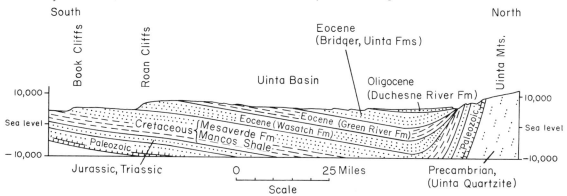

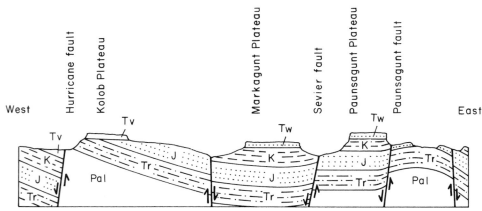

Figure 15.14   *The central part of the High Plateaus Section. The High Plateaus are between the Hurricane and Paunsagunt faults. To the east is the Canyon Lands Section (figure shows north end of the Kaibab Upwarp); to the west is the Basin and Range Province.* **Pal**, *Paleozoic;* **Tr**, *Triassic;* **J**, *Jurassic;* **K**, *Cretaceous;* **Tv**, *Tertiary volcanics;* **Tw**, *Tertiary sedimentary formations. Length of section, about 65 miles.*

including the Uinta Mountains, San Rafael Swell, Kaibab, Monument, Defiance, and Zuni upwarps, and folds at the Zuni Mountains, San Juan Mountains, and Uncompahgre Plateau (Fig. 15.15,B). On many or most of these folds movement was later renewed.

At the San Juan Mountains a pile of volcanic eruptives, probably accompanied by upwarping, had started accumulating in latest Cretaceous time and continued to grow during the Paleocene. This highland shed volcanic sediments (Animas Formation, Table 15.1) southward onto the Plateau in the San Juan Basin. Paleocene formations in the Uinta Basin indicate that mountains were forming to the east and to the west of that basin, and also at the Uinta Mountains. Probably there were mountains of this age in central Arizona that shed sediments northward onto the area of the Plateau. The site of the Colorado Plateau in Paleocene time was a basin, or series of basins, surrounded by newly formed mountains draining into it. The Plateau area must have been at or near sea level.

During the Eocene the downwarping that had formed Flagstaff Lake spread eastward to the foot of the Rocky Mountains at the site of the Uinta Basin, and there was downwarping in Wyoming.

This produced Green River Lake (Fig. 15.15,C), in which the tremendous oil shale deposits of the Green River Formation accumulated. Some environmentalists wish this had never happened because of the expected impact on the landscape when production begins. The catchment area of the Colorado Plateau part of the Green River Lake probably was about the same in kind and extent as that of Flagstaff Lake.

Green River Lake came to an end in middle Eocene time, in part perhaps because of uplift and in part because of filling by the 3,000 feet of sediments that had been deposited (Table 15.1). Thereafter, streams deposited some additional thousands of feet of sediments, forming the Bridger and Uinta formations in what is now the northern part of the Plateau. In late Eocene time, uplift of the Uinta Mountains was renewed along an anticline that marks the northwestward extension of the Uncompahgre Upwarp, and probably at the San Rafael Swell. Whether this renewed uplift was synchronous with deposition of the Uinta and Bridger formations is not clear, but the uplift did deform the Green River Formation. The Nacimiento Upwarp in New Mexico was elevated at this time too, and presumably there was uplift at the other folds also.

During the Oligocene the Uinta Basin became a playa, and thereafter the basins began to overflow. At about the same time, block faulting began in the Basin and Range Province south and west of the Plateau; the Basin and Range Province had previously been mountainous and was undergoing erosion while the Colorado Plateau was receiving sediments. Beginning in the Oligocene, conditions reversed. The Colorado Plateau is without Oligocene deposits (except for the Duchesne River Formation in the Uinta Basin) and almost without Miocene deposits. Presumably during Oligocene time the Plateau began being uplifted relative to the basins in the Basin and Range Province, and in places exterior drainage could commence. During Miocene time, however, the Colorado River had been ponded in the Rocky Mountains at such structural basins as the Middle Park, State Bridge syncline, and the basin of the Gunnison River east of the Black Canyon, as already noted (p. 390). Any overflow from those basins probably became contained in the much larger structural basins downstream on the Colorado Plateau—the Henry Mountains structural basin and that of the Kaiparowitz Plateau. The Green River did not cross the Uinta Mountains and join the Colorado River system until after the Browns Park Formation had been deposited—that is, in early Pliocene time. The drainage from the north continued to be ponded.

By middle Miocene time the Colorado Plateau had been uplifted to within 3,500 feet of its present structural height (Fig. 15.16). The evidence for this is the dry canyon that breaks through the southwest rim of the Plateau at Peach Springs, Arizona. The Precambrian rocks forming the floor of that canyon at an altitude of about 3,500 feet must have been above sea level when the canyon was eroded. The sediments partly filling that canyon include volcanic ash dated as 18 million years old (middle Miocene). These relationships also show that the stretch of Grand Canyon just upstream from there had already been eroded to half its present depth by that time.

The stream that did this cutting presumably was the Little Colorado River. Through Miocene time (Fig. 15.15,D) the Little Colorado River collected drainage from mountains in central Arizona that still were attached to the Colorado Plateau. Gravels from these mountains are strewn northward from the present south rim of the Plateau all the way to the Little Colorado. In late Miocene or early Pliocene time those mountains were detached from the Plateau, faulted downward, and the drainage northward from them disrupted. The valley of the Little Colorado River is unique among those on the Plateau in that it is very broad and open with long parallel tributaries from the south and north. It even looks old compared to the young-looking canyons of the streams draining from the north. According to this interpretation, the first half of the canyon cutting at Grand Canyon was by the Little Colorado River before it lost its water sources by downfaulting and breaking away of the highlands south of the Plateau. The later erosion at Grand Canyon occurred when the drainage from the north reached there.

During the middle Miocene, extrusive volcanics began accumulating around the west, south, and east sides of the Plateau, and the laccolithic intrusions, or at least some of them (e.g., La Sal Mountains), formed at this time; some apparently were intruded earlier. At the time the laccolithic mountains formed, the Colorado Plateau was still covered by the Cretaceous formations—a landscape of badlands and mesas. This is indicated by the fact that all the laccolithic mountains intrude the Cretaceous formations, even those on uplifts where the Cretaceous away from the mountains has been removed by erosion. The colorful painted deserts formed by the Jurassic and Triassic were largely restricted to the valley of the Little Colorado River. This provides a measure of the amount of erosion that has occurred on the Plateau since the middle Miocene—namely, a volume about equal to the Cretaceous formations that once extended southward from the Book Cliffs in Utah to Black Mesa in Arizona.

Other evidence of the former Cretaceous landscape is revealed by outcrops along the west rim of the canyon of the north-flowing Dolores

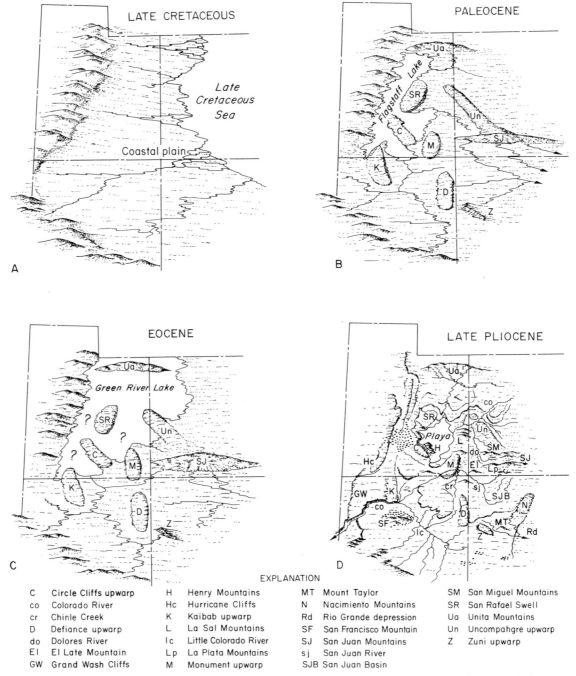

Figure 15.15 (A) *The Colorado Plateau area in Late Cretaceous time. The area was part of a coastal plain that extended eastward from the foot of mountains in central Arizona and central Utah. The edge of the Late Cretaceous Sea was to the east in Colorado. (B) The Colorado Plateau area in Paleocene time. Flagstaff Lake was formed along the western edge of the Plateau area. (C) The Colorado Plateau area in Eocene time.*

(Continued)

EXPLANATION

C	Circle Cliffs upwarp	H	Henry Mountains	MT	Mount Taylor	SM	San Miguel Mountains
co	Colorado River	Hc	Hurricane Cliffs	N	Nacimiento Mountains	SR	San Rafael Swell
cr	Chinle Creek	K	Kaibab upwarp	Rd	Rio Grande depression	Ua	Unita Mountains
D	Defiance upwarp	L	La Sal Mountains	SF	San Francisco Mountain	Un	Uncompahgre upwarp
do	Dolores River	lc	Little Colorado River	SJ	San Juan Mountains	Z	Zuni upwarp
El	El Late Mountain	Lp	La Plata Mountains	sj	San Juan River		
GW	Grand Wash Cliffs	M	Monument upwarp	SJB	San Juan Basin		

River about west of the San Miguel Mountains (Fig. 15.17). Gravel was deposited on the rim before the river had cut into its canyon, but now the rim drains southwestward to the San Juan River! Clearly, when the Dolores River was at that position, there were hills of Cretaceous shale and sandstone west of there that kept the Dolores flowing north, otherwise it too would have turned southwestward to the San Juan. South of there the Dolores River makes a sharp bend northward as if it originally flowed southwestward to join the San Juan. Such a course could have been interrupted and the river turned northward by the laccolithic intrusions at El Late (Ute) Mountain. Volcanism was extensive during the Pliocene. Evidence that it continued into the Holocene is provided by the fresh-looking lavas in valley bottoms and the eruptives around Sunset Crater.

The compositions of the igneous rocks at the big volcanoes and at the laccolithic mountains average about the same, but for reasons that are obscure the compositions changed in quite different ways as the igneous activity progressed. At the laccolithic mountains, the silica-poor dioritic rocks (Table 2.3) were first to form and the silica-rich rhyolitic rocks the last, whereas at the volcanoes, the silica-rich rocks were the first to form and the silica-poor rocks the last. Perhaps when the volcanic vents reached the surface, pressure was relieved sufficiently to cause the molten magma to froth off the silica rich fraction, like the froth on newly opened ale.

The distribution of igneous centers on the Colorado Plateau (Fig. 15.18) illustrates some important principles about the occurrence of volcanic and other centers of igneous activity. One would suppose that volcanoes would be concentrated where there is much faulting, but instead of being concentrated in the highly faulted neighboring parts of the Basin and Range Province, the volcanic centers are concentrated on the uplifted but otherwise little-deformed rocks of the plateau. Mount Taylor and the basaltic volcanoes around it are on the plateau 25 miles or more west of the highly faulted west edge of the Rio Grande depression. No two of the laccolithic mountains have the same structural setting. The Henry Mountains intruded a structural basin, the Abajos intruded an uplift, the LaSals intruded salt anticlines, Ute Mountain intruded an area of gentle and uniform dips, the La Plata Mountains are at the base of the big uplift at the San Juan Mountains, and the San Miguel laccoliths are high on the flank of that uplift.

Likewise, we have seen that the volcanic field in the Raton Mesa Section of the Great Plains is as extensive or more so than the volcanics in the nearby parts of the Southern Rocky Mountains. The laccolithic intrusions in Montana are numerous on the little-disturbed Missouri Plateau rather than in the nearby much-deformed Rocky Mountains.

Yet from the perspective of outer space it is to be noted that Cenozoic volcanism was concentrated in the western part of the continent; evidence of Cenozoic igneous activity is almost wholly lacking in the central and eastern parts. This distribution tells us something about the structure of the continent, but what? The message is not clear.

Seismic Activity

The Colorado Plateau, which is even now a highly elevated block of the crust, may still be rising, as is suggested by the fact that its edges

---

Downwarping of the Uinta Basin produced the Green River lake, which covered most of the northern part of the Plateau area. Most of the uplifts, like the San Rafael Swell, probably stood higher than the lake and shed sediments into it. (D) The Colorado Plateau in late Pliocene time. The laccolithic mountains were formed, and there were eruptions at Mount Taylor, San Francisco Mountain, and at the volcanic pile in the central High Plateaus. The main streams were already superimposed on the uplifts, but these streams shifted monoclinally in adjustment to the intrusions. The valley of the Little Colorado River was in about the same position and about as deep as it is today. A considerable canyon had already formed in Grand Canyon. [After U.S.G.S.]

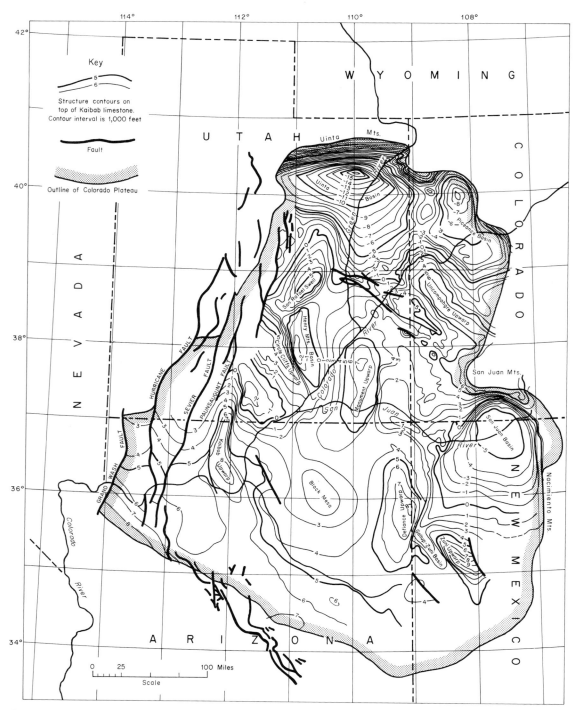

Figure 15.16 *Structure contour map of the Colorado Plateau. Contours drawn on a geologic formation reveal its changes in altitude and dip and bring out the locations, shapes, and dimensions of folds and faults. [After U.S.G.S. Prof. Paper 669.]*

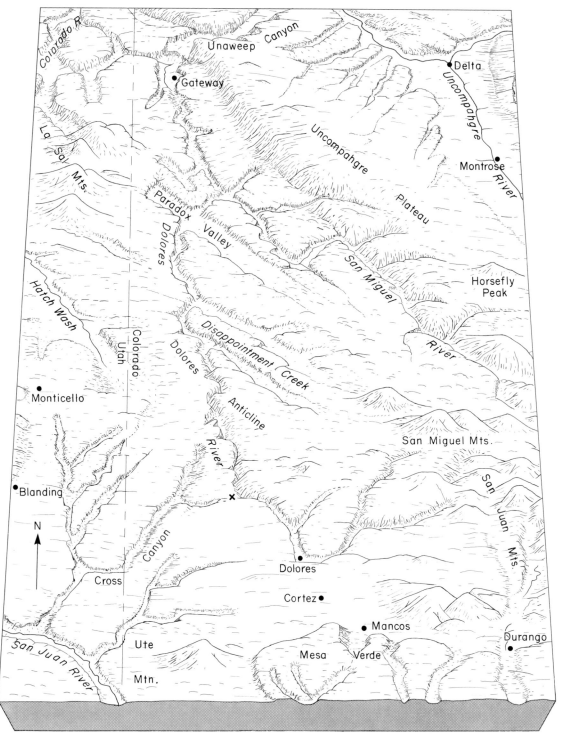

Figure 15.17 *Dolores River drainage basin. The headwaters of the river probably originally flowed southwest from Dolores to join the San Juan River; they may have been turned northward by the early Miocene doming at Ute Mountain. A gravel deposit (N) on the west rim of the north-trending canyon forms the divide between Dolores River and drainage to the southwest. When the Dolores River deposited the gravel, there must have been hills of Cretaceous shale at the site of Cross Canyon and the canyons northwest of it. [After U.S.G.S. Prof. Paper 669.]*

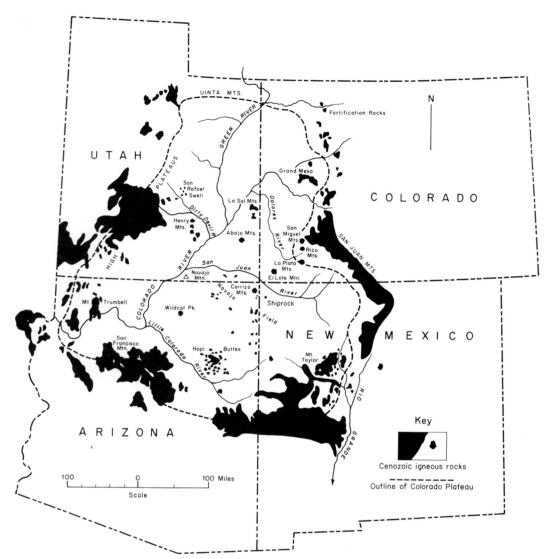

Figure 15.18 *Map illustrating distribution of Cenozoic igneous rocks on the Colorado Plateau. The laccolithic mountains are mostly in the interior of the plateau; the volcanic centers are mostly around the edges of the plateau.*

coincide with belts of more than average seismic activity. The epicenters of major earthquakes are alined along the western edge of the plateau, and along its southeastern edge in the Rio Grande Valley. Epicenters of minor earthquakes also are alined along the southwestern edge of the plateau and along its north and east sides, where it joins the Rocky Mountains. The foci of only a few minor earthquakes have been recorded from beneath the Plateau.

This seismic record, together with the geology, suggests that not much differential earth movement is occurring within the Plateau, but that the province as a whole may be moving with respect to its neighbors, and is perhaps being tilted to the northeast. In accord with this interpretation is the fact that the area around Lake Mead, which lies southwest of the Plateau, is undergoing measurable southwestward tilt at the present time (p. 507).

Earthquakes have been most frequent and most intense along the west edge of the Plateau, which, as already noted, is the western boundary of the stable continental platform and the eastern boundary of the cordilleran geosynclines.

Meteor Crater

Meteor Crater is a hole in the ground about a mile in diameter and more than 500 feet deep in nearly horizontal Permian and Triassic formations. The rim rock is Triassic Moenkopi Formation, and below that, in succession, is Kaibab Limestone, Toroweap Sandstone, and Coconino Sandstone. The bottom of the pit is concealed by Quaternary, Wisconsinan and younger alluvial and lacustrine deposits. The wall rocks, very much shattered, are thrust upward and blanketed by debris thrown out of the crater. This debris is layered in the reverse order of the formations in the wall; blocks of Coconino and Toroweap rest on blocks of Kaibab Limestone, which rests on the Triassic. This feature was long thought to be the result of a volcanic explosion, but opinion today is that it was formed by impact of a meteorite. No fragments of the meteorite have been found, but there has been found a strange mineral, *coesite,* which has the same composition as quartz but a different crystal structure attributed to physical shock, such as meteorite impact.

The origin of meteorites must remain a mystery as long as we do not know the origin of the earth, the moon, and the other planets. Nevertheless, meteorites can help provide understanding of our earth if the simplistic view is taken that they represent the last fragments that were moving through space and that were largely gathered together 4.6 billion years ago to form the earth. Some meteorites are given radiometric ages twice as old as the oldest rocks in the shields; other meteorites are given younger dates than some of our earthly rocks, perhaps because of impact and fusion while our earth has been evolving.

Meteorites are of two principal kinds, iron and stone. As is true of all classifications, there are intermediate kinds of meteorites, called stony irons. The iron meteorites average more than 99 percent iron and nickel with traces of cobalt, phosphorus, sulfur, and other elements. The proportion of iron to nickel varies widely, but averages about 10 to 1. The stones average about 25 percent iron and nickel, and the proportion of iron to nickel averages about 20 to 1. The intermediates have an average composition of about 35 percent oxygen, 20 percent silica, 15 percent magnesium, less than 2 percent each of aluminum and calcium, with only traces of sodium and potassium—very different proportions from those of the earth's crust. Yet the minerals found in meteorites mostly occur naturally on earth and likewise most of the earthly minerals occur in meteorites. The exceptions are certain easily oxidized minerals in meteorites (e.g., ferrous chloride, calcium sulfide) that do not occur naturally on earth because of the presence of water and oxygen, and certain minerals that crystallized from aqueous solutions on earth but are not found in meteorites.

In all the world about 1,500 meteorites have been discovered; about half are stones, a third are irons, and the rest are stony-irons. Most meteorites are about pea size. The largest stone meteorite weighs about half a ton; the largest iron meteorite weighs more than 50 tons.

The irons may be compared with the composition of earth's core, and the stones compared with that of the mantle. Another class of meteorites with high silica content may be compared with the composition of earth's crust. These are silica-rich, globular, or spindle-shaped glassy bodies known as *tectites.* They once were molten. They occur in clusters at widely separated localities around the earth. Individually they are small, mostly less than half an inch in diameter, but they occur by the millions and their bulk may be considerable.

Climate

The saucer-like form of the Colorado Plateau is expressed also in the climatic maps, because precipitation is greater and evaporation less along the rims than in the interior (Fig. 15.19). In much of the interior, the average annual precipitation is less than 10 inches, whereas along the high southwest rim it exceeds 20 inches. One reason for the aridity of the interior is the rain shadow caused by the High Plateaus.

Much of the province is arid because of the high evaporation rate. The effective moisture is even less than the average precipitation would suggest, and especially so during the growing season. Probably 95 percent of the precipitation is lost by evaporation, transpiration, and seepage into the ground.

Summers are hot and winters cold. The frost-free period lasts about 200 days along the Colorado River, about 160 days in most of the uplands in the interior of the Plateau, and 100 days or less on the rims and mountains. Climatic maps more detailed than Figure 15.19 would show that each of the laccolithic mountains and large volcanoes receives more rainfall than the surrounding areas and that temperatures and rates of evaporation are lower there.

Figure 15.19 *Average annual precipitation in Colorado, Utah, Arizona, and New Mexico (Colorado Plateau shown by heavy line).* [From U.S.D.A.]

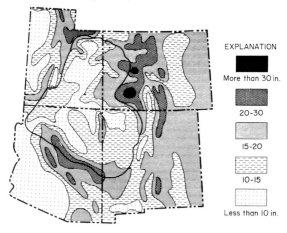

EXPLANATION

More than 30 in.

20–30

15–20

10–15

Less than 10 in.

Late Quaternary climatic changes have left their mark on the Colorado Plateau by altering the processes operating in that now-arid region. During dry periods erosion was dominant, as it is now; during wet periods alluvium was deposited on the floodplains, and colluvium accumulated on the hillsides. During the Pleistocene some mountain tops were glaciated, others subjected to severe freeze and thaw (periglacial). These features may be seen on mountain tops that today are without perennial snow banks.

A geologically recent climatic change of special interest occurred at the end of the thirteenth century, which, according to tree-ring studies, was a dry period. During that time many Pueblo settlements were abandoned, and the Pueblo Indians moved to the Rio Grande Valley.

Vegetation

Vegetation on the Colorado Plateau, like the climate, also reflects the saucer-shaped form of the plateau surface. The rims of the plateau, and the isolated mountains, are forested; the interior supports desert shrub or grassland (Fig. 15.20,A).

The Lower Sonoran Zone, characterized by creosote bush and mesquite, extends into the Colorado Plateau along the bottom of Grand Canyon below about 2500 feet; most of the plateau is in the Upper Sonoran Zone, which extends to altitudes of about 7,500 feet.

The Upper Sonoran Zone is represented by several kinds of plant stands, most of which reflect differences in the availability of moisture. The effective moisture for a given rainfall within the zone is controlled chiefly by differences in the kind of ground, which in turn are caused by differences in the geology, but partly by altitude (evaporation is less at the higher and cooler elevations). Gravel-covered terraces at upper elevations generally support sagebrush and grama grass, whereas similar ground at lower altitudes is covered by shadscale and curly grass. Very sandy ground at upper elevations supports a variety of shrubs and even some scrub oak, whereas this kind of ground at lower elevations has mostly blackbrush. Impermeable ground on shaley formations supports a low-growing plant, mat saltbush (Fig. 8.20,C). Areas with loam tend to be grassy. Cracks and crevices on rocky benches or ledges have juniper, mountain ash, scrub oak, and bitterbrush—all xerophytes.

At the top of the Upper Sonoran Zone is a woodland of pinyon and juniper, the lower boundary of which is the so-called arid timberline. Below this is treeless land with desert shrubs; above are the forested, higher-altitude zones.

Where groundwater is available in the Upper Sonoran Zone there are stands of phreatophytes, and the kinds depend on the quality of the water. Where the water is alkaline and fairly deep, as along many alluvial floodplains, the principal plant is greasewood. Where the groundwater is alkaline but shallow, the most common plant is saltgrass. Where the quality of groundwater is good, there is cottonwood, rabbitbrush, and sacaton grass.

The vegetation maps, of which Figure 15.20,A is an example, are misleading, because probably a quarter of the Canyon Lands Section is bare rock. This bare rock includes surfaces along the walls and rims of the canyons, and it includes badlands and flats in the shale formations.

Above the pinyon and juniper woodland of the Upper Sonoran Zone are forests of the higher zones: first, the Transition Zone, with yellow pine and Douglas fir from about 7,500 to about 9,500 feet; then the Canadian and Hudsonian zones, with spruce and fir to about 11,500 feet; and finally, above timberline, the Alpine Zone, with small herbs and grasses. The forests of these zones are like those in the Southern Rocky Mountains. In the Grand Canyon Section there is lumbering.

The distribution of vegetation on gravel-covered benches (p. 467) around the foot of some of the mountains illustrates the close response of the vegetation to slight differences in availability of ground moisture (Fig. 15.20,B). For example, where a stream leaves the Henry Mountains and flows into the gravel, the water seeps into the ground. It then percolates along the base of the

gravel; where it reappears in springs, there are stands of cottonwood, willow, rabbitbrush and other phreatophytes. Dry channels, which collect a little runoff, are marked by lines of pinyon and juniper extending down into the sagebrush zone and by lines of sagebrush and grama grass extending down into the zone of shadscale.

The Colorado Plateau is used mostly for grazing—winter grazing at the lower altitudes and summer grazing on the mountains and high plateaus. But the carrying capacity of the land is low. Even the forested areas of the Transition Zone and higher zones support only about 25 cows per square mile; the shrubland and grassland of the Upper Sonoran Zone will support only 5 or 6 cows per square mile, less than 5 percent of the productivity of an equal area in the central United States (Fig. 9.7). Is it in the national interest to expose such poor land to overgrazing? Or to invest in "range improvement" programs that still cannot match the native productivity of the more easterly physiographic regions? The answer is political.

Hydrology

WATER SUPPLY

More than nine-tenths of the Colorado Plateau drains to the Colorado River at Grand Canyon. Only narrow strips along the southern and western edges drain elsewhere.

The average annual discharges (in acre feet) of streams on the Colorado Plateau are:

Colorado River, above mouth of Dolores River	6,000,000
Dolores River, near the mouth	870,000
Green River, at mouth	5,100,000
San Juan River, near mouth	2,100,000
Colorado River, above junction with Little Colorado	14,400,000
Little Colorado River, near the mouth	240,000
Colorado River, at Grand Canyon	13,000,000

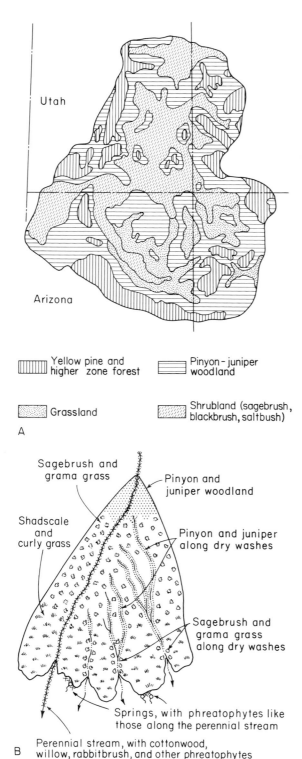

Yellow pine and higher zone forest

Pinyon-juniper woodland

Grassland

Shrubland (sagebrush, blackbrush, saltbush)

A

Sagebrush and grama grass

Pinyon and juniper woodland

Shadscale and curly grass

Pinyon and juniper along dry washes

Sagebrush and grama grass along dry washes

Springs, with phreatophytes like those along the perennial stream

B   Perennial stream, with cottonwood, willow, rabbitbrush, and other phreatophytes

These measurements cannot be compared closely because the records are for different numbers of years and the annual discharge fluctuates widely. For example, records from Lees Ferry—a station just above the junction with the Little Colorado—show that the discharge has ranged from a minimum of less than 4 million acre-feet to more than 23 million acre-feet.

What is important is the fact that the sum of the discharges of the rivers above Grand Canyon nearly equal, or may even slightly exceed, the discharge at Grand Canyon, which indicates that runoff from the central Colorado Plateau is less than is lost by evaporation and seepage.

The amount of water lost by evaporation can be illustrated in another way. The annual discharge of the Colorado River at Grand Canyon has been as low as 4,000,000 acre feet, as high as 23,000,000 acre feet, and has averaged about 13,000,000 acre feet. Lake Powell in Glen Canyon has an area of about 250 square miles, 160,000 acres. The evaporation rate in Glen Canyon probably averages more than 6 feet per year, which means that more than 1,000,000 acre feet of water is lost annually by evaporation from that one reservoir—enough water to supply a metropolitan area as large as Denver. In addition, there are seepage losses. Many feel that this dam should not have been built. Certainly if more dams and reservoirs are built along the Colorado

Figure 15.20 (A) *Vegetation map of the Colorado Plateau. 1 = yellow pine and higher-zone forest; 2 = pinyon-juniper woodland; 3 = grassland; 4 = shrubland (sagebrush, blackbrush, saltbrush). [After U.S.D.A.] (B) Distribution of vegetation on gravel-covered benches at the foot of the Henry Mountains indicates altitudinal zoning within the Upper Sonoran Zone and the response of the vegetation to slight differences in moisture availability. The lower parts of the fans have shadscale and curly grass. Above this is a belt of sagebrush and grama grass. Pinyon and juniper grow at the apex of the fan. Perennial streams and springs are marked by phreatophytes. Dry washes, which collect a little runoff, are marked by xerophytes that extend from the upper zones downward into the lower zones.*

River, the evaporation and seepage losses will exceed the flow of the river, and it will become necessary to import water to maintain the river flow. Yet in the face of this, there have been proposals to build dams even in Grand Canyon.

Most streams that rise on the Colorado Plateau are intermittent. A few streams on mountains are perennial for short distances, but the annual discharge of even the largest is no more than a very few thousand acre feet. These streams, even when in flood, rarely extend far from the foot of the mountains. In crossing the deserts their water is lost by seepage and evaporation. The Dirty Devil River is classed as perennial, although in dry periods it fails to flow in some stretches. At the other extreme, floods in that stream may have peaks as high as 15,000 cfs.

Springs are important water sources on the Plateau and differ in size, quality, and mode of occurrence. Springs in the mountains are most numerous. Many are perennial and may yield several gallons per minute; their water is uniformly good. Many such springs are at the toe of boulder fields. Snow that collects between the boulders melts slowly and feeds streams underneath that lose almost no water by evaporation. Springs in the foothill belt are fewer and generally smaller than those in the mountains, and their water, although generally potable, commonly contains considerable dissolved solids. Most of these springs occur at the edge of gravel benches and are recharged by underflow from streams draining the mountains (Fig. 15.20,B). Springs in the desert are few and small. Their discharge rarely amounts to more than seepage, and many of them, perhaps a third, are too alkaline or saline for use.

Another important source for water is provided by natural tanks (p. 141). The Waterpocket Fold was so named by the Powell Survey because of its many water-bearing tanks—natural depressions in the rocks.

Additional water supplies on the Colorado Plateau have been obtained locally by drilled wells. In some of the structural basins, aquifers have been found within a few hundred feet of the surface, but this groundwater is of limited supply and of uncertain quality. Much is too alkaline for use.

Municipal water supplies vary widely in quality, depending upon the source. Cities that obtain their supplies from the mountains have excellent water with little more than 100 ppm tds (parts per million total dissolved solids). Towns in the desert obtain their water from wells or streams, and water from these sources commonly contains 800 to 1,000 ppm tds and has a hardness of 250 to 300.

DEVELOPMENT OF THE
COLORADO RIVER

Below Glenwood Canyon in the Rocky Mountains (see p. 387), the Colorado River crosses the eastern tip of the Uinta Basin. Its deep valley there is due partly to antecedence because the northeast flank of this part of the Uinta Basin was involved in the late Tertiary uplift of the White River Plateau, and part of the uplift of the southwest flank of the Basin occurred during late Tertiary or Quaternary time. On Grand Mesa, lavas 5,000 feet higher than the river are dated as 10 million years old; under the lavas are river gravels. The deep valley of the Colorado River across the Uinta Basin has been cut during Pliocene and Quaternary time; this involves an average rate of canyon cutting of about 500 feet per million years.

At Grand Junction the Colorado River is joined by the Gunnison in a valley along the north side of the Uncompahgre Plateau (Fig. 15.21). Formerly there was drainage across the structure at Unaweep Canyon (see chapter frontispiece). River gravels at each end of the abandoned canyon, some faulted, indicate that the canyon has been uplifted a thousand feet since the gravels were deposited. The river now crosses the northwest tip of the uplift at Ruby and Westwater canyons.

Green River flows south across the Wyoming Basin, bumps into the Uinta Mountains, turns east along Browns Park, which is a structural valley containing Miocene or Pliocene sediments (Browns Park Formation, Table 15.1), and then

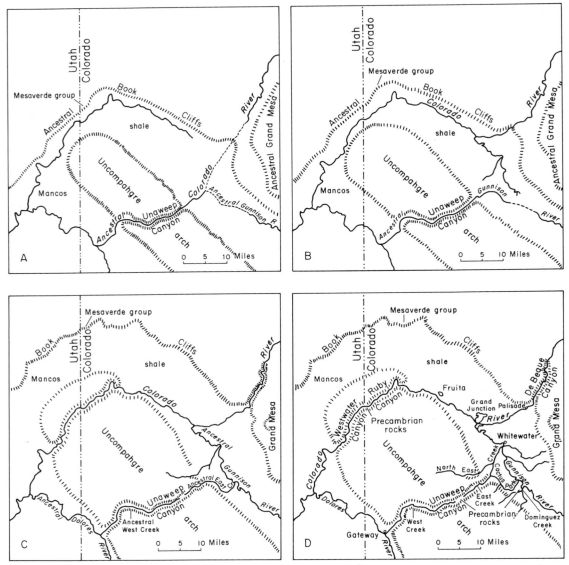

Figure 15.21 *Maps of part of western Colorado and eastern Utah, showing probable drainage pattern and topographic features at four successive stages of development. Broken drainage lines are hypothetical. (A) Just before capture of ancestral Colorado River. (B) After capture of ancestral Colorado River and just before capture of ancestral Gunnison River. (C) After capture of ancestral Gunnison River. (D) Present drainage pattern, after renewed uplift of the Uncompahgre arch and capture of East Creek. [After U.S.G.S. Prof. Paper 451.]*

turns into the mountains and crosses them at Lodore Canyon (Fig. 15.22). South of the Uinta Mountains, Green River crosses the Uinta Basin; its valley is presumably, due partly to anteced-

ence, as is the valley of the Colorado River across that big structure.

Powell attributed the Lodore Canyon of Green River to antecedence; in his view the river maintained its course as the Uinta Mountains were uplifted. But part of the uplift dates back to early Tertiary time and the river cannot be that old because the canyon is in bedrock no lower than the Miocene surface of the Miocene-Pliocene fill in Browns Park. But neither can the canyon be due wholly to superposition from fill that buried the Uinta Mountains. The fill would have to extend across most of the Wyoming Basin to the north and the Uinta Basin to the south, which is too much fill to be removed in so little time, and there is not that much sediment in the delta. Another possibility that has been suggested infers piracy by a stream eroding headward across the range; more likely, there were windgaps at the heads of streams draining southward, and the Green River could have been diverted through one of these by superposition from fill deposited in Browns Park

Probably a third of the canyon cutting in the Uinta Mountains can be attributed to Pliocene and later uplift of the Mountains, another third can be attributed to general lowering of the Browns Park Surface by later erosion, and the remaining third could represent the depth of the windgap before capture. In any case, Green River did not join the Colorado River system until after the Browns Park Formation had been deposited; this important fact bears on interpretations of the geologic history of Grand Canyon.

From the Uinta Basin southward, both the Green and Colorado Rivers flow against the dip. In 60 miles there is about 15,000 feet of structural rise (Fig. 15.16), and part of this tilting is no older than middle Tertiary because Oligocene formations are involved. Part surely is Pliocene or Quaternary, as suggested by the record of uplift at the Uncompahgre Plateau. During Miocene time, before the Green River crossed the Uinta Mountains, the Colorado River was ponded, at least intermittently, in the structural basins at Middle Park and State Bridge (p. 387). The Gunnison may have been the first river to discharge to the central part of the Colorado Plateau (Fig. 15.23), and it would probably have been ponded at the huge Henry Mountains structural basin.

In northern Arizona, on the Kaibito Plateau about 25 miles east of Marble Canyon, are river gravels composed of Precambrian rocks, Tertiary volcanic rocks, and cherts were almost certainly derived from the San Juan Mountains. The gravels are probably older than the nearby Pliocene Bidahochi Formations and certainly are no younger. The deposits are within 50 miles of the head of Grand Canyon and project 1,500 feet below the canyon rim. Either Grand Canyon was 1,500 feet deep when the gravels were deposited, or there has been 1,500 feet of uplift of the Kaibab Plateau since their deposition. The evidence seems compelling that the San Juan River had made it across the Monument Upwarp and was discharging into Grand Canyon by late Miocene or early Pliocene time. The Colorado and Green probably had not yet reached that far south.

Looking next at the Little Colorado River, it follows a broad strike valley in Triassic formations and collects drainage off the high south rim of the Plateau. This is a stripped surface on Paleozoic formations, and this stripping was completed by the end of Miocene time because in this part of the valley the widespread Bidahochi Formation (tuffaceous sediments and lavas) dates back to early Pliocene time. The Little Colorado River has cut downward only about 500 feet since the Bidahochi Formation was deposited.

On the stripped plain south of the Little Colorado River are gravel deposits derived from mountains in central Arizona that have been faulted off the south rim of the Colorado Plateau. The Little Colorado River was a much larger stream when it was draining those mountains, which broke away from the Plateau in late Miocene and early Pliocene time.

This brings us to the grand problem of the Colorado River, the age of Grand Canyon. Grand Canyon probably was started by the Little Colorado River when it was a much larger stream than it is now. In late Miocene time it seems to have been joined by the San Juan River. The main stem of the Colorado River and the Green probably did not reach Grand Canyon until Pliocene time. Moreover, lavas on the floor of Grand Canyon show that the canyon was within 50 feet

456

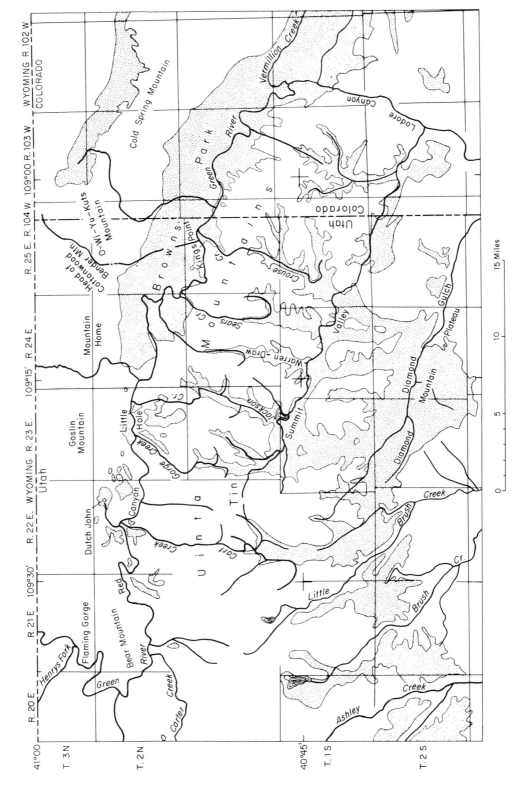

Figure 15.22 *Eastern part of Uinta Mountains, showing Lodore Canyon, Browns Park, Diamond Mountain Plateau and barbed drainage in northern part of mountains. Distribution of Browns Park Formation shown by stippled pattern. [After Hansen, et al., 1960.]*

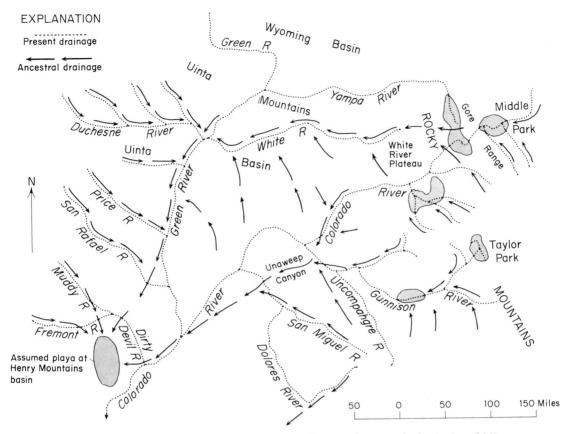

Figure 15.23   *Probable drainage system in the upper Colorado River basin at the beginning of Miocene time, before the intrusions of the laccolithic mountains. Present drainage dotted; inferred ancestral drainage dashed. The Green and Yampa Rivers still were north of the Uinta Mountains, perhaps discharging to the east, and did not join the Colorado River system until latest Miocene or early Pliocene time. When the Uinta Basin overflowed, that drainage probably was ponded temporarily in the Henry Mountains structural basin. Most of the rivers in the Rocky Mountains became interrupted, at least temporarily, by the basins and ranges that began developing there in latest Oligocene time.*

of its present depth 1.5 million years ago, and at Peach Springs (Fig. 15.6) is an abandoned dry canyon, surely a former segment of Grand Canyon, that is partly filled with volcanics and sediments dated at 18 million years old, or middle Miocene.

Grand Canyon crosses a series of north-trending structures, including the Kaibab Upwarp (Fig. 15.6). At the Hurricane Fault the river turns southward, and at Peach Springs it turns 135 degrees northwestward to leave the Plateau via the Lower Granite Gorge. The dry canyon at Peach Springs continues south along the Hurricane Fault and extends to the rim of the Plateau. This dry canyon shows that most of the uplift of this rim of the Plateau and most of the canyon cutting there occurred before the middle Miocene.

Lower Granite Gorge is young, for there is good evidence that the Colorado River did not discharge there until Pliocene time. Miocene fill in Grand Wash, at the mouth of the Lower Granite Gorge, is local fill and not Colorado River sediment, and it is overlain by a thousand feet of embankment limestone that is probably of

Pliocene age. The limestone (Hualpai) records a lake vastly larger than Lake Mead; it has a center at about the mouth of the Lower Granite Gorge and is without a clastic delta.

The ancestral river could have been dammed at a time when the Little Colorado River lost its headwaters because of faulting at the south side of the plateau (p. 503) and before the Colorado and Green Rivers had reached that far. The damming could have been caused by the volcanics and sediments preserved in the dry canyon at Peach Springs. Such a dam would allow water to seep into the cavernous limestone formations, there, which dip 2,000 feet to the foot of Grand Canyon. Such seepage could help keep the river from overflowing until the Colorado and Green rivers joined the system, and the seepage would supply the water and the carbonate need to deposit the Hualpai Limestone. By this interpretation, Lower Granite Gorge resulted from capture of the ancestral drainage by underground stream piracy.

DRAINAGE PATTERNS

Because of the aridity and because of the considerable differences in rainfall within short distances on and off the mountains, the drainage has developed nearly every type of pattern imaginable. The great variety of drainage patterns on the Colorado Plateau (Fig. 15.24) results primarily from the many differences in structure, although a few drainage patterns are due mainly to process and stage.

Differences in process and stage are represented by changes in drainage pattern as gravel fans are built onto the pediments at the foot of the mountains. Drainage patterns on the gravel-free pediments are dendritic. When a stream draining from the mountains is captured and diverted onto such a pediment, a gravel fan is deposited and the drainage pattern on the gravel at that stage becomes braided. When the slope of the fan has been built to a grade sufficient for the stream to continue to transport the gravel, the drainage lines become nearly parallel (Fig. 15.25).

Drainage patterns attributable to structure are more common. On the steeply dipping, east flanks of the upwarps, the drainage has developed trellis patterns (Fig. 15.24,A). Trellis patterns have also developed in the block-faulted High Plateaus and in the faulted salt anticlines. At the laccolithic mountains and volcanoes the drainage patterns are radial (Fig. 15.24,B). On the badlands the drainage is dendritic. On gently dipping sandstone formations, bare rock surfaces are extensive, and at such places minor joints in the sandstone cause the drainage to be parallel. On the sandy deserts, drainage courses become clogged with windblown sand, and the drainage there is disintegrated, with closed depressions between the sand dunes and up valley from them. On some lava-capped plateaus, especially in the High Plateaus and Datil Sections, the drainage is sluggish and meanders widely on the upland flats. On young lava flows the surfaces are exceedingly rough and are referred to by the Spanish term *malpais,* meaning bad country. In such areas much of the drainage is underground.

Some canyons, controlled by joints or faults and having small streams, are nearly straight, and deviate only a few hundred feet in several miles. Canyons of the larger streams meander widely and this meandering takes two forms. The main canyons of streams like the Dirty Devil River are straight, but within the main canyon is an inner gorge and this and the river in it meander widely, almost wildly. The main canyons of other rivers meander as widely as the inner gorges and the streams within them. This is true along much of the Colorado, Green, Dolores, and San Juan rivers. As a general rule, the larger the stream the wider its meander belt (Fig. 15.26); this seems to be true of the canyons as well (Fig. 15.27).

The origin of the meandering canyons on the Colorado Plateau has been a subject of wide interest and much discussion: but since present-day stream meanders in general are not well understood and since the meandering canyons must represent ancient features that have been modified as canyon cutting progressed, not much has come of the discussion. The varied shapes of alcoves show that some meanders have wid-

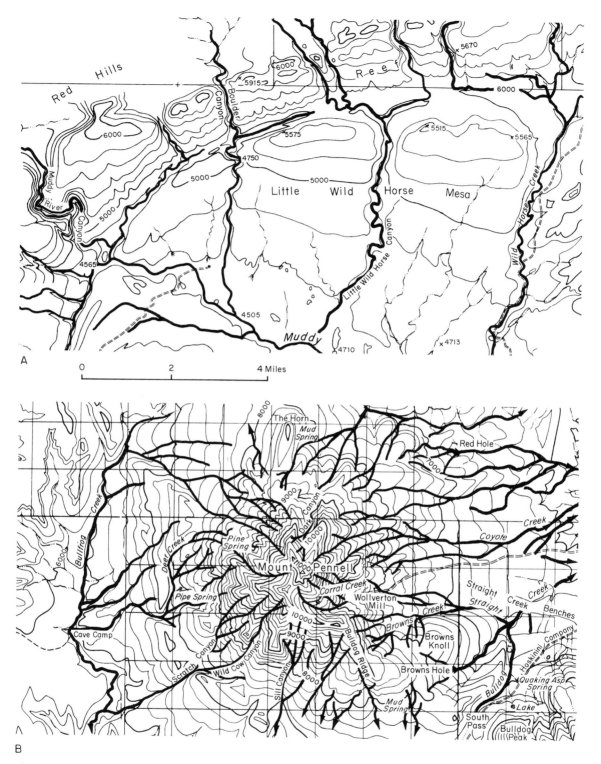

Figure 15.24 *Examples of differences in drainage patterns on the Colorado Plateau. The trellis pattern (A) is developed along a monoclinal fold (reef) at the southern end of the San Rafael Swell, Utah. The radial pattern (B) developed on Mount Pennell in the Henry Mountains.*

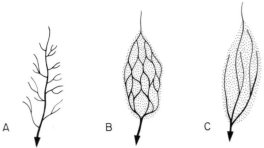

Figure 15.25 *Changes in drainage patterns on pediments and gravel fans attributable to differences in process and stage. On gravel-free pediments the drainage is dendritic (A). When a stream from a mountain is diverted onto a pediment, it builds a gravel fan there and the drainage pattern is braided (B) while the fan is being aggraded. When the fan has been built steeply enough so that new additions of gravel can be transported across its surface, the drainage pattern becomes parallel and consequent (C).*

ened as down-cutting progressed (Fig. 15.42,A); other evidence shows that lateral widening of some meanders was interrupted by vertical down-cutting (Fig. 15.42,B), and that others were produced only after a long period of vertical erosion (Fig. 15.42,C).

At many places the comparatively small tributary streams have anomalous courses. Price River heads in the High Plateaus and flows eastward to join the Green River, but instead of following an open shale valley around the south side of the Book Cliffs, this river continues eastward in a deep canyon across the southern rim of the Uinta Basin and joins the Green River in Desolation Canyon. The San Rafael and Muddy rivers, which head in the High Plateaus, cross the uplift at the San Rafael Swell. The San Juan River crosses the Monument Upwarp.

Other drainage anomalies are found along certain intermittent tributaries. Hall Creek follows a structurally controlled valley along the Waterpocket Fold, but at two places the creek leaves the open valley and turns westward into canyons cut into the sandstones turned up in the fold. Chinle Creek flows northward in a broad valley, but joins the San Juan River by turning

into a canyon on the flank of the Monument Upwarp (Fig. 15.28). The Chaco River, in New Mexico, follows a similar course. The perennial Gunnison River, like Hall Creek, winds out of its strike valley into canyons cut into the northeast flank of the Uncompahgre Uplift.

Surface Deposits and Soils

GLACIAL AND
PERIGLACIAL DEPOSITS

Glacial deposits on the Colorado Plateau exist only on parts of the High Plateaus, the La Sal Mountains, San Francisco Mountain, and at the White Mountains on the south rim of the Plateau in east-central Arizona—the only four areas known to have been glaciated. In each of these areas the moraines and other deposits attribut-

Figure 15.26 *River meanders in canyons. The canyon of the Dirty Devil River is as deep and as wide as Labyrinth Canyon, but the flow is small compared to that of the Green River. The flow of the San Juan River is greater than that of the Dirty Devil.*

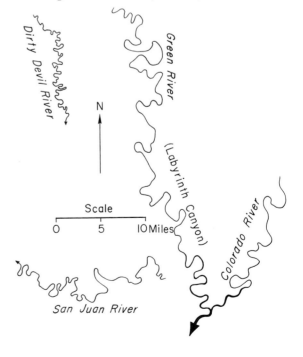

Figure 15.27 *Looping meanders of the Colorado River incised into late Paleozoic red beds at Canyonlands National Park.*

able to the Wisconsin stage of glaciation are well developed, and there are deposits representing earlier glaciations. Although the Colorado Plateau had few glaciers, the effects of the several climatic changes were expressed there in several ways. Mountain tops that were not glaciated were subjected to intensive frost action that developed extensive boulder fields. Travel even on foot across these boulders can be difficult. Their origin was explained in graphic terms a hundred years ago by a British geologist (Jukes, 1853):

> Any one who ascends the mountains . . . will often be surprised at the multitude of angular fragments and fallen blocks he sees scattered over their summits. . . . Of these many, if not most, have been detached by the action of frost causing the water in the joints and crevices to expand and rend them asunder, just as in a cold winter's night the jugs and water-bottles are apt to be burst by the frost in our bed-rooms.

The effects of the intensive Pleistocene frost action, referred to as periglacial effects, are very

well illustrated at the Henry Mountains. The mountain tops there not only have extensive boulder fields, but the tops are so smoothly rounded that the structural geology is obscured. The frost action has broken down the igneous rocks as completely as the sedimentary rocks. The lower half of those mountains, however, were below the periglacial zone, and the landforms there admirably reflect the structural geology of the laccoliths and the sedimentary formations domed by them.

On northern exposures in parts of the plateau, notably along some escarpments west of the Abajo Mountains, so much snow collected at times during the Pleistocene that debris avalanches developed at time of thaw; some of these are about a mile long and scores of feet high. They are related to colluvial deposits that are widespread on shale slopes at the sides of mesas and canyons. Evidently, as a result of climatic changes, the stages during which colluvium accumulated alternated with stages during which erosion of the colluvium was accelerated. In

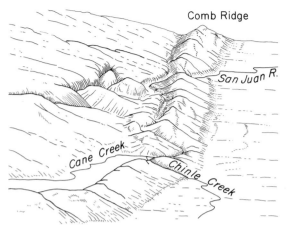

Figure 15.28 *Drainage relationships where the San Juan River crosses Comb Ridge to enter the Monument Upwarp. A tributary, Chinle Creek, flows north in a strike valley east (right) of Comb Ridge, but turns out of that lowland and into the Ridge to join the San Juan River in its canyon. Cane Creek follows a strike valley at the foot of Comb Ridge, but leaves that strike valley and joins Chinle Creek along Comb Ridge. This drainage must be superimposed, and probably from a surface only a few hundred feet higher than the present streams.*

many places colluvial deposits of two or more ages may be distinguished (Fig. 15.29).

Meltwaters from the extensive Pleistocene glaciers in the Rocky Mountains, both to the east and to the north, swept down the Colorado River and deposited in it thick fills of gravel. Subsequently this gravel fill was partly re-excavated and the gravel left as terraces high above the river. These Pleistocene terraces are numerous up to about 500 feet above the river; the few terraces located at higher altitudes seem to be Tertiary.

SAND, SOIL, LOESS

Extensive upland areas on the Colorado Plateau are covered by sand dunes, which occur in crescentic forms and as linear ridges (Fig. 15.30). Most of the active sand dunes overlie older dune sand that is stabilized, and the two generations of dune sand can be distinguished. Sand in the active dunes is loose; the underlying and older dune sand is iron stained and slightly consolidated. The older dune sand, which is of early Holocene or perhaps late Pleistocene age, is the source of the sand in the active dunes. The dunes are developed where poorly consolidated sandy formations are exposed. As the dunes migrate from those formations into areas where shaley formations are exposed, they become smaller and finally disappear.

Soils on the Colorado Plateau have received very little study because of their slight agricultural use. Most are classed as lithosols—that is, soils derived from parent materials that have been only slightly weathered. Nevertheless, as in other physiographic provinces, three very different kinds of soils representing three quite different geologic ages can be distinguished.

The oldest and most weathered of these soils developed in pre-Wisconsinan time. In the upper layers of these soils, as in the Red and Yellow Podzols previously described, pebbles, even of granite, are weathered to clay. The upper clayey layer is a few feet thick where fully preserved. Below this is a layer in which the rocks retain their shape and structure but have been altered to clay and can be cut by a knife. In this layer, and in some lower layers, there is a thick accumulation of lime carbonate, called *caliche*. Below the caliche is fresh parent material. Agriculturally important pre-Wisconsinan soil occurs along the Utah-Colorado boundary. This soil, is a Chestnut Soil, developed on an ancient loess deposit, (Fig. 6.1); both the loess and the soil are overlapped by Wisconsinan gravel deposits.

Whereas most loesses in the United States (p. 124) were derived from glacial meltwater deposits during the Pleistocene, the loess on the Colorado Plateau was derived from deserts—those to the west and southwest. The Colorado Plateau loess therefore resembles those in the Near East and North Africa, similarly derived from deserts.

On most of the Plateau the soils are alkaline, but on the mountains, where there is more rainfall and more vegetation, the soils are acid. On the mountain tops, where the ground is churned by freezing and thawing, the soils are like those of the arctic; they are not layered but have the organic and mineral fractions mixed throughout the weathering profile.

The soils of Wisconsinan age, exemplified by those developed on early Wisconsinan glacial deposits and their gravel outwash, have a leached layer at the top that is a foot or two thick. Pebbles in this layer are fresh, but are likely to be deeply stained with iron oxide, as are the sand and silt. Holocene soils show little or no signs of oxidation, and the leached layer is no more than a few inches thick. Wisconsinan and Holocene soils are farmed along some flood plains.

ALLUVIAL DEPOSITS AND THE
PROBLEMS OF ARROYO-CUTTING

Alluvial deposits on the Colorado Plateau are of two kinds. Flood plains along some valleys have been built up by the main stream overflowing its banks and spreading a deposit of silt across its valley floor. Such alluvial deposits are rather homogeneous along the valley, regardless of the kind of formations being crossed, and flood plain surfaces are nearly level.

A second kind of alluvial deposit is formed where the main stream is not competent to carry away all of the sediment brought to it by its tributaries, and the deposits consist of coalescing fans built into the main valley by the tributaries. These alluvial deposits are not homogeneous, for they reflect the kind of sediment being transported by each tributary, and the surface of the flood plain is not flat but consists of broad low fans apexing at each tributary. The two kinds of alluvial deposits clearly reflect quite different stream regimens. They are small-scale, rather obvious models of the differences in the flood plain along the Mississippi River, the first kind being like the flood plain in the Mississippi Embayment, and the second kind being like the river's valley through the Driftless Area (p. 357).

The streams are now incised in arroyos cut into the alluvium. Arroyos are deep, steep-walled, flat-bottomed channels of ephemeral streams. They may be 5 to more than 50 feet deep

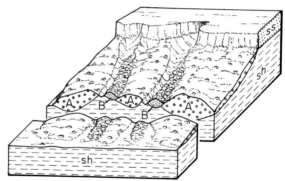

Figure 15.29 *Colluvium (A and B) on the Colorado Plateau forms apron-like deposits on shale (sh) slopes below rims of sandstone (ss). The older of the deposits (A), a thick accumulation containing boulders from the cliff, was eroded by gullies that cut into underlying shale. In these gullies a younger, thinner, and less bouldery colluvium (B) accumulated. Present gullies are cutting into the shale along the contacts between the deposits, and even the youngest colluvium is being eroded.*

and a few feet to a few hundred feet wide (Fig. 15.31). The alluvium consists mostly of fine-grained sediments but may include lenses of gravel or sand. The silty facies is broken by vertical fissures; the banks collapse along these fissures and, like the banks in loess, are generally vertical or nearly so. Because of this, the arroyos are difficult to cross, although in time they may weather to more rounded slopes. Surface water getting into the vertical fissures back from a bank

Figure 15.30 *Sand dunes on the Colorado Plateau. The wind direction is from the left. The arcuate dunes are called barchane dunes.*

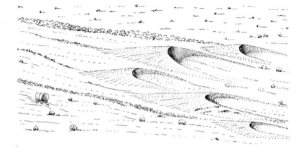

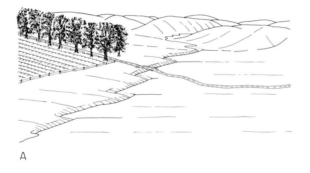

A

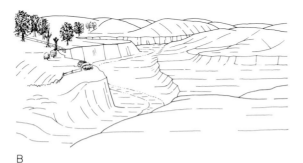

B

Figure 15.31 *Pleasant Creek, Utah, in the western part of the Henry Mountains area before arroyo cutting (A) and in 1935 (B). The arroyo, about 20 feet deep, was eroded between 1900 and 1935. [After U.S.G.S.]*

discharges underground to the bed of the arroyo; this process is known as piping, and the pipes may extend tens of feet back from the arroyo bank. Their roofs are subject to collapse and can be treacherous for livestock.

The arroyos are small box canyons, and they head at a vertical bank of alluvium. They maintain this vertical headwall as they extend themselves headward.

In most valleys three ages of alluvium can be recognized. The oldest is late Pleistocene, and contains bones of such Pleistocene animals as the elephant, the camel, the horse, and the long-horned bison. A younger alluvium was deposited during the middle Holocene, which was a comparatively wet period in the southwestern deserts. This alluvium contains bones of the modern

fauna, excluding the horse, which became extinct in North America at the end of the Pleistocene; it was reintroduced by the Spaniards. With these bones are numerous hearths and some stone artifacts of prehistoric Indians who had not yet learned to use the bow and arrow or to make pottery. They are sometimes referred to as basket-makers; they sealed their baskets with pitch and could use them to heat water by placing heated stones in the water. As a consequence their fireplaces are conspicuous because of the abundant broken rock. They used the atlatl (throwing stick) and spear rather than the bow and arrow. These Indians were succeeded in about A.D. 500 by the ancestral Pueblo Indians, referred to as the Anasazi, who developed one of the most advanced cultures north of Mexico. Their town and camp sites are on top of the middle Holocene alluvium and are clearly younger.

The youngest of the three alluvial deposits accumulated during the period of the Spanish occupation and contains historic artifacts.

Intervening between these periods of alluviation were periods of arroyo-cutting, and most of the arroyos were wider and deeper than the present ones. Depending upon the thickness of the alluvial deposits and the width and depth of the arroyos cut into them, the stratigraphic relationships between the deposits may vary greatly, and there may be one terrace or three, as is illustrated in Figure 15.32.

These alternating episodes of alluviation and arroyo-cutting reflect, at least in part, the alternation of wet and dry periods. That the alluvial deposits formed during wet periods is shown by the correlation of those deposits with others in shallow lakes (playas in the Basin and Range Province); that the arroyos formed chiefly during dry periods is indicated by the historic record and by dune sand that partly fills the arroyos and is preserved under the younger alluvial deposits.

This bears on the important and very practical question about the degree to which the present cycle of arroyo-cutting and other erosion should be attributed to climatic change or to overgrazing and other land use. The record is clear that there have been periods of alluviation that alternated

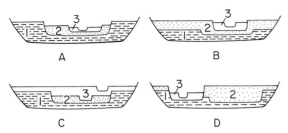

Figure 15.32 *Diagrammatic sections illustrating some common stratigraphic relationships in the alluvial deposits in the western states. 1, late Pleistocene alluvium; 2, pre-pottery, Recent alluvium; 3, historic alluvium. (A) From old to young, the alluvial deposits are progressively thinner, and the arroyos in which they were deposited are progressively smaller. (B) The second alluvium has overtopped the first. (C) The third alluvium has overtopped the older ones. (D) An example of a large number of complicated relationships that occur locally.*

with periods of arroyo-cutting, and the evidence is pretty good that these can be equated with changes of climate. But there also is good evidence that land use at least triggered the present cycle of arroyo-cutting, because the date of settlement differs for each valley, and so does the date of onset of the erosion. In almost every valley, the cutting began 10 to 15 years after it was first settled. The land that was settled was surrounded by public lands and there were no restrictions; settlers were free to graze as much livestock as they could possess, without considering the carrying capacity of the range. There can be no question but that the lands were seriously overgrazed. But even if use of the land were to stop, would the erosion heal itself without the return of wetter conditions?

Before the erosion began, at least some of the streams were in small, meandering, and even braided, channels. Figure 15.33 illustrates changes in the channels on the alluvium and the arroyos cut into them. Erosion during the past half century has clearly been severe, but the amount of downcutting can easily be exaggerated. For example, banks may be 20 feet high, but the actual downcutting less than half that because the arroyo eroded laterally into a high bank of alluvium. The present channel is very

much wider than the one that was on the alluvium, and such erosion not only destroys towns, homes, fields, and roads, but also lowers the water table under the alluvium. This loss of water supply in the desert is one of the most damaging effects of arroyo-cutting.

The general extent of such erosion on the Colorado Plateau is shown in Figure 7.1. Erosion is slight on the western and southern rims of the plateau, chiefly because those areas have extensive flat benchlands of resistant rock, but also because they are well forested and have been protected by inclusion within national forests. The areas subject to severe erosion that are outside the Indian reservations have received some protection from the Bureau of Land Management, but that agency has never had adequate funds and staff to take proper care of so much public land.

A case can also be made for attributing the arroyos that antedate the historic alluvium to the practice of agriculture and other disturbing uses of the land by the prehistoric Indians. Again, the evidence is clouded, for there was climatic change too. For example, tree-ring studies show that there was a drought that lasted a decade or so at the end of the thirteenth century. Along two streams, Cane Wash in Monument Valley and Bull Creek at the north end of the Henry Mountains, Utah, there is evidence that the centers of Indian occupation had been gradually shifted upstream, apparently in response to drying of the streams. At Cane Creek (Fig. 15.34,A) the earliest occupation site was downstream at a playa, or dry lake, where the stream had been dammed by dune sand. Today that playa is hardly an enticing place to reside. The population shifted progressively upstream from there, apparently due to drying of the stream, which would have lowered the water table and increased the difficulty of obtaining water for irrigation. At Bull Creek (Fig. 15.34,B), there is geologic evidence that stream flow diminished; in late Pleistocene time Bull Creek, draining from the Henry Mountains, was capable of transporting coarse gravels to the Dirty Devil River, 20 miles to the north. During the Holocene the flow has so diminished that Bull

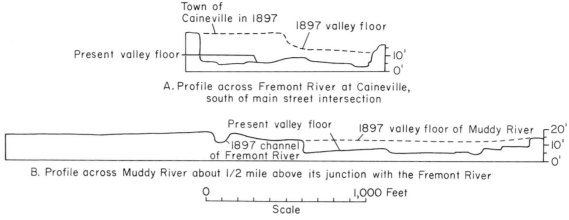

Figure 15.33 *Profiles across the Fremont River, showing the amount of erosion since 1897. [After U.S.G.S.]*

Creek today carries gravel only half way to the river. Agricultural Indians contemporaneous with the Anasazi, at Cane Wash, referred to as the Fremont Culture, farmed the floodplain of Bull Creek. The center of population shifted upstream, probably in response to diminution of flow of Bull Creek. Not only has Bull Creek cut itself an arroyo, but the surface of the floodplain there has been lowered a foot or so by erosion. Remains of Indian fireplaces form mounds that stand a foot above the alluvial surface because they have been protected against erosion by the stones in the fireplaces and by the baking of the alluvium. Camp sites and fireplaces are buried under silty dunes held in place by shrubs, and remnants of the occupation layer are a foot or so higher than the surrounding alluvial surface. The lowering of the alluvial surface evidently began as wind erosion and has been continued by sheet wash. The Indian sites are on alluvial pedestals capped by mounds of wind-blown sand and silt. The relationships strongly suggest that this erosion is attributable to land use by the Indians.

The arroyos on the Plateau can be thought of as small canyons, but it would be erroneous to think of the canyons as big arroyos. They differ not only in scale but in terms of the mechanisms that formed them. Uplift that steepens stream gradients causes the streams to cut downward,

and the canyons are attributed to the downcutting caused by regional uplift of the Plateau. The general progress of canyon-cutting no doubt was accompanied by alternating episodes of alluviation and arroyo-cutting in response to changes in stream regimen caused by fluctuations in the climate. The main cause of the canyons was uplift of the Plateau, dating back to the Oligocene; the main cause of the arroyo-cutting has been fluctuating runoff caused by changes in climate.

PAINT ON THE CANYON WALLS— DESERT VARNISH

Canyon walls in the Colorado Plateau are decorated picturesquely with colorful patterns formed by a stain of iron and manganese oxides called desert varnish. Along the Colorado River in Glen Canyon the effects are like tapestry. The desert varnish is not limited to the canyons, but occurs widely on all kinds of rock surfaces, including gravels, boulder fields, and stones or boulders on hillsides. It is found at all altitudes from canyon bottoms to mountain tops.

How the stain was deposited is not entirely clear, but the iron and manganese must have been in solution in water. Some may have been leached from within the rock formations and deposited at the surface. At other places the iron and manganese must have been brought from farther away by surface water or by groundwater.

Iron and manganese oxides are being deposited today at seeps along the canyon walls, but these are minute areas compared to the dry areas of desert varnish. Furthermore, the desert varnish is being removed from these dry areas, and the fresh rock once again is being exposed. This desert varnish is older than the cliff dwellings and other prehistoric remains dating back at least to A.D. 500, for the dwellings are built against stained cliffs (Fig. 15.41). Apparently, most desert varnish is an ancient deposit dating from a wetter time.

Desert Landforms

PEDIMENTS AND BADLANDS

Around the foot of the mountains and along the base of escarpments on the Colorado Plateau are extensive benches that have been planed by erosion of the bedrock. Most of these are partly covered by gravel. Such surfaces are particularly well developed on shale formations, and their origin is clearly revealed along the foot of the Book Cliffs and around the foot of the Henry Mountains (Fig. 15.35). The processes that developed these surfaces have operated at numerous other places in the United States—for example, the Great Plains (p. 360).

Where streams that head in mountains discharge into an area of lower rainfall, water is lost by seepage and by evaporation. As the volume of water in such a stream is reduced, so is its power to transport its load; the gravel being transported from the mountains becomes deposited, and the lower stretch of the stream course becomes aggraded.

Streams rising within the desert carry water infrequently, as when heavy rains cause local floods. At such times these streams can erode their beds, particularly if they are in easily eroded formations, such as shale not protected by gravel. The bed can be eroded below that of a gravel-ladened stream draining from the moun-

tains, in the same way that Bear Creek has eroded its bed below that of Rock River on the Great Plains (Fig. 13.35). In time, the stream draining from the mountains will be left perched, and sooner or later captured and turned into the lower stream valley. When the stream originating in the mountains is turned into the lower valley, the new channel and associated pediment, which have been free of gravel, become the dumping ground for gravel being transported by the captured stream. Gravel is deposited at the point of capture, and a gravel fan begins to form and gradually spreads downstream from the point of capture and covers the pediment. The gravel is younger than the erosion surface on which it rests, and it was not transported by the stream that eroded the channel and planed the pediments. As erosion progresses and as more streams cut downward, the gravel-covered pediments are left as gravel-capped benches high above the drainage lines.

Around the foot of the Henry Mountains are examples of every stage in the process—incipient capture (Fig. 15.35), capture that occurred recently enough such that the gravel fan only partly covers the pediment, and capture that occurred long enough ago such that the pediment has been completely buried by gravel and side streams have begun to cut below the stream from the mountain (Fig. 15.36).

Gravel resists erosion. The gravel-capped pediments are remnants of benches reduced by erosion that attacks the sides of the benches and undermines the gravel cap. The streams that cut downward almost invariably have incised themselves along the edges of the gravel fills, with the result that gravel benches on one side of a valley are at different heights from those on the opposite side.

Ordinarily a main stream has a flatter gradient than its tributaries, but the reverse is true of streams draining from areas of high rainfall to areas of low rainfall. The main streams from the mountains have steeper gradients than their tributaries (Fig. 15.37).

These diversions at the base of mountains in the desert can cause marked changes in the major

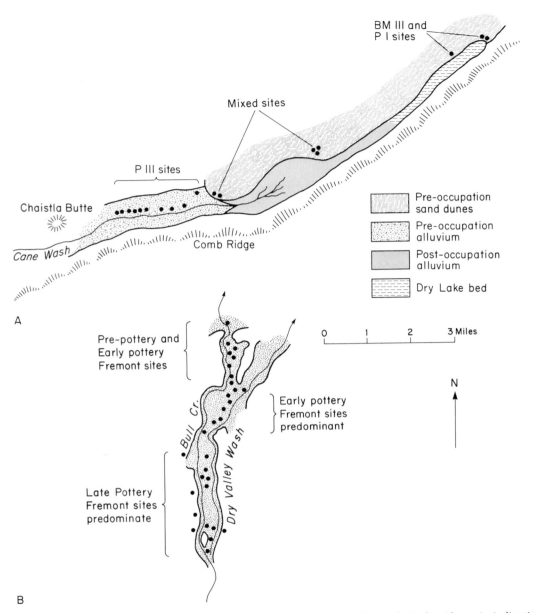

Figure 15.34 *The archeological record at numerous places supports the geological evidence in indicating that the flow of springs and streams in the western United States has diminished during the past 2,000 years. For example, Cane Wash in Arizona (A) was ponded by sand dunes that antedate the archeological occupations there, and the wash has subsequently built an alluvial fan upstream from there. The once-ponded area is now a dry lake bed. Basketmaker III–Pueblo I sites that date from about A.D. 700 are situated on pre-occupation dunes at the edge of the dry lake. Upstream, on pre-occupation alluvium near Chaistla Butte, are Pueblo III sites that date from about A.D. 1200. Between these and the dry lake sites are mixed sites of intermediate age. Probably the population shifted up the valley as flow in Cane Wash diminished. [After Hunt, 1955.] Bull Creek, north of the Henry Mountains, Utah (B), originally discharged northeastward via Dry Valley Wash, and was subsequently turned northward. Diminishing flow of Bull Creek is indicated by drying of springs and by the incapacity of the creek to transport gravels as far as it formerly did. Apparently, part of the drying occurred while this stretch of the valley was occupied by the Fremont Indians, because most of the later sites are situated upstream, as if the population shifted in that direction. These sites date from the general period A.D. 500 to A.D. 1100.*

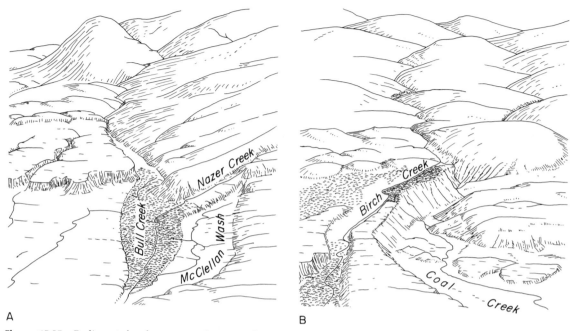

A   B

Figure 15.35 *Pediment development and stream diversions at the foot of the Henry Mountains, Utah. Streams draining from the mountains, like Bull Creek and Nazer Canyon (A) and Birch Creek (B), are aggrading their courses and depositing gravel where they emerge at the foot of the mountains. Streams rising in front of the mountains, like McClellan Wash (A) and Coal Creek (B), are free of gravel and have cut their courses much below the more watered streams from the mountains. McClellan Wash is 20 feet lower than Bull Creek and 55 feet lower than Nazer Creek. Coal Wash is 400 feet lower than Birch Creek. The divide holding Nazer Creek on its gravelly perch is only 5½ feet high, and any major flood may breach it. The divide holding Birch Creek at its height above Coal Creek is 10 feet high. When these divides are breached the streams from the mountains will deposit gravel on the pediments. The benches along each side of the streams are gravel-covered pediments that record a complex series of more ancient episodes of such pediment-cutting and burial beneath gravel because of stream diversion.*

drainage. For example, the largest canyon tributary to the Dirty Devil River from the west was eroded by streams draining from the Henry Mountains. But that canyon now receives no drainage from the mountains, the streams having been diverted to other drainage courses north and south of it. The nearly dry canyon is another example of an underfit stream.

Erosion on the pediment surfaces is exceedingly slow. A thirty-year photographic record of a surface in southeastern Utah shows almost no change in the depth or position of small rills only a few inches wide and an inch deep. No change was noted in the positions of small stones scattered on the surface. Yet the badland hills at the

head of such pediments are severely eroded during each rainstorm. These shales have a high content of swelling clay, a kind that expands when water enters its crystal structure. On slopes of such shale, flakes break off to collect in a layer of loose material a few inches thick. This highly porous layer is not much denser than cotton, and a slight rain may wet it enough to develop numerous small slides. A harder rain washes off the loose material along rills. The slopes retreat rapidly, and the sediment is transported across the pediment sloping from the foot of the badlands. The energy of the water on the pediment is evidently fully consumed in transporting its load of mud from the badlands and it is not capable of

Figure 15.36 *Sloping from the foot of high escarpments and around the foot of mountains on the Colorado Plateau are smooth gravel-covered plains. These are erosion surfaces in shale formations mantled by gravel deposited there by streams draining from the higher country. Streams discharging to the deserts from the wetter, high areas lose their water by seepage and evaporation and deposit their load of sediment. The aggraded gravel benches are dissected by desert washes along which pediments may develop (as in Fig. 15.40); the gravel-laden streams from the mountains become captured by the desert washes and deposit their load there. View is of the southwest side of Mt. Hillers in the Henry Mountains (see Fig. 15.10). [Photograph by Fairchild Aerial Surveys for U.S.G.S.]*

cutting into the shale underlying the pediment.

The shale formations are the ones that supply most of the sediment to the streams on the Colorado Plateau and practically all that sediment is derived by erosion of the steep slopes in the badlands; the vastly greater area of pediment contributes little to the sediment until it becomes gullied by arroyos, which start a new cycle of badlands.

In terms of age, the oldest and highest level, gravel-capped pediments around the Henry Mountains were eroded when the nearby canyons, including that of the Colorado River, were within about 500 feet of their present depth. The pediments extend into the canyons. Probably the oldest pediments that are preserved (because of

their gravel cap) are of earliest Pleistocene or late Pliocene age.

In the driest parts of the Colorado Plateau, where annual precipitation is no more than about 5 inches, the shale formations that ordinarily erode to badlands may have short stretches of vertical shale bluffs. Most of these have a sloping base quite like the steep slopes at the sides of badland hills. The vertical bluff evidently develops by spalling along steep fissures in the shale; it receives no washing, only the beating of wind-directed raindrops or hail. The slope at the base has an easily eroded active layer that erodes as rapidly and in the same way as the slopes on the badland hills. Where spalling at the vertical face is slow, that face becomes higher as the sloping face is reduced; where spalling is rapid, the landform becomes a badland hill. Such vertically faced shale bluffs or monuments do not develop in the wetter parts of the Plateau.

There have been two quite different schools of thought about the manner of retreat of slopes in arid and semiarid regions (Fig. 15.38,A). According to one view, the slope lessens as erosion progresses; according to the other, the slope of the hillside and the slope from the base of the hill remains constant as erosion progresses. So far as the badlands and pediments on the Colorado Plateau are concerned, the second process prevails. The steep slope at the sides of badlands and the width of the narrow crest on top remain about the same, regardless of the height of the badland hills, at least until a hill is reduced to a height no greater than its width; after that the side slopes are reduced and the hill becomes broadly convex. Moreover, pediment slopes are essentially constant on particular shale formations, regardless of the length of the pediments.

Hogbacks on the Colorado Plateau, where water is scarce, are curiously rough and dissected by comparison with those in the Appalachians, where water is plentiful (Fig. 15.38,B). The two regions of course have had very different geologic histories, but why the landforms, which reflect similar structures, are so different is not at all clear.

MESAS, CUESTAS, HOGBACKS

Probably nowhere else in the world is structural control of landforms better displayed than on the Colorado Plateau. Soil and other cover is thin or lacking. Vegetation is sparse, and the rock formations are extensively exposed. The Cretaceous formations consist of massive units of shale 500 to more than a thousand feet thick, and they erode easily. Interbedded with the shale are layers of sandstone 50 to more than 100 feet thick that erode slowly. Where the formations are flat or nearly so, the sandstones cap flat-topped mesas (Fig. 15.39). The slopes retreat by erosion of the shale undercutting the sandstone cap, which collects as talus on the slopes. But the

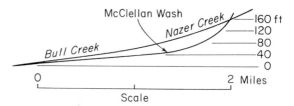

Figure 15.37 *Most master streams have flatter gradients than their tributaries, but the reverse is true along streams draining from areas of high rainfall to areas of low rainfall. Bull Creek and Nazer Creek are perennial streams that rise in the Henry Mountains; their courses are clogged with gravel and are steeper than the course of the tributary, McClellan Wash, which is usually dry but rises in the desert and is free of gravel. Compare with Figure 15.31,A. [After U.S.G.S.]*

broken fragments of sandstone that collect on the slope weather and disintegrate faster than the slope retreats and do not collect there as an armor plate. At the foot of the shale slope are badlands, and sloping from them are the pediments. Where the formations are gently dipping, the sandstones form cuestas; where dips are steep they form hogbacks (Fig. 15.40).

The Jurassic and Triassic formations also are shale and sandstone, and they too form mesas, cuestas, and hogbacks. Whereas the Cretaceous shale is mostly steel gray, the Jurassic and Triassic formations are brightly colored, mostly red but variegated with greens, purples, yellows, and browns. In the Upper Triassic and Lower Jurassic is a thick sequence of sandstone, the Glen Canyon Group, about 1,200 feet thick. The formation owes its name to the fact that these sandstones form the walls of Glen Canyon. They also form the big hogbacks and cuestas, that outline such broad folds as the San Rafael Swell, Circle Cliffs Uplift, and Monument Upwarp. These are asymmetrical folds with steep flanks marked by hogbacks on the east and gentle flanks marked by cuestas on the west (Fig. 15.8).

Lava flows also cap many mesas, especially in the Datil and High Plateaus sections. One of the pioneering geologists, Clarence Dutton, described the Mt. Taylor volcanic field as "mesa, mesa everywhere; nothing but mesa."

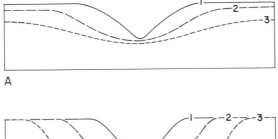
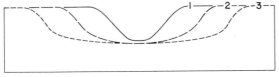

Figure 15.38 *Contrasting views of how slopes retreat in arid and semiarid landscapes. In one view (A) slopes are reduced as erosion lowers the hills and causes the side to retreat. In the other view (B) hills maintain their slopes and height as their sides are eroded back.*

ALCOVES, ARCHES, BRIDGES, AND TANKS

Overhanging cliffs in the sandstone formations are commonplace and almost a characteristic feature of the Colorado Plateau. Some are so small that they can be used only for nests by cliff swallows; others are large enough to have afforded protection to the cliff dwellings of the prehistoric Pueblo Indians. (Fig. 15.41). Some of the large alcoves beneath such cliffs in the Henry

Mountains area are 600 feet long, 150 feet deep, and 200 feet high. They form in at least three ways, as illustrated in Figure 15.42.

An alcove arch that develops along the outside of a meander may evolve to a natural bridge as at Rainbow Bridge or the Natural Bridges National Monument. Where the meanders in a canyon are closely spaced, they may cut through an alcove and thereafter flow through it and under the arch that remains (Fig. 15.43). Arches also develop away from streams, by weathering on uplands (Fig. 15.44).

Among other erosional features of the plateau are the depressions in sandstone surfaces, referred to locally as "tanks," for they fill with water after rains. The tanks are important in the water economy of the plateau; in some parts of the plateau desert travelers must depend on these natural cisterns for water. Some are as large as swimming pools.

The tanks are of at least three kinds. Some were formed as plunge pools below waterfalls (Fig. 15.42,D); others, as potholes in the sandstone beds of rivers that are now dry. Still others are on upland surfaces and probably formed as standing water dissolved the cement in the sandstone and enabled the wind to blow away the loosened sand grains once the water had evaporated.

The alcoves, arches, bridges, tanks, and other unusual landforms on the Plateau commonly are

Figure 15.39 *Diagram illustrating contrast in landform and the structural geology controlling it at a mesa, where the beds are flat; at a cuesta (Skyline Rim), where the beds are gently inclined; and at a hogback (Caineville Reef), where the beds are steeply inclined.*

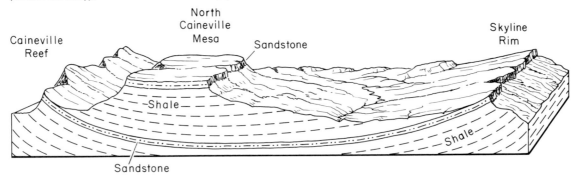

Figure 15.40 *Vertical aerial photograph of some cuestas, badlands, and mesas on the Colorado Plateau. Compare with frontispiece to Chapter 3, which is a nearly oblique view. In the upper left is the meandering course of the Fremont River. In left center is a cuesta facing west and sloping east. In right center are badlands in Cretaceous shale with pediments sloping from their base, and at lower right is mesa capped by resistant sandstone. Width of the view is approximately 5 miles. [U.S.G.S.]*

attributed to wind erosion, but in general the wind merely removed the grains of sand that became loosened by water that dissolved the cement holding them together. Moreover, these

erosion forms, obviously older than the cliff dwellings, probably date from the Pleistocene. During periods when the climate was less arid, the rate of erosion by streams and the rate of

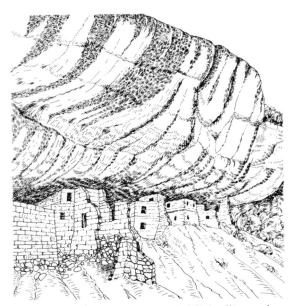

Figure 15.41 *Prehistoric Anasazi cliff dwelling under an overhanging cliff at Mesa Verde National Park. The Anasazi ruins at Mesa Verde and elsewhere on the Colorado Plateau were built during the period A.D. 500 to A.D. 1300. They were abandoned at the end of the thirteenth century after a period of drought. Streaks of desert varnish antedate the ruins.*

dissolution were greater than it is today, and the whole process took place at a correspondingly greater rate.

PEDESTAL ROCKS, MONUMENTS

Pedestal rocks (Fig. 15.45) are abundant where resistant sandstone crops out from between thicker beds of massive, earthy, easily eroded sandstone to form caps. Some of the caps are wide, like the one known as Mexican Hat. Rain that falls on the cap runs off the top, but it adheres to the bottom side of the cap for a short distance in from the rim and then drips to the ground, forming a drip curtain. The splash of this drip curtain forms a little trench or moat around the foot of the pedestal rock. Back of the drip curtain one can stay dry. A pedestal rock without a drip curtain may not be a satisfactory umbrella.

Water does move farther in from the rim, but only as a film that travels along the base of the

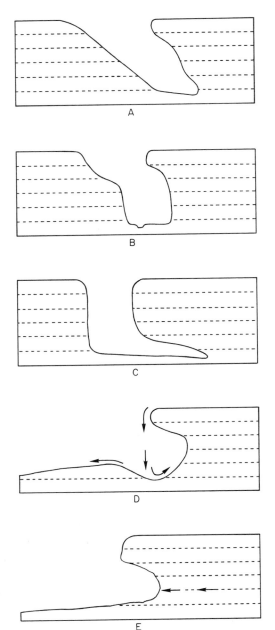

Figure 15.42 *Some alcove arches are formed by lateral cutting of streams (A, B, C). The forms depend on the relative progress of vertical and lateral cutting by the stream. Other arches are formed by the splash behind the plunge pool under waterfalls (D). Still others are due to groundwater softening the cement in the sandstone, which permits loosened grains to be blown away (E). These are the kind that the prehistoric Anasazi used for their cliff dwellings.*

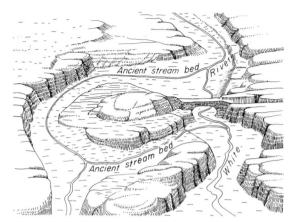

Figure 15.43 *How natural bridges are formed by a stream cutting off a meander in a canyon. [After U.S.G.S.]*

caprock and down the upright. It is this water that does most of the eroding for it dissolves the cement that holds the sand grains together, and the loosened grains can be blown away. Pedestal rocks are shaped, in part, by wind, but there is little or no sandblasting.

Monuments, like the many big ones in Monument Valley, have developed where formations of massive sandstone a few hundred feet thick are broken by many steep fissures, or joints. The monuments are of resistant rock that forms cliffs. These retreat as the sandstone breaks at the joints and spalls away. The blocks that topple may be only a few feet wide yet a few hundred feet long. They break into small pieces when they strike ground at the base of the cliff. With so much rock surface exposed, disintegration by weathering is accelerated. For some reason, the slopes at the base of the monuments are almost lacking in talus blocks of sandstone.

Mineral Deposits

Most mineral resources on the Colorado Plateau (Fig. 15.46) come from the sedimentary formations, and uranium and mineral fuels account for most of the production.

Coal is extensive in Cretaceous formations in the Navajo Section, the High Plateaus, and the Uinta Basin; some less extensive deposits occur in the Canyon Lands Section. These were important coal fields when the railroads used steam locomotives, but production has waned. Lately coking coal has been produced to supply steel plants in the western states, and there is strip mining to supply steam plants that generate electricity.

Oil and gas have been produced in the San Juan Basin part of the Navajo Section and in the Uinta Basin; recent discoveries have been made in the central part of the Canyon Lands Section. Near Price, Utah, carbon dioxide gas has been produced for the manufacture of dry ice.

Vast deposits of oil-shale that underlie the Uinta Basin are an important resource for the future. These deposits are estimated to contain

Figure 15.44 *Delicate Arch, an erosion remnant of sandstone at Arches National Park. [Courtesy Utah Travel Council.]*

50 times as much oil as the combined total of oil already produced and oil in reserve. At present, however, oil-shale cannot profitably compete with other sources of petroleum, and the demand for the scanty water that is available appears excessive.

The plateau is an important source of uranium. For ten years it was the scene of mad scrambling for uranium prospects, a true uranium rush, and the effort led to the discovery of several major deposits. Now that these deposits have been brought into production, the rush is over.

Production of other minerals has been minor, but important deposits of potash and other salts underlie the salt anticlines southwest of the Uncompahgre Upwarp.

Land Use

Indian Reservations comprise a large part of the Colorado Plateau, roughly a third. Among them are:

    1. Navajo, Hopi, Jicarilla Apache, and Ute Mountain Indian Reservations, which cover more than half the Navajo Section.

    2. Zuni, Laguna, Acoma, Puerto Cito, and Mescalero Apache Reservations, which cover about a quarter of the Datil Section.

Figure 15.45 *Pedestal rocks on the Colorado Plateau. Many of the pedestals have thin caps that form broad rims over pedestals, which suggests the name "Mexican hat."*

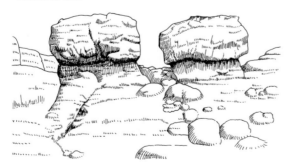

    3. Kaibab and Hualpai Indian Reservations in the northwest part of the Grand Canyon Section.

    4. Uinta and Ouray Indian Reservations along the northern and southern edges of the Uinta Basin.

Nearly half the plateau is public domain. This half is used chiefly for grazing, and much of it has been severely overgrazed but is recovering as corrective measures to curtail grazing are taken. We have already noted erosion in connection with prehistoric land use (p. 468). The mountains are grazed in summer; the lower parts, which are desert, are used as winter range. Most of the rest of the Plateau is in national forests.

Private lands make up a small fraction of the Plateau. The two principal farming areas are the flood plain formed by the Colorado and Gunnison rivers in the Grand Junction area (peaches, melons, apples, and vegetables) and the loessial belt in southwest Colorado and southeast Utah (pinto beans). Other valley areas also are farmed, notably in the vicinity of Farmington, New Mexico, and Moab, Green River, and Price, Utah.

Towns are few and widely separated. Farmington, the largest, has a population of less than 25,000. The total population on the plateau probably is less than 500,000.

CAPITALIZING ON ARIDITY

The Colorado Plateau illustrates that aridity can be an asset, for given a humid climate the plateau would have lost most or all of its spectacular features. Grand Canyon and the other canyons along the Colorado River would become as drab as Hells Canyon of the Snake River—still vast, but without the impressively distinctive sculpturing and without the color. The uplands would be grassed over and perhaps have trees and scenery not much different from that of the Appalachian Plateaus. The painted deserts would be gone, and Monument Valley would be a collection of rounded hillocks. There would be

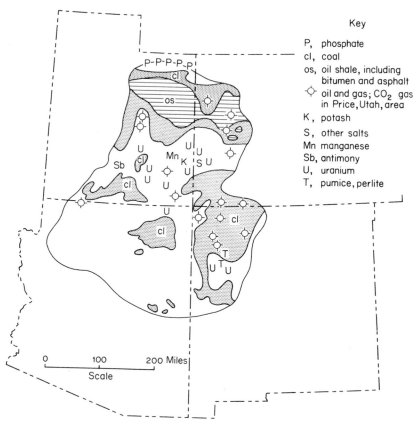

Key

P, phosphate
cl, coal
os, oil shale, including
      bitumen and asphalt
⬦ oil and gas; CO$_2$ gas
      in Price, Utah, area
K, potash
S, other salts
Mn manganese
Sb, antimony
U, uranium
T, pumice, perlite

Figure 15.46 *Principal mineral deposits on the Colorado Plateau.*

no Rainbow Bridge or other natural bridges, arches, or alcoves. There would be more agriculture, more industry, and the land would be as crowded with people as is the rest of the country and would be largely in private hands.

Instead, thanks to aridity, a spectacularly beautiful segment of our country remains public land available to 200,000,000 of us who annually or on weekends seek to escape from offices, industry, and urban crowds. To make best use of the Colorado Plateau requires further capitalizing on the aridity and the advantages it has brought.

This land, like the Rocky Mountains, is suitable for grazing in moderation. The new highways necessary to make maximum use of the incomparable scenery need not be like the Arizona segment of U.S. Highway 66—cluttered with billboards, stands selling imported "Indian" souvenirs (including Japanese varieties), "zoos with real live animals," automobile morgues, and other roadside monstrosities wholly out of keeping with the rich Indian tradition of that beautiful painted desert. The plateau is large enough to provide wilderness areas for those who can afford the luxury of pack train and guide, but many, many more miles of that spectacular canyon country could be made accessible to the vastly more numerous families who want to take the kids camping too, and cannot afford packtrains and guides. The wilderness should not be restricted to the wealthy. One way to achieve this would be to make the Canyonlands and parts of other sections of the Plateau an outdoor museum.

POTENTIALITIES OF AN
OUTDOOR MUSEUM

The Canyonlands Section of the Colorado
Plateau embraces some of the finest scenery in
North America. The landforms are spectacular;
the colorful geological formations are so well
exposed that their story can be understood by
nongeologists; the archeological history is easy to
see and easy to understand, and the varied as-
semblages of plants there illustrate many kinds
of plant adaptation. The area north of the San
Juan and Paria rivers could well be classified as
dominantly for recreational uses; compatible
secondary uses would be agriculture in small
areas, general grazing, lumbering on the isolated
mountains, and mining (including oil and gas
development). Some parts of the Canyonlands
already have been designated as special purpose
areas—as parks, monuments, or recreational
areas. The rest of the area, most of which is
managed by the Bureau of Land Management but
includes some National Forest, could be used as
a vast outdoor museum coordinated with the
already existing parks and monuments. Such an
outdoor museum could serve both educational
and recreational purposes.

Part of the traveling public has only a casual
interest in the natural features of the environment, but many in this group *become interested
when the features are explained.* These interests
could be met by roadside signs and leaflets call-
ing attention to and briefly describing various
natural features. A second group consists of those
who have a greater interest and ample time to
satisfy at least part of their curiosity. For this
group, there could be self-guided tours with
numbered stations and guidebooks (sold at cost)
giving many details. The self-guided tours could
be organized by means of numbered stops illustrating particular interests: e.g. bedrock geology,
erosional history, plant ecology, wildlife, history,
and archeology. For dedicated amateurs, specialized students, and even professionals, there could
be provided, in addition to the guidebooks, semi-
technical but comprehensive summaries of the
various fields of interest.

The Canyonlands Section offers recreation of
several kinds. In dry weather, for the kids, there
are many square miles of dune sand on the Green
River Desert; in wet weather, even more square
miles of hub-deep mud just to the north. Sand
or mud, the Section has it. The Green and Colorado rivers offer fishing, but so also do many of
the mountain streams. The mountains already are
popular with those who hunt deer by rifle or bow
and arrow. On the Henry Mountains is a herd
of bison.

Camp sites could be established at numerous
places along the rims of the canyon where people
would be able to observe the spectacular views
and the marvelous color changes as the sun
travels across the sky. As this is written, the
region has only one, at Hatch Point, overlooking
much of Canyonlands National Park, a view
matched only by the more accessible overlook at
Deadhorse Point State Park. Many or most of
these camp sites would have to be dry camps.
Numerous camp sites have already been developed in the mountains, where water is available.

The present system of roads was developed
with consideration only for highway economics,
and the result is a series of routes most people
regard as dull. Not even an enthusiastic desert
environmentalist would be enthralled by the
drive from Grand Junction to Green River, Utah,
and south to the marinas on Lake Powell, unless
he thinks only of the presently inaccessible spectacular country along both sides of that highway.
The Canyonlands are by no means plagued with
too many roads; rather, they have too many roads
in the wrong places. Besides the present highways, we need a substantial number of stub
roads and loop drives to provide access to the
scenic canyons, cliffs, hogbacks, mesas, badlands,
and dune areas. Most of these stub roads and
loop drives could be built in conjunction with
camp sites, because most of the places to be
visited would be of wide interest. Such roads
need not be paved; they need merely to be graded
enough for modern automobiles, most of which
are pretty helpless where roads are primitive,
despite the advertisements from Detroit. Additional primitive roads are needed for jeep trails

that would enable many more people to enjoy the ledges of the inner canyons. Beyond the jeep trails, there still would be miles and miles of room for the hikers and those traveling by pack train. The Canyonlands have plenty for everyone; there is no need to rob Peter to pay Paul there.

They embrace an area about equal to that of *all* park service lands in the contiguous United States. The development of those lands for educational and recreational services could help relieve congestion at the parks, and still retain their multiple uses.

References

Crampton, C. G., 1964, Standing up country: New York, Alfred A. Knopf.

Cross, Whitman, 1894, The laccolitic mountain groups of Colorado, Utah, and Arizona: U.S. Geol. Survey Ann. Rept., pt. 2, pp. 157–241.

Dutton, C. E., 1880, Geology of the High Plateaus of Utah: U.S. Geog. and Geol. Survey Rocky Mountain Region Rept.

———, 1882, The Tertiary history of the Grand Canyon district: U.S. Geol. Survey Mon. 2.

Gregory, H. E., 1916, Geology of the Navajo country: U.S. Geol. Survey Prof. Paper 93.

———, 1938, The San Juan country: U.S. Geol. Survey Prof. Paper 183.

———, 1950, Geology and geography of the Zion Park region, Utah and Arizona: U.S. Geol. Survey Prof. Paper 220.

———, 1951, The geology and geography of the Paunsagunt region, Utah: U.S. Geol. Survey Prof. Paper 226.

Hunt, A. P., 1953, Archeological survey of the La Sal Mountain area, Utah: Univ. Utah Anthropological Papers No. 14.

Hunt, Chas. B., and others, 1953, Geology and geography of the Henry Mountains region, Utah: U.S. Geol. Survey Prof. Paper 228.

———, 1956, Cenozoic geology of the Colorado Plateau: U.S. Geol. Survey Prof. Paper 228.

———, 1969, Geologic history of the Colorado River: U.S. Geol. Survey Prof. Paper 669, pp. 59–130.

Powell, J. W., 1875, Exploration of the Colorado River of the West, 1869–72: New York, Smithsonian Inst. Ann. Rept.

Robinson, H. H., 1913, The San Francisco volcanic field, Arizona: U.S. Geol. Survey Prof. Paper 76.

Wormington, H. M., 1947, Prehistoric Indians of the Southwest: The Denver Museum of Natural History, Popular Series No. 7, 9th printing, 1969.

The Basin and Range Province consists of rough, rocky mountains formed by northerly trending fault blocks. The blocks, commonly faulted on the west and tilted east, are separated by broad, down-faulted valleys partly filled by debris eroded from the bordering mountains. This debris consists of gravel fans sloping from the foot of the mountains and ending at alluvial flood plains or playas. This view is southeast across the south end of Death Valley. Across the valley at the left is the faulted west front of the Black Mountains. [Photograph by Warren Hamilton, U.S.G.S.]

16

BASIN AND RANGE PROVINCE— FRAGMENTED PART OF THE CRUST

The Basin and Range Province, covering about 300,000 square miles—about 8 percent of the United States—consists of desert basins and ranges that, on the average, are drier than the Colorado Plateau and that, in most places, have less vegetation. Altitudes of the basins range from below sea level (at Death Valley and Salton Sea) to about 5,000 feet above sea level. Many of them are closed and contain dry lake beds. The mountain ranges, numbering more than two hundred, tend to form parallel ridges. The crests generally are jagged and 3,000 to 5,000 feet higher than the bases. Most of the summits are less than 10,000 feet in altitude, but some reach a maximum of more than 13,000 feet. The ranges typically are 50 to 75 miles long and 10 to 25 miles wide; the basins are wider than the ranges.

The population, totaling about 3,500,000, is distributed very unevenly. The few places having water are densely populated; most of the rest of the province is open and unfenced desert. The population is concentrated in a few areas: along the Rio Grande between Santa Fe and El Paso; in the Tucson-Phoenix area, Arizona; in the Las Vegas and Reno areas, Nevada; along the Hum-

boldt River, Nevada; in the area about Salt Lake City, Utah; and in the Yuma and Salton Sea areas.

The wide valleys are interconnected across low divides, a feature that has greatly favored transportation routes. The province is gridded with good highways in all directions, and five railroads cross the province. The Western Pacific and Southern Pacific Railroads, connecting Salt Lake City and San Francisco, cross the northern part. The Union Pacific runs southwestward from Salt Lake City to Los Angeles. The Santa Fe and Southern Pacific railroads cross the southern part of the province and lead to Los Angeles.

National Parks and Monuments in the Basin and Range Province that illustrate its physiographic features include Death Valley and Joshua Tree National Monuments, California; Lake Mead Recreational Area, Nevada and Arizona; Saguaro Cactus, Organpipe Cactus, and Chiricahua National Monuments, Arizona; White Sands National Monument and Carlsbad Caverns, New Mexico; Big Bend National Park, Texas; and Lehman Cave National Monument, Nevada. Others could well be added: Great Salt Lake and parts of the salt desert around it; Carson Sink and parts of the mountains bordering it; and some of the other lakes, basins, and ranges near the foot of the Sierra Nevada. Also, in my judgment, parks at some of the abandoned mining camps to illustrate early mining technology and the history of mining would be both educational and popular.

Other outstanding features of the Basin and Range Province include its

1. Complex geology and recency of faulting; despite the complex geology, the topography has considerable homogeneity because of the recency of the faulting.

2. Structural rather than erosional valleys.

3. Warm desert climate.

4. Numerous and extensive Pleistocene lake beds.

5. Three quite different kinds of ground in every valley—gravel fans rising from valleys to the base of bordering mountains, dry lake beds or floodplains in the central parts of valleys, and rocky bordering mountains.

6. Deposits of various kinds of salts in the playas.

7. Metal resources, especially copper.

8. Picturesque vegetation, especially the cacti and yuccas.

9. Extensive use of adobe (mud brick) construction.

The Basin and Range Province, although distinct from the surrounding provinces, is gradational with each of them, and its boundaries are more arbitrary than most dealt with thus far. Similarly, the five sections into which the province has been divided (Fig. 16.1) are separated by arbitrary boundaries.

Structural Relationship to the Rest of the Continent

The northern and western parts of the Basin and Range Province are in the mobile part of the continent that became geosynclinal during late Precambrian, Paleozoic, and early Mesozoic time. In fact, the boundary between the Basin and Range Province and the western edge of the Colorado Plateau and Middle Rocky Mountains very nearly coincides with the structural break that marks the western edge of the stable platform of the craton. This structural break and the contrast between the provinces are illustrated in Figure 16.2. The Paleozoic formations, for example, thicken from about 5,000 feet on the Colorado Plateau to more than 40,000 feet in the Basin and Range Province.

The southern and eastern parts of the Basin and Range Province, however, extend diagonally across what had been stable platform; in fact, this part extends across the southwestern extension of the Transcontinental Arch (Fig. 14.3,B). The uniform thinness of the Paleozoic across this part of the Basin and Range Province is illustrated by four stratigraphic sections between Grand Canyon and El Paso (see Table 16.1).

On the other hand, the Arizona part of the Basin and Range Province does correspond to one or more Precambrian geosynclines that extend diagonally northwestward across the southwest corner of the Colorado Plateau at Grand Canyon. It appears that the Precambrian geosyncline was east of the Paleozoic one and that the Paleozoic geosyncline was east of the early Mesozoic geosynclines (Triassic and Jurassic) that once existed along the western edge of the Basin and Range Province, and extended diagonally across the Sierra Nevada to the Pacific. The downwarping along the west edge of the continent seems to have progressed westward. The Paleozoic and younger geosynclines, like the Appalachian geosyncline, were in two belts. Bordering the craton was a belt of miogeosynclinal deposits of limestone, shale, and sandstone; a tectonically active ridge separated this trough from a deeper one farther from the craton, in which poorly sorted conglomerate and other coarse clastic sediments were mixed with volcanics of all kinds. The sediments that accumulated in these several geosynclines aggregate a thickness of 30 miles, but they were offset and

Table 16.1

Paleozoic Formations Across the Southern Part of the Basin and Range Province

	Grand Canyon	Central Arizona	Southeastern Arizona	El Paso
Permian	Kaibab Limestone 525 feet Coconino Sandstone 350 feet Hermit Shale 225 feet	Kaibab Limestone 250 feet Coconino Sandstone 1,100 feet	Naco Group 3,000 feet	Top eroded
Pennsylvanian and Permian	Supai Formation 825 feet	Supai Formation 2,000 feet		Hueco Limestone 900 feet
Mississippian	Redwall Limestone 500 feet	Redwall Limestone 100 feet	Escabrosa Limestone 700 feet	Absent
Devonian	Temple Butte Limestone 0–40 feet	Martin Limestone 400 feet	Martin Limestone 400 feet	Absent
Silurian	Absent	Absent	Absent	Fusselman Limestone 300 feet
Ordovician	Absent	Absent	Absent	Montoya Limestone 60–120 feet El Paso Limestone 300 feet
Cambrian	Tonto Group 875 feet	Tapeats Sandstone 100 feet	Abrigo Limestone 800 feet Bolsa Quartzite 400 feet	Bliss Sandstone 0–90 feet
Total thickness	3,200 feet	4,000 feet	5,300 feet	2,500 feet (?)

not stacked above one another. (Section 2 in Fig. 16.3).

A major episode in the development of the present landscape occurred during the Cretaceous, when the Basin and Range Province was folded, faulted, and uplifted. The resulting mountains were the source of the sediments washed into the Cretaceous geosyncline to the east. The Cretaceous record of the Basin and Range Province is therefore one of erosion.

The deformation continued into the early Tertiary, but beginning in the Oligocene the Basin and Range Province became block faulted. It is this faulting that broke that part of the continent into basins and ranges. Whereas valleys on the stable platform and in the much older mountains of the Appalachians are erosional, the valleys in the Basin and Range Province are structural in origin. In many, the earth movements are continuing, and the topographic relief between the basins and ranges is continuing to increase.

Several mechanisms have been suggested to account for the block faulting that produced the so-called basin and range structure. The faulting seems to be the result of tension and extension of the crust, whereas the earlier structural movements seem to result from compression and shortening of the crust. One of the earliest expla-

Figure 16.1 *Physiographic map of the Basin and Range Province.*

Idaho

1. Portneuf Range
2. Bannock Range
3. Deep Creek Mts.
4. Sublett Range
5. Cotterell Range

Utah

1. Promontory Mts.
2. Raft River Mts.
3. Hogup Mts.
4. Newfoundland Mts.
5. Lakeside Mts.
6. Cedar Mts.
7. Stansbury Mts.
8. Oquirrh Mts.
9. Tintic Mts.
10. Deep Creek Range
11. Fish Springs Range
12. Confusion Range
13. House Range
14. Canyon Mts.
15. Cricket Mts.
16. Mineral Mts.
17. San Francisco Mts.
18. Wah Wah Mts.
19. Needle Range
20. Bull Valley Mts.
21. Pine Valley Mts.

Nevada

1. Pilot Range
2. Toana Range
3. Pequop Mts.
4. Blanchard Mtn.
5. Independence Mts.
6. Ruby Mts.
7. Sulphur Springs Range
8. Cortez Mts.
9. Tuscarora Mts.
10. Shoshone Mesa
11. Shoshone Range
12. Battle Mt.
13. Sonoma Range
14. Osgood Range
15. Santa Rosa Range
16. East Humboldt Range
17. Humboldt Range
18. West Humboldt Range
19. Trinity Range
20. Calico Mts.
21. Granite Range
22. Virginia Mts.
23. Stillwater Range
24. Clan Alpine Mts.
25. Desatoya Mts.
26. Toiyabe Range
27. Toquima Range
28. Simpson Park Mts.
29. Monito Range
30. Diamond Mts.
31. White Pine Range
32. Egan Range
33. Schell Creek Range
34. Snake Range
35. Wilson Creek Range
36. Grant Range

(Key continued on next page.)

37. Pancake Range
38. Hot Creek Range
39. Wassuk Range
40. Gillis Range
41. Excelsior Mts.
42. Silver Peak Range
43. Cactus Range
44. Kawich Range
45. Reveille Range
46. Belted Range
47. Mormon Mts.
48. Virgin Mts.
49. Muddy Mts.
50. Sheep Range
51. Spring Mts.
52. McCollough Range

California

1. Warner Range
2. White Mts.
3. Inyo Mts.
4. Panamint Range
5. Funeral Mts.
6. Black Mts.
7. Avawatz Mts.
8. Ord Mts.
9. Bullion Mts.
10. Bristol Mts.
11. Providence Mts.
12. Chemehuevi Mts.
13. Whipple Mts.
14. Turtle Mts.
15. Chocolate Mts.

Arizona

1. Black Mts.
2. Cerbat Mts.
3. Hualpai Mts.
4. Chemehuevi Mts.
5. Harcuvar Mts.
6. Santa Maria Mts.
7. Bradshaw Mts.
8. Harquahala Mts.
9. White Tank Mts.
10. Gila Bend Mts.
11. SH Mts.
12. Kofa Mts.
13. Dome Rock Mts.
14. Trigo Mts.
15. Castle Dome Mts.
16. Gila Mts.
17. Cabeza Prieta Mts.
18. Mohawk Mts.
19. Grover Mts.
20. Sanceda Mts.
21. Sand Tank Mts.
22. Maricopa Mts.
23. Sierra Estrella
24. Salt River Mts.
25. Comobabi Mts.
26. Baboquivari Mts.
27. Sierrita Mts.
28. Tumacacori Mts.
29. Patagonia Mts.
30. Santa Rita Mts.
31. Huachuca Mts.
32. Whetstone Mts.
33. Rincon Mts.
34. Santa Catalina Mts.
35. Pinal Mts.

36. Superstition Mts.
37. Mazatal Mts.
38. Sierra Ancha
39. Gila Mts.
40. Santa Teresa Mts.
41. Galiuro Mts.
42. Pinaleno Mts.
43. Natanes Mts.
44. Peloncillo Mts.
45. Dos Cabezas Mts.
46. Chiricahua Mts.
47. Mule Mts.

New Mexico

1. Peloncillo Mts.
2. Animas Mts.
3. Big Hatchet Mts.
4. Big Burro Mts.
5. Summit Mts.
6. Pinos Altos Range
7. Mogollon Mts.
8. Black Range (Mimbres Mts.)
9. San Mateo Mts.
10. Sierra de las Uvas
11. Florida Mts.
12. Organ Mts.
13. San Andres Mts.
14. Caballo Mts.
15. Fra Cristobal Mts.
16. Magdalena Mts.
17. Sierra Ladron
18. Manzano Mts.
19. Sandia Mts.
20. Ortiz Mts.
21. Pedernal Hills
22. Gallinas Peak
23. Sierra Oscura
24. Capitan Mts.
25. Sacramento Mts.

Texas

1. Franklin Mts.
2. Hueco Mts.
3. Quitman Mts.
4. Sierra Diablo
5. Guadalupe Mts.
6. Delaware Mts.
7. Apache Mts.
8. Davis Mts.
9. Sierra Vieja
10. Glass Mts.

KEY TO LAKES AND PLAYAS

Utah
a. Utah L.
b. Sevier L.

Nevada
a. Franklin L.
b. Carson Sink
c. Black Rock Desert
d. Smoke Creek Desert
e. Pyramid L.
f. Winnemucca L.
g. Goshute Valley
h. Antelope Valley
i. Cave Valley
j. Railroad Valley

k. Gabbs Valley
l. Walker L.
m. Teels Marsh
n. Columbus Marsh
o. Clayton Valley
p. Penoyer Valley
q. Garden Valley
r. Coal Valley
s. Desert Valley
t. Dry Lake Valley
u. Indian Spring Valley
v. Pahrump Valley
w. Ivanpah Valley
x. Lake Mead

Oregon
a. Klamath Lakes
b. Summer L.
c. Abert L.
d. Goose L.

California
a. Deep Springs Valley
b. Eureka Valley
c. Saline Valley
d. Owens L.
e. Panamint Valley
f. China L.
g. Searles L.
h. Coyote L.
i. Soda L.
j. Bristol L.
k. Cadiz L.
l. Danby L.
m. Palen Dry L.
n. Salton Sea

Arizona
a. Lake Mohave
b. Red L.
c. Havasu L. (Parker Dam. Res.)
d. Theo. Roosevelt L.
e. San Carlos Res.
f. Wilcox Playa (Sulphur Springs Valley).

New Mexico
a. Alkali Flat
b. Plains of San Augustin
c. Elephant Butte Res.
d. Caballo Res.
e. Estancia Basin

Texas
a. Salt Basin

KEY TO NATIONAL PARKS AND MONUMENTS

LC, Lehman Cave Nat. Mon., Nev.
     Death Valley Nat. Mon., Death
     Valley, Calif.
JT, Joshua Tree Nat. Mon., Calif.
LM, Lake Mead Recreational Area,
     Ariz.-Nev.
SC, Saguaro Cactus Nat. Mon., Ariz.
OP, Organpipe Cactus Nat. Mon., Ariz.
CH, Chiricahua Nat. Mon., Ariz.
WS, White Sands Nat. Mon., N. Mex.
     Big Bend Nat. Park, Big Bend, Texas

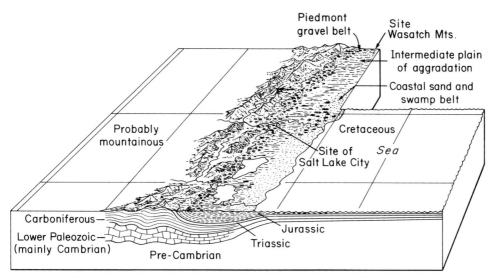

Figure 16.2 *Diagram of early Cretaceous paleogeography in northern Utah, with cross section about through central Utah, showing the Paleozoic geosynclinal belt along the eastern edge of the Basin and Range Province and the stable platform to the east. [From U.S.G.S. Prof. Paper.]*

nations visualized the province as being the crest of a broad arch that collapsed. Another interpretation supposed collapse into a liquid substratum that was the source of the abundant volcanics erupted during the Cenozoic. A third interpretation supposes lateral transfer eastward of subcrustal material, perhaps by convection, to elevate the Colorado Plateau and permit collapse of the Basin and Range Province. Still a fourth possibility is rifting as a result of the western edge of the continent drifting northwestward away from the craton. This last possibility is also suggested by the present-day faulting along the Pacific Border (see Chapter 18). These are by no means mutually exclusive interpretations; they may all have contributed to the block faulting.

Geologic History

Figure 16.3 illustrates diagrammatically the evolution of the structure and topography of the Great Basin. In late Precambrian time there was a geosyncline in the southern part of the Great Basin, where at least 30,000 feet of sediments accumulated. Only the edge of this geosyncline is indicated in Figure 16.3, because the Precambrian rocks are buried in most parts of the Great Basin, and the limits of the geosyncline are poorly known.

In Paleozoic time a second geosyncline occupied much of what is now the Great Basin, and in it another 30,000 feet or more of sediments accumulated (Fig. 16.3, stage 1). In the Central Area and to the east there are formations of carbonate rocks (limestone and dolomite) and shale; toward the west there are formations derived in part from volcanic eruptives. Some folding and faulting took place at various times during the Paleozoic, but the resulting structures are not shown in Figure 16.3.

In Early Mesozoic time (stage 2) a third geosyncline developed and another 30,000 feet or so of sediments accumulated. These sediments, also derived in large part from volcanic eruptives, overlap the west flank of the Paleozoic geosyncline.

In middle and late Mesozoic time (stage 3) a batholith formed at the site of the Sierra Nevada (not shown), and the Mesozoic and Paleozoic formations in the Great Basin were folded, thrust faulted, and uplifted to form the mountains from

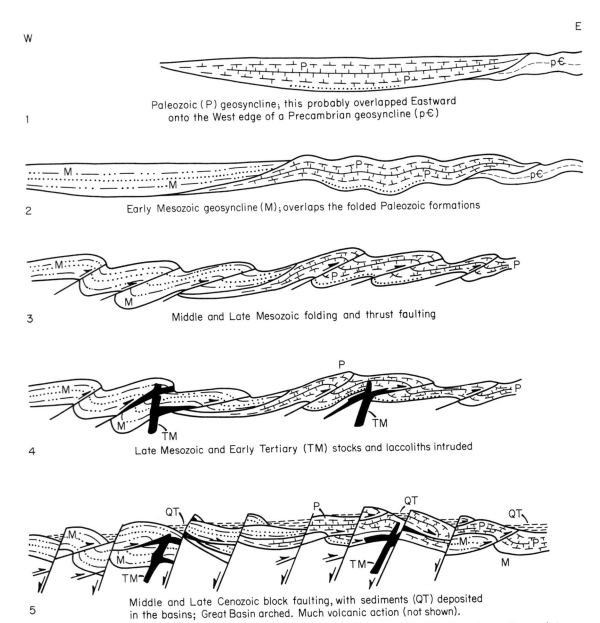

W

E

1   Paleozoic (P) geosyncline; this probably overlapped Eastward
onto the West edge of a Precambrian geosyncline (pЄ)

2   Early Mesozoic geosyncline (M); overlaps the folded Paleozoic formations

3   Middle and Late Mesozoic folding and thrust faulting

4   Late Mesozoic and Early Tertiary (TM) stocks and laccoliths intruded

5   Middle and Late Cenozoic block faulting, with sediments (QT) deposited
in the basins; Great Basin arched. Much volcanic action (not shown).

Figure 16.3 *Evolution of the structure and topography of the Great Basin. Three geosynclines—Precambrian, Paleozoic, and early Mesozoic—are imbricated, with the younger ones progressively farther west. During each geosynclinal stage, there were many episodes of folding and faulting. The block faulting that developed the basins and ranges as we know them is still continuing.*

which sediments were shed eastward into the Cretaceous geosyncline that had occupied the site of the Rocky Mountains and Great Plains. Later (stage 4), the igneous activity that had begun much earlier in the Sierra Nevada spread eastward; and stocks and laccoliths were intruded into the deformed Mesozoic and Paleozoic rocks.

In middle Tertiary time the Great Basin began to be block faulted, and this faulting has continued to the present time (stage 5). Volcanism (not shown), which was sporadic during the early Tertiary, became extensive during the stage of block faulting. Along the north side of the Great Basin, lavas and other eruptives completely buried the faulted and folded older rocks. As block-faulting progressed, sediments derived from the up-faulted blocks were deposited in the basins. In some, the fill is enormously thick. Death Valley, for example, is estimated to contain 8,000 feet of fill. Death Valley therefore has been down-faulted 2 miles below sea level, but has been kept nearly filled with sediments derived by erosion of the neighboring uplifted blocks.

A northwest-trending belt of volcanic rocks extends across the middle of the Great Basin from the southern part of the Colorado Plateau to the northwest corner of the Basin. These volcanic deposits include a high percentage of glassy, rhyolitic, pyroclastic material that is welded together by volcanic glass and is known as "welded tuff." The mass of angular, glassy fragments and particles of stone and minerals is cemented together (welded) by contorted layers of glass. They are the result of eruptions of the Peléan type, which produce glowing avalanches of incandescent volcanic dust and fragments of the glassy shells of burst bubbles. Associated with the tuffs are basaltic lavas to the northwest, in the Harney Basin of the Columbia-Snake River Plateau, and to the southeast, on the south rim of the Colorado Plateau, the eruptives are largely basaltic. Perhaps the three areas of volcanism are connected, and the Peléan mode of eruption across the Great Basin could be due to widespread frothing of the subterranean magmas as

a result of the extensive middle Tertiary faulting in the Great Basin.

The rocks in the mountains bordering Death Valley represent all the great eras of geologic time, the Precambrian, Paleozoic, Mesozoic, and Cenozoic (Fig. 16.4, Table 16.2). Precambrian rocks exposed there include at least 3,000 feet of metamorphic rocks belonging to the crystalline basement plus a sequence of much younger and only slightly metamorphosed sedimentary rocks (Pahrump Series; see Table 16.2) that total roughly 10,000 feet in thickness. Overlying the Pahrump are three more Precambrian formations, the Noonday Dolomite, Johnnie Formation, and Stirling Quartzite, totalling about 7,000 feet thick.

All periods of the Paleozoic, from Cambrian to Permian, are represented by a sequence 30,000 feet thick, which consists mostly of carbonates. Triassic formations nearby, totalling 8,000 feet thick, include carbonate rocks, siltstone, and volcanic rocks.

The metamorphic rocks belonging to the crystalline basement are samples of the older part of the continental crust of North America. The rocks look impressively massive and strong where they form the bold front of the Black Mountains south of Badwater, but in fact, beginning in late Precambrian time they were part of the fragile western margin of the crust of North America and were repeatedly bent downward to form troughs (geosynclines) many miles deep, scores of miles wide, and hundreds of miles long. The site of Death Valley was in the geosynclines; the site of Grand Canyon was east of them, on a stable shelf of the continent.

The stable shelf at Grand Canyon remained so from the late Precambrian to the Paleozoic and beyond. That shelf extends under the entire central United States, and the rocks forming it are widely exposed in the Canadian Shield.

Death Valley has been part of the unstable, mobile edge of the continent. The contrast in geology between Death Valley and Grand Canyon illustrates the broader-scale structure of our continent. At Grand Canyon the formations are

Table 16.2

Rock Formations Exposed in the Death Valley Area

System	Series	Formation	Lithology and Thickness	Characteristic Fossils
Quaternary	Holocene		Fan gravel; silt and salt on the floor of the playa; less than 100 feet thick.	
	Pleistocene		Fan gravel; silt and salt buried under the floor of the playa; thickness perhaps 2,000 feet.	
		Funeral Fanglomerate	Cemented fan gravel with interbedded basaltic lavas; gravels cut by veins of calcite (Mexican onyx); perhaps 1,000 feet thick.	Diatoms, pollen
Tertiary	Pliocene	Furnace Creek Formation	Cemented gravel; silty and saliferous playa deposits; various salts, especially borates: thickness more than 5,000 feet.	Fossils, scarce
	Miocene	Artist Drive Formation	Cemented gravel; playa deposits; much volcanic debris; thickness perhaps 5,000 feet.	Fossils, scarce
	Oligocene	Titus Canyon Formation	Cemented gravel; mostly stream deposits; thickness 3,000 feet.	Vertebrates, e.g., titanotheres
	Eocene and Paleocene		Granitic intrusions and volcanics; not known to be represented by sedimentary deposits.	
Cretaceous and Jurassic			Not represented; area was being eroded.	
Triassic		Butte Valley formation of Johnson (1957)	Exposed in Butte Valley are 8,000 ft of meta-sediments and volcanics.	Ammonities, smooth-shelled brachiopods, belemnites, and hexacorals.
Carboniferous	Pennsylvanian and Permian	Formations at east foot of Tucki Mountain	Conglomerate, limestone, and some shale. Conglomerate contains cobbles of limestone of Mississippian, Pennsylvanian, and Permian age. Limestone and shale contain spherical chert nodules. Abundant fusulinids. Thickness uncertain on account of faulting; estimate 3,000 ft + ; top eroded.	Beds with fusulinids, especially *Fusulinella*.
	Mississippian and Pennsylvanian(?)	Rest Spring Shale	Mostly shale, some limestone; abundant spherical chert nodules. Thickness uncertain because of faulting; estimate 750 ft.	None.

Period	Age	Formation	Lithology	Fossils
Carboniferous (Continued)	Mississippian	Tin Mountain Limestone and younger limestone.	Mapped as one unit. Tin Mountain Limestone, 1,000 ft thick, is black with thin-bedded lower member and thick-bedded upper member. Unnamed limestone formation, 725 ft thick, consists of interbedded chert and limestone in thin beds and in about equal proportions.	Mixed brachiopods, corals, and crinoid stems. *Syringopora* (open-spaced colonies). *Caninia* cf. *C. cornicula.*
Devonian	Middle and Upper Devonian.	Lost Burro formation	Limestone in light and dark beds 1–10 ft thick give striped effect on mountainsides. Two quartzite beds, each about 3 ft thick, near base; numerous sandstone beds 800–1,000 ft above base. Top 200 ft is well-bedded limestone and quartzite. Total thickness uncertain because of faulting; estimated 2,000 ft.	Brachiopods abundant, especially *Spirifer, Cyrtospirifer, Productilla, Carmarotoechia, Atrypa*. Stromatoporoids. *Syringopora* (closely spaced colonies).
Silurian and Devonian	Silurian and Lower Devonian.	Hidden Valley Dolomite.	Thick-bedded, fine-grained, and even-grained dolomite; mostly light color. Thickness 300–1,400 ft.	Crinoid stems abundant, including large types. *Favosites.*
Ordovician	Upper Ordovician	Ely Springs Dolomite.	Massive black dolomite; 400–800 ft thick.	Streptelasmatid corals: *Grewingkia, Bighornia.* Brachiopods.
	Middle and Upper(?) Ordovician.	Eureka Quartzite	Massive quartzite, with thin-bedded quartzite at base and top; 350 ft thick.	None.
	Lower and Middle Ordovician.	Pogonip Group	Dolomite, with some limestone, at base; shale unit in middle; massive dolomite at top. Thickness, 1,500 ft.	Abundant large gastropods in massive dolomite at top: *Palliseria* and *Maclurites*, associated with *Receptaculites*. In lower beds: *Protopliomerops, Kirkella*, Orthid brachiopods.
Cambrian	Upper Cambrian	Nopah Formation	Highly fossiliferous shale member 100 ft thick at base; upper 1,200 ft is dolomite in thick alternating black and light bands about 100 ft thick. Total thickness of formation 1,200–1,500 ft.	In upper part, gastropods. In basal 100 ft, trilobite trash beds containing: *Elburgia, Pseudagnostus, Homagnostus, Elvinia, Apsotreta.*
	Middle and Upper Cambrian.	Bonanza King Formation.	Mostly thick-bedded and massive dark-colored dolomite; a thin-bedded limestone member 500 ft thick 1,000 ft below top of the formation; 2 brown-weathering shaly units, about 200 and 500 ft, respectively, below the thin-bedded member. Total thickness uncertain because of faulting; estimated about 3,000 ft in Panamint Range; 2,000 ft in Funeral Mountains.	The only fossiliferous bed is the shale below the limestone member that occurs near the middle of the formation. This shale contains linguloid brachiopods and trilobite trash beds with fragments of "*Ehmaniella.*"

Table 16.2 (Continued)

System	Series	Formation	Lithology and Thickness	Characteristic Fossils
Cambrian (Continued)	Lower and Middle Cambrian.	Carrara Formation.	An alternation of shaly and silty members with limestone members; transitional between the underlying clastic formations and the overlying carbonate ones. Thickness about 1,000 ft but variable because of shearing.	Numerous trilobite trash beds in lower part yield fragments of olenellid trilobites.
	Lower Cambrian	Zabriskie Quartzite.	Quartzite, mostly massive and granulated due to shearing; locally in beds 6 in. to 2 ft thick; not much crossbedded. Thickness more than 150 ft; variable because of shearing.	No fossils.
Cambrian and Cambrian(?)	Lower Cambrian and Lower Cambrian(?).	Wood Canyon Formation	Basal unit is well-bedded quartzite about 1,650 ft thick; shaly unit above this 520 ft thick contains lowest olenellids in the section; top unit of dolomite and quartzite 400 ft thick.	A few scattered olenellid trilobites and archaeocyathids in the upper part of the formation. *Scolithus?* tubes.
		Stirling Quartzite	Well-bedded quartzite in beds 1–5 ft thick comprising thick members of quartzite 700–800 ft thick separated by 500 ft of purple shale; crossbedding conspicuous in quartzite. Maximum thickness about 2,000 ft.	None.
		Johnnie Formation	Mostly shale, in part olive brown, in part purple. Basal member 400 ft thick is interbedded dolomite and quartzite with pebble conglomerate. Locally, tan dolomite near the middle and at the top. Thickness more than 4,000 ft.	None.
Precambrian		Noonday Dolomite	In southern Panamint Range, dolomite in indistinct beds; lower part cream colored, upper part gray. Thickness 800 ft. Farther north where mapped as Noonday(?) Dolomite, contains much limestone, tan and white, and some limestone conglomerate. Thickness about 1,000 ft.	*Scolithus?* tubes.
		Unconformity		
		Kingston Peak(?) Formation	Mostly conglomerate, quartzite, and shale; some limestone and dolomite near middle. At least 3,000 ft thick.	None.

Pahrump Series	Beck Spring Dolomite	Blue-gray cherty dolomite; thickness estimated about 500 ft.	None.
	Crystal Spring Formation	Total thickness about 2,000 ft. Consists of a basal conglomerate overlain by quartzite that grades upward into purple shale and thinly bedded dolomite; upper part, thick-bedded dolomite, diabase, and chert. Talc deposits where diabase intrudes dolomite.	None.
	—Unconformity—		
	Rocks of the crystalline basement	Metasedimentary rocks with granitic intrusions.	None.

Source: From U.S. Geological Survey Professional Paper 494-A.

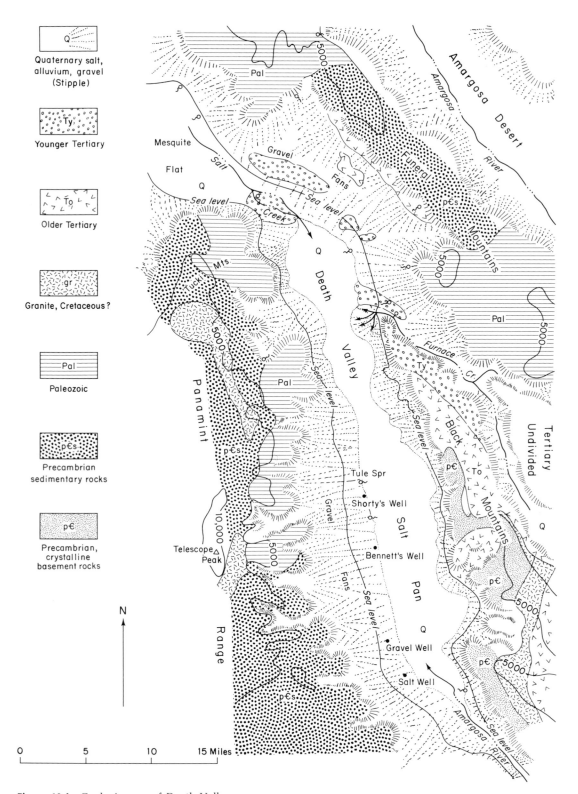

Figure 16.4 *Geologic map of Death Valley.*

thin and nearly horizontal; at Death Valley they are thick and greatly deformed by folding and faulting; igneous activity melted some rocks, and these formed granitic intrusions and volcanic eruptions.

The later Precambrian and the Paleozoic and Triassic rocks began as marine sedimentary deposits; they were deposited in the ancient seas that flooded the geosynclines along the mobile belt at the edge of the stable part of the continent. Subsequently they were uplifted, folded, faulted, and altered by igneous activity.

During the Jurassic and Cretaceous, Death Valley was greatly elevated, and the deformed rocks were eroded. In early Tertiary time volcanism and granitic intrusions reached a maximum, and the eruptive rocks and the sediments derived from them collected in structural basins similar to those of today. The later Cenozoic formations are mostly playa and fan-gravel deposits eroded from the mountains and washed into the basins as we know them.

Structural Framework and Topography

GREAT BASIN

The Great Basin, which makes up about half of the Basin and Range Province, centers in Nevada but extends into the adjoining states. The Great Basin consists typically of linear, roughly north-south mountain ranges separated by valleys, many of which are closed basins. Only three small parts of the Great Basin drain to its exterior: a small part of the northeast corner of the section drains north to the Snake River; Pit River, a tributary of the Sacramento River, drains Goose Lake and part of the northwest corner of the section; part of the southeast corner drains to the Virgin River, which joins the Colorado at Lake Mead.

The relief between the valleys and adjoining mountains only locally exceeds 5,000 feet, although altitudes in the Great Basin range from below sea level, at Death Valley, to more than 13,000 feet. Five subdivisions of the Great Basin may be distinguished on the basis of their struc-

ture, topography, hydrography, and kind of ground (Fig. 16.5). These are:

1. The Central Area of elevated basins and ranges;

2. The Bonneville Basin east of the central area;

3. The Lahontan Basin west of the central area;

4. The Lava and Lake Area at the northwest corner of the Section;

5. The Southern Area.

The Central Area is characterized by valleys that are mostly 5,000 feet in altitude. Some are closed, but none contain perennial lakes. Dry lake beds and alluvial flats make up about 10 percent of the Central Area. The remaining part is about equally divided between the mountains and the gravel fans sloping from them. A large part of the Central Area drains to the Lahontan Basin by way of the Humboldt River.

The mountain ranges in the eastern and northern parts of the Central Area are linear ridges (Fig. 16.6) of complexly deformed miogeosynclinal Paleozoic rocks consisting in large part of limestone. To the west the rocks are mostly eugeosynclinal sandstone, siltstone, and shale derived from volcanic rocks. The eugeosynclinal facies has been overthrust eastward onto the miogeosynclinal facies. Block faulting of these folded and faulted rocks produced the basins and ranges. At about the time this block faulting started, there were extensive eruptions of lavas and tuffs in the southwest part of the Central Area, and these blockfaulted, volcanic rocks form the ranges there. The downfaulted blocks throughout the Central Area are buried under the debris washed into the valleys by erosion of the uplifted blocks. The block faulting has continued into historic time, and in many valleys the gravel fans and other valley fill are faulted along with the bedrock. This recent faulting and tilting of the block mountains has contributed to some of the drainage anomalies to be described later. (p. 523).

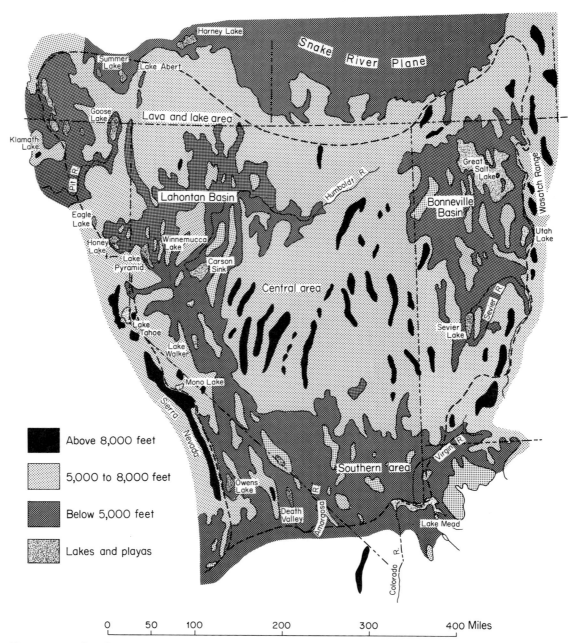

Figure 16.5 *Altitudes and subdivisions in the Great Basin. The central area is high; the Bonneville and Lahonton basins are low. The Great Basin appears to be arched.*

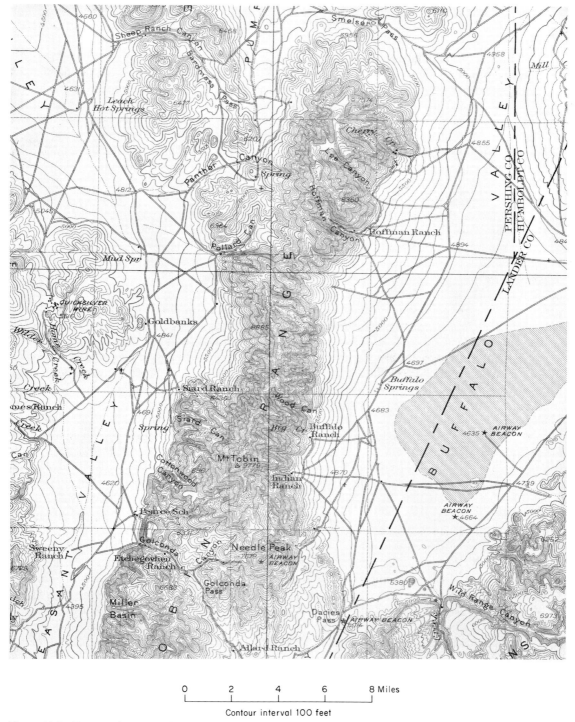

0   2   4   6   8 Miles

Contour interval 100 feet

Figure 16.6 *Topographic map of typical north-south basins and ranges in the Great Basin. There are three major kinds of ground in the Province: mountains, gravel fans sloping from them, and dry lake beds or alluvial flats in the middle of the basins. Compare with Figure 14.39. [From U.S.G.S. Sonoma Range, Nevada, Quadrangle.]*

The Bonneville Basin, the eastern subdivision of the Great Basin, covers most of western Utah. It is structurally similar to the Central Area but lower. In most of this subsection the basins are less than 5,000 feet in altitude. They are slightly higher in southwestern Utah. Great Salt Lake, the lowest part of the subsection is at an altitude of 4,200 feet. In the Bonneville Basin, playas and alluvial flats are extensive and make up about 40 percent of the basin. The mountains cover about a quarter of the basin, and gravel fans cover the rest—a proportion very different from that in the Central Area, probably because the Bonneville Basin is so much lower.

In structure and composition, most of the mountain ranges in the Bonneville Basin are like those in the northeastern part of the Central Area. The ranges are mostly complexly folded and faulted miogeosynclinal Paleozoic rocks that were later divided into structural blocks by late Tertiary and Quaternary block faulting. To the south, volcanic rocks form some mountain ranges; in the north, the volcanic rocks are young and occur mostly in the basins.

The Bonneville Basin lacks exterior drainage and has three major lakes within it—Great Salt Lake, Utah Lake, and Sevier Lake. Sevier Lake is dry much of the time now, but would be perennial if it received the water that is consumed for irrigation.

The Lahontan Basin, between the Central Area and the Sierra Nevada, is structurally and topographically similar to the Bonneville Basin. The greater part is alluvial flat and playa, and it too contains some large lakes—Pyramid Lake, Lake Winnemucca, Walker Lake, and the playa at Carson Sink at the mouth of the Humboldt River. The mountain ranges are fault blocks of Triassic and Jurassic formations and Tertiary volcanic rocks. The Triassic and Jurassic formations are complexly folded and faulted in much the same way as are the Paleozoic formations in the Central Area and Bonneville Basin.

The Lava and Lake Area northwest of the Lahontan Basin is topographically higher than the Lahontan Basin. It is a block-faulted lava plateau with numerous high volcanic cones. The lavas probably bury complexly folded and faulted Jurassic and Triassic formations that are structurally lower than those in the Lahontan Basin. Several lakes—Honey Lake, Eagle Lake, and others in the Klamath area—are crowded against the foot of the mountains at the edge of the Great Basin. There is exterior drainage from Goose Lake via the Pit River and from Klamath Lakes via the Klamath River.

The topographic grain of the Lava and Lake Area has much less linearity than the other parts of the Great Basin because the thick, extensive lava flows and volcanic cones are young, in large part of Quaternary age, and they partly mask the block faulting, which in large part is of late Tertiary age.

The Southern Area bears some structural resemblances to the Central Area but is lower, both structurally and topographically. Toward the south, the mountain ranges trend northward, but they are separated from the ranges in the Central Area by a northwest-trending belt of mountains and hills, most of which are small and have very irregular outlines. This belt, which parallels the diagonal southwest border of Nevada, extends from the vicinity of Lake Mead to the vicinity of Walker Lake. It coincides with a zone of shearing, the Las Vegas shear zone, along which there seems to have been some miles of lateral movement; the blocks on the southwest side of the shear zone have moved northwestward relative to the blocks on the northeast side. The displacement seems to decrease northwestward.

The rocks that form the mountain ranges in the Southern Area include complexly folded and faulted Paleozoic and Precambrian rocks, some small masses of equally deformed Triassic and Jurassic rocks, granitic intrusions (some related to the Sierra Nevada batholith and some much younger), and a thick series of Tertiary and Quaternary sedimentary and volcanic rocks. All these were block faulted during middle and late Tertiary time and during the Quaternary, as was the rest of the Great Basin.

Along the western boundary of the Southern Area, at the foot of the Sierra Nevada, are Mono Lake and Owens Lake. Death Valley, which in-

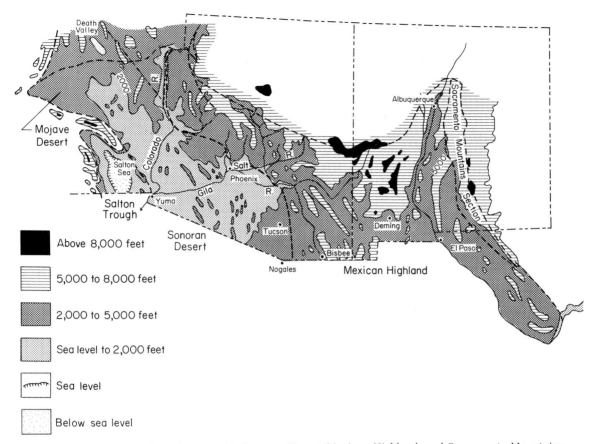

Figure 16.7 *Altitudes in the Salton Trough, Sonoran Desert, Mexican Highland, and Sacramento Mountains Sections of the Basin and Range Province.*

cludes more than 200 square miles that are more than 250 feet below sea level, collects the runoff from almost 9,000 square miles of surrounding area, but is rarely flooded. Most of the time it is a dry, salt-encrusted playa. The southeastern part of the Southern Area drains to the Colorado River.

SONORAN DESERT

The Sonoran Desert Section, which includes the Mojave Desert in southeastern California and the deserts in southwestern Arizona, extends far southward into Mexico along the east shore of the Gulf of California, and is named for the State

of Sonora, in Mexico. Except where the province joins its higher neighbors, altitudes rarely exceed 3,000 feet and are mostly less than 2,000 feet (Fig. 16.7). Total relief and local relief are very much less than in the Great Basin, and much of the faulting may be older.

The Mojave Desert and southwest Arizona are structurally higher than the Great Basin. The rocks are mostly metamorphic. Some are of Precambrian age; some are younger. Presumably much of the metamorphism occurred in late Mesozoic and early Cenozoic time, when the Great Basin was intensely deformed and intruded by satellites of the Sierra Nevada batholith. Some of the granitic rocks in the Sonoran Desert Section are late Mesozoic and early to middle Cenozoic in age, like those in the Great Basin, but some are of Precambrian age.

Possibly some of the granite is hybrid—that is, Precambrian granite that become partly recrystallized during the structural deformation and igneous activity that took place in late Mesozoic and early Cenozoic time. Some minerals in such hybrid granite may be relict, and date from Precambrian time; others are new minerals dating from the metamorphism that formed the granite.

Block faulting in the Sonoran Desert Section, as in the Great Basin, probably started in middle or early Tertiary time and continued until Pleistocene time, but the amount of Holocene faulting has been less except in the Mojave Desert. The block mountains, however, are irregular in outline, perhaps indicating a greater frequency of transverse faults that divide the main blocks. The structure seems to consist of a series of horsts and grabens without dominant tilting in one direction. In the southern part of the section there is northwest linearity in the grain of the topography. In the north-central part the linearity is northerly. In the Mojave Desert the outlines of the ranges are irregular, although the major block faults there trend northwest.

Mountains make up about 40 percent of the section; basins, about 60 percent. The mountain ranges, however, are short compared to those in the Great Basin. The Arizona part has through drainage to the Gila and Colorado Rivers (Fig.

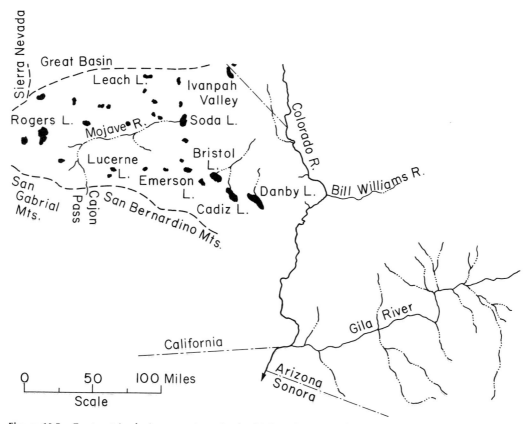

Figure 16.8 *Contrast in drainage systems in the Mojave Desert and in the parts of the Sonoran Desert Section that lie within Arizona. (A) Southwest Arizona has through drainage to the Colorado and Gila rivers and their tributaries. (B) Drainage in the Mojave Desert is broken up by a series of closed basins containing dry lakes.*

16.8); there are few closed basins. The Mojave Desert part, however, lacks through drainage and consists of a series of closed basins.

For more than 100 miles eastward from the Sierra Nevada, the boundary between the Mojave Desert and the Great Basin is along the Garlock fault—a major transverse fracture with many miles of displacement. The block on the Mojave Desert side of the fault has moved eastward relative to the block on the Great Basin side. The southern boundary of the Sonoran Desert Section is along the San Andreas and related faults at or near the foot of the San Gabriel and San Bernardino mountains, and the Mojave block has moved eastward relative to them too. The Mojave Desert, therefore, is a pie-shaped structural block that has moved relatively eastward. It has also moved upward relative to the Great Basin.

Because of the scarcity of datable Mesozoic and older formations in the Sonoran Desert Section, the structural history is poorly known. In Cretaceous time this area was probably part of the upland from which sediments were shed eastward and northeastward to the geosyncline that extended across the site of the Colorado Plateau and Rocky Mountains. This area is now structurally and topographically lower than the Colorado Plateau. The structural displacements that reversed the structural and topographic relationship by raising the Colorado Plateau high above the Basin and Range Province occurred during the Cenozoic (see Chapter 15).

Volcanism was widespread in the Sonoran Desert Section during Tertiary and Quaternary time, and some volcanic activity occurred during late Quaternary time. Structural movements in the Mojave Desert occurred recently enough for the drainage to be broken up into small closed basins (Fig. 16.8). Presumably the deformation there continued on a considerable scale for a longer time than it did farther east.

SALTON TROUGH

The Salton Trough is the emerged part of the thousand-mile-long trough occupied by the Gulf of California. Three major faults extend north-

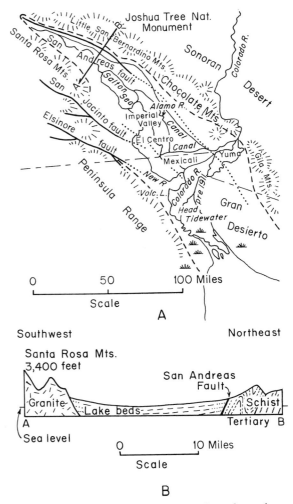

Figure 16.9 (A) *Salton Trough (boundary shown by broken line) and some of the principal faults outlining it. (B) Cross section north of Salton Sea.*

westward into California from this structural and topographic depression—the San Andreas, San Jacinto, and Elsinore faults (Fig. 16.9).

The northeast side of the trough is fairly straight and is marked topographically by the Gila Mountains, Chocolate Mountains, and the mountains near Joshua Tree National Monument. The southwest side has offsets along the San Jacinto and Elsinore faults. Horizontal movement along these faults has been substantial, and along each one the block on the southwest side has moved northwestward relative to the block on the northeast side. This horizontal displacement between the two sides of the trough may amount to scores of miles.

The Gulf of California and its northern extension, the Salton Trough, have been variously interpreted. One theory is that the gulf occupies a graben that has been faulted downward between the mainland and Baja California. Another theory is that Baja California has been torn northwestward from the mainland and that the gulf and the trough are underlain shallowly by rocks belonging to the subcrust, an interpretation suggested by the fact that the underlying rocks are more dense than those that form the mountains on each side of the trough (Fig. 2.21).

The Colorado River is about 140 feet above sea level at Yuma, Arizona, near the apex of an alluvial fan that extends 50 miles southwestward across the trough. Where the fan joins the far side, the altitude is about 30 feet above sea level. From here the surface slopes southeastward about 15 miles to tidewater and northward about 50 miles to the Salton Sea, 235 feet below sea level.

Along the edges of the Salton Trough are marine deposits of late Tertiary age that contain pebbles derived from older formations in the adjoining mountains, showing that the Trough was in existence in the late Tertiary and was inundated by the Gulf of California at that time. North of Yuma, marine or brackish-water deposits of Pliocene (?) age occur along the Colorado River 300 feet above sea level. In the Salton Trough, late Tertiary marine beds are overlain by playa deposits, also of late Tertiary age, but apparently no marine deposits of Quaternary age have been found, which suggests that the gulf was excluded from the trough at about the beginning of Quaternary time, presumably by the formation of the Colorado River delta. Since then, during the Quaternary, the trough has been sinking, and the neighboring fault blocks, which include the Tertiary strata, have been rising. The mountains reach heights above 5,000 feet.

The trough and the delta have been downwarped during the Holocene Epoch. The presence of fresh fault scarps north of Salton Sea and the frequent occurrence of earthquakes attest to continued structural movement. Associated Holocene volcanic activity is indicated by deposits of volcanic ash (pumice) interbedded with lake beds, by the occurrence of mud volcanoes that emit sulfurous steam, and by hot springs.

A prehistoric lake, called Lake Cahuila, filled the trough to the level of the top of the delta. The beach line, which is marked by sand containing fresh-water shells and is distinct around much of the Salton Trough, varies in altitude from 30 to 57 feet above sea level, indicating at least 27 feet of warping since the lake features formed. Lake Cahuila may be only a few hundred years old.

An elaborate set of irrigation canals (Fig. 16.9) takes Colorado River water to the farmed land in the Imperial Valley, which is the area south of Salton Sea. In 1904 the River flooded and turned northward into the Salton Sea by way of old courses along the Alamo and New rivers. The steep slope northward favored those courses rather than the direction southward to the gulf. The depth of Salton Sea was doubled and a vast area inundated. The flooding was not checked until 1907, and in a few years after that evaporation had reduced the water to approximately its present level.

MEXICAN HIGHLAND SECTION

The Mexican Highland Section, which includes the Rio Grande Valley, is varied, both structurally and topographically. It grades westward into the Sonoran Desert Section, which is much lower, and it grades northward into the Colorado Plateau, which is much higher.

South of the Gila River and along the Rio Grande Valley, the section consists of well-defined mountain ranges separated by wide valleys. The mountains make up only a quarter or a third of the area; valleys occupy the rest. The mountain ranges consist of fault blocks. Along the Rio Grande Valley they trend north, but west of there they trend northwest. The direction of

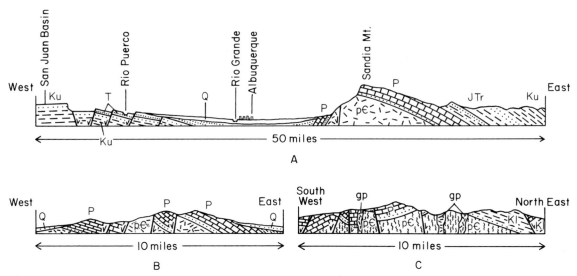

Figure 16.10 *Structural cross sections in the Mexican Highland Section. (A) Sandia Mountain and the Rio Grande Valley at Albuquerque, New Mexico. (B) Florida Mountains, New Mexico. (C) Mule Mountains at the Bisbee mining district, Arizona. pℇ, Precambrian; P, Paleozoic; JTr, Jurassic and Triassic; Kl, Lower Cretaceous; Ku, Upper Cretaceous; T, Tertiary; Q, Quaternary; gp, granitic intrusions. [After U.S.G.S.]*

the tilting and faulting are variable. Many ranges tilt east and are down-faulted on the west side; others tilt west and are down-faulted on the east side (Fig. 16.10). The valleys are mostly between 4,000 and 5,000 feet in altitude, and the mountains are 3,000 to 5,000 feet higher.

The drainage system is moderately well developed. Most of the Arizona portion drains to the San Pedro and Gila rivers. Most of the New Mexico and Texas portions drain to the Rio Grande. A few basins, however, are closed and contain playas; in New Mexico, several valleys that are not topographically closed are long, and they are so broad and flat that they are not crossed by streams. The basins, like others in the province, are filled, or nearly so, with debris eroded from the mountains.

The structural history of the Mexican Highland Section is as complex as that of the Great Basin. Major deformation occurred in southern Arizona early in the Mesozoic, and at that time erosion stripped the Paleozoic formations from some areas of Precambrian rocks (Fig. 16.10,C). Some granitic intrusions were emplaced at this time and are overlapped by 15,000 feet of marine

sedimentary formations of Early Cretaceous age. These formations include some volcanic debris, which suggests that the igneous activity may have continued into Early Cretaceous time and that some of the intrusions reached the surface and erupted.

In Early Cretaceous time this part of the Basin and Range Province must have been lower than the Colorado Plateau area, because the Lower Cretaceous formations thin toward the plateau. But in Late Cretaceous time the situation reversed. The southern part of the Mexican Highland Section was raised to become part of the upland that contributed sediments to the Upper Cretaceous sea that extended across the Colorado Plateau, the Rocky Mountains, and the Great Plains. Uplift of this part of the Mexican Highlands must have continued intermittently during Late Cretaceous time. The Lower Cretaceous formations are cut by granitic intrusions, some of which may be Late Cretaceous in age; others are of Tertiary age. In Tertiary time structural movements once again dropped the Mexican Highland Section below the Colorado Plateau. It was this displacement in late Miocene and Pliocene time that cut off the headwaters of the Little Colorado River (see p. 458).

The faulting that outlined the mountain ranges and basins apparently began in early or middle Tertiary time, as it did in the Great Basin. There was faulting before the deposition of the Santa Fe and other late Tertiary formations along the Rio Grande, but these formations were involved in later movements along the faults (Fig. 16.10,A). Some volcanism occurred about this time also. The faulting here seems to have ceased earlier than it did in the Salton Trough, Mojave Desert, and Great Basin, as is suggested by the integration of the drainage and the scarcity of fresh fault scarps. However, the belt of earthquake epicenters that extends northward along the Rio Grande Valley (Fig. 2.17) suggests that earth movement is still going on.

Along its northern boundary, the Mexican Highland Section grades into the Colorado Plateau, both structurally and topographically. In New Mexico, the northern part of the Highland is a block-faulted lava plateau that grades northward into the lava-covered Datil Section of the Colorado Plateau. The relationship is very similar to that along the northern edge of the Great Basin, where block-faulted lavas grade northward into the lava-capped plateaus there.

In Arizona, the northern boundary of the Highland is a dissected escarpment of Precambrian rocks capped by Paleozoic formations and Tertiary lavas. The escarpment is several thousand feet high, faces south, and extends 500 miles from the Colorado River to the Rio Grande Valley. The escarpment has acted as a structural hinge along which the country lying to the south has alternately been bent upward and downward relative to the country to the north. The country south of the escarpment was structurally lower than the country to the north during Early Cretaceous time. It was higher during late Cretaceous times and again during early and middle Tertiary time, when gravels were shed northward onto the Colorado Plateau. Today it is lower (Fig. 16.11).

SACRAMENTO MOUNTAINS SECTION

The Sacramento Mountains Section (Figs. 16.7, 16.12), which forms the eastern border of the Basin and Range Province and adjoins the Great

Figure 16.11 *Edge of the Colorado Plateau, near the mouth of the Grand Canyon, where the plateau overlooks the Basin and Range Province. The Joshua tree, Spanish bayonet, cholla, and prickly pear represent the Lower Sonoran Life Zone.*

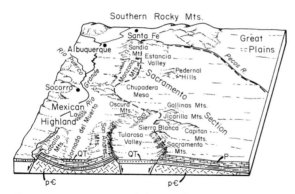

Figure 16.12 *Diagram of the Northern part of the Sacramento Section and of the structural basins along the Rio Grande in New Mexico.*

Plains, bears little resemblance to either province. It contains structural basins that are closed topographically; these basins seem to be due as much to downwarping as to faulting. Moreover, the structure of the fault blocks is not at all complex, for the formations in them have gentle dips suggestive of fault blocks on the Colorado Plateau. In addition, there are dome mountains with exposed cores of Precambrian rocks, and other dome mountains produced by the intrusion of stocks and laccoliths into the gently dipping sedimentary formations. The area of the section is small, but it comprises several distinctly different parts.

At the north is the Estancia Basin, which occupies a syncline between the Sandia-Manzano Mountains uplift on the west and an uplift of Precambrian rocks in the Pedernal Hills to the east. The basin is 50 miles long and 20 miles wide. A series of playas in the low part of the basin, near its southern end, are about 6,000 feet in altitude. The Sandia and Manzano mountains to the west exceed 10,000 feet; the Pedernal Hills to the east are about 7,500 feet in altitude. The basin is filled with Quaternary (and Tertiary?) deposits. The Paleozoic formations rise eastward and westward from under the fill. Beyond the Pedernal Hills the formations dip gently eastward under the head of the Pecos River Valley and under the Great Plains.

South of Estancia Valley is Chupadera Mesa, an east-sloping plateau formed by gently dipping Paleozoic formations that lie 1,500 to 2,000 feet above Estancia Valley. East and southeast of Chupadera Mesa are several mountains—the Gallinas, Jicarilla, and Capitan mountains, and Sierra Blanca (Fig. 16.11). Sierra Blanca Peak is about 12,000 feet in altitude; Capitan Peak, more than 10,000 feet. The mountains are formed of intrusive stocks and laccoliths, like the laccolithic mountains on the Colorado Plateau, but they also include volcanic rocks. Most of the igneous activity probably occurred during Tertiary time, but the volcanism continued into Quaternary time. A volcanic center near the southeast edge of Chupadera Mesa erupted a basaltic lava flow 40 miles long and 1 to 4 miles wide that descended 1,500 feet from the mesa into Tularosa Valley. The flow is young, like some in the northern part of the Datil Section.

South of these igneous centers is the Sacramento Range, which extends more than 80 miles to the Texas border. This is a block of late Paleozoic formations that dip gently eastward under the broad valley of the Pecos River. The west side of the range is an escarpment 4,000 feet high, evidently formed by a fault that raised the mountain block above the Tularosa Basin. Southward, in Texas, the Sacramento Mountains become the Guadalupe (Fig. 16.13) and Delaware mountains; although structurally similar to the Sacramento Mountains, they are more faulted and they dip more steeply eastward. The high part of the Guadalupe Mountains, between Guadalupe Peak and El Capitan, now a National Park, is an exhumed, fossil limestone reef. The Carlsbad and other caverns, a few miles to the northeast, were eroded in the limestone during the Quaternary.

The Tularosa Basin contains white sand that is composed of gypsum dissolved from Permian formations and redeposited in saline playas in the valley. At White Sands National Monument the sand covers an area of 250 square miles with dunes averaging about 20 feet high. There, seemingly dry ground has phreatophytes rooted in shallow groundwater.

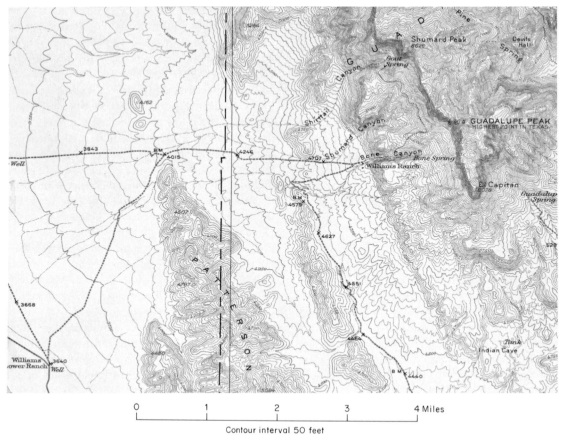

Figure 16.13 *Guadalupe Mountains, Texas, southern part of the Sacramento Mountains Section. The mountains are a block of late Paleozoic limestone faulted upward on the west and tilted east. The ridges at the west are other fault blocks partly buried by the coalescing alluvial fans. [From U.S.G.S. Guadalupe Peak, Texas, quadrangle.]*

Seismic Activity and Present-day Earth Movements

At least three quite independent lines of evidence show that the Basin and Range Province is undergoing considerable earth movement (structural deformation) at the present time. These are:

1. The numerous earthquake epicenters in and around the province;

2. The numerous Holocene fault scarps and warped or faulted Pleistocene and Holocene shorelines; and

3. The measurable displacement of benchmarks and measurements by tiltmeters.

The distribution of earthquake epicenters in and around the Basin and Range Province (Fig. 2.17) suggests that the province as a whole may be moving relative to its neighbors, but that the interior of the province either is relatively stable or is being arched without the kind of fracturing that produces earthquakes.

Earthquake data show a concentration of epicenters along the western and eastern parts of the Great Basin, and a few are distributed across its north and south borders. Few epicenters have been recorded in the interior of the Great Basin.

Epicenters are concentrated also in the Salton Trough and along the western part of the Sonoran Desert; a moderate number of epicenters of minor earthquakes, not shown on Figure 2.17, are aligned across the north and east sides of the Sonoran Desert and roughly outline that section.

In the Mexican Highland Section epicenters are concentrated in the Rio Grande depression, and there are several along the hinge line that joins this section with the Colorado Plateau. A few epicenters have been recorded in west Texas.

The southern third of the combined area of Arizona and New Mexico has few epicenters; apparently this is a stable area. It had been unstable during the late Precambrian, stable during the Paleozoic and early Mesozoic, and unstable during the Tertiary. Few parts of the continent have varied so in stability.

In general, the frequency of Holocene fault scarps and of faulted or warped Quaternary shorelines accords with the frequency of earthquake epicenters. These obviously Holocene displacements are most common along the western part of the Basin and Range Province, which is

the most active area seismically. Such features are common but less well developed along the eastern part of the Great Basin, where the shorelines of Pleistocene lakes have been warped and faulted (Fig. 16.31). They are even less well developed elsewhere in the province (Fig. 16.14, 16.15).

Present-day earth movements also are indicated by three kinds of surveys. Precise level surveys made at Lake Mead show that the lake basin has sunk a few millimeters, presumably because of the weight of water on that part of the crust. At Las Vegas, Nevada, the same surveys show more than 2 feet of sinking attributable to withdrawal of groundwater under that basin. The surveys also show that the entire area around Lake Mead has been regionally tilted a few millimeters southwestward since the surveys were begun in 1935.

In Death Valley, tiltmeters (Fig. 16.16) installed on various fault blocks show that tilting of the blocks is continuing. In general, the blocks are

Figure 16.14 *Recency of faulting is a feature of many parts of the Basin and Range Province. The west front of the Black Mountains in Death Valley was faulted recently enough to form hanging valleys (hourglass valleys) in the upfaulted Tertiary volcanics. The faulting also has dragged upward the top of an old fan (the fan surface stained dark with desert varnish).*

Figure 16.15 *Gravel fan (center skyline). This one is in Death Valley at the foot of the Black Mountains. The double terrace crossing the left part of the fan is a Holocene fault scarp representing about 10 feet of displacement caused by the most recent increment of downfaulting of the valley.*

being tilted in the direction in which the formations dip. The rate of tilting is variable, and when there are earthquakes nearby the direction of tilting may reverse, as if the blocks were settling back. There may be considerable vertical and horizontal displacement too, but neither has been measured.

Level-line surveys across various structures in the Basin and Range Province also reveal differences in altitude when the lines are resurveyed. Topographic engineers and geodosists generally attribute these differences to errors in the surveys, but geologists point out that the indicated changes in altitude all too often are in the direction the crustal blocks have been moving, and that the surveys are more accurate than the engineers have supposed.

Differences in the frequency of seismic activ-

ity and of Holocene faulting and warping may be due to differences in the rate and severity of the displacements, to differences in the depth of the earth movements, or to differences in the kind of movement. If more were known about the measurable displacements now going on in the Basin and Range Province we would be far better equipped to understand the processes of crustal deformation. The matter is of more than academic interest, as any survivor of an earthquake disaster can testify, and the Basin and Range Province, which is known to be actively moving, is one of the outdoor laboratories where the necessary research should be undertaken. The causes and cures of earthquakes have been the subject of accelerated studies undertaken since the 1964 disaster at Anchorage, Alaska; these studies have, understandably, been concentrated

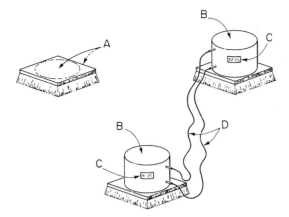

Figure 16.16 *Principle of tiltmeter used to measure earth tilt. Three concrete stands, approximately level, are arranged to form a triangle about 80 to 100 meters on a side. On top of each stand is a finely tooled brass plate (A) onto which pots (B) can be attached. The pots are half filled with water, to the height of a window (C) in the side, sealed, and 2 hoses (D) connect the water and the air in the two pots. The height of the water in the pots is measured by a finely calibrated screw at the base of each pot that can be viewed through the window when it touches the water surface. A series of readings are made between each pair of the concrete stands, and closures can be read to less than 10 microns. Readings are made annually or at other intervals to determine if the triangle has been tilted. In a short period of time the tilt may be less than the error of closure, but the readings can show accumulated tilt over a longer period of time.*

in the densely populated areas along the Pacific Coast, but much basic information applicable there could as well be obtained through intensive studies of earth movement in the Basin and Range Province.

Climate

The present climate in the Basin and Range Province is arid. Except on a few mountain summits, annual precipitation averages less than 20 inches, and in about three-quarters of the province, less than 10 inches (Fig. 16.17). This extreme aridity accounts for the scarcity of perennial streams and the abundance of playas. It also explains

why the large rivers flowing through the province all head elsewhere.

In the northern part of the Great Basin winters are cold, partly because of the northerly latitude and partly because of the high altitude. Summers are hot. The west side of the Great Basin is in the rain shadow of the Sierra Nevada and averages less than 5 inches of precipitation per year. Even in the eastern part, the average precipitation is barely twice that.

The southern part of the Great Basin and the sections south of it have very mild winters that have made these areas attractive to winter visitors. But summers there are very hot. To reverse the old saying, "It's not the humidity, it's the heat!" It has been said that, in the summer, mules bray only at midnight, that birds flying across the valleys have died of desiccation, and that when the Devil visited this area he took off his coat, exclaiming "It's a dry heat."

Death Valley represents the extreme. July temperatures there *average* above 100°F, and a maximum of 134°F has been recorded. Ground-surface temperatures of 190°F have been recorded there in summer. Winters, though, are mild and at that time of year the valley is packed with people. Freezing temperatures are very un-

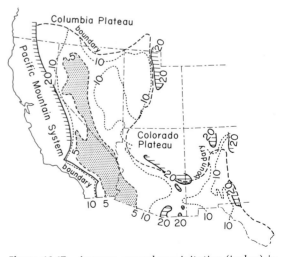

Figure 16.17 *Average annual precipitation (inches) in small areas of higher than average precipitation on some of the higher mountains. [After U.S.D.A.]*

common. The average January temperature is above 50°F, which is about the same as the average *annual* temperature across the central United States! The average annual rainfall in Death Valley is only a little more than 1.5 inches; evaporation, if there were anything to evaporate, would take place at the rate of about 150 inches annually.

In the Mohave Desert and Salton Trough the annual precipitation averages less than 5 inches, and most of that precipitation comes during the winter. Eastward, in the Sonoran Desert, the annual precipitation increases to more than 10 inches; that precipitation is biseasonal and about equally divided between the summer growing season and winter.

Temperatures in the Mexican Highland Section average considerably cooler than those in the Sonoran Desert and only slightly warmer than those in the northern part of the Great Basin. In much of this section the average annual precipitation is between 10 and 20 inches.

The valleys along the Rio Grande, sometimes referred to as the Chihuahuan Desert, named for the State of Chihuahua in Mexico, average less than 10 inches of precipitation annually, but the seasonal distribution differs from that of the deserts farther west, as most falls during the summer growing season.

High parts of the Sacramento Mountains Section receive more than 20 inches of annual precipitation. Even the Estancia Basin, on the lee side of the Sandia and Manzano mountains, receives an average of 12 inches annually. On account of the altitude, the average temperature in the Sacramento Mountains Section is lower and the growing season shorter than in most of the Basin and Range Province.

The Basin and Range Province was not always a desert. In Pleistocene time the climate was wet enough to develop lakes hundreds of feet deep (p. 92). The shorelines of some of these are conspicuous topographic features (Fig. 16.32, 16.33). Other products of the past climates are some of the soils and caliche deposits, including travertine deposits marking old springs that have dried (Fig. 16.18).

Water Supply

Supplies of surface water and groundwater in the Basin and Range Province are meager, for the rivers are few and small, and they become even smaller as they cross the province. In many of the basins both the surface water and the groundwater are saline. In most parts of the province the water table is deep and the water is of doubtful quality. Demand for water in the Basin and Range Province exceeds the supply.

The largest river, the Colorado, discharges between 10 and 15 million acre feet of water annually. Water from the river is used extensively for irrigation and other supplies in the Imperial Valley, and some of it is taken to the Los Angeles metropolitan area. There is little irrigation along the river because most of the valley is narrow and lacks a broad flood plain. Water is pumped from the river to irrigate land south of Yuma.

There is irrigation along the Rio Grande, but this river has an average annual discharge of only about a million acre feet in the vicinity of Albuquerque, and the discharge has decreased by nearly half by the time the river reaches El Paso. Where the Rio Grande discharges into the San Luis Valley from the San Juan Mountains, it contains about 134 ppm total dissolved solids (tds). At Santa Fe the tds is increased to 180 ppm, at El Paso 780 ppm, and at Ft. Quitman, 100 miles below El Paso, 1,780 ppm. Below that point, the Rio Grande is joined by the Pecos River, which crosses Permian salt beds, and at Carlsbad, New Mexico, that river contains 2,380 ppm of dissolved solids. Nevertheless, the freshening effect of tributaries from Mexico reduces the tds on the Coast Plain above Brownsville to 525 ppm.

The Rio Grande Basin embraces about 182,000 square miles, of which 89,000 are in the United States and the remainder in Mexico. The average annual discharge has been estimated to be about 9,000,000 acre-feet, most of which is consumed for irrigation and most of that by the United States. Before 1874, the river was navigable by small steamboats to Rio Grande City at the mouth of the San Juan, but a hurricane in 1874 so changed the lower course that it has not been usable for navigation since.

The Gila River, which has an annual flow of about 200,000 acre-feet, and its tributary Salt River, which is three times as large, are used for irrigation along their valleys.

Irrigation is intensive and extensive along the eastern border of the Great Basin, where considerably more than a million acre feet is available annually in the several rivers (Bear, Weber, Provo, and Sevier) draining to the basin from the Middle Rocky Mountains and High Plateaus. These water supplies already are highly developed and effectively so. Their development dates from 1848, when the Mormons, ending their trek across the Great Plains and Wyoming Basin, descended the well-watered canyons of the Wasatch Mountains, and came onto the fertile, irrigable benches that overlook Great Salt Lake.

Rivers entering the western part of the Great Basin (Truckee, Carson, Walker, and Owens rivers) also deliver considerably more than a million acre feet annually. Owens River is diverted for municipal supplies at Los Angeles. The others are used for irrigation and other supplies in their drainage basins.

The Humboldt River has an average discharge of perhaps 500,000 acre feet per year. Most of the water is consumed for irrigation, and the discharge in the lower stretch is barely 100,000 acre feet per year. Water in the river contains 300 to 600 ppm of salts; the water in Humboldt Lake contains at least 1,000 ppm.

Springs and groundwater are used to irrigate limited acreage in several of the basins in the central part of the Great Basin. Groundwater supplies are being overdrawn in several basins. At Las Vegas, Nevada, the water level in the wells is declining and the land surface there has settled about 6 inches as a result of groundwater withdrawals (Fig. 9.11). In the basins west of Las Vegas, at Pahrump Valley, and in the Amargosa Desert, groundwater is being pumped to irrigate cotton, and the groundwater levels there are falling. When tilled, those desert valleys are frightful dust bowls, yet they are being used to produce a crop that is already overproduced. Such misuse

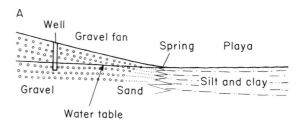

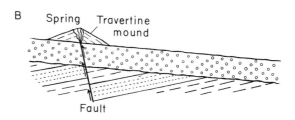

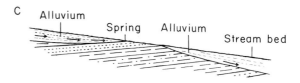

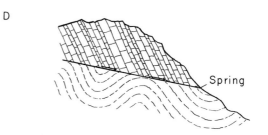

Figure 16.18 *Some of the ways in which groundwater occurs in the Basin and Range Province. (A) Water tables under gravel fans are deep, but may be reached by wells. The water table slopes gently toward the basin. Where the gravel and sand grade to silt and clay the water movement is checked and reaches the surface in a spring zone at the edge of the dry lake. (B) Water moving along high-angle faults may build mounds of travertine. These waters usually are warm. (C) Underflow in alluvium along a stream bed is forced to the surface where a bedrock ridge is crossed. (D) In the mountains, perched water tables occur along faults and other structural discontinuities, and springs develop where these reach the surface.*

of the land and water resource is compelling argument why such lands should be held in the public domain.

Overdrafts of groundwater also are indicated in some of the basins near Phoenix and Tucson, Arizona, and along the Rio Grande Valley in Texas.

One of the chief needs for water in the Basin and Range Province is for livestock. Water is obtained largely from wells, but some is obtained from springs. Some common kinds of springs are diagrammed in Figure 16.18.

The limit of salinity for water to be used for irrigation or for livestock is about 4,000 ppm, and the water in the middle of many of the desert basins exceeds this limit. The decrease in stream flow across arid and semiarid regions is accompanied by an increase in salinity. Irrigation contributes to the increase, but salinity increases even where there is no irrigation, as along the Amargosa River (Fig. 16.19). Along with the increase in total dissolved solids in the Amargosa River there is an increase in the proportion of

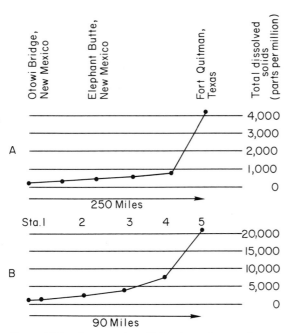

Figure 16.19 *Increase in salinity downstream along the Rio Grande River (A) and the Amargosa River (B).*

chloride, from about 30 percent at station 1 to about 70 percent at station 5; most of the remaining salts are sulfates.

Vegetation

The Basin and Range Province is mostly shrubland and has few trees. Nevada is called the Sagebrush State, and Figure 16.20 shows why. The sagebrush extends over the Great Basin as a nearly continuous blanket covering thousands of square miles. Moreover, extensive areas contain no other shrubs. This land is highly aromatic, and pleasantly so, particularly after rains.

The sagebrush and the pinyon-juniper woodland together constitute the Upper Sonoran Zone. This zone embraces most of the Great Basin, whereas the Lower Sonoran Zone embraces most parts of the southern sections of the Basin and Range Province. High mountains support some yellow pine and Douglas fir, representing the Transition Zone, and a few of the highest mountain tops support spruce and fir, representing the Canadian Zone. The Upper Sonoran and higher zones are similar to those on the Colorado Plateau except at the salt flats and salt marshes, such as the extensive ones in Great Salt Lake Desert and the many smaller ones in the Great Basin and in the Mojave Desert. Only salt-tolerant plants grow in these places, the species depending on the kind and amount of salts.

The Mexican Highland Section, which is also Upper Sonoran, supports several distinctive oaks, some of them evergreen. These oaks range far southward into Mexico and northward to the foot of the escarpment under the south rim of the Colorado Plateau. Yuccas mixed with cacti are common.

The Lower Sonoran Zone is more extensive in the Basin and Range Province than in any other part of the southwestern United States. It is characterized by the creosote bush (Fig. 16.20), although many other species with different water requirements are associated with it. This is the land where the picturesque cacti and yucca (Fig. 8.11) are most abundant.

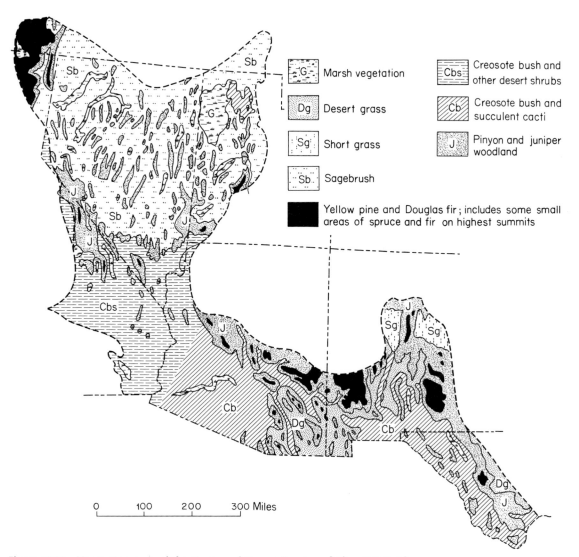

Figure 16.20 *Vegetation map of the Basin and Range Province. [After U.S.D.A.]*

Creosote bush, which may be taken as the norm for the Lower Sonoran Zone, grows extensively on the sandy and gravelly parts of the basins, where slopes rise from playas or alluvial floodplains to the mountains. The plant grows from 3 or 4 feet to 10 or 12 feet high. The density and height of stands vary widely, depending on size of catchment area and kind of ground.

Where somewhat more moisture is available than at the usual site for creosote bush, other species—such as burrowweed, encelia, yucca,

and various cacti—may grow along with it. Where the moisture is less than is needed by the creosote bush, there may be stands of desert holly or, in some places, desert saltbush. If the available moisture is still less, there may be no vegetation at all, as on some gravel benches having small catchment areas and smooth surfaces covered by closely spaced pebbles (desert pavement), which facilitate runoff of the little rain that falls.

Because the xerophytes differ in drought resistance from one species to another, plant geography in the Lower Sonoran Zone is controlled chiefly by the availability of moisture, which in turn is controlled by the kind of ground. Some ground is permeable; some impermeable. Some areas receive runoff from neighboring areas; others receive only the rainwater that falls on them. Some permeable ground is underlain at shallow depths by impermeable layers that catch and hold the moisture; some is permeable to great depth, and water seeping into it goes too deep for use by the plants. Such differences are reflected in the distribution of the various species of xerophytes.

The importance of slight differences in the availability of moisture in an arid climate can be illustrated by the growth of xerophytes along highways. Highways commonly are lined by a luxuriant growth of species that are much less developed away from the road, because the shoulders and edges, even where they are not ditched, collect some extra runoff from the pavement.

Differences both in the amount and *seasonal* distribution of the rainfall also are reflected in differences in the distribution of the various xerophytes in the Lower Sonoran Zone. In the Mojave and other deserts west of the Colorado River, precipitation averages less than about 5 inches annually, and most of it falls during the winter; those deserts have extensive stands of the creosote bush with Joshua tree, a tree-size yucca, on the higher benches of gravel. Eastward in the Sonoran Desert, where the precipitation is greater and is distributed *biseasonally,* the creosote bush is accompanied by numerous succulent cacti, plants capable of storing water. Some of these, like the saguaro cactus, have an accordion-like structure and measurably swell when there is water to be absorbed.

A consequence of this water-storing property is that the plants are senitive to differences in exposure at the limits of their ranges. Because they store water, they are limited by freezing temperature; they may be killed by severe freezes of short duration or by protracted periods of temperatures only moderately below freezing. At

Organ Pipe Cactus National Monument, the organ pipe cactus is at its northern limit, and there it prefers the warm, south-facing hillsides. The saguaro cactus there grows equally well on north slopes, but 200 miles farther north in Arizona, at the northern limit of its range, it too prefers south-facing hillsides. This generally is true of all species at the northern limit of their ranges, but conspicuously so for the big cacti. Conversely, species at the south limit of their ranges tend to prefer the cooler north slopes.

The Chihuahuan Desert, east of the Mexican Highlands, has about the same annual precipitation as the Sonoran Desert, but most of it falls during the growing season. This desert is characterized by yuccas, so much so that one of them has been adopted as the state flower of New Mexico. It could also be called the red chili desert, for this is the land where colorful strings of red chilis hang decoratively around so many of the adobe houses.

Two transects illustrating differences in the distribution of xerophytes between the lower, fine-grained, and the upper, coarse-grained, parts of the alluvial fans in these deserts are given in Figure 16.21.

At some places, such as near springs, or along certain washes where groundwater is shallow, there are distinctive stands of phreatophytes (Fig. 8.21). The different species of phreatophytes have different salt tolerances, and their distribution reflects the quality of the groundwater. In Death Valley, for example, where groundwater contains more than about 0.5 percent (5,000 ppm) of salts, honey mesquite cannot tolerate the salinity, but other phreatophytes can. Where the salinity increases toward the salt pan (Figs. 8.22,B, 16.22,B), arrowweed and salt grass form a stand panward from the mesquite and extend to where the groundwater contains about 3 percent of salts. Higher salinities exceed the tolerance of those species, and the arrowweed and salt grass give way to pickleweed, which can tolerate 6 percent of salts (twice the salinity of sea water) in the water around its roots. At the temperatures of Death Valley, no flowering plant can tolerate more than 6 percent of salts in the

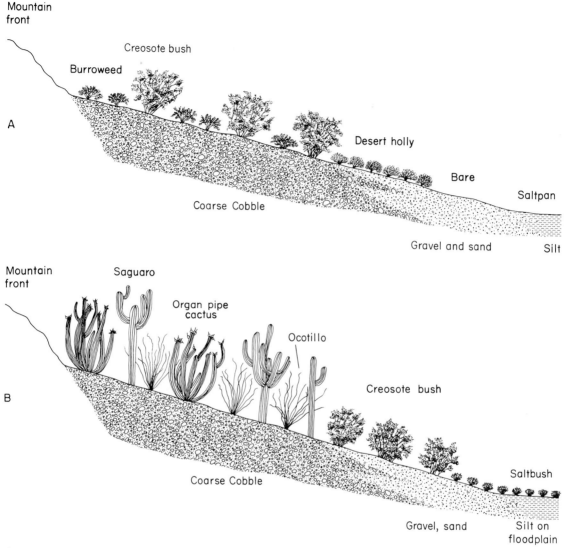

Figure 16.21 *Transects illustrating differences in distribution of xerophytes on gravel fans in the southern part of the Basin and Range Province. (A) Transect in Death Valley. (B) Transect in Organ Pipe Cactus National Monument. The species characteristic of the lower plant stands may range to the high parts of the fans; consequently, the number of species increases upward on the fans. Each transect is 5 to 10 miles long.*

soil water. In the plant itself the water presumably becomes more concentrated because of the water lost by transpiration. Where groundwater contains more than 6 percent of salts, the ground is barren; a few hardy algae, fungi, and bacteria may grow in such ground, but these plants also have limits to the salinity they can tolerate and

are zoned with respect to salinity in much the same way as are the flowering plants.

The spread of tamarisk (salt cedar), an attractive phreatophyte of tree size that was introduced into the United States in the 1850's, poses a serious problem in the Southwwest. It has spread along streams and irrigation ditches

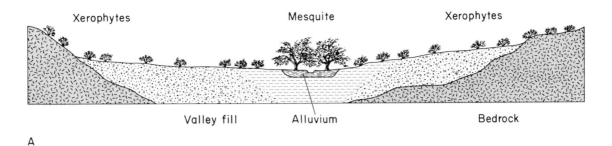

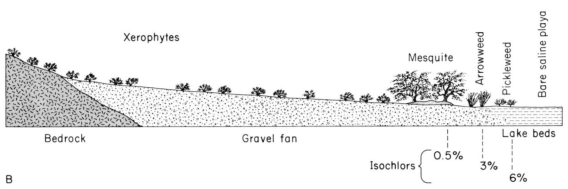

Figure 16.22 *Diagrams illustrating how groundwater conditions are indicated by stands of phreatophytes in the Lower Sonoran zone. (A) Mesquite growing where groundwater discharges in alluvium along a stream. The valley sides, which receive only the rainwater that falls on them and a small amount of runoff from uphill, support stands of xerophytes. (B) Saline playas are without vegetation even though groundwater may be near the surface. At the edges of the playas where the salinity is less, there are stands of phreatophytes zoned with respect to their salinity tolerances. The gravel fans and mountainsides, where groundwater is deep, support only xerophytes.*

throughout the Southwest and even beyond. Its dense stands crowd out native plants and consume vast amounts of water that can ill be spared. Tamarisk is especially abundant along the Colorado River and the Rio Grande and their tributaries, and along streams to the east on the plains. It has spread into the Rocky Mountains and into Death Valley, growing wherever there is some water.

Surface Deposits and Soils

Soils in the Basin and Range Province are classed as Gray Desert Soils in the Great Basin and as Red Desert Soils in the southern Sections. These soils are very limy beginning a few inches below the surface, and even the surface layers are only slightly leached. Although the subsoils are lighter

in color than the surface soils, organic surface layers are thin or absent. The Gray and the Red Desert Soils occur mostly on the gravel fans and pediments. Alluvial soils are extensive in the Salton Trough and along the rivers. The alluvial soils along the Rio Grande and the Virgin River are subject to severe erosion. Most of the soils can be highly productive if irrigated, but generally this is possible only on the flood plains. Most of the land is used for grazing.

In the Mexican Highland Section, above 3,000 feet and up to about 6,000 feet, are some Red Brown Soils. Some of these, apparently the younger ones, are only slightly leached and have no layer of lime accumulation. The older soils have leached upper horizons and a thick zone of lime accumulation 3 to 6 feet below the surface. At still higher elevations in that area, the soils are reddish, clayey, and commonly leached of their lime carbonate. Some of these soils are evidently of pre-Wisconsinan age.

The lime-cemented layers, which may be a few inches or many feet thick, may be nearly as hard as concrete, or they may be friable. The lime may occur in layers or as nodules. Where well developed, the deposits are known as caliche, and they originate in at least four ways, only one of which is strictly a soil process.

Lime layers attributable to soil processes are the result of leaching by water filtering into the ground, dissolving lime carbonate in the upper layers, and transporting it downward (Fig. 16.23,A). But in deserts there is not enough water to wet more than the upper foot or so of the soil, and when that soil dries, the lime carbonate is deposited in the subsoil. This is the general process by which alkaline soils are formed.

A second kind of caliche deposit forms in the capillary fringe above a water table (Fig. 16.23,B).

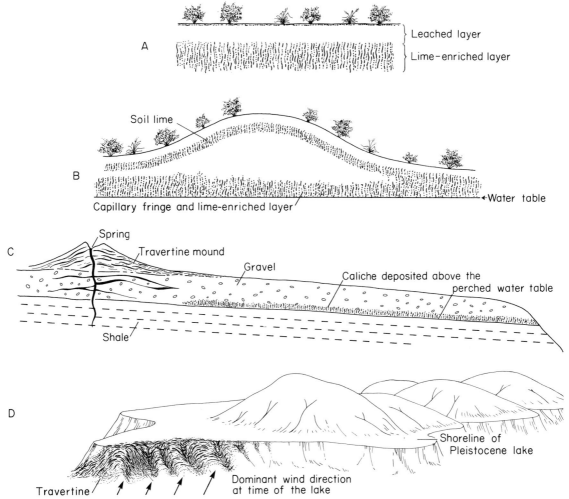

Figure 16.23 *Four kinds of caliche deposits in the Basin and Range Province. (A) Lime deposited by the soil process as a result of leaching of the surface layers and deposition of the lime in the subsoil. (B) Lime carbonate deposited in the capillary fringe above a water table. These deposits bear little or no relation to the topography. (C) Lime carbonate deposited as travertine at a spring and in the aerated zone above the perched water table. (D) Lime carbonate deposited at headlands along a Pleistocene shoreline.*

In general, these deposits are thicker and more strongly developed than those attributable soil processes. Moreover, where the deposits are formed by downward filtration of water, the veinlets of calcium carbonate branch downward; where they are formed by a rising capillary fringe, they branch upward. Unfortunately, the branching may be obscured by changes that have occurred since the deposit was formed, and in such cases the distinction may be based on whether the deposit conforms to a topographic surface, as do soil horizons, or to subsurface levels that are unrelated to topography, as are most water tables.

A third kind of caliche deposit in the Basin and Range Province occurs at springs that are charged with calcium carbonate. The springs deposit travertine on and below the surface (Fig. 16.23,C). Well-developed deposits of this kind are easily enough identified, but those that are weathered and eroded must be identified by relating them to existing or dried springs and to the surface and underground water courses draining from them.

A fourth kind of caliche in the Basin and Range Province was formed along the shorelines of the Pleistocene lakes (Fig. 16.23,D). These deposits commonly occur at headlands or other exposed places along old shorelines, and are apparently due to aeration by wave action of the carbonate-charged waters.

Another kind of surface deposit characteristic of the Basin and Range Province is known as desert pavement, which is a smooth surface built of pebbles on gravelly surfaces. These are often as smooth as a carefully laid pebble or cobble pavement, and they slope with the gravel fan or other surface. A cross section of desert pavement shows a layer of porous loam, a few inches thick, under a single layer of cobbles protecting the surface (Fig. 16.24). The origin of the surfaces and of the layering is not at all clear. Wind erosion could remove the silt and sand and allow the gravel to accumulate in a layer that protects the surface from further erosion, but some other processes must have operated where a layer of loam exists beneath the gravel layer. Perhaps

volume changes due to wetting and drying, and heaving by salt crystals, cause the pebbles to work upward and the sandy silt to settle downward.

Alluvial Fans and Pediments

A typical basin in the Basin and Range Province consists of two kinds of ground. At the center is a playa or alluvial flat of clayey or silty ground, with or without a crust of salts, and surrounding this are gravel fans that rise from the flats to the foot of the bordering mountains. Many of the fans are several miles long and more than a thousand feet high (Figs. 16.6, 16.25). They consist of coarse debris, mostly gravel and sand deposited at the mouths of canyons by streams flowing from the mountains.

The apexes of some alluvial fans are located at the mouths of canyons; the apexes of other fans have been extended up canyons into the mountains, as have those illustrated in Figure 16.26. Where a fan extends far into a canyon it may engulf and largely bury the foothills, which then project above the surface of the fan as isolated rock hills (Fig. 16.27). These differences in form reflect differences in the histories of the fans.

Four major factors affect the composition and form of gravel fans: (1) structural movements taking place while the fan is building; (2) stream flow, present and past; (3) kind and size of debris transported to the fan; and (4) length of time the fan has been building—that is, stage. The problem of deciphering in detail the history of a particular fan is complicated by the fact that each

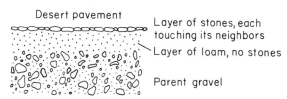

Figure 16.24   Cross section of desert pavement. A layer of closely set stones overlies porous loam a few inches thick, which rests on the parent gravel deposit.

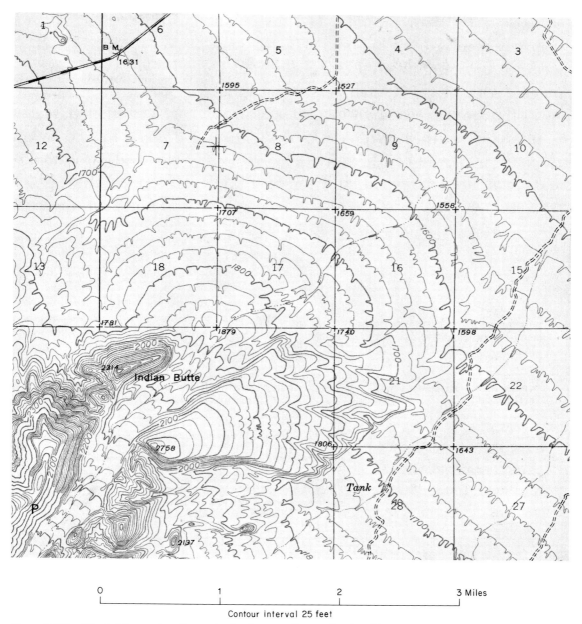

Figure 16.25   *Alluvial fan and pediment in the Sonoran Desert Section. [From U.S.G.S. Antelope Peak, Arizona, quadrangle.]*

of these factors is a variable, as may be illustrated by some examples.

A small fan at the base of a mountain (Fig. 16.26,A) may be a young fan, or it may be only the top of a much larger and older fan that has been subsiding structurally and is largely buried. The fans that extend into the canyons (Fig. 16.26,B), and large ones that isolate foothills (Fig. 16.27), may represent an advanced stage of development where conditions have been stable or

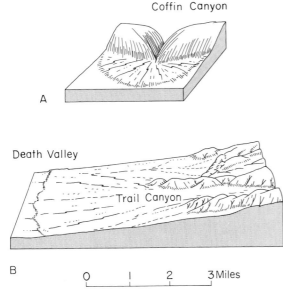

Figure 16.26 *Some different forms of gravel fans (see also Fig. 16.27). (A) A small fan at the straight front of a mountain range. (B) A fan that extends into the canyons. [After U.S.G.S.]*

they may be the result of tilting while the fan was being built.

Along newly formed fault escarpments there first develop steep, short fans, and as these become extended downslope, the head of the fan becomes trenched. The slope of the fan decreases as its length increases. On most fans the slope is more than 100 feet per mile, and many have slopes of 500 feet per mile. In general, the coarser the gravel, the steeper the slope; but there are exceptions, particularly where there has been recent tilting.

In general the gravel at the surface of fans in this province is well rounded, like typical stream gravel, but some fan surfaces are so old that the boulders and cobbles have disintegrated into a new crop of angular rock fragments. Younger gravel, not old enough to have been broken up by weathering, is darkly stained with desert varnish; some cobbles may have a weathered rind. The youngest gravel is well-rounded and without desert varnish.

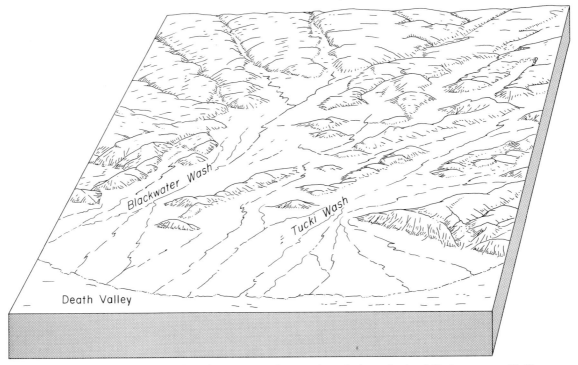

Figure 16.27 *Some fans deeply embay the mountain front and partly bury the foothills (compare with Fig. 16.26). [After U.S.G.S.]*

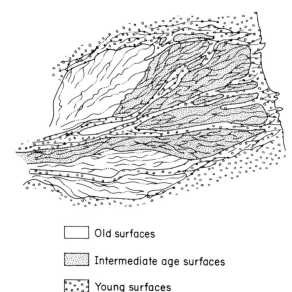

☐ Old surfaces

▨ Intermediate age surfaces

▨ Young surfaces

Figure 16.28 *Orderly differences in drainage pattern on different parts of a gravel fan. Old surfaces (white areas) that are high above the drainage and not subject to flooding have parallel drainage. Surfaces of intermediate age (stippled) and of intermediate height are flooded infrequently and have a mixed dendritic and braided drainage pattern. The youngest surfaces (circle pattern), which are subject to seasonal washing, have a braided drainage pattern. The example is Death Valley Canyon in Death Valley.* [After U.S.G.S.]

In places there are orderly differences in drainage patterns on these different surfaces (Fig. 16.28), reminiscent of the differences in drainage patterns of fans built on pediments on the Colorado Plateau (Fig. 15.25). On the old and weathered surfaces, the drainage is parallel. Surfaces that are flooded infrequently have a dendritic and braided drainage pattern. On the youngest surfaces the drainage is braided.

Around the foot of the mountains in the Sonoran Desert and Mexican Highland Sections, pediments as well as gravel fans are extensive (Fig. 16.22). The pediments, which are surfaces of erosion as contrasted with the constructional or depositional surfaces on the alluvial fans, are in some ways similar to the pediments on the Colorado Plateau (p. 467) and in other ways different. One difference is that some of the extensive Sonoran Desert and Mexican Highland pedi-

ments have developed around the foot of low, small mountains where the rainfall is little, if any greater than in the surrounding basin. These streams lack the change in regimen that characterizes the drainage on the pediments on the Colorado Plateau. The pediments in both areas have dendritic drainage patterns, and the gravel fans being built on them have braided patterns. They are also alike in that many streams rising on the pediments have lower gradients than the master streams transporting gravels from the mountains (Fig. 15.37). This relationship has been used in a practical way at the copper mine at Ajo, where a large arroyo draining from the mountain to the mine pit was turned through a tunnel to a neighboring and lower stream course that does not head in the mountain.

Sand Deserts

Despite the aridity of the Basin and Range Province, sand dunes are not particularly abundant or characteristic. Much of the stony ground is protected by an armor plate of desert pavement. Other ground is too saline, and the sand is anchored with salt. Still there are a dozen or so places where the winds have built substantial areas of active dunes.

One such area is north of Winnemucca, Nevada, and another is south of the Carson Desert. At both places the dunes are actively migrating. Other dune fields in the Great Basin are near Delta, Utah. In California, active dunes are climbing the northeast side of the Big Maria Mountains. One of the better known dune fields in the region is between the Colorado River and the Salton Sea; this area is known as the Algodones Dune Belt. Other dunes are at Mesquite Flat, in Death Valley, and near Kelso, southeast of Soda Lake in the Mojave Desert. Dunes at White Sands National Monument in New Mexico are unusual in that they are composed mostly of grains of gypsum. Farther north in New Mexico, in a small dune field on the west side of the Rio Grande north of Socorro, the dunes appear to be migrating northeastward into the river valley.

All these are popular areas, particularly for

vacationing families. Sand dunes are a favorite medium for working off energy stored in restless youngsters.

Rivers and Lakes, Wet Ones and Dry Ones

PERENNIAL LAKES

Despite their aridity the Great Basin and the Mojave Desert are curiously lands of lakes. They contain about two dozen fairly large perennial

lakes and more than 100 dry ones. In wetter times, during the Pleistocene, these lakes stored a lot of water. At the present time their water surface totals almost 5,000 square miles, and the water lost by evaporation from these surfaces equals the recharge by the streams draining into them—an amount roughly equal to the average annual discharge of the Colorado River.

Lakes along the east side of the Great Basin (Fig. 16.29) are recharged by streams from the Rocky Mountains and High Plateaus in Utah. As already noted, Sevier Lake, fed by Sevier River,

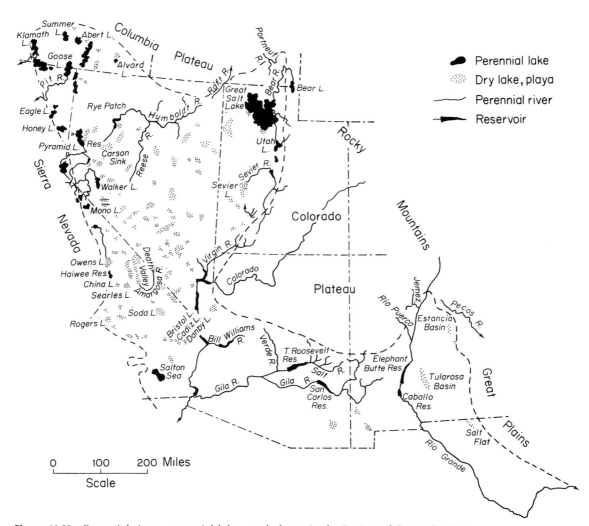

Figure 16.29 *Perennial rivers, perennial lakes, and playas in the Basin and Range Province.*

would be a perennial lake but for the water taken from it for irrigation. Utah Lake, fed by the Provo River, is a fresh-water lake that overflows into Great Salt Lake by way of the Jordan River. Great Salt Lake, fed chiefly by the Jordan, Weber, and Bear rivers, covers about 2,000 square miles and has a maximum depth of about 30 feet. Having no outlet, and receiving the salts brought by the rivers, the lake water has become a brine containing more than 20 percent of salts, mostly sodium chloride and sodium sulfate. The lake has been estimated to contain 400 million tons of sodium chloride and 30 million tons of the sulfate. Some salt is produced from salt pans at the edge of the lake; potash is produced from the western salt flats.

Lakes along the west side of the Great Basin are numerous but mostly small. The waters of these lakes contain about 1,000 ppm of dissolved solids. Pyramid Lake and Walker Lake, which collect water from the Truckee, Carson, and Walker rivers, contain about 3,000 ppm of salts. The rivers contain 200 to 300 ppm of salts. Summer Lake and Abert Lake, Oregon, contain brines with 1 percent or more of dissolved solids.

RIVERS

HUMBOLDT RIVER.   The rivers in the Great Basin, especially those issuing from the Rocky Mountains and the Sierra Nevada, have excellent water, and the drainage map (Fig. 16.29) illustrates why the California Trail followed the course it did (Fig. 14.48). To avoid the desert west of Great Salt Lake, the trail followed Bear River, Snake River, and Raft River and then crossed low passes to the head of the Humboldt River. By this route perennial streams could be followed almost all the way from the Wyoming Basin to the Sierra Nevada. The importance of the Humboldt River to the 1849 California gold rush has been well summarized by the historian Bancroft (1890, History of Nevada, Colorado, and Wyoming, p. 15):

In the progress of westward-marching empire few streams on the North American continent have played a more important part than the Humboldt

River of Nevada. Among the watercourses of the world it can lay claim neither to great beauty nor to remarkable utility. Its great work was to open a way, first for the cattle train and then for the steam train, through a wilderness of mountains, through ranges which otherwise would run straight across its course. It is the largest river of this region, and the only one hereabout running from east to west. Most of the others are with the mountains, north and south.

The Humboldt is not a mighty stream, but it has been and still is a mighty important one.

The Humboldt River crosses one important structural barrier, about 30 miles below Elko, where the river flows through a gorge cut through a fault block of late Tertiary volcanic and sedimentary rocks. The rest of the course winds around the major uplifts rather than crossing them. The ancestral Humboldt River may have drained to the Pacific, perhaps by way of a wind-gap at the head of the Feather River (p. 578).

AMARGOSA RIVER.   One of the driest rivers in the Great Basin is the Amargosa. After following a southward course this river makes a U-turn northward into Death Valley. Most of the time the river bed is dry. The average annual discharge probably is no more than a few hundred acre feet. In the rare times when it flows throughout its 150-mile course, enough water is lost by evaporation to increase the salinity progressively as the river approaches the floor of Death Valley. At the mouth of the river the water is twice as salty as sea water.

RIO GRANDE.   The wide Rio Grande begins as springs and snowbanks above 12,000 feet in the San Juan Mountains in southwestern Colorado. It first flows east and discharges into the San Luis Valley at an altitude of about 7,500 feet. This valley, in the Southern Rocky Mountains, is a structural valley separating the volcanic pile at the San Juans from the upfolded and upfaulted Sangre de Cristo Mountains on the east. The depth of the fill is not given on the tectonic or basement maps of the United States, but one estimate gives it as 8,000 feet.

The river has built a broad, low fan where it discharges into San Luis Valley, and this has created a broad, undrained sump on the north side. The overflow of irrigation water into this sump has developed saline ground. Where the river enters New Mexico, it is incised into a canyon eroded in basaltic lavas. Where it leaves this canyon, it enters the Basin and Range Province at an altitude of about 5,500 feet. In the next 300 miles from there to El Paso, the river descends another 2,000 feet (to about 3,600 feet at El Paso), and in the next 300 miles below El Paso it descends to an altitude of about 2,000 feet, where it makes the big bend at Big Bend National Park. In these 600 miles across the Basin and Range Province, the river parallels the structural uplifts and troughs rather than cutting across them. At the Big Bend, the river escapes from the Basin and Range Province by cutting across the block-faulted ranges in canyons 1,500 to 1,700 feet deep. Cutting across these structures, the river descends another 1,000 feet within 100 miles and enters the Coastal Plain Province at an altitude of about 1,000 feet. In crossing the Coastal Plain, the river descends 1,000 feet in 400 miles; its delta extends about 25 miles into the Gulf of Mexico.

Development of the Rocky Mountains drainage system, as already noted (p. 387), can be divided into four principal stages. In the earliest stage, late Cretaceous to Eocene, the mountains began to be uplifted, but their bases remained near sea level, and sediments that were eroded from the newly formed mountains collected in lake and other basins that remained near sea level. In the second stage, the Oligocene, the basins began to overflow, partly by being filled and partly because regional uplift had begun. In the third stage, Miocene, the drainage from the Southern Rocky Mountains became interrupted by renewed faulting and folding, and this tectonic activity disrupted the ancestral Rio Grande too. The ancestral Rio Grande may have had an easterly or southeasterly course but Miocene deposits attributable to the Rio Grande are lost. Whatever its original course, the River was eventually turned southward into the structural troughs between Albuquerque and El Paso. The river apparently found its way southward by overflowing from one basin to the next and finally dissipated itself on the broad desert, the Messila Basin, southwest of El Paso. Meanwhile, a tributary of the Rio Conches captured the basins below El Paso, and at some time, perhaps as late as the Pleistocene, captured the Rio Grande and turned it through the gap at El Paso. The main stem of the Rio Grande, like the main stem of the Colorado River, seems to have been a "Johnnie-come-lately" in the system. The Rio Conchos apparently played a major role in the development of the Rio Grande system, just as the Little Colorado seems to have played a major role in the development of the Colorado River system.

The Rio Conchos was probably superimposed across the block mountains at Big Bend at a time when they were much lower than they are now, perhaps in the Miocene. One needs to account for the absence, or at least scarcity, of deltaic sediments older than Quaternary at the mouth of the Rio Grande. Perhaps the river was ponded by Miocene and Pliocene uplift of those mountains, much as the Colorado River was ponded by uplifts across its course. The coarse sediment could be contained in the structural basins upstream from the barriers. If this process were repeated enough times during middle and late Tertiary time, the river could have eroded its 1,800 foot canyons in slow and easy stages as the block faulting progressed.

COLORADO RIVER. The Colorado River follows an anomalous course; after leaving Grand Canyon, the river course is westward across three structural uplifts and as many basins. Turning southward at Hoover Dam it crosses four more uplifts and basins before entering the Gulf. These structural features are late Tertiary and Quaternary in age. The basins contain deposits derived from the uplifts, and the deposits themselves are involved in the later structural movements. The river originally may have been superimposed across the uplifts during their early stages, while

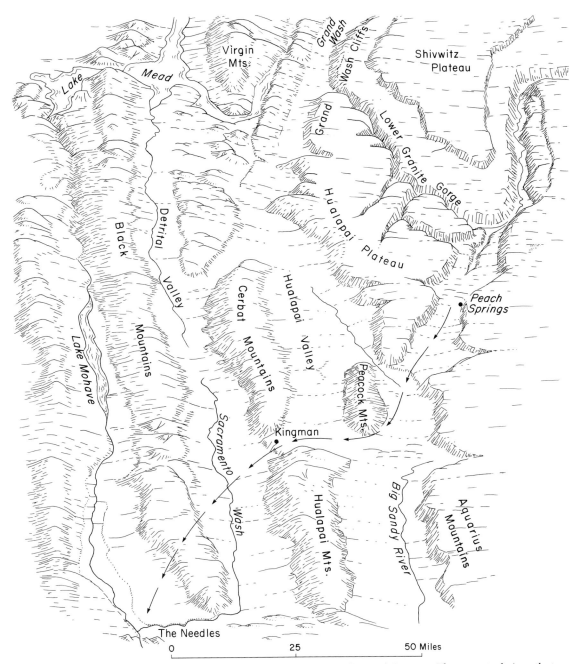

Figure 16.30 *Diagram of basins and ranges west and southwest of Grand Canyon. The ancestral river that discharged via the canyon at Peach Springs may have gone through the lava-filled gap at Kingman and the valley now clogged by the volcanic pile at the south end of the Black Mountains.* [After U.S.G.S.]

they were still low, but the canyons that have been cut into the uplifts must be the result of antecedence.

The Colorado River enters the Basin and Range Province at the block-faulted Grand Wash trough, between the Virgin Mountains on the west and the rim of the Colorado Plateau on the east (Fig. 16.30). The river arrived here no earlier than middle Pliocene and perhaps later (p. 457). Continuing west, the river crosses the structural trough, where it is joined by the Virgin River, and then crosses the Black Mountains in a canyon. When the Black Mountains first began being uplifted is uncertain, but the uplifting (by block faulting and tilting) has continued because Pleistocene gravels are turned up around the base of the mountains. Evidently the Colorado River was superimposed across that barrier when it was structurally lower; subsequent uplift deformed the Pleistocene gravels, and the canyon became deepened by antecedence.

At Hoover Dam the river turns south in Boulder Canyon. After leaving it, the river first is narrowly confined in a gorge between uplifted gravel fans, and farther on it enters a broad floodplain that buries the ends of those fans. These threefold changes in kind of valley—rocky canyon, gravelly gorge, and floodplain—are repeated four times between Boulder Canyon and the delta, suggesting southward tilting of a series of the longitudinal valleys.

There is substantial evidence of at least three kinds of major late Cenozoic structural movements along this part of the course of the Colorado River. First, estuarine deposits that contain Gulf of California fossils no older than middle Pliocene (and probably younger) occur on gravel fans high above the Colorado River upstream, nearly to the mouth of the Bill Williams River. Second, the Colorado River marks the boundary between structurally unstable ground to the west and structurally stable ground to the east. Earthquake epicenters are abundant west of the river and almost lacking east of it (Fig. 2.17). Third, species of small fish at springs along the Mojave River (and even in Death Valley!) are related to those in the Colorado River, indicating that the

Mojave River and the Amargosa River, including Death Valley, were formerly tributaries to the Colorado. The ancestral river course, disrupted by Quaternary earth movements, probably is marked by the Bristol, Cadiz, and Danby playas (Fig. 16.8).

The Colorado River is noteworthy not only for its uncertain past but also for its load of silt, which, until so many dams were built, averaged about 20,000 ppm of suspended load. This amounts to 100,000 acre-feet of mud annually. If a cup of water were dipped from the river, a measurable layer of silt would quickly settle to the bottom, but the water would not lose its brown color or clayey taste.

GILA RIVER. The Gila River and its tributaries cross structural barriers in the Mexican Highland Section, but in the Sonoran Desert Section the Gila winds around the uplifts rather than crossing them. If the flow of water had been less, this drainage very likely would have been disintegrated like that on the Mojave Desert. If the flow had been greater than it has been, the river might very well have maintained an antecedent course across one or another of the structural uplifts.

PLEISTOCENE LAKES, PLAYAS

During Pleistocene time the Great Basin and the Mojave Desert had numerous, large lakes (Fig. 16.31), with a total water surface of at least 50,000 square miles, which is ten times that of the present lakes. Assuming the evaporation rate then was half what it is now, roughly five times as much water must have drained into the basins. But it is doubtful if rainfall was five times greater. Probably the additional water came partly from greater rainfall and partly from water stored as ice in the glaciers. By this reasoning we might infer that the Pleistocene climate had half the present evaporation rate and twice the present precipitation; if so, it would still have been semiarid!

Largest of the Pleistocene lakes was Lake Bonneville, which covered 20,000 square miles in northwestern Utah; Great Salt Lake covers 2,000 square miles. Lake Bonneville had a maximum depth of nearly 1,000 feet; Great Salt Lake is only 30 feet deep. The shorelines of Lake Bonneville, more than 2,500 miles long at the high-water stage, are unmistakably impressed on the sides of the bordering mountains (Figs. 16.32 and 16.33). The highest beach line is at an altitude ranging from about 5,100 to 5,200 feet, the difference in height being due to later warping of the shoreline as a result of structural movements (Fig. 16.34).

At the level of the Bonneville shoreline, the lake overflowed to join the Snake River, and rapidly eroded alluvial fill at the divide. At a depth of 300 feet, bedrock was encountered and further downcutting checked. The lake stood for a long time at this lower level, the Provo level,

Figure 16.32 *Beach deposits of Lake Bonneville at the south end of Salt Lake Valley. The highest beach (B), the Bonneville shoreline, is about 300 feet higher than the Provo shoreline (P) and nearby a thousand feet higher than Great Salt Lake.*

and during this stage large deltas were built at the mouths of the rivers draining from the mountains. Most of the cities in this part of Utah, including Salt Lake City, are situated on deltas built at the Provo level.

Prehistoric men may have viewed this lake along with the Pleistocene elephants and camels, for paleo-Indians are known to have been in this country in late Pleistocene time. But the Pleistocene fauna became exterminated as the lake dropped to within 300 feet of the level of Great Salt Lake, and the first men known to have entered the basin arrived when the lake surface was less than 50 feet higher than the surface of Great Salt Lake. They lived in caves (Danger Cave, Hogup Cave) on the west side of Great Salt Lake Desert. According to radiocarbon dating these caves were occupied 11,000 years ago, and since that time the lake has not risen high enough to flood the caves, and the lowest is only 50 feet higher than Great Salt Lake.

Structural movements since the time of Lake Bonneville have warped the shorelines a total of 300 feet. Part of this warp appears to be the result of doming centered in the lake basin (Fig. 16.34) as if the crust had risen when the load of water was removed—the opposite of what has happened recently at Lake Mead (p. 507). In addition to being warped, the shorelines have been faulted at a number of places (Figs. 16.34, 16.35).

As the Pleistocene drew to a close, evaporation increased, and the level of the lake gradually lowered. There was another short stillstand at a level 300 feet below the Provo; this level, referred to as the Stansbury shoreline, marks the end of Lake Bonneville. Great Salt Lake is all that remains of the lake today.

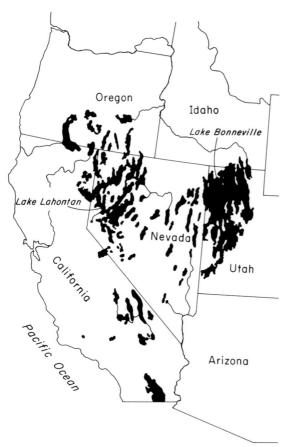

Figure 16.31. *Pleistocene lakes in the Great Basin and Mohave Desert. [From Geol. Soc. America.]*

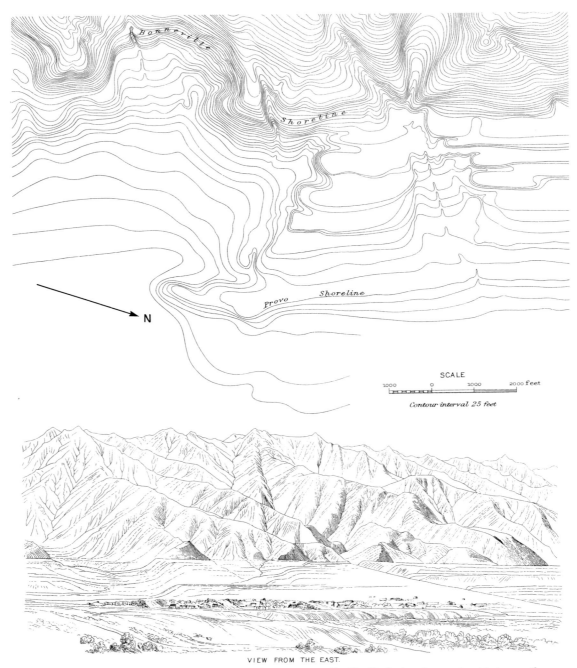

Figure 16.33 *Shore bars, terraces, and mountain front near Wellsville, Utah showing contrast between the littoral topography and the subaerial topography on the mountains above the old beach of Lake Bonneville.* [By G. Thompson and W. H. Holmes.]

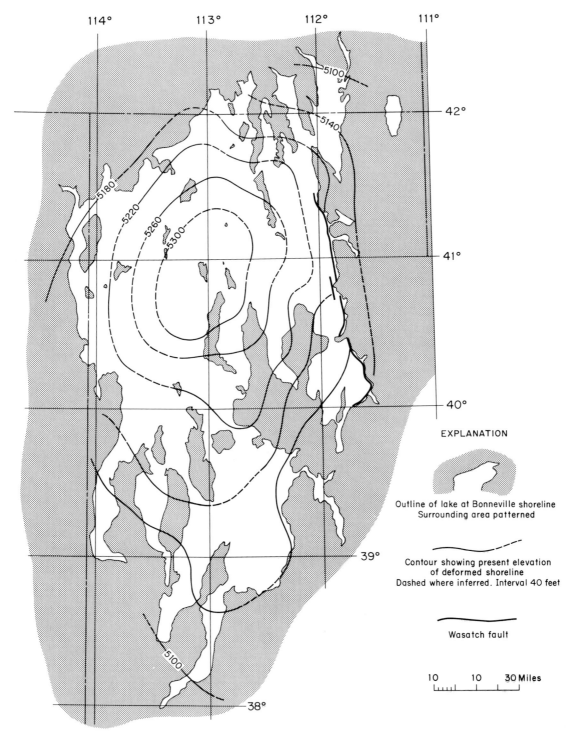

Figure 16.34 *Map of Lake Bonneville. The faults indicated are those that disrupted the shorelines; the contours show how the shorelines have been warped. [After U.S.G.S.]*

Figure 16.35 *Fault scarps crossing a Lake Bonneville delta. [After U.S.G.S.]*

The lake was contemporaneous with the glaciers in the Wasatch Mountains, for the lake beds are interbedded with moraines and glacial outwash. Some basaltic volcanoes erupted during the time of the lake, but none within the basin has erupted since.

Another major lake in the Great Basin, with a history similar to that of Lake Bonneville, centered at Carson Sink and extended nearly to the foot of the Sierra Nevada. It is known as Lake Lahontan (Fig. 16.31).

Sometime during the Holocene Epoch, apparently between 2,000 and 5,000 years ago, many of the dry lakes were flooded by shallow lakes or ponds. Death Valley, for example, contained a lake that was 30 feet deep, and it was in this lake that the salt pan was deposited. The deposits

that formed in this shallow lake are overlain by sand dunes containing Indian artifacts—early pottery and arrow points. In the 2,000 or so years since this Holocene lake was formed, the floor of the Valley has been tilted to the east; the eastern shoreline is 20 feet lower than the western one (Fig. 16.36). This tilting was accompanied by faulting, and the kind and amount of deformation closely duplicates that at Hebgen Lake, Montana, which resulted from the 1959 earthquake there (p. 414).

Some of the other playas have salt crusts similar to the one in Death Valley. Deposits at Searles Lake, about 40 miles southwest of Death Valley, and on the desert west of Great Salt Lake are commercially important sources for several kinds of salts. Most of the salts produced, however,

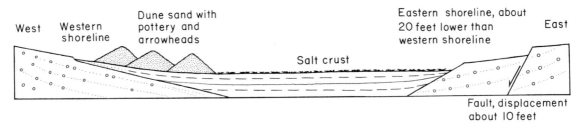

Figure 16.36 *Cross section of the floor of Death Valley. The salt pan, 5 to 6 miles wide, is represented by a crust of salts as much as 3 feet thick. These salts were deposited as a result of evaporation of a Holocene lake.*

come from brines under the surface rather than from the crusts. Still other playas are simply bare clay flats without salt crusts.

These different kinds of playas reflect differences in the hydrologic regimen. Playas consisting of clay flats without a salt crust are subject to frequent flooding by muddy streams draining into them. The salts in these basins are distributed throughout the muds and do not form a crust because there is very little standing water. Playas covered by a salt crust were either lakes or marshes.

In Pleistocene time, Death Valley contained a lake 600 feet deep, one of a chain of lakes that extended to the foot of the Sierra Nevada. At the foot of the Sierra was Owens Lake, fed by the Owens River (Fig. 16.29). This overflowed into China Lake, located between Owens and Searles lakes. China Lake, in turn, overflowed into Searles Lake, which overflowed into the Panamint Valley, a playa west of Death Valley. The Panamint Valley may have overflowed into Death Valley.

Water also spilled into Death Valley from the Mojave River, which empties into the playa at Soda Lake. In Pleistocene time this playa contained Lake Mojave, and it overflowed northward into the south bend of the Amargosa River and to Death Valley. The Mojave River at one time may have drained to the Colorado River, perhaps along the course marked by the playas at Emerson, Bristol, Cadiz, and Danby lakes. But there has not been sufficient flow in the stream to maintain its course across the structural blocks while they were being warped and faulted.

Mineral Resources

Mines and mining, a major activity in the Basin and Range Province, have centered on many kinds of deposits, but those of copper, gold, silver, lead, zinc, and salines are mined on a sufficient scale to be of national interest.

The Basin and Range Province has yielded about 70 percent of the copper produced in the United States. Most of the deposits, the so-called

Figure 16.37 *Open-pit prophyry copper mine at Bingham Canyon, Utah. Some of the open-pit copper mines are a mile wide and hundreds of feet deep. Power shovels capable of handling many tons with each scoop operate on the terraces, which also serve as road beds for railroad trains into which the ore is loaded by the shovels.*

porphyry deposits, are mined by power shovel at vast open pits (Fig. 16.37). The ores are low grade, containing as little as 0.5 percent copper, but production is feasible because the deposits are huge, and the open-pit mining methods allow vast quantities to be handled. The principal deposits are at Bingham Canyon, Utah; Ely, Nevada; Ajo, Bagdad, Bisbee, Clifton-Morenci, Globe-Miami, Jerome, Ray, and Superior, Arizona; and Santa Rita, New Mexico (Fig. 16.38).

The deposits in these districts are much alike. They are associated with granitic stocks about a mile in diameter that have been thoroughly shattered. The stocks and the limestones intruded by them have been altered by hydrothermal solutions. The primary ore mineral, chalcopyrite (copper-iron sulfide), together with pyrite, occurs as isolated grains and as veins disseminated throughout the shattered and altered rocks.

The upper parts of the shattered intrusions have been weathered and the metallic minerals redeposited in zones, much like those of a soil profile, but scores of feet deep. In the ideal case, the copper and sulfur have been leached from the uppermost layer. Below this is an oxidized layer in which the leached copper was redeposited as carbonate (azurite and malachite), as oxides (cuprite, tenorite), and as silicate (chrysocolla). This layer is analogous to the limy

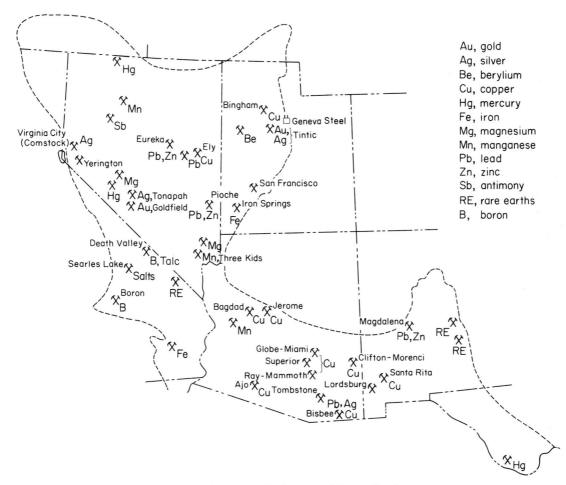

Figure 16.38 *Some important mining districts in the Basin and Range Province.*

B-horizon of the soils in that region. Below the carbonate layer the downward-percolating solutions deposited both copper and sulfur as the sulfide chalcocite. Below this is unweathered parent material—the shattered, hydrothermally altered rock containing primary chalcopyrite and pyrite.

The conversion of ore to metal at the huge open-pit copper deposits takes four steps: mining, concentrating, smelting, and refining. At Bingham Canyon, the mining is done in tiers. The rock is loosened by blasting, and electric shovels with a 25-ton capacity load the rock into trucks. For each ton of ore, $2\frac{1}{2}$ tons of weakly mineralized

rock must be removed, and the trucks haul this to dumps outside the mine. An acid solution percolates through the dumps to dissolve copper in the lean rock, and this solution goes to a precipitation plant, where the copper is recovered. At Bingham Canyon about 6,000 tons of copper is recovered by the precipitator every month. This copper then goes to the smelter.

The ore is hauled by train to concentrator plants, where it is crushed dry to about $\frac{3}{4}$-inch size and then mixed with water and milled to the consistency of fine sand. This mixture goes to flotation tanks, where waste material is separated from the copper minerals. The concentrate contains about 27 percent of copper; the waste, which totals more than 100,000 tons *daily,* is taken to a disposal area covering 8 square miles.

The concentrate goes to the smelter, where it is mixed with the copper recovered by the precipitator plants and heated in reverberatory furnaces to 2,700°F, producing copper matte containing 40 percent copper. The molten matte goes to a converter, where air is blown through the melt, removing more impurities and producing blister copper containing 98.6 percent of the metal. The molten blister copper is deoxygenated and brought to about 99.5 percent pure copper. This goes to a refinery, where, by passing electric plates, the metal is further refined to 99.96 percent copper.

Copper is not the only product of these porphyry ores. Other metals are present in minor amounts, but the quantity of ore mined and concentrated is tremendous, and some by-product metals—molybdenum and lead for example—are produced in large amounts.

In general, silver is obtained primarily from the mining of copper ores, but at Virginia City (the Comstock Lode) and at Tonopah, Nevada, silver was the principal metal sought. The Comstock Lode, discovered in 1859, produced enough silver to affect the nation's monetary system. The important deposits of silver at Tonopah were discovered in 1900. The gold camp at Goldfield, Nevada, was discovered in 1903.

These mines, and the porphyry copper ores, were for the most part discovered as a result of prospecting for placer gold. But placer gold production from the Basin and Range Province has not been large.

A complete map of the mining districts in the Basin and Range Province would show more than 500 districts; Figure 16.38 shows fewer than 50. Those indicated were selected to show the large porphyry copper mines (Cu) and some of the principal districts that have been productive or that contain considerable reserves of minerals other than copper. The province contains a great variety of mineral deposits, and the list given in the figure could be greatly expanded.

Although salts are omnipresent in the Basin and Range Province, there has been little production of common salt (sodium chloride) except from some salt pans adjacent to Great Salt Lake. Other salts have been important to the national economy, notably borax. This salt was first produced in quantity from Death Valley about 1882, and the deposits there were made famous by the well-advertised 20-mule teams that were used to haul borax from the valley to the railroad—a 10-day trip. The Death Valley borax mines are now closed, and production has shifted to more valuable deposits in the Mojave Desert.

Other salts produced from brines at Searles Lake, California, and Great Salt Lake Desert include potassium salts and such sodium salts as glauber's salt (sodium sulfate) and soda ash (sodium carbonate).

The Death Valley area has also been a major source of talc, obtained from underground mines in Precambrian rocks. Important deposits of some of the rare earths occur in the Mojave Desert, although these have not yet been developed for production in large quantities.

More About the Resources

Aridity in the Basin and Range Province is not an asset, as it is on the Colorado Plateau, because few areas there have colorful rocks and picturesque landforms. Only confirmed denizens of the desert find it beautiful, and for them it does indeed have attractions, especially for those seeking solitude.

Mild winters in the Lower Sonoran zone of the southern part of the province have made that area a popular winter resort area. In addition to the pleasant climate, there is also the intangible asset of the colorful influence of Mexico and of the Indian cultures, ancient and modern. And the vegetation is exotic.

As a consequence of the many and varied mineral deposits in the Basin and Range Province, abandoned mining camps and ghost towns are legion. This is the land of the purple bottle, and the abandoned camps are increasing by pop-

Figure 16.39 *Abandoned mine camps are another feature of the Basin and Range Province. This example is in the Davis Mountains State Park, in TransPecos Texas. [Courtesy of Texas Parks and Wildlife Department.]*

ular places for collecting not only glass that has turned purple, but mineral and rock specimens. Abandoned mines and mills have a special lure, including those that were more productive of stock issues than of ore. In a national park or national monument abandoned mines are of historic interest, for they have again become part of the wilderness, and visitors are guided to them. But a productive modern mine at the site would be deplored for marring the wilderness.

References

Benson, L., and others, 1969, The cacti of Arizona: 3rd ed., Univ. Arizona Press. Bull. No. 4.

Blackwelder, E., and others, 1948, The Great Basin, with emphasis on glacial and postglacial times: Bull. Univ. Utah v. 38, n. 20.

Butler, B. S., 1920, The ore deposits of Utah: U.S. Geol. Survey Prof. Paper 111.

Browne, J. Ross, 1864, A peep at Washoe: New York, Harper and Bros., p. 309–436.

Chalfant, W. A., 1953, Death Valley, the facts: Stanford Univ. Press.

Gilbert, G. K., 1890, Lake Bonneville: U.S. Geol. Survey Mon. 1.

Hunt, A. P., 1960, Archeology of the Death Valley saltpan, California: Univ. Utah Anthropological Papers No. 47; reprinted 1971, Johnson Reprints.

Hunt, Chas. B., 1966, General geology of Death Valley, California: U.S. Geol. Survey Prof. Paper 494.

————, 1966, Plant ecology of Death Valley, California: U.S. Geol. Survey Prof. Paper 509.

Nolan, T. B., 1943, The Basin and Range Province in Utah, Nevada, and California: U.S. Geol. Survey Prof. Paper 197-D, pp. 141–196.

Rickard, T. A., 1932, A history of American mining: New York, McGraw-Hill.

Russell, I. C., 1885, Geological history of Lake Lahontan: U.S. Geol. Survey Mon. 11.

———, 1889, Quaternary history of Mono Valley, California: U.S. Geol. Survey Ann. Rept. 8, pp. 261–394.

Shreve, F., 1951, Vegetation of the Sonoran Desert: Carnegie Inst. Wash., Publ. 591.

Flows of flood basalt exposed along the Columbia River near Vantage, Washington. The cliff is 1,100 feet high. [Photograph by the Washington Department of Conservation and Development.]

17

....

COLUMBIA-SNAKE RIVER PLATEAUS— LAND OF LAVA

The Columbia-Snake River Plateau (Fig. 17.1), embracing a little more than 100,000 square miles, includes most of the Northwest's lava fields, the most distinctive features of the province. In most of the plateau the lavas are nearly horizontal, but in some areas they are folded. The surface of the plateau, which averages about 3,000 feet high (Fig. 17.2), is surmounted by ridges where the lavas have been folded or faulted, and by irregular mountains where older rocks protrude through the lavas. Southward the plateau grades into the Basin and Range Province, and includes closed basins where drainage is ponded. The climate is semiarid, for the plateau is in a rain shadow of the high Cascade Range.

Altitudes average much lower than on the Colorado Plateau. The Walla Walla Section is below 2,000 feet and extends below 500 feet in altitude. The Harney and Payette sections and the Snake River Plain are all below 5,000 feet, except for a few small, isolated mountains not shown in the figure. Most of the Blue Mountains Section, which could be included in the Northern Rockies, lies below 8,000 feet, but at least one peak reaches to 10,000 feet.

The Columbia-Snake River Plateau has a population of almost 1½ million, largely concentrated along the Snake River in Idaho and along the rivers that drain into the plateau from the Northern Rocky Mountains and from the Cascades.

Outstanding features of the Columbia-Snake River Plateau are the

1. Great extent of the lavas and their prevailing near-horizontality.

2. Semiarid climate.

3. Vegetation, which, except on the few mountains, consists chiefly of shrubs and grasses rather than trees.

4. Two great rivers, the Columbia and the Snake, and the reservoirs along them.

5. Extensive plain along the Snake River in Idaho.

6. Canyons in Washington and Oregon.

7. Great extent and thickness of ancient, weathered loess, known as Palouse soil.

8. Bare, stream-worn lava surfaces (scabland) in Washington, where the loess was

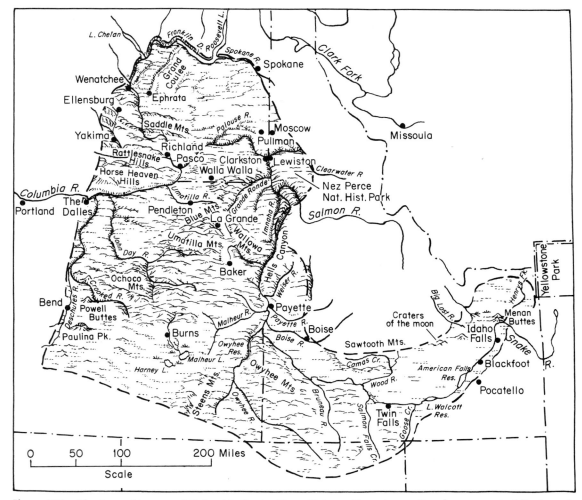

Figure 17.1 *Physiographic map of Columbia-Snake River Plateau. There is a national monument at Craters of the Moon, a National Recreational Area at Grand Coulee, and a national historical park at Nez Perce; the latter has no boundary but links 22 federal, state, county, Indian, and privately owned historical sites pertaining to the Nez Perce Indians and the Lewis and Clark expedition.*

eroded from the land between rivers by extraordinary floods during Pleistocene time.

9. Dry canyons (coulees) and dry falls that were eroded by the Pleistocene floods.

10. Hydroelectric power at the numerous dams along the Columbia and Snake Rivers.

The land is used chiefly for farming and ranching. The principal crops are wheat, hay, and other forage, and Idaho's potatoes. Much of the farming is dry farming—that is, without irrigation. The chief livestock raised are beef cattle and sheep. Although the plateau is covered mainly by shrubs and grassland, sawmills are numerous around its edges, the logs being hauled from the bordering mountains. Except for some minor coal beds the plateau is without mineral fuels, and other mineral resources have not been important in its economy.

The rivers once were an important source of

salmon, especially for the Indians. But the dams have reduced the salmon runs despite attempts to devise ways for the salmon to pass them. Current studies show, however, that stocking more favorable streams with fertilized eggs might reverse this trend.

Separated from the Columbia-Snake River Plateau, yet related to it, are the lava fields at the Stikine and Interior plateaus in British Columbia (Fig. 18.2). On the Stikine Plateau is Mt. Edziza, a complex cone rising to 9,143 feet in altitude. Level Mountain is a shield volcano that

covers 700 square miles and rises to 7,101 feet in altitude. Some volcanoes erupted in the midst of the Pleistocene ice; these, known as tuyas, are flat-topped. On the Interior Plateau, south of the Stikine, are three large shield volcanoes.

Structural Framework and Topography

The relation of the Columbia-Snake River Plateau to the lava fields in the Pacific Northwest is illustrated in Figure 17.3. The northern bound-

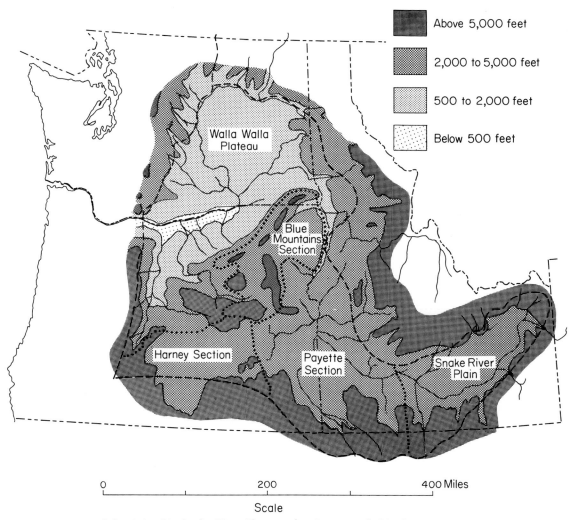

Figure 17.2 *Map of the Columbia-Snake River Plateau, showing general altitudes.*

Figure 17.3 *Middle and late Cenozoic plateau basalts and related volcanics in the Pacific Northwest. White areas are nonvolcanic and mostly prevolcanic rocks. Along the Cascades are Quaternary composite cones built on top of Tertiary shield volcanoes. The Snake River Plain is largely Pleistocene plateau basalt. Harney Lake Basin and the Yellowstone Plateau are mostly late Tertiary and Quaternary. The Columbia River Basin is mostly middle and late Tertiary plateau basalt; the Interior Plateau in British Columbia is also middle and late Teriary but includes broad shield volcanoes as well as plateau basalt.*

ary of the Province, from eastern Idaho to central Washington, is the contact along which the plateau lavas overlap the older rocks forming the Northern Rocky Mountains and the northern end of the Cascade Range. South of Puget Sound, the Cascade Range is composed of lavas and other volcanic rocks, but its structure is anticlinal, with towering volcanoes aligned along the crest of the anticline. Both structurally and topographically, this mountain range differs markedly from the plateau to the east, and the two are separated by a sharp break in the topography.

On the east, the Yellowstone Plateau, included in the Middle Rocky Mountains, could as well be included in the Columbia Plateau, for it is continuous with the Columbia Plateau and resembles it as much as it does the Rockies. On the south, the lavas and other volcanic rocks extend from the Columbia Plateau into the northern part of the Basin and Range Province, where they are disrupted by block faults and form north-trending ridges. Structurally and topographically, the Columbia Plateau grades into the Basin and Range Province, and the boundary between them is arbitrary.

Structurally the Columbia-Snake River Plateau is a basin some miles deep between the Idaho Batholith and the Cascade Range, and the basin extends eastward along the south side of the Idaho Batholith and other Northern Rockies to join the Yellowstone Plateau.

WALLA WALLA SECTION

The Walla Walla Section is a structural basin that was downwarped while the lavas were being erupted. The first eruptions, which occurred in early Tertiary time, ponded the drainage. Lavas filled the central part of the sinking basin, and lakes developed around its edges. Deposits of sandstone and shale accumulated in the lakes to a thickness of several thousand feet (Swauk and Roslyn formations, Eocene). Away from the basin these deposits overlap the older crystalline rocks, and toward the basin they are interbedded with the lavas. To the west, in the Cascade Range, these deposits contain abundant plant remains, including some coal beds.

The downwarping and eruptions continued through Eocene time and into Oligocene time, and the deposits (Clarno Formation) contain a great deal of volcanic ash and other sediments of volcanic origin. The downwarping continued through the end of Oligocene time and into Miocene time, and a lake was formed along the south edge of the basin against the flank of the Blue Mountains uplift. Lake and stream deposits,

which accumulated in the lake to a thickness of about 1 mile (John Day Formation) contain both animal and plant remains; basinward these sediments are interbedded with lavas. Similar deposits, formed later in Miocene time (Ellensburg and Mascall Formations), contain much volcanic debris, including a great accumulation of lavas called the Columbia River Basalt (Table 17.1). These lavas, about a mile thick, extended farther and farther onto the flanks of the basin with each renewal of eruption. The total volume of these lavas may be as great as 100,000 cubic miles.

Despite the great volume and great extent of the lavas, the Walla Walla Section is without volcanic cones. The eruptions were from fissures, now marked by swarms of dikes, especially along the south and west sides of the Section.

In Pliocene time (represented by the Dalles and Rattlesnake formations) the volcanic activity in this Section began to wane, although it continued as vigorously as ever in the Snake River Plains, in the southern Columbia Plateau, and in the Cascade Range. The Cascades became a high anticline at this time, and as uplift progressed a series of southeast- and east-trending folds developed along the northwest edge of the Walla Walla Section (Fig. 17.4).

The older Columbia River Basalts differ from the younger in their content of glass and of olivine (Table 17.1). Younger Quaternary basalts to the west in the Cascade Range and farther south in Oregon are rich in olivine. These differences have been interpreted as due to different sources of the lavas rather than differentiation from one parent magma.

As the Walla Walla basin was downwarped, the lavas and lake beds were folded. The anticlines are curiously persistent folds, longer than most in the Valley and Ridge Province of the Appalachian Highlands. They form ridges with smooth crests, 1,500 to 3,000 feet higher than the broad basins that separate them. The smooth crests of the ridges coincide with the axes of the anticlines, unlike the ridges in the Valley and Ridge Province, most of which formed by erosion of the flanks of folds.

These folds, as a group, diverted the Columbia

Table 17.1

Stratigraphic Section of Columbia River Lavas

Series	Formation	Lithology and Thickness
Pliocene	Ellensburg Formation	Pebble conglomerate, sand, and mudflows; 1,800 feet thick. Upper 500 feet basaltic and contains coarse brown sand; remainder andesitic. Beds of fine ash in lower part.
Pliocene or Miocene		Gradational zone in which the lower part of Ellensburg grades laterally into the upper part of the Columbia River Basalt.
Miocene	Columbia River Basalt — Yakima Basalt	*Most of the Yakima Basalt is glassy without much olivine except in the upper flows.* Saddle Mountains Member: one or more basalt flows about 400 feet thick; some flows of agglomerate, some pillow lava. Priest Rapids Member: four basalt flows 220 feet thick. Quincy Diatomite Bed: diatomite with lenses of silt and clay; thickness to 35 feet. Roza Member: two basalt flows 200 feet thick. Squaw Creek Diatomite Bed: diatomite grading westward to sand, silt, and clay; 17 feet thick. Frenchman Springs Member: six basalt flows 375 feet thick. Vantage Sandstone Member: quartz, feldspar, mica sand or tuffaceous silt, sand. Lower Basalt Flows: pillow lavas common; more than 1,000 feet thick.
	Columbia River Basalt — Picture Gorge Basalt	Mostly crystalline rather than glassy basalt with about 5 percent olivine.

River a hundred miles eastward into the basin; otherwise the river presumably would have continued its course along the edge of the lava field. Yet the Columbia River and the Yakima River, a tributary, have cut gorges across the folds (Fig. 17.18) and are antecedent. Repeated uplift at these anticlines is recorded by the overlap of some lavas and sedimentary rocks against the flanks of the folds.

The structurally lowest part of the Walla Walla Section is the Pasco Basin, in which the Columbia River is joined by the Snake. There the lavas are buried under many hundreds of feet of silt, sand, and gravel, and their upper surface is below sea level. This buried lava surface was the ground surface when the lavas were erupted, and its position below sea level is due to continued basinward sinking since the eruptions. This area may still be sinking, but the measurements needed to confirm this have not been made.

The Columbia River enters the Walla Walla Section from the north, and after being joined by the Spokane River, flows westward in a deep canyon along the northern edge of the lavas. Grand Coulee Dam and Franklin D. Roosevelt Lake are along this stretch. The canyon, in places more than 2,000 feet deep, turns south at the northwest corner of the lava basin, crosses an anticlinal fold and ridge (Saddle Mountains) and then turns southeastward, in the direction of the Pasco Basin (Fig. 17.4). From there to the gorge through the Cascade Range the river is only a few hundred feet below the plateau surface.

The Snake River enters the Walla Walla Section in a canyon about 2,000 feet deep, but the plateau surface slopes westward and the canyon

becomes less and less deep in that direction. In
the Pasco Basin the lavas are buried under lake
beds, and both the Snake and Columbia rivers
flow through open valleys, one of the few open
stretches west of the Snake River Plain.

Between the two rivers much of the plateau
surface is scabland. Enormous floods during
Pleistocene time (p. 558) overtopped the canyon
walls of the Columbia and Spokane rivers and
discharged southwestward across the plateau.
The surface was stripped of its soil along a network of channels (Fig. 17.5). Some valleys cut in

the lavas are tremendous; Grand Coulee is one
of them (Fig. 17.21).

The Pasco Basin ends downstream at an anticline that is breached by the Columbia River.
After crossing this uplift the river enters Umatilla
Basin (Fig. 17.4), and skirts its northern edge.
From here the lavas rise westward onto the uplift
of the Cascade Range, and the Columbia River
enters its gorge through that Range.

The lavas also rise southward toward the
Ochoco-Blue Mountains uplift. Three tributaries
of the Columbia River in this part of the section

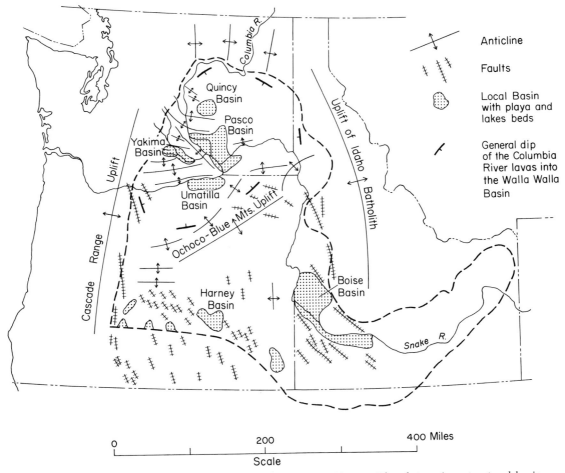

Figure 17.4 *Structural framework of the Columbia-Snake River Plateau. The plateau is a structural basin
located between the Idaho Batholith and the Cascade Range. The lavas north of the Ochoco-Blue Mountains
Uplift are folded, especially at the northwest edge of the basin. Southward the lavas are faulted, and the
structure grades into that of the Basin and Range Province.*

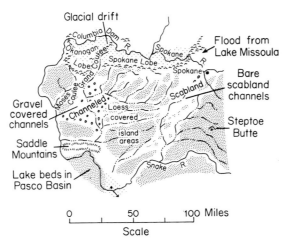

Figure 17.5 *Braided pattern of scabland channels on the Columbia-Snake River Plateau between the Columbia and Snake rivers.* [*After Amer. Assoc. Geog.*]

are the Umatilla, John Day, and Deschutes rivers. The Umatilla River crosses the Umatilla Basin in an open valley to join the Columbia. The John Day River, which heads in the Ochoco-Blue Mountains, has eroded a canyon about 1,000 feet deep through stream beds in the shallow western end of the Umatilla Basin and exposed the underlying lavas where they begin their rise westward to the Cascades. Throughout its course this river flows through a canyon in which Tertiary lake and stream beds, interbedded with the Columbia River basalt and other basalts are extensively exposed. The Deschutes River flows through a canyon more than 1,000 feet deep. The Deschutes, however, drains north along the east base of the Cascade Range and joins the Columbia at the western end of the Umatilla Basin. The drainage basin includes much Quaternary lava and many volcanic cones. Long stretches of the canyon are incised into the young lavas. The uplands are extensively mantled with volcanic ash from the nearby volcanic centers and from the larger ones on the Cascades.

BLUE MOUNTAINS SECTION

The Blue Mountains Section is formed by an uplift of a complex of eugeosynclinal Paleozoic and Mesozoic sedimentary rocks (Table 17.2) and intrusive Cenozoic rocks. The structure and topography of this uplift have more in common with the Northern Rockies than with the Columbia Plateau, and this section could be considered a part of the Northern Rocky Mountains that projects westward into the Columbia Plateau. The rocks represent a segment of the Paleozoic and early Mesozoic eugeosynclines that extended northward across the central and western parts of the Great Basin; similar rocks reappear in British Columbia between the Rocky Mountain Trench and the Coast Mountains. The mountains, which antedate the eruptions on the Columbia Plateau, once stood as islands in the sea of lavas, but they were further uplifted while the lavas were being erupted. Extensive areas, especially in the Umatilla and Blue mountains (Fig. 17.6), are elevated plateaus of basalt. These lavas are more than a mile higher than the lavas in the central part of the Walla Walla Section, and most or all of this difference in altitude represents uplift since the eruptions.

Tertiary sedimentary rocks and interbedded volcanics in the John Day Basin provide a remarkably complete record, not only of the structural and volcanic history of the region, but also of the history of climatic and vegetational changes during the Tertiary (see p. 564). One of the swarms of dikes that fed the Columbia River Basalt is exposed along the north fork of the John Day River; other dike swarms are exposed along the Grande Ronde and in the eastern Wallowa Mountains. These dike swarms are several miles wide and up to 45 miles long.

Briefly, the structural history recorded by the rocks described in Table 17.2 is: (1) marine sedimentation from the Permian to the Jurassic (source of sediments was from the west); (2) major deformation and intrusion of granite in the late Jurassic and in the Cretaceous; (3) erosion during the Cretaceous; (4) Eocene volcanism accompanied by saprolitic weathering; (5) continued volcanism, folding, and faulting from the Oligocene to the Pliocene; (6) Quaternary erosion.

The Snake River crosses the uplift in Hells Canyon, which is deeper than Grand Canyon

(Figs. 17.7, 17.9). The river enters this canyon from the Payette Section at an altitude of about 2,100 feet (Fig. 17.8), and here the lavas of the Columbia-Snake River Plateau are at river level. Fifty miles downstream the lava surface is at about 6,500 feet, and the altitude of the river is 1,300 feet. On the west wall of the canyon, the base of the lavas is between 3,000 and 4,000 feet; on the east wall, a mountain of older rocks, known as the Seven Devils, projects above the lavas and reaches a peak of 9,410 feet. He Devil

Mountain (Fig. 17.9), only six miles from the river, reaches an altitude of 8,000 feet.

A short distance north of the mouth of the Grande Ronde (Great Roundabout) River, the Snake River leaves the uplifted area and enters the Walla Walla Basin. The base of the lavas dips downstream and passes below the bed of the river at an altitude of about 800 feet. The surface of the lavas and the rim of the canyon here are about 2,000 feet higher.

The Seven Devils and Wallowa mountains

Table 17.2

Tertiary and pre-Tertiary rocks in the Blue Mountains Section of the Columbia Plateau

Series	Formation	Lithology and Thickness
Pliocene	Rattlesnake Formation	Gravel, tuff and rhyolite, 900 feet thick, thought to have been deposited in ancestral valley of the John Day River. Correlative beds to the west and northwest are the Madras and Dalles Formations containing pumiceous andesite, olivine basalt, ash beds, mud flows, conglomerate, and diatomacous beds.
		——————Angular unconformity——————
Miocene	Mascall Formation	Clay, sand, volcanic ash and tuff; 800 to more than 1,000 feet thick. Correlative with the Yakima Basalt.
	Picture Gorge Basalt	Crystalline basalt without much olivine; flows average 70 feet thick and aggregate more than 1,000 feet thick. In places these lava flows are unconformably overlain by Quaternary olivine basalt flows that evidently were more fluid because the Quaternary flows average only about 20 feet thick.
		——————Angular unconformity——————
Early Miocene and Late Oligocene	John Day Formation	Tuff, lapilli tuff, rhyolitic ash flows, rhyolitic lava and rhyolite domes; 4,000 feet thick. Richly fossiliferous.
		——————Angular unconformity——————
Eocene	Clarno Formation	Lava flows, volcanic breccia, tuff, and tuffaceous sandstone mostly of andesitic composition. Thin layers of red saprolite in and at top of the formation. About 6,000 feet thick.
		——Major unconformity; much deformation and intrusion of granite——
Triassic		Shale, limestone, volcanics; thickness uncertain.
		——————Unconformity?——————
Permian	Clover Creek Greenstone	Altered flows and pyroclastic rocks with some conglomerate, limestone, and chert; more than 4,000 feet thick. Oldest proved fossils in this region.
Pennsylvanian(?)	Elkhorn Ridge Argillite	Argillite, tuff, and chert, some limestone and greenstone; more than 5,000 feet thick.
Pre-Carboniferous	Burnt River Schist	Greenstone, quartz schist, conglomeratic schist, limestone, slate, quartzite; more than 5,000 feet thick.
?		Biotite gneiss of sedimentary origin.

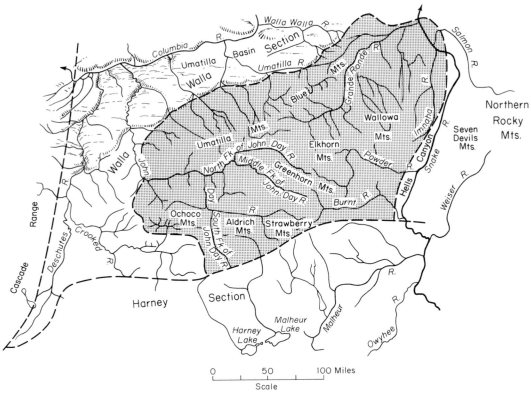

Figure 17.6 *Drainage pattern in and around the Blue Mountains Section (shaded area). The John Day River and its tributaries form a trellis drainage pattern; other streams are dendritic.*

have peaks higher than 9,000 feet. Most of the rest of the section, although mountainous, is below 6,000 feet. The Wallowa Mountains were glaciated.

HARNEY LAKE SECTION

The Harney Lake Section, a volcanic plain at the southwest corner of the Columbia-Snake River Plateau, has the least distinct boundaries of any section of the plateau. It grades northward into the Ochoco and Umatilla mountains and into the Walla Walla Section, southward into the Great Basin, and eastward into the Payette Section.

The Harney Lake Section, located along a swarm of northwest-trending faults, is a plain with little local relief except at the volcanic cen-

ters. Variously referred to as the Great Sand Desert and as the Great Sage Plain, it is composed of nearly horizontal lava flows, mostly Quaternary in age, largely covered with loose

Figure 17.7 *Hells Canyon of the Snake River, at the east edge of the Columbia-Snake River Plateau, is deeper than Grand Canyon, but its walls are not as colorful or as steep as those in Grand Canyon.*

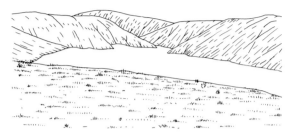

Figure 17.8 *View downstream at Farewell Bend, where the Snake River leaves the Payette Section (foreground) and enters Hells Canyon to cross the Ochoco-Blue Mountains Uplift.*

volcanic ash and surmounted by hundreds of volcanic cones, a landscape wholly unlike that of the Walla Walla Section. Many of the lavas and cones are composed of fresh rock and cinders, for the volcanism is very young. Between the cones and the lava benches are short dry washes, most of which end in dry lakes. There is no exterior drainage except at the edges of the section.

Volcanic cones are most numerous and highest in the northwest part of the section (Fig. 17.10). Southeastward the cones are lower, the flows more extensive, and the playas more numerous and larger. At the southeast end of the section, the basins culminate in a large marshy tract containing two lakes, Harney Lake and Malheur Lake. These lakes formerly overflowed to the Snake River by way of the Malheur River, but

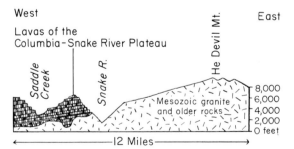

Figure 17.9 *Snake River at Hells Canyon. Here the westward-dipping lavas have been stripped from the east side of the canyon, and older rocks form the mountains there. The lavas rest on a rough, mountainous surface.*

a lava flow has dammed the outlet; now the lakes overflow only in very wet times.

These lakes, the lowest part of the section, lie at altitudes slightly above 4,000 feet. The highest peak, Paulina Peak at Newberry Volcano (Fig. 17.11), a little higher than 8,000 feet in altitude, is at the west end of the section. Only a few volcanic mountains are more than 2,000 feet high, and most are only a few hundred feet higher than the plain. The topography has a striking northwest-southeast grain, reflecting the faulting and dominant direction of flow of the lavas.

NEWBERRY VOLCANO AND ENVIRONS

At the western edge of the Harney Lake Section, near Bend, Oregon, is the Pleistocene Newberry Volcano (Fig. 17.11), a shield volcano 4,000 feet high covering about 700 square miles and rising to a summit altitude of about 8,000 feet. Most of the volcano is basaltic, and flows on the outer flanks slope roughly 4 percent, about 200 feet per mile. The flanks are studded with more than 100 basaltic cinder cones and some domes and flows of rhyolite.

Late in the history of the volcano, increasing amounts of rhyolite were erupted, and a cone of alternating basalt and rhyolite was built about 3,000 feet high. The apex collapsed along a series of arcuate fractures to form a caldera about 5 miles in diameter, which is now occupied by two lakes. The north wall rises in a series of fault steps, and just north of the caldera rim two lines of cinder cones mark arcuate fractures along which sliding was incipient. The caldera opens westward and is straight-walled like the summit graben at Haleakala in Hawaii.

A lake formed in the caldera, and was divided by renewed basaltic eruptions across the original lake bottom; as the lava contacted the water, it chilled to glass, broke into small particles, and built a broad ridge of the loose particles. When this was built above water, a series of eruptions added a higher cone of pumice, and these last eruptions showered the eastern, downwind flank of the volcano with pumice as thick as 20 feet. This ash covers many of the older cinder cones

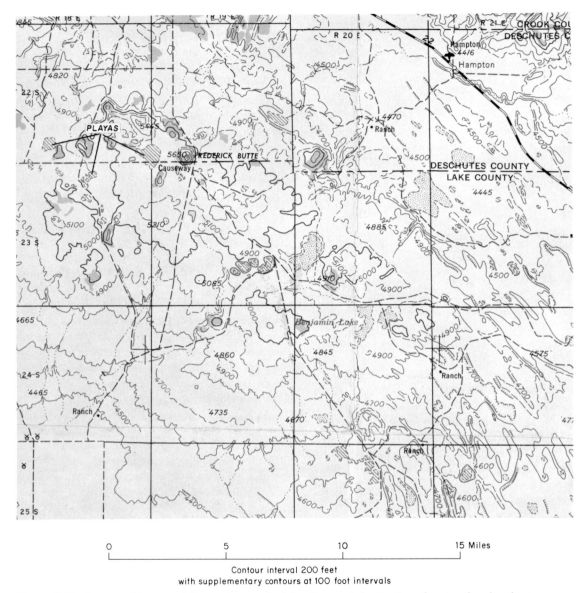

Figure 17.10 *Topographic map of the western part of the Harney Lake Section, showing the abundant volcanic cones and playas. [From Crescent, Oregon, 1/250,000 quadrangle.]*

on the flanks of Mt. Newberry, and some still younger cones have been built on top of it.

Some of the ash is about 2,000 years old; the younger cinder cones may be only a few hundred years old. Hot springs issue from fractures at the east side of the caldera and at places on the flanks of the shield. Newberry Volcano may only be dormant, not dead.

Also nearby are maar-type volcanic centers, represented by Hole in the Ground (Fig. 17.11). The geometry and dimensions of this feature are about the same as those of Meteor Crater on the Colorado Plateau, but Hole in the Ground is the result of volcanic explosion. While Newberry Volcano was active, a lake filled Christmas Lake Valley to a maximum depth of about 150 feet. The lowest shoreline, about 50 feet lower, has been dated by the radiocarbon method as 13,000 years old, or latest Wisconsinan.

During the highest stage, the groundwater table was high, and at the topographic saddle west of the lake and about south of Newberry Volcano, heated lavas came in contact with the groundwater, causing steam explosions that blasted deep cone-shaped craters and produced Hole in the Ground. The extruded material accumulated as blocky breccia around the vent and partly refilled the crater. Around Hole in the Ground are blocks 3 to 10 feet in diameter, composed of various volcanic rocks, some of which are not to be seen in the crater walls and are obviously from depth. The breccia is stratified, indicating a series of explosions, not just one big one. Moreover, unlike Meteor Crater, each layer contains a mixture of all kinds of rocks; they are not sorted, as at Meteor Crater.

PAYETTE SECTION

The Payette Section (Fig. 17.12) consists of northwest-trending structural and topographic

units. At the north a structural basin occupied by the Snake River lies between two uplifts, the Idaho Batholith on the northeast and the Owyhee Mountains on the southwest. A second basin is south of the Owyhee Mountains.

The structural trough of the Snake River in the Payette Section is deeply buried under lake, playa, and stream deposits that were deposited upstream from Hells Canyon. The deep fill of sediments in the trough evidently resulted from repeated ponding of the Snake River as the uplift was raised during Cenozoic time. The river maintained its course across the uplift by overflowing along its old channel each time it was raised by the folding. Moreover, the lake beds are dissected and form benches a few hundred feet higher than the rivers.

The Snake River enters the Payette Section below Twin Falls (Fig. 17.13) at an altitude of about 2,800 feet and follows the boundary between lava fields of the Snake River Plain and stream and lake beds of the Payette Section. For more than 50 miles the river flows through a gorge 500 feet deep. Below the main gorge, where the Snake is joined by the Bruneau River, the

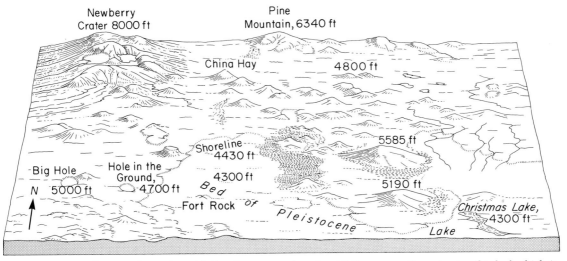

Figure 17.11 *Newberry Volcano is a shield volcano covering about 700 square miles, about a third of which is shown in the northwest corner of the figure. The top of the volcano collapsed to form a caldera. The landscape includes a wide variety of landforms: the shield volcano, its caldera, cones on the flank of the shield, benches of lava, ice caves, maar type volcanos, flats of volcanic cinders and ash, Pleistocene lake features, and alkaline flats.*

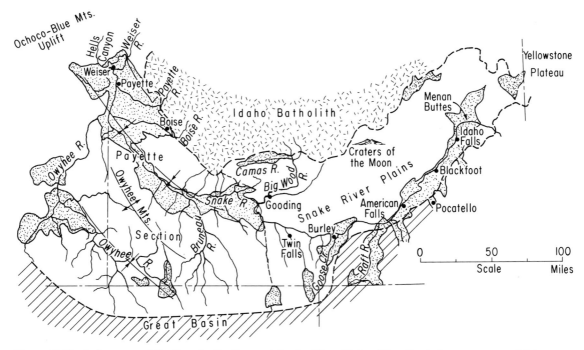

Figure 17.12 *Index map of the Payette Section and Snake River Plains. The stippled areas represent lake, playa, and stream deposits of Cenozoic age. The white areas in the sections are almost entirely lavas and related volcanic rocks.*

altitude of the river drops to about 2,450 feet. Here the surface of the lavas lies a few hundred feet higher than the lake beds. Westward, the river valley gradually becomes more open. The Snake River crosses the lavas (Fig. 17.12) in a gorge 500 feet deep and then follows an open, flat-bottomed valley several miles wide between benches of lake beds that form the divides be-

Figure 17.13 *Twin Falls of the Snake River, Idaho. The falls, almost 200 feet high, now are greatly reduced in volume because the water is used to produce hydroelectric power.*

tween the Snake, Boise, Payette, and Weiser rivers. By the time the Snake River reaches the entrance to Hells Canyon it has dropped to an altitude of about 2,100 feet. The gradient here is only half as steep as it is where the river enters the Payette Section.

The northern edge of the Payette Section, marked by the overlap of the lake beds and lavas onto the Idaho Batholith, is topographically and structurally distinct. At Boise, the mountains of the batholith rise above the plain nearly 5,000 feet in about 8 miles. Much of the uplift of the batholith occurred after the Columbia River Basalts of Miocene-Pliocene age were erupted, for those lavas are turned up along the west flank of the batholith (Fig. 17.9). But the lavas of the Snake River Plain and those of the Payette Section, are younger than the Columbia River basalts and are involved only in the latest structural movements.

The northern boundary of the Payette Section

appears to be a major crustal break trending northwest and having at least 2½ miles of displacement and probably very much more. Gravity data indicate that the basaltic rocks under the Payette Section are at least 2½ miles thick, and may be as much as 7 miles thick. These dense rocks have been displaced downward against the less-dense rocks of the Idaho Batholith. Late Tertiary and Quaternary formations that extend across the boundary are displaced downward toward the Snake River, and the amount of displacement is progressively less in the younger deposits. About 2,000 feet of the displacement occurred during the Quaternary, another 2,000 feet in late Pliocene time, and about 5,000 feet earlier in the Pliocene; an unknown amount of deformation took place at a still earlier time. Southward from the Snake River Plain the lava surface rises onto the uplift at the Owyhee Mountains.

Where the Owyhee River turns north it cuts across the Owyhee Mountains in a gorge 50 miles long and, for much of its length, is about 1,500 feet deep. The river, incised in the uplifted Tertiary and Quaternary lavas and lake beds, is at an elevation of about 3,000 feet where it enters the gorge, and is at about 2,300 feet where it emerges on the Snake River Plain. Owyhee Dam, near the lower end of the gorge, forms a reservoir that extends most of the way across the uplift. This reservoir provides a good datum for determining whether uplift across the gorge is continuing at the present time.

The southern boundary of the Payette Section is south of the Owyhee River trough, where the flank of that northwest-trending syncline is interrupted by the northerly trending block mountains of the Great Basin. The boundary is an arbitrary line through a zone almost 50 miles wide, where the two structures, although very different, grade into one another. In general, the Payette Section is a northwest-trending structural basin separating the structurally higher Great Basin from the still higher Idaho batholith. Downwarping of the Payette Section in late Cenozoic time apparently was contemporaneous with the block faulting in the Great Basin.

SNAKE RIVER PLAIN

The Snake River Plain (Fig. 17.12) represents a vast field of late Cenozoic (mostly Quaternary) lavas. The plain is a continuation of the structural trough represented by the Payette Section, but under the plain the trough is narrower and lacks the subsidiary anticlines and synclines that characterize the Payette Section. Structurally the trough narrows and becomes shallower eastward toward the Yellowstone Plateau. The boundary is drawn where the lake beds of the Payette Section abut against the lavas of the Snake River Plain. The plain is about 3,000 feet in altitude at the west, and rises eastward to about 5,000 feet. The north side, formed by the mountainous Idaho batholith, is about 5,000 feet high. The Snake River flows along the southern edge of the plain, which is about 500 feet lower than the northern edge. For most of its course along the plain, the river flows on top of the lavas, but for 30 miles below American Falls it is incised in the lavas and flows through a shallow gorge, impressive because of the size of the river (Fig. 17.14).

The plain is interrupted by many volcanic cones—among them Craters of the Moon, a national monument. Two unusually striking cones, the Menan Buttes, are above Idaho Falls. Figure 17.15 illustrates one of them.

The transition between the synclinal trough of the Snake River Plain and the north-trending fault-block mountains of the Great Basin is concealed under the lavas of the plain. The lavas at the surface are mostly Quaternary in age and

Figure 17.14 *Gorge of the Snake River in the plain below American Falls, Idaho.*

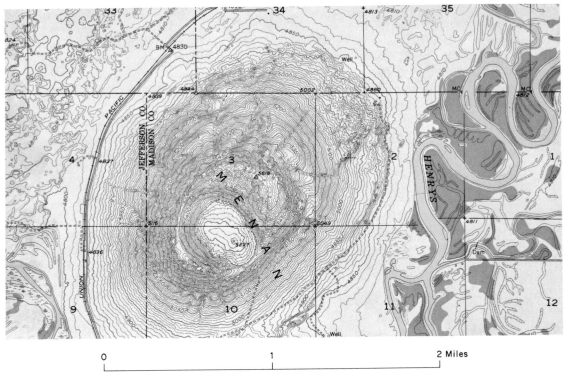

Figure 17.15 *Topographic map of the north Menan Butte, a volcanic cinder cone near the head of the Snake River Plain, Idaho. East of the butte is the floodplain of the Henrys River. Note the cutoff meanders. To the west is lava plain. [From U.S.G.S. Menan Buttes, Idaho, quadrangle.]*

are younger than most of the block faulting, but downwarping of the syncline may have progressed contemporaneously with the block faulting.

East of the Snake River Plain is the Yellowstone Plateau, where the volcanic deposits are even younger than those on the plain. Volcanism still continues in the form of hot springs and other fumarolic activity.

Present-day Earth Movements

The Columbia-Snake River Plateau has not been subject to frequent or to severe earthquakes, but, like the Colorado Plateau, is partly ringed by a belt of earthquake epicenters (Fig. 2.17). Gravity measurements indicate that the Plateau is under-

lain by a thick sequence of dense rocks that contrast with the light rocks under the adjoining provinces to the north and south. The boundaries between the dense and light rocks are marked by earthquake epicenters and correspond to the northern boundary of the Columbia-Snake River Plateau and to most of its southern boundary.

The distribution of these epicenters, together with evidence of tremendous displacement along at least part of the boundaries in late Tertiary and Quaternary time (p. 551), suggests that the plateau as a whole is still moving downward relative to the neighboring provinces. During the last 10 million or so years the Snake River Plain has been sinking, relative to the Idaho Batholith, and the displacement amounts to an average rate of a few inches every hundred years. There is no reason to suppose that movement has ceased. It probably is continuing, perhaps as rapidly as ever, and measurements are much needed to determine this displacement.

A few earthquake epicenters have been recorded along the Snake River trough; along the Ochoco-Blue Mountains Uplift, where it is crossed by the Snake River; and north of the uplift, in the southeastern part of the Walla Walla Section.

Plateau Basalts

The Columbia-Snake River Plateau is one of the few places in the world where vast quantities of basaltic lava were erupted quietly along fissures (now marked by dike swarms), accumulated to great thicknesses, and spread for great distances from their sources. Each continent has such a lava field of basalt, as if they were some essential part of continental structure. Plateau basalt covers the Parana Basin in South America, the Deccan Traps of western India, the north-central Siberian Plateau, the Ethiopian Plateau, and 200,000 square miles in the north Atlantic, including Iceland, the Antrim Plateau in northeastern Ireland, the Inner Hebrides, Faeroe Islands, and southern Greenland. All of these areas are comparable in their volume of basaltic lavas that form plateaus; actually, each is an accumulation of plateaus built by successive lava flows.

The basaltic, or mafic, rocks are those without much silica, generally less than 52 percent. Granitic rocks are those with considerable silica, 65 to 70 percent or more; their melts contained considerable silica, and the rocks are referred to as salic.

The plateau basalts illustrate that basaltic rocks are chiefly extrusive, whereas the neighboring Idaho batholith, the Sierra Nevada, and the batholiths of the Coast Ranges of Canada illustrate that the granitic rocks are chiefly intrusive. A major reason for this difference in habit of the two kinds of rocks is the great difference in viscosity of their melts. Basaltic lava is fluid; granitic magma and its eruptive equivalent, rhyolite, are viscous. Basaltic magma therefore rises more easily than granitic magma through the crustal rocks, and at the surface can spread widely in thin sheets.

The chronology of Cenozoic volcanic and related events on the Columbia-Snake River Plateau are summarized below.

Eocene and Paleocene: Deposition of coarse, clastic sediments and eruption of volcanics near the base of the Cascade Range, forming the Clarno Beds in eastern Oregon and the Swauk Conglomerate, Kachess Rhyolite, Teanaway Basalt, and the Manastash and Roslyn formations in Washington.

Oligocene: Eruption of the main part of the Keechelus Volcanics in eastern Washington and deposition of the volcanically derived John Day Formation in eastern Oregon.

Miocene: Columbia River Basalt erupted in eastern Washington and eastern Oregon; Mascall Formation and Payette Formations of volcanics and lake beds deposited in eastern Oregon while lavas continued being erupted farther north in Washington.

Pliocene: In eastern Washington, Ellensburg Formation deposited in lake, followed by more lavas; in eastern Oregon and on Snake River Plains, lavas and ash.

Pleistocene: In early Pleistocene, deposition of loess in eastern Washington; subsequent erosion of scablands by overflow of Lake Missoula in Montana (p. 415); eruptions of lavas and ash in the Harney Basin and at Craters of the Moon on the Snake River Plains.

Holocene: Continuation of fumarolic activity at east end of the volcanic belt, at Yellowstone Park; latest eruptions at Craters of the Moon, Newberry Volcano, and others nearby.

Drainage Features

The drainage systems on the Columbia-Snake River Plateau have several interesting features: (1) the course of the Columbia River, which is guided in places by the structural rim of the basin but also crosses it; (2) the course of Snake River across the Blue Mountain uplift at Hells Canyon; (3) contrasts between straight and meandering courses of tributaries; (4) the channel scablands and dry canyons in the Walla Walla Section produced by Pleistocene floods; (5) floods on the Snake River Plain, caused by overflow of Lake Bonneville; and (6) landsliding at reservoirs in poorly consolidated lake beds.

COURSES OF THE COLUMBIA AND SNAKE RIVERS

Although the Columbia and Snake rivers make some large bends in crossing the Columbia Plateau, their general positions are structurally controlled. Hells Canyon is the outstanding anomaly, but the rest of the course of the Snake River accords with the structure. The Columbia River crosses some folds at Frenchman Hills and Saddle Mountain (Fig. 17.19), but except for these its course also accords with the structure. Between the big bends the river courses are straight. The only stretches that suggest meandering are the stretch of the Columbia River upstream from its gorge through the Cascade Range and the stretches of the Snake River upstream from its junction with the Columbia and upstream from Hell's Canyon.

Whereas the Colorado River flows against the dip of the saucer-like structure of the Colorado Plateau, the Columbia River first winds around the rim of the Columbia Plateau and then down into the center. The Columbia does not flow against the regional dip until it approaches the east flank of the Cascade uplift.

The Columbia River has a southward course in northern Washington and reaches the north rim of the Columbia River Basalt just west of Spokane, where the river turns west and follows the rim of the lavas around the northwest side of the Walla Walla Section until, near Wenatchee, it turns southeastward into the Pasco Basin, the structurally and topographically lowest part of the Walla Walla Section. It crosses an anticline of Columbia River Lavas at Wallula Gap, and

another where it leaves the Pasco Basin. Some attribute the river bend at Wenatchee to folding of the lavas; others think the river course is more ancient and antecedent across the anticlines. At the base of the Ellensberg Formation (Pliocene) are gravels derived from Precambrian Belt formations, which means that the Columbia River has been discharging to the Walla Walla Section at least since early Pliocene time. It could have discharged there while the Columbia River lavas were being erupted, and its course would have been repeatedly diverted as the lavas accumulated.

The history of Hells Canyon is obscure. In the Payette Section, at the head of the canyon, Miocene-Pliocene lake beds more than 1,500 feet thick clearly record ponding of the river. The Miocene deposits, referred to as the Payette Formation, are interbedded with Columbia River lavas; the Pliocene Idaho Formation is interbedded with Snake River lavas. The Payette Formation unconformably overlaps northward onto a steeply sloping, eroded surface of granite of the Idaho Batholith. At its maximum extension, the lake surface was at the present 4,200 foot contour, Hells Canyon is thought to be at least as old as the Miocene lakes, because they appear to have been repeatedly drained, presumably because Snake River overflowed a divide along Hells Canyon.

A Miocene divide may have been a windgap at the head of a stream draining northward, or perhaps a strike valley at the east edge of a flow of the Columbia River Lavas, or perhaps an uplifted section of a still older (Oligocene?) Hells Canyon. Another possible interpretation is that the Micocene lakes were drained by overflowing to the south or west. Such an ancient river course is indicated by the occurrence of Snake River gravels under Columbia River Basalt in the Baker area.

Deposition of the Idaho Formation, several thousand feet thick, is surely the result of repeated increments of uplift at the structural arch crossed by Hells Canyon at the Seven Devils and Wallowa Mountains (Fig. 17.16). The crest of that arch is at the deepest part of Hells Canyon. The

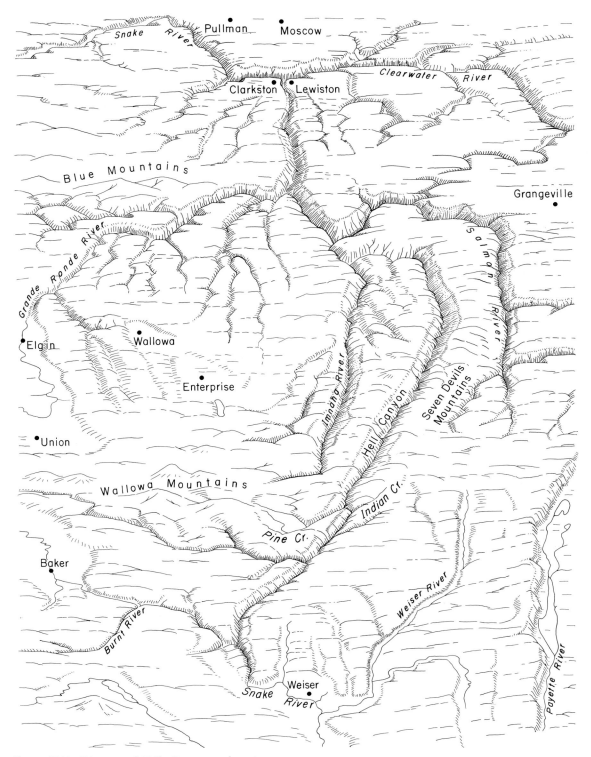

Figure 17.16 *Diagram of Hells Canyon and environs.*

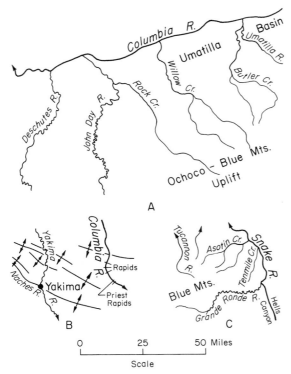

Figure 17.17 *Sketch maps illustrating some meander patterns on the Columbia-Snake River Plateau. (A) Columbia River and its principal tributaries at the western edge of the plateau. (B) Yakima River and Columbia River where they cross anticlinally folded lavas. (C) Snake River and tributaries at the lower end of Hells Canyon and north flank of the Blue Mountains.*

uppermost of the Columbia River lavas are about 6,000 feet in altitude along the west rim of the canyon, and their base is at about 3,500 feet. Southward these lavas plunge under the Payette Section and intertongue with the lake beds of the Payette Formation, below 4,000 feet. We may conclude that at least 2,000 feet of the uplift at the arch is post-Payette; probably more. Since that time there has been at least 2,000 feet of downcutting into the base of the lavas and the underlying rocks, and the Payette Section has been structurally lowered sufficiently to accommodate several thousand feet of Pliocene and early Pleistocene lake beds, alluvial deposits, and lavas. Probably, each increment of uplift along

the arch crossing Hells Canyon was accompanied by sinking at the Payette Section, ponding of Snake River, followed by overflow via the uplifted segment of the temporarily abandoned canyon. Each 50 feet of uplift at the arch, accompanied by 50 feet of sinking at the Payette Section, would accommodate a 100-foot-deep lake. Downcutting at the point of overflow would have been slow, because the river would not have had the bed load of gravel with which to erode the channel. By this interpretation, the fill of sediment would about keep pace with structural deformation and would be succeeded by downcutting in the canyon.

Courses of Tributaries

Tributaries of the Columbia and Snake rivers have a curious mixture of straight and meandering courses (Fig. 17.17). The John Day River has perhaps the most sinuous course of any on the Columbia Plateau (Fig. 17.17,A). In the lower 50 miles, its canyon, which is about 1,500 feet deep, makes about 25 U-turns. The Deschutes River, 25 miles to the west, is more than twice the size of the John Day River but also has a meandering course. One of its tributaries is appropriately named Crooked River. Both the Deschutes and John Day rivers join the Columbia where the lavas begin their rise onto the Cascade Mountains.

Other tributaries joining the Columbia River in the Umatilla and Pasco basins have nearly straight courses. Willow Creek, 25 miles east of the John Day, and Umatilla River, 35 miles farther east, meander very little (Fig. 17.17,A). These comparatively straight streams and their straight tributaries drain northward to the central part of the structural basin.

The Yakima River has closely spaced meanders where it crosses anticlines north of Yakima (Fig. 17.17,B) and downstream where it emerges onto the broad plain of fill in the structural trough. The Columbia River has rapids (Priest Rapids) where it crosses the same set of anticlines, but its course is almost straight (Fig.

17.17,B). This difference probably reflects the difference in the volume and eroding power of the two streams.

Tributaries of the Snake River flow in straight courses down the north flank of the Blue Mountains. The Grande Ronde River, however, which flows east to join the Snake River in a canyon about 2,000 feet deep, makes a U-turn every mile in the last 20 miles of its course (Fig. 17.17,C).

Hell's Canyon is straight, but immediately

upstream is one of the few stretches along which the Snake River has developed meanders. The relationship of meanders to structure suggests that the uplift across Hells Canyon was sufficiently rapid to impede this river. Burnt River and Weiser River, the principal tributaries of the Snake River in this area, drain southward off the uplift to join the Snake at the head of Hells Canyon, forming a barbed drainage pattern. Their general courses are straight, although they have

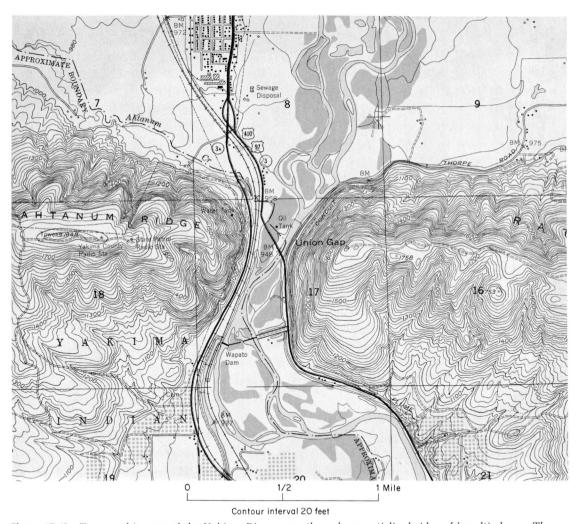

Figure 17.18 *Topographic map of the Yakima River gorge through an anticlinal ridge of basaltic lavas. The axis of the anticline is along the crest of the ridge. The river, antecedent across the fold, was repeatedly ponded as the fold rose, but each pond overflowed through the gap and maintained the channel through it. Compare with Figs. 11.29, 14.15, 14.35. [From U.S.G.S. Yakima East, Washington, quadrangle.]*

Figure 17.19 *Water gaps on the Columbia-Snake River Plateau (A) formed where rivers cross the anticlinally folded lavas. The landforms are similar topographically to the water gaps in the Valley and Ridge Province (B) but the structural geology is very different.*

developed small meanders within their valleys. The Payette, Boise, and Owyhee rivers meander on the floodplain in this area, as does the Snake.

Between this area and the eastern part of the Snake River Plain, the Snake River does little meandering. Above American Falls, however, the river has developed a moderately meandering course, and the meanders have short radii and are closely spaced; meanders at the head of Hells Canyon have long radii and are correspondingly widely spaced. The difference may reflect the westward increase in size of the Snake River.

The straightness or degree of meandering of streams on the Columbia-Snake River Plateau seems to correlate with the geologic structure. Streams draining down the dip tend to have straight courses; those flowing along the strike, or against the dip, tend to meander. But whether a stream develops meanders across an obstruction, such as a rising anticline, also seems to depend on the capacity of the stream to erode its channel. This is controlled by such factors as gradient, volume of water, roughness of the channel, and load. An additional complication is the likelihood that some drainage patterns are

relicts of conditions that no longer exist, such as the floods that carved Grand Coulee.

PLEISTOCENE FLOODS

GRAND COULEE AND THE SCABLANDS. The scablands (Fig. 17.5), which extend across the Walla Walla Section from the Spokane and Columbia rivers southward to the Snake River, are the result of several major floods during Pleistocene time, when ice dammed the Columbia River (Fig. 17.20). One ice lobe, the Okanogan lobe, dammed the Columbia River at the big bend below Grand Coulee Dam. Earlier, the Spokane lobe had dammed the Spokane River. The meltwaters overflowed across the plateau, producing many anomalous features.

The most impressive is the Grand Coulee (Fig. 17.21). This canyon cut into the lavas is about 50 miles long, almost 1,000 feet deep, and about 1 mile wide. It contains cataracts higher than Niagara Falls, plunge pools more than 100 feet deep, and river bars about 150 feet high. Until water

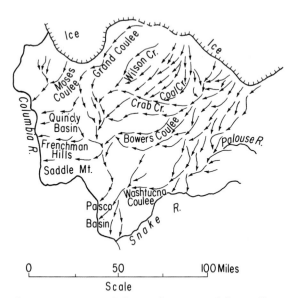

Figure 17.20 *Map of the northern part of the Walla Walla Section, showing the direction of flow of Pleistocene meltwaters across the plateau surface during the period in which the rivers at the north were dammed by glacial ice.*

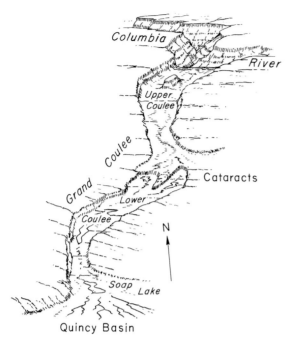

Figure 17.21 *The Grand Coulee, Washington. The coulee heads at the rim of the canyon of the Columbia River. Grand Coulee Dam, not shown, is at the bend in the canyon just west of the head of the coulee. The walls of the Upper Coulee, which is about 25 miles long, reach heights of about 800 feet. They decrease in height southward, and the Upper Coulee ends in a set of cataracts 400 feet high that mark the head of Lower Coulee. The Lower Coulee, also about 25 miles long, crosses a monocline in the lavas. The west wall is higher than the east wall.*

from above Grand Coulee Dam was turned into it, the canyon was without water except for intermittent streams and small alkaline lakes. The canyon was cut by the Columbia, when it was dammed by ice and swollen with meltwaters; when the glaciers receded, the floods subsided and the river returned to its canyon.

The Grand Coulee crosses a monocline in a set of dry cataracts more than 3 miles wide and about 400 feet high that divide the canyon into two parts. The upper canyon is cut in the elevated beds west of the monocline, and the lower canyon follows the fold, with the result that its west wall is higher than the east wall. At the mouth, in the Quincy Basin, are huge gravel fans.

The Grand Coulee heads in a wind gap in the south rim of the canyon of the Columbia River, just above Grand Coulee Dam. The rims on each side of the gap are about 800 feet higher than the floor of the coulee, which is about that much higher than the Columbia River (Fig. 17.22).

Eastward from Grand Coulee to the Palouse River is a network of braided scabland channels. These broad channels are about 50 to 100 feet deep and are separated by uplands mantled with loess. Some have bars, others have cataracts, many have potholes. In many places the floods that developed these channels had to overflow high divides to get from one channel to another, and some of these divides are hundreds of feet high. The Palouse River crosses a divide hundreds of feet high to join the Snake River. Where canyons were not incised across divides, the floodwaters eroded scabland surfaces on the lavas.

Valleys draining westward to the scabland area—even the valley of the Snake River—contain remnants of deltaic deposits having foreset beds that dip upstream—that is, to the east. A delta built eastward into the Palouse River where it enters the scabland is more than 75 feet thick. Another built eastward up the Snake River from the mouth of the Palouse is 260 feet thick and extends about 5 miles up valley. These deltaic deposits indicate a reversal of stream flow, and are attributed to floods that backed up into the valleys from the scabland area.

Vast quantities of water were required to erode the scablands and to deposit the deltas and huge bars. Some geologists have doubted that the melting glaciers alone could have produced the necessary floods, and have postulated a catastrophic release of water from glacial Lake Missoula (Fig. 14.44), along Clarks Fork, in Montana. The ice front extended from near Spokane northeastward across the Spokane River and Clarks Fork. If water stored in Lake Missoula had been released suddenly by failure of the ice dam, the resulting flood would have discharged into the scabland part of the Columbia Plateau. There may have been a succession of such floods. Lake Missoula may have alternately filled and over-

Figure 17.22 *A part of the Dry Falls precipice, Grand Coulee, looking upstream. Note the scouring of the basalt surface and potholes (right foreground). [From Geology Illustrated by John S. Shelton. W. H. Freeman and Company. Copyright © 1966.]*

flowed, thereby cutting an escape channel in the ice, which could have been sealed again by the ice when the flood had subsided.

OVERFLOW OF LAKE BONNEVILLE.   When Lake Bonneville overflowed (p. 527), it quickly cut downward about 300 feet to a bedrock rim, and the flood of water caused by the sudden lowering of the lake swept down the Snake River Plain, depositing a mass of basaltic boulders about the size of watermelons. The deposit is appropriately known as the Melon Gravel, and roadside signs suggest sending mother-in-law a melon. Figure 17.23 shows the path of the Bonneville flood.

Landslides Along the Rivers

Several hundred landslides have developed along the Columbia River around the north and west sides of the Walla Walla Section (Fig. 17.24); landslides have developed also along the river gorge through the Cascade Range. The Bonneville Dam abuts against a landslide that covers several square miles; a major earthquake in that area could cause a disaster.

Many of the slides have occurred in Pleistocene and Holocene stream and lake deposits of silt, sand, and gravel, like those upstream from Grand Coulee Dam that were laid down in the lake dammed by the Okanogan lobe of glacial ice. Some sliding dates back to the time of these Pleistocene lakes, but the number of landslides has greatly increased as a result of the newly built reservoirs. The slides, due partly to the lubricating effect of the water, partly to the weight of water, and partly to the water undercutting unstable formations, are of four major kinds.

Most commonly a block or series of blocks have slid on a surface that is concave toward the slid block, and the blocks have rotated backward along that surface (Fig. 17.25,A). The top of the

block is a slumped mass; the lower end may be an earthflow. In the next most common kind of slide, the block or blocks rotate forward (Fig. 17.25,B). A third kind of slide develops where the slip surface is a series of scoops that develop alcoves along the rim above the slid blocks (Fig. 17.24). The alcoves originate as parts of one slide, but they grow by slump. A forth kind of landslide consists of mudflows in which the material moves as a pasty fluid (Fig. 17.25,C). Considerable property damage has resulted from the landslides, some of which are more than a mile long.

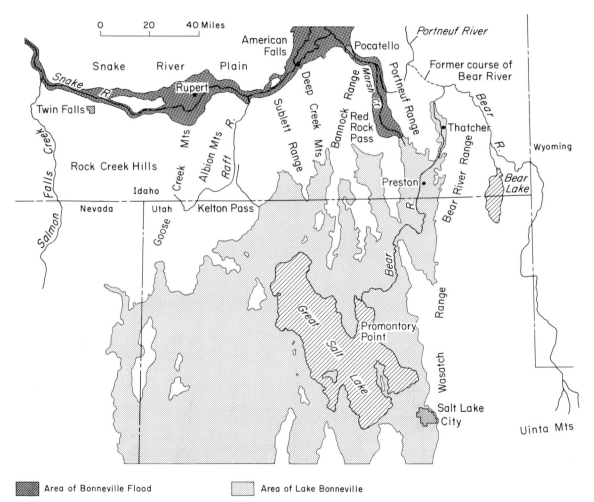

Figure 17.23 *Northern part of Lake Bonneville, nearby part of Snake River Plain, and path of the Bonneville Flood from Red Rock Pass to Twin Falls. The path of the Bonneville flood is marked by Melon Gravel, a bouldery gravel in bars more than 200 feet thick and forming terrace deposits 300 feet or more above the present canyon floor. [After U.S.G.S. Prof. Paper 596.]*

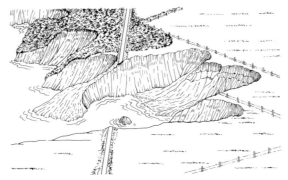

Figure 17.24 *Landslide along the shore of Franklin D. Roosevelt Lake on the Columbia River. In three days a multicove slide here severed the highway (foreground), which was located 2,000 feet back from the original lakeshore. The sliding created large waves on the lake; the largest reached a height of 65 feet on the opposite shore.*

Climate

The climate on the Columbia-Snake River Plateau is semiarid and cool. Except on the mountains, the average annual temperature is about 50°F. The average January temperature is about 32°F; the average July temperature about 70°F. The average annual minimum is −10°F, and the maximum is more than 100°F. Despite the altitude and latitude the temperatures in the Walla Walla Section are moderate, and the growing season is long (Fig. 17.26) because the surrounding mountains shelter the section against cold winter winds.

Average annual precipitation is less than 10 inches in the west, in the rain shadow of the Cascade Range. Eastward from there precipitation increases to more than 20 inches on the mountains (Fig. 17.26). The precipitation is fairly evenly distributed throughout the year, except during the summer months, when there is little rain. During many summers the rainfall may amount to only a half inch. Average annual snowfall on the mountains is as high as 100 inches, but on most of the plateau the average is about 2 feet. Snow cover usually exceeds 1 inch for about 60 days each year.

Thunderstorms and hail storms are infrequent in the western part of the plateau, but they are not uncommon in the eastern part. There is considerable cloudiness and fog in the semiarid Walla Walla and Payette sections.

The semiarid climate is new to the Columbia-Snake River Plateau. Here as elsewhere during Pleistocene time the climate was very different, but it was also different during most of Tertiary time, before the Cascades had been raised to their present height. Until Miocene time the climate was like that along the Pacific Coast. Not until Pliocene time did it become semiarid as it is today. In Pleistocene time the climate was alternately warm-dry and cold-wet. Two important effects of these Pleistocene climates are the scablands (p. 559) and the Palouse Soils (p. 566).

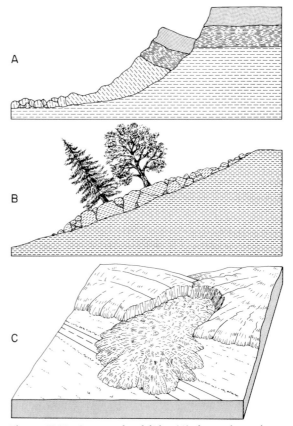

Figure 17.25 *In some landslides (A) the surface of sliding is concave toward the slid block, which rotates backward. In others (B) the slide surface is not concave, and the slid block rotates forward. Other slides (C) consist of mudflows.*

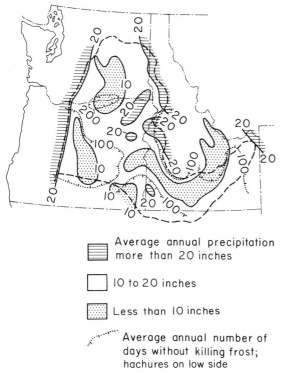

Average annual precipitation
more than 20 inches

10 to 20 inches

Less than 10 inches

Average annual number of
days without killing frost;
hachures on low side

Figure 17.26 *Average annual precipitation and average annual number of days without killing frost on the Columbia-Snake River Plateau. [From U.S.D.A.]*

Vegetation

In about half the Columbia-Snake River Plateau, the natural vegetation is sagebrush. About a quarter is grassland and another quarter woodland and forest (Fig. 17.27). West and north of the plateau are forested mountains; to the south is the sagebrush land of the Great Basin.

Two species of sagebrush grow on the Columbia-Snake River Plateau. The predominant species, the common one that grows so abundantly in the Great Basin, grows on land suitable for farming, especially if it can be irrigated. The other species, low growing and gnarled, grows in the scablands, which are not suited for agriculture. In most of the sagebrush lands the average annual precipitation is less than 10 inches—they are the driest parts of the plateau.

Areas that receive more than about 10 inches of rain per year have an open cover of bunch grass, which reflects both the amount of rainfall and its seasonal distribution. If more water were available during the growing season, the bunch grass would be replaced by denser stands of grasses. If the available moisture were any less, the bunch grass would be replaced by sagebrush. Associated with the grasses is a great profusion

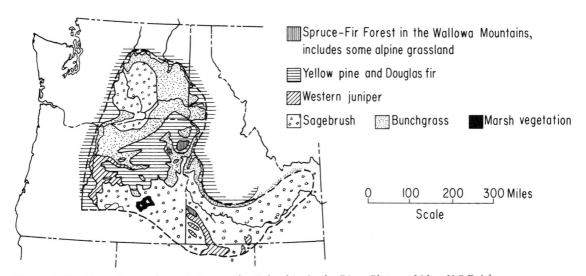

Spruce-Fir Forest in the Wallowa Mountains, includes some alpine grassland

Yellow pine and Douglas fir

Western juniper

Sagebrush   Bunchgrass   Marsh vegetation

0   100   200   300 Miles
Scale

Figure 17.27 *Map of natural vegetation on the Columbia-Snake River Plateau. [After U.S.D.A.]*

of flowering plants. These lands are excellent for raising wheat.

Marsh grasses and shrubs grow along the edges of sloughs and lakes, especially around Harney and Malheur lakes, and at some of the playas that are frequently wet. Along the valleys are willows and cottonwoods. Alkaline ground supports greasewood.

A woodland of western juniper grows in the area of low rainfall in central Oregon (Fig. 17.27). Juniper grows widely in the sagebrush and grassland country, but only locally in stands that can be called woodland, and most of these cover very small areas where runoff is collected or evaporation reduced so that more moisture is available than on the surrounding shrubland and grassland.

Forests of western yellow pine and Douglas fir grow mostly in the areas with more than 15 inches of annual precipitation. These are important sources of lumber, and are favored by vacationists because the summer climate is highly agreeable and the forest stands are open with an understory of grasses like a park. Other trees in these forests are the western white pine, aspen, Rocky Mountain juniper, and white fir (Fig. 17.28).

The Wallowa Mountains are high enough to extend into the Canadian Zone of Engelmann spruce and alpine fir and the highest peaks reach to alpine grassland. Timberline here is at a little over 7,000 feet.

The vegetation, as well as the climate, is new to the Columbia Plateau. In early Tertiary (Eocene) time, before the Cascades had been raised, the vegetation was uniform all the way to the coast, and the common trees were tropical or subtropical types, including palms. There were few conifers.

In the John Day Basin in eastern Oregon, the Clarno Formation (Eocene) has yielded fossil plants representing such forms as:

laurel (most abundant)	tropical ferns
aguacatillo (a tropical family)	oak
fig	yew
palm	cycads like some
ancestor of the sycamore	in Mexico

Figure 17.28   *The west edge of the Columbia Plateau, near the base of the Cascade Range (skyline), is forested with pine. This scene is at Tumalo State Park, north of Bend, Oregon, looking west toward the Three Sisters volcanoes. [Courtesy of the Oregon State Highway Dept.]*

This assemblage is rather similar to that of today's tropical Central American forests, which receive heavy rainfall and rarely freeze; the assemblage extended nearly to the coast. Moreover, the saprolitic weathering of the Clarno Formation (Table 17.2) indicates that tropical or semitropical conditions prevailed in Eocene time. The region that was to become the sagebrush country of the John Day Basin must have looked very different then.

The fossil record of the John Day formation, indicates that during the Oligocene, the sagebrush-covered John Day Basin supported redwood forest. Elevation of the Cascade Range had barely begun, and the forest extended, without much change in character, nearly to the west coast. Besides redwood, the forest included:

walnut	sycamore	beech
birch	horn-beam	
		chestnut
alder	maple	sweet gum
elm	oak	katsura (known today from Japan and China)

Species that lived along the coast—swamp cypress, avocado, lancewood, catalpa, and palm—suggest that temperatures were rather mild there. Away from the coast, the subtropical forest of the Eocene had been replaced by one that had a good many of the features of the present-day hardwood forest in the eastern United States.

The Oligocene forest on the Columbia-Snake River Plateau included many species that grew in the forest at Cook Inlet, Alaska, during the Eocene. How did the migration of species occur? It is easy to visualize migration of trees whose seeds can be carried widely by wind or by birds or insects. Seeds of such trees as walnut, oak, and chestnut, however, would have to be transported by squirrels or other rodents. One estimate indicates that such transport could take place at a rate of about a mile in a thousand years. Since millions of years were available during the late Oligocene and early Miocene, the distance, less than 2,000 miles, could have been managed at a migration rate of very much less than 1,000 feet in a thousand years. This is another example of how slow processes accomplish great changes because of the vastness of geologic time.

The Miocene forests of the Columbia-Snake River Plateau (Mascall Formation in Oregon; Latah Formation in eastern Washington and Idaho) included several species now confined to eastern North America—beech, swamp cypress, a black oak, elm, hickory. Two other species are confined today to eastern Asia, the ginkgo and the dawn redwood. Other species in the Mascall Formation that seem related to forests in eastern North America include a cottonwood that is similar to the swamp cottonwood of the lower Mississippi River valley, a birch that resembles the paper birch in New England and the maritime provinces of Canada, and hop hornbeam and chestnut oak. Altogether 35 species of trees in the

Mascall Formation have living equivalents in eastern North America, 34 have equivalents in east Asia, and 24, including a sycamore, have equivalents in western North America. The similarities between the American and Asian forests suggests that the two continents had a common ancestral forest in northeastern Asia and northwestern North America.

By Pliocene time the Cascade Range had been raised anticlinally, but it still evidently was not a high barrier. Pliocene formations on the Columbia Plateau contain fossil evidence of:

willow	cherry	fir
oak	aspen	spruce
sycamore	cottonwood	maple
box elder	elm	pine

West of the Cascades the Pliocene formations include fossils of some of these species plus sweet gum, persimmon, and sequoia.

By the end of Pliocene time the High Cascades were being built by eruptions at the big volcanoes aligned along the anticlinal ridge of middle Tertiary lavas. And the volcanoes were built higher and higher during the Quaternary. During the Pleistocene the altitudinal ranges of the forests and other vegetative zones must have shifted upward and downward as the climate alternately chilled and warmed during the glacial and interglacial stages, but the record of such shifting is complicated by the structural movements and by the building of the high volcanoes that imposed topographic effects on the climate.

Today the vegetation is wholly different on the two sides of Cascades. Immediately east of the Cascades, in the rain shadow, the vegetation is chiefly sagebrush, with willows and cottonwoods along the streams and juniper scattered on the hills. In the Blue-Ochoco Mountains and on the eastern slope of the Cascades are:

Douglas fir	Englemann spruce
Lodgepole pine	larch
Ponderosa pine	alder
Western white pine	aspen
True firs (as distinct from Douglas fir)	

The western slope of the Cascades and the Coast Ranges have high rainfall and are characterized by tremendous stands of Douglas fir. Those forests have at least two dozen tree species that do not grow on the Columbia-Snake River Plateau.

Surface Deposits and Soils

Surface deposits on the Columbia-Snake River Plateau are mostly loessial. In the Harney Lake Section, except where there are lavas, the surface deposits are mostly volcanic ash of varying textures. Soils are alkaline in the dry areas, especially toward the west, in the rain shadow of the Cascades. The higher areas in the east have acid soils. The loesses are mostly Pre-Wisconsinan, and are deeply weathered. Many of the lavas are young and relatively unweathered but even the young deposits of volcanic ash are likely to show signs of weathering because the glasses, especially if fine grained, weather easily.

In the Walla Walla Section, loess deposits are as much as 150 feet thick. Soils developed on them are called Palouse Soils; they are zoned like the soils in the central United States (Fig. 17.29). In the lowest, driest, and hottest areas, the weathering is slight, as in Desert Soils, and the soil horizons are only weakly developed. Bordering this area is a belt of Brown Soils, also loessial, which is in turn bordered by belts of loess on which Chestnut, Chernozem, and Prairie soils have developed. The loess deposits and soils are missing in the channeled scablands but are preserved on the divides where they overlie the basalt. Where they are 2 feet or more deep, these soils may be cultivated.

The weathering of these loesses represents the superimposed effects of several different climatic conditions, for most of the loess is ancient, antedating the last glaciation, as does much or most of the weathering. The dark, organic-rich, surface layers are Recent, but the limey zones may be ancient. These soils probably represent a complex of loessial deposits of different ages, and part of the alteration and layering is attributable

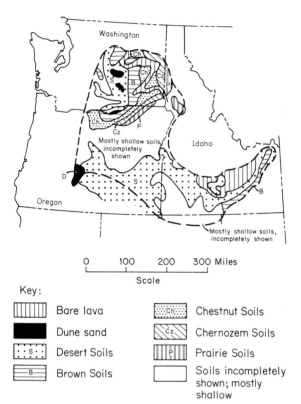

Figure 17.29 *Soils in the basin areas of the Columbia-Snake River Plateau. [After U.S.D.A.]*

to soil processes under climatic conditions and vegetative cover that differed considerably from those of the present time.

The loessial soils in the Walla Walla Section and along the Snake River are subject to severe erosion, both by gullying and by wind. The farmed lands produce clouds of dust.

Soils on the hilly and mountainous parts of the Columbia-Snake River Plateau are shallow and are not shown in Figure 17.29. They are derived in part from alluvial, colluvial, and related surface deposits, but mostly they are wind-deposited volcanic ash from the Cascades and other volcanic centers, and loessial dust from the desert basins. Presumably there are podzolic soils under the yellow pine and higher-altitude forests.

Soils in the Harney Basin Section are Desert Soils largely developed on loamy or sandy volcanic ash 25 to 50 feet deep. The soils are thin

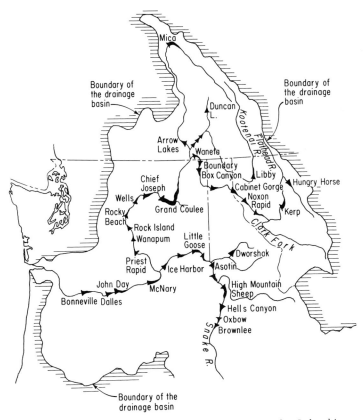

Figure 17.30 *Network of dams and reservoirs along the Columbia River and its principal tributaries.*

and weakly developed, for the ash is young and not deeply weathered. The organic layer is thin or lacking. At many playas the soils are alkaline or saline.

The Payette Section and Snake River Plain are mantled with loess 2 to 10 feet deep, and these soils also have weakly developed profiles and are classed as Desert Soils. In places, however, there are Brown Soils with distinct soil horizons. On the north side of the Snake River Plain extensive areas are bare lava.

Water Resources

Despite being semiarid the Columbia-Snake River Plateau has abundant water supplies, both as surface water and as groundwater. The Co-

lumbia River enters the province with an average annual discharge greater than the Missouri River. Where it leaves the province and enters the Cascade Range the discharge is nearly half that of the Mississippi River at Memphis. Its principal tributary, the Snake River, has a discharge 3 or 4 times that of the Colorado River.

A network of dams and reservoirs has been constructed along the Columbia River (Fig. 17.30). The largest, the Grand Coulee Dam, partly takes the place of the Pleistocene ice dam of the Okanogan glacial lobe. The dam is 550 feet high and more than 4,000 feet long. The Franklin D. Roosevelt Lake above it stores nearly 20,000,000 acre-feet of water, some of which is pumped to a storage reservoir in Grand Coulee, where it is distributed for irrigation in Quincy Basin (Fig. 17.21).

Where the Columbia River enters the United States its average annual discharge is about 71 million acre feet. By the time it leaves the Columbia Plateau and enters the Cascade Range, its discharge has doubled (Fig. 5.1). The total water-power potential in the Columbia Plateau is very much greater than that of the Tennessee Valley and Colorado River combined.

The Snake River enters the Snake River Plain above Idaho Falls, and from there to the mouth of the Boise River (Fig. 17.12), more than 300 miles, it has few tributaries. The Wood (Malad)

River is the only stream from the mountains north of the plain that reaches the Snake River. Water from these streams is lost by seepage into the lavas and by evaporation. The tributaries from the south rise on the north rim of the Great Basin and are small. Despite the lack of large tributaries the volume of water in the Snake River increases greatly as it flows westward to the Payette Section, for it is supplied by ground-water. The annual discharge from one group of springs along a 40-mile stretch near Twin Falls is about 4,000,000 acre feet (Fig. 17.31).

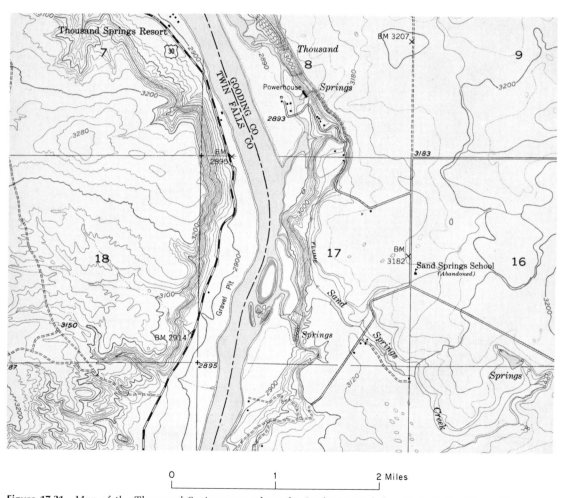

Figure 17.31 *Map of the Thousand Springs area along the Snake River, below Twin Falls, Idaho. These springs are large enough and high enough to supply a power plant. [From U.S.G.S. Thousand Springs, Idaho, quadrangle.]*

The basaltic lavas through which the groundwater moves vary greatly in permeability. Some are dense and nearly impermeable; others have open lava tubes through which groundwater moves freely. Some permeable lavas overlie impermeable sedimentary beds, and the groundwater is perched. Figure 17.31 illustrates the setting of some of the springs that discharge to the Snake River in this area.

Groundwater supplies in the Snake River Plain and in the Payette Section are large, but heavy drafts are being made on that resource, and the surface waters are largely already allotted.

As the Snake River leaves the Payette Section and crosses the Ochoco-Blue Mountains Uplift, it is joined by several tributaries. On the west are the Owyhee River, Malheur River, Willow Creek, Burnt River, and Pine Creek. On the east are the Boise, Payette, Weiser, and Wildhorse rivers. More large tributaries join the Snake where it leaves the uplift and enters the Walla Walla Section. On the west are the Imnaha and Grande Ronde rivers; on the east the Salmon and Clearwater rivers. These tributaries more than triple the volume of the river along a 200-mile stretch.

The importance of groundwater to the flow of Snake River, as contrasted to the Columbia, is illustrated also by the difference in the quality of their water. Snake River at Twin Falls, Idaho, contains nearly 300 ppm of dissolved solids. It is an alkaline, calcium-magnesium bicarbonate water with a hardness of nearly 200. The Columbia River, above the mouth of Snake River, contains only 100 ppm of total dissolved solids (tds). It is slightly alkaline, and the hardness is well under 100.

Most towns on the Snake River Plain obtain their water from wells rather than from the river, because for much of its length the river flows in a gorge. Most of the wells are 100 to 500 feet deep, but one well at Idaho Falls is 1,600 feet deep. The total dissolved solids in this groundwater is commonly around 300 ppm, but locally exceeds 500 ppm. This is an alkaline, bicarbonate water that contains a moderate amount of sulfate. Where the content of alkalis (Na and K) equals that of alkali earths (Ca and Mg), the water is only moderately hard, but where there is much calcium and magnesium the hardness may be as high as 350.

Towns in the Payette Section also use groundwater rather than river water for their municipal supplies. The wells are 100 to 600 feet deep, and the water is of better quality than that farther east. Groundwater in the Payette Section generally contains less than 200 ppm dissolved solids. The water is mostly bicarbonate water but contains enough sulfate and alkalis to class most of it as a soft water with a hardness of less than 100.

The quality of water is excellent in those tributaries of the Columbia and Snake rivers that rise in the Cascades, in the Northern Rocky Mountains, and in the Ochoco-Blue Mountains uplift. These waters have less than 75 ppm of dissolved solids, and commonly less than 50. By contrast, the southern tributaries of the Snake, which head in the rim of the Great Basin, have hard, alkaline waters containing more than 250 ppm tds.

In brief, water problems in the parts of the Columbia Plateau drained by the Columbia and Snake rivers relate to water distribution and floods, and both of these problems are gradually being eliminated by the dams and reservoirs that have been and will be constructed. Quantity, quality, and seasonal variability pose no problems. Nor has pollution been a problem, although it could become one if wastes escape from the atomic plant near Pasco.

Water supplies in the Harney Lake Section, are like those of the Great Basin. The playas are saline or alkaline, and the streams draining to them are intermittent. Harney Lake is generally too saline to be used by humans or livestock. Malheur Lake, which occasionally overflows to Harney Lake, is fresher, but even it is little used. Groundwater from bedrock formations, though not abundant, generally contains less than 700 ppm of dissolved solids and is satisfactory for irrigation, but some of this groundwater contains more than 2,000 ppm of dissolved solids and is not suitable.

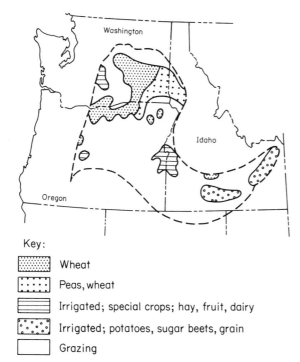

Key:

▒ Wheat

⋮ Peas, wheat

▤ Irrigated; special crops; hay, fruit, dairy

⋰ Irrigated; potatoes, sugar beets, grain

☐ Grazing

Figure 17.32 *Land utilization in the Columbia-Snake River Plateau.*

Other Resources

The principal produce from the Columbia-Snake River Plateau is agricultural. About 20 percent is arable land (Fig. 17.32) and the remainder is chiefly grazing land. About half the arable land is irrigated; the rest is dry-farmed.

The value of the agricultural produce exceeds a half billion dollars yearly. Almost half the produce consists of wheat and small grains; fruits account for about a quarter, and the remainder is about equally divided between livestock (including some dairying) and other crops, especially potatoes and sugar beets.

The grazing lands on the plateau are some-what better than in the Great Basin, yet the three southern sections—Harney Basin, Payette, and Snake River Plain—on the average cannot support even a dozen cows per square mile (about 50 acres per cow). Grazing lands are much better in the mountain sections.

Salmon fishing, formerly considerable, has declined because the dams and reservoirs have obstructed the salmon runs.

Sawmills are numerous, especially in the Spokane area. There is little manufacturing, although this is changing because of the availability of ample hydroelectric power. At Richland, in southeastern Washington, is the government's huge Hanford plant and reservation for separating plutonium from uranium. The plant stands on the site of the former village of Hanford.

The mineral production and resources of the Columbia-Snake River Plateau have not been nationally significant. Considerable chromite has been found in the Ochoco and Blue mountains, and undeveloped deposits of clay with a high alumina content are extensive in a belt of Palouse Soil extending 75 miles southeast from Spokane. Some of these clays are residual deposits (ancient soils) resulting from the weathering of the Columbia River basalts. Others, similar to those on the basalts, developed on the granitic rocks of the Idaho batholith. Still others are transported deposits derived by erosion of the residual ones. The deposits could become an important source of aluminum ore when methods are found for economically extracting the metal from the clay.

Other mineral deposits on the Columbia-Snake River Plateau are minor. Some antimony, mercury, gold, and silver have been found in the Ochoco and Blue mountains. Small zinc deposits are known in the Owyhee Mountains, but the future of the mineral industry in the Columbia Plateau depends on someone finding a use for that black rock known as basalt.

References

Bowen, N. L., 1928, The evolution of the igneous rocks: Princeton Univ. Press; reprinted 1956 by Dover Publications.

Bretz, J. H., 1928, The channeled scabland of eastern Washington: Geog. Rev. v. 18, n. 3, pp. 446–477.

———, 1932, The Grand Coulee (Washington): Am. Geog. Soc. Spec. Publ. 15.

Chaney, R. W., 1936, The succession and distribution of Cenozoic floras around the northern Pacific Basin—Essays in geobotany; Berkeley, Univ. California Press, pp. 55–85.

———, 1956, The ancient forests of Oregon: Eugene, Ore., Univ. Oregon Press, Condon Lecture Publ.

Daly, R. A., 1914, Igneous rocks and their origin: New York, McGraw-Hill.

Hansen, H. P., 1947, Postglacial forest succession, climate, and chronology in the Pacific Northwest: Am. Philosophical Soc. Trans., v. 37.

Williams, H., 1953, The ancient volcanoes of Oregon: Eugene, Ore., Univ. Oregon Press, Condon Lecture Publ.

Mount Hood, one of the central-type volcanoes forming the High Cascades. [Photograph by the Oregon State Highway Commission.]

18

PACIFIC MOUNTAIN SYSTEM— WESTERN EDGE OF THE CONTINENT

The Pacific Mountain System (Figs. 18.1, 18.2) comprises about 360,000 square miles along the Pacific Coast of United States, Canada, and the southeastern panhandle of Alaska. The mountain system extends eastward to the deserts of the Basin and Range Province and Columbia-Snake River Plateau in the United States, and to the Intermontane Plateaus and Rocky Mountains of Canada. The mountains are responsible for the deserts to the east in the United States, for they wring the moisture from air moving inland from the Pacific Ocean.

Parks and monuments are numerous in the Pacific Mountains. In the Alaska Panhandle are Glacier Bay and Sitka national monuments. In British Columbia are Tweedmuir, Garibaldi, Strathcona, and Ernest C. Manning provincial parks. Along the Cascades are North Cascades, Mount Ranier, Crater Lake, and Lassen Peak national parks and Lava Beds national monument. The Sierra Nevada has Yosemite, Sequoia, and Kings Canyon national parks and Devils Post Pile national monument. In the Lower California province is the extensive Anza-Borrego state park. The coastal mountains have Olympic and Redwood National Parks and Oregon Caves, Muir Woods, Pinnacles, Channel Islands and Cabrillo national monuments, the Point Reyes national seashore, and the San Diego state beaches.

The Pacific Crest Trail, which extends from the mountains of the Lower California Province through the Sierra Nevada and the Cascades to Manning Provincial Park in Canada, is the analog of the Appalachian Trail in the eastern part of the United States.

Structurally and topographically the mountains are of five kinds:

1. Granitic mountains, represented by the batholiths in the Lower California Province, the Sierra Nevada, the Klamath Mountains, some ranges in the northern part of the Cascades, and the Coast Mountains of Canada and the southeast panhandle of Alaska.

2. Volcanic mountains, represented by the Cascade Range.

3. Mountains composed of complexly folded and faulted eugeosynclinal formations that are mostly pre-Tertiary in age, repre-

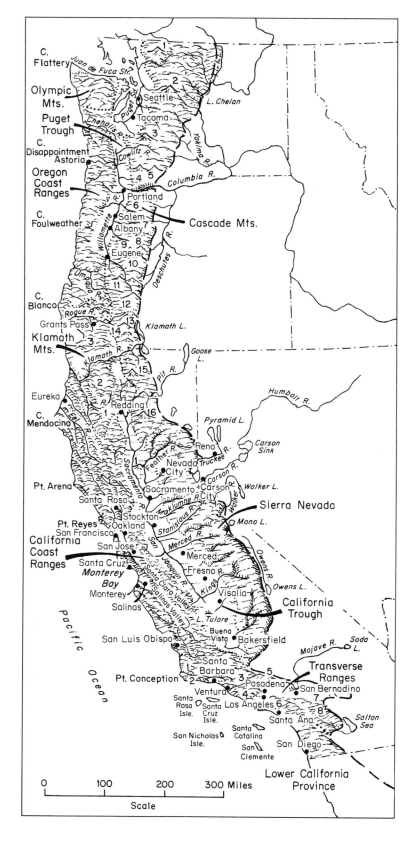

Volcanic Peaks Along
the Cascade Range

1. Mt. Baker
2. Glacier Peak
3. Mt. Rainier
4. Mt. St. Helens
5. Mt. Adams
6. Mt. Hood
7. Mt. Jefferson
8. Black Butte
9. Belknap Crater
10. Three Sisters
11. Diamond Peak
12. Mt. Thielsen
13. Crater Lake
14. Mt. Loughlin
15. Mt. Shasta
16. Lassen Peak

Mountains in the Klamath
Mountains Province

1. Trinity Mts.
2. Salmon Mts.
3. Siskiyou Mts.

Mountains in the
California Trough

1. Marysville Buttes

Mountains in the
Transverse Ranges

1. San Rafael Mts.
2. Santa Ynez Mts.
3. Topatopa Mts.
4. Santa Monica Mts.
5. San Gabriel Mts.
6. Santa Ana Mts.
7. San Bernardino Mts.
8. San Jacinto Mts.

Figure 18.1 *Physiographic map
of the Pacific Mountain System.*

Figure 18.2   *Physiographic diagram of southern British Columbia.*

sented by the Transverse Ranges, California Coast Ranges north of San Francisco Bay, Olympic Mountains, some of the ranges at the north end of the Cascades, Vancouver Island, and other islands to the north.

4. Mountains composed of moderately folded but much-faulted formations that are mostly Tertiary in age and easily eroded, represented by the Oregon Coast Range and by the California Coast Ranges south of San Francisco Bay.

5. Dome mountains, represented by the Marysville Buttes in the Central Valley of California near Sacramento.

The mountains in this system are arranged like three links of a chain. The northern link—formed by the south end of the Coast Mountains in British Columbia, the Cascade Range, the Oregon Coast Range, and the Olympic Mountains—is joined at the south by the Klamath Mountains. The Puget Trough, which includes the Willamette Valley in Oregon, forms the hole in the northern link.

South of the Klamath Mountains the Central Valley of California forms the hole in the middle link, which is made up of the Sierra Nevada and the California Coast Ranges. These mountains are joined at the south, where the Sierra curves westward. The southern link is formed by the

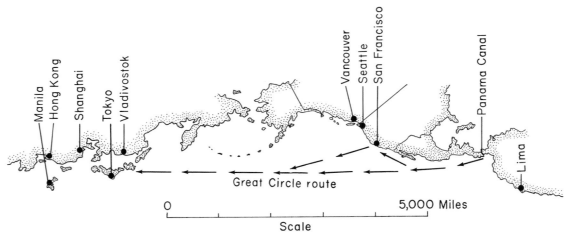

Figure 18.3 *Position of San Francisco relative to the Great Circle route between the Panama Canal and Asiatic ports.*

Transverse Ranges, the Lower California Province, and the Salton Trough.

Perhaps the two most distinctive features of the Pacific Mountain System are its variety and the number of its extremes, for it is a land of superlatives. It has mountains that are among the highest, roughest, and most scenic in the United States, but the troughs between the mountains are superlatively low, flat, and monotonous. Part of the land is as densely populated as any part of the continent, yet other parts are wilderness. Average annual rainfall ranges from less than 10 inches to more than 150 inches. Some parts are hot; others are the site of glaciers. Some areas have desert shrubs, whereas other areas have dense forests of giant redwoods. And it includes some of the sunniest and some of the foggiest and smoggiest parts of the continent.

The mountainous coast, which contrasts sharply with the broad coastal plain along the Atlantic seaboard, is part of the circum-Pacific volcanic belt and has been the site of volcanic eruptions in historic time, at Mount Lassen. It also is part of the seismically active belt bordering the Pacific and is subject to frequent, severe earthquakes.

The resources are richly productive and var-

ied. Energy resources include hydroelectric power, a little coal, and tremendous quantities of petroleum. Of the metals there is iron and mercury, and gold was once important in California's economy. Among the nonmetals there is substantial salt production. Agricultural products include fruits of all kinds, vegetables, and grains. Lumbering is a major industry; so too are fishing and wine-growing (in California). San Francisco has one of the world's finest harbors, and it is most favorably located midway along the Pacific Coast and beside the great circle route from the Panama Canal to the Asiatic ports (Fig. 18.3). Other important harbors are at Vancouver, Seattle, and Los Angeles. Crude petroleum and petroleum products account for about 75 percent of the tonnage shipped and received at California ports. Other important commodities carried by the coastal traffic are lumber and wood products, which are shipped from a number of small ports along the coast and received at the major ports.

The population is concentrated near the harbors and on the plains of the Great Valley of California and the Puget Trough. The rest of the region is ruggedly mountainous and is sparsely inhabited.

Structural Framework and Topography

SIERRA-CASCADE MOUNTAINS

The Sierra Nevada and the Cascade Mountains are combined as a physiographic province 1,000 miles long and 50 to 100 miles wide. These are the highest mountains discussed thus far, and they form a barrier that can be crossed at only a few places.

Structurally the mountains are an uplift, in places surmounted by volcanoes and lavas. The highest parts of the uplift are at the ends—at the south end of the Sierra Nevada and at the north end of the Cascades. At these ends of the province granitic rocks and older metamorphosed sedimentary formations are exposed. A sag in the uplift is represented by the Southern Cascades Section, and the old rocks there are buried under young volcanoes and lavas. This sag is the site

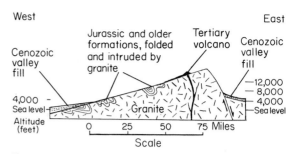

Figure 18.5 *Cross section illustrating the general structure of the Sierra Nevada. It is a block mountain of late Jurassic and Cretaceous granite, faulted on the east side and tilted to the west. (Compare with Fig. 2.20)*

of two streams that cross the uplift, Klamath River and Pit River. Besides the mighty Columbia, they are the only rivers that do. The Feather River, at the north end of the Sierra Nevada, extends very nearly across the barrier.

This elongate uplift marks a sharp western boundary of the Great Basin and Columbia Plateau. The west side of the uplift is marked by narrow structural and topographic troughs, except at the Klamath Mountains, which adjoin the sag at the Southern Cascades Section.

SIERRA NEVADA. The Sierra Nevada is a westerly tilted and northward plunging Cenozoic fault block that cuts obliquely across a late Mesozoic batholith. About 350 miles long and roughly 60 miles wide, it was raised by faulting on the east and tilted westward (Figs. 18.4, 18.5). The fault-block structure is similar to that in the Great Basin, but the Sierra stands apart because it is so very large and is composed chiefly of granite (Fig. 18.6).

The Sierra Nevada reaches its maximum height along the eastern fault scarp, only 5 to 10 miles from the eastern foot of the mountains (Fig. 18.7). Altitudes along the eastern foot are between 4,500 and 5,000 feet; the summit is 9,000 feet higher. From the summit, the mountains slope westward for more than 50 miles and pass under the Tertiary fill in the California Trough at an altitude of about 1,000 feet (Fig. 18.4).

Figure 18.4 *Diagram of the Sierra Nevada, the Great Valley, and the California Coast Ranges.*

Figure 18.6 *Granite terrain in the Sierra Nevada. Scene is at D. L. Bliss State Park. [Courtesy of California Dept. of Parks and Recreation.]*

Because of this structure, the mountains drain mostly to the west, and the dozen or so major rivers have cut deep valleys, some nearly a mile deep, into the granite. Yosemite Valley is the best known of these. The sediments derived by erosion of these valleys have been deposited as huge alluvial fans at the edge of the California Trough, and as older fill within it.

Caboniferous, Triassic, and Jurassic eugeosynclinal formations are extensive along the western foot of the Sierra, especially toward the north, and they form a belt 25 miles wide that extends diagonally across the Sierra just north of the latitude of Sacramento (Fig. 2.1). These formations, all folded, faulted, and considerably metamorphosed, were intruded by, and form the roof of, the granite batholith.

The eroded top of the granite batholith dips northward as well as westward. To the north, the granite passes under lavas and other volcanics at the southern end of the Cascades. The recency of the northward structural tilt is shown by the progressive northward decrease in the altitudes of passes across the mountains. The lowest pass, at the head of the Feather River, at an altitude of 5,218 feet, is used by the Western Pacific Railroad and Alternate U.S. Highway 40. Altitudes of the passes and the roads that cross them are, in order from north to south (Fig. 18.7):

Donner Pass, northwest of Lake Tahoe; U.S. 40 and Southern Pacific Railroad; 7,089 feet.
Emerald Pass, south of Lake Tahoe; U.S. 50; about 7,100 feet.

Carson Pass, north of the North Fork of the
  Mokelumne River; Route 88, 8,573 feet.
Ebbets Pass, into the North Fork of the Stanis-
  laus River; Route 4; 8,730 feet.
Sonora Pass, into South Fork of the Stanislaus
  River; Route 108; 9,626 feet.
Tioga Pass, north of Yosemite Valley; Route
  120; 9,941 feet.

For 150 miles south of Tioga pass no road crosses
the Sierra Nevada. Toward the south end, the
range slopes southward. Walker Pass, crossed by
Route 178, between the Kern River and Owens
River, is at an altitude of 5,250 feet. Tehachapi
Pass, crossed by U.S. Highway 466 and the rail-
roads between the Central Valley and Mojave
Desert, is at an altitude of 3,988 feet.

The Sierra Nevada, a truly formidable barrier
(Fig. 18.8), is unusual among major mountain
ranges in that its great length is not crossed by
any river. The Feather River, which extends almost across it, heads in an open, lava-filled valley
at a wind gap at about 5,000 feet in altitude. The
wind gap at the head of that valley is only 200
feet higher than the Great Basin drainage a mile
to the east. Almost certainly the Humboldt River
and other streams in the Great Basin once discharged westward through this wind gap and
across the Sierra Nevada by way of the Feather
River. This drainage probably was disrupted in
late Quaternary time as a result of a few scores
of feet of displacement of the Sierra block, cou-

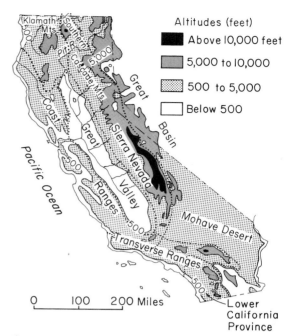

Figure 18.7   *Altitudes in the southern provinces of the Pacific Mountain System.*

pled perhaps with lava flows that may have contributed to the damming of drainage courses.

The granitic (actually grandiorite) batholith
extends discontinuously beyond the Sierra
Nevada fault block—southward to Lower California and northeastward across the northwest
corner of the Great Basin. The batholith consists
of a complex of plutons separated by narrow

Figure 18.8   *Eastern front of the Sierra Nevada, overlooking the Great Basin in the vicinity of the Owens River. The summit, 11,000 to 14,000 feet in altitude, is 6,000 to 8,000 feet higher than the Owens Valley (foreground). This is the faulted, east side of the Sierra; the displacement is at least as great as the topographic relief and may be two or three times that amount.*

septa of metamorphic rocks or of very basic rocks. The batholith began forming in late Jurassic time, and the Jurassic and older sedimentary formations that formed the roof were folded, faulted, and metamorphosed, and granitic masses were intruded into them in late Jurassic and in Cretaceous time. The Sierra Nevada segment of the batholith is in the Triassic eugeosyncline; Jurassic eugeosynclinal formations parallel the Sierra on the west. Paleozoic formations bordering the Sierra are miogeosynclinal on the east and eugeosynclinal on the west. The batholith evidently is somehow related to these ancient structures (see below). Veins of gold-bearing quartz were deposited in the fractured rocks in a belt almost parallel to the range and near its western base. This belt of veins later became known as the Mother Lode; the placer deposits that were eroded from them led to the great gold rush of 1849.

During Cretaceous time, parts of the Sierra were high enough to have been the source of thick sediments (Chico Formation) that were deposited in basins parallel to the coast and just west of the batholith. The basins were shallow, but continually sank, and a total thickness of 25,000 feet of sediments was deposited. The upper part of the Chico contains increasingly larger amounts of potassium feldspar, like the feldspar in the Sierra granite, indicating that erosion had cut through the roof and into the batholith. The present Great Basin also was a mountainous area at this time (p. 487), for it shed sediments into the Cretaceous sea that flooded the sites of the Colorado Plateau, the Rocky Mountains, and the Great Plains. The ancestral Sierra Nevada formed the western edge of that mountainous area.

Parts of the Sierra Nevada batholith are younger than the Chico Formation. The plutons forming the highest part of the Sierra are of late Cretaceous age (90 to 79 m.y.) and must have been forming (or perhaps cooling) while the Chico Formation was being deposited. Just west of the present summit is a belt of plutons that formed during the early Cretaceous; along the east and west base of the Sierra, there are plutons of Juras-

sic age. Small plutons at the east base are dated as Triassic. Two hundred and fifty age determinations of the granite in and near the Sierra Nevada suggest that that part of the batholith developed in five stages, each of which lasted 10 to 20 million years and was separated by periods of quiescence lasting twice that long. Although individual parts developed in stages, probably the batholith as a whole developed continuously during its long history.

In early Eocene time, the ancestral Sierra remained high enough to shed sediments westward, but the western edges of the granite and the roof rocks were submerged. The sedimentary deposits, about 7,500 feet thick (Martinez, Meganos, Capay, and Tejon formations), were largely derived from the erosion of the granitic batholith. Coal beds not of commercial quality) developed where swamps formed along the ancient shore, now the western foot of the Sierra.

During the Oligocene Epoch the Sierran granite and other rocks probably were deeply weathered, as were rocks elsewhere in the Pacific Mountains, and as has been noted, in the Columbia-Snake River Plateau, where the Eocene Clarno Formation underwent a similar deep weathering. Sediments eroded from the weathered Sierran granite were deposited in troughs farther west that those of the Eocene.

In Miocene time the Sierra Nevada was largely buried under volcanic ash and lava flows. The erosion of this volcanic cover and of the underlying rocks resulted in the deposition of 12,000 feet of sediments in marine basins to the west (Vaqueros, Temblor, Monterey, and Santa Margarita formations). By this time, though, the Great Basin, which had begun to break up as a result of faulting in Oligocene time, was sufficiently broken to disrupt much drainage across the ancestral Sierra, and the physiographic provinces began to take the forms we know today.

The Sierra Nevada appears to have become a distinct fault block during Pliocene time. The summit, presently 11,000 to 14,000 feet high, is thought to have reached a height of about 7,000 feet during the Pliocene, and canyons about 1,000 feet deep were cut into the western slope. These

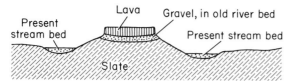

Figure 18.9 *Inverted topography at Table Mountain, California. A lava flow down an old valley crowded the drainage to either side. Today, the old valley, with its cap of lava, forms the divide between two stream courses.*

structural movements were accompanied by volcanism, and lava flows poured down some of the canyons. The Pliocene deposits west of the Sierra Nevada (Jacalitos, Etchegoin, and Tulare Formations) are 10,000 feet thick, but only parts of them were derived by erosion of the Sierra; some of these sediments were derived from highlands that lay farther to the west.

It was in Pleistocene time that the Sierra became raised and tilted to its present height and position. The mountain tops were glaciated at least three times, and the canyons were eroded to their present depths. In places the topography has become inverted (Fig. 18.9), for some of the Tertiary lavas that had flowed down canyons now form ridges, because erosion has reduced the surrounding granitic terrain to lower levels than the lava.

The glaciers deepened some valleys so much that tributaries were left as hanging valleys, like the many examples in Yosemite Valley (Fig. 18.10). The glaciers extended down the faulted east side of the Sierra to the desert basin below, depositing huge terminal moraines at the mouths of canyons at altitudes of about 6,000 feet. On the wetter west side the glaciers extended down to about 3,000 feet. The summit is scored with cirques. Many contain lakes, and some sheltered ones contain ice fields.

As a result of this history, there are two quite different ages and kinds of topography in the Sierra Nevada (Fig. 18.10). The older topography, represented by the uplands between the canyons, was and still is a surface without great local relief and without steep slopes. Subsequent uplift and westward tilting of that surface enabled the gla-

ciers and rivers to cut deeply into it and to develop a younger and very rugged topography between the remnants of the older surface. Such differences in kind and age of landforms are referred to as *topographic unconformities.* They are characteristic of recently elevated mountains, and are prominent in the Klamath and Northern Cascade mountains as well as of the Sierra Nevada.

CASCADE MOUNTAINS. The Cascade Range is divided into three sections (Fig. 18.11). The Southern Cascades mark the lava-covered structural sag in the Sierra-Cascade uplift, and they end southward where the granitic and older rocks of the Sierra Nevada rise southward from beneath the lavas. The structure rises northward too, and the Middle Cascades consist of an uplift of middle Tertiary lavas surmounted by huge volcanic cones of Pleistocene age. The Northern Cascades, structurally the highest part of these mountains, are like the Sierra Nevada in that they are composed of granitic batholiths and older metamorphosed, eugeosynclinal sedimentary formations. Some of these granitic masses are Tertiary, and hence much younger than the Sierra.

Much of the lava field of the Southern Cascades is less than 5,000 feet in altitude. It extends eastward far into the Great Basin and westward to the west side of the Great Valley of California. Its surface is studded with volcanic cones (Fig. 18.12), many of them a few thousand feet high. Two of the high ones are Mount Shasta, which exceeds 14,000 feet (Fig. 18.13), and Mount Lassen, which reaches to about 10,500 feet. Mount Lassen, which erupted in 1914 and 1915, has been made a national park. Although the Southern Cascades are crossed by the Klamath and Pit rivers, much of the drainage has been disrupted by the flows. Lakes are numerous, but many are dry because the lavas are porous.

In the Middle Cascades Section early and middle Tertiary lavas rise northward from under the late Tertiary and Quaternary ones. As the uplifted lavas rise northward, the Quaternary lavas decrease in extent but form an imposing row of huge Quaternary volcanoes (Fig. 18.14).

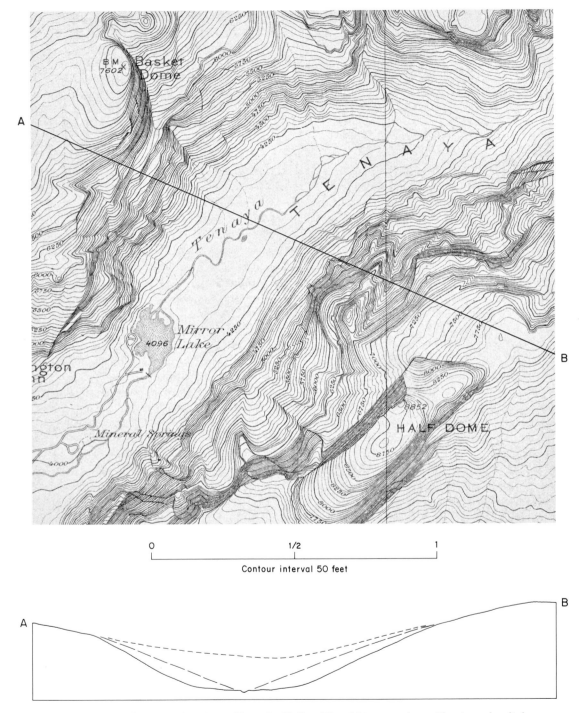

Contour interval 50 feet

Figure 18.10   *Topographic unconformity at Yosemite Valley. The old topography, without much relief, had broad open valleys (dotted line in the cross profile). A deeper V-shaped valley (broken line) evolved from this as a result of downcutting due to westward tilting of the Sierra. When glaciated, this valley became U-shaped.*

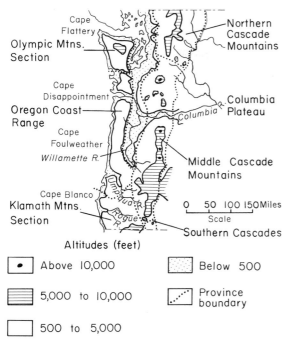

Altitudes (feet)

●	Above 10,000	▦	Below 500
≡	5,000 to 10,000	⬚	Province boundary
☐	500 to 5,000		

Figure 18.11 *Altitudes in the Washington and Oregon parts of the Pacific Mountain System.*

The high part of the mountains is near the east side, overlooking the Columbia-Snake River Plateau. This crest, which is marked by a row of Quaternary volcanoes, is the High Cascades; the mountainous west slope, composed almost wholly of dissected early and middle Tertiary lavas, is the Western Cascades. The Western Cascades are so eroded that no trace remains of their original volcanic landscape.

Uplift had begun by Miocene time, and by the end of that epoch the mountains were high enough to cut off moisture from the Columbia Plateau, which became increasingly arid. The uplift was accomplished partly by arching of the Miocene lavas and partly by faulting along the east side (Fig. 18.15,B). The Miocene lavas were highly fluid basalt and formed broad, low, shield volcanoes; the later eruptives were more viscous andesite, which built high, steep-sided cones of interlayered volcanic ash and lavas on the broad shield volcanoes (Figs. 18.15,C, 18.16).

Crater Lake, another national park, once was a high volcanic cone, Mount Mazama. It was not unlike Mount Rainier and was once probably as high, but an eruption about 7,000 years ago fractured the cone, ejected great quantities of ash, and caused the remaining part to collapse into the throat of the volcano, forming a *caldera* (Fig. 18.15,D). The lake that partly fills it is about 2,000 feet deep.

During Pleistocene time glaciers formed on all the peaks of the High Cascades above 9,000 feet, and some still remain on the high peaks. These have greatly modified the volcanoes, but the conical forms are still clearly preserved. On Mount Mazama, glacial till truncated by the collapse of the caldera provides evidence of the former great height of the original volcano.

Only one river, the Columbia, crosses the Middle Cascades (Figs. 18.17, 18.18). Since the present course of the river is almost the same as it was in Miocene time, the river is essentially antecedent across the Miocene and later uplifts. Lake beds on the Columbia Plateau side of the gorge indicate that the river was ponded at times, probably by a combination of lava flows and uplift of the channel. But the tremendous discharge of the river caused it to overflow each time along its former elevated course.

North of Mount Rainier the Cascades were greatly uplifted. The mountains there are composed of granitic batholiths that intrude older metamorphosed sedimentary rocks, and resemble the Northern Rocky Mountains to the east, except that the Cascades are several thousands of feet higher. The rocks and structures of the Northern Cascades are like those in the Sierra Nevada, and the landforms are of two ages and of two kinds, as are those in the Sierra. The upland is an old surface without much relief, and incised into it are steep-sided, deep valleys that developed as a result of the uplift. In addition, the Northern Cascades are surmounted by Quaternary volcanic cones like those in the south. One of these is Mount Baker (altitude 10,750). The summits are glacially sculptured (Fig. 18.19).

The geologic history of the volcanoes of the High Cascades is illustrated by that of Mount Rainer National Park. During the Eocene the area

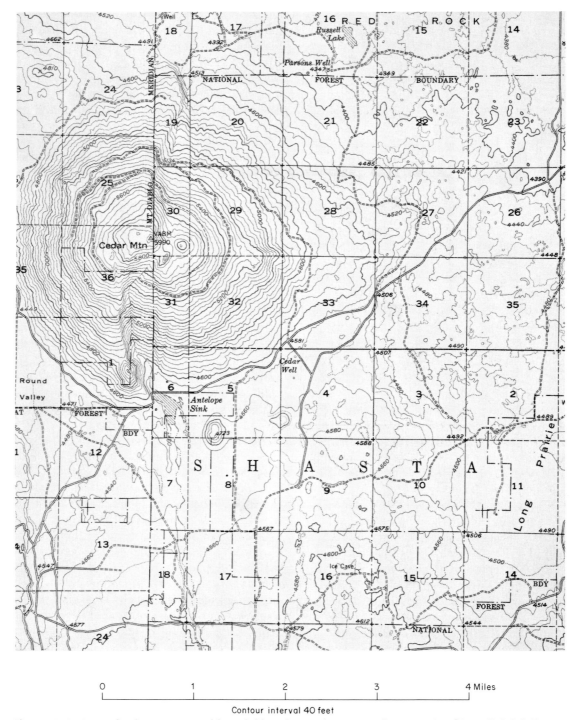

Figure 18.12 *Map of volcanic cone and lava field in the Southern Cascade Mountains. [From U.S.G.S. Bray, California, quadrangle.]*

Figure 18.13 *Mount Shasta, California, a volcano in the Southern Cascades. The volcanic cone is about 2 miles high. The altitude of the base is about 3,500 feet; the peak is above 14,000 feet. The upper limit of plant growth is about 13,000 feet; timberline is at about 9,000 to 9,500 feet. The base of the mountain is in the Transition Zone, here characterized by sugar pine.*

was at or near the edge of a deep marine trench; terrestrial deposits with coal beds were formed to the east, whereas the trench accumulated volcanic clastic rocks—tuff breccias, subaqueous volcanic mudflows, sandstone and siltstone of volcanic debris, and some lavas. These deposits make up the Ohanapecosh Formation, which is more than 10,000 feet thick. In the Oligocene, the Ohanapecosh deposits were folded, uplifted, deeply weathered, eroded, and buried under 3,000 feet of massive rhyolitic or dacitic ash flows (Stevens Ridge Formation of Oligocene or early Miocene age) that represent Peléan type erup-

tions, or glowing avalanches. The weathering of Ohanapecosh had developed saprolite, and the glowing avalanches that violently moved across the surface incorporated saprolitic mud in the lower parts of the flows. The volcanic activity culminated in the eruption of 5,000 feet of basaltic lavas (Fifes Peak Formation), including related mudflows and minor amounts of rhyolitic ash. By that time, an ancestral ridge had been built at the Cascades.

Further uplift occurred during the late Miocene when a granitic pluton, the Tatoosh pluton, a small batholith, worked its way upward and eventually reached the surface. It injected a complex of sills into the older uplifted Ohanapecosh and Stevens Ridge formations, and in places broke through them to erupt at the surface and contribute pumiceous debris eastward to the Ellensburg Formation of early Pliocene age. The top of the pluton became dissected by canyons as deep as 4,000 feet before the first Mount Rainier eruptions took place in the Pleistocene. The canyons were filled and the topography smoothed by andesitic lavas from Mount Rainier. The cone continued to grow by eruptions of lava, breccia, tuff breccia, and pumice until the summit was a thousand feet higher than it is today. The top has subsequently been lowered, apparently by explosions that caused cauldron subsi-

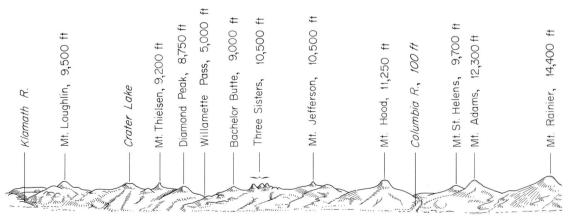

Figure 18.14 *Diagram of the middle Cascade Mountains as seen from the east. The mountains are an anticlinal uplift of early and middle Tertiary lavas surmounted by volcanic cones of late Tertiary and Quarternary age.*

A. Early Tertiary shield volcanoes.

B. Middle Tertiary. Shield volcanoes continue to grow, and the lavas become arched and faulted upward.

C. Late Tertiary and Quaternary. Shield volcanoes continue to be arched and faulted upward; steep sided cones of andesitic lavas and ash are built on the arch.

D. Late Quaternary at Crater Lake. An eruption destroys the top of the ancient volcano, Mt. Mazama, and deposits a layer of ash over the Pacific Northwest; collapse of the cone into the throat of the volcano develops a caldera, which contains Crater Lake.

Figure 18.15 *Cross sections of the Middle Cascades, illustrating the arching of the early and middle Tertiary lavas, faulting along the east side of the mountains, and the late Tertiary and Quarternary volcanic cones built on top of the earlier structures.*

Figure 18.16 *Mt. Rainier viewed from the west. The base of the cone of Mt. Rainier is about 5,000 feet in altitude and about 15 miles in diameter; the peak is at 14,410 feet.*

Figure 18.17 *Gorge of the Columbia River across the Cascade Mountains (view up river). The mountains are formed by Miocene and Pliocene lavas that were raised anticlinally across the River's course. The altitude of the upper surface of these lavas is 4,500 to 5,000 feet, and at least that amount of uplift has occurred.*

dence. The volcanic activity appears to have destroyed glaciers that must have formed there during the early and middle Pleistocene. Some of the explosive activity and mudflows may have been caused when the hot lavas encountered ice and meltwaters. The present glaciers survive because the volcano is quiescent. The most recent eruption took place about A.D. 1,400. The poorly consolidated volcanic rocks that form the cone are now being rapidly eroded.

The Cascades in Washington include granitic plutons of two ages. The younger, like the

Figure 18.18 *Gorge of the Columbia River through the Cascade Range. View is west near the east foot of the range. The river is antecedent across the broadly arched middle and late Tertiary lavas.*

Figure 18.19   *Eldorado Range in the North Cascades National Park; head of Boston Glacier.*

Tatoosh Pluton at Mount Rainier, the Snoqualmie Pluton to the north, and the Cloudy Pass batholith at Glacier Peak, are middle Tertiary. The older, which include the Colville, Osoyoos, Similkameen and Chelan plutons (Fig. 18.20) or batholiths, are late Mesozoic.

LOWER CALIFORNIA (PENINSULAR RANGE) PROVINCE

The Lower California Province, situated between the Salton Trough and the coast, is the northern end of Baja California. The province is a batholith of granite that, in part at least, is of Cretaceous age, intrusive into Lower Cretaceous formations and overlain by younger, Upper Cretaceous ones. The granite forms a westward-tilted plateau, the east front of which is a tremendous east-facing escarpment, like the east front of the Sierra Nevada. San Jacinto Peak at the north end is more than 11,000 feet in altitude and overlooks Salton Trough, which extends below sea level. Northwest-trending faults extend obliquely across the escarpment and divide it into a series of northwest-trending mountains.

Along the coast are wave-cut marine terraces of Pleistocene age (Fig. 18.21). These terraces, some of which are as much as 1,300 feet above sea level, record a series of Pleistocene uplifts. The terraces are warped, for the uplift was irregular.

Similar terraces on the coasts of some of the offshore islands are further evidence of different amounts of uplift on different structural blocks. San Clemente Island is terraced practically to its summit (1,480 feet). Santa Catalina Island has only a few poorly developed terraces, even though it lies between San Clemente Island and the Palos Verdes Hills, both of which are prominently terraced.

PACIFIC BORDER PROVINCE

GREAT VALLEY OF CALIFORNIA.   The Great Valley of California, situated between the Sierra Nevada and the Coast Ranges, is a structural trough—part of a Tertiary and Quaternary geosyncline. In the south, where the structural depth is greatest, Tertiary and younger formations bury the granitic batholith and its roof rocks to a depth of at least 3 miles. The axis of the trough is near the western edge of the Great Valley, where the base of the geosynclinal sediments has not been reached by even the deepest drill holes. Most of the sedimentary deposits were derived by erosion of the Sierra Nevada; the youngest form long, low alluvial fans that slope westward from the foot of the Sierra. The sedimentary formations in the trough, are richly petroliferous, especially toward the south, and some of California's principal oil fields are producing from them.

Figure 18.21 *Wave-cut marine terraces along the coast of the Peninsular Range about 50 miles north of San Diego. A conspicuous low terrace and remnants of several higher ones, cut into Tertiary formations and veneered with marine deposits of Pleistocene age, record a series of uplifts of this part of the coast during Pleistocene time.*

Figure 18.20 *Exposed Jurassic, Cretaceous, and Tertiary granitic intrusions (black) along the Pacific Coast of North America. Probably there is much more granitic rock shallowly buried under the country rocks, which are left white. The country rocks are mostly Cenozoic in the United States and mostly Paleozoic and late Precambrian eugeosynclinal rocks in Canada and Alaska. What happens to these granitic masses with depth? By one interpretation, they increase in extent. By a second, their shapes and positions change, but proportions remain about the same. A third interpretation holds that the intrusions are bubble-shaped and taper downward.*

Most of the Great Valley of California is below 500 feet in altitude, and about a third is less than 100 feet in altitude. The northern part is drained by the Sacramento River. Most of the southern part drains to the San Joaquin River, but the southernmost quarter is a closed basin containing two playas, Tulare and Buena Vista lakes. This basin probably is due chiefly to structural sinking, but may be due in part to deposition of an alluvial fan at the mouth of Kings River.

The Marysville Buttes, situated between the Sacramento and Feather rivers, about 50 miles north of Sacramento, are about 10 miles in diameter and about 2,000 feet higher than the surrounding plain. They are dome mountains caused by the intrusion of stocks and laccoliths. As the igneous activity continued, the intrusions broke through to the surface, erupting as volcanoes.

CALIFORNIA COAST RANGES. The California Coast Ranges (Fig. 18.4) consist of a series of ridges and valleys trending about northwest and about parallel to the coast. The summits of most ridges are below 5,000 feet, and many are below 3,000 feet (Fig. 18.7). Along some of the coast there are four ranges separated by three valleys; most ranges and valleys are short and interrupted by offsets.

North of San Francisco Bay the rocks of the Coast Ranges are complexly folded and faulted

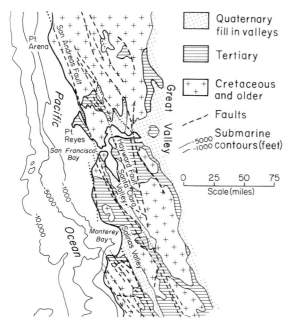

Figure 18.22 *Geologic map of part of the California Coast Ranges, illustrating the fault system. Note that Monterey Bay has a submarine canyon; San Francisco Bay does not. [Generalized from U.S.G.S. and A.A.P.G.]*

Mesozoic eugeosynclinal formations, mostly Cretaceous and older. These formations continue in the ranges south of the bay, but along with them are younger formations that are also folded and faulted, although less so than the older rocks (Fig. 18.22).

One of the principal faults controlling the Coast Ranges is the San Andreas fault (Fig. 18.34). Displacement along this fault is mostly right lateral; the block on the west is moving northward relative to the one on the east. Since Cretaceous time this displacement may have been more than 100 miles; this could have been accomplished at a rate of only 15 to 20 feet in every thousand years. The displacement at the time of the 1906 earthquake was as much as 20 feet. Some effects of geologic structure on topography are strikingly illustrated by the San Andreas fault near point Reyes, 20 miles northwest of San Francisco Bay (Fig. 18.23).

Because of the geologic structure, drainage in

the Coast Ranges has developed a trellis pattern. Many streams, after following a strike valley, turn and cut across one or more structural ridges. Russian River (Fig. 18.4) is an example. Drainage from the Great Valley crosses the Coast Ranges only at San Francisco Bay.

There is some question about how long the Sacramento and San Joaquin rivers have discharged into the Pacific Ocean through the Golden Gate. The absence of a submarine canyon off San Francisco Bay, and the existence of a sizable one off Monterey Bay (Fig. 18.21), suggests that drainage into San Francisco Bay may once have discharged by way of the Santa Clara Val-

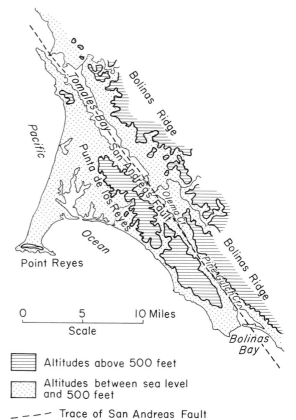

Figure 18.23 *Trace of San Andreas Fault in the vicinity of Point Reyes. The northwest-trending ridges and valleys in the California Coast Ranges are structurally controlled, like the valley between Bolinas Ridge and Point Reyes. (From U.S.G.S. Point Reyes, California, quadrangle.)*

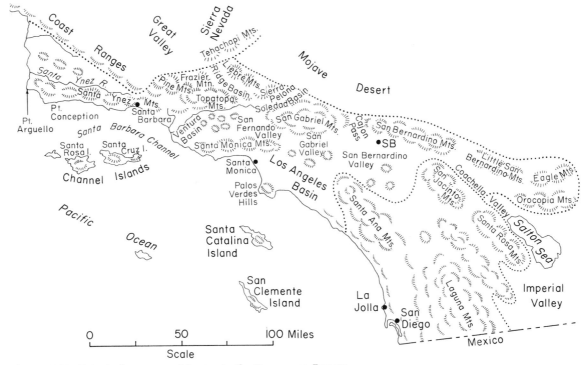

Figure 18.24 *Principal ranges and basins in the Transverse Ranges.*

ley, which now drains northward, and then across the divide separating the Santa Clara and Salinas valleys (Fig. 18.4) and into the ocean at Monterey Bay. On the other hand, most submarine canyons are not at the mouths of rivers and are generally attributed to submarine erosion.

TRANSVERSE RANGES.   The Transverse Ranges (Fig. 18.24), classed as a section of the Pacific Border Province, consist of ranges and basins trending nearly east and transverse to the southeasterly trends of the adjoining areas, as in the Sierra Nevada, Great Valley, and Coast Ranges at the north, and in the Lower California, or Peninsular, Province at the south. The transverse structures also control the easterly trending coast between Point Conception and Santa Monica, the Santa Barbara Channel, and the Channel Islands. The ranges are mostly faulted anticlines, struc-

turally rather like the Coast Ranges to the north, and the basins are faulted synclines. The Channel Islands are peaks on the otherwise submerged parts of the uplift at the Santa Monica Mountains, and the Santa Barbara Channel is the still-submerged western extension of the Ventura Basin (Fig. 18.25).

Toward the west the mountains consist mostly of marine formations of Tertiary age; those to the east are higher and consist mostly of older rocks, including much granite, some of it Precambrian and dated at 1.3 billion years. The basins contain thick Tertiary deposits buried under Quaternary fill, much of it marine.

The highest ranges in this section—the San Gabriel and San Bernardino mountains—are separated by the San Andreas fault. Both reach altitudes of more than 10,000 feet. They consist partly of Precambrian granite and older, highly metamorphosed sedimentary and volcanic rocks.

The San Gabriel Mountains also include some Miocene granitic plutons. Both ranges are bounded by faults.

The Los Angeles Basin, a coastal lowland covering about a thousand square miles, is the only part of the Pacific Border Province that might be referred to as a coastal plain. Its structure, though, is quite unlike that of the Atlantic or Gulf Coastal Plains, for the structural floor of the basin is buried under 30,000 feet of folded and faulted Cretaceous, Tertiary, and Quaternary deposits. In Miocene time the basin extended beyond its present limits, but it became smaller as it filled. Today, only the western part remains submerged. Many anticlines in the Los Angeles Basin are marked by rows of hills, some of which are sites of oil fields.

KLAMATH MOUNTAINS. The Klamath Mountains Section of the Pacific Border Province (Fig. 18.26) is a mountainous coastal area between the Coast Ranges of California and Oregon. Its rocks and their structures are like those of the Sierra Nevada. Paleozoic and early Mesozoic eugeosynclinal formations, much deformed and metamorphosed, were intruded by late Mesozoic granite, and the older rocks and structures were further modified during Tertiary and Quaternary time by uplift and other deformation that has elevated the mountains to their present position.

The uplifted formations plunge gradually southward and extend under the California Coast Ranges, the northern parts of which are composed of Mesozoic formations. The general southward plunge continues to the southern California Coast Ranges, which are composed chiefly of Tertiary formations. To the north, the Klamath Mountains uplift plunges sharply under the Oregon Coast Range, composed of Tertiary formations, and eastward the uplift extends be-

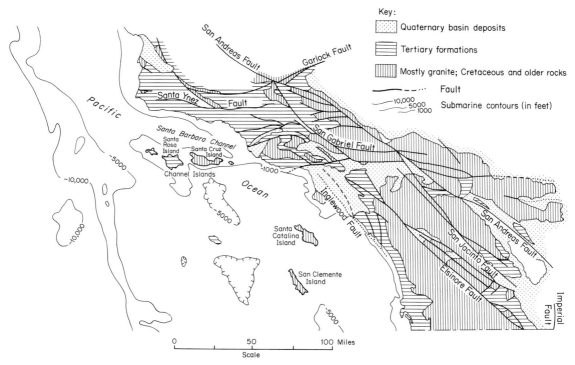

Figure 18.25 *Transverse Ranges and Lower California Province, showing the fault pattern that controls those ranges and basins. This is the widest stretch of continental shelf along the Pacific Coast of North America, and it evidently is much faulted.* [Generalized from U.S.G.S. and A.A.P.G.]

Figure 18.26 *Orientation map of the Klammath Mountains Section in the Pacific Border Province.*

neath the Quaternary lavas at the Cascade Mountains.

Klamath River and Rogue River, antecedent across the uplift, follow meandering gorges incised 1,500 to 2,500 feet into an old erosion surface preserved across the uplands. The high peaks, mostly between 5,000 and 7,500 feet in altitude, are monadnocks that rise above it.

The geologic structures in the granitic and older rocks of the Klamath Mountains Section are arcuate in plan. At the south, where the folds and

faults emerge from beneath the California Trough and the lavas of the Southern Cascades, the trends are northwest. Followed northward, these structures curve first to the north, and then, in the northern part of the section, to the northeast where they extend under the Middle Cascades. If projected southward, the trends would connect with those of the Sierra Nevada; if projected northeastward, they would connect with the Ochoco-Blue Mountains uplift on the Columbia Plateau (p. 544). The uplifts at the Sierra Nevada, Klamath Mountains, and Ochoco-Blue Mountains may be one continuous, sinuous structure.

OREGON COAST RANGE.   The Oregon Coast Range consists of irregular hills and low mountains along the coast of Oregon and southwestern Washington. The highest summits are a little more than 3,000 feet high; the relief is generally less than 2,000 feet (Fig. 18.11). Hillsides are rounded and the valleys are open. The topography resembles that of some parts of the Appalachian Plateaus.

Some valleys head within 15 miles of the coast and flow eastward to the Willamette Valley; others head within 5 miles of the edge of that valley and flow westward to the coast. The mouths of the valleys are drowned, and increasingly so northward, which suggests that the most recent structural movement has involved northward tilting.

The rocks are Tertiary in age and form a plateau structure interrupted by open, short folds and without much faulting. The east base of the range is the Willamette Valley, which is the south end of the Puget Trough, a structural as well as topographic trough. In Eocene time the entire area was a depression, and the ocean shore was along the site of the Cascade Mountains, about 100 miles inland from its present position (Fig. 18.27). The Klamath Mountains were an upland of pre-Tertiary rocks. The site of the Cascades was one of extensive volcanism and lay near sea level. Later, in Oligocene time (Fig. 18.27), the influx of volcanic debris and other sediments exceeded the rate of subsidence of the basin, and the shore was pushed seaward. By Miocene time

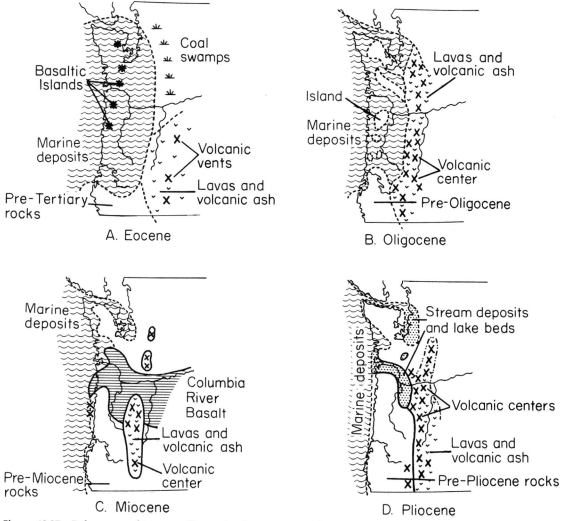

Figure 18.27 *Paleogeographic maps illustrating four stages in the development of the landscape in the northern part of the Pacific Mountain System. [Generalized from Washington Div. Mines and Geol.]*

the shore had almost reached its present position, and the Cascades were greatly elevated. Uplift and warping continued during the Pliocene while the Cascade Mountains were being built higher. Uplift that continued into Quaternary time is recorded by wave-cut bluffs along the coast and by a series of marine terraces as high as 1,500 feet above sea level. (Fig. 18.28).

OLYMPIC MOUNTAINS. The Olympic Mountains in northwestern Washington (Fig. 18.11) are

formed by a domal structural uplift much higher than that of the Oregon Coast Range, and the mountains are very much higher topographically, reaching to altitudes above 8,000 feet. The core of the uplift consists of resistant pre-Tertiary rocks around which Tertiary formations, including thick Eocene pillow lavas, are turned up to form the flanks. During early Eocene time the site of the Olympic Mountains was below sea level, but uplift had produced a low peninsula by late Eocene time. Uplift continued throughout the rest

Figure 18.28 *Cape Foulweather, on the Oregon coast. Besides the fog, the coast is characterized by uplifted marine terraces (two in this view) and by Sitka spruce.*

of the Tertiary Period, and the mountains reached their present height during the Quaternary. During Pleistocene time the Olympic Mountains were glaciated, and many cirques still contain glaciers. Glacial deposits at the foot of the mountains are folded and tilted, indicating the recency of uplift, which is probably still continuing.

PUGET TROUGH.   The Puget Trough, a partly submerged lowland that is less than 500 feet in altitude in the emerged part, is the southern end of a structural and topographic depression that extends from the Willamette Valley in Oregon northward for about 1,500 miles into Washington, and along the coast of British Columbia. It forms the famous Inside Passage to Alaska. At the south the trough forms a lowland 200 miles long and barely 25 miles wide between the Oregon Coast Range and the Cascade Mountains. Northward, the trough is partly filled with glacial outwash. It slopes under Puget Sound, and where it is incompletely submerged, it forms hundreds of islands. Farther north, along the coast of British Columbia and Alaska, the trough is deeply sub-

merged and bordered by steep mountainsides.

In Pleistocene time even the lowland at the south was submerged. Glaciers dammed Puget Sound, and their meltwaters discharged to the Pacific Ocean around the south side of the Olympic Mountains. The Columbia River was a strait across the Coast Range, and it built an extensive delta in the quiet water that flooded the lower part of the Willamette Valley. During late Pleistocene and Holocene time, this lowland has risen a few hundred feet; at Puget Sound and farther north the trough has remained submerged, showing northward tilting like that of the ranges along the coast.

The emerged part of the Puget Trough covers only about 10,000 square miles, a little more than 5 percent of the area of Washington and Oregon, but half the population of those two states lives in this section of the Pacific Border Province.

COAST MOUNTAINS OF
BRITISH COLUMBIA AND ALASKA

The Coast Mountains, about 1,000 miles long, have many summits higher than 10,000 feet in altitude. The mountains are composed largely of late Mesozoic granitic, batholiths—by far the greatest of the batholiths along the Pacific Coast of North America, 1,000 miles long and in places more than 100 miles wide. At many places the western base of the mountains descends abruptly to oceanic depths some thousands of feet below sea level; the relief, therefore, is much greater than the mountainous heights one sees. At Vancouver and Queen Charlotte islands and the islands of southeastern Alaska are comparative lowlands formed of Paleozoic and Mesozoic eugeosynclinal sedimentary formations. The many islands are separated by deep trenches, most of them fault valleys. The summits are very jagged with numerous matterhorns and aretes between the ice-filled cirques. Many or most of the glaciers extend to within 500 feet of the sea and some reach the sea. The deep, steep-walled valleys that extend into the mountains form spectacular fjords. During the Pleistocene, glaciers from the Coast Mountains crossed the Strait of Georgia and extended onto Vancouver Island.

East of the Coast Mountains are interior mountain ranges, mostly under 8,000 feet altitude, and mostly formed of folded Mesozoic eugeosynclinal formations. Associated with these ranges are extensive plateaus capped by lavas. The most extensive of these extends the southern half of British Columbia covering about 15,000 square miles along each side at an altitude of about 3,000 to 4,000 feet. It covers much of the south half of British Columbia. The lava-capped plateau, at an altitude of 3,000 to 4,000 feet, has three large shield volcanoes near the middle of the west side. The lavas are Tertiary to Holocene in age. They overlie folded and faulted eugeosynclinal sedimentary formations, including Paleozoic rocks on the east and Mesozoic on the west. The canyon of the Frazer River is incised into the plateau and reaches the Strait of Georgia in a valley that curves around the south end of the Coast Mountains (Fig. 18.29).

Uplift of the Coast Mountains began in Jurassic time, and during the Cretaceous Period this was part of a mountainous area west of the geosynclinal sea that connected the Gulf of Mexico and the Arctic Ocean (Fig. 2.14,C; p. 378). Structural deformation and igneous activity have continued to the present time. One volcano, Mount

Figure 18.29 *Valley of the Columbia River in British Columbia, between the Monashee (left) and Selkirk mountains (right). [Courtesy of British Columbia Dept. of Travel Industry.]*

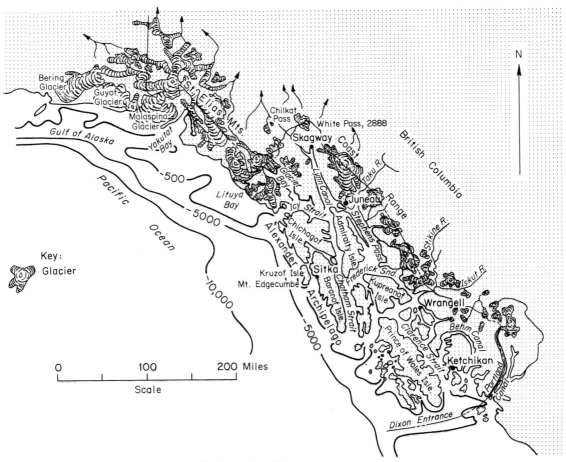

Figure 18.30 *Map of the southeastern Alaska panhandle.*

Edgecumbe on Kruzof Island, west of Sitka (Fig. 18.30), has been active during the Holocene. Frequent and severe earthquakes indicate that structural movements are continuing (Fig. 19.13). In 1899 the Yakutat Bay area experienced a major earthquake during which the shore was greatly elevated; at one fault there was vertical displacement of 49 feet. In 1958 another earthquake in that area caused a slide that created huge waves (p. 638). This area, like much of the Pacific Mountain System, could serve as laboratory for studying directions and rates of present-day earth movement.

Unlike the Cascades and Sierra Nevada, the Coast Mountains are crossed by several trans-verse river valleys. Two rivers, the Stikine and Taku, cross the Coast Mountains and discharge into the Alexander Archipelago. The Stikine River heads on the west slope of the Canadian Rockies and, after crossing the Coast Mountains, discharges to an inlet about 15 miles north of Wrangell. The Taku River also heads east of the Coast Mountains, crosses them, and discharges into an inlet south of Juneau and at the head of Stephens Passage. At Taku Inlet there is a glacier a mile wide and 100 to 300 feet high at its terminus. Here, as along other ice fronts, tidal changes break icebergs from the front of the glacier. Farther south, in British Columbia, the Coast Mountains are crossed by the Iskut, Nass, and Skeena

Rivers and the Dean Channel. Some of these valleys are 9,000 feet deep and would dwarf Grand Canyon or even Hell's Canyon.

The panhandle of southeastern Alaska, including the islands, is a mountainous uplift of late Mesozoic and early Cenozoic granitic rocks flanked on the west by Paleozoic and Mesozoic sedimentary rocks. The axis of the uplift is in the Coast Range along the boundary between the panhandle and British Columbia (Fig. 19.1,A). Paleozoic and Mesozoic eugeosynclinal formations and some outliers of the granitic intrusions form the coast and the islands, which form the Alexander Archipelago.

The mountains rise precipitously from the sea to altitudes of about 9,000 feet along the crest of the Coast Mountains. The coast and archipelago are cut by an intricate network of deep, narrow fjords. (Fig. 18.31) at the north end of the famous inside passage from Seattle to Alaska. This inside passage occupies a structural trough that was probably once like the Rocky Mountain Trench but which is now submerged. The connecting waterways are variously referred to as canals, passages, sounds, and straits. Many are long and straight like Lynn Canal and Chatham Strait, and evidently mark fault lines. The patterns of fjords are as varied as patterns of streams, for they are drowned valleys. Fjords may be straight and parallel. They may have a trellis or dendritic pattern. Some that extend into cirques have circular headwalls.

The Alexander Archipelago, representing the partly submerged western foothills of the Coast Range, consists of hundreds of islands. The large ones are 3,000 to 5,000 feet high with steep sides, and where the slopes are not too steep, are cov-

Figure 18.31 *Alaskan fjord. Heavily forested mountains rise directly from sea level.*

ered with dense forests. Northward, at Glacier Bay, are the lofty St. Elias Mountains, where several peaks reach to more than 15,000 feet in altitude. Offshore from the archipelago the submarine surface slopes steeply to a depth of about 7,500 feet and then more gradually to a depth of about 10,000 feet (Fig. 19.3).

Many hundreds of alpine glaciers fill the valleys of the Coast Mountains, and many extend down valley to the sea. One of the best known, Muir glacier, is only about 20 miles long but is fed by numerous tributaries and covers 350 square miles. The front of the glacier—about a mile wide and 100 to 200 feet high—has receded despite the fact that the ice advances at the rate of a few feet per day. Melting and the breaking off of icebergs where the glacier enters the sea exceed the rate of ice advance. Many of the glaciers are receding.

GRANITE, BATHOLITHS.   Whereas the Frazer, Columbia, and Snake River Plateaus are largely basalt, the Coast Mountains of British Columbia, southeastern Alaska, and northern Cascades, as well as the Sierra Nevada and Lower California Province, are in large part granite (Fig. 18.32). Trying to explain vast granite batholiths is as difficult as trying to explain the vast plateau basalts. Presumably the difference in mode of occurrence—intrusion versus extrusion—reflects the greater fluidity of silica-poor melts as compared to silica-rich ones.

Batholiths are like stocks, only larger and defined arbitrarily as larger than 30 square miles. Large ones may exceed a thousand square miles. They consist of a complex of individual intrusions—plutons—some of which have uniform composition; others are differentiated in concentric zones having different compositions.

The individual plutons are partly concordant with the adjacent folded formations and partly cut irregularly across them. Most have steeply inclined side walls, and between the individual plutons there may be slabs of very different, highly metamorphosed and sheared country rock. Some plutons contain blocks of the country rocks that were broken from the roof or walls and

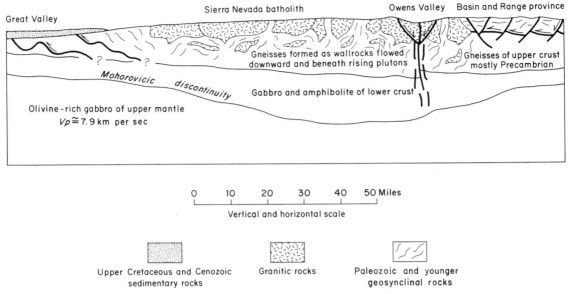

Great Valley   Sierra Nevada batholith   Owens Valley   Basin and Range province

? ——— ?

Gneisses formed as wallrocks flowed
downward and beneath rising plutons

Gneisses of upper crust
mostly Precambrian

Mohorovicic   discontinuity   Gabbro and amphibolite of lower crust

Olivine-rich gabbro of upper mantle
$Vp \cong 7.9$ km per sec

0   10   20   30   40   50 Miles
Vertical and horizontal scale

Upper Cretaceous and Cenozoic   Granitic rocks   Paleozoic and younger
sedimentary rocks   geosynclinal rocks

Figure 18.32 *Geologic and crustal section through the Sierra Nevada of California. Plutons of granitic magma melted in the upper mantle and lower crust, rose through crust and coalesced at the surface to form the Sierra Nevada batholith. In the Basin and Range Province, late Precambrian, Paleozoic, Mesozoic, and Cenozoic rocks slide westward via the Amargosa thrust, then broke into normal-fault blocks. [Modified after U.S.G.S. Prof. Paper 554-C.]*

floated in the intruding mass. Locally the country rock is melted and partly or wholly assimilated by the granite. The granitic rock is coarsely crystalline (as compared to the fine-grained or even glassy volcanic rocks) and the composition may be that of true granite or of quartz rich rocks without much potash feldspar, such as quartz diorite, granodiorite, quartz monzonite, etc.

Although batholiths are associated with geosynclines, not all geosynclines have batholiths, and there is great variation in the degree of development of granite at the various geosynclines.

The granite in the Pacific Border Province developed in the eugeosynclinal Triassic and Jurassic belts; the batholiths seem to be slightly oblique to the Paleozoic geosynclines, being east of the Paleozoic eugeosyncline toward the south but in it at the north. There were at least three episodes of development of these granitic masses. Some are Precambrian; other are Mesozoic and mostly late Mesozoic (sometimes referred to as Nevadan); still others are early Tertiary (sometimes refered to as Laramide); finally, some are mid-Tertiary.

THE COAST AND CONTINENTAL SHELF

Unlike the Atlantic seaboard, most of the Pacific Coast is mountainous. Toward the south the coast has recently been uplifted and is characterized by steep bluffs and highly elevated marine terraces. Uplift seems to be continuing. At the Los Angeles Basin a coastal plain slopes from the foot of the mountains to the sea, but from there to the Puget Trough there are only about a half dozen plains, all small and all at the mouths of broad valleys.

Most of the geologic formations along the coast from Washington to California are nonresistant and readily erode to form bluffs. The shorelines are straight, fully exposed to the surf, and without barrier beaches and lagoons. At Puget Sound and north to Alaska, the coast has been downwarped, and far more so than the north end of the Atlantic seaboard.

Southward as far as Point Conception the continental shelf off the Pacific Coast (Fig. 18.33) is barely 50 miles wide, and is mountainous. South of Point Conception the width of the shelf increases to about 150 miles. The offshore islands there are peaks of mountains that have as much relief as those on the land.

There is practically no continental shelf opposite the Coast Mountains. Many of the straits there are deeper than 600 feet. Off Queen Charlotte Islands the rim of the shelf descends 3,000 feet within 4 miles of the shore.

Two major structurally controlled mountain ridges, each with relief about equal to that of the Sierra Nevada, extend about 1,500 miles westward from the coast into the Pacific Ocean (Fig. 20.1). The more northerly of these joins the coast at Cape Mendocino, where the San Andreas fault extends into the ocean. This submerged ridge, called the Mendocino Mountains, is seismically active and may be a westward continuation, or branch, of the San Andreas fault. There sub-

merged mountains form a southward-facing escarpment. To the south the ocean averages about a half mile deeper than to the north.

The more southerly ridge, known as the Murray Mountains, extends westward from the Transverse Ranges. These submerged mountains form a north-facing escarpment. The ocean bottom north of the Murray Mountains is deeper that it is to the south.

The steep edge of the continent along the Pacific Coast has numerous submarine canyons, like those incised into the edge of the Atlantic Continental Shelf. Some are V-shaped with tributaries. Most are cut into easily eroded Tertiary formations, but at least one is in granite and another is in basalt. Some of the canyons are not at all related to present drainage. The canyons probably are due mostly to erosion by submarine currents, but their origin, like that of those along the Atlantic coast, continues to be a mystery.

Seismic Activity

The mountains of the Pacific Mountain System are young and still growing. Earthquakes are frequent. This seismically active area is part of the circum-Pacific belt of volcanic and seismic activity that extends 15,000 miles along the Pacific coasts of South America, North America, and Asia (Fig. 2.25). On maps this belt appears strongly arcuate, but on the globe it is much less so and for long distances is nearly straight, like the great circle route shown in Figure 18.3.

The seismically active belt is interrupted between northern California and the Puget Trough by an area with few seismic epicenters (Fig. 2.17). This quiet area corresponds to the belt of Cenozoic lavas at and west of the Columbia Plateau. The coast from Puget Trough northward and westward through the Aleutian Islands is seismically active.

The California segment of the seismically active belt is best known because it is heavily populated, but this segment is by no means the most active part of the circum-Pacific seismic belt. Yet in 100 years California has experienced about 200 earthquakes classed as destructive or nearly de-

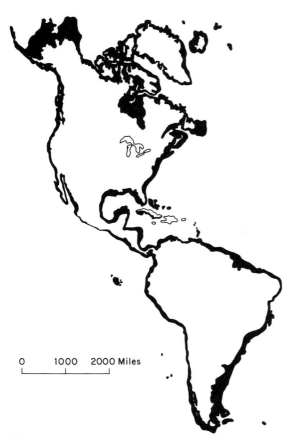

Figure 18.33 *The continental shelves of the Americas.* [*After U.S.G.S.*]

Table 18.1

Surface Faulting During Historical Earthquakes in California Region

Date	Fault	Estimated or Recorded Magnitude (Richter scale)	Surface Effects
1836	Hayward	About 7.0	Ground breakage
1838	San Andreas	About 7.0	Ground breakage
1852	Big Pine	No data	Ground breakage
*1857	San Andreas	About 8.0	Right-lateral slip, possibly as much as 30 ft.
1861	Calaveras	No data	Ground breakage
1868	San Andreas	No data	Long fissure in earth at Dos Palmas
1868	Hayward	About 7.0	Strike slip
*1872	Owens Valley fault zone	8.3±	Right-lateral slip, 16–20 ft., left-lateral movement may also have occurred; vertical slip, down to east, 23 ft.
1890	San Andreas	No data	Fissures in fault zone, railroad tracks moved, railroad bridge displaced
1899	San Jacinto	About 6.6	Surface evidence questionable
1901	San Andreas	About 6.3	Ground breakage
*1906	San Andreas	8.3	Right-lateral slip, 16 ft.
1922	San Andreas	6.5	Ground breakage
1934	San Andreas	6.0	Ground breakage
1934	San Jacinto fault zone in Colorado River Delta	7.1	Distinct fault trace on 1935 aerial photographs
1940	Imperial	7.1	Right-lateral slip, 19 ft.
1947	Manix	6.4	Left-lateral slip, 3 in.
1950	Unnamed fault along west edge of Fort Sage Mountains	5.6	Vertical slip, down to west 5–8 in.
1951	Superstition Hills	5.6	Right-lateral slip, slight
1952	White Wolf	7.7	South-dipping reverse fault; left-lateral slip, 2 ft; upthrown 2 ft.
1956	San Miguel	6.8	Right-lateral slip, 3 ft.; vertical slip, down to southwest 3 ft.
1966	Imperial	3.6	Right-lateral slip, 1½ cm.
1966	San Andreas	5.5	Right-lateral slip, several inches
1968	Coyote Creek Superstition Hills Imperial, and San Andreas	6.5	Right-lateral slip, up to 38 cm. on Coyote Creek; right-lateral slip, 1–2 cm. on Superstition Hills, Imperial, and San Andreas
1971	San Fernando Valley; San Gabriel fault system	6.6	50 cm vertical slip and 50 cm horizontal
	Faults Showing Continuous or Intermittent Creep San Andreas fault from San Juan Bautista to Cholame Hayward fault Calaveras fault zone from near Dublin to Hollister Imperial fault. Possible creep after 1940 Imperial Valley earthquake Manix fault Garlock fault		

Source: Pre-1971 data after U.S. Geological Survey.

*Three largest earthquakes.

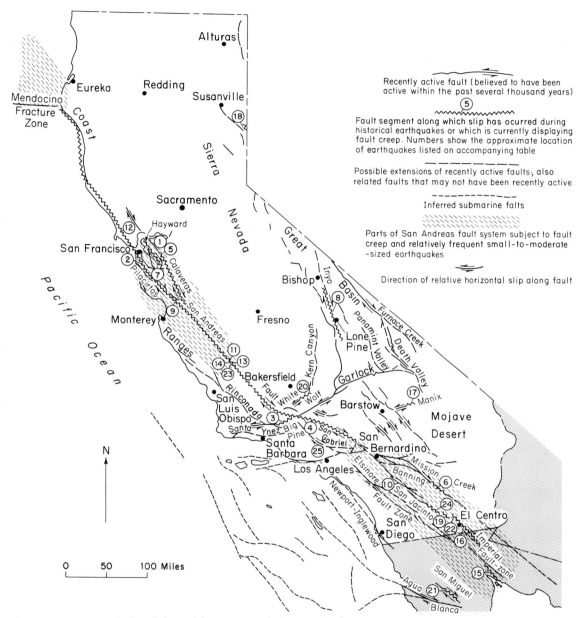

Figure 18.34   *Active faults of the California region [After U.S.G.S.]*

structive. There have been, of course, countless other minor tremors detected only by seismographs. Some of the principal earthquakes (the three largest are marked by an asterisk) have been the following (Table 18.1; Fig. 18.34):

The destructiveness of an earthquake is not directly related to the magnitude of the shocks. The Long Beach earthquake in 1933, for example, was not of great magnitude seismically, but it was one of the most destructive earthquakes in United States history because it centered in a densely populated area. Conversely, the Owens

Valley earthquake of 1872, at the east foot of the Sierra Nevada, like the New Madrid Earthquake in the Mississippi Valley in 1811 (p. 229), was of major magnitude but damage was slight because the affected area was sparsely populated.

The average rise of sea level along the Pacific Coast, between 2 and $2\frac{1}{2}$ inches in the last half century, is only one-half to one-quarter as great as that along the Atlantic seaboard and the Gulf of Mexico (p. 91). This difference is very possibly due to uplift of the Pacific Coast at a rate only slightly less than the rate of rise of sea level. If we assume sea level has risen 5 to 6 inches in 50 years, which is roughly the average for the Atlantic seaboard, we might infer that the Pacific Coast has been uplifted 3 to 4 inches in that time. This would amount to 5 or 6 feet of uplift per thousand years—a rate quite commensurate with the record of mountain building along the Pacific Coast during late Tertiary and Quaternary time. Some areas, the San Gabriel Mountains for example, are known to be rising at two or three times that average rate.

When will crustal strains along the Pacific Coast again be relieved by sudden movement and cause the next earthquake? Nobody knows, and, unfortunately, we have only recently begun systematic observations and measurements that may serve as the basis for forecasting. The problem has practical as well as theoretical interest, because parts of the Pacific Coast, especially California, are crowded and becoming more so. The land must be used, but care could be taken in selecting building sites. It is questionable, for example, whether buildings should be constructed on very low land subject to submergence, such as the land adjoining San Francisco Bay. Bluffs along the southern coast of California are notorious for landsliding. Such lands could be better used for parks rather than for residences.

At least four kinds of observations and measurements can be made to locate actively moving ground and to determine the directions and rates of movement:

1. Install tiltmeters at critical locations (Fig. 16.16).

2. Make precise level surveys of selected areas, of the kind made at Lake Mead (p. 507).

3. Determine precise azimuth and relative heights across selected geologic structures to detect local differential movement.

4. In seismically active areas reappraise previous leveling surveys on the assumption that corrections that have been applied are due to earth movement rather than to engineering error (p. 508).

We cannot hope to stop the mountain-making forces, but we can live with them more safely if we adapt ourselves to their ways.

The U.S. Geological Survey has pointed out that most earthquake casualties result from falling objects and debris. Earthquakes may also trigger landslides and generate tsunamis, which can cause great damage.

Climate

Almost every type of climate is represented in the Pacific Mountain System: warm-dry, temperate-wet, cold-dry, and cold-wet. The differences (Fig. 18.35) reflect the great length of the area, more than 26 degrees of latitude; its altitudinal range, from sea level to more than 14,000 feet; its proximity to the ocean; and the effects of the mountain ranges paralleling the coast. If the Coast Ranges were as high as the Sierra Nevada and the Cascade Mountains, most of California would be semiarid, like the Columbia-Snake River Plateau and Great Basin.

The maps in Figure 18.35 illustrate how the climate is affected by differences in latitude (A, H), altitude (B, E, H), and proximity to the ocean (C, D, F, G). Some effects of differences in exposure and altitude are illustrated in Figures 18.36, 4.8, and 8.17. Average annual precipitation in the Sierra Nevada increases about a half inch with every 100-foot increase in altitude.

Not brought out by the maps is the highly seasonal distribution of the rainfall, which, in contrast to the Middle West and eastern seaboard (Fig. 4.4), takes place mostly during the fall, win-

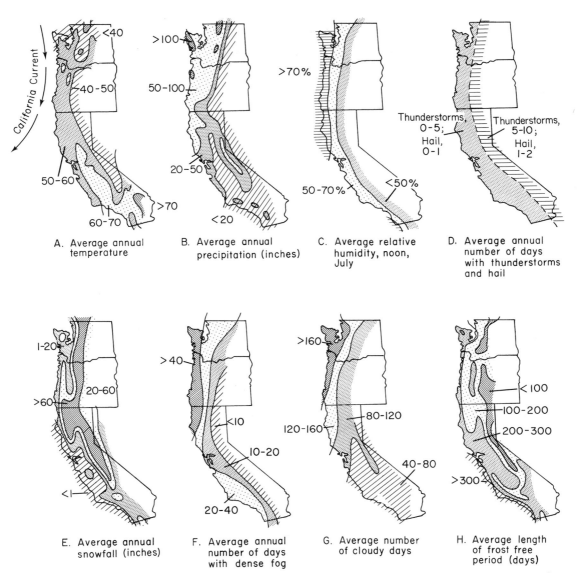

Figure 18.35 *Climatic maps of the Pacific Mountain System. Principal factors affecting the differences in the climates are the range in latitude, oceanic currents (especially the California Current), and the topography.* [*Generalized from U.S.D.A.*]

ter, and spring. Summers are dry. During the winter, southwesterly winds bring warm ocean air over the cold land; during the summer, winds from the northwest bring cold ocean air over warm land (Fig. 4.8,C). As a result, there are two seasons: one wet, the other dry. Forests that are soaked and dripping in the wet season become dry as tinder and highly susceptible to forest fires

in the dry season. Forest fires are a major hazard in the region (Fig. 8.30). In summer, California's grasslands become golden brown, and in allusion to this, the state is sometimes referred to as the "Golden Bare." Fortunately, thunderstorms, which could cause forest fires, are far less frequent than in other physiographic provinces (Fig. 4.7).

Vegetation, Agriculture, Lumbering

Because of the great variety in climate, all the vegetation zones from Lower Sonoran to Alpine are represented in the Pacific Mountain System, and each has a humid and semiarid facies.

The Lower Sonoran Zone is represented by grasslands in the Great Valley and in some inland valleys south of the Transverse Ranges. In these areas of bunch grass and greasewood (Fig. 18.36) the rainfall is greater and the temperature ranges less extreme than in the Lower Sonoran Zone deserts farther inland and leeward of the mountains, and the floras are correspondingly different. In the Great Valley and other areas near the coast, the Lower Sonoran Zone is characterized by annual plants. The lower parts of the Great Valley along the rivers are alkaline flats with greasewood, pickleweed, salt grass, and shadscale.

The Upper Sonoran Zone supports two kinds of plant stands—chaparral, and oak and grass (Fig. 18.36). Chaparral is a mixture of stout woody shrubs and small trees that grow in almost impenetrable thickets. It has peculiarities that are attributed to repeated burning, including fires in prehistoric time. Some shrubs develop horizontal roots that sprout again after the tops are burned; others can reseed freely after fire and re-establish themselves in the burned area. Along the coast of southern California the chaparral extends upward to about 5,000 feet altitude; northward, where there is more rainfall and fog, the chaparral gives way to redwood forests.

The redwood (*Sequoia sempervirens*) is an unusual tree not only because of its great size but also because of its ability to withstand fire and flooding. Floods in the Eel River have destroyed several hundred of them, but many survived the deep burial of their bases under silt. New roots grow vertically from the buried ones, and new lateral roots grow from the buried part of the trunk. The trees withstand fire because thick bark protects the tissue beneath; if the crown burns, a new one grows from adventitious buds along the main trunk and the branches. Moreover, the redwood has no insect enemies. These

traits give the redwood definite advantage over competitors like Douglas fir, tan oak, grand fir, and bay, which are easily killed by fire or siltation.

Still another feature of the redwood tree is its ability to correct for tilt. Trees growing to heights of 250 feet need this! When tilt occurs gradually, as on slumping ground, the tree base grows faster on the downslope side to build a buttress elongated in the direction of tilt. The long diameter may be three times the shorter one.

The Transition Zone descends to sea level along the coast of Washington and Oregon. Inland, along the Sierra Nevada, it begins at about 3,000 feet in altitude. This zone is the great forest region of northwestern United States and comprises four main kinds of forests, each with numerous subtypes.

In the north is the forest of Douglas fir, the most important lumber tree in the Pacific states and perhaps the most important in the whole continent. This forest, which extends from sea level to about 5,000 feet along the western slope of the Cascade Mountains, also includes western hemlock, white fir, grand fir, western red cedar, maples, and oaks. Sitka spruce grows along the coast.

Southward along the coast redwood forest extends from sea level to about 2,500 feet in altitude. Associated with the redwood are Douglas fir, western hemlock, grand fir, and tideland spruce. Redwood and Douglas fir are the tallest American trees; some are about 400 feet high.

Inland from the coastal redwood forest is a forest of sugar pine, a 5-needle pine with tremendous cones 12 to 24 inches long. This forest, which includes white fir, lies mostly between 2,000 and 5,000 feet in altitude. The more arid parts support yellow pine, incense cedar, and sagebrush. In the south, on the west slope of the Sierra Nevada, this forest includes the giant sequoia stand at Sequoia National park.

The fourth forest of the Transition Zone, composed chiefly of western yellow pine, grows along the dry, eastern slope of the Sierra Nevada and Cascades. Its lower limit along the foot of the

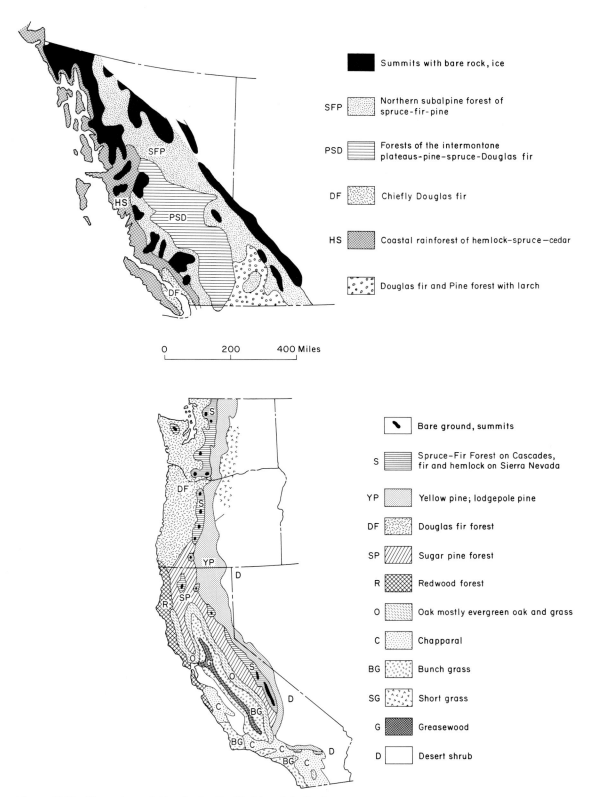

Figure 18.36 *Natural vegetation in the Pacific Mountain System.*

Sierra is at about 5,500 feet, but it descends to 500 feet along the east foot of the Cascades at the Columbia River.

The forests of British Columbia and southern Alaska consist of spruce, cedar, and hemlock rain forest near the coast and spruce, fir, and pine at higher altitudes.

Forests above the Transition zone in the Cascade Range consist of Engelmann spruce, western white pine, whitebark pine, lodgepole pine, white fir, and subalpine fir. In the south the forests consist mostly of Shasta red fir, Jeffrey pine, western white pine, and lodgepole pine. Timberline rises southward from about 6,000 feet in the northern Cascades to about 10,500 in the southern Sierra Nevada. Upward from timberline is the Alpine Zone, which supports various shrubs and herbs.

The southern provinces in the Pacific Mountain System include major agricultural areas. The acreage harvested, most of which is irrigated, is only about 2 percent of the United States total, but the value of the produce, more than $10 billion annually, is 10 percent of the United States total. The per-acre value of the farmland there is higher than in any other part of the country except around New York City. Important crops include barley, cotton, dry beans, potatoes, rice, sugar beets, wine grapes, citrus fruits, figs, avocados, walnuts, and olives. One of the incredible features of our civilization is the classification of California olives, the tiniest being classified "Big." Honey is another important product; a bee ranch may produce 150,000 pounds of honey a year. That takes a lot of busy bees!

Agriculture in California began with the Franciscan Missions, the first western ranches. Beginning in 1769 the friars established 21 missions, located about one day's travel apart, from San Diego to San Francisco Bay (Fig. 18.37). They produced fruits, cereals, vegetables, and herds of sheep, cattle, and horses. Each was self-sufficient, utilizing Indians as serf labor while Christianizing them. After Mexico obtained independence from Spain in 1821, the Indians were freed and the Missions declined.

The first orange grove was started at San Gabriel Mission in 1804, and by 1841 oranges were being raised commercially. Since 1900 citrus-growing has passed cereals in importance. Irrigation projects were undertaken along the San Joaquin and Kings rivers as early as 1872.

Today fruit-farming is big business. A large-scale fruit farm covers thousands of acres, has its own packing house, may employ thousands of pickers and packers at peak season, manufactures its own crates, owns tractors and trucks by the dozen, and ships fruit by the carload. At the other extreme are small orchards operated part time by retired families.

Lumber and timber production from the Pacific Mountain System totals about 15 billion board feet annually, and is valued at around $600,000,000. This is about half the United States production, and three quarters of it is from the Douglas fir forests in Oregon and Washington; the remainder is from the Transition Zone forests in California. The forests in California, except the

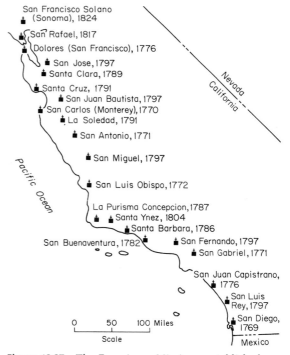

Figure 18.37 *The Franciscan Missions, established along the coast of California from 1769 to 1824, were the first western ranches.*

redwood forests, are also used for stock grazing, but the Douglas fir forests from Oregon north are used very little for grazing.

Stands of old-growth timber in the Pacific Northwest, when logged, may yield 50,000 board-feet per acre. Some logging is selective— that is, individual trees are removed from a stand. This method is common along streams because it minimizes damage to the water and the fish, and it is the usual practice along highways to preserve the forest scenery. Selective logging, though, may not be economical. It requires many roads, and much logging equipment presently available cannot be used. Moreover, the logging debris left on the ground, referred to as slash, must be left there.

Clearcutting commonly is more economical. The slash can be burned, reducing both the fire hazard and helping to prevent the spread of diseases and pests, such as dwarf mistletoe. Burning also prepares the ground for replanting, but if the burning is too hot and bakes the ground it increases erosion and decreases infiltration. Burning also causes loss of certain nutrients, notably nitrogen. After burning, clearcut areas commonly are planted with 2-year-old Douglas fir spaced about 12 feet apart, approximately 300 per acre. In 10 years the trees may be 25 to 30 feet high. Steep ground may have to be seeded. After planting, the ground may need to be fertilized to replace nutrients lost by the burning.

Surface Deposits and Soils

Residual deposits due to deep weathering of various rocks are extensive in the mountains along the coast north of San Francisco Bay, on the wet west slopes of the Cascades and Sierra Nevada, and in Puget Trough, where they are overlapped by glacial outwash of Wisconsinan age. The residuum, deep-red clay, is older than the Wisconsinan glaciation; some of it dates from the Tertiary. Soils developed on it are classed with the Red and Yellow Podzols.

This residuum is mostly below 4,000 feet in altitude. At higher altitudes the surface deposits

and soils are mostly late Pleistocene and Holocene in age and are Gray-Brown Podzols developed on moraines, colluvium, and other deposits of Wisconsinan and Holocene age.

The Puget Trough contains lake beds, alluvium, and glacial deposits; along the coast are beach deposits and dunes.

The California Trough contains broad alluvial floodplains along the rivers, and alluvial fans with gravel rise from the floodplains to the base of the bordering mountains. Soils developed on these deposits, especially in the warm, dry southern part, are varied. Figure 18.38 illustrates some of the principal soil differences along a transect from the coast to the Sierra Nevada.

Along the ocean side of the Coast Ranges of California the soils are mostly slightly acid Prairie Soils with well-developed, organic-rich, brown to black surface layers about 10 inches thick. The subsoils, 18 to 30 inches thick, are light-brown, blocky, and slightly alkaline. The Prairie Soils are not well dated, but seem to be no older than late Pleistocene. In some places older, residual deposits have developed from hard rocks and consist of deep-red clays like the pre-Wisconsinan residuum.

Along the dry inland side of the Coast Ranges, Rendzina Soils have developed on the limy formations. These soils have a surface layer like that on the Prairie Soils except that it is less acid even though it is lime-free. The subsoil is brown, clayey, and very limy. Eastward, near the edge of the Great Valley, the subsoils are more calcareous, and the surface soils slightly calcareous and not so dark.

The Rendzina Soils end at the edge of the Great Valley at about 500 feet in altitude, where the Coast Range formations are overlapped by alluvium deposited by streams discharging eastward to the San Joaquin River. Desert Soils have developed here, for annual rainfall is only 10 inches or less. The deposits are young, the soil processes are weak, and the profiles weakly developed and very limy throughout. These Desert Soils grade eastward into the equally young alluvial soils along the San Joaquin River.

East of the River is a belt of saline soils subject

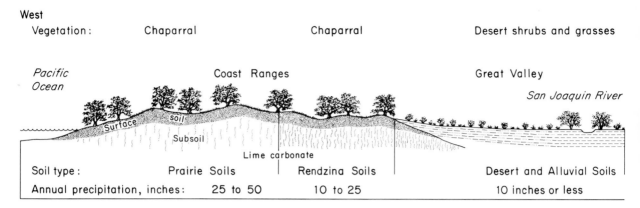

Figure 18.38   *Cross sections illustrating differences in soils from the coast of California to the Sierra Nevada.*

to flooding by streams from the Sierra Nevada. Through frequent wetting and drying, the soils have accumulated soluble salts and local salt crusts.

Eastward the land is better drained. It rises to roughly 600 feet in altitude at the foot of the Sierra Nevada and consists of low ridges and broad valleys. The surface deposits are fan gravels and alluvium whose soils, other than those in the valley bottoms, are planosols, related to the Prairie Soils (Table 6.1) but having well-defined clayey hardpans. These are acid soils. The surface layers, about 5 inches thick, are brown and contain little organic matter. The subsoil is lighter in color and is compact and clayey. One to 3½ feet below the surface is brownish-red hardpan cemented with iron and silica. Some of these soils must be as old as late Pleistocene.

On the western slope of the Sierra Nevada, as on the western slope of the Cascades, there is a lower belt of ancient soils and an upper belt of young soils. The younger soils, Gray-Brown Podzols, occur on the higher parts of the Sierra that were subjected to glacial erosion or intensive frost action during late Pleistocene time. They are only a foot or two thick, with an ashy-gray leached layer over a compact and gray-brown subsoil. The ancient soils, Red and Yellow Pod-

Figure 18.39   *The ground in much of the Coast Ranges is unstable, and slides are numerous each winter when the rains come. In summer, the same ground becomes parched dry and is subject to brush fires. This scene is in the Berkeley Hills, between Orinda and Oakland, California. [Photograph by Bill Young, courtesy of the San Francisco Chronicle.]*

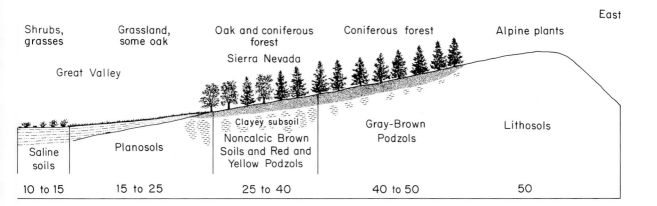

zols and noncalcic Brown Soils, occur in a belt along the foot of the mountains. These soils are red-brown clay and may be many feet deep. The parent materials are the granitic or volcanic rocks. All these soils have thin surface layers of forest litter.

Glaciers, Rivers, and Lakes

Glaciers—relicts from the Pleistocene ice ages—and perennial snow and ice cover the greater part of the Coast Ranges of Canada and Alaska, and about 500 square miles of the high parts of the Sierra Nevada, the Cascades, and the Olympic Mountains. Ice is most extensive on Mount Rainier, in the Northern Cascades, and on the Olympic Mountains. Both areas are preserved as national parks. The lower limit of perennial snow and ice, controlled both by temperature and precipitation, is determined by the relative rates of accumulation and removal, the chief modes of removal being melting and evaporation. In the Sierra Nevada the lower limit is around 12,000 feet but varies with the exposure; in the Northern Cascades the limit is perhaps 8,000 feet, although at Mount Rainer glacial tongues extend down the valleys to about 4,500 feet. During the glacial periods the lower limit of perennial snow and ice was about 5,000 feet lower than it is today, and the glaciers extended correspondingly farther down the valleys. Pleistocene glaciers also devel-

oped on some of the southern ranges, such as the San Bernardino Mountains. In Pleistocene time, the area covered by snow and ice in the Pacific Mountain System was probably a hundred times greater than it is today.

Along with the southward decrease in snow and ice in the mountains, there is a corresponding southward decrease in the size of the streams discharging from the mountains. No large rivers drain from the southern 250 miles of the Pacific Mountains (Fig. 18.40; see also Fig. 5.1). North of the latitude of San Francisco, however, large streams are the rule; such rivers as the Sacramento, Klamath, and Willamette are larger than the Colorado River, although they are short and drain small areas.

Lakes are numerous in the Cascades and in the Sierra Nevada. Many of the glacial cirques contain lakes, and other lakes are formed by morainal dams. One of the largest is Lake Chelan in Washington, which is contained by a morainal dam. The dam is east of the mountain front, and the lake, which is 65 miles long, extends far back into the glaciated valley in the mountains. The altitude of the lake surface is almost 1,100 feet, but the lake is 1,400 feet deep, and its bottom is below sea level. Most of the great depth is due to glacial gouging, but it may have been lowered too by the northward tilting that drowned the northern part of the Puget Trough (p. 594).

Among the high-altitude lakes in the Cascade Range is Crater Lake (altitude 6,239 feet), which

Figure 18.40 *Discharge of principal California Rivers (millions of acre feet per year).*

has had a complex history involving both volcanism and glaciation (Fig. 18.15,D). Lake Tahoe, in the Sierra Nevada, is at about the same altitude as Crater Lake. It was formed when its valley was dammed by a lava flow, but its history is complicated by glaciation too. Yosemite Lake, in the bottom of Yosemite Valley, is also dammed by a moraine.

Water-power resources of the Pacific Mountains are considerable, and, combined with the tremendous hydroelectric power resources along the Columbia, Snake, and Colorado rivers, amount to more than half the total water-power resources of the United States.

Fish and Wildlife

Fish and wildlife were the first resources to be exploited in the Pacific Northwest. Astoria, Ore-

gon, was founded in 1811 by the Pacific Fur Company. Large game included elk, deer, and bear. Smaller game included beaver, badger, mink, weasel, raccoon, and various rabbits. Among the predatory animals were timber wolf, mountain lion, wild cat, red fox, and coyote. Fur trading declined after 1840, and about 50 years later fishing became a major industry.

Best known of the Pacific Coast fish is the amazing salmon, which leaves the sea in breeding season and ascends the rivers for hundreds of miles. The favorite variety is the sockeye (red) salmon, which commonly weighs 5 pounds. It is most abundant in the north. Another favorite is the chinook (king) salmon, which commonly weighs 25 pounds and may reach 100 pounds. It was common along the Columbia River and its tributaries, but has been decreasing since the construction of the many dams that obstruct its migration upstream. Other varieties are the chum, pink, and silver salmon, all mostly around 5 pounds. The Indians who lived on salmon preserved their fish by drying them. During the 1830's the white settlers began preserving fish by salting them in kegs; canning was started during the 1860's.

Marine environments along the Pacific Coast, like those along the Atlantic (p. 245), are zoned latitudinally and at right angles to the shore. The boundary between the northern and southern faunas, the analogue of Cape Cod, is near Point Conception.

Off the northern Pacific Coast the most important fisheries are for salmon, flounder, halibut, albacore (tuna), crab, and rockfish. Other northern fishes are two trout (close relatives of the salmon) that also live in the ocean and ascend the rivers to spawn. These are the steelhead, an ocean-dwelling rainbow trout, and the dolly varden. Other fish are the mackerel, smelt, and candlefish, so named because it was used by Indians as a source for fuel oil. Shad, a herring, was introduced to the Pacific Coast in about 1870 and has become a major commercial fish. Marine mammals of the northern fauna include the northern sea lion, Alaska fur seal, and sea otter.

Along the southern Pacific Coast the principal

commercial fish are pilchard (sardines), tuna, and mackerel. Other fishes characteristic of the southern coast are the striped marlin (300 to 400 pounds), giant sea bass, skipjacks, anchovies, and the shell fish abalone. With these live the California sea lion, Guadalupe fur seal, and elephant seal—all mammals.

Of the total quantity of Pacific Coast fish produced annually, about 1½ billion pounds, more than half are sardines.

Some Resource Problems— Exemplified by California

During the 1850's, the decade following the discovery of gold in California, that state's population grew at the rate of 50,000 per year. A hundred years later, during the 1950's, the increase in population averaged 10 times the earlier rate. The 1950 population of California was about 10 million; in 1960 it was about 15 million. The present California growth rate is about twice the growth rate of China or India.

With increased population atmospheric pollution must increase except as drastic means are taken to minimize the causes. So it may be said:

Once upon a time there was an idyllic land of beautiful mountains beside the sea. It had clear streams and brooks with trout and salmon, and blue skies bright with sunshine. It was called California. The people who lived there bragged about their environment and derided the crowded, dirty, noisy, smog-ridden cities at the other side of the continent. They so advertised the blessings of California that many people and industries moved there. California then became the most populated state in the nation, and now it too is crowded, dirty, noisy, and smog-ridden. The man-made smog problem still awaits solution.

California's farms, forests, fisheries, and hydroelectric plants can, however, continue or even increase their present high rate of productivity. Oil and gas production will continue at a high level for a long time to come, but the petroleum supply sooner or later will be depleted. Offshore fields may become the chief sources of the future.

WATER SUPPLIES—AND LAND SUBSIDENCE

The Pacific Mountain System in British Columbia, Washington, Oregon, and northern California has plentiful water. Water problems there are due to pollution and floods, not to inadequate supply. In quality, the water is some of the best, with total dissolved solids generally less than 100 ppm and hardness less than 10.

Because California receives most of its rainfall in winter rather than during the growing season, crops have to be irrigated. The southern provinces are short of water, the annual precipitation is deficient and the seasonal distribution unfavorable. Total annual requirements exceed 2 million acre feet, and about half of this must be brought long distances. The imported supplies are obtained from the Colorado River (about 600,000 acre feet in 1960). Canals are being constructed to transport water from the northern rivers to the southern provinces.

Not only is water scarce in the southern provinces, but the local supplies are not of good quality. Well water with 650 ppm of dissolved solids and a hardness of almost 400 is used by some cities in the Los Angeles Basin. Figure 18.41 shows the differences in the quality of water from various sources in the basin.

Besides canals, the water needs may be met by desalinization of sea water, for the populous areas are only a little above sea level. Desalinization of sea water, already technologically feasible, will become economically feasible when there is great enough demand.

The Great Valley of California contains huge supplies of groundwater, which are especially important in the San Joaquin Valley, where surface-water supplies are small. The Great Valley is a structural valley that began forming during the Cretaceous as an embayment of the Pacific Ocean. It gradually filled with clay, silt, sand, and gravel, and the sea was expelled. Freshwater sediments, laid down on top of the older marine ones, are porous and saturated with groundwater supplied by Sierran rivers. In pre-Spanish days the valley contained extensive marshes and two

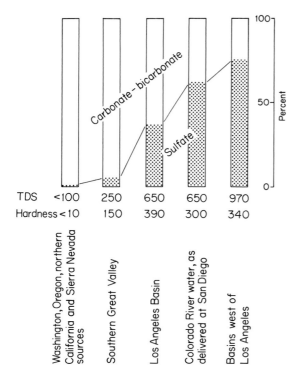

Figure 18.41 *Diagram illustrating differences in quality of water used for municipal supplies in various parts of the Pacific Mountain System. The chloride content is generally less than 10 percent and is not included. Compare Figure 5.18.*

lakes, Kern and Buena Vista lakes, in which the water table was above the ground surface. As this highly productive agricultural land became more settled and developed, increasing numbers of water wells were drilled and the water table was lowered. The lakes have dried. A crisis began developing about 1946, and in the 10 years since then the amount of water pumped from the underground reservoir has increased fourfold to more than 2 million acre-feet annually, and the water table in places has been lowered more than 100 feet.

Besides exhausting the water supply, this pumpage causes the land to settle, and to the degree that it settles, the sediments become more compacted and incapable of holding as much groundwater as they formerly contained. The underground reservoir becomes smaller.

The problem reaches beyond the Great Valley. In the Santa Clara Valley (Fig. 18.42), with-

drawals of groundwater increased fourfold from 1920 to 1960. The pumpage amounting to 180,000 acre-feet per year in the 1960's, has caused the artesian pressure head to fall as much as 250 feet, and the ground at San Jose by 1967 had subsided 8 feet. This compaction has caused a volume loss in the groundwater reservoir that amounts to 500,000 acre-feet. At the south end of San Francisco Bay this subsidence has amounted to 4 feet and has necessitated construction of levees to prevent flooding of bayshore land.

If misery loves company, Californians can cite similar land subsidence problems at Houston, Texas, Mexico City, Venice, Italy, and at Osaka and Tokyo, Japan.

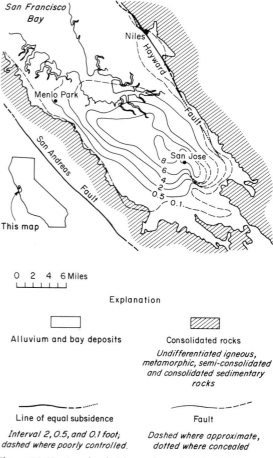

Figure 18.42 *Land subsidence from 1934 to 1967, Santa Clara Valley, California [Modified from an open-file map of the U.S. Geological Survey.]*

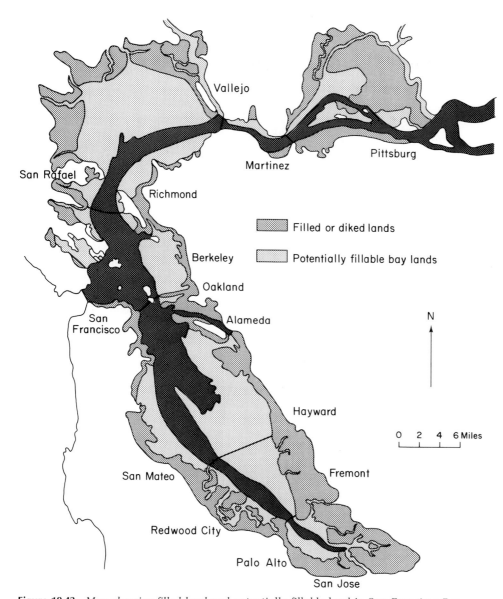

Figure 18.43 *Map showing filled land and potentially fillable land in San Francisco Bay.*

SAN FRANCISCO BAY — TO SAVE OR
NOT TO SAVE

Some of the environmental problems concerning Chesapeake, Delaware, and other bays along the Atlantic seaboard were discussed in Chapter 10. The Pacific Coast has its problems too, notably at San Francisco Bay (Fig. 18.43). In 1850, when Californians were interested chiefly in

gold, San Francisco Bay (including San Pablo and Suisun bays) totaled about 680 square miles. Since then, 280 square miles around the shores have been diked off from open water or filled in, with trash and dry fill, to make land for airports, freeways, industrial developments, apartments, and housing tracts. Thus what was once marshland (haven for ducks, but also haven for mosquitoes) is now valuable real estate. This is known as "reclamation."

Of the remaining 400 square miles of water surface, slightly more than half is less than 12 feet deep and has been described by the Army's Corps of Engineers as "susceptible of reclamation," or filling. If that land were to be filled, the Bay would consist of only 187 square miles, and in some places it would be little more than a river. As the San Francisco Bay Conservation and Development Commission has expressed it, "You'll wonder where the water went if you fill the Bay with sediment." Fortunately, too, for San Francisco Bay, the Corps of Engineers has claimed jurisdiction over all tidelands below mean high tide, and diking or filling in those areas can now be done only by permit. Granting of permits is not automatic, but follows public notice and consideration of environmental impact. It is hoped that similar consideration will be given to tidelands elsewhere—for example, along the Atlantic and Gulf coasts.

Unlike the bays on the Atlantic seaboard, San Francisco Bay lies within the jurisdiction of but one state. However, the shores are in nine counties crowded with 15 municipalities, and a development that one municipality might wish may be injurious to a neighboring one. About a quarter of the Bay bottom is privately owned, another quarter owned by the municipalities or other local governmental units, the state owns about 50 percent and the Federal government about 5 percent. The problem, of course, is to devise a mechanism for developing the Bay as a unit in order to reconcile conflicting interests. Steps have been taken to develop such planning, by creating a Bay Commission for that purpose. Another recent step forward was the creation of the San Francisco Bay National Wildlife Refuge in the southern part of the bay; most of the salt ponds there now lie in the refuge.

The conflicting interests around San Francisco Bay uses include (see also p. 245):

1. Port development for shipping.

2. Water-related industrial development, such as manufacturing.

3. Water-related recreational development.

4. Airport and freeway development.

Filling the Bay, or even diking, destroys tidal zone habitat. The estuarine zone, where salt water mingles with fresh water, is this earth's most biologically productive acreage. It is a complex system contributing to life both on land and in the sea. A highway on solid fill rather than on pilings interferes with the tidal zone as effectively as a dike at a salt pond.

Filling the Bay increases the difficulty of combating the increasing problem of water pollution. Most of the municipal, industrial, and agricultural wastes now going into the Bay are treated before being discharged, and San Francisco Bay is now freer of pollution than most other waterways. The problem of disposing of increasing amounts of waste becomes aggravated, however, if the volume and surface area of the bay are reduced.

Filling the Bay can seriously affect the weather in the Bay area. The daily tidal flow is $3\frac{1}{2}$ times the daily discharge of the Mississippi River, and this serves as an air conditioning system. Reducing the volume of water and extent of its surface adversely affects the system and increases the frequency and intensity of temperature-inversions which are the prime causes of air pollution and smog.

The fill in the Bay rests on bay muds, and is not safe ground in the event of earthquakes. By anticipating the hazard, the risk to life and property can be minimized, but the geological setting is very much like that at Anchorage, Alaska, where block after block of buildings slid toward Cook Inlet because of an unstable clay subbase.

Another problem at San Francisco Bay concerns the extensive diked areas that make up salt ponds. Much salt is produced there by evaporation. Salt ponds maintain the water surface and help maintain the natural air conditioning; the problem here relates to the future use of that wet land when salt production becomes uneconomical. It has been pointed out that buying the land and returning it to the Bay represents California's last opportunity to enlarge the Bay rather than shrink it.

The San Francisco Bay metropolitan area has a population approaching 5 million. In another 25 or 30 years the population may be twice that, which means doubling the demand for public parks, beaches, fishing piers, hiking pathways and other playgrounds. At the present time only 10 to 15 miles of the 275-mile shoreline around the Bay is permanently open to the public.

MINERAL RESOURCES

One of the significant events in United States history, and certainly one the most colorful, was the discovery of gold in California in 1848. Until that time, settlement and development of the Pacific mountains and valleys had been slow; when gold was discovered the westward trickle of emigration became a flood.

Only minor deposits of gold had been worked in California while it was part of Mexico. In January 1848, less than two weeks before the signing of the Treaty of Guadalupe Hildalgo, James W. Marshall discovered gold in a sawmill flume near Sacramento. Within a year the rush was on. The discovery of gold in California and the subsequent discovery of silver in Nevada greatly increased interest in all minerals. Prior to those discoveries iron and lead were the only industrial metals of importance in United States commerce. The importance of the precious metals, gold and silver, in the national economy of that period is illustrated perhaps by the fact that our first mineral resources inventory was sponsored by the Treasury Department.

The principal California lode gold deposits are in the Mother Lode belt near the western foot of the Sierra Nevada. This belt is about a mile wide and about 100 miles long. The productive ground consists of quartz veins in steeply dipping slates and altered volcanic rocks of late Paleozoic and Jurassic age. The ore consists of native gold and gold-bearing pyrite accompanied by minor other sulfides. A total of about $2 billion in gold has been produced, about three-quarters from placers and the remainder from lode mines, some of which are about a mile deep.

The discovery of gold contributed to the development of quicksilver deposits in the Pacific Mountains, because quicksilver was used for recovering gold by amalgamation. The highest production came from the New Almaden mine, south of San Francisco Bay. The mine, named after Almaden, Spain, which has the world's richest deposits of quicksilver, was first opened in 1845. The New Almaden mine has produced a third of the total production of the United States. The mercury occurs as cinnabar (mercury sulfide) accompanied by metallic mercury and various sulfides of iron, copper, lead, and antimony.

California, our second largest oil-producing state, has numerous productive fields in the San Joaquin Valley, Los Angeles Basin, and Coast Ranges. Most of the production has come from Miocene and Pliocene formations, but the Eocene and Cretaceous deposits also contain petroleum. The state's first oil well, drilled by hand in 1875 to a depth of 30 feet at a tar pool near Los Angeles, produced for more than half a century!

The oil fields in the Los Angeles Basin are aligned along northwest-trending zones (Fig. 18.44). In the San Joaquin Valley the principal fields produce from anticlines and other structures along the valley, especially near the foot of the Coast Ranges. Other fields are located along the coast northwest of Los Angeles.

Figure 18.44 *Oil fields in the Los Angeles Basin are aligned along the northwest-trending zones. The Wilmington field has dropped below sea level because of oil withdrawals.*

Other mineral production in the Pacific Mountains has been comparatively minor. Mines in British Columbia have produced copper, silver, and zinc; copper has been produced in Washington, and a large deposit in the Northern Cascades has been the subject of controversy between those who would keep that country as wilderness and those who would mine the copper. Gold accompanied by silver, copper, and lead has been produced in the Klamath Mountains and Northern Cascades. From the Tertiary formations, in California, there has been production of diatomite, glass sand, and clay. Coal has been produced chiefly in Washington.

OIL SPILLS

In January of 1969, Santa Barbara, California, became the focal point of a major confrontation between the extremists who would preserve the environment by forbidding any mineral production that might be at all hazardous to the environment and those who would produce a mineral resource regardless of such possible hazard. The issue developed when oil began escaping from an offshore well on federal land in the Santa Barbara Channel, part of a tract that had been leased a year before to twenty-six oil companies for a total of $603,000,000. Gas began escaping from one of the wells at the platform and with it was crude oil with a flow estimated by the company (probably conservatively) at 500 barrels (21,000 gallons) a day. It took 10 days to plug the well, and by that time not less than a quarter of a million gallons of oil had spilled to the surface. In the next week or two, other breaks occurred in relief wells drilled in an attempt to relieve the pressure and in fissures near the platform. More oil flowed to the surface.

The oil slick spread in great streams northward to the beaches and marinas at Santa Barbara, southward to the Channel Islands, east-ward along the coast to Santa Monica, and westward around Point Conception. Attempts were made to contain the slick with log booms, by spraying with chemical dispersants, by pumping the oil into tank trucks, and by spreading straw on the oil, which could be gathered up after it had soaked up oil. Much of the oil was picked up by birds and various shore organisms—sand fleas, sand crabs, red worm, and shell fish, large numbers of which were killed. Seals on Santa Cruz Island apparently stayed ashore while the oil slick was there, and seem to have escaped unharmed. Citizens of Santa Barbara were outraged.

The issue is not peculiar to Santa Barbara; it is general, and concerns such pipelines as the Alaska pipeline, oceanic transport of petroleum, locations of refineries, locations of nuclear power plants, ways and means of disposing of atomic wastes, strip mining, lumbering, and pulp mills—in fact almost any kind of industrial development. Surely the answer is not "either, or." The choice between black and white in a real world is not always possible, and as populations explode we need increasingly to preserve our natural environment while at the same time we need to increase utilization of our energy resources. Seventy-five percent of tonnage shipped and received at California ports is petroleum or petroleum products, so the risk of oil spill is not confined to Santa Barbara. Confronted with such risks, should we close the harbors?

The outraged people in Santa Barbara and elsewhere have become accustomed to central heating, washing machines, dishwashers, even air conditioners, and a host of other energy driven appliances. Somehow we have to find the way to utilize our energy resources while protecting against the kind of castastrophe that struck Santa Barbara channel in January 1969. We want fire for warmth, but we have fire departments for the times when a fire gets out of control.

References

Anderson, C. A., 1941, Volcanoes of the Medicine Lake Highland, California: Univ. Calif. Dept. Geol. Sci., Bull. v. 25, pp. 347–422.

Bakker, Elna, 1971, An island called California: An introduction to its natural communities: Berkeley, Univ. California Press.

California Div. Mines, 1948, The Mother Lode Country: San Francisco, Calif. Div. Mines Bull. 141.

————, 1951, San Francisco Bay counties guidebook: San Francisco, Calif. Div. Mines Bull. 154.

————, 1954, Geology of southern California: San Francisco, Calif. Div. Mines Bull. 170, Ten chapters and Five guidebooks.

Crowell, J. C., 1962, Displacement along the San Andreas fault, California: Geol. Soc. America Spec. Paper 71.

Gilbert, G. K., 1917, Hydraulic mining debris in the Sierra Nevada: U.S. Geol. Survey Prof. Paper 160.

Irwin, W. P., 1960, Geologic reconnaissance of the northern Coast Ranges and Klamath Mountains, California, with a summary of the mineral resources: San Francisco, Calif. Div. Mines Bull. 179.

Douglas, R. J. W., and others, 1968, Geology of western Canada, in Geology and Economic Minerals of Canada: Canada Geol. Survey, pp. 365–488.

Jepson, W. L., 1951, A manual of the flowering plants of California: Berkeley, Univ. California Press.

Lawson, A. C., 1914, San Francisco folio: U.S. Geol. Survey Folio 193.

Little, H. W., and others, 1968, Economic minerals of western Canada, in Geology and economic minerals of Canada: Canada Geol. Survey, pp. 489–546.

Mackin, J. H., and Cary, A. S., 1965, Origin of the Cascade landscapes: Wash. Div. of Mines and Geol. Inf. Circular 41.

Matthes, F. E., 1930, Geologic history of the Yosemite Valley: U.S. Geol. Survey Prof. Paper 160.

McKee, Bates, 1971, Cascadia—The geologic evolution of the Pacific Northwest: New York, McGraw-Hill.

Oakeshott, G. B., 1971, California's changing landscape—a guide to the geology of the state: New York, McGraw-Hill.

Reed, R. D., 1951, Geology of California: Tulsa, Oklahoma, Am. Assoc. Petrol. Geologists.

Snavely, Parke D., Jr., and Wagner, H. C., 1963, Tertiary geologic history of western Oregon and Washington: Wash. Div. Mines and Geol. Investigations No. 22.

Sunset Staff and Iacopi, R., 1971, Earthquake country: Menlo Park, California, Lane Book Co.

Woodring, W. P., and others, 1940, Geology of the Kettleman Hills oil field, California: Stratigraphy, paleontology, and structure: U.S. Geol. Survey Prof. Paper 195.

————, 1946, Geology and paleontology of the Palos Verdes Hills, Calif., U.S. Geol. Survey Prof. Paper 207.

Williams, Howel, 1932, Geology of the Lassen Peak Volcanic National Park, Calif.: Univ. California Dept. Geol. Sci. Bull. v. 21, pp. 195–385.

————, 1941, Crater Lake—the story of its origin: Berkeley, Univ. California Press. (Also available as Carnegie Inst. Wash. Publ. 540.)

————, 1948, Ancient volcanoes of Oregon: Eugene, Ore., Univ. Oregon Press, Condon Lecture Publ.

Snowfields above the head of a valley glacier in Alaska. Although Alaska has spectacular mountains and alpine glaciers, less than half the state was glaciated during the Pleistocene. [U.S. Air Force photo.]

19

....

ALASKA, AND CANADA WEST OF THE MACKENZIE RIVER—FRONTIER LAND

Alaska (Fig. 19.1,A) covers an area of 586,000 square miles, almost one-fifth that of the United States (Fig. 19.2). In Canada, the Yukon Territory and Northwest Territories eastward to the Mackenzie River (Fig. 19.1,B) embrace about 175,000 square miles. The population in these parts is scanty. In 1970 only five towns, all of them in Alaska, had populations greater than 5,000. The total population of Alaska and the two Canadian territories is less than 350,000, less than the number of people crowded into the inner parts of the average industrial city.

The vast terrain is highly varied but can be divided into eight physiographic provinces:

1. Southeastern panhandle of Alaska and Coast Mountains of Canada, included in Chapter 18; a mountainous coastal area with numerous islands and fjords.

2. South-central Alaska; a coastal and inland belt consisting of arcuate mountains and lowlands that curve around the Gulf of Alaska.

3. Alaska Peninsula and Aleutian Islands; the southwestern panhandle of Alaska, formed by a volcanic arc and bordered on the south by the Aleutian Trench, an active, present-day geosyncline.

4. Yukon Basin: includes the plateaus and lowlands along the Yukon River and its tributaries, the delta, the Kilbuck-Kuskokwim Mountains, some mountain ranges in the Yukon Territory, and the Tintina and Shakwak Trenches.

5. Seward Peninsula and Bering Coast Uplands: a roughly dissected plateau with low mountains, forming a projection westward to Bering Strait.

6. Brooks Range and mountains extending eastward into Yukon Territory.

7. Arctic Slope, the coastal plain bordering the Arctic Ocean, including the Mackenzie River delta and plains bordering the Mackenzie River.

8. Mackenzie Mountains and neighboring ranges in the Yukon.

Looking at the region as a whole, its outstanding features include its:

1. Great relief. Mount McKinley (altitude 20,300 feet) is the highest point in North America; the Aleutian Trench (Fig. 19.3), 25,000 feet below sea level, is the lowest continental edge of North America.

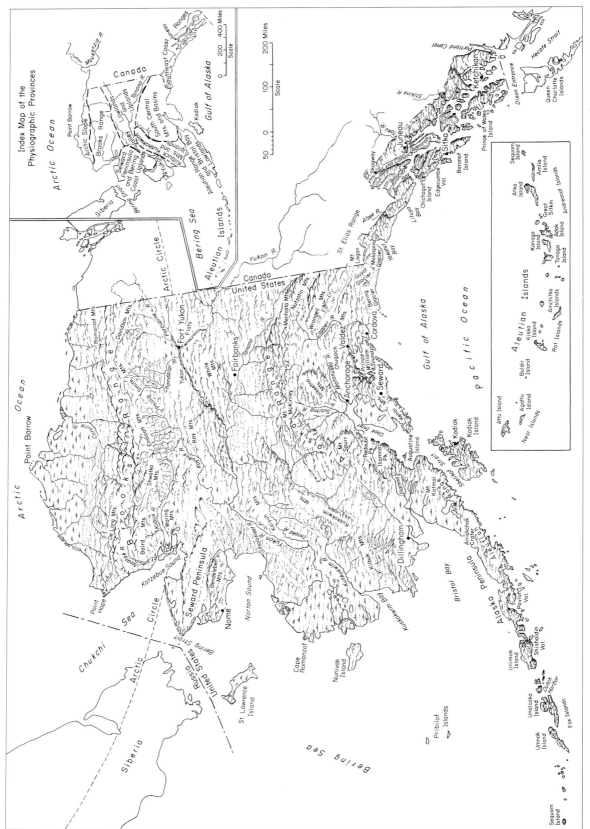

Index Map of the
Physiographic Provinces

A

Figure 19.1 *Physiographic map of Alaska (A) and the Yukon Territory (B).*

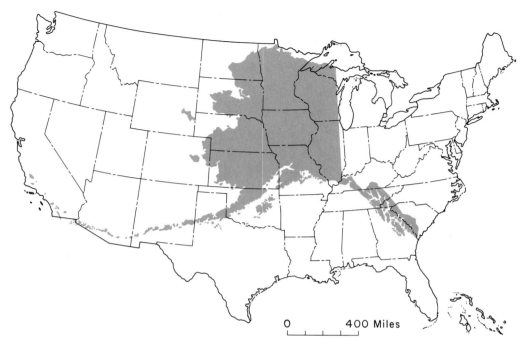

Figure 19.2 *Alaska is immense, far bigger than little old Texas. If Alaska were moved a bit, and oriented as shown here, with Point Barrow occupying the position of Lake of the Woods, the southeastern tip of the Panhandle would be at the mouth of the Savannah River, and the westernmost Aleutian Island would be west of Los Angeles. [After U.S.G.S.]*

2. Hundreds of volcanoes.

3. Thousands of glaciers. One, the Malaspina, is larger than the state of Rhode Island. Glacier Bay in Southeastern Alaska is a national monument—a fjord with glaciers at the head.

4. Vast extent of permanently frozen ground, perhaps as much as 350,000 square miles.

5. Extreme range of climate. The southern coast, warmed by the Kuroshio (Japan) Current, rarely has temperatures below 0°F, but winter lows in the interior may reach 78°F below zero and summer highs 100°F above. The southeast coast, one of the rainiest parts of the continent, receives more than 150 inches annually; the Arctic slope, one of the driest, receives less than 5 inches.

6. Frequent and severe earthquakes along the south coast, sometimes accompanied by giant waves.

Other outstanding features are the mosquitoes and bear stories. Alaskans make fun at the small size of Texas. A burger shop advertises Alaskan-size burgers at 50¢ and Texas-size burgers at 15¢.

The principal industry is fishing, especially for salmon, halibut, and herring. Mining, particularly of gold, was important in the past, but activity is now slight. Southeast Alaska contains large forest resources. Lumber production has been slight, but there are large pulp mills near Ketchikan and Sitka. The inside passage makes travel to and from Seattle easy. The Alaska Highway crosses the southern Yukon Territory to Whitehorse and continues west to the Tanana River valley and to Fairbanks.

South-central Alaska holds about half of the region's population. The economy includes farming as well as fishing, oil production, and mining. Production of oil on the Kenai Peninsula is the most important effort in the minerals field. Coal is mined, and there has been mining for gold, silver, copper, chromite, fluorspar, and zinc.

Valdez is destined to become an important shipping center when (and if) the Alaska pipeline is constructed. The plan is to move oil by pipeline from the big fields on the Arctic Slope to Valdez and to ship oil by tankers from there. Rivers draining the Alaska Range are large, but are swift and turbulent and only the lower courses are navigable. At the heads of the rivers, passes across the Alaska Range provide access to the Yukon River Basin.

The Alaska Peninsula and Aleutian Islands are thinly populated. They have a rich fauna of fish, sea fowl, and fur-bearing animals, especially seal, sea otter, and blue fox. Report of these by the explorer Bering caused the Siberian fur hunters and fishermen to move eastward into Alaska, bringing it under Russian control. Hunting, fishing, and domestic raising of fox have been major economic activities. Agriculture and mining have not been important.

Despite the lack of population, this area poses knotty international problems. Is the Bering Sea beyond the 12-mile limit a part of the United States, or is it part of the Pacific and, therefore, international water? The United States owns the islands, which are the home of the fur seals, but does it own the seals when they go to sea? The questions still are not resolved, but conservation of the resources is greatly improved as a result of international agreements beginning with the Bering Sea Arbitration in 1893. Still to be settled is the question of national ownership and regulation of activities over the continental shelf areas, not only off the coast of Alaska but off all coasts. The shelf area in the Bering Sea is more than half the size of all Alaska (Fig. 19.3).

Interior Alaska holds about a quarter of the region's population, mostly in a single basin along the Tanana River near Fairbanks. In that area there is some agriculture, mostly root crops, cabbage, oats, and barley. Many thousands of square miles in the other basins also are suitable for agriculture, but they are not likely to be developed until the markets expand and the trans-

Figure 19.3 *Altitudes in Alaska. Note the scale. The Coastal Plain at Point Barrow is as wide as the Atlantic Coastal Plain, and the delta of the Yukon is about twice as large as the delta of the Mississippi River!*

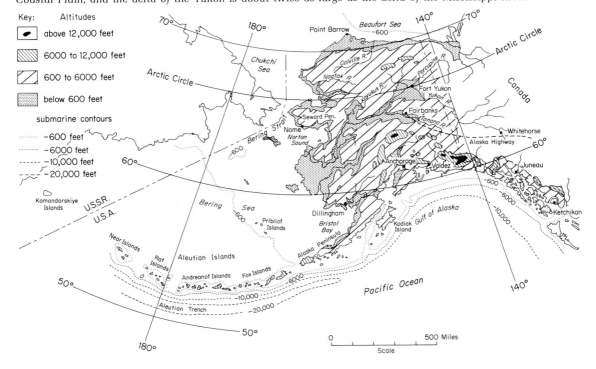

portation system is extended. Fur animals are raised, and there is hunting for big game. The region has produced much gold; the Fairbanks area alone has produced a third of Alaska's placer gold. There are important reserves of antimony, mercury, and tungsten, and some silver and molybdenum. Along the coast fishing is important; Bristol Bay has been one of the world's foremost fishing centers, and has contributed a major part of Alaska's salmon pack.

The Seward Peninsula and Bering Coast Uplands are thinly populated. Nome, the principal town, had a population of 2,300 in 1960. For eight months of the year Nome and the surrounding area are frozen in and inaccessible to shipping.

The Arctic Slope is even more thinly populated. It is free of ice and open to shipping only about one month each year, but it is of economic interest because of its oil and gas reserves, especially at Prudhoe Bay. It is also the breeding ground for many species of wild fowl. This area is a long way from the Gulf of Mexico, but many of the fowl that breed along the Arctic Slope of Alaska winter along the shores of the Gulf of Mexico.

When Alaska was made a state in 1959, only 0.2 percent of the land was privately owned. Alaska was allowed 25 years to select more than 100 million acres from the public domain—an action that has a parallel in the cessation of the Northwest Territories to the federal government by the original states. Eskimos and Indians, however, are objecting to the selection of lands by the State by pressing their rights to vast tracts that include much of the Yukon Flats and the oil-rich Arctic Slope.

The controversial Alaska pipeline would extend 600 miles southward from Prudhoe Bay on the Arctic Coast to the port of Valdez on the Gulf of Alaska. Because the route crosses permanently frozen ground on the Arctic Slope and in the Brooks Range, the engineering problems posed by a heated pipeline in frozen ground are major. Large rivers in the Yukon Basin require bridges, and the pipeline must cross active faults at the base of and in the mountain ranges of south-central Alaska. At the harbor at Valdez, as much

as possible of the terminal facilities must be constructed above the reach of the tsunamis that threaten that coast.

Structural Framework and Topography

RELATION TO CONTINENTAL STRUCTURES

The plains, mountains, and plateaus west of the Mackenzie River adjoin the Great Plains, which extend southward 2,500 miles from the Arctic Ocean to the Rio Grande. The Mackenzie River is only 200 miles west of the Canadian Shield. The craton ends at the river; to the west are mountains and plateaus composed of highly folded and faulted geosynclinal formations. A cross section of these mountains and plateaus is rather like a cross section of the Coast Mountains farther south (Fig. 19.4), and the geological history is similar.

Along the coast are tightly folded Paleozoic eugeosynclinal rocks consisting of graywacke, argillite, conglomerate, and basaltic and andesitic lava flows and tuffs, quite like the eugeosynclinal formations southwest of the Coast Mountains in the Alaska Panhandle (Chapter 18). Moreover, they are intruded by granite batholiths, mostly of Cretaceous age but some Tertiary. Batholithic rocks are relatively less abundant than they are to the south.

North of the Alaska Range is the Yukon Plateau, whose rocks and structure are like those of the intermontane plateaus between the Coast Mountains and Canadian Rockies. The rocks include Precambrian, Paleozoic, and early Mesozoic eugeosynclinal formations. Northward, in the Brooks Range, the Paleozoic and younger formations become miogeosynclincal, and they are overlain by miogeosynclinal Cretaceous formations. The older rocks are thrust northward onto the Cretacous (Fig. 19.4), in much the same way as those in the Canadian Rockies. These miogeosynclinal formations extend northward under the Arctic Slope and overlap a stable shelf at the Arctic Platform (Fig. 19.4).

North of the Arctic Slope is continental shelf, barely 100 miles wide, and mostly less than 200 feet deep. It breaks off under the Beaufort Sea to an abyssal plain more than 2 miles deep. This plain has been variously interpreted as a fragmented and sunken block of shield rocks and as a segment of oceanic crust.

Off the Pacific Coast, the structure also differs from that of the Coast Mountains because of the broad continental shelf in the Gulf of Alaska; beyond the shelf is the active Aleutian Trench. Both the Arctic Shelf and the shelf under the Gulf of Alaska are mantled by Tertiary and Quaternary deposits.

SOUTHEASTERN COAST MOUNTAINS

The Southeastern Coast Mountains of Alaska have been described with the Coast Mountains of British Columbia as part of the Pacific Coast System (Chapter 18).

GLACIERED COAST

North of Glacier Bay the uplift increases at the St. Elias Mountains, where several peaks are higher than 15,000 feet; Mount Logan, in the Yukon Territory, is nearly 20,000 feet high. Rivers are few; most precipitation is snow, which discharges as glacial ice. The system of glaciers in this province so completely covers the ground that not much is known about the geologic structure. Along the coast are Tertiary formations, and, toward the west, they have yielded some petroleum.

One river, the Alsek, crosses the St. Elias Mountains, providing a drainage anomaly as baffling as the Taku and Stikine, which cross the Coast Mountains farther south. The river course can hardly be superimposed across so high a mountain range, nor is it likely antecedent. In the absence of evidence, it seems simplest to assume that the river was superimposed across the mountain range when it was much lower than it is now, and that the canyon has been deepened by antecedence during repeated late Tertiary and Quaternary uplift.

SOUTH-CENTRAL ALASKA

South-central Alaska (Fig. 19.5) includes the coast from the Copper River west of Shelikof Strait. Along the eastern segment are the Chugach Mountains, and farther inland the Wrangell and Talkeetna Mountains and the Alaska Range. To the west is the Aleutian Range.

The structural and topographic grain consists of a series of huge arcs around the Gulf of Alaska (Fig. 19.11), reflecting nearly parallel arcuate geosynclines of different ages. Two arcs, one represented by the Alaska Range and another by the Matanuska-Cook Inlet-Shelikof Strait, were geosynclines during most of Mesozoic time and were separated by the Talkeetna geanticline. In late Mesozoic time another geosyncline formed along the Kodiak-Kenai-Chugach Mountains arc. In Tertiary time the Alaska Range and the Kodiak-Kenai-Chugach arc were uplifted, but the Matanuska-Cook Inlet-Shelikof Strait arc remained low and was partly filled with Tertiary sediments. In late Tertiary time the Aleutian Trench developed, and during Quaternary time its eastern part, extending into the Gulf of Alaska, was largely filled with sediments.

Throughout its geologic history this section has been the center of much igneous activity, and the geosynclines include considerable volcanic sediments. In the uplifted areas, large granitic intrusions probably accompanied the uplift. Igneous activity today is represented by active volcanoes at Mount Wrangell and at a half dozen centers in the Aleutian Range north of Mount Katmai (Fig. 19.6).

The Aleutian Range, bordering Shelikof Strait and Cook Inlet, is transitional between this section and the volcanic arc that forms the Alaska Peninsula and the Aleutian Islands. The Aleutian Range is a structural uplift of Mesozoic formations and granitic intrusions and is topographically continuous with the Alaska Range. The volcanoes in the range mark the eastern end of the volcanic arc, which extends about 2,000 miles to the west.

The Tertiary formations in the structural troughs are many thousands of feet thick and

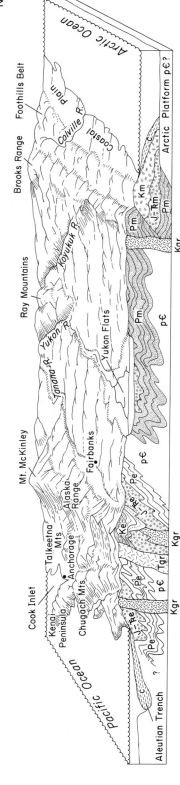

Figure 19.4 Block diagram illustrating the topography and geologic structure of Alaska. The Yukon Basin, between the Alaska and Brooks ranges, is structurally the highest part of Alaska. It exposes the oldest rocks (Precambrian, *pC*). It has been a geanticline since early Paleozoic time, separating eugeosynclinal Paleozoic (*Pe*), Jurassic-Triassic (*J-Tre*), and Cretaceous (*Ke*) formations in the south from miogeosynclinal Paleozoic (*Pm*), Jurassic-Triassic (*J-Trm*), and Cretaceous (*Km*) formations in the north. Intensity of folding and metamorphism decreases northward. Granitic batholiths were intruded in the folded belts during the Jurassic-Cretaceous (*Kgr*) and during the Tertiary (*Tgr*). Cenozoic shelf deposits (*C*) have been deposited on the coasts and continental shelfs. Not shown are the Tertiary and Quaternary volcanoes. Length of section about 700 miles.

intensely folded and faulted. They are in part coal-bearing, and where the deformation is slight, as along Cook Inlet, the coals are lignite, but where the formations are strongly folded along Matanuska Valley the coal is bituminous (Fig. 11.42).

Deformation of the structural trough at Shelikof Strait, Cook Inlet, and Susitna River is continuing, as is indicated by the frequency of severe earthquakes originating in that area (Fig. 19.12).

ALASKA PENINSULA AND ALEUTIAN ISLANDS

The Alaska Peninsula and Aleutian Islands form an arc consisting of more than 75 volcanoes, about half of which are known to have erupted during the last 200 years (Fig. 19.6). The volcanic belt extends 1,500 miles from Mount Spurr, opposite Cook Inlet, to Buldir Volcano between the Rat Islands and Near Islands.

The volcanoes are aligned along a structural uplift that plunges southwestward from the Alaska Range. The highest volcanoes are at the high, northern end of the uplift. Altitudes of the peaks decrease southwestward from 11,000 feet at Mount Spurr to 10,200 feet at Mount Redoubt, 10,000 feet at Mount Iliamna, and 7,500 feet at Mount Katmai. Most of the other volcanoes on the Peninsula are below 6,000 feet except Pavlof Volcano, which is almost 9,000 feet high. Mt. Shishaldin on Unimak Island is more than 9,000 feet in altitude, but farther west the volcanoes are lower (below 4,000 feet). Other volcanoes are submerged.

Several kinds of volcanic structures are represented along the arc. Shield volcanoes, the earliest to form, are composed of thin lava flows that spread widely and built broad, low cones. Somewhat younger than these are the steep-sided cones, composed both of lavas and of fragmental material. Some of these are still active. The superposition of steep-sided volcanoes on broad, low ones makes for a structure that is similar to that of the Cascade Mountains. Volcanic domes were formed where steep-sided, bulbous masses

of viscous lava were partly extruded at vents (Fig. 19.7). Cauldrons, formed by subsidence accompanying Peléan eruptions, are represented by Katmai and the Valley of Ten Thousand Smokes.

Mount Katmai and the nearby Valley of Ten Thousand Smokes are situated on the Alaska Peninsula at Shelikof Strait, near the southern limit of Alaska's forests. The mountain and the valley are both in the Katmai National Monument, which covers about 1,700 square miles. Katmai was inactive before 1912, but in June of that year it suddenly exploded with a Peléan eruption. An avalanche of incandescent rhyolitic pumice and glass dust erupted from swarms of fissures and poured down the Valley of Ten Thousand Smokes. All vegetation was burned by the glowing cloud; native houses were filled with pumice, and some were buried. What had been a river became a braided network of channels clogged with volcanic mud, and the wet ground under the hot layer of sand and dust erupted in millions of steam jets, some rising more than a thousand feet into the air and hundreds rising 500 feet high. The volume of volcanic mud that poured down the valley has been estimated at more than a cubic mile.

Not only was there a glowing avalanche; immediately thereafter, Katmai erupted vast quantities of pumice from the summit. The total volume of material erupted has been estimated at about 4.75 cubic miles. The rhyolitic eruption created a caldera 3 miles in diameter bounded by cliffs 3,700 feet high in what had been a cone of andesitic lavas. The original top of the cone must have been at an altitude of about 10,000 feet; the present rim of the caldera is at an altitude of 6,700 feet. Collapse of the cauldron has been attributed to melting and solution of the andesitic lava by rising rhyolitic magma. The collapse engulfed about $1\frac{1}{2}$ to 2 cubic miles of the top of the cone and beheaded several glaciers that had been there before the eruption.

The older rocks in the uplift under the volcanoes are poorly exposed along the Aleutian Islands. But the narrowness of the long volcanic belt, the frequency of earthquakes along the arc, and the fact that earthquakes along the south

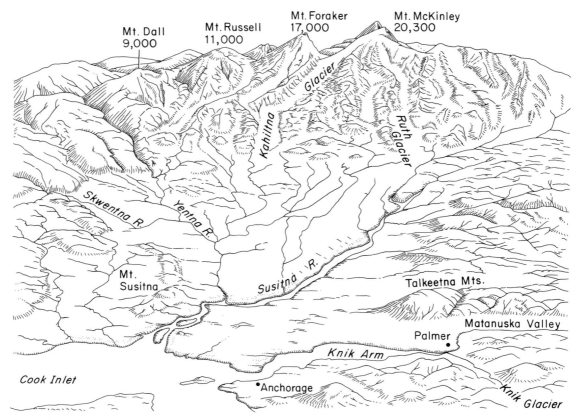

Figure 19.5 *Diagrammatic view of South-central Alaska looking from above Cook Inlet to Mount McKinley. The glaciers are small remnants of the Pleistocene ice sheet, which covered these mountains and filled the valleys, including Cook Inlet.*

side of the arc originate at shallower depths than those along the north side all suggest that the arc may represent the upper plate of a north-dipping fault whose trace is along the Aleutian Trench (Fig. 19.8).

Not much of the land on the islands or on the peninsula is level. Steep slopes prevail all the way to the water's edge. Shores are rocky and craggy (Fig. 19.9). A continental shelf borders the Alaska Peninsula and Unimak Island (Fig. 19.3), but the rest of the islands are emerged peaks on a narrow ridge that is mostly submerged. South of the islands the submarine topography to a depth of about 150 feet consists of valleys and ridges, whereas from 150 down to 325 feet the slope is smooth. This contrast in submarine topography suggests that sea level once stood about 150 feet lower than it does now. Beyond a depth

of 325 feet the slope steepens and the submarine topography suggests faulting.

The Aleutian Trench, a kind of geosyncline undergoing present-day deformation, is a deep, narrow, submarine trough south of the Aleutian Islands and Alaska Peninsula (Fig. 19.3), but becomes shallower in the Gulf of Alaska and finally disappears. This shallowing is thought to be due to filling of the trough by Quaternary sediments. The deep western part receives little sediment because the land area draining to it is small. Gravity measurements indicate that the trench is underlain by light rock between masses of heavier rock that form the higher ground on each side of the trench.

The Pribilof and other islands in the Bering Sea are, like the Aleutians, composed largely of Quaternary eruptives, but unlike the Aleutians these are isolated mountains rising from a plain—the continental shelf under the Bering Sea. The Pribilof Islands are important as the breeding ground of the Alaska fur seal. Blue and white foxes, native to these islands, are also sought for their furs.

The Aleutian Chain was discovered in 1741 by Vitus Bering. Between 15,000 and 20,000 Aleuts were distributed throughout the island arc over 1,200 miles. The coastal waters and those of the Bering Sea are highly productive, and provided the basis for their settlements. Pacific Ocean water moving northward through the straits between the islands leads to complex mixing with the Bering Sea water, including upwelling. Sea mammals, fish, and birds lived well there as did the Aleuts.

YUKON BASIN

The Yukon Basin consists of the tremendous area lying between the Alaska Range on the south and the Brooks Range and MacKenzie Mountains Region on the north. It includes most of the drainage basin of the Yukon River, one of

the world's longest rivers, which is about 2,000 miles long and is navigable by river steamer most of the way to its headwaters in Canada. Its general trend is northwest in Yukon Territory. Its altitude is only 900 feet where it enters Alaska. Its principal tributaries in Alaska are the Koyukuk, Tanana, and Porcupine rivers. In Canada it is joined by the Klondike River at Dawson, where the discovery of placer gold in 1896 led to a rush of prospectors into the region. The Kuskokwim, the other major river in the Basin, rises in the Alaska Range, flows southwest, and is navigable by steamer for about 600 miles.

The lower Yukon and lower Kuskokwim rivers, for about 150 miles, cross an extensive, low, deltaic flat containing numerous large swamps. Tidewater extends about 100 miles up the rivers. Topographically this area is like the Mississippi Delta, but is twice as large.

Upstream from the deltaic lowland the river gradients remain low; at Fort Yukon (Fig. 19.10,A) the river is little more than 400 feet above sea level; Fairbanks, on the Tanana, is 450 feet above sea level. Here the Yukon and its tributaries have cut into a dissected plateau 1,000 to 2,000 feet

Figure 19.6 *Volcanoes on the Alaska Peninsula and Aleutian Islands. Almost all these volcanoes have been active during the Holocene; about 36 have erupted since 1760.*

1. Mt. Spurr
2. Mt. Redoubt
3. Mt. Iliamna
4. Augustine Volcano
5. Mt. Douglas
6. Mt. Katmai
7. Aniakchak Crater
8. Pavlof Volcano
9. Mt. Shishaldin
10. Bogoslof Volcano
11. Great Sitkin Volcano
12. Little Sitkin Volcano

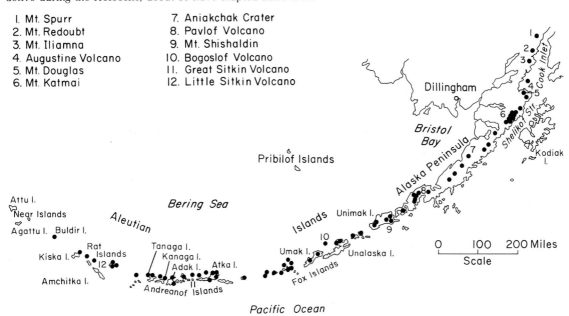

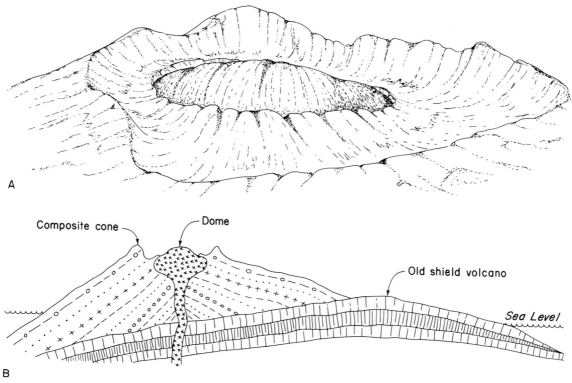

Figure 19.7 *Great Sitkin Volcano. (A) View of the crater and the basalt dome within it. The crater is about 0.75 mile in diameter and about 4,000 feet in altitude. The basaltic dome formed in 1945. (B) Cross section illustrating the structure of the Great Sitkin Volcano. Composed of lavas and volcanic ash, the volcano is built on the flank of a broad, low shield volcano of basaltic lavas. [Generalized after U.S.G.S.]*

higher than the rivers, which are in wide valleys bordered by bluffs a few hundred feet high (Fig. 19.10,B). Northward and southward from the Yukon River the plateau slopes upward and joins the bordering mountain ranges at altitudes around 3,000 or 4,000 feet. The plateau, however, is not a structural surface; it is an erosion surface that truncates complex structures in resistant Precambrian, Paleozoic, and Mesozoic eugeosynclinal rocks and granitic rocks intrusive into them: numerous monadnocks rise above its surface.

Most valleys are narrow and deeply incised into the plateau surface, but this terrain is interrupted by about a dozen structural basins, in which the rivers meander across vast flats. One of these, the Yukon Flats (Fig. 19.10,A), extends

150 miles along the river in the vicinity of Fort Yukon and covers 10,000 square miles. Downwarping of the basins began in the Tertiary and apparently continued into the Quaternary, for the basins are filled to unknown depths with glacial outwash.

During the geologic past, much of this area was geanticlinal and shed sediments northward and southward to bordering geosynclines. The southwest courses of the Kuskokwim, Koyukuk, and lower part of the Yukon rivers are controlled by southwest-trending structures inherited from two geosynclines and an intervening geanticline.

The Yukon Basin in Canada includes two great linear valleys, which are shorter but otherwise similar to the Rocky Mountain Trench. These are the Tintina and Shakwak trenches, 300 and 200 miles long, respectively. Both trend about northwest, and end near the Alaskan border. Their width varies from about 1 to 10 miles. Where narrow and straight, these are impressive structural features.

North of the Yukon Basin is the Brooks Range, which reaches altitudes of more than 8,000 feet at its eastern extreme near the Mackenzie River delta, and decreases to less than 5,000 feet altitude in the west, where it marks the boundary between a Mesozoic miogeosyncline on the north and a geanticline on the south. The Mesozoic formations thicken greatly northward from the mountains to the coast. Uplift of these old rocks formed the Brooks Range during Tertiary and Quaternary time. This uplift is separated from that at the Seward Peninsula by the Quaternary Selawik Basin.

SEWARD PENINSULA AND BERING COAST UPLANDS

The Seward Peninsula and the Bering Coast Uplands are part of an uplift that extends westward into Siberia and is breached at the Bering Strait. Uplift has been progressing for a long time;

Quaternary uplift is recorded by marine terraces of Quaternary age along the narrow coastal plain. The surface truncates complex structures in resistant Paleozoic formations and granite bodies that intrude them. It is a rough plateau, with monadnocks rising 1,500 to 2,000 feet above the general surface; steep-walled canyons have been incised into it. Most of this ground is permanently frozen.

ARCTIC SLOPE

The Arctic Slope is a nearly featureless coastal plain, which is as much as 100 miles wide and extends from the delta of the Mackenzie River westward about 750 miles to within 100 miles of Point Hope (Fig. 19.1). The plain is not much above sea level. The ground is permanently frozen to great depths. During the brief summer the surface is dotted with lakes and ponds. Point Barrow is the northernmost point in the United States; Canada's islands extend 750 miles farther north.

The Arctic Slope is underlain by Mesozoic and Paleozoic miogeosynclinal deposits that contain tremendous petroleum resources. Developing the

Figure 19.8 *Possible structure under the Aleutian Islands. Composite volcanoes of lavas and volcanic ash have built high, steep-sided cones on broad, low shield volcanoes that overlie complexly deformed Tertiary and older rocks. Earthquakes south of the islands are shallow compared to those north of the islands and are thought to identify the position of the subduction frictional zone where the basaltic oceanic crust is being dragged northward under the island arc by the mantle.*

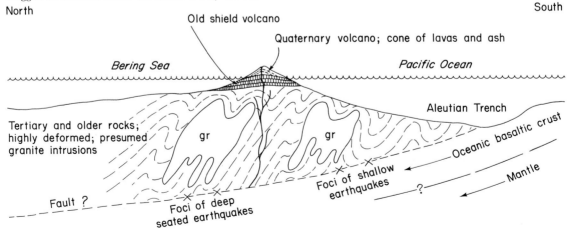

Figure 19.9 *View west of Kanaga Island, one of the Andreanof group, a typical view of the Aleutian Islands except for absence of fog. Width of foreground about 12 miles. Kanaga Volcano is a steep-sided cone, 4300 feet high, composed of lavas and volcanic ash. Round Head, at the northeast corner of the island, is an older volcano composed of basaltic lava. Its vent is submerged and lies northeast of the island; the Kanaga Volcano is built on the southwest flank of the older volcano.*

resource poses major environmental problems because of the permanently frozen ground. The ground is an enormous marsh during the summer, when the active layer of the frozen ground has melted; it freezes over again in the winter.

The Arctic Slope is a stable coast and records some changes in sea level during the past 2,000 years. Raised beaches, attributed to eustatic rise of sea level but possibly due to surges during storms, having been dated at between A.D. 265 and 500 and between A.D. 1000 and 1100. Beginning at about A.D. 500, sea level fell to about 2 meters below the present sea level, when an Eskimo town was built near sea level. It was subsequently flooded by the rise of the sea between A.D. 1000 and 1100. The present sea level is about a meter below the high level. Inland are Pleistocene beaches as high as 45 feet.

MACKENZIE MOUNTAINS REGION.   In the Mackenzie Mountains region we include several mountain ranges and plateaus that are situated along the northeast side of the Yukon Basin and that separate it from plains along the Mackenzie River and from there eastward to the Shield. The mountains and plateaus that form the headwaters of the Porcupine River overlook the Arctic Slope and extend westward to the Brooks Range. The geology is like that of the Brooks Range (Fig. 19.4). The Porcupine Plateaus, which extend southeastward along the west side of the Rich-

Figure 19.10 *Topography along the Yukon River. (A) Yukon Flats. For 150 miles in the vicinity of Fort Yukon, the River meanders with a braided pattern across a vast alluvial flat, built partly of alluvium deposited by the Yukon and partly of alluvial fans deposited by its tributaries. (B) For much of its course the river flows between bluffs a few hundred feet high. The bluffs shown in this view are at the head of the gorge below the Yukon Flats.*

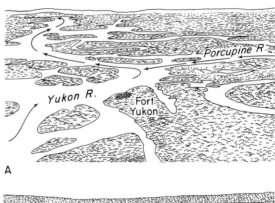

A

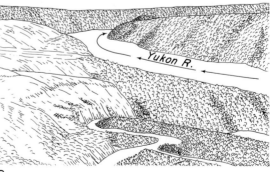

B

ardson Mountains, are composed of Lower and Upper Cretaceous formations that are folded and overthrust toward the east. The Upper Cretaceous formations are in large part coastal plain deposits that overlapped northeastward onto the marine lower Cretaceous.

The Richardson Mountains to the east consist of Paleozoic formations that are also folded and thrust eastward. The Porcupine Plateaus and the Richardson Mountains together form a projecting spur that connects the Brooks Range with the Mackenzie and Selwyn mountains, which are arcuate in plan and bulge toward the northeast. These mountains consist of complex folds and faulted sheets of Precambrian and Paleozoic formations thrust toward the northeast.

During the Pleistocene, there were rather minor alpine glaciers on the tops of the higher mountains in this region, but the continental ice sheet, pushing northwestward from the Keewatin center, reached the mountains and in places extended onto them.

The plateaus and plains extending eastward from the foot of the mountains to the Mackenzie River consist of Cretaceous formations resting on Devonian and older shelf strata that overlap the Canadian Shield.

Geologic History

The geologic history of Alaska and the Yukon is very much like that of the Coast Mountains of southeastern Alaska and British Columbia if one includes the Intermontane Plateaus east of the Coast Mountains and the Canadian Rockies still farther east. The oldest rocks are tightly folded and highly metamorphosed sedimentary rocks of Precambrian age, the Birch Creek Schist in the Yukon-Tanana Uplands of the Yukon Basin. Moreover, the Yukon Basin, in which the oldest rocks are exposed, is similar to the Intermontane Plateaus east of the Coast Mountains in having been a geanticline.

During the Paleozoic, much if not all of Alaska and the Yukon Territory was submerged, and there were two geosynclinal belts (Fig. 19.4). To-

ward the Pacific there was a eugeosyncline that collected volcanics and volcanically derived sediments mixed with poorly sorted clastic deposits forming graywacke, chert, and sandstone. In this belt, deformation progressed as the geosyncline sank. Northward, at the Brooks Range, these eugeosynclinal deposits grade into miogeosynclinal limestone, sandstone, and shale; these rest unconformably on the folded and metamorphosed Precambrian formations, thus recording a late Precambrian episode of folding and metamorphism. Angular unconformities in the Devonian and older Paleozoic formations also record deformation that took place during the first half of the Paleozoic. This is reminiscent of the more fully documented history of the geosyncline far to the south in the Basin and Range Province.

Beginning in the Mississippian and continuing through the Pennsylvanian, Permian, and Triassic, southern Alaska became a submarine lava field. These lavas form extensive greenstone formations. North of the Yukon they grade into miogeosynclinal and shelf deposits.

The Jurassic was characterized by repeated folding and faulting and batholithic intrusion; it was activity of this sort that was responsible for the so-called Nevadan Orogeny in the Coast Mountains. In the Matanuska-Cook Inlet-Shelikof Strait arc (Fig. 19.11) there was a geosyncline in which 10,000 to 20,000 feet of an andesitic flows and tuffs and related sediments (Talkeetna Formation) were deposited. This deposition extended to the north flank of the arc formed by the Kodiak-Kenai-Chugach Mountains. The Talkeetna batholith, which extends from the Talkeetna Mountains through the southern Alaska Range to the Aleutian Range, was intruded at this time. The Brooks Range was uplifted, and miogeosyncline or shelf deposits were laid down on the Arctic Slope.

Mountain-building and batholithic intrusion continued in southern Alaska during the Cretaceous; deposition continued in the geosyncline along the Matanuska-Cook Inlet-Shelikof Strait arc and on the Arctic Slope north of the Brooks Range. By the end of the Cretaceous, Paleozoic

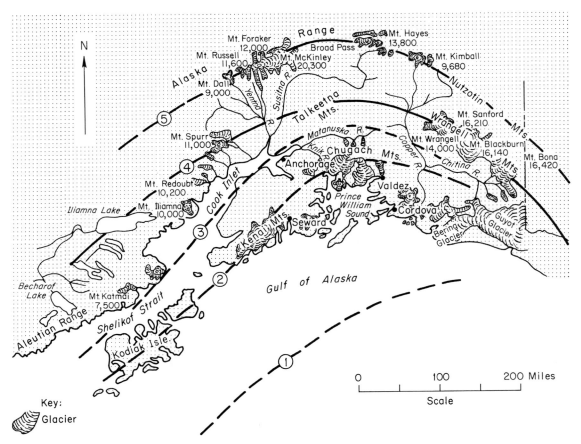

Key:

 Glacier

1. Aleutian Trench—a Quaternary geosyncline.

2. Kodiak-Kenai-Chugach Mountains arc—a geosyncline during Cretaceous time; uplifted to form mountains during Tertiary and Quaternary time.

3. Matanuska-Cook Inlet-Shelikof Strait arc—a geosyncline during Mesozoic and early Tertiary time; partly filled with Tertiary and Quaternary sediments; now a structural trough between uplifts 2 and 4.

4. Talkeetna-Aleutian Range arc—an uplifted belt of Paleozoic and older rocks intruded by granitic batholiths; probably a geanticline during most of the Mesozoic and Cenozoic.

5. Alaska Range arc—a geosyncline during most of Mesozoic time; intruded by granitic batholiths in Mesozoic and Tertiary time; uplifted in late Tertiary and Quaternary time.

Figure 19.11 *Map of South-central Alaska, showing five major structural elements that control the topographic grain of the area, and the principal active glaciers. [Generalized from U.S.G.S.]*

rocks in the Brooks Range were pushed northward and thrust onto the Cretaceous rocks (Fig. 19.4).

During the Cenozoic, Alaska and the Yukon Territory were dry land, and volcanism has continued, notably in the Aleutian Islands and Alaska Peninsula. Marine sediments were deposited on the continental shelves along both the Arctic and Pacific coasts, and folding and faulting, which continue to the present time, are manifested by the many earthquakes in that region; these are discussed in the next section of this chapter. The extent and effects of Pleistocene glaciations are discussed on page 644.

Earthquakes and Tsunami

Severe earthquakes are uncommon in the Yukon Territory, but are frequent in two belts in Alaska. One forms an arc along the Aleutian Islands, the Alaska Peninsula, and across the Alaska Range to the vicinity of Fairbanks. The other begins in the St. Elias Mountains and extends southeastward along the southeastern panhandle and the coast of British Columbia to the Puget Trough. The area between these two belts is comparatively quiescent (Fig. 19.12), but the structural grain indicated by the seismic epicenters differs from the exposed structural geology shown in Figure 19.11, and probably the earthquake belts parallel the structure more than is indicated.

In any year, Anchorage may experience a half dozen earthquakes that are strong enough to rattle dishes. On March 27, 1964, a major earthquake shook Prince William Sound, causing 115 deaths and $300 million in property damage. The earthquake lasted 3 to 5 minutes. Displacements as great as 50 feet occurred along reactivated faults from Cordova to Kodiak and along others on the ocean floor (Figs. 19.13, 19.14).

The earthquake triggered many landslides and avalanches; more than 2,000 were counted in an area of 2,000 square miles. Streams were dammed and temporarily diverted. Railroads and highways were blocked. Many slides terminated on glaciers. Submarine slides contributed to the tsunamis and other water surges (seiches).

The theory that such avalanches may move on a cushion of air was confirmed by studies at a slide in the Chugach Mountains, at what is now known as Shattered Peak. A substantial part of the mountain slid onto the Sherman Glacier. It crossed a 450-foot-high ridge like a skier going off a jump, leaving the forest on the lee side undamaged. The avalanche of broken rock rode almost 4 miles across the glacial ice at 100 miles per hour. Yet delicate features on the surface of the glacier were preserved under the layer of debris that finally settled to its surface.

At lakes the initial shocks developed parallel cracks through 4 feet of winter ice. Oscillation of lake waters by the seismic waves in places

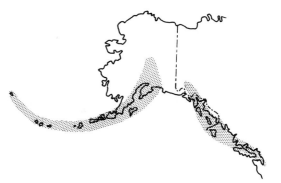

Figure 19.12 *Earthquake belts (stippled areas) in Alaska. One belt extends from the Alaska Range southwestward along the Alaska Peninsula, and westward along the Aleutian Islands and Trench. The western end of the belt connects with one extending from Kamchatka to Japan. The other belt of earthquakes in Alaska extends southeastward along the St. Elias Mountains and along the Panhandle and coast of British Columbia to Puget Trough. [From U.S.C.G.S.]*

completely broke the ice, wave-tossed chunks of which scarred trees along the shore to heights of 30 feet. Slumps in delta deposits generated waves great enough to destroy shore buildings. Some coastal freshwater lakes became inundated by sea water and some still are saline. Some surges of water were large enough to produce, in sand, ripples 2 feet high and 50 feet apart. Other lakes were temporarily lowered as a result of spilling caused by seiches, although most of these were recharged by spring meltwaters. Some were permanently lowered by seepage along open fractures and fissures. At Kenai Lake a 50-ton block of deltaic sediment was washed onto the shore, and bridge piles 27 feet long were moved without being tilted.

Along streams there was not much breakup of the winter ice; and spillage was evidently minor. The discharge of many streams was temporarily reduced because of damming by slides; the flow of one stream was reduced from 550 to 70 cubic feet per second. Sediment load of the streams greatly increased during the month following the earthquake, chiefly as a result of slides. The load of the Matanuska River increased

Figure 19.13 *During the 1964 earthquake, some parts of Alaska were uplifted and other parts downwarped. Shown in this figure is an elevated part of the sea floor (white area). In other places, the encroachment of salt water is killing trees. [Photograph by George Plafker, U.S.G.S.]*

fivefold over normal for the month of April 1964, but the load returned to normal by summer.

Groundwater was affected by the earth shocks. At Anchorage, artesian wells rose rapidly at the initial shocks, then fell sharply. For more than 8 hours they fluctuated, some as much as 24 feet. Shallow wells became turbid and intermittently ejected sand, mud, and water. In general, well levels were lowered, artesian pressures

decreased, and spring discharges diminished. Near the coast the water quality was affected by increased chloride attributed to invasion by sea water as a result of a 4-foot drop of the water table.

Where groundwater was shallow and overlain by impermeable frozen ground, the initial shocks caused increases in groundwater pressures, which broke the frozen layer and allowed sedi-

Figure 19.14 *The 1964 earthquake caused some bridges to collapse as if the stream banks had been pulled apart (above), and others buckled as if the banks had been pushed together (below). [Photographs by U.S.G.S.]*

ment, which in places was as much as a foot thick, to be ejected from the ground. Where the frozen layer did not fracture, pressure ridges were formed. Sediment ejection took place mostly on outwash plains, toes of alluvial fans, and deltas—those places were unconsolidated surficial deposits are saturated and under moderately thick crusts.

Water levels were affected in other parts of the world too. At a reservoir in Michigan there was a seiche 1.8 feet high. A well in South Dakota fluctuated 23 feet. Water was sloshed out of swimming pools in Texas. A well in Puerto Rico fluctuated $3\frac{1}{2}$ feet, and one in Australia fluctuated $2\frac{1}{4}$ feet. Such fluctuations took place widely around the world, and the timing leaves little doubt about their correlation with the seismic waves generated by the Anchorage earthquake. Most wells and standing bodies of water showed no fluctuation.

Other curious features of the earthquake developed because the ground was frozen. Tidal waves removed railroad tracks but left the ties frozen in place. In places groundwater rose quietly inside buildings, leaving a high water mark on the *inside* of windows, yet not causing violent flood damage.

Unsatisfactory foundation conditions were primarily responsible for the tremendous property damage. Anchorage is situated on a glacial outwash plain resting on an impermeable clay formation. The shaking by the earthquake caused sliding on the wet clay formation. The shaking by the earthquake caused sliding on the wet clay. Many residences along the bluffs overlooking Cook Inlet were carried to destruction by landslides (Figs. 19.15, 19.16).

The landslides were not all of the same kind. Some were rotational (Fig. 19.14,A), with the soles concave upward, the mass moving down at the head and out at the toe. Attempts to excavate the toe and backfill the head only aggravate such slides. Other slides move along a horizontal sole (Fig. 19.17,B) on sand or clay made liquid by the shaking. Some houses on such slides were moved a few hundred feet without serious damage.

What damage occurred was caused by development of horsts and grabens; the fracture along the side of one graben passed under a school building and caused it to topple over intact but upside down on the floor of the graben. Some houses moved as much as 600 feet seaward and 200 feet laterally, and then came the legal question: whose land is that? The house and the block of land under it moved onto a neighbor's tract.

Earthquakes that center near the coast of Alaska are commonly accompanied by huge waves, erroneously called "tidal waves." One kind, tsunamis, can cross the Pacific in a matter of hours and cause destruction on distant shores. Tsunamis generated off Alaska reach the Hawaiian Islands, about 2,500 miles away (see Chapter 20). The 1964 earthquake that so heavily damaged Anchorage created a tsunami that caused loss of life and property damage along the coast of California.

The tsunami are apparently caused when the ocean bottom is suddenly raised or dropped. A network of specially equipped seismological stations provides warnings when the kind of earthquake occurs that may generate a tsunami. The stations are operated around the Pacific in a cooperative venture by several countries.

Another kind of destructive sea wave is caused by slides. These may be generated in the fjords, where the combination of shaking and avalanches, whether of rock or glacial ice, creates waves not unlike those that children create by sliding in a bathtub. In Lituya Bay, about 100 miles southeast of Yakutat Bay, an avalanche accompanying an earthquake in 1958 created a wave 100 to 200 feet high that surged onto the shore with sufficient force to strip all the forest from a promontory 1,720 feet high (Fig. 19.18).

Climate

Climatic data for Alaska and the Yukon Territory are woefully inadequate. Few stations have records that date back more than 25 years, and inasmuch as these were kept in the principal towns, the data are not evenly distributed areally

Figure 19.15 *In most earthquakes the greatest damage occurs where the foundation conditions are unsatisfactory. This view shows how ground composed of glacial outwash and related deposits broke as a result of sliding on a buried layer of wet clay. The foreground pulled away from the background, and a school (top center) was toppled.* [Photograph by U.S.G.S.]

or altitudinally. The climatic map (Fig. 19.19) leaves much to be desired.

In the Southeast Coast Ranges, despite the many glaciers, the climate near the coast is surprisingly mild, with average winter temperatures at about 32°F and minimums about 0°F. The waterways remain open during the winter. Summer temperatures average in the 50's (°F) and maximums are in the 90's. The growing season lasts 4 months or more.

The precipitation is heavy, generally averaging more than 80 inches annually and in places more than 150 inches. Inland from the coast the climate becomes increasingly severe, partly because of increased distance from the ocean but chiefly because of the increase in altitude. It is the to-

pography, together with the high precipitation, that maintains such a huge volume of ice in the mountains that the glaciers extend down to sea level despite the mild temperatures there. Above 3,000 feet there is perennial ice. Above 8,000 feet most storms, even during summer, are accompanied by snow.

Temperatures along the coast of south-central Alaska during the winter average about 5°F lower than in southeastern Alaska; summer temperatures average little if any lower. The growing season is 2 to 3 weeks shorter, except on islands like Kodiak, where the growing season is about as long as in southeastern Alaska. Inland from the coast the range in temperature greatly increases with summer maxima around 90°F and

Figure 19.16 *Unsatisfactory foundation conditions were responsible for much of the property damage at Anchorage in the 1964 earthquake. Homes on the bluffs overlooking Cook Inlet (back of the observer) were tumbled down in landslides resulting from the shaking. The landslid blocks in this view have the structure illustrated in Figure 19.17,A.*

winter minima around −40°F. The growing season lasts about 3 months. Average annual precipitation along the coast is 50 to 70 inches and increases southeastward. Inland the average annual precipitation greatly decreases, ranging from 15 to 30 inches, depending on relation to nearby mountains.

Temperatures in the Aleutian Islands are about the same as in the islands along the southeast coast of Alaska. Winters are slightly warmer and summers slightly cooler. Annual precipitation is less, averaging about 50 inches on Unalaska, but the islands are almost constantly shrouded by fog. Records are not at hand, but the islands are fog-covered probably 90 percent or more of the year. Islands in the Bering Sea are very much colder than the Aleutian Islands, and their annual precipitation is much less.

Lowlands and uplands in the Yukon Valley have a continental climate, with long, cold winters and short, hot summers. Fort Yukon has recorded a minimum of 78°F below zero and a maximum of 100°F. The growing season is less than 3 months. The region is semiarid, with average annual precipitation less than 20 inches, and in much of the region less than 15 inches. At Fort Yukon the average is 7 inches. Despite the low temperatures and long winters, the valleys of the Yukon and Kuskokwim were not glaciated during the Pleistocene (Fig. 19.20), probably because of insufficient precipitation.

On the Seward Peninsula, Nome has recorded a minimum of −47°F and a maximum of 84°F. The average January temperature is about 3°F and the average July temperature less than 50°F. The growing season is less than 2 months. Average annual precipitation is about 18 inches.

North of the Brooks Range and northeast of the Mackenzie Mountains winters are long and cold. January temperatures at Point Barrow average 17°F below zero; July temperatures average about 40°F. The growing season lasts about 2 weeks. Average annual precipitation is less than 5 inches. During the Pleistocene the summit of the Brooks Range and mountains in the Mackenzie Mountains area were glaciated, but the glaciers did not extend far down the sides (Fig. 19.20). Because of the low precipitation, the mountains have only small glaciers.

Glaciers, Glacial Deposits, and the Glacial Process

With so many glaciers and so much permanently frozen ground, Alaska and the Yukon Territory seem less removed from the Pleistocene than

Figure 19.17 *Two kinds of landslides that cause very different kinds of damage. Some slides are rotational (A); buildings on such ground are toppled and the ground continues to be unstable. Other slides (B) move along a horizontal layer, and the slid block divides into horsts (h) and grabens (g). Such slides may move buildings several hundred feet without seriously damaging them.*

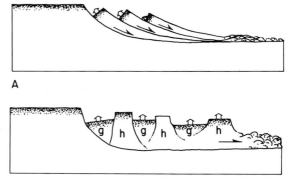

A

B

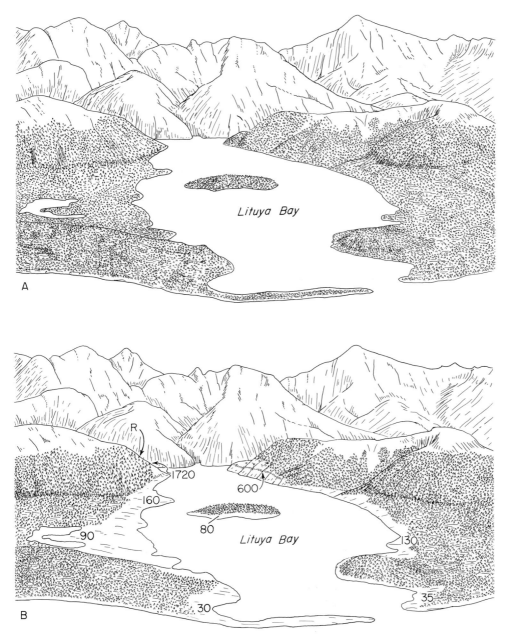

Figure 19.18   *Views of Lituya Bay, southeastern Alaska, before (A) and after (B) the destructive great wave of 1958. The lower slopes of the mountains, from sea level to about 2,500 feet, are heavily forested. Higher up, the mountains are bare. Glaciers descend each of the valleys in the mountains (Fairweather Range) at the head of the bay. A rock slide at R, triggered by the 1958 earthquake, created a wave that completely destroyed the forest up to the altitudes shown (feet). At the promontory across from the slide the wave swept away forest to a height of 1,720 feet. Three boats were in the bay at the time of the wave. One, behind the island, rode out the wave. Another was washed into the ocean across the top of the sand spit at the mouth of the bay. A third was destroyed. (Data from U.S.G.S.)*

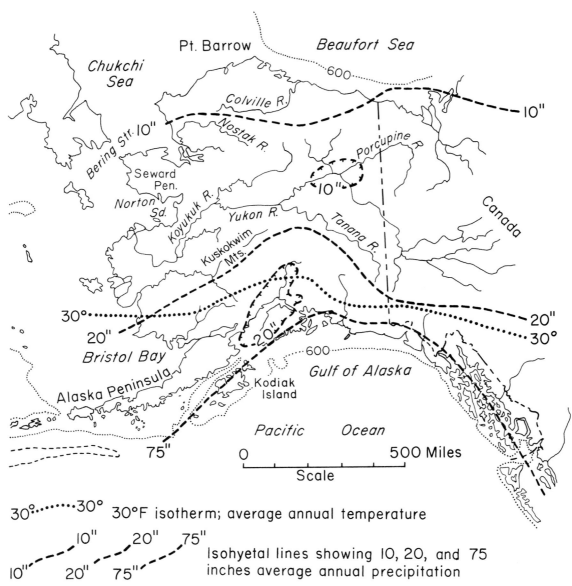

Figure 19.19 *Climatic map of Alaska. South of the 30° isotherm the average annual temperature is above 30°F; to the north the average is below 30°F. Along the coast precipitation is at a maximum during the fall; in the interior and in northern Alaska, there is precipitation throughout the year. In winter a low pressure area forms over the Gulf of Alaska, bringing southwesterly winds to the Panhandle; in summer a high-pressure area forms over the gulf, bringing westerly winds to the southern and southeastern coasts.*

most of the rest of North America, and the effects of the past climates are less noticeable there. In the Coast Mountains of southeast Alaska, glaciers are numerous, especially along the Gulf of Alaska. From Yakutat Bay west to Copper River the mountains are largely covered by glacial ice.

Along the flanks of the mountains from Glacier Bay to Copper River, a distance of more than

250 miles, glaciers several thousands of feet thick are almost continuous. The large Malaspina, Guyot, and Bering glaciers are piedmont glaciers that extend onto flat country beyond the foot of the mountains and form ice plateaus up to 1,500 feet high, but sloping to sea level. They are fed by valley glaciers that head above the snowline, which is at an altitude of about 2,500 feet. The snowline is 5,000 feet higher on the dry, northeast side of the coastal mountains.

This system of glaciers is the largest in the world outside Greenland and the Antarctic ice caps. In Alaska and Canada the ice-covered area probably exceeds 5,000 square miles, about one-third the area of Switzerland.

The edges of the ice plateaus are covered with moraines that support forests. The edge of the huge Malaspina glacier is so heavily forested that it was not identified as a glacier until 1880. The interior of the plateau, however, is clear ice with

Figure 19.20   *The surprisingly limited extent of Pleistocene glaciers (stippled area) in Alaska and the Yukon Territory provides a good example that considerable precipitation as well as low temperature is necessary for glaciations. Compare Figure 20.16. (After U.S.G.S.)*

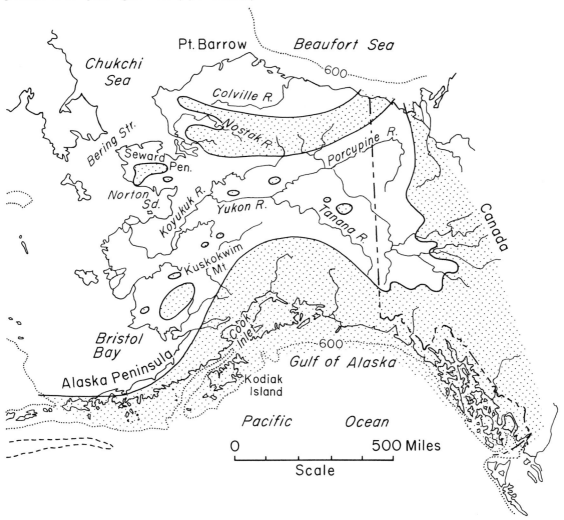

a gently undulating but crevassed surface. Streams flow on this ice until they discharge into a crevasse and join the subglacial drainage.

In south-central Alaska valley floors are covered by Pleistocene glacial drift, including till, glacial outwash, and lake and estuarine deposits, all mantled by loess. Much of Matanuska Valley is covered by loess, and is well suited for agriculture. At least three ages of Pleistocene glacial deposits have been recognized, and they record that all of this part of Alaska was covered by ice during the Pleistocene (Fig. 19.20).

The valleys, filled with the glacial deposits, have level or gently rolling floors flanked by steep mountains (Fig. 19.5). The valley sides were steepened by downfaulting or downwarping of the troughs, and have been further steepened by glacial erosion.

The upper 18,000 feet of Mount McKinley is in the zone of perennial ice (Fig. 8.10). Above 12,000 feet, there is probably no rain—only snow. But despite this, glaciers in the Alaska Range are small compared to those in southeast Alaska because of the difference in precipitation, which is only 30 inches at valley stations on the Susitna River below Mount McKinley, and less than 20 inches in the valleys north of the Range.

The lowlands and uplands in the Yukon River valley were not glaciated during Pleistocene time, but glacial effects are considerable because the rivers received the meltwaters from the glaciers in the mountains to the north, east, and south. The sediments deposited by these meltwaters built the alluvial flats in the structural basins, like Yukon Flats, and the floods must also have contributed greatly to enlarging the delta, which has probably had a history similar to that of the Mississippi River, where the river course has continually shifted across the growing front of the delta.

The alluvial flats were the source of loess deposited across the uplands, quite like the loesses bordering the lee sides of rivers in the central United States (p. 352). The loess blanket on the uplands north of the Tanana River in the Fairbanks area is more than 100 feet thick in places, but it thins northward away from the river. Interbedded with this loess are layers of volcanic ash as much as 6 inches thick.

Extensive as Alaska's glaciers are, they are only small remnants of those that formed during the Pleistocene (Fig. 19.20). Two glacial advances in Alaska are thought to be of Wisconsinan age, and there were at least two earlier, pre-Wisconsinan glacial advances. Alaska's existing glaciers illustrate three quite different ways in which glaciers occur. Where the ice is thick enough to bury the mountains as well as the valleys, the glaciers form *ice sheets*. The world's most extensive ice sheets are in Greenland and in the Antarctic, but small ones bury some Alaska mountaintops, especially east of Copper River. *Valley glaciers*, the most common kind in Alaska, are confined to valleys, and descend them without overtopping the ridges. *Piedmont glaciers*, like the mighty Malaspina, form where glaciers emerge at the foot of a mountain and spread like viscous dough on the piedmont flat.

In the collecting area above the snowline, the snow compacts into granules, known as *firn*, and the granules in turn compact into massive ice. This compaction is due to alternate melting and freezing of the particles. Solid ice will flow on a flat surface under its own weight if the thickness exceeds about 250 feet. On sloping surfaces, however, much lesser thicknesses move easily under their own weight. Many Alaskan glaciers are more than 1,000 feet thick, and advance several feet per day, although generally less. This movement of the ice takes place partly by shearing, partly by recrystallization, and partly by granulation.

Below the snowline is a zone of seasonal melting, the *ablation zone*, where the ice is reduced by meltwater runoff. If the melting exceeds the recharge by flow of ice from above the snowline, the glacier front retreats. If recharge exceeds the melting, the glacier front advances. Most Alaskan glaciers have retreated during the last few decades. Between 1936 and 1950 the rate of retreat of the Muir glacier averaged 1,500 feet per year.

In advancing down a valley the ice erodes its base and sides, partly by plucking and partly by abrasion. Debris that moves down the valley walls as a result of washing and slow creep collects along the sides on the ice surface and forms lateral moraines. Where two valley glaciers join, two of these moraines come together to form a *medial* moraine. At the front of the ice, a terminal moraine is deposited. The morainal material and debris within the ice are carried from the front by meltwaters and deposited as glacial outwash.

Erosion is active at the very head of a glacier, too, and produces the cirques so characteristic of glaciated mountains. This erosion involves several processes. In the warm season the ice moving down valley pulls away from the country rock, forming an arcuate crevasse (*bergschrund*) along which the exposed rock wall becomes subject to accelerated frost action because it is alternately soaked by meltwaters, and frozen, and then thawed. In the next cold season the crevasse fills with snow which compacts to firn and then to solid ice. In the next warm period the rocks loosened by frost heaving are pulled from the wall as the bergschrund opens. Retreat of the head wall, combined with lowering of the floor, produces the highly characteristic, steep-walled cirque.

Water, Permanently Frozen Ground

Alaska has plenty of water, but the people have a frontier attitude about protecting it. None of the cities or military establishments has had adequate water-treatment facilities, although some starts have been made. Because Alaska's population is small, municipalities have always been able to get away with dumping raw sewage into the rivers or straits.

Pulp mills and seafood canneries dump their wastes into estuaries. Oil spills have been numerous, and if production becomes really major, as seems likely, this problem will become worse.

The solution to Alaska's pollution problems lies in overcoming the difficulties posed by the permanently frozen ground (Fig. 19.21), the general aspects of which were discussed in Chapter 12. Figure 19.22 illustrates diagrammatically the

kinds of differences in permafrost that can be expected between the Arctic Slope and the Pacific Coast.

In some parts of Alaska the permafrost has receded, partly because of an apparently slight climatic warming trend and partly because forests have been cleared for agriculture. The ground ice melts irregularly, producing a hummocky, pitted togography not unlike that in limestone karst regions. The phenomenon is referred to as "thermokarst." Drainage is disrupted, and many of the depressions develop small lakes or ponds. Where the bodies of water provide further insulation and the melting continues, *thaw lakes* develop, some of which may be a mile or more in diameter and 10 to 20 feet deep. As the melting continues, thaw lakes may coalesce and develop new, integrated drainage. Thaw lakes are especially common on silt plains of former lake beds or other fine-textured ground.

Soils and Vegetation

Soils most suitable for farming are those developed on glacial outwash in the valleys and basins, and those developed on loessial deposits on rolling uplands. The upper layers of these soils contain considerable volcanic ash. The farmed soils are podzolic, and most are Holocene in age.

Numerous unusual ground features in the arctic result from the extreme environmental conditions. Among these are features related to the permafrost, such as patterned ground, that is, the systematic development of polygons, circles, or other ground forms resulting from the sorting action by the frequent and intense freezing and thawing (see Chapter 12). Mounds called "pingoes" are caused by the surface layer becoming bulged by water that freezes as it is squeezed from the active layer over permafrost. Thermokarst lakes occurs along the coastal plain as a result of irregular melting of ice in the ground. In the mountains, the thawing of loose ground creates lobes of earth that move down the slope, solifluction lobes. A particular kind of such moved ground occurs along the Colville River,

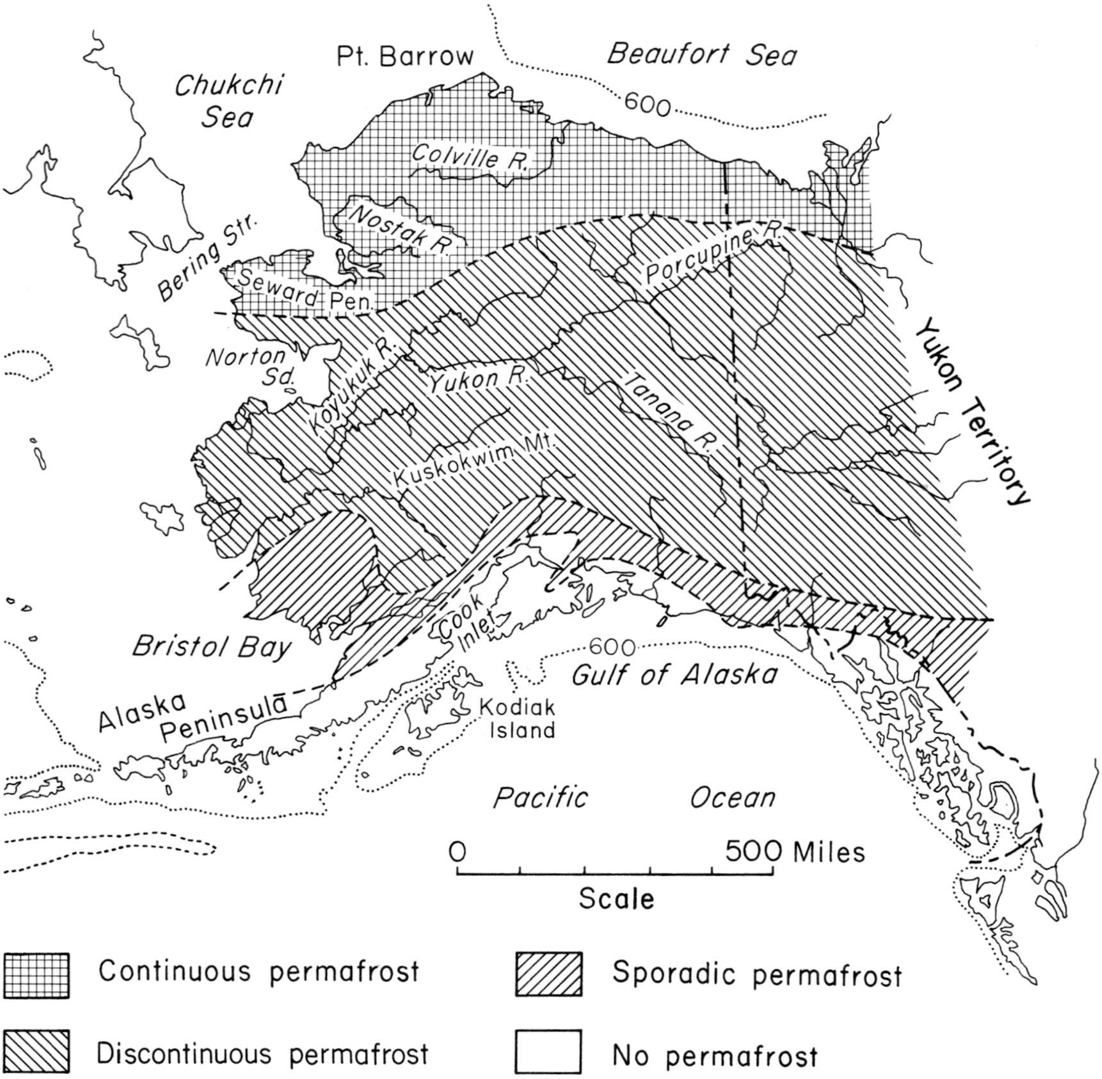
Pt. Barrow
Beaufort Sea
Chukchi Sea
600
Colville R.
Nostak R.
Bering Str.
Seward Pen.
Porcupine R.
Norton Sd.
Koyukuk R.
Yukon R.
Tanana R.
Yukon Territory
Kuskokwim Mt.
Cook Inlet
Bristol Bay
600
Gulf of Alaska
Alaska Peninsula
Kodiak Island
Pacific Ocean
0
500 Miles
Scale
Continuous permafrost
Sporadic permafrost
Discontinuous permafrost
No permafrost

Figure 19.21 *Distribution of permanently frozen ground in Alaska and Yukon Territory. [After U.S.G.S.]*

where bentonitic Cretaceous shale becomes hydrated and the clayey ground flows on low slopes during prolonged rain or during snowmelt.

More than half of Alaska is treeless (Fig. 19.23). In southeastern and south-central Alaska the treeless ground is bare rock, glacial ice, and snowfields. The southern slopes of the Alaska Range, the Alaska Peninsula, and the Aleutian Islands are grassland with some sedge and dwarf willows. The east coast of the Bering Sea, the north flank of the Brooks Range, and the coastal plain along the north coast have short, cool summers; the ground supports tundra vegetation, which averages about 30 percent lichens. There is wet tundra, dry tundra, and rock ridge tundra. Some tundra is shrubby with willow, alder, and dwarf birch. Some is herbaceous, with sedge and grass. In the north some well-drained ground is rock desert, with various shrubs and herbs growing amid the rubble. Tundra-like vegetation in swampy areas is *muskeg*. The lichens, sedges, shrubs, and mixed grasses, weeds, and mosses are the summer feed for the reindeer; in winter their diet consists almost entirely of a branching lichen a few inches high, known as reindeer moss and regarded as the most characteristic plant of the tundra. Lichens require 15 to 40 years to re-establish themselves after a fire.

Alaska has only about 30 species of trees; they grow in two principal kinds of forests. Along the coast, where winters are mild, the forest is Sitka spruce and hemlock. About 70 percent is hemlock, 25 percent spruce, and the remaining 5 percent mostly Alaska cedar, western red cedar, white birch, alder, and lodgepole pine. In the interior, where winters are severe, forests consist chiefly of white spruce and birch. White spruce occupies the better-drained ground; black spruce occupies swampy ground. Cottonwood, aspen, alder, and willows grow along the streams. Other trees in the interior forest include the balsam poplar, larch, and tamarack. The interior forests are dense along the valley bottoms and in the several basins, but more open on the uplands.

Forests of Engelmann spruce and lodgepole pine that grow in the Northern Cascades and Rocky Mountains do not extend northward beyond the latitude of Juneau (Fig. 19.23).

The vegetation is an aid in estimating the depth of the active layer over permanently frozen ground. Where tall willows grow on a floodplain, the active layer is generally more than 8 feet thick. Under white spruce, it is generally at least 2 or 3 feet thick, but under Black Spruce may be as shallow as 1 foot.

Volcanic Ash

The parts of Alaska that are subject to ash falls are of special ecological interest because a major volcanic eruption may deposit a widespread thick blanket of ash. The eruption of Mt. Katmai in 1912 deposited a few feet of ash near the volcano and a foot of ash on Kodiak Island a hundred miles to the east. An eruption at Mount Spurr in 1953 deposited ash at Valdez, 200 miles away. The effects of such ash falls on the vegetation may be zoned as follows:

Zone 1, near the volcanic center: vegetation incinerated by incandescent ash;
Zone 2, heavy ash fall: trees killed, herbage killed by burial;

Figure 19.22 *Diagrammatic section illustrating permanently frozen ground in Alaska. In the north the permafrost is about 1,000 feet thick; the active layer is about 3 feet thick. Southward the permafrost thins and becomes discontinuous; the active layer thickens. Unfrozen ground underlies the permafrost, and unfrozen layers may lie between the permafrost and the active layer.*

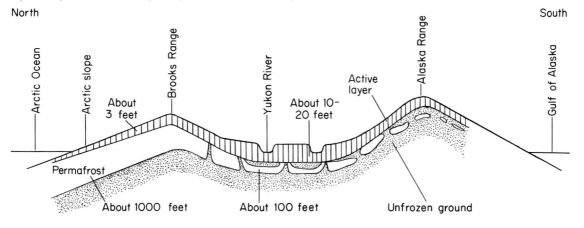

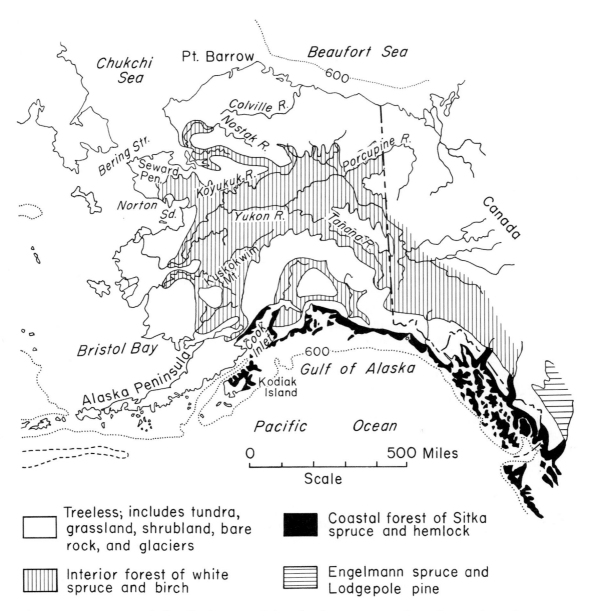

Figure 19.23 *Forests in Alaska. The forests are believed to be moving onto the treeless arctic tundra.* [*Generalized from U.S.G.S. and U.S.D.A.*]

Zone 3, moderate ash fall: trees killed but grasses recover;

Zone 4, lighter ash fall: trees and shrubs little affected; small plants damaged;

Zone 5, farthest from the center: plants locally affected by acid rains but not otherwise damaged.

The rates of weathering, revegetation, and other recovery of these zones involves a complex of factors. The ash, composed of minerals and glass shards, changes texture and composition rapidly because of compaction, washing by rains, and high susceptibility to erosion. The soil acidity and content of soluble elements change as weathering progresses; moisture retention is changed by compaction and by erosion. Moreover, plants differ in their resistance to damage by ash falls. Conifers may yield under ash without damage, as they do under snow. Plants differ in their resistance to damage by sandblasting, which is an important process on fresh volcanic ash. Plants also differ in their moisture requirements and in their need for or tolerance of the available soluble elements. In general, liverworts have been the first to grow on fresh surfaces of volcanic ash in Alaska; lichens generally are first on lava surfaces, but no simple succession of plants follows these pioneers.

An equally complex array of factors controls the rates and order of weathering and revegetation of deposits laid bare by retreating glaciers. Figure 19.24 illustrates one kind of succession in such environments.

Bering Land Bridge

The land bridge across the Bering Strait and the Bering Sea has long been supposed to be the route by which man reached North America from Asia. The concept, which is doctrine in archeology, may be right, but it could be wrong and merely a durable fallacy.

Alaska was connected with Siberia through much of Cenozoic time. Fossil marine molluscs in late Tertiary deposits on the north coast of Alaska are North Atlantic species. In that area the oldest fossils of Pacific species are early Pleistocene, during which time the Bering Strait was apparently opened. During the Pleistocene, crustal movements and eustatic changes in sea level caused alternate emergence and submergence of the land bridge. There is no question about the existence of the land bridge, but the degree to which it was used by man is questionable.

The land bridge evidently was not a satisfactory route between the continents, because during much of Tertiary time the vertebrate fauna of North America did not mix with the fauna of the eastern hemisphere. Paleontologists tell us that faunal interchanges between the two hemispheres took place during early Eocene, late Eocene, early Oligocene, late Miocene, and middle to late Pliocene time. At other times during the Tertiary the faunas were separated and speciated differently. The marine molluscs indicate that the bridge was there during much if not all of Tertiary time, but the vertebrate animals seem to have used it very little if at all. The earliest known remains of man in North America are late Pleistocene; man did not use the bridge before that time, if then.

No other intercontinental route is evident, but perhaps another should be sought in view of the lack of paleontological or archeological evidence indicating use of the Bering Bridge either by man or the other mammals.

Resources for the Future

Resources of the north country are mostly for the future, because they have been little developed. Fisheries, the principal basis of the present economy, produce mostly salmon but include considerable herring, halibut, shrimp, and crab. The

Figure 19.24 *Environmental zones in front of a retreating glacier (compare Fig. 8.14).*

Spruce or
fir needles
Deposits containing:
alders and willows
sedges
mosses

Barren gravel

Ice

fishing is mostly in the Gulf of Alaska and Bristol Bay.

Besides gold, Alaska has important deposits of copper and some lead and zinc, especially in the coastal mountains bordering the Gulf of Alaska. Coal is available in many parts of the country, and supplies local needs. Petroleum, the principal mineral product, occurs on the Kenai Peninsula, along the Cook Inlet, and on the Arctic Slope.

Fur animals, another major resource, were overexploited until measures were adopted to preserve the herds of seal, sea otter, and other fur-bearing animals. Besides the sea animals there are fox, marten, mink, bear, beaver, weasel (ermine), muskrat, and caribou. Some of these are bred and raised for their furs.

Farmlands probably total less than 100 square miles, but at least fifty times as much is suitable for farming. Agriculture will probably increase at least in so far as supplying many local needs as the population increases and the transportation system is extended.

Timber resources are huge. It has been estimated that the annual forest crop could supply the pulpwood for a million tons of newsprint annually, and the estimate is probably conservative.

Unique scenery and unique natural phenomena such as the volcanoes and glaciers are other Alaska resources that should attract increasing thousands of visitors annually. The fjords are equal to those of Norway. The glaciers of Switzerland are minor compared to those of Alaska; Mount McKinley is a mile higher than the Alps and closer to New York. And why go to Africa for big game?

Alaska could become a major world competitor in attracting vacationers from the other states. If Alaska were to advertise what it can offer, and if our airlines were to reduce rates there, travel could be diverted from the trans-Atlantic routes. It might also be in the national interest to give less subsidy to the trans-Atlantic luxury liners and more to the Alaska coastal lines.

On the debit side are the fogs, mosquitoes, and charges for tourist facilities that are hardly commensurate with the services rendered. The last could be corrected by drawing more capital to Alaska by advertising its attractions. The fogs will remain, but fog has not been a handicap to some California Chambers of Commerce. Ingenuity will be taxed, however, to make the mosquitoes into an asset.

References

Alaska Glacial Committee, 1965, Map showing extent of glaciations in Alaska: U.S. Geol. Survey Miscel. Geol. Inves. Map I-45.

Berg, H. C., and Cobb, E. H., 1967, Metalliferous lode deposits of Alaska: U.S. Geol. Survey Bull. 1246.

Black, R. F., 1951, Eolian deposits of Alaska: Artic v. 4, pp. 89–111.

Cederstrom, D. J., 1952, Summary of ground-water development in Alaska, 1950: U.S. Geol. Survey Circ. 169.

Cederstrom, D. J., P. M., and Subitsky, Seymour, 1953, Occurrence and development of ground water in permafrost regions: U.S. Geol. Survey Circ. 275.

Coulter, H. W., Hopkins, D. M., Karlstrom, T. N. V., Pewe, T. L., Wahrhaftig, Clyde, and Williams, J. R., 1965, Extent of glaciations in Alaska: U.S. Geol. Survey Misc. Geol. Inv. Map I-415, scale 1:2,500,000.

Davis, T. N., and Echols, Carol, 1962, A table of Alaskan earthquakes, 1788–1961: Alaska Univ. Geophys. Inst. Research Dept. no. 8.

Dutro, J. T., and Payne, T. G., 1957, Geologic map of Alaska: U.S. Geol. Survey, scale 1:2,5000,000.

Eckel, E. B., 1970, The Alaska earthquake, March 27, 1964—Lessons and conclusions: U.S. Geol. Survey Prof. Paper 546.

Ferrians, O. J., Jr., 1965, Permafrost map of Alaska: U.S. Geol. Survey Misc. Geol. Inv. Map I-445, scale 1:2,500,000.

Ferrians, O. J., Jr., Kachadoorian, Reuben, and Greene, G. W., 1969, Permafrost and related engineering problems in Alaska: U.S. Geol. Survey Prof. Paper 678.

Hopkins, D. M., Karlstrom, T. N. V., and others, 1955, Permafrost and ground-water in Alaska: U.S. Geol. Survey Prof. Paper 264-F, pp. 113–146.

Johnson, M. S., and Hartman, C. W., 1969, Environmental atlas of Alaska: Fairbanks, Univ. of Alaska.

Karlstrom, T. N. V., and others, 1964, Surficial geology of Alaska: U.S. Geol. Survey Misc. Geol. Inv. Map I-357, scale 1:1,584,000.

Kellog, C. E., and Nygard, I. J., 1951, Principal soil groups of Alaska: U.S. Department of Agriculture Mon. 7.

Muller, S. W., 1943, Permafrost or permanently frozen ground and related engineering problems: U.S. Geol. Survey Spec. Rept., Strategic Eng. Study 62, 2d ed., Military Intelligence Div. Office, Chief of Engineers, U.S. Army; 1947, Ann Arbor, Mich., Edwards Brothers.

Payne, T. G., 1955, Mesozoic and Cenozoic Tectonic elements of Alaska: U.S. Geol. Survey Misc. Geol. Inv. Map I-84.

Sigafoos, R. S., 1958, Vegetation of northwestern North America, as an aid in the interpretation of geologic data: U.S. Geol. Survey Bull. 1061-E, p. 165–185.

Smith, P. S., 1939, Areal geology of Alaska: U.S. Geol. Survey Prof. Paper 192, 100 p.

U.S. Geological Survey, 1965, The Alaska earthquake, March 27, 1964: U.S. Geol. Survey Prof. Papers 542 and 543.

Wahrhaftig, Clyde, 1965, Physiographic divisions of Alaska: U.S. Geol. Survey Prof. Paper 482.

Washburn, A. L., 1956, Classification of patterned ground and review of suggested origins: Geol. Soc. America Bull., v. 67, n. 7, pp. 823–865.

Williams, Howel (ed.), 1958, Landscapes of Alaska—Their geologic evolution: Berkeley, Univ. California Press.

Williams, J. R., 1970, Ground water in the permafrost regions of Alaska: U.S. Geol. Survey Prof. Paper 696.

For the Yukon, see various sections in Canada Geological Survey, 1968, Geology and economic minerals of Canada.

The Hawaiian Islands are volcanoes at various stages of erosion. The older and most eroded islands are at the northwest; the younger and still active volcanoes are at the southeast. This is Oahu, at the middle of the island group, and intermediate in age and dissection. The view is southwest toward Honolulu (distance), looking across the eroded remnants of a Tertiary volcanic series that forms the great Pali or northeast cliff of the island. [Photograph by Agatin T. Abbott, Hawaii Institute of Geophysics.]

20

HAWAII, PUERTO RICO—
SAMPLES OF OCEANIC PHYSIOGRAPHY

Hawaii and Puerto Rico occupy tropical oceanic positions just south of the Tropic of Cancer. The Hawaiian Islands, situated near the middle of the Pacific Ocean, jut upward from a northwest-trending ridge that separates two oceanic deeps, each of which descends more than 18,000 feet below sea level (Fig. 20.1). The islands are merely peaks along the ridge; the highest are more than 13,000 feet above sea level, resulting in a total relief of more than 6 miles. Puerto Rico is one of the easternmost peaks of a partly submerged mountain range composed of Cretaceous and older rocks. This mountain range forms the Greater Antilles and extends eastward to the Virgin Islands (Fig. 20.2); the Lesser Antilles, which form an arc at the east side of the Caribbean, are largely Cenozoic volcanoes, some of them still active. The Hawaiian Islands are true oceanic islands, both in the geographic sense and in composition; they are almost wholly basalt, like the crust under the ocean. Puerto Rico is not basaltic; it is composed of continental rocks approximating granite in composition. It is a fragment of the North American continent.

Listed below are some of the islands' outstanding features:

1. Mountainous topography.

2. The Hawaiian Islands are a ridge separating two oceanic abysses; Puerto Rico is a mountain range of folded rocks paralleled on the north by the Puerto Rico Trench, which is 6 miles deep.

3. Oceanic climate. Both groups of islands have little seasonal change in temperature; both are in the belt of trade winds, and their windward, northeastern sides are wet, whereas the leeward southwestern sides are semiarid.

4. Puerto Rico is subject to hurricanes generated east or west of the Lesser Antilles; Hawaii is spared this hazard.

5. Hawaii is subject to tsunamis generated in the trenches surrounding the Pacific Ocean; Puerto Rico is spared this hazard.

6. Because of their isolation, both islands have meager but unique faunas. Hawaii, for example, has no snakes and few other reptiles. Both are fringed in part with coral reef.

7. Both islands have tropical rain forest and tropical fruits; before man's arrival, many species were endemic.

8. The soils are largely lateritic.

9. Mineral resources are scanty. Puerto Rico has considerable hydroelectric power; Hawaii does not, because the basaltic lavas are too porous to provide much runoff. Both economies are based in large part on agriculture and

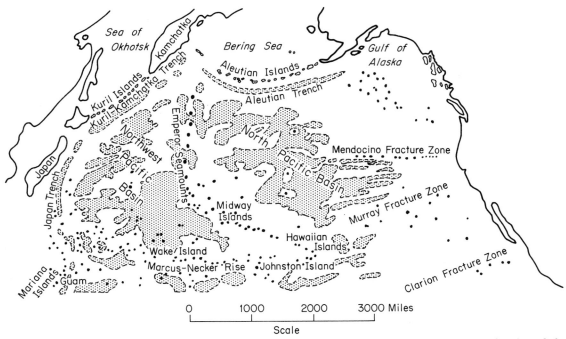

Figure 20.1 *Diagram of the North Pacific Ocean, showing the basins that are deeper than 18,000 feet (stippled area) and the general distribution of seamounts, guyots, and islands (dots) along the ridges separating the basins. [Generalized from Scripps Institute of Oceanography and National Geographic Society.]*

on tourism; Hawaii "benefits" from major military establishments.

10. Puerto Rico has half the area (3,400 square miles) and four times the population (almost 3 million) of Hawaii. In Hawaii every racial group is a minority, and racial integration is probably more advanced than it is anywhere else in the world. Puerto Rico, like the continent of which it is a fragment, has racial tensions.

Hawaii was formally annexed to the United States by the voluntary action of its people and by a joint resolution of Congress in 1898. That same year, Puerto Rico was ceded to the United States by Spain. It was established as a commonwealth in 1952. It has most of the powers and responsibilities of a state except that its citizens are not subject to United States taxes and have neither voting representation in the Congress nor the right to vote for President.

Structural Framework and Topography

HAWAII

There are five principal Hawaiian Islands and four smaller ones (Fig. 20.3), all basaltic volcanoes. Volcanic activity began in the west and moved eastward, so the youngest islands and the ones with the highest peaks are toward the east. Hawaii, the most easterly and the largest of the islands, has peaks more than 13,000 feet in altitude, and some volcanoes there still are active. This island is not flanked by coral; the older islands, more reduced and lower, are flanked by coral reefs. Farther west, between Kauai and Midway, are shoals and small islands of coral, some with basaltic remnants; these islands are even older.

The islands are hilly and mountainous, especially toward the east. About a fourth of the area is below 650 feet in altitude; a half is between 650 and 2,000 feet, and a fourth is above 2,000 feet. The coast lines are mostly rocky and rough. Erosion at the exposed, windward (northeast) shores in places has produced seacliffs 3,000 feet high. Only Oahu and Niihau have much coastal plain. There is only one harbor, Pearl Harbor, which is west of Honolulu, and there is a bay at Hilo.

The Hawaiian volcanoes developed during the Tertiary and seem to have been built above sea level late in Tertiary time. Most of the parts that are built above sea level were formed during late Tertiary and Quaternary time. The older islands, such as Oahu (Fig. 20.4), have been reduced by

erosion, some coastal plain has been built, and the shores are fringed with coral reefs.

On the big island, Hawaii, the volcanoes at Mauna Loa and Kilauea are still active and erupt every few years; three other volcanoes are dormant. One of these, Mauna Kea, had alpine glaciers in late Pleistocene time.

PUERTO RICO

At Puerto Rico the total relief of the mountain range forming the Greater Antilles is almost 35,000 feet. To the north, the base of the island lies 75 miles away in the Puerto Rico Trench (Fig.

Figure 20.2 *Index map of the West Indies, showing the location of Puerto Rico at the east end of the Greater Antilles. Arrows show ocean currents.*

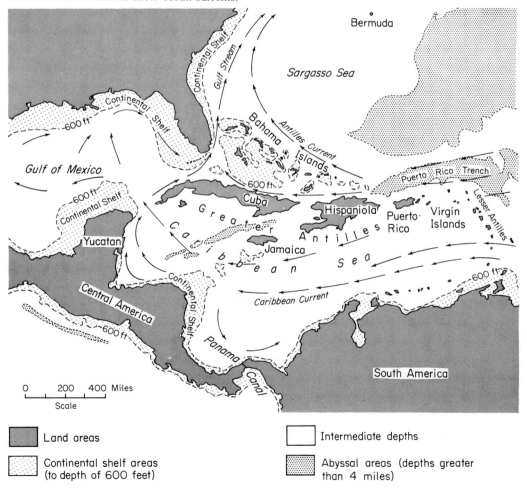

Land areas

Continental shelf areas (to depth of 600 feet)

Intermediate depths

Abyssal areas (depths greater than 4 miles)

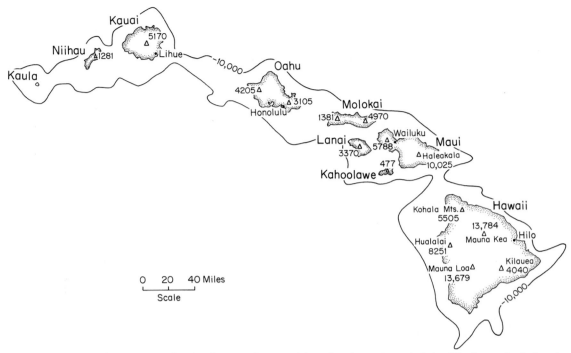

Figure 20.3 *Map of Hawaiian Islands, showing the principle volcanic cones and their altitudes and relation to the −10,000-foot submarine contour. [After U.S.G.S.]*

20.5) and is 6 miles below sea level. To the south, the base of the island lies in the Caribbean Sea about 3 miles below sea level. The east-west trending ridges and peaks forming the backbone of the island, the Cordillera Central (Fig. 20.6) make up about a third of the island. Local relief is considerable, and slopes are steep. The crest is crowded toward the south side of the island. Sierra de Luquillo, an isolated high mountain in the northeast corner of the island, lies slightly north of the eastern extension of the Cordillera Central. About 20 miles southeast of the island, along the eastern extension of the Cordillera Central, is Vieques Island. The rocks forming the mountains are mostly Cretaceous lavas and sedimentary formations derived from volcanic sources (Fig. 20.5). They are cut by granitic intrusions of Cretaceous and Tertiary age. This terrain is flanked by Tertiary marine limestone that forms low plateaus having karst topography pitted with scattered caverns and sinkholes and

surmounted by peculiar, steep-sided, haystack-like hills of limestone. In the limestone country, some rivers disappear underground and reappear near the coast. The Cretaceous formations and granitic intrusions had been uplifted and folded before the limestone was deposited. Further uplift in late Tertiary time raised the limestones to form the plateaus. In latest Tertiary and in Quaternary time there was further uplift and faulting: Puerto Rico was arched, tilted northeastward, and on the west became separated from Hispaniola by downfaulting in the strait between the two islands.

Puerto Rico lies in a seismically active belt that extends southeastward along the volcanic arc of the Lesser Antilles and westward to South America by way of Hispaniola and the trench between Jamaica and Cuba (Fig. 20.2), yet aside from a severe shock that was centered near Puerto Rico's west coast in 1918, earthquakes have been minor. Shore features (p. 678) indicate

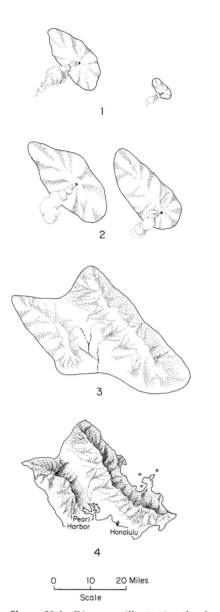

Figure 20.4 *Diagrams illustrating the development of a volcanic island. The example is Oahu. Stage 1: late Tertiary time; two volcanoes appear above sea level. Stage 2: late Tertiary or early Quaternary time; the volcanoes are built high above sea level. Stage 3: Quaternary time; the volcanic mountains are joined, and the activity has ceased. Stage 4: late Quaternary time; the mountains are reduced by erosion; they are fringed by coastal plain and in places by coral reef. Erosion has been particularly vigorous on the northeast side, which is to the windward. The northeast coast is very rocky.* [After U.S.G.S.]

that there has been little if any structural movement in the last several thousand years.

The subcrustal structure responsible for the island uplift and for the trench might be low-angle faulting directed northward, similar to the structure inferred under the Aleutian Islands (Fig. 19.8).

Relation to Other Oceanic Features; A Note on Plate Tectonics

The mountains in the Pacific Ocean seem to be mostly of volcanic origin, but they are of three principal types. The first, represented by the Hawaiian Islands, includes the conical, active or extinct volcanoes that have been topographically reduced by erosion (Fig. 20.7). Many are bordered by coral reefs, and the submerged parts of the mountain sides are steep. The second type (Fig. 20.7) includes the submerged mountains with irregular summits (*seamounts*) and those with tops that are smooth and flat, as if planed by erosion (*guyots*). Seamounts and guyots may be flanked by coral reefs (Fig. 20.7). The third type, referred to as banks, includes the broad, submerged plateau-like mountains (Fig. 20.7).

Many of the coral reefs extend to depths that are excessive for growth of coral. Those growths at depths of a few hundred feet probably reflect eustatic changes in sea level during the glacia tions and interglaciations of the Pleistocene. But at some islands, notably Eniwetok, drilling has shown coral extending as deep as 4,000 feet and underlain by basaltic lavas having textures and structures like the lavas erupted above sea level. This is strong evidence for sinking of the ocean floor, as postulated by Charles Darwin in 1839.

Seamounts, guyots, and the submerged parts of the Hawaiian Islands have steep sides, steeper than the sides of subaerial volcanoes and attributed to rapid cooling of submarine lavas. Guyots may be seamounts that have been planed by wave erosion when their tops were at sea level. If so, their submergence may be due to downwarping of the ocean floor. Supporting this view is the fact that where guyots are grouped together

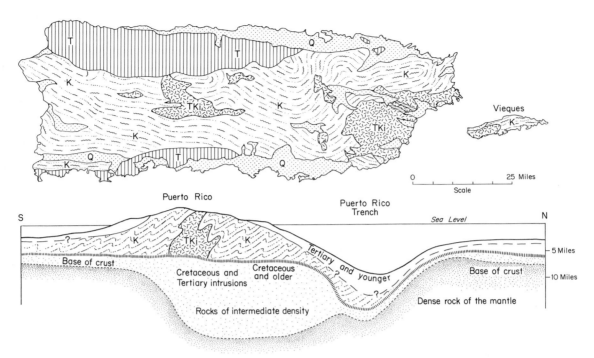

Figure 20.5 *Geologic map and cross section of Puerto Rico. The island is an uplift of Early Tertiary and Cretaceous (K) rocks invaded by Cretaceous and early Tertiary intrusions (TKi) and flanked by middle Tertiary limestone (T). Quaternary deposits include coral reefs, dunes and beach sand in part cemented to eolianite and to beachrock along the shores, and alluvium along valley bottoms. The axis of the uplift parallels the Puerto Rico Trench, which is underlain by a thick mass of light crustal rock. The dense rock of the mantle is very much shallower under the shelf north of the trench and under the Caribbean Sea.*

their depths are about the same. Some guyots, however, may be due to explosive submarine eruptions, which can produce steep-sided but flat-topped, plateau-like volcanic piles. The process seems to depend upon violent blasting of highly porous, vesiculated debris into the water, and this slowly settling debris may be spread widely by the turbulence caused by the eruption.

Rocks dredged from these submerged mountains are almost entirely basalt. Some coral has been found at depths greater than 150 feet, which is about the lower limit of coral growth. Deeply submerged reefs seem to indicate considerable downwarping or rise of sea level. Shallow, live reefs may form atolls or fringe reefs.

The Puerto Rico Trench separates the island itself from the North American Basin. Figures 20.8, 20.9 illustrate the physical geography of the ocean floors and the relationships to them of the major structural features on the continents.

The volcanic, mid-Atlantic Ridge divides the Atlantic Ocean Basin into eastern and western series of basins, each more than 3 miles deep. The Puerto Rico Trench is the deepest hole in the entire Atlantic Basin. The mid-Atlantic Ridge is 1 to 2 miles higher than the basins, and in places projects above sea level to form islands—the Azores in the North Atlantic, and St. Paul, Ascension, Tristan da Cunha, and Bouvet islands in the South Atlantic. All these are of volcanic origin, and the whole ridge seems to be also. The ridge connects northward with the Reykjanes Ridge, which is part of a vast lava plateau centering at Iceland and extending from Greenland to the British Isles.

The Pacific Ocean has twice the area and more than twice the volume of the Atlantic Ocean. It too is divided into broad basins separated by volcanic ridges, many of them trending north-westerly. Depths in these basins are generally between 16,000 and 23,000 feet, but there are several deep, narrow troughs—trenches, like the Puerto Rico Trench—in which depths greater than 35,000 feet have been recorded. Most of the ridges have scattered islands along them.

Where depths exceed 3 miles (roughly half of the ocean floor), the bottoms are floored with red clay, much of it with admixed manganese nodules. Shallower basins and the flanks of the deep ones are largely covered with ooze composed of the calcareous tests of Globigerinae. On submarine ridges, there may be calcareous ooze with pteropod molluscs. Ooze composed of the siliceous tests of Radiolaria may be mixed with the Globigerina ooze; far south of the equator in both oceans are extensive deposits of diatomaceous ooze, which also is siliceous.

Off the northwest coast of Africa, the bottom sediments include a great deal of fine sand and silt blown offshore from the deserts. At high latitudes the bottom sediments include ice-rafted rocks, many of them showing glacial scratches.

Continental Drift

Almost 100 years ago (1885) Eduard Suess suggested that the continents in the southern hemisphere had been joined in one large continental mass that he named Gondwanaland. In 1915 Alfred Wegener assembled considerable evidence that the continents had been joined and had drifted apart (Fig. 20.10). That the continents once were joined was suggested first by the jig-saw-puzzle fit of the coastlines on opposite sides of the Atlantic Ocean. Subsequently it was found that in late Paleozoic time three major climatic and vegetational belts could be fitted across what is now the Atlantic Ocean. At the south was a belt of glaciation, and north of this a belt with

Figure 20.6 *Map of Puerto Rico, showing the east-west-trending mountain range, the Cordillera Central, that forms the backbone of the island. [After U.S.D.A.]*

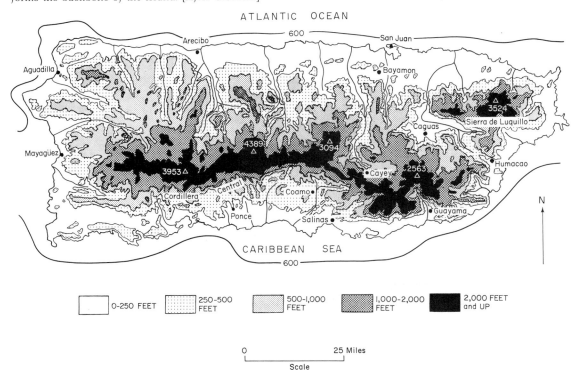

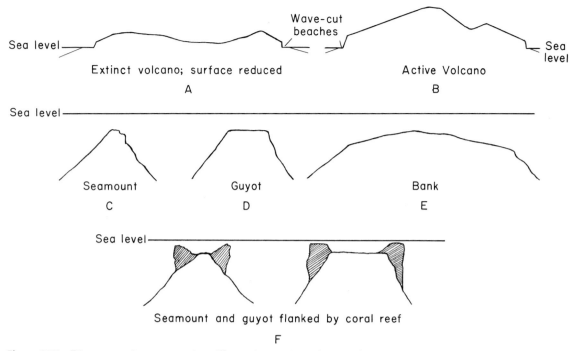

Figure 20.7 *Diagrammatic cross sections illustrating various shapes of oceanic mountains. Guyots flanked by coral form atolls, which consist of a deep central body of clear, quiet water partly enclosed by a crescentic series of coral islands. The enclosure may be many miles in diameter. Seamounts that form islands may similarly be flanked by a crescentic series of coral islands forming a deep moat of clear, quiet water around the central island.*

coal beds containing fossils of an identical fern, *Glossopteris*, that once grew in South America, South Africa, Madagascar, India, Australia, and New Zealand. Still farther north, in North America and Europe, there were desert deposits with salt beds. In addition, it was found that the major geologic structures along the west coasts of Europe and Africa fitted with those along the east coasts of North and South America.

Continental drift had been suggested independently by F. B. Taylor in 1910 to explain the arcuate mountain ranges along the west coasts of North and South America and in southern Europe and southern and southeastern Asia. In 1937 A. L. Du Toit suggested there had been two supercontinents, Gondwana in the southern hemisphere and Laurasia in the north, and that they had been separated by an east-west Tethyan geosynclinal trough.

A number of species of extinct animals have also been found to be indigenous to the opposite coasts. A recent discovery is a fresh-water amphibian that lived in Antarctica, South America, and Africa during the Triassic. Those three areas had to be connected at that time.

The theory of continental drift attributes the Mid-Atlantic and other oceanic ridges (Fig. 2.16) to upwelling of the mantle, presumably at the boundary between rising parts of convection cells. According to this theory the ocean floor under the Atlantic is spreading and the continents are being pushed apart.

PALEOCLIMATE

Tillites are known in Devonian and Permian formations, the *Devonian* occurrences are in South America and South Africa. By contrast, in

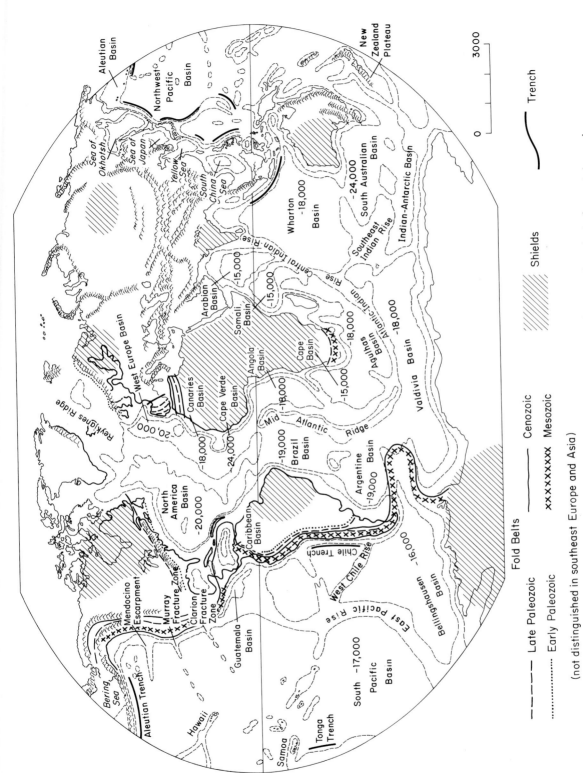

Figure 20.8 Major mountain ranges and basins (depths in feet) of the oceans, and their relation to the principal mountains and shields on the continents.

Fold Belts

——— Late Paleozoic   ——— Cenozoic

············ Early Paleozoic   xxxxxxxx Mesozoic

(not distinguished in southeast Europe and Asia)

Shields

——— Trench

0   3000

662

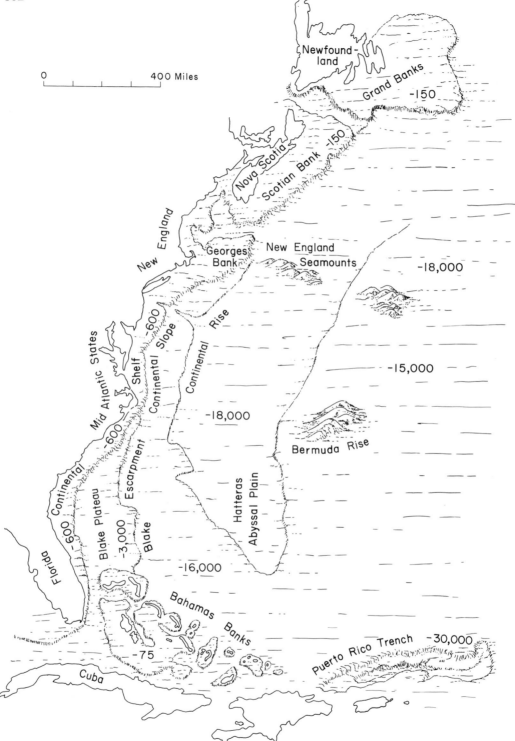

Figure 20.9 *Major geomorphic features of the bottom of the Atlantic Ocean off the eastern seaboard. The banks off New England, Nova Scotia, and Newfoundland were glaciated, and their surfaces are mantled with gravelly glacial deposits, morainal and outwash.*

North America, Europe, southeast Asia, and Australia, the marine Devonian contains *coral limestone*. This has led to the suggestion that the poles or continents have shifted such that the south pole was in what is now the South Atlantic Ocean near 20° west longitude and 40° south latitude. The north pole would have been in the north part of the Pacific Ocean. The equator, according to this reconstruction, would have been near the south coast of Australia and would have extended through the Arabian Peninsula, Central Europe, and eastern North America and back across the Pacific southwesterly to Australia.

Permian tillite is widely distributed in southern South America, southern Africa, India, and Australia. These deposits are associated with a distinctive flora (*Glossopteris* flora) that is indicative of a *cool climate*. The Pennsylvanian and Permian fern forests of Europe and North America, source of the rich coal deposits on those continents, are suggestive of a warm climate. The Permian climate map was somewhat like that for the Devonian.

The parallelism of the east coast of the Americas with the west coast of Europe and Africa long excited the temptation to fit them together as in a jigsaw puzzle. The temptation became very real in 1915 when Alfred Wegener marshalled paleontological and structural geological evidence suggesting that the continents bordering the Atlantic had indeed once been joined together. His theory, continental drift, was received with skepticism; it seemed easier to send requisitions down to the Devil whenever the rock record required that the furnaces be lit to produce magma or other earth movement, and the skepticism could be expressed in verse:

"Continents sliding, n'er colliding! Hully Gee!"

Since Wegener's time, knowledge about the form, composition, and structure of the ocean basins and the deeper parts of the continents has increased tremendously, today, going far beyond Wegener, the theory holds that not only the continents but the ocean basins too are adrift. The concept, now known by the name "plate tecton-

ics," envisions convection cells in the mantle turning over as illustrated in Figure 20.11. Lava, generated between the cells, rises along a crack in the ocean basin and builds a volcanic ridge. The upper part of the mantle, flowing away from the crack, drags with it the lavas erupted on the ocean floor. Lavas far from the crack are older than those near it, and in this way the continents are moved apart.

The lavas on the ocean floor show reversals of relict magnetism (p. 47) that are paired. These can be dated back only to about 4,000,000 years ago, but pairs beyond the ones that can be dated are interpreted as indicating contemporaneity. The indicated rates of movement so determined and spreading of the ocean floor and continued separation of the Americas from Africa and Europe range from 2 to 6 centimeters per year.

Plate tectonics considers the earth's crust as being divided into major plates of stable crust that are moving with respect to one another. New crust is being formed at the lava ridges, and the basaltic crust forming the ocean floor is pushed aside. Lateral movement of the top of the cell in the mantle drags this crust under the light crust of the continents at what are called "subduction zones," where the basaltic crust is dragged downward under the leading edge of a continental slab. A trench is developed in the subduction zone. Interaction of the two crustal slabs generates lava that is composed partly of the basalt slab and partly of the more acidic and lighter continental rocks, producing volcanoes that are more silicic and more explosive than those that are generating oceanic crust. The volcanoes at Hawaii are basaltic, and erupt quietly; those of the Lesser Antilles and the Aleutian Islands are more acidic and erupt violently.

The theory of plate tectonics divides the crust into six major plates and several smaller ones (Fig. 20.12). The boundaries between the plates are of at least three kinds: (1) tensional boundaries as at the mid-Atlantic Ridge, where there is spreading; (2) compressional subduction zones characterized by trenches, volcanism, and earthquakes; and (3) shear zones where adjoining plates are sliding past one another.

1. Permian – 225 million years ago

2. Triassic – 200 million years ago

3. Jurassic – 135 million years ago

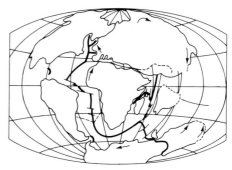

4. Cretaceous – 65 million years ago

Figure 20.10 *Continental drift and plate tectonics. At the end of the Paleozoic, the continents were united in one continental plate. During the Triassic the continental plates began to break apart (see Fig. 2.16,A). The continents became almost wholly separated plates by the end of the Cretaceous, and have continued drifting apart during the Cenozoic.*

Volcanoes, Volcanic Eruptions

In most parts of the world, people flee when volcanoes erupt, but in Hawaii people travel to the scenes of the eruptions to watch the display. In a century and a half only one person has been killed by a volcano. Indeed, the volcanoes have been made into a National Park! Hawaiian eruptions are quiet effusions of highly fluid, molten, basaltic lava, and not at all explosive. The active volcanoes are Mauna Loa and Kilauea on the island of Hawaii.

On the other hand, volcanoes of the Lesser Antilles, just east of Puerto Rico, and those associated with the trenches at subduction zones, are violently explosive. In fact, in contrast to volcanoes of the Hawaiian type, the most explosive type is named for Mt. Pelée in the Lesser Antilles.

There are all gradations between these extreme types, for volcanic eruptions are of many kinds. The Greeks and Romans, familiar with the explosive kinds, interpreted them as conflict between the primitive elements—air, fire, and water.

By the end of the eighteeenth century it became recognized that the products of volcanism are not the products of ordinary combustion. Experimental remelting of lavas in glass furnaces showed that when the melted lavas were again chilled quickly, they formed glasses, whereas melts that were chilled slowly became crystallized. It was observed that eruptions give off gases, and that some lavas are made porous by gas bubbles, which form *vesicles*. The common gases that accompany eruptions are hydrogen sulfide, carbon dioxide, and steam (additional water is combined with some of the minerals). These volatiles are part of the original melt; they are not merely the result of absorption at or near the surface. Volcanic eruptions are the ejection of heated gases, fluids, and solid matter from the earth, and the proportions and combinations of these constituents largely determine the process and kind of eruption.

The most viscous eruptives and the most violently explosive, the *Peléan* type, are so named for the volcanic mountain 400 miles southeast of Puerto Rico. The lavas are so viscous that they become bulged upward in a dome over the vent, and when such domes explode they produce superheated steam clouds ladened with incandescent and molten dust particles, a heavy sort of mist with temperatures well over a thousand degrees centigrade. Such a glowing avalanche moves down the mountainside close to the ground at hurricane speed, overwhelming everything in its path.

Less devastating, but still explosive, are the volcanoes of the Lipari Islands north of Sicily. The *Vulcanian* type, named for the southernmost island, erupts explosively at frequent but irregular intervals. Most of the material ejected is solid;

most of the rest is angular rock fragments, and some is pasty lava. Much of the material is glass. The explosions are accompanied by clouds of steam and fine ash rising 2 to 4 miles.

Volcanoes of the *Strombolian* type, named for the northernmost of the Lipari Islands, are in almost continuous eruption, and have been throughout historic time. Not much lava is extruded, but the molten lava in the vent is explosively thrown into the air every few minutes. The pasty clots form various shapes of *volcanic bombs* (Fig. 20.13) and frothy hunks of clinker.

Still less violent are the Hawaiian type of eruptions.

In the last two hundred years Mauna Loa has erupted about 35 times; about half of these eruptions occurred at the summit, the other half occurred along rifts on the flanks (Figs. 20.14, 20.15). Kilauea, which has produced about a dozen flank eruptions, has intermittently maintained a lake of active lava at the summit. A volcano observatory is operated by the U.S. Geological Survey in Hawaii National Park.

The start of an eruption may be announced by earthquakes focused about 35 miles below the surface, and located by seismographs distributed

Figure 20.11 *Diagram illustrating the mechanics envisioned in the concept of plate tectonics. For explanation, see text.*

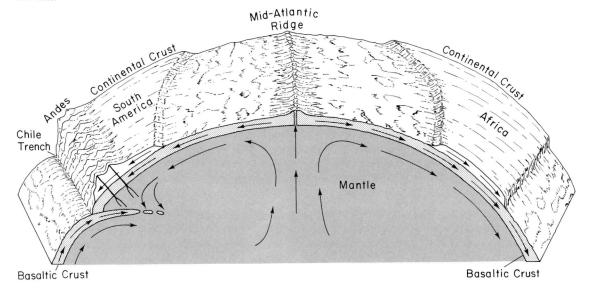

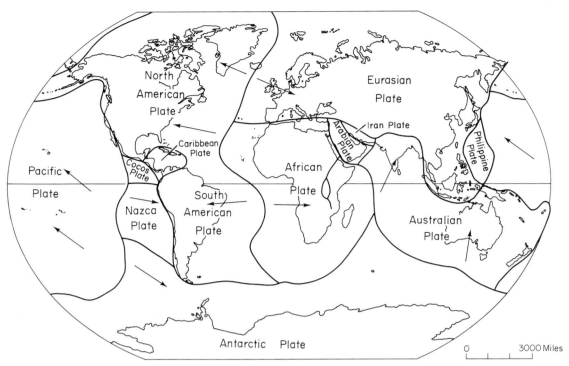

Figure 20.12   *Principal plates of the earth's crust that are believed to be moving relative to one another.*

over the island. In a matter of weeks (or months) the earthquake focus rises to within a few miles of the surface, and the flanks of the volcano bulge outward (detected by tiltmeters). Attempts to predict the time of eruptions have thus far been only partly successful, but a high degree of success has been achieved in predicting the place of eruption—that is, which volcano and where— on the summit or the flank?

The eruptions usually occur along a few miles of a fissure and begin as fountains of molten lava. At first the molten spray of the fountains forms a "curtain of fire," sometimes as high as 800 feet. The falling, cooling spray builds ramparts along the fissure. Gradually the activity becomes concentrated at a few places along the fissure, and the fountains at these centers build cones of spatter and cinder. Most of the erupted lava, however, moves downslope like rivers confined between banks of their own construction or forms a lake in the summit caldera. The hottest lavas come to rest with a smooth surface of quenched

vesicular glass (*pahoehoe*); cooler lavas have a rough spiny surface of crystallized clinker (*aa*).

Hawaii's volcanoes illustrate the principle that eruptions are preceded or accompanied by local, minor earthquakes, but on the other hand very few earthquakes and almost none of the very destructive ones are accompanied by volcanism. Volcanic activity causes earth movement, but earth movement is not necessarily accompanied by volcanism or other igneous activity.

Tsunamis

Hawaii, and indeed all the shores of the Pacific, are exposed to tsunamis, commonly but erroneously called tidal waves. They are generated not by tides but by earth movements on the ocean floor, most commonly in or near the trenches. For example, an earthquake might cause a mass of ocean bottom to slide into a trench and create a surge of water, very much like that generated

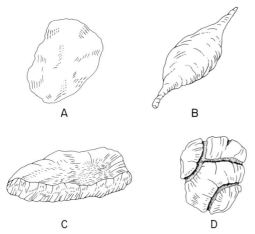

Figure 20.13 *Shapes of volcanic bombs. The plastic mass develops a rounded shape due to spinning in the air (A). Others, possibly more liquid, develop spindle shapes (B). Many are flattened by impact when they hit the ground (C). Vesicles may be elongated and develop a spiral pattern. Some have a dense or glassy selvage and a vesicular interior. Crusts may become fractured as a result of interior swelling of the gases (D). Some bombs are hollow; crusts may be rough or smooth.*

by a child sliding into a bathtub. As the wave crosses the Pacific, its amplitude is not high but its wavelength is long; as it approaches shore and is slowed, the wavelength decreases, but the amplitude greatly increases. The first effect is likely to be a withdrawal of water from the shore, sufficient to ground large ships, followed by a wave tens or scores of feet high. Figure 20.18 shows the heights reached by the tsunamis of 1946 and 1960 at the Hawaiian Islands.

The height and intensity of waves caused by a tsunami are not uniform along the coast, and are controlled by several factors. In general, the greatest heights are reached on the side facing the wave's origin. The shape of the island has an effect in refracting the waves, and lee sides of round islands like Kauai experience higher waves than do the lee sides of angular or elongate islands, like Molokai. Waves on the lee sides are likely to be highest where the waves meet after being refracted around the two sides of the island. Exposure is an important factor because

storm waves, which are most frequent and generally highest on the windward side, are carried shoreward by the tsunami. The near-shore submarine topography affects the waves because shallow water slows a wave and increases its height. Fringing reefs, however, reduce the intensity of the waves.

A tsunami generated by the Alaska earthquake of 1964 (Chapter 19) lashed the California coast. One in 1969 struck the west coast of Celebes in Indonesia and demolished four villages and killed more than 600 persons.

Because of the hazard, a tsunami warning system has been established around the Pacific. The system can provide a few hours warning of the possible approach of a tsunami, because it takes a few hours for such a wave to cross the Pacific. At this stage, however, the warning system is only partly successful, because not all earthquakes at or near the trenches generate tsunamis, and too many alarms defeat the purpose.

Climates

Both Hawaii and Puerto Rico have pleasant tropical climates. The surrounding oceans and the highly persistent northeast trade winds maintain almost uniform climatic conditions throughout the year. At any given location temperature and precipitation are nearly uniform through the year but both vary greatly with altitude and exposure. At sea level in the Hawaiian Islands the average January temperature is about 70°F; the average July temperature is about 75°F. At San Juan, on the north coast of Puerto Rico, the January average is about 75°F; the July average is about 80°F. The south coast averages roughly a degree warmer.

Temperatures decrease about $3\frac{1}{2}$°F for each 1,000 feet of altitude. Frost in the Hawaiian Islands is rare below 4,000 feet and has never been recorded below 2,500 feet. Puerto Rico is similar. On the very high peaks of the Hawaiian Islands, however, snow may fall during any month of the year, and there is permanent ice in deep cracks.

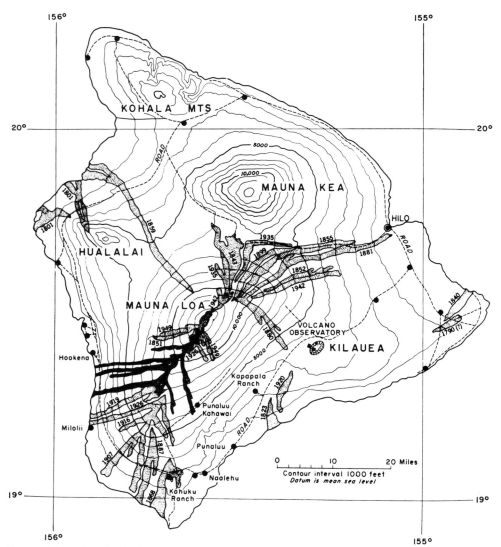

Figure 20.14   *The island of Hawaii, showing the five major volcanic mountains and the historic lava flows to 1953. [After U.S.G.S.] The eruptions of Mauna Loa are centered along the rift that crosses the summit; the eruptions of Kilauea occur at the summit and on the flanks, but the lava flows are mostly from flank eruptions. Note that Kilauea is low on the east flank of Mauna Loa.*

Figure 20.19 illustrates the variations in precipitation for Puerto Rico and the islands of Oahu and Hawaii. Precipitation is heaviest on the windward sides of the islands; lee slopes are semiarid. In Puerto Rico, for example, the trade winds, blowing from just slightly north of east, first reach the Sierra de Luquillo, and annual

rainfall there averages more than 200 inches. Rainfall is considerable in the Cordillera Central, especially in the western part of the island. Leeward of Sierra de Luquillo is rain shadow. Annual rainfall on the north coast, at San Juan, averages 61 inches; on the south coast, which is leeward of the Cordillera, the rainfall is much less, and at Ponce averages 35 inches. The rainfall occurs mostly as showers, but on some windward slopes these may occur daily.

A second major effect of the winds is evaporation. Humidity is high, averaging above 75 percent throughout the day. As a consequence, areas protected from the wind are uncomfortably muggy, but exposed areas are pleasantly cool. Because winds are persistent, evaporation rates are high and the effective moisture is far less than seems indicated by the amount of precipitation. Areas with less than 35 inches of annual rainfall are semiarid.

Puerto Rico is in the belt of hurricanes, which originate in the eastern part of the Caribbean Sea and in the ocean farther east. The hurricane season is mostly July 1 to November 1. July and October hurricanes generally form over the eastern Caribbean, and these rarely attain maximum intensity until they pass Puerto Rico. August and September storms form farther east, over the ocean, and these may develop into major storms by the time they reach the island. Hurricane winds may exceed 100 miles per hour and be accompanied by torrential rain. The storms usually move at 5 to 15 miles per hour.

The Hawaiian Islands are free of tornadoes and typhoons. Thunderstorms are infrequent and never severe. Hail is rare. The windward sides are cloudy (Fig. 20.20) but the clouds are high and fogs rarely interfere with shipping or airplane schedules.

Despite the oceanic setting, the climate was different during the Pleistocene, when glaciers formed on Mauna Kea. The lateritic soils (p. 671), which are ancient deposits, possibly formed under climatic conditions different from those of the present.

Vegetation

The native flora of the Hawaiian Islands is unique. Not only does it differ from that of the continents surrounding the Pacific, but it differs from the other islands in the Pacific. When the Hawaiian Islands first appeared above sea level

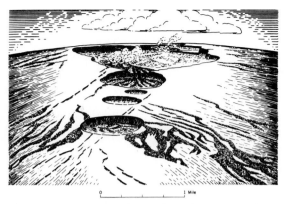

Figure 20.15 *View northeast along the summit of Mauna Loa, showing the large caldera on the summit and the adjoining pit craters. The summit caldera is 9,000 feet wide. [From U.S.G.S.]*

in late Tertiary time, a few millions of years ago, they were barren lavas. Seeds were transported there, perhaps by floating, perhaps in part by birds, and the islands became covered with vegetation. But in isolation from their parent stocks these plants evolved into different forms. Before man arrived on the islands, about 85 percent of the flora consisted of endemic species—species that have so changed from their parent stock that they now are peculiar to the islands. The older the island, the larger the number of endemic species. The remaining 15 percent are indigenous species that retain characteristics of these species elsewhere. Almost all the flowering trees and shrubs and food-producing plants have been introduced by man, and have spread at the expense of the indigenous plants. Stands of native plants on the islands include shrub, forest, bog, and moss-lichen.

Most of the shrub land is along the coastal lowlands, on the lee sides of the mountains, but extends to considerable altitudes where the rainfall is slight. Such areas are Hawaii's deserts.

Forests grow above the shrub land on the lee sides of the mountains, but extend to sea level on the windward side. There are at least five kinds of forest, reflecting differences in moisture availability. One kind occurs on the dry lands on the lee sides of the mountains up to about 2,500

Figure 20.16   *The Kohala shield volcano at the northwest tip of the island of Hawaii is younger than the volcanoes forming Oahu, and it still retains its shield form. This view, southwest across the northwest flank of the shield, shows how shore erosion has formed sea cliffs in the older parts of the volcanic pile (lower left), whereas younger flows (right) still slope to the sea. [Photograph courtesy of Agatin T. Abbott, Hawaii Institute of Geophysics.]*

feet. Wetter areas, up to about 6,000 feet, support a forest that includes one of the principal lumber trees, *Ohia*. With it are tree-like ferns. A third kind of forest is found above the *Ohia* forests on Maui and Hawaii up to about 9,500 feet in altitude. A fourth kind of forest is characterized by the koa tree, which is the largest Hawaiian tree, growing 60 feet high and attaining diameters up to 12 feet. These four kinds of forests consist of native plants; the fifth kind of forest is composed predominantly of introduced species.

Shrubs mixed with scattered trees grow on the upper slopes of the high mountains. Bogs with a distinctive plant growth are common in areas of high rainfall, mostly between 4,000 and 6,000 feet in altitude. Mosses and lichens grow above timberline on the summits of the highest mountains, where rainfall is low and frost is frequent. The relationship of the vegetation to the topography and soils is illustrated in Figure 20.21.

The agricultural crops are principally sugar and pineapple, but various other special crops are becoming important: coffee, banana, papaya, citrus fruits, mango, macadamia nut, and avocado. Native woods are used for cabinet making or other special uses.

Puerto Rico, like Hawaii, has rain forest on the wet north slopes of the mountains and dry forest on the south side. Mangrove grows in swamps along much of the coast.

Most of Puerto Rico is under cultivation, and the natural vegetation is undisturbed in only a few places. Areas with high rainfall, like Sierra de Luquillo, are covered by dense forest (Fig. 20.22), including such trees as mahogany, ebony, mamey, tree ferns, sierra palm, mango, Spanish cedar, sandalwood, and rosewood. Growing with these are orchids, jungle vines, and matojo grass.

The southern slope of the island, which is semiarid, supports dry forest consisting of acacia, royal palm, yucca, cacti, and dry grasses. Mangrove grows along much of the coast. Mangrove swamps include bogs with reeds, sedges, cattails, ferns, and grasses.

Agriculturally the island consists of a coastal belt planted chiefly in sugar cane, supplemented with coconut and sea island cotton. Of the alluvial areas, about 85 percent is planted in sugar cane and 10 percent in a grass (malojilla) used for forage and hay. The remaining 5 percent is bog. The lower foothills are planted in citrus fruits, pineapple, and various subsistence crops; some are used for pasture. The north sides of the higher hills are used for growing tobacco, and the highest for coffee. The wood of the mangrove and other trees is burned for charcoal and used for fuel.

The meager fauna reflects the island's long isolation. Offshore there is considerable coral (Fig. 20.26) and sports fish, but not much food fish.

Surface Deposits and Soils

Surface deposits in Hawaii include, at one extreme, the glacial deposits on Mauna Kea; at the other, the saline deposits in some of the desert areas. The soils include, at one extreme, the highly leached soils of the rain forests; at the other, the calcareous (alkaline) soils in the deserts. Deep lateritic soils are widespread on old lavas forming the older islands, whereas young lavas on the younger islands are still bare rock.

Calcareous desert soils are found at low altitudes—below 2,500 feet—where the annual rainfall averages less than 20 inches. The layer of carbonate accumulation is 2 to 20 inches thick and 15 to 24 inches below the surface. The surface layers have little organic matter and are reddish. The sparse vegetation consists mostly of shrubs.

Calcareous grassland soils in Hawaii resemble those on the Great Plains (Chapter 6). They occur on the lee sides of the mountains, but the average annual rainfall may be as great as 65 inches, and the soils extend to about 4,000 feet in altitude. These soils have organic-rich surface layers a foot thick. Although the rainfall may be considerable, the year-round growth of grasses suffices to return bases to the surface soil.

In general, the bulk composition of these calcareous soils is like that of the parent rocks—the lavas and volcanic ash. The calcareous soils are developed mostly on volcanic ash, which is more extensive and thicker on the lee sides of the volcanoes than on the windward sides. These deposits and the soils on them are young, for ash has been repeatedly added to them.

The lateritic soils in Hawaii, which contrast strikingly with the calcareous soils, are the result of intensive leaching of the bases and silica. They are open-system, acid soils. There has been residual enrichment of iron, titanium, and aluminum because of the removal of other elements, but there is no horizon in which elements have accumulated that were leached from another layer. Four varieties of these soils are distinguished.

One kind, found in dry or moderately humid areas, has little organic matter, and is slightly acid. The soil is residually enriched in iron, titanium, and aluminum; the matrix is mostly the clay mineral kaolin. Manganese dioxide has accumulated in the upper part of these soils and forms nodules in the lower part. These soils have developed on all the islands where the average annual precipitation is 10 to 80 inches, but where there is a dry season. The vegetation consists of

shrubs and grasses. These are known as low-humic laterites, and at least those in the driest areas probably are relicts of an ancient soil that developed when there was more moisture and different vegetation than there is today. It seems doubtful that time has been sufficient for even the volcanic ash to be so weathered in areas that receive as little as 10 inches of rain and in areas where the acidity is so slight.

A second kind of laterite is found at altitudes up to 3,000 feet, where the rainfall averages 40 to 150 inches. These support a considerable growth of shrubs, grasses, or forest, and since there is considerable organic matter in the soil, they are more acid. More silica and aluminum have been lost from these soils than from the low-humic laterites, and they contain little or no manganese dioxide.

A third kind of laterite occurs under the rain forests, and is very acidic. These soils, which occur where the rainfall is considerable and where there is no dry season, are continually wet. They are porous and retain much water, but when dried they become very hard and are difficult to wet again.

The fourth kind of laterite, apparently the oldest, seems to represent the most advanced kind of weathering. This laterite is characterized by upper layers strongly enriched in iron and titanium oxides. In places these layers form crusts. These ferruginous lateritic soils are not found on Hawaii, the youngest of the islands; they are best developed on Kauai, the oldest of the islands. They are found where the present rainfall is as low as 25 inches annually and as high as 150 inches, and at altitudes up to 4,000 feet. In the low-rainfall areas these soils probably are ancient ones that formed when the rainfall was greater than it is now.

Differences between the four kinds of laterite reflect differences in their degree of weathering or stage of development. The least developed, and probably the youngest of these soils, is the low-humic laterite; weathering is most advanced in the ferruginous laterite, which probably is the oldest. The differences are strikingly shown by differences in their chemical composition. Analyses show progressive depletion of silica, alkalis, and alkali earths and residual enrichment in iron and alumina (Fig. 20.23). Even the low humic laterites are more altered than is the residuum, or saprolite, that is parent material for the Red and Yellow Podzols on the continent (see Chapter 6).

Other soils in Hawaii include some that are so young and unweathered that the parent material still dominates the profile. Others, still younger, have no profile and are simply unweathered surface deposits, whether alluvium, volcanic ash, volcanic cinders, coral sand, basaltic beach sand, or lavas. In places these are young surface deposits; in other places they are old deposits that have been freshly exposed by erosion. Soils in poorly drained areas are classed as bog or paddy soils. Some near the coast are saline. Salts also have accumulated locally in some of the desert soils.

Surface deposits in Puerto Rico include alluvium in valley bottoms, and beach sand, dune sand, and swamp deposits along the coasts. North coast sands at and near the shore are cemented with calcium carbonate to form eolianite and beachrock (see p. 678). Much of the island is covered by thick residual soils, including various laterites, Red and Yellow Podzols, Gray-Brown Podzols, Rendzina Soils, and a series of alkaline soils that include Chernozem, Reddish-Chestnut, and Brown Soils. The acid, open-system Lateritic

Figure 20.17 *The volcanic activity is continuing in the southeastern part of the island of Hawaii, and the volcanoes and lavas there retain their volcanic forms. In the upper view, lavas can be seen issuing from a fissure on the east flank of Kilauea volcano and cascading across fault scarps. In the distance is Mauna Kea volcano, and at the left is the northeast flank of the shield volcano at Mauna Loa. The lower view shows the caldera at Kilauea volcano, the northeast flank of Mauna Loa on the left, and Mauna Kea on the skyline. [Photograph by Agatin T. Abbott, Hawaii Institute of Geophysics.]*

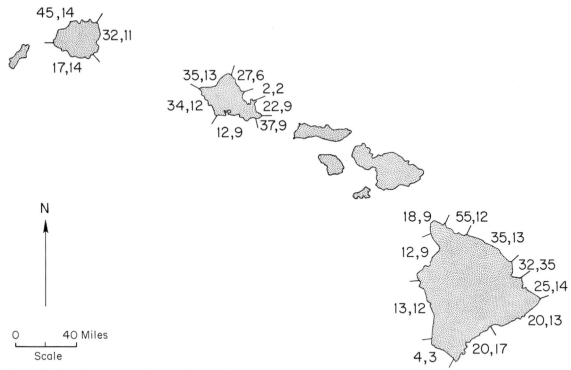

Figure 20.18 *Maximum heights reached by the 1946 tsunami (first figure) and the 1960 tsunami (second figure) along some coastal sections of Hawaii. The 1946 tsunami originated in the Aleutian Trench, to the north; the 1960 tsunami came from the direction of Chile, southwest* [Data from University of Hawaii.]

and the Red and Yellow Podzolic Soils are as much as 80 feet deep and are developed on the wet, windward side of the island; the closed-system, alkaline soils are thinner and are developed on the dry, leeward side (Fig. 20.24). The Rendzina Soils are developed on the plateaus of Tertiary limestone. The thick, well-developed, residual soils, especially the laterites and the Red and Yellow Podzols, are paleosols and are of Pleistocene age or older, for they are overlapped by Pleistocene surface deposits.

Where developed on Cretaceous volcanic rocks or Tertiary limestone, the lateritic soils are yellow, brown, or red, acid and clayey to a depth of 40 feet, and the clay is aggregated to give a granular and loamy texture. On granitic rocks the surface soil is bright red and clayey; this grades downward to disintegrated rock and is as much

as 80 feet deep in places. On serpentine the soil is a deep-red, iron-rich laterite that grades to yellow with depth, is 30 or more feet deep, and, like the parent rock, contains considerable nickel and chromite. Along the coast, these lateritic soils are overlain by Pleistocene terrace deposits about 100 feet above sea level.

Elsewhere the granitic rocks have weathered to a dense, granular material like sand, but composed of the minerals of the parent rock in varying stages of decomposition. These soils are younger than the laterite, and the mineral alteration is less advanced.

The Gray-Brown Podzols also are developed on the granitic intrusions and on the Cretaceous volcanic rocks. They are shallow soils, 1 to 2 feet thick, granular, and well drained. Surface layers are gray-brown to black clay, slightly acidic and

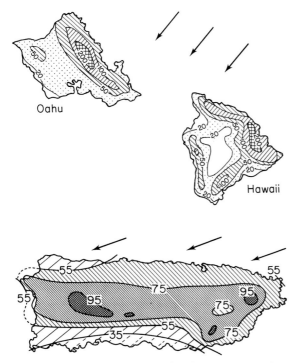

Figure 20.19 *Isohyetal maps of Oahu, Hawaii, and Puerto Rico. Direction of trade winds shown by arrows. Maximum precipitation is on the windward side of the islands. [Bottom map after U.S.D.A.]*

about 6 inches thick. Below these layers there is a brown, slightly acidic, silty clay layer that is 8 to 18 inches thick.

The Rendzina Soils have a black, calcareous surface layer 4 to 10 inches thick that grades downward into parent rock, which is soft white limestone or marl.

The alkaline soils have surface layers ranging from brown to black. All are calcareous mixtures of sand and clay. The subsoils are clayey and highly calcareous, being the layer of lime accumulation. Other soils included with these have no layer of lime accumulation and are Prairie Soils; others have clay hardpans like planosols.

The alluvial deposits are by far the most productive ground on the island. The ground is irrigated where rainfall averages less than about 60 inches. The lateritic soils are leached of most of

their bases and other plant nutrients and require fertilizer. Moreover, the old lateritic and Red and Yellow Podzolic soils are highly susceptible to erosion, like the Red and Yellow Podzolic soils in the United States (see Chapter 6).

Water Supply

Despite the very high annual rainfall in much of the Hawaiian Islands, the water supply is not abundant, because the ground, being composed of lavas, is highly porous, and most of the rainwater runs through it and all the way to the base of the island, where it collects in a lense over salt water (Fig. 20.25). Salt water is about $\frac{1}{40}$th heavier than fresh water, and the fresh water can float on the salt water. A lens of fresh water projects above the salt water table $\frac{1}{40}$th the thickness of the lens in the same way that only a small part of an iceberg protrudes above sea level. The freshwater lens, however, contains a brackish zone in which the two waters mix.

The brackish zone is a very important factor in developing supplies of groundwater from such a lens, because overdrafts by wells cause salt water to rise in cones into the fresh-water lens and contaminate it (Fig. 5.13). The water that can be supplied by such a lens without disturbing the salt-water—fresh-water boundary is equal to the annual recharge by infiltration. To preserve the supply, water must be skimmed from the top of the lens rather than pumped from lower down.

Figure 20.20 *Airplane view south to the peaks on Hawaii, with clouds banked against the windward (north) side by the northeast trade winds. Hualalai has no trade wind clouds, but the west slope has clouds at midday due to landward breezes.*

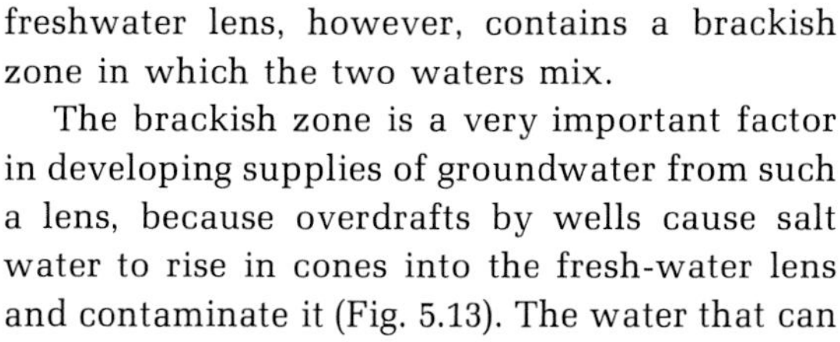

Mauna Kea	Mauna Loa	Kohala	Hualalai
13,800	13,700	5,500	8,250

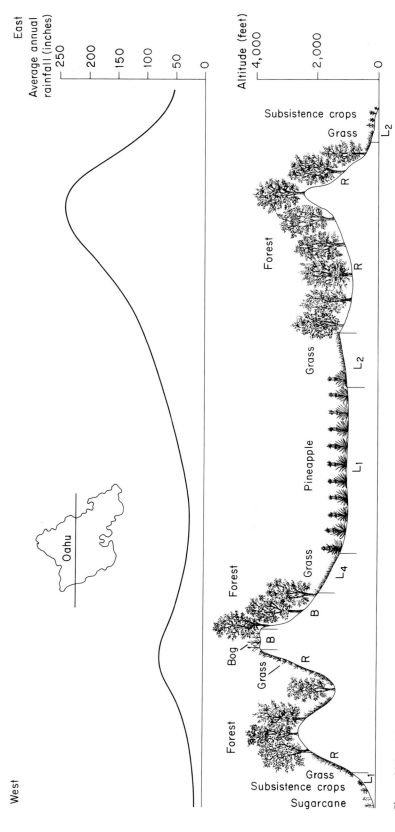

Figure 20.21 *West to east transect across the island of Oahu, illustrating some relationships between topographic position, rainfall, vegetation, soils, and land use. L_1, low-humic laterite; L_2, humic laterite; L_4, ferrugenous laterite; B, bog soil; R, stoney ground. [After U.S.D.A.]*

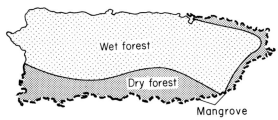

Figure 20.22 *Distribution of three types of forest in Puerto Rico. (After U.S.D.A.] Most of the island is under cultivation, and little forest remains. On the windward (north) slope there is wet forest; on the leeward (south) slope, dry forest. Mangrove forest (greatly exaggerated in figure) grows along the coast in an interrupted belt less than a mile wide.*

This skimming is done by tunnels with infiltration galleries, and these are replacing wells in the Hawaiian Islands. Most of this water is soft; the average hardness of water in the municipal systems is about 50.

On the high parts of the islands the depth to this basal lens of groundwater makes drilling uneconomic. Some water is obtained from groundwater perched on impervious beds, but these supplies are limited. Most water supplies on the mountains are obtained by collecting rain water in cisterns. It seems strange, in such a high-rainfall area, to see no surface water and to see buildings equipped with cisterns and storage tanks for collecting water!

Differences in the geology introduce considerable differences in the mode of occurrence of the water supplies. For example, Kauai is exceptional in that more than half of its rainfall is discharged in streams. On the other islands, large areas have practically no runoff.

Water supplies in Puerto Rico are obtained both from surface water and from groundwater. Because of the abundant limestone, most of the water is hard; in municipal systems the hardness

Figure 20.23 *Graph showing the progressive depletion of silica (SiO_2) and of alkalis ($K_2O + Na_2O$) and alkaline earths ($CaO + MgO$) and the changes (mostly increases) in iron (Fe_2O_3) and alumina (Al_2O_3) in Hawaiian lateritic soils. Percentages refer to total of constituents illustrated in the graph; other constituents in the parent rock total less than 10 percent; in the lateritic soils they may total 30 percent and are mostly water and organic matter.*

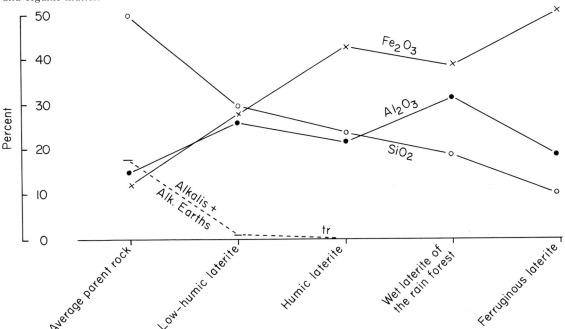

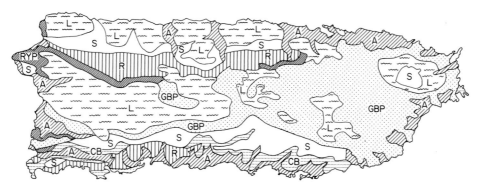

Figure 20.24   *Soil map of Puerto Rico. L, lateritic soils; RYP, Red and Yellow Podzols; GBP, Gray-Brown Podzols; R, Rendzina Soils; CB, mostly pedocals—Chernozem, Reddish Chestnut, and Reddish-Brown Soils with small areas of Reddish Desert and Reddish Prairie Soils; A, alluvial soils; S, mostly shallow soils. [After U.S.D.A.]*

averages about 125, which is much higher than in Hawaii, because those islands are mostly lavas and not carbonates.

Groundwater supplies in Puerto Rico are obtained principally from the Tertiary and Quaternary formations; Cretaceous formations have not been important sources. The intrusive igneous rocks yield the softest water, but the supplies are small. Much of the developed water, both surface water and groundwater, is used for irrigation.

Shore Features

Puerto Rico's shore features exhibit considerable variety. The northeast coast, highly indented and dotted with small islands, has a pattern like that of the New England coast. This might suggest submergence and drowning of the valleys, but the bottom offshore is a shallow, nearly level bank with coral reefs, and is not at all suggestive of submergence.

Along the southeastern coast rocky headlands, built chiefly of granitic rocks (Fig. 20.5), are separated by broad, alluviated valleys fronted by long, arcuate beaches of quartz sand. The configuration of this stretch of shore seems to be controlled by the structural geology of the old rocks, whose surface here slopes eastward below sea level. The relation between topography and

structural geology is similar on the west side of the island and western end of the south coast, except that the headlands there are mostly Cretaceous formations.

The central part of the south coast is mostly alluvial plain with beaches composed of sand from the Cretaceous volcanic formations in the mountains. The western part of the north coast is a cliff of Miocene limestone (Fig. 20.26) 150 to 200 feet high; the eastern part of that coast is broad alluvial plain with swamps and lagoons. The reason for this difference is obscure, but may be due to eastward tilting.

Beach sands along the north coast are quite different from those at the south. Instead of quartz sand, they are mostly carbonate—shell fragments, fragments of coral, calcareous algae, and grains of limestone. Along much of this coast the beach sand in the intertidal zone is cemented with calcium carbonate to form *beachrock* (Fig. 20.26). Dune sand is similarly cemented but to depths below low tide and to heights about 100 feet above high-tide level. In the spray zone above high-tide level the cemented dune sand is roughened with solution pits and residual pinnacles and is terraced with erosional platforms in the intertidal zone.

The origins of the calcium carbonate cement in beachrock and related deposits are obscure. In Puerto Rico the cemented deposits are largely limited to limestone areas, yet the calcium carbonate content of the ocean water at such places is very little greater than where there is no limestone. Moreover, in other parts of the world, similar deposits formed where there is no limestone. Such deposits can form rapidly; in many places trash only a few years old is firmly cemented. Some deposits may be due to physical-chemical precipitation, others may be due to biochemical activity of organisms.

Curiously, the coral around Puerto Rico grows along shores that are away from the limestone and beachrock (Fig. 20.26). This has been attributed partly to the turbidity of the water along the north coast when the rivers flood. The muddy water, which inhibits coral growth, drifts westward; the coral grows toward the east. Moreover, the ocean floor off the north coast is sandy as well as exposed to strong waves, and the foundation may be unsuitable for the growth of young coral.

Recent studies of shoreline details around Puerto Rico indicate that there has been little variation in sea level during the last 2,000 years. Four thousand years ago sea level may have been about 12 feet lower than it is now. This suggests crustal stability in this area during that time.

Puerto Rico has only two harbors, one at San Juan on the north coast and another at Ponce on the south. The west end of the island, however, is sheltered from the prevailing winds, and two shipping ports, Aguadilla and Mayaguez, are located there.

Hawaiian beaches illustrate the contrast in composition between ocean basins and continents. Quartz is abundant on continents, for the rocks are siliceous relative to those in the ocean basins. Quartz is scarce on oceanic volcanic islands like the Hawaiian Islands; there is no excess silica, as it has all been consumed to make silicate minerals. The sand of Hawaiian beaches is not the quartz sand familiar to those residing on the continent.

Some of the Hawaiian beaches are composed of grains of calcium carbonate derived by breakup of beachrock or by erosion of offshore reefs, which washes the coral and shell fragments

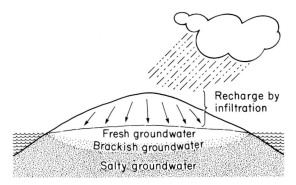

Figure 20.25 *Diagram illustrating occurrence of groundwater on the Hawaiian Islands. Because the islands are composed largely of very permeable lavas, surface water is scanty and a large fraction of the annual rainfall infiltrates the ground and sinks to nearly sea level. It collects at the base of the islands as a lens of fresh water floating on salt water. The groundwater is brackish in a zone where the two waters are mixed.*

onto shore. Examples are the widely advertised beach at Waikiki, and another on the northeast (windward) shore of Oahu, at Kailua. Other carbonate sand shores are at Kihei on the south side of Maui and at Hapuna Beach on the island of Hawaii.

Other Hawaiian beaches are composed of black sand, and these are of several kinds. Some consist of glassy volcanic debris; others are concentrates of heavy black minerals, such as magnetite and ilmenite, which weather from the basaltic rocks; others consist of fragments of the lavas; still others, composed largely of crystals of olivine, are greenish.

Figure 20.26 *Map of Puerto Rico shows principal areas of limestone (stippled), beachrock (black), and coral reef (wavy pattern). [After U.S.G.S.]*

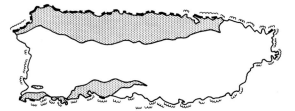

Considerable stretches of the Hawaiian shores consist of cliffs eroded into the lavas. Sea stacks are common, and there are sea caves and arches.

Resources

The economies of both Hawaii and Puerto Rico are largely dependent upon agriculture and tourism, the basis of which is the pleasant and otherwise highly satisfactory climate that both offer the tourist. Mineral resources are of no importance. Puerto Rico has considerable hydroelectric power; conceivably, Hawaii could develop steam power by circulating water in the heated ground at the volcanoes, but the possibility seems remote. The semiarid areas might be suitable places for experimenting with the harnessing of solar energy, but the probabilities are that energy needs in the near future will be met by importing fuels, fossil or nuclear.

Although largely agriculturally based, less than 10 percent of the Hawaiian Islands is cultivated, and almost all of the cultivated land is used for raising sugar cane and pineapple. About half the land is in pasture, about 30 percent is forest reserve, and 5 percent is in national parks. Most of the rest is wasteland. There is considerable livestock, but beef production meets only two-thirds of the local demand. The carrying capacity of the range land averages about one beef animal per 10 acres.

Also important to the islands' economy is the income from the armed forces stationed there. This income exceeds that obtained from sugar and pineapple production, and without this subsidy the islands might be another depressed area, which is a sad commentary on our system.

Puerto Rico's greatest resource problem is shortage of land for its large and growing population. Despite the overcrowding and the limited resources, the commonwealth has successfully reduced illiteracy and has raised per capita income and the general standard of living. One wonders how long this can be continued if the population continues to increase. Progress has been substantial, although much remains to be done to relieve poverty that persists in city slums as well as in rural areas away from the luxurious tourist centers.

References

Cline, M. G., and others, 1955, Territory of Hawaii: U.S. Dept. Agriculture Bureau of Soil Survey, ser. 1939, n. 25.

Dana, J. D., 1890, Characteristics of volcanoes: New York, Dodd, Mead and Co.

Degener, Otto, 1945, Plants of Hawaii National Park, illustrative of plants and customs of the South Seas: Ann Arbor, Mich. Edwards Bros.

Kaye, C. A., 1959, Coastal geology of Puerto Rico: U.S. Geol. Survey Prof. Paper 317.

Keen, M. J., 1968, An introduction to marine geology: New York, Pergamon Press.

Macdonald, G. A., and Orr, J. B., 1950, The 1949 summit eruption of Mauna Loa, Hawaii: U.S. Geol. Survey Bull. 974-A, pp. 1–33.

Macdonald, G. A., and Abbott, A. T., 1970, Volcanoes in the sea—the geology of Hawaii: Honolulu, University of Hawaii Press.

Stearns, H. T., 1946, Geology of the Hawaiian Islands: Terr. Hawaii, Div. Hydrography.

Wentworth, C. K., and Macdonald, G. A., 1953, Structures and forms of basaltic rocks in Hawaii: U.S. Geol. Survey Bull. 994.

APPENDIX A

●●●●●●●●●●●●●●●●●●●●●●●

TOPOGRAPHIC MAPS

Topographic maps have many uses as fundamental tools for planning and executing projects that are necessary to our modern way of life. They are of prime importance in planning airports, highways, dams, pipelines, transmission lines, industrial plants, and countless other types of construction. Topographic maps are an essential part of geologic and hydrologic research, of mineral investigations, and of studies on the quantity and quality of water. They greatly facilitate the study and application of flood control, soil conservation, and reforestation. Intelligent and efficient development of our natural resources depends on the availability of adequate topographic maps.

In addition, the rapidly growing list of map users now includes many who have discovered the advantages of topographic maps in the pursuit of outdoor activities such as hunting, fishing, and vacationing. Reliable maps showing relief features, woods, clearings, and watercourses are of inestimable value to the serious hiker. There is, in fact, very little of our outdoors that cannot be better understood and appreciated with the aid of topographic maps.

The greater part of this material has been taken from publications of the United States Geological Survey and the Geological Survey of Canada.

United States Topographic Maps

The National Topographic Map Series includes the several quadrangle and other map series published by the United States Geological Survey. A map series is a family of maps conforming generally to the same specifications or having some common unifying characteristic such as scale. Adjacent maps of the same quadrangle series can generally be combined to form a single large map. The principal United States map series and their essential characteristics are given in the following table.

The National Topographic Map Series also includes other special-purpose maps that are prepared from standard quadrangles but do not follow the standard quadrangle format. Metropolitan Area Maps, at 1:24,000 scale, have been prepared for many cities and published in one or more sheets, according to the size of the area shown. The National Park Series, at various scales, covers national parks, monuments, and historic sites. Many of these maps are available with shaded-relief overprinting on which the topography is made to appear three dimensional by the use of shadow effects. State base maps at scales of 1:500,000 (1 inch represents approximately 8 miles) and 1:1,000,000 (1 inch represents

Table A.1

United States Topographic Maps

Series	Scale	1 inch represents	Standard quadrangle size (latitude-longitude)	Quadrangle area (square miles)	Paper size E–W N–S width length (inches)
7½-minute	1:24,000	2,000 feet	7½ × 7½ min.	49 to 70	[1]22 × 27
Puerto Rico 7½-minute	1:20,000	about 1,667 feet	7½ × 7½ min.	71	29½ × 32½
15-minute	1:62,500	nearly 1 mile	15 × 15 min.	197 to 282	[1]17 × 21
Alaska 1:63,360	1:63,360	1 mile	15 × 20 to 36 min.	207 to 281	[2]18 × 21
U.S. 1:250,000	1:250,000	nearly 4 miles	[3]1° × 2°	4,580 to 8,669	[4]34 × 22
U.S. 1:1,000,000	1:1,000,000	nearly 16 miles	[3]4° × 6°	73,734 to 102,759	27 × 27

[1]South of latitude 31° 7½-minute sheets are 23 × 27 inches; 15-minute sheets are 18 × 21 inches.
[2]South of latitude 62° sheets are 17 × 21 inches.
[3]Maps of Alaska and Hawaii vary from these standards.
[4]North of latitude 42° sheets are 29 × 22 inches. Alaska sheets are 30 × 23 inches.

approximately 16 miles) are available for all States except Alaska and Hawaii, which are covered by maps at other scales. For some States, topographic and shaded-relief editions are also available.

Maps of the United States are available in sizes and scales ranging from letter size, 1:16,500,000 scale, to a two-sheet wall map, 1:5,000,000 scale. In addition, topographic maps of special format are produced for many principal rivers and their flood plains.

Although most of the maps of the National Topographic Map Series are produced by the Geological Survey, other Federal agencies—the Army Map Service, Coast and Geodetic Survey, Tennessee Valley Authority, Forest Service, and the Mississippi River Commission—also prepare topographic maps in connection with their regular activities that are incorporated in the National Topographic Map Series and published by the Geological Survey. For some mapping projects, State or local agencies share the cost of mapping equally with the Federal Government. These cooperative projects expedite the mapping of areas of particular interest to the cooperating agency, and help to complete the National Topographic Map Series.

Control Surveys are required to present map features in correct relationship to each other and to the earth's surface. Two kinds of control are required: horizontal and vertical. Horizontal control is needed to develop and maintain correct scale, position, and orientation of the map. For this purpose, latitude and longitude of selected points within the area to be mapped must be determined by field surveys. Similarly, vertical control is needed to determine the correct position of the contours which show the shape and elevation of the terrain. To obtain this, the elevation of selected points must also be determined in the field. Control points so located become the framework on which map detail is assembled. This framework determines the accuracy with which the positions and elevations of map features can be shown. Maps of abutting quadrangles join without a break in the continuity of map detail.

Permanent control points in the United States are usually marked on the ground by metal tablets 3¾ inches in diameter set in rock or masonry, and many are shown on the maps by appropriate symbols (Fig. A.1). Some marks serve for both horizontal and vertical control. Because such data are useful for many other purposes, the re-

Figure A-1

sults of control surveys are published for sale in tabulated lists, each covering a 15-minute quadrangle.

Mapping procedures have changed considerably since the time when all topographic maps were sketched by hand in the field, using an alidade and a planetable. Today, most maps are compiled in the office by photogrammetric methods, using stereoscopic plotting instruments and aerial photographs. These complex instruments provide three-dimensional optical models of the terrain from which the compiler makes precise measurements for accurate delineation of contours, drainage, woodland, and culture. Nevertheless, field surveys are still required to establish the geodetic framework on which aerial photographs are assembled and to add detail not obtainable from photographs. In areas obscured by dense foliage or heavy shadows, map features are plotted by planetable methods. Place names and political boundaries are determined, and roads, water features, and buildings are classified in the field. These field surveys may be done either before or after the map manuscript is compiled from aerial photographs. Before publication, each quadrangle map is edited for content, legibility, accuracy, and spelling and placement of names.

National standards for the horizontal and vertical accuracy of topographic maps in the United States were adopted in 1941, and maps that meet these standards carry a statement to that effect in the lower margin. The standards for horizontal accuracy require that at least 90 percent of the well-defined map points shall be plotted correctly within one-fiftieth of an inch on the pub-

lished map. This tolerance corresponds to 40 feet on the ground for 1:24,000-scale maps and about 100 feet on the ground for 1:62,500-scale maps. The standards for vertical accuracy require that at least 90 percent of the elevations interpolated from the contour lines shall be correct within one-half the contour interval.

Symbols are the graphic language of maps—their shape, size, location, and color all have special significance. On topographic maps published by the Geological Survey the colors in which symbols are printed indicate the general classes of map features they represent. Symbols for water features are printed in blue; man-made objects—roads, railroads, buildings, transmission lines, and many others—are shown in black; and green is used to distinguish wooded areas from clearings. The symbols that show the shape and elevation of the land surface—the distinguishing characteristic of topographic maps—are printed in brown.

Some map symbols are pictographs, which resemble the objects they represent, but the brown contour lines are abstractions that have no counterpart in nature; they are an effective device for representing the third dimension on flat paper. Practice and imagination are required to visualize hills and valleys from the contours of a topographic map; but once this ability is acquired, the topographic map presents a third dimension that is useful in many ways.

Some of the features depicted on a topographic map are illustrated in the accompanying bird's-eye view of a river valley and the adjoining hills (Fig. A.2). The river flows into a bay which is partly enclosed by a hooked sandspit. On both sides of the valley are terraces through which streams have cut gullies. The hill on the right has a smoothly eroded form and gradual slopes above a wave-cut cliff, whereas the one on the left rises to a steep slope from which it falls off gently and forms an inclined tableland crossed by a few shallow gullies. An unimproved dirt road and bridge provide access to a church and two houses situated across the river from an improved light-duty road which follows the seacoast and curves up the river valley.

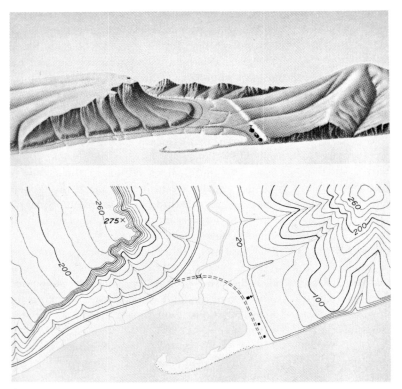

Figure A-2

The lower illustration shows the same features represented by symbols on a topographic map. Elevations are represented by contour lines; the vertical difference between contours in this illustration is 20 feet. To understand the contour symbol, think of it as an imaginary line on the ground which takes any shape necessary to maintain a constant elevation above sea level. The shoreline shown on the map illustration is, in effect, a contour representing zero elevation or sea level. If the sea should rise and cover the land, the shoreline would trace out, in turn, each of the contour lines shown on the map. Since the vertical difference in elevation between contours in this example is 20 feet, the shoreline would coincide with a new contour each time sea level rose 20 feet.

For easier reading, index contours (every fourth or fifth contour, depending on the contour interval) are accentuated by making the lines heavier. Supplementary contours, used to depict features which the basic contours do not adequately portray, are shown as dashed or dotted lines. Figures in brown at intervals along contour lines give the elevations of the lines above sea level. The elevation of any point can be read directly, or interpolated between contours. Map users who are concerned with quantitative measurement of terrain features can determine this basic data from map contours.

To the map user who is not concerned with exact ground elevations but only with the general appearance and shape of the land, maps with relief shading are useful. The pictorial effect of contoured topographic features is emphasized by simulating the appearance of sunlight and shadows. By overprinting the conventional map with shading, the illusion of solid, three-dimensional land surface is given. Such maps are usually selected for areas of special topographic or recreational interest.

Water features are printed in blue and are

generally classified as either perennial or intermittent. Perennial water features contain water most of the year (except for infrequent and extended periods of drought), and are shown by solid lines. Intermittent water features contain water only part of the year and are indicated by broken lines. Single lines represent rivers, streams, canals, and ditches less than 40 feet wide on $7\frac{1}{2}$-minute quadrangle maps, or less than 80 feet wide on 15-minute maps. Larger streams and rivers are shown to scale, with double lines. Large bodies of water usually are shown with a light blue tint.

The blue line marking the limits of the coastal waters represents mean high water, always at a higher level than the contour reference datum, mean sea level. Quadrangle maps that include seacoasts and tidal waters sometimes show depth curves, soundings, some obstructions to navigation, and other marine detail of interest. These maps, however, should not be used for navigation, because the marina features are incomplete; for submarine topography, maps by the U.S. Coast and Geodetic Survey should be used.

Two classes of buildings are distinguished by symbols on quadrangle maps. Buildings intended to shelter human activities are shown by a solid or a crosshatched symbol; those intended for the protection of machinery, animals, or materials are shown with an open-outline or a hatched symbol. Buildings such as sheds, smaller than the average dwelling, are not shown.

On some maps heavily built-up city areas, larger than approximately three-fourths of a square mile, are shown with a red-tint overprint. Within the tinted area only the streets and landmark buildings are shown, such as schools, churches, public buildings, and other structures that are prominent because of their outstanding size, design, or historic associations. The limits of the tinted area usually do not coincide with the legal boundary of the municipality.

Maps published by the Geological Surveys are intended to give a picture of the terrain that is as complete as can be legibly reproduced at the selected publication scale. Relatively unimportant features are sometimes omitted, and many small but important features are exaggerated in

size to make them readable. Some features are mapped because of their relative importance on a regional basis, such as wells and springs in the West; other features, such as windmills and fence lines, are mapped for their value as landmarks.

Geographic names are recognized as an integral and important part of a quadrangle map. Much effort is made to establish correct map nomenclature, which is based primarily on present-day local usage. In the United States name controversies are referred to the Board on Geographic Names, an interdepartmental agency established by law to determine choice, spelling, and application of geographic names for Federal usage.

The map margin, the space outside the projection lines on published maps, is used to identify and explain the map. The marginal information corresponds somewhat to the table of contents and introduction of a book, telling briefly how the map was made, where it is located, what agency prepared it, and other information to make the map more useful.

Map revision is needed to show changes in man-made features, such as new roads, buildings and reservoirs, and changes in the shape of the terrain. The rate and amount of change varies greatly from urban to remote areas, therefore maps are not all revised at definite intervals and to the same extent. The needs of map users for up-to-date maps that meet modern standards are considered in selecting maps for revision. Revision methods vary, but usually are a combination of photogrammetric, field, and cartographic procedures designed to bring the map content up to date and to maintain or improve the original accuracy of the map.

Topographic Maps of Canada

Canada is divided into numbered primary quadrangles, each 4 degrees of latitude by 8 degrees of longitude (Fig. A.3). These areas are assigned numbers which become higher from east to west and from south to north. The beginning point is 00, somewhere in the Atlantic Ocean well to the

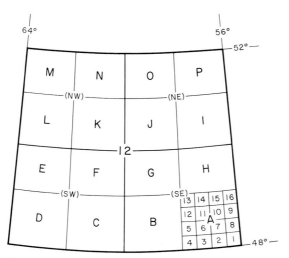

Figure A-3

southeast of Newfoundland and Nova Scotia. By convention the righthand digit shows the north-south spread—for example, 32 lies north of 31. The digits representing tens and hundreds show the east-west spread, thus 42 lies west of 32 and 22 lies east of 32. In a general way, then, the smaller the number of the primary quadrangle the farther southeast in Canada is the area represented by the map. Parts of quadrangle 01 represent southeastern Newfoundland while parts of quadrangle 117 are in the northwest corner of Yukon Territory.

Map sheets representing the primary quadrangles are issued on a scale of 1:1,000,000, or roughly 1 inch to 16 miles.

The primary quadrangles are divided in turn into quarters, which are designated by the addition of letters indicating the northwest (NW), northeast (NE), southwest (SW) or southeast (SE) quarter. Thus 42NW is the upper left-hand or northwest corner of primary division number 42. Maps illustrating these smaller areas belong to the 1:500,000 series, or approximately 1 inch to 8 miles.

Each of the quarters is further divided into four parts so that the primary unit is now divided into sixteen parts. Each of these is assigned a

letter beginning with "A" in the southeast corner and traversing westward to B, C and D along the bottom row of the primary quadrangle; then north and back eastward across the next row, E, F, G, H; then north to the next row and westward across I, J, K, L; finally north and traversing eastward again, M, N, O, P. Thus map sheet 12A would be a 1:250,000 sheet, approximating 1 inch to 4 miles, in the southeast corner of area No. 12, which, one can see from the number, lies somewhere well down in the southeastern part of Canada. Similarly 12M would be in the upper left or northwest corner and 12F would be a little south and west of center of area 12.

Each one of the lettered blocks is again subdivided, this time into sixteen squares with the numbers arranged in the same way as the letters of the larger subdivisions were—i.e., starting in the southeast corner and going 1, 2, 3, 4 to the southwest corner, etc. Thus 12A/1 would be a small division of 12 in the extreme southeast corner, and 12A/16 would be in the northeast corner of the letter block in the southeast corner of primary division 12.

Most map sheets of Canada are given a name as well as a number. This usually comes from a prominent city, river, mountain or other feature within the area mapped. Thus we have the Ottawa map area, 31G/5. Most commonly used map sheets in Canada now are 1:50,000-scale maps which represent one half (east and west) subdivisions of the numbered subdivisions of the lettered subdivisions of the primary quadrangles. Thus if you were to look for the City of Ottawa and its environs you would find it straddling two map sheets, 31G/5 E and 31G/5 W.

The subdivisions in the Canadian system, being bounded by latitude and longitude lines, make for complications because meridians of longitude converge toward the north pole. This means that a map sheet in northern Canada will be long and narrow compared to a map sheet farther south. Consequently, Canada north of latitude 60° has modified subdivisions of the primary quadrangles.

APPENDIX B

Altitudes of the 25 Largest Cities in the United States and Canada

City	State or Province	Rank	Altitude (feet) High	Altitude (feet) Low
New York	New York	1	410	Sea level
Chicago	Illinois	2	673	577
Los Angeles	California	3	5,074	Sea level
Philadelphia	Pennsylvania	4	441	Sea level
Detroit	Michigan	5	672	573
Montreal	Quebec	6	At airport, 117	
Houston	Texas	7	83	Sea level
Baltimore	Maryland	8	489	Sea level
Dallas	Texas	9	686	390
Washington	District of Columbia	10	410	1
Indianapolis	Indiana	11	845	664
Cleveland	Ohio	12	1,050	570
Milwaukee	Wisconsin	13	799	577
San Francisco	California	14	934	Sea level
Toronto	Ontario	15	At airport, 569	
San Diego	California	16	823	Sea level
San Antonio	Texas	17	1,000	505
Boston	Massachusetts	18	330	Sea level
Memphis	Tennessee	19	335	195
St. Louis	Missouri	20	614	385
New Orleans	Louisiana	21	25	− 5
Phoenix	Arizona	22	1,160	1,058
Columbus	Ohio	23	893	685
Seattle	Washington	24	520	Sea level
Jacksonville	Florida	25	Business dist., 20	Sea level

APPENDIX C

Altitudes of Named Summits Over 14,000 Feet Above Sea Level

Summit	State or Province	Quadrangle	Rank	Altitude (feet)
Mt. McKinley South Peak	Alaska	Mt. McKinley A-3	1	20,320
Mt. Logan	Yukon	115, B-C	2	19,850
Mt. McKinley	Alaska	Mt. McKinley A-3	3	19,470
Mt. St. Elias	Alaska	Mt. St. Elias	4	18,008
Mt. Foraker	Alaska	Talkeetna	5	17,400
Mt. Lucania	Yukon	115, F-G	6	17,147
Mt. King	Yukon	115, B-C	7	17,130
Mt. Steele	Yukon	115, F-G	8	16,664
Mt. Bona	Alaska	McCarthy B-2	9	16,500
Mt. Blackburn	Alaska	McCarthy C-7	10	16,390
Mt. Sanford	Alaska	Gulkana A-1	11	16,237
South Buttress	Alaska	Mt. McKinley A-2	12	15,885
Mt. Wood	Yukon	115, F-G	13	15,885
Mt. Vancouver	Alaska-Yukon	Mt. St. Elias	14	15,700
Mt. Churchill	Alaska	McCarthy B-2	15	15,638
Mt. Fairweather	Alaska-British Columbia	Mt. Fairweather	16	15,300
Mt. Hubbard	Alaska-Yukon	Mt. St. Elias	17	[1]15,015
Mt. Bear	Alaska	McCarthy B-1	18	14,831
Mt. Walsh	Yukon	115, F-G	19	14,780
East Buttress	Alaska	Mt. McKinley A-2	20	14,730
Mt. Hunter	Alaska	Talkeetna D-3	21	14,573
Mt. Alverstone	Alaska-Yukon	Mt. St. Elias	22	[1]14,565
Browne Tower	Alaska	Mt. McKinley	23	14,530
Mt. Whitney	Calif.	Mt. Whitney	24	[2]14,494
Mt. Elbert	Colo.	Mt. Elbert	25	[2]14,433
Mt. Massive	Colo.	Mt. Elbert	26	14,421
Mt. Harvard	Colo.	Mt. Harvard	27	14,420
Mt. Rainier	Wash.	Mt. Rainier	28	14,410
Mt. Williamson	Calif.	Mt. Whitney	29	14,375
La Plata Peak	Colo.	Mt. Elbert	30	14,336
Blanca Peak	Colo.	Huerfano Park	31	[2]14,317
Uncompahgre Peak	Colo.	Lake City	32	14,309
Crestone Peak	Colo.	Hooper No. 1	33	14,294
Mt. Lincoln	Colo.	Mt. Lincoln	34	14,286

Summit	State or Province	Quadrangle	Rank	Altitude (feet)
Grays Peak	Colo.	Grays Peak	35	14,270
Mt. Antero	Colo.	Poncha Springs	36	14,269
Torreys Peak	Colo.	Grays Peak	37	14,267
Castle Peak	Colo.	Hayden Peak	38	14,265
Mt. Evans	Colo.	Mt. Evans	39	14,264
Quandary Peak	Colo.	Mt. Lincoln	40	14,264
Longs Peak	Colo.	Longs Peak	41	14,256
McArthur Peak	Yukon	115, B-C	42	14,253
Mt. Wilson	Colo.	Mt. Wilson	43	14,246
White Mountain	Calif.	White Mountain	44	[1]14,246
North Palisade	Calif.	Mt. Goddard	45	14,242
Mt. Cameron	Colo.	Mt. Lincoln	46	14,238
Shavano Peak	Colo.	Poncha Springs	47	14,229
Mt. Belford	Colo.	Mt. Harvard	48	14,197
Mt. Princeton	Colo.	Poncha Springs	49	14,197
Mt. Yale	Colo.	Mt. Harvard	50	14,196
Crestone Needles	Colo.	Trinidad	51	[3]14,191
Mt. Bross	Colo.	Mt. Lincoln	52	14,172
Kit Carson Mtn.	Colo.	Hooper No. 1	53	14,165
Mt. Wrangell	Alaska	Gulkana A-1	54	14,163
Mt. Shasta	Calif.	Shasta	55	14,162
Mt. Sill	Calif.	Mt. Goddard	56	14,162
El Diente Peak	Colo.	Dolores	57	14,159
Maroon Peak	Colo.	Maroon Bells	58	14,156
Tabeguache Mtn.	Colo.	Garfield-Poncha Springs	59	14,155
Mt. Oxford	Colo.	Mt. Harvard	60	14,153
Mt. Sneffels	Colo.	Montrose	61	14,150
Point Success	Wash.	Mt. Rainier	62	14,150
Mt. Democrat	Colo.	Mt. Lincoln	63	14,148
Liberty Gap	Wash.	Mt. Rainier	64	14,133
Capitol Peak	Colo.	Capitol Peak	65	14,130
Mt. Lindsey	Colo.	Huerfano Park	66	[3]14,125
Pikes Peak	Colo.	Pikes Peak	67	14,110
Snowmass Mountain	Colo.	Snowmass Mountain	68	14,092
Windom Peak	Colo.	Needle Mountains	69	14,087
Mt. Russell	Calif.	Mt. Whitney	70	14,086
Mt. Eolus	Colo.	Needle Mountains	71	14,084
Columbia Peak	Colo.	Mt. Harvard	72	14,073

(Continued)

Altitudes of Named Summits Over 14,000 Feet Above Sea Level (Cont.)

Summit	State or Province	Quadrangle	Rank	Altitude (feet)
Mt. Bierstad	Colo.	Mt. Evans	77	14,060
Sunlight Peak	Colo.	Needle Mountains	78	14,059
Mt. Augusta	Alaska	Mt. St. Elias	73	14,070
Culebra Peak	Colo.	Trinidad	74	[3]14,069
Missouri Mountain	Colo.	Mt. Harvard	75	14,067
Humboldt Peak	Colo.	Hooper No. 1	76	14,064
Split Mountain	Calif.	Big Pine	79	14,058
Handies Peak	Colo.	Handies Peak	80	14,048
Middle Palisade	Calif.	Big Pine	81	14,040
Little Bear Peak	Colo.	Huerfano Park 3	82	14,037
Mt. Sherman	Colo.	Mt. Sherman	83	14,036
Redcloud Peak	Colo.	San Cristobal	84	14,034
Mt. Langley	Calif.	Lone Pine	85	14,028
Conundrum Peak	Colo.	Hayden Peak	86	14,022
Mt. Tyndall	Calif.	Mt. Whitney	87	14,018
Pyramid Peak	Colo.	Maroon Bells	88	14,018
Wetterhorn Peak	Colo.	Ouray SE	89	14,017
Wilson Peak	Colo.	Mt. Wilson	90	14,017
Mt. Muir	Calif.	Mt. Whitney	91	14,015
North Maroon Peak	Colo.	Maroon Bells	92	14,014
San Luis Peak	Colo.	Creede	93	14,014
Huron Peak	Colo.	Mt. Harvard	94	14,005
Mount of the Holy Cross	Colo.	Holy Cross	95	14,005
Sunshine Peak	Colo.	San Cristobal	96	14,001

[1]Elevation determined in 1966. Not shown on Mt. St Elias Quadrangle.
[2]Coast & Geodetic Survey.
[3]Colorado Mountain Club.

APPENDIX D

Extreme and Mean Altitudes of the States and Provinces

State or province	Highest point		Lowest point		Approx. mean Altitude (feet)
	Point	Altitude (feet)	Point	Altitude (feet)	
Alabama	Cheaha Mountain	2,407	Gulf of Mexico	Sea level	500
Alaska	Mount McKinley, South Peak	20,320	Pacific Ocean	Sea level	1,900
Alberta	Mt. Columbia	12,294	Liard River	1,000	5,000
Arizona	Humphreys Peak	12,633	Colorado River	70	4,100
Arkansas	Magazine Mtn.	2,753	Ouachita River	55	650
British Columbia	Mt. Fairweather	15,300	Pacific Ocean	Sea level	5,000
California	Mount Whitney	14,494	Death Valley	−282	2,900
Colorado	Mount Elbert	14,433	Arkansas River	3,350	6,800
Connecticut	Mt. Frissell, on South Slope	2,380	Long Island Sound	Sea level	500
Delaware	On Ebright Road	442	Atlantic Ocean	Sea level	60
District of Columbia	Tenleytown	410	Potomac River	1	150
Florida	Sec. 30, T. 6 N., R. 20 W.	345	Atlantic Ocean	Sea level	100
Georgia	Brasstown Bald	4,784	Atlantic Ocean	Sea level	600
Hawaii	Mauna Kea	13,796	Pacific Ocean	Sea level	1,990
Idaho	Borah Peak	12,662	Snake River	710	5,000
Illinois	Charles Mound	1,235	Mississippi River	279	600
Indiana	Franklin Township	1,257	Ohio River	320	700
Iowa	Ocheyedan Mound	1,675	Mississippi River	480	1,100
Kansas	Mount Sunflower	4,039	Verdigris River	680	2,000
Kentucky	Black Mountain	4,145	Mississippi River	257	750
Louisiana	Driskill Mountain	535	New Orleans	−5	100
Maine	Mount Katahdin	5,268	Atlantic Ocean	Sea level	600
Manitoba	Baldy Mountain	2,727	Hudson Bay	Sea level	1,200
Maryland	Backbone Mtn.	3,360	Atlantic Ocean	Sea level	350
Massachusetts	Mount Greylock	3,491	Atlantic Ocean	Sea level	500
Michigan	Mt. Curwood	1,980	Lake Erie	572	900
Minnesota	Eagle Mtn.	2,301	Lake Superior	602	1,200
Mississippi	Woodall Mtn.	806	Gulf of Mexico	Sea level	300
Missouri	Taum Sauk Mtn.	1,772	St. Francis River	230	800
Montana	Granite Peak	12,799	Kootenai River	1,800	3,400
Nebraska	Johnson Township	5,426	SE corner of State	840	2,600
Nevada	Boundary Peak	13,140	Colorado River	470	5,500
New Brunswick	Mt. Carleton	2,690	Gulf of St. Lawrence	Sea level	1,200

(Continued)

Extreme and Mean Altitudes of the States and Provinces (Continued)

State or province	Highest point		Lowest point		Approx. mean Altitude (feet)
	Point	Altitude (feet)	Point	Altitude (feet)	
Newfoundland (island)	Lewis Hills	2,672	Atlantic Ocean	Sea level	1,200
Newfoundland	Torngat Mountains	5,500	Atlantic Ocean	Sea level	2,200
New Hampshire	Mount Washington	6,288	Atlantic Ocean	Sea level	1,000
New Jersey	High Point	1,803	Atlantic Ocean	Sea level	250
New Mexico	Wheeler Peak	13,161	Red Bluff Res.	2,817	5,700
New York	Mount Marcy	5,344	Atlantic Ocean	Sea level	1,000
North Carolina	Mount Mitchell	6,684	Atlantic Ocean	Sea level	700
North Dakota	White Butte	3,506	Red River	750	1,900
Northwest Terr.	Baffin Island	8,500	Atlantic Ocean	Sea level	1,000
Nova Scotia	North Barren	1,747	Atlantic Ocean	Sea level	500
Ohio	Campbell Hill	1,550	Ohio River	433	850
Oklahoma	Black Mesa	4,973	Little River	287	1,300
Ontario	Tip Top Mountain	2,120	Hudson Bay	Sea level	500
Oregon	Mount Hood	11,235	Pacific Ocean	Sea level	3,300
Pennsylvania	Mount Davis	3,213	Delaware River	Sea level	1,100
Puerto Rico	Cerro de Punta	4,389	Atlantic Ocean	Sea level	2,200
Quebec	Mt. Jacques Cartier	4,160	Hudson Bay	Sea level	2,000
Rhode Island	Jerimoth Hill	812	Atlantic Ocean	Sea level	200
Saskatchewan	Cypress Hills	4,546	Slave River	600	1,000
South Carolina	Sassafras Mtn.	3,560	Atlantic Ocean	Sea level	350
South Dakota	Harney Peak	7,242	Big Stone Lake	962	2,200
Tennessee	Clingmans Dome	6,643	Mississippi River	182	900
Texas	Guadalupe Peak	8,751	Gulf of Mexico	Sea level	1,700
Utah	Kings Peak	13,528	Beaverdam Creek	2,000	6,100
Vermont	Mount Mansfield	4,393	Lake Champlain	95	1,000
Virginia	Mount Rogers	5,729	Atlantic Ocean	Sea level	950
Virgin Islands	Crown Mtn.	1,556	Atlantic Ocean	Sea level	750
Washington	Mount Rainier	14,410	Pacific Ocean	Sea level	1,700
West Virginia	Spruce Knob	4,862	Potomac River	240	1,500
Wisconsin	Timms Hill	1,952	Lake Michigan	581	1,050
Wyoming	Gannett Peak	13,785	Belle Fourche River	3,100	6,700
Yukon	Mt. Logan	19,850	Arctic Ocean	Sea level	3,500

PLACE INDEX

SUBJECT INDEX